The Essays of
Virginia Woolf

VOLUME V

THE ESSAYS OF VIRGINIA WOOLF

Volume I: 1904–1912
Volume II: 1912–1918
Volume III: 1919–1924
Volume IV: 1925–1928

The Essays of Virginia Woolf

VOLUME V

1929–1932

EDITED BY

STUART N. CLARKE

Houghton Mifflin Harcourt

BOSTON   NEW YORK

2010

First U.S. edition

Text by Virginia Woolf copyright © Anne Olivier Bell and Angelica Garnett
1927, 1928, 1930, 1931, 1933, 1938, 2009

Introduction and editorial notes copyright © Stuart N. Clarke 2009

www.hmhbooks.com

First published in Great Britain by The Hogarth Press, 2009

Library of Congress Cataloging-in-Publication Data is available.

ISBN 978-0-547-38534-1

Printed in the United States of America

DOM 10 9 8 7 6 5 4 3 2 1

Contents

Introduction

Looking at this substantial volume, casual readers might think that it represents much of Virginia Woolf's writing during the four-year period, 1929–32. They would be wrong, however. Certainly Woolf took her essays and reviews seriously: 'these articles, all architecture, a kind of cabinet work, fitting parts together, making one paragraph balance another; are such hard labour in the doing that one cant read them without remembering the drudgery. One starts full tilt; one sees a scene in a flash; but the working out is almost (with me) unbelievably laborious.'[1] Then one has only to look at Woolf's reading notes and drafts to realise the amount of work that lies behind these very readable essays. Finally, 'Phases of Fiction', originally devised as a book in the *Hogarth Lectures on Literature* series, took an unbelievable amount of time over a number of years; a transcription of its drafts would fill a book.[2]

For Woolf, of course, the core of her working life was writing fiction, and during this period she wrote *The Waves* from July 1929 until she finished correcting the proofs on 18 August 1931. By 21 July 1931 at the latest she had begun writing *Flush: A Biography* as a relief from 'the last screw of The Waves'.[3] Writing *Flush* – 'that abominable dog'[4] – continued into 1933. The essays fertilised the fiction, and *vice versa*, and occasional echoes and parallels have been footnoted in the essays. In 1931 William Empson wrote that in 'Time Passes' in *To the Lighthouse* (1927) 'it seems as if Mrs Woolf herself was not so much remembering [Mrs Ramsay's shawl from 'The Window'] as finding her way about the book as if by habit; it is this sort of small correspondence, used so often, that makes up a full and as it were poetical attitude to language such as would gain by an annotated edition'.[5]

Although Empson was writing shortly before *The Waves* was published, his comments about Woolf's 'poetical attitude to language' apply even more to that novel written in the most poetic prose. On 10 January 1931 Woolf was stirred by rereading her essay 'Poetry, Fiction and the Future',[6] and on 16 August she concluded: 'It is a good idea I think to write biographies; to make them use my powers of representation reality accuracy; & to use my novels simply to express the general, the poetic. Flush is serving this purpose.'[7] During these years Woolf was often thinking about poetry and prose and the relationship between them. In the *Arcadia* Sidney 'bethinks himself, one must not use the common words of daily speech'; and 'it is not to be denied that two of the novelists who are most frequently poetical – Meredith and Hardy – are as novelists imperfect'. It is not by chance that the last section of 'Phases of Fiction' deals with 'The Poets'. If 'time to come lies far beyond our province', nevertheless the 'poet is always our contemporary'.[8] No wonder, when Woolf read *Aurora Leigh* 'with great interest for the first time the other day',[9] she wanted to write about it. Elizabeth Barrett Browning's attempt to put daily life into poetry was not so different from Woolf's attempt to poeticise the novel. In her essay on *Aurora Leigh* she throws down the gauntlet for her own experiment. *The Waves* takes it up and confutes her own conclusion at the end of that essay: 'We have no novel-poem of the age of George the Fifth.'

In this volume we also see evidence of Woolf's feminist preoccupations. 'Women and Fiction' leading to *A Room of One's Own* and 'Women and Leisure' all appeared in 1929. Even if the women were not from her own class, writing 'Memories of a Working Women's Guild' (and its revisions) reminded her in 1930 of the discrimination against and the subjection of women. Then on 29 January 1931: 'I have this moment, while having my bath, conceived an entire new book – a sequel to a Room of Ones Own – about the sexual life of women: to be called Professions for Women perhaps – Lord how exciting! This sprang out of my paper to be read on Wednesday to Pippa's society . . . I'm very much excited.'[10] This would occupy her for a number of years and develop into *The Years* (1937) and *Three Guineas* (1938).

Virginia Woolf wrote essays primarily as a relief from fiction and as a means of making money:

Writing articles is like tying one's brain up in neat brown paper parcels. O to fly free in fiction once more! – and then I shall cry, O to tie parcels once more! – Such is life – a see-saw – a switch back.[11]

This last half year I made over £1800; almost at the rate of £4000 a year; the salary almost of a Cabinet minister; & time was, two years ago, when I toiled to make £200. Now I am overpaid I think for my little articles ... Well, after tomorrow I shall close down article writing, & give way to fiction for six or seven months – till next March perhaps.[12]

Above all, Woolf had to keep writing: 'The only way I keep afloat is by working. A note for the summer I must take more work than I can possibly get done. <I am> – no, I dont know what it comes from. Directly I stop working I feel that I am sinking down, down.' Referring to taking on too much work, she added in the margin of her diary two months later: 'This vow I kept'.[13]

This volume and its predecessor contain the two pillars of Virginia Woolf's essays: her two *Common Reader* volumes of 1925 and 1932. Because of the duplication and revision of essays previously published, Volumes IV and V are misleading if looked at superficially. 'Phases of Fiction' and the postcard on George Eliot in this volume, for example, can hardly be equated. Suffice it to say that Volumes IV and V, each covering a four-year period in Woolf's working life, comprise a significant amount of work. And neither can the amount of work involved in the revisions be underestimated: 'Why did I ever say I would produce another volume of Common Reader? It will take me week after week, month after month. However a year spent ... in reading through English literature will no doubt do good to my fictitious brain. Rest it anyhow. One day, all of a rush, fiction will burst in.'[14] Yet only four of the essays in *The Common Reader: Second Series* were written especially for that volume, while the remaining twenty-two were revised to a greater or lesser extent. Woolf was trying to bring imagination and cohesion to a disparate collection, unified only by her approach and personality. We can see from her revisions increasing cross-references between the essays, and this is most significant in the much-revised final essay, 'How Should One Read a Book?': 'the CR I confess is not yet quite done. But then – well I had to re-write the last article, which I had thought so good, entirely. Not for many years shall I collect another bunch of articles'.[15] Georgia Johnston remarks about *The Common Reader* that when 'we read the volume as a whole, circularly, the last essay, "How It Strikes a Contemporary," informs the first, "The Common Reader," as if Woolf had conceived of the volume as a loop'.[16] Beth Rigel Daugherty develops this insight: 'When Woolf adds *The Second Common Reader* to her first, she enlarges the loop, seeing the *two* volumes as a whole.'[17] Nevertheless, Woolf remained dissatisfied:

I am working very hard – in my way, to furbish up 2 long Elizabethan articles to front a new Common Reader: then I must go through the whole long list of those articles. I feel too, at the back of my brain, that I can devise a new critical method; something far less stiff & formal than these Times articles. But I must keep to the old style in this volume. And how, I wonder, could I do it? There must be some simpler, subtler, closer means of writing about books, as about people, could I hit upon it.[18]

The Common Reader: Second Series was published by the Hogarth Press on 13 October 1932 and as *The Second Common Reader* by Harcourt, Brace on 27 October 1932. Reviews were almost universally favourable.[19]

The *Times Literary Supplement*, as with a number of the reviews, considered Winifred Holtby's *Virginia Woolf* together with *The Common Reader: Second Series*, and this offered an opportunity to look back at Woolf's achievements in fiction as well as at her essays. Naturally, those 'who enjoyed Mrs Woolf's first series, or the other essays which have appeared in these columns and are reprinted here, will renew their enjoyment'. Or, as the editor, Bruce Richmond put it: 'I was constantly purring and saying "Ha ha! This first appeared in the Supplement".' The *TLS* chose 'Dr Burney's Evening Party' as the 'gem' of the collection.[20]

The Times itself saw Woolf as 'a novelist deliberately using her creative imagination' and praised her for 'conduct[ing] us not into the classroom but out of it',[21] with particular reference to 'The Strange Elizabethans'. E. J. Scovell in the *New Statesman and Nation* stated that 'most readers . . . will be enchanted by [the essays], whether or not they have read what she is writing about' and perceptively noted that Woolf regretted 'the limiting nature of fact, the impossibility of knowing the truth about it'.[22] Dilys Powell in the *Sunday Times* found 'in these essays an extraordinary insight into the creative mind; and . . . a series of brilliant pictures of the characters'.[23] Gerald Bullett in the *Week-end Review* considered Woolf's potted biographies to be 'her best and most characteristic' essays. He noted that she did not confuse biography with criticism: 'She does not ask us to read the novels of Geraldine Jewsbury: Geraldine is worth attention for her own sake.'[24]

Vita Sackville-West in the *Listener* strongly recommended the book, comforting her readers (and those who listened in to her talk on the BBC) that, 'although you may have found difficulty in following some of Mrs. Woolf's novels, I assure you that you will find no difficulty at all in following her critical essays. They are wholly delightful. They are sensitive, acute, picturesque, humorous, and yet severe.'[25] Basil de Selincourt in the *Observer* took a similar view but expressed it more wittily, while taking a swipe at 'a disposition at the back of our minds to believe that criticism must be scientific'.[26]

Stephen Spender in the *Criterion* thought that 'what interests her chiefly is the artist's development, rather than the actual word' and that she 'feels her dead historic characters protest that they are alive'. He concluded: 'it is not often in this book that we are aware of an effect that is too deliberate, and even when we are so aware, it is an effect of which we do not tire'.[27]

John Sparrow in the *Spectator* wondered what was Woolf's secret of success, and answered himself: 'she writes vividly because she reads vividly'. He was one of the few reviewers to single out for praise 'How Should One Read a Book?',[28] although Theodora Bosanquet in *Time and Tide*, noting that it was 'a paper read at a school', commented 'fortunate school'.[29] Roger Pippett in the *Daily Herald* chose 'George Gissing': 'A miraculous achievement! And an everyday occurrence with Mrs. Woolf! You ignore such an exciting writer at your peril.'[30] And Rebecca West in the *Daily Telegraph* alighted on '*Robinson Crusoe*': 'Is there anybody writing anywhere in the world at this moment who could surpass the essay . . . so beautifully moulded into a form appropriate to its content that what is an authentic critical masterpiece seems as light on the mind as a song?'[31]

Yvonne ffrench gushed in the *London Mercury*: 'the apotheosis of Mrs. Woolf as an essayist has begun' with these 'flawless' essays. She considered that, unlike the first series, this time Woolf had 'followed a definite plan'.[32] By contrast, Denys Thompson in *Scrutiny* thought that '*The Common Reader: First Series* was a contribution to criticism and the *Second Series* is not', because 'an interest in amiable eccentrics has become almost exclusive'.[33] Perversely, Geoffrey Grigson in the London *Bookman* linked Woolf to Felicia Hemans. Surprisingly, he also connected her with Sir Henry Newbolt: 'you find unending curiosity, continual liveliness, but the same absence of thought (to be inquisitive is not to be thoughtful), the same urbanity, the same good taste'.[34]

On the other side of the Atlantic, there was the same enthusiasm. In the *New York Times* of 13 November 1932 the review, entitled 'Mrs. Woolf Uncommon Reader', by Percy Hutchinson was extremely laudatory. It began by describing VW as '[a]mong the foremost stylists of the present day', commented that Woolf's 'deserved reputation is enhanced by the second of these collections' – as for '"I am Christina Rossetti"', 'what felicity of phrasing! What absolute exactness in discovering and characterizing the distinguishing note!' – and concluded: 'In all ways . . . does Virginia Woolf become as nearly perfect as Heaven grants it to the critic to be, for while the wisest of guides and the most felicitous of writers, she makes no effort to usurp our judgments . . .'[35] Horace Gregory placed the book and Virginia Woolf ('one of the great writers of our time') in a world 'after a great war': her 'immediate purpose is not critical; the purpose is to make the [literary] tradition come alive, to select all that remains vital in our inheritance'.[36] V. S. Pritchett in the *Christian Science Monitor* thought 'Geraldine and Jane' was 'a masterpiece', 'The Niece of an Earl' was 'a most amusing piece', while as a writer himself, although he considered it 'a counsel of perfection [in 'How Should One Read a Book?'] to say that reading must be an act of equipped coöperation between reader and author', he endorsed Woolf's view as 'an axiom of criticism'.[37] William J. Gorman in the *New Republic* compared Woolf with Edmund Gosse, to the latter's disadvantage: the book 'is refined, but not sallow, eclectic but not mediocre'.[38] Typically, Gerald Sykes in the New York *Nation* was one of the few to equivocate. He concluded: 'Her polished, amiable book offers fireside pleasures which in this rude day the most apostolic opponent of archaism cannot altogether resist.'[39]

Some of the reviewers noted that in the second *Common Reader* there was no equivalent of 'How It Strikes a Contemporary' which concluded the first *Common Reader*. Indeed, if we look through the whole of this volume we find few contemporary writers. Her mind, Woolf wrote, 'over which I have little control, is leading me away from contemporary life in the direction of the Elizabethans'.[40] Even in 1932 Augustine Birrell, Edmund Gosse and Thomas Hardy were figures from the past. The review of André Maurois' *Climats* (1928) in 'On Not Knowing French' was perhaps an anomaly. Only 'A Letter to a Young Poet' deals with contemporary English writing, but it would lead on to 'The Leaning Tower' in 1940 (see *VI VW Essays*). Similarly, there are fewer 'lives of the obscure' than in previous volumes. The two obvious exceptions are 'Jack Mytton' and the two parsons, James Woodforde and John Skinner. The Rev. William Cole (the subject of two essays) was also obscure, but he was the friend of Horace Walpole, and both would be revisited at the end of the 1930s with 'Two Antiquaries: Walpole and Cole' and 'The Humane Art' (see *VI VW Essays*). Genuinely obscure were the women of the Women's Co-operative Guild and, if Woolf admitted that perhaps her approach to her introduction to *Life as We Have Known It* had been too literary,[41] the terrible sufferings and privations that they had undergone would remain with her and inform her political views in the years to come: 'Some horror become visible: but in human form... What a system.'[42] Woolf's criticism of the social system in this volume will principally be found in 'The "Censorship" of Books' and in the six 'London Scene' essays in a subtly muted form suitable for the readers of *Good Housekeeping*.

According to Woolf, there was a special reason for collecting and revising essays for inclusion in a book: 'I must go on with the C. Reader – for one thing, by way of proving my credentials.'[43] There were, however, at least two issues with her 'credentials'. On the one hand there was the problem of the imaginative handling of facts, the 'granite and rainbow'[44] of biographical criticism. Her view may be symbolised by her comment to Margaret Llewelyn Davies about her revisions to the draft of the introductory letter to *Life as We Have Known It*: 'I brought in a few cigarettes in Lilians ash tray – do they matter? A little blue cloud of smoke seemed to me aesthetically desirable at that point.'[45] In a letter of 24 January 1924 to Edmund Blunden about George Dyer (the friend of Charles Lamb), she wrote: 'What I said in my article is, I think, substantially true; but I may have arranged it a little, to suit my purpose.'[46] Similarly, Woolf's attitude to errors of fact was often cavalier. In *A Room of One's Own*, Lady Stephen's *Life of Miss Emily Davies* was corrected to *Emily Davies and Girton College* from the fourth Hogarth Press impression onwards.[47] It was never corrected in America. Again, when Donald Brace informed her that a 'woman writes us from Los Angeles, California, to complain that... the correct title of Mrs. Greville's poem is "A Prayer for Indifference." She says it is not an "Ode" at all. If you would like a correction made here, will you let me know?',[48] there seems to have been no response. When Woolf broadcast on the

BBC that after 16 May 1816 Beau Brummell 'never set foot in England again', Berry the wine merchants wrote in to contradict her. Instead of altering her essay when she revised it for *The Common Reader: Second Series*, she appended a note at the end. Following the publication of 'Geraldine and Jane' in the *Times Literary Supplement*, several correspondents wrote in, praising the essay but supplying additional information about Geraldine Jewsbury.[49] When the essay was revised for *The Common Reader: Second Series*, this sentence remained unchanged: 'Until she was twenty-nine we know nothing of her except that she was born in the year 1812, was the daughter of a merchant, and lived in Manchester, or near it.' Most egregious of all were the minor errors in 'George Gissing', the subject of a kind of one-sided running battle with Gissing's son.[50] This was one of Woolf's most revised essays, yet the errors were never corrected.

Here we may consider in passing the distinct impression that Woolf gives of a comparative indifference to her American readers: 'I always write things twice over, and let the Americans, who are in a hurry, have the first version.'[51] What she says is literally true – there was no direct airmail service between Britain and the United States until 1939 – but in actual fact Woolf never stopped revising. For example, she published 'Dr Burney's Evening Party' in the *New York Herald Tribune* in July 1929, revised it for Desmond MacCarthy's *Life and Letters* in September, and would revise it yet again for *The Common Reader: Second Series*. Meanwhile, her American publishers wanted to include it in an anthology that they published in 1931, and for this they used the *Life and Letters* revision which seems to indicate that Woolf was conscious of her transatlantic audience and her own reputation there. Incidentally, the essay was introduced thus:

Virginia Woolf possesses a surprising variety of styles. Each new book is different from those that have gone before; we behold with some astonishment the same author's name on the title page of *Jacob's Room*, *The Voyage Out*, *A Room of One's Own*, and *Orlando*. The reader decides that he may classify her as an experimental writer, and then, picking up a recent magazine, discover that she has performed a fine bit of antiquarian reconstruction in 'Doctor Burney's Evening Party.' . . .[52]

As indicated above, Virginia Woolf's most revised essay in this volume is 'George Gissing': its first version appeared in the *New Republic* on 2 March 1927 and with variations in the *Nation &*

Athenæum on 26 February. It was revised as the introduction to *Selections Autobiographical and Imaginative from the Works of George Gissing*, published on 11 September 1929 by Jonathan Cape, and then was revised again for *The Common Reader: Second Series*. Finally, it appeared as the introduction to Gissing's *By the Ionian Sea*, which was published by Cape on 6 March 1933. She wrote to Cape on 18 October 1932 about her introduction to *By the Ionian Sea*: 'I would suggest that you should print from the version just issued in the second series of my Common Reader. I have altered it to a certain extent. I do not think that I could alter it any further.'[53] Nonetheless, when she returned the proofs to Cape's office on 25 November 1932 she had made a few more revisions.

Another issue was Woolf's fear of professionalism. She insisted to Donald Brace, her American publisher, that 'one might describe' *The Common Reader: Second Series* 'as an unprofessional book of criticism',[54] and the phrase, 'unprofessional criticism', appeared as part of the blurb on the Hogarth Press dust-jacket. She must have agreed with Tolstoy:

The following are the chief obstacles which hinder even very remarkable men from creating true works of art: first, professionalism – that is, a man ceases to be a man, but becomes a poet, a painter, and does nothing but write books, compose music, or paint pictures; wastes his gift on trifles and loses the power of judging his work critically. The second, also a very serious obstacle, is the school. You can't teach art, as you cannot teach a man to be a saint. True art is always original and new, and has no need of preconceived models. The third obstacle, finally, is criticism, which, as some one has justly said, is made up of fools' ideas about wise men.[55]

This reluctance to be professional is not just modesty, but a belief in the importance of the partnership between the reader and the writer.[56] At this time the modern university-trained professional literary critics as we know them today were beginning to emerge. Woolf resisted this development. As she concluded in 'All about Books': 'The time has come to open *Scrutinies* and begin to read – no, the time has come to rake out the cinders and go to bed.' Her own criticism was different. Hermione Lee points out that, as 'a pioneer of reader-response theory, Virginia Woolf was extremely interested in the two-way dialogue between readers and writers'.[57] Woolf's criticism was democratic, as we see in 'How Should One Read a Book?' in particular, and the reviewers' reactions to this essay are often revealing. While we shall observe in Volume VI an increasing emphasis on democracy not only in literature but in life, it is enough to end here with her comments on Hazlitt that apply so appropriately to her own essays: 'if such criticism is the reverse of final, if it is initiatory and inspiring rather than conclusive and complete, there is something to be said for the critic who starts the reader on a journey and fires him with a phrase to shoot off on adventures of his own'.[58]

1 – IV VW *Letters*, no. 2215, 2 August [1930], to Ethel Smyth. And see V VW *Letters*, no. 2628, 6 September [1932], to Ottoline Morrell: 'That is why one gets so sick of essay writing. I feel sticky all over when I've done, measuring, fitting and using glue.'
2 – See p. 84, n. 1, below and Appendix II for a discrete section.
3 – IV VW *Diary*, 7 August 1931; and see Berg, M 13.
4 – *Ibid.*, 3 January 1933.
5 – William Empson, 'Virginia Woolf', in *Scrutinies*, compiled by Edgell Rickwood (Wishart, 1931), p. 207; reprinted in *M&M*, p. 303.
6 – See IV VW *Diary* and IV VW *Essays*.
7 – IV VW *Diary*.
8 – 'The Countess of Pembroke's Arcadia', 'Phases of Fiction', 'How Should One Read a Book?'
9 – IV VW *Letters*, no. 2340, 25 March 1931, to Helen McAfee.
10 – IV VW *Diary*; and see Appendix V.
11 – IV VW *Letters*, no. 2346, 9 April 1931, to Ethel Smyth.
12 – III VW *Diary*, 30 June 1929; and see Appendix VIII below and WSU. Cf. VW's resolution on 2 January 1931 to 'care nothing for making money' (IV VW *Diary*): only five new essays were published in 1931.
13 – III VW *Diary*, 23 June 1929. 'I am' was cancelled by VW.
14 – IV VW *Diary*, 8 February 1932.
15 – *Ibid.*, 6 July 1932.
16 – Georgia Johnston, 'The Whole Achievement in Virginia Woolf's *The Common Reader*', in *Essays on the Essay: Redefining the Genre*, ed. Alexander J. Butrym (University of Georgia Press, 1989), p. 153.
17 – Beth Rigel Daugherty, 'Readin', Writin', and Revisin': Virginia Woolf's "How Should One Read a Book?"', in *Virginia Woolf and the Essay*, ed. Beth Carole Rosenberg and Jeanne Dubino (Macmillan, 1997), p. 173, n. 4.
18 – IV VW *Diary*, 16 November 1931.
19 – In addition to those cited below, see also the following briefer reviews: 'Virginia Woolf', *Glasgow Herald*, 20 October 1932, p. 4; 'Bloomsbury Unbends', *Punch*, 26 October 1932, p. 474; Peter Renny, 'Unprofessional Criticism', *Empire Review*, November 1932, pp. 303–4; *Booklist* (Chicago),

vol. xxix (December 1932), p. 109; *Forum* (New York), December 1932, p. ix; H. V. Routh, 'The Nineteenth Century and After', *Year's Work in English Studies*, vol. xiii (1932), at p. 307; Jack Isaacs, 'Literature', *Annual Register* (1932), part ii, at p. 11; Samuel C. Chew, *Yale Review*, vol. xxii (Winter 1933), p. 390; Herschel Brickell, *North American Review*, vol. ccxxxv (January 1933), p. 95. The *Book Review Digest* (1932), pp. 1046–8, includes excerpts from numerous reviews. *M&M* do not include any reviews of *CR2*.

20 – A. S. McDowall (unsigned), 'The Method of Mrs. Woolf', *TLS*, 20 October 1932, p. 755. Winifred Holtby, *Virginia Woolf* (Wishart, 1932). Bruce Richmond to VW, n.d. [1925?] (MHP, III, Box Nash–Rylands).

21 – 'A Portrait Gallery', *The Times*, 28 October 1932, p. 17, col. e.

22 – E. J. Scovell, 'Virginia Woolf, Critic', *NS&N*, 15 October 1932, pp. 454, 456.

23 – Dilys Powell, 'Virginia Woolf', *Sunday Times*, 16 October 1932, p. 12; reprinted in *Virginia Woolf: Critical Assessments*, ed. Eleanor McNees (Helm Information, 1994), vol. ii, pp. 93–4.

24 – Gerald Bullett, 'Mrs. Woolf's Essays', *Week-end Review*, 5 November 1932, p. 548.

25 – V. Sackville-West, 'Books of the Week', *Listener*, 26 October 1932, p. 610; and see *V VW Letters*, 18 [October 1932], no. 2645, to V. Sackville-West.

26 – Basil de Selincourt, 'Disinterested Criticism', *Observer*, 23 October 1932, p. 8.

27 – Stephen Spender, *Criterion*, vol. xii (April 1933), pp. 522–4.

28 – John Sparrow, 'The Common Reader', *Spectator*, 4 November 1932, pp. 634, 636. Another critic who saw the key to Woolf's approach in 'How Should One Read a Book?' was Ælfric Manson in the *Dublin Review*, July 1933, pp. 135–7.

29 – Theodora Bosanquet, 'Virginia Woolf's Reality', *Time and Tide*, 15 October 1932, pp. 1111–12.

30 – Roger Pippett, 'Books You Should Read: Who Will Write Our Great Story?', *Daily Herald*, 13 October 1932, p. 13.

31 – Rebecca West, 'A Human Problem Eight Centuries Old', *Daily Telegraph*, 4 November 1932, p. 6.

32 – Yvonne ffrench, 'Belles-Lettres', *London Mercury*, vol. xxvii (December 1932), pp. 173–4.

33 – Denys Thompson, *Scrutiny*, vol. i, no. 3 (1932–3), pp. 288–9; reprinted in *Virginia Woolf: Critical Assessments*, vol. ii, pp. 95–6; he particularly objected to 'How Should One Read a Book?', especially as the 'advice was given to a school'. By the end of 1933, 'Mrs. Woolf's latest phase' had become a 'deterioration and collapse': see T. R. Barnes, 'Lytton Strachey', *Scrutiny*, vol. ii (December 1933), pp. 301–3, at p. 303.

34 – Geoffrey Grigson (1905–85), 'Sir Henry Newbolt and Mrs. Woolf',

Bookman, November 1932, pp. 121–2. Presumably, Wyndham Lewis was referring to Grigson when he wrote about VW in his letter to the *Spectator*, 2 November 1934, p. 675: 'here we *have* not a Jane Austen – a Felicia Hemans, rather, as it has been said; for there are some even more "malicious" than I am, I am afraid'; reprinted in *M&M*, p. 342.

35 – P. H. [Percy Hutchinson], 'Mrs. Woolf, Uncommon Reader', *New York Times*, 13 November 1932, sec. v, p. 2.

36 – Horace Gregory, 'In a Room of Her Own', *New York Herald Tribune*, 30 October 1932, Books sec. x, pp. 1–2.

37 – V. S. P. [V. S. Pritchett], '"Becoming" an Author', *Christian Science Monitor*, 3 December 1932, p. 7.

38 – William J. Gorman, 'An Uncommon Sensibility', *NR*, 8 February 1933, p. 357.

39 – Gerald Sykes, 'Ex-Modernist', *Nation*, 4 January 1933, p. 25; reprinted in *Virginia Woolf: Critical Assessments*, vol. ii, pp. 97–8. Cf. his wholly negative review of *The Waves*: 'Modernism', *Nation*, 16 December 1931, pp. 674–5; reprinted in *Virginia Woolf: Critical Assessments*, vol. iv, pp. 10–11, and in *M&M*, pp. 284–6.

40 – *IV VW Letters*, no. 2399, 2 July 1931, to Helen McAfee.

41 – See *ibid.*, no. 2322, 1 February [1931], to Margaret Llewelyn Davies.

42 – *V VW Diary*, 20 March 1936.

43 – *IV VW Diary*, 16 February 1932.

44 – 'The New Biography', *IV VW Essays*; and see *O*, ch. ii, p. 73, and *O Holograph*, MS 58.

45 – *IV VW Letters*, no. 2322, 1 February 1931.

46 – Uncollected letter in *VWB*, no. 26 (September 2007), p. 5; and see *IV VW Essays*, p. 121.

47 – *Room*, ch. i, p. 31, n. 1.

48 – Letter of 24 February 1933 (LWP Ad. 18) about 'Dr Burney's Evening Party'.

49 – See letters from O. H. T. Dudley, Edith J. Morley, Ella Hepworth Dixon and W. H. Hutton, *TLS*, 7 March 1929, p. 185, and from E. H. Woodruff, *TLS*, 4 April 1929, p. 276.

50 – See pp. 541–3 below.

51 – *IV VW Letters*, no. 2212, [27 July 1930], to Margaret Llewelyn Davies.

52 – Robert Silliman Hillyer *et al.*, *Prose Masterpieces of English and American Literature* (Harcourt, Brace, 1931), p. 444. VW was paid £4 for the reprint.

53 – *V VW Letters*, no. 2646.

54 – Letter of 5 November 1931 (copy in LWP Ad. 18); quoted in *The Second Common Reader* (Pelican Books, no. A132, Penguin Books, 1944), p. [2]; and see p. 333 below.

55 – Quoted in A. B. Goldenveizer, 'Talks with Tolstoi', 2 August 1897, in *Translations from the Russian*, by Virginia Woolf and S. S. Koteliansky (Virginia Woolf Society of Great Britain, 2006), pp. 194–5.

56 – See Katerina Koutsantoni, 'Issues of Authority and Authoritarianism in *The Common Reader: Second Series*', VWB, no. 17 (September 2004), pp. 35–43.

57 – Hermione Lee, 'Virginia Woolf's Essays', in *The Cambridge Companion to Virginia Woolf*, ed. Sue Roe and Susan Sellers (Cambridge University Press, 2000), p. 91.

58 – 'William Hazlitt', *CR2* below.

Editorial Note

The present volume is compiled upon the principles already established for the edition. Of the fifty-nine pieces it includes (excluding the appendices), twenty-six make up *The Common Reader: Second Series*, published by the Hogarth Press on 13 October 1932; and seven are earlier versions of essays appearing therein; of the remaining twenty-six ('Memories of a Working Women's Guild' and 'Introductory Letter to Margaret Llewelyn Davies' are counted as two essays), three are reprinted for the first time. Variants are provided here from articles (signalled by headnotes in Volume IV) which were included in *The Common Reader: Second Series* with relatively little revision – this view proved to be over-optimistic in the case of 'George Gissing' (see Appendix I). Headnotes are similarly given in this volume for two 1929 essays revised for inclusion in *The Common Reader: Second Series*.

The question of variants also arises in the case of those essays that found publication on both sides of the Atlantic (see Appendix VIII). This issue is discussed in the Introduction, but an article (such as 'Dorothy Wordsworth') that appeared more or less simultaneously in the UK and the USA and then in *The Common Reader: Second Series* usually has three versions, and it is clear that the US predates the UK version. Accordingly, it has often been found practicable and necessary to print the US version in its chronological place, while the UK periodical version, which formed the basis of *The Common Reader: Second Series* revision, appears as footnotes in *The Common Reader: Second Series*. Endnotes are only provided on the first appearance of an essay, unless new material occurs in the later version. It is intended to include a separate index in Volume VI to all the essays in the edition, and this will help in tracking down these different versions.

As in the previous volumes the contents follow the listing in Section C of the late B. J. Kirkpatrick's bibliography (4th ed., 1997), with the insertion of the following: 'Foreword to *Recent Paintings by Vanessa Bell*' (p. 137); 'On Being Ill' (p. 195); 'Introductory Letter to Margaret Llewelyn Davies' (p. 225); the postcard, 'George Eliot, 1819–1880' (p. 247); and 'The Love of Reading' (p. 271).

Every effort has been made, using Woolf's manuscript reading notes, to trace references to sources in the editions Woolf used, or at the very least in the editions the Woolfs owned. A great deal is known on this subject thanks to the labours of Brenda Silver, Elizabeth Steele and Andrew McNeillie, but a number of mysteries remain. In a very few cases it has been impossible to discover the work from which a quotation derives, let alone the relevant edition, and these failures are acknowledged in the notes.

Manuscript drafts of a number of articles survive and, where these have been identified, they have been listed under the essays to which they refer.

The following general changes to the text have usually been made throughout: double quotation marks have been changed to single, and *vice versa*; the full stops after Dr, Messrs, Mr, Mrs, and St have been omitted, except in quotations; M-dashes changed to spaced N-dashes; American spellings have been changed to British; book-titles have been italicised; and words ending in -ize changed to -ise. However, the question of regularising quotations inside or outside punctuation has not been addressed. It is debatable whether articles in journals have been treated with too much or too little respect, as errors (e.g. 'Middlesborough') have usually been allowed to stand. In dealing with quotations made by Woolf, significant discrepancies are drawn attention to in the notes, but errors of punctuation have usually been ignored. Particular care has been taken with the text of 'On Being Ill' and the 'Introductory Letter to Margaret Llewelyn Davies', as both were published by the Woolfs' Hogarth Press. The former was one of the last of their hand-printed books, but as will be seen that was no guarantee of complete perfection. A more stringent practice has been employed with *The Common Reader: Second Series*. No specific changes have been made to the text, except those listed in Appendix VII. Here again, significant discrepancies in the quotations are drawn attention to in the notes.

Acknowledgements

First of all, I wish to thank Andrew McNeillie for agreeing to pass the last third of his task over to me in the middle of 2006, when it became clear that he would not have time to complete Volumes V and VI of *The Essays of Virginia Woolf* in the following few years. He also handed over his photocopies of Virginia Woolf's articles; having added them to my collection, I have hardly had to photocopy any source material in preparing this volume. He very generously offered to let me use the annotations in his *The Common Reader: Second Series* (Hogarth Press, 1986), and I have greatly (and very gratefully) depended on these as the basis for my notes. Other debts of this nature will be found listed in the Abbreviations and the Bibliography.

Secondly, I thank Anne Olivier Bell, the Society of Authors (Jeremy Crow) as the Literary Representative of the Estate of Virginia Woolf, and the Hogarth Press (Random House UK: Alison Samuel, Poppy Hampson) for entrusting me with this task. Copy-editor Lindeth Vasey undoubtedly improved my draft. I also thank the Society of Authors as the Literary Representative of the Estate of Vanessa Bell for permission to print an extract from an unpublished letter and the University of Sussex and the Society of Authors as the Literary Representative of the Estate of Leonard Woolf for permission to reprint the article in Appendix IV.

No one has spent more time helping me than my partner, Brian Evans. I recorded *The Common Reader: Second Series* onto cassette tapes, so that I could check the various texts of the book (see Appendix VII), but Brian read article after article aloud to me as I checked the many different versions that were published by Woolf.

Stephen Barkway read the computer print-out of the whole book, and made a number of helpful suggestions and criticisms – including suggestions for improving the Introduction – for which I am extremely grateful.

Karen V. Kukil of the Mortimer Rare Book Room, William Allan Neilson Library, Smith College, has generously provided me with photocopies of articles and manuscripts and has been generally supportive.

The late Julia Briggs lent me microfilms, and I also benefited from discussions with her.

Roger Phillips told me about the London Borough of Camden's Virtual Library, and this saved me a lot of work by enabling me to access from home the *DNB, ODNB, OED, The Times Digital Archive* and the *TLS Centenary Archive*.

I also owe thanks to Aileen Christianson, Vanessa Curtis, Mary Ellen Foley, Diane F. Gillespie, Sarah M. Hall, Brenda Helt (and, through her, to Andrew Elfenbein), Julia Paolitto, David Philps, Jane Roberts, Sheila M. Wilkinson and Henry Woudhuysen.

I am also grateful to the following institutions: Harry Ransom Humanities Research Center, University of Texas at Austin; Houghton Library (Denison J. Beach), Harvard University; Manuscripts, Archives and Special Collections, Washington State University Libraries; and Rare Books Department (Nicholas Smith), Cambridge University Library.

I wish to acknowledge the resources of the British Library (especially at St Pancras but also at Colindale), the periodicals department at London University Library, Special Collections at Sussex University Library and the Library Archives (Archives of The Hogarth Press, MS 2750) of the University of Reading.

It is clear from the photocopies I have inherited that I must also thank Elizabeth Inglis for her help prior to her retirement from Sussex University Library. There are bound to be others who assisted Andrew McNeillie, and to them I apologise for the *lacunae*.

Abbreviations

Berg	Henry W. and Albert A. Berg Collection, New York Public Library
CDB	*The Captain's Death Bed and Other Essays*, ed. Leonard Woolf (Hogarth Press, London, 1950; Harcourt Brace Jovanovich, New York, 1950)
CDML	*The Crowded Dance of Modern Life, Selected Essays: Volume Two*, ed. Rachel Bowlby (Penguin Books, London, 1993)
CE	*Collected Essays*, ed. Leonard Woolf (4 vols, vols 1–2, Hogarth Press, London, 1966, Harcourt Brace & World Inc., New York, 1967; vols 3–4, Hogarth Press, London, and Harcourt Brace & World Inc., New York, 1967)
CR	*The Common Reader*: 1st series (Hogarth Press, London, and Harcourt Brace & Co., New York, 1925; annotated edition by Andrew McNeillie, 1984); 2nd series (Hogarth Press, London, and Harcourt Brace & Co., New York, 1932; annotated edition by Andrew McNeillie, 1986)
CSF	*The Complete Shorter Fiction*, ed. Susan Dick (Hogarth Press, London, and Harcourt Brace Jovanovich, New York, 1985)
DNB	*Dictionary of National Biography*
DoM	*The Death of the Moth and Other Essays*, ed. Leonard Woolf (Hogarth Press, London, and Harcourt Brace & Co., New York, 1942)
G&R	*Granite and Rainbow*, ed. Leonard Woolf (Hogarth Press, London, and Harcourt Brace & Co., New York, 1958)

Kp4	B. J. Kirkpatrick and Stuart N. Clarke, *A Bibliography of Virginia Woolf* (4th ed., Clarendon Press, Oxford, 1997)
L&L	*Life and Letters*
LSc	*The London Scene* (Frank Hallman, New York, 1975; Hogarth Press, London, and Random House, New York, 1982; Snowbooks, London, n.d. [2004]; Ecco [HarperCollins], New York, n.d. [2006])
LW	Leonard Woolf
LWP	Leonard Woolf Papers, Sussex University Library
M&M	*Virginia Woolf: The Critical Heritage*, ed. Robin Majumdar and Allen McLaurin (Routledge & Kegan Paul, London, 1975)
MHP	Monks House Papers, Sussex University Library
MoB	*Moments of Being*, ed. Jeanne Schulkind (2nd ed., Hogarth Press, London, and Harcourt Brace Jovanovich, New York, 1985)
Mom	*The Moment and Other Essays*, ed. Leonard Woolf (Hogarth Press, London, 1947; Harcourt Brace & Co., New York, 1948)
N&A	*Nation and Athenaeum*
NR	*New Republic*
NS&N	*New Statesman and Nation*
NYHT	*New York Herald Tribune*
O	*Orlando: A Biography* (Hogarth Press, London, 1928)
O Holograph	*Orlando: The Original Holograph Draft*, ed. Stuart Nelson Clarke (S. N. Clarke, London, 1993)
OBEV	*The Oxford Book of English Verse, 1250–1900*, ed. Arthur Quiller-Couch (Clarendon Press, Oxford, 1900)
ODNB	*Oxford Dictionary of National Biography*
OED	*Oxford English Dictionary*
PA	*A Passionate Apprentice: The Early Journals, 1897–1909*, ed. Mitchell A. Leaska (Hogarth Press, London, and Harcourt Brace Jovanovich, New York, 1990)
Room	*A Room of One's Own* (Hogarth Press, London, 1929)
TLS	*Times Literary Supplement*
VW	Virginia Woolf
VW Diary	*The Diary of Virginia Woolf*, ed. Anne Olivier Bell (5 vols, Hogarth Press, London, and Harcourt Brace Jovanovich, New York, 1977–84)

VW Essays	*The Essays of Virginia Woolf*, 6 vols
VW Letters	*The Letters of Virginia Woolf*, ed. Nigel Nicolson and Joanne Trautmann (6 vols, Hogarth Press, London, and Harcourt Brace Jovanovich, New York, 1975–80)
VWB	*Virginia Woolf Bulletin*, Virginia Woolf Society of Great Britain
VWRN	Brenda R. Silver, *Virginia Woolf's Reading Notebooks*, (Princeton University Press, Princeton, 1983)
W&F	*Women & Fiction: The Manuscript Versions of 'A Room of One's Own'*, ed. S. P. Rosenbaum (Blackwell Publishers for the Shakespeare Head Press, Oxford, 1992)
W&W	*Women and Writing*, ed. Michèle Barrett (The Women's Press, London, 1979)
WE	*A Woman's Essays, Selected Essays: Volume One*, ed. Rachel Bowlby (Penguin Books, London, 1992)
WSA	*Woolf Studies Annual*
WSU	Virginia Woolf's account book of payments received July 1928–July 1937, Holland Library (MASC Cage 4661), Washington State University

The Essays

1929

On Not Knowing French

One scarcely dare say it, but it is true – nobody knows French but the French themselves. Every second Englishman reads French, and many speak it, and some write it, and there are a few who claim – and who shall deny them? – that it is the language of their dreams. But to know a language one must have forgotten it, and that is a stage that one cannot reach without having absorbed words unconsciously as a child. In reading a language that is not one's own, consciousness is awake, and keeps us aware of the surface glitter of the words; but it never suffers them to sink into that region of the mind where old habits and instincts roll them round and shape them a body rather different from their faces. Thus a foreigner with what is called a perfect command of English may write grammatical English and musical English – he will, indeed, like Henry James, often write a more elaborate English than the native – but never such unconscious English that we feel the past of the word in it, its associations, its attachments.[2] There is an oddity in every page that Conrad[3] wrote. Right in themselves, the words come together somehow incongruously.

Thus, though the number of French books read every year by English people is probably very large, their version of them, if submitted to the French critics, would often seem strangely out. In the same way, it is always amusing to see what takes the French taste in contemporary English literature, or to receive back from their critics some queer, a little lopsided version of English reputations, some brilliant but fantastic

3

vision of English character. The extreme vivacity of M. Maurois' lives of Shelley and Disraeli rose in part from the novelty with which he endowed them.[4] And this novelty was the more striking because there was perhaps a grain of truth that custom had overlaid.

It is novelty, and the strangeness, and the very fact that we are conscious and not unconscious that make the habit of reading French books so widely spread among the English; that make French literature so stimulating, so refreshing, so new to our minds. It is a delight, after mumbling over the old stories of our old memoirs in the familiar English atmosphere of joints and butlers and port and Parliament and Queen Victoria on the throne, to flash instantly into the brilliance of Mérimée and the court of Napoleon and the Empress Eugénie.[5] After trudging through muddy lanes and damp shrubberies we seem to tiptoe a little self-consciously upon polished floors under crystal chandeliers. And all our ramblings round and about this figure and that, as we pick our way through the ramifications of French memoirs, are full of surprises and excitements – of terrifying encounters with great ladies more severe than our own, of interviews with dukes and diplomats who seem (such is the prestige of the French) more pompous, more polite than our local nobility. Our ramblings lead us into *châteaux* that have much more than the formality of our country houses; into villages perched on hillsides with strange swift streams in the valleys and wild boar, or wolves perhaps, in the forests. The priest blesses the hounds. The hunt is different. The very foxes are different. The talk is of incredible distinction. With an awe that is absent from our visits to the court of Charles the Second under the guidance of Pepys, we find ourselves at Versailles waiting with the Duc de Saint Simon for the King to pass.[6] It is a formidable civilisation, more articulate, less homely than our own.

And if it is a delight to have a change of scene, it is also a delight to have a change of tongue. Habit has made English – the ordinary daily English of which most books are made – as colourless, as tasteless as water. French, even the French of daily use, has wine in it; it sparkles; it tingles; it has its savour. Here and there, in Saint Simon, for instance, a curious word, unknown and therefore uncoloured by habit, emerges, so that we can feel it and see it apart from the text, and wonder for a moment what sort of meaning we shall fill it with when we have looked it up in the dictionary. The sentence, too, takes a different curve. The old swing of the wrist, going up and down the page sowing phrases as mechanically as a man sowing seed, is altered.

It takes a spirited, unusual pace which makes us wake and attend. With all these advantages and a vocabulary of desirable words – how, for example, one longs to pilfer words like *amertume* and *pierreries*,[7] and there are a thousand others – the French, it would seem, can hardly fail to write better than the English.

That they do write better is an illusion perhaps, an illusion born of unfamiliarity and glamour, but it is an illusion that is always winning support. Take *Climats*, for example, the new novel by M. Maurois. It would be difficult to find a fellow to it in English. One cannot bring to mind at the moment any living English writer so intelligent, so dextrous, so accomplished as M. Maurois. There are, it is true, a dozen with more of one quality – imagination, perhaps, or originality – but the one quality overpowers the rest, so that the result is unequal. We race through half a dozen chapters at top speed; then we yawn. But in *Climats* the balance is so even, one gift comes so pat to the help of another, that we are supported evenly and lightly from end to end. The predominating quality is, no doubt, intelligence. The book is a study of a man and his relations with two women. In the first part the man gives his own version of his character and his relations with his wife; in the next the mirror is held up at a different angle by his second wife, and the two pictures join with all the neatness of expert carpentry – there is Philippe before us in the round. Nor is it simply as a piece of craftsmanship that the book is admirable. Look into those two pictures and one will find, more particularly in the first, things noticed, perceptions seized, and so subtle a use of suggestion that the presence of the first wife permeates the second part and thus bridges what might, with the change of persons, have been a break in the continuity. But it is over the intelligence that the English reader will ponder, for it is perhaps the rarest quality in our own fiction. Intelligence is not easy to define. It is not brilliance; nor is it intellectual power; it is perhaps the sense that the interest of life does not lie in what people do, nor even in their relations to each other, but largely in the power to communicate with a third party, antagonistic, enigmatic, yet perhaps persuadable, which one may call life in general. That is what makes the people in *Climats* so reasonable. Isabelle's words express this relationship. 'Ce que j'ai compris de très important, depuis un an, c'est que, si l'on aime vraiment, il ne faut pas attacher trop d'importance aux actions des êtres qu'on aime. Nous avons besoin d'eux; eux seuls nous font vivre dans une certaine "atmosphère" (votre amie Hélène dit "un climat" et c'est très juste) dont nous ne pouvons nous passer. Alors, pourvu que nous puissions les garder, les conserver, le reste, mon Dieu, qu'est-ce que cela peut faire? Cette vie est si courte, si difficile.'[8]

The French words, in their lucidity, in their intelligence, seem to break through our island mists and to lie before us serene in sunshine. Yet perhaps the quality which M. Maurois calls 'un idéalisme de magazine anglo-saxon'[9] is too stubborn to be persuaded out of existence so easily. Human beings are not reasonable to this extent; nor so exacting, nor so clear-sighted.

'En apparence, j'ai fait un métier. En fait, ma seule occupation a été de poursuivre un bonheur absolu que je croyais atteindre à travers les femmes et il n'y a pas de poursuite plus vaine.'[10] This conclusion, which is so aptly rounded by Philippe's death a few pages later, would have been disturbed, in nine out of ten English novels, by cheerfulness in some form or other breaking in – perhaps an idea, perhaps a sight – something, at any rate, that would have made a mess of the book and given scope for one or other of our English habits – the love of preaching, or the love of poetry.

But the word poetry reminds us of our precarious foothold in these parts. Just as one is secretly persuaded that no Frenchman, Russian, German,[11] has the instinct for English poetry in him – he can acquire everything but that – so confidence fails us when we try our wings in this particular form of flight. In reading poetry, it may be, one reads in phrases, running the words together, so that they must be malleable and flexible all through, whereas in prose each word is taken separately into the mind. The ear, too, collects a thousand hints and suggestions from one's own tongue which escape it in another. At any rate, in reading French prose even, it is curious how far out one finds one's self, looking for poetry where poetry is not, finding it absurdly where nothing of the sort was intended. It is enough for Odile to walk in Compiègne for the irrational belief to possess us that Compiègne is not like Richmond, reached by the electric train; it is a forest of infinite charm, in which flowers, earlier and more elegant than our homely violets and primroses, grow in clumps, like those in pictures. And then Odile has only to hold her grey fur to her throat to accentuate to our insular eyes the grace of the Latin, her elegance, her distinction. When we are thus susceptible, when influences and suggestions of this kind have such power over us, who can say how insidiously our critical sense may not be seduced and the object of criticism transformed? The French, we think, are wrong to attribute such importance to Byron and Poe.[12] Our verdicts have been arrived at, perhaps, by the same misunderstandings, and are just as false. But none the less we take our stand on it – *Climats* is an admirable piece of fiction.

1 – A signed review in the *New Republic*, 13 February 1929, (*Kp4* C308), of *Climats* (Bernard Grasset, 1928) by André Maurois (1885–1967). Maurois, Anglophile and man of letters, wrote a preface to the French translation of *Mrs Dalloway*, published in 1929 (*Kp4* D22), where he called VW 'un grand écrivain' and with approval quoted (translated into French) the now-famous passage from 'Modern Fiction', beginning 'Is life like this?' (see *IV VW Essays*, pp. 160–1). His biographies were influenced by Lytton Strachey's, as VW implied: see *ibid.*, p. 475.

In April 1924 VW could not 'swallow quick enough Ariel by [Ethel Sands's] friend Maurois' (*III VW Letters*, no. 1460). She read his *La Vie de Disraëli* in August 1927 (*ibid.*, nos 1793, 1806). At the end of December 1928 she was 'reading M: Maurois for an article, which . . . will be printed in England France and America, simultaneously' (*ibid.*, no. 1976). It was not published in the UK, but a French translation appeared in *Le Figaro* on 10 February 1929 (*Kp4* D50). In a letter dated 9 December 1928, she promised to send the editor, André Chaumeix, what was to become 'Quand on ne sait pas le français . . .' the following month (see Appendix VIII). This was the first of nine articles to appear in *Le Figaro* between 1929 and 1932. Reading Notes (Berg, RN 1.13) (*VWRN XIII*). Holograph draft, dated 30 December [1928] (MHP, B 6e).

Nine years later a letter from VW, (*Kp4* C352.1), thanking the editor of *Impressions* for the tribute to be paid to her work in the issue of January–February 1938 (nos 19–20), was printed on p. 4 of that issue: 'I am naturally honoured that you should think of devoting some space in your paper to a consideration of my work. I have the highest admiration for French literature, and any pleasure that I can give to French readers by my work is but a very slight repayment of the debt that I owe to them. ¶ I shall read what you have to say with interest and respect, and would ask you to accept thanks for the honour you are doing me.' The editor, Yves Picart, wrote in his 'Avant propos' that VW was 'une des premières de l'Angleterre contemporaine': 'Dans les pages suivantes, l'aspect profondément nouveau de son talent sera analysé avec minutie et subtilité par nos éminents collaborateurs qui s'attacheront surtout au dernier aspect de son oeuvre, plus caractéristique des tendances essentielles' (p. 2).

2 – This comment provoked an acerbic correspondence in the *New Republic*. As VW put it on 5 May 1929: 'I am in trouble in America for saying that Henry James didn't write English' (*IV VW Letters*, no. 2026). Letters from Harriot T. Cooke, VW and Edmund Wilson appeared on 24 April 1929

under the heading 'The American Language'. It was Cooke who referred to Choctaw, implied that Henry James was born in Boston rather than in New York and referred to a '"certain condescension" which the English display towards us poor benighted Americans'. VW wrote (*Kp4* C310.1): 'I hasten to submit to your correspondent's correction and to retract my opinion that because Henry James was born in Boston he therefore did not write English like a native. I will do my best to believe that the language of Tennyson and the language of Whitman are one and the same. But may I explain that the responsibility for my error rests with Walt Whitman himself, with Mr Ring Lardner, Mr Sherwood Anderson, and Mr Sinclair Lewis? I had been reading these writers and thinking how magnificent a language American is, how materially it differs from English, and how much I envy it the power to create new words and new phrases of the utmost vividness. I had even gone so far as to shape a theory that the American genius is an original genius and that it has borne and is bearing fruit unlike any that grows over here. But in deference to your correspondent I hasten to cancel these views and will note for future use that there is no difference between England and America; climate and custom have produced no change of any sort; America is merely a larger England across the Atlantic; and the language is so precisely similar that when I come upon words like boob, graft, stine, busher, doose, hobo, shoe-pack, hiking, cinch and many others, the fact that I do not know what they mean must be attributed to the negligence of those who did not teach me what is apparently my native tongue. ¶ Having thus admitted my error, may I "just as a matter of curiosity" [used by Cooke in his letter] ask to be enlightened on another point? Why, I wonder, when I say that Henry James did not write English like a native is it assumed that I intend an insult? Why does your correspondent at once infer that I accuse the Bostonians of talking Choctaw? Why does he allude to "condescension" and refer to "us poor benighted Americans" and suppose that I look upon them as "newcomers to the English language" when I have said nothing of the sort? What have I done to make him angry? Lowell's essay "On a Certain Condescension in Foreigners" (for such he apparently thought the English) should, I think, have for pendant "On a Certain Touchiness in" – dare I say it? – "Americans." But may I implore you, Sir, if I use that word, not to infer that I thereby imply that you wear a pigtail and paint your forehead red? If I speak of "Americans" it is merely because our common ancestors some centuries ago agreed, for reasons best known to themselves, to differ.' The controversy dragged on in the correspondence pages for months, although VW made no further contribution.

While some of the words that VW says she does not know are now easily understood, others are more obscure but may be found in *You Know Me Al* (1916), first published in the *Saturday Evening Post* (NY) in 1914, by Ring Lardner (1885–1933), and which she described as 'a story written often in a language which is not English' (see 'American Fiction', *IV VW Essays*). Glossary: a 'boob' is a person who makes mistakes rather than the mistakes themselves; to 'graft' is to obtain profit by shady or dishonest means (to sponge off someone, according to *You Know Me Al*); a 'stine' is Jack Keefe's misspelling of a stein (of beer) (ch. iii, letter of 'Januery 3'); a 'busher' is a bush leaguer, one who plays in a minor baseball league (*passim*); a 'dirty doose' is a term of abuse (ch. iii, letter of 27 December, and ch. v, letter of 4 October); a 'hobo' is a professional tramp, one who spends his life travelling from place to place, especially stealing rides on trains, and begging for a living; a 'shoe-pack' is a kind of moccasin; 'hiking' probably means working upwards or out of place, especially referring to clothes; a 'cinch' is something done or obtained without difficulty (a near certainty).

Alfred, Lord Tennyson (1809–92). For Walt Whitman (1819–92), Sherwood Anderson (1876–1941) and Sinclair Lewis (1885–1951), see 'American Fiction', *IV VW Essays*. James Russell Lowell (1819–91) was United States Minister to Great Britain 1880–5 and VW's 'sponsor' rather than 'godfather' (see *IV VW Essays*, p. 279, n. 3); his 'On a Certain Condescension in Foreigners' (1869) was collected in *My Study Windows* (1871).

VW's letter was reprinted in *Congenial Spirits: The Selected Letters of Virginia Woolf*, ed. Joanne Trautmann Banks (Hogarth Press, 1989), no. 2022a, and in Andrew McNeillie, 'Virginia Woolf's America', *Dublin Review*, no. 5 (Winter 2001–2), pp. 41–60, at pp. 49–50.

3 – Joseph Conrad (1857–1924).

4 – Maurois' lives of Percy Bysshe Shelley (1792–1822) and Benjamin Disraeli (1804–81) were *Ariel* (1923) and *La Vie de Disraéli* (1927), respectively.

5 – Queen Victoria (1819–1901; reigned from 1837); Prosper Mérimée (1803–70); Napoleon III (1808–73; President of France 1849–52, Emperor 1852–70); Empress Eugénie (1826–1920). Ch. iv of *Vignettes of Memory* by Lady Violet Greville, the only work footnoted by VW in 'Phases of Fiction' (see p. 46 and n. 12), describes the court of Napoleon III at Compiègne.

6 – Charles II (1630–85; reigned nominally from 1649, actually from 1660); the *Diary* of Samuel Pepys (1633–1703) covers the years 1659–69. The *Mémoires* of the Duc de Saint-Simon (1675–1755) describe the French Court during the closing years of Louis XIV (1638–1715; reigned from 1643).

7 – 'bitterness' and 'jewels', respectively.

8 – *Climats*, pp. 276–7.

9 – *Ibid.*, p. 177, which continues: 'Surtout un refus de voir et d'accepter la vie telle qu'elle est; un idéalisme . . . une sentimentalité agaçante'.

10 – *Ibid.*, p. 268.

11 – The French translation reads: 'pas de Français, de Russe, d'Allemand ou d'Américain'.

12 – George Gordon, Lord Byron (1788–1824); Edgar Allan Poe (1809–49).

Geraldine and Jane

Geraldine Jewsbury would certainly not have expected anybody at this time of day to bother himself about her novels. If she had caught any one pulling them down from the shelf in some library, she would have expostulated. 'They're such nonsense, my dear,' she would have said. And then one likes to fancy that she would have burst out in that irresponsible, unconventional way of hers against libraries and literature and love and life and all the rest of it with a 'Confound it!' or a 'Damn it all!' for Geraldine was fond of swearing.

The odd thing about Geraldine Jewsbury was the way in which she combined oaths and endearments, sense and effervescence, daring and gush. '... Defenceless and tender on the one hand, and strong enough to cleave the very rocks on the other'[2] – that is how Mrs Ireland, her biographer, puts it. Or, again: 'Intellectually she was a man, but the heart within her was as womanly as ever daughter of Eve could boast'.[3] Even to look at, there was, it would seem, something incongruous, queer, provocative about her. She was very small and yet boyish, very ugly, yet attractive, qualities that are almost extinguished, in the only portrait we have of her, by the flowing skirts and the sweeping table-cloth of the professional photographer. There she sits, reading, with her face half-turned away, defenceless and tender at the moment rather than cleaving the very rocks.

But what had happened to her before she sat at the photographer's table, reading her book, it is impossible to say. Until she was twenty-nine we know nothing of her except that she was born in the year 1812, was the daughter of a merchant and lived in Manchester or near it. In the first part of the Nineteenth Century a woman of twenty-nine was no longer young. She had lived her life or she had missed it. And though Geraldine was in many ways an exception, still it cannot be doubted that something very tremendous had happened in those dim years before we know her. Something had happened in Manchester. An obscure male figure looms in the background – a faithless but fascinating creature who had taught her that life is treacherous, life is hard, life is the very devil for a woman. A dark pool of experience had formed in the back of her mind into which she would dip for the consolation or for the instruction of others. 'Oh! it is too frightful to talk about! For two years I lived only in short respites from this blackness of darkness',[4] she exclaimed from time to time. There had been seasons 'like dreary, calm November days when there is but one cloud, but that one covers the whole heaven'.[5] She had struggled, 'but struggling is no use'.[6] She had read Cudworth[7] through. She had written an essay upon materialism before giving way. For, though the prey of so many emotions, she was also oddly detached and speculative. She liked to puzzle her head with questions about 'matter and spirit and the nature of life'[8] even while her heart was bleeding. Upstairs there was a box full of extracts, abstracts and conclusions. Yet, what conclusion could a woman come to? Did anything avail a woman when love had deserted her, when her lover had played her false? No – it was useless to struggle; one had better let the wave engulf one, the cloud close over one's head. So she meditated, lying often on the sofa with a piece of knitting in her hands and a green shade over her eyes. For she suffered from a variety of ailments – sore eyes, colds, nameless exhaustion; and Greenheys, the suburb outside Manchester where she kept house for her brother, was very damp. 'Dirty, half-melted snow and fog, a swampy meadow, set off by a creeping cold damp'[9] – that was the view from her window. Often, she could hardly drag herself across the room. And then there were incessant interruptions; somebody had come unexpectedly for dinner; she had to jump up and run into the kitchen and cook a fowl with her own hands. That done, she would put on her green shade and peer at her book again, for she was a great reader.

She read metaphysics, she read travels, she read old books and new books – Carlyle's books among them. She gave little parties where she discussed literature rather boldly, with a cigar in her mouth, and life and morality, for she was always being loved or not being loved – whichever it was; passion played a great part in her life.

Early in the year 1841 she came to London and secured an introduction to the great man whose lectures she had so much admired. She met Mrs Carlyle. They must have become intimate with great rapidity. In a few weeks Mrs Carlyle was 'dearest Jane'. They must have discussed everything. They must have talked about life and the past and the present and certain 'individuals' who were sentimentally interested or were not sentimentally interested in Geraldine. Mrs Carlyle flung off anecdote after anecdote; how she had worked; how she had baked; how she had lived at Craigenputtock. For directly Geraldine returned to Manchester, she began writing long letters to Jane which echo and continue the intimate conversations of Cheyne

Row. 'A man who has had *le plus grand succès* among women, and who was the most passionate and poetically refined lover in his manners and conversation you would wish to find, once said to me . . .[10] "It may be that we women are made as we are in order that they may in some sort fertilise the world. We shall go on loving, they (the men) will go on struggling and toiling, and we are all alike mercifully allowed to die – after a while." I don't know whether you will agree to this, and I cannot see to argue, for my eyes are very bad and painful.'[11]

Probably Jane agreed to very little of all this. For Jane was eleven years the elder. Jane was not given to abstract reflection upon the nature of life. Jane was the most caustic, the most concrete, the most clear-sighted of women. But it is perhaps worth noting that when she first fell in with Geraldine, she was beginning to feel those premonitions of jealousy, that uneasy sense that old relationships had shifted and that new ones were forming themselves, which had come to pass with the establishment of her husband's fame. No doubt in the course of those long talks in Cheyne Row, Geraldine had received certain confidences, heard certain complaints and drawn certain conclusions. Besides being a mass of emotion and sensibility Geraldine was a clever, witty woman who thought for herself and hated what she called 'respectability' as much as Mrs Carlyle hated what she called 'humbug'. In addition Geraldine had from the first the strangest feelings about Mrs Carlyle. She felt 'vague undefined yearnings to be yours in some way. . . .[12] You will let me be yours and think of me as such, will you not?'[13] she urged again and again. 'I think of you as Catholics think of their saints,'[14] she said. '. . . You will laugh, but I feel towards you much more like a lover than a female friend.'[15] No doubt Mrs Carlyle did laugh; but she could scarcely fail to be touched by the little creature's adoration.

Thus, when Carlyle himself early in 1843 suggested unexpectedly that they should ask Geraldine to stay with them, Mrs Carlyle, after debating the question with her usual candour, agreed. She reflected that a little of Geraldine would be 'very enlivening',[16] but on the other hand much of her would be very exhausting. Geraldine dropped hot tears on one's hands; she watched one; she fussed one; she was always in a state of emotion. Then, 'with all her good and great qualities', Geraldine had in her 'a born spirit of intrigue'[17] which might make mischief between husband and wife, though not in the usual way; for, Mrs Carlyle reflected, her husband had the habit of preferring her to other women, 'and habits are much stronger in him than passions'.[18] On the other hand, she herself was getting lazy, intellectually; Geraldine loved talk and clever talk; with all her aspirations and enthusiasms it would be a kindness to let her come; and so she came.

She came on the first or second of February, and she stayed till Saturday, the eleventh of March. Such were visits in the year 1843. And the house was very small, and the servant was inefficient. Geraldine was always there. All the morning she scribbled letters. All the afternoon she lay fast asleep on the sofa in the drawing room. She dressed herself in a low-necked dress to receive visitors on Sunday. She talked too much. As for her reputed intellect – 'she is sharp as a meat axe, but as narrow'.[19] She flattered. She wheedled. She was insincere. She flirted. She swore. Nothing would make her go. The charges against her rise in a crescendo of irritation. Mrs Carlyle almost had to turn her out of the house. She was unable to hide her annoyance. At last they parted. Geraldine was in floods of tears but Mrs Carlyle's eyes were dry. Indeed, she was immensely relieved to see the last of her visitor. Yet, when Geraldine had driven off and she found herself alone, she was not altogether easy in her mind. She knew that her behaviour to a guest whom she herself had invited had been far from perfect. She had been 'cold, cross, ironical, disobliging'.[20] Above all, she was angry with herself for having taken Geraldine for a confidante. 'Heaven grant that the consequences may be only *boring* – not *fatal*,'[21] she wrote. But it is clear that she was very much out of temper, and with herself as much as with Geraldine.

Geraldine was well aware that something was wrong. Estrangement and silence fell between them. People repeated malicious stories to which she half listened. But Geraldine was the least vindictive of women; 'very noble in her quarrels',[22] as Mrs Carlyle herself admitted, and, if foolish and sentimental, neither conceited nor proud. Above all, her love for Jane was sincere. Soon she was writing to Mrs Carlyle again 'with an assiduity and disinterestedness that verge on the superhuman',[23] as Jane commented with a little exasperation. She was worrying about Jane's health and saying that she did not want witty letters, but only dull letters telling the truth about Jane's state. For – it may have been one of the things that made her so trying as a visitor – Geraldine had not stayed for four weeks in Cheyne Row without coming to conclusions which it is not likely that she kept entirely to herself. 'You have no one who has any sort of consideration for you,'[24] she wrote. 'You have had patience and endurance till I am sick of the virtues, and what have they done for you? Half-killed you.'[25] 'Carlyle', she burst out, 'is much too grand for every-day life. A sphinx does not fit in comfortably to our parlour life arrangements.'[26] But she could do nothing. 'The more one loves, the more helpless one feels,'[27] she moralised. She could only watch from Manchester the bright kaleidoscope of her friend's existence and compare it with her own prosaic life, all made up of little odds and ends, but, somehow, obscure though it was, she no longer envied Jane the brilliance of her lot.

Had it not been for the Mudies, they might have gone on indefinitely corresponding in a desultory way at a distance – 'I am tired to death of writing letters into space', Geraldine had exclaimed, 'one only writes, after a long separation, to oneself, instead of one's friend'.[28] The Mudies and Mudieism, as Geraldine called it, played a vast, if almost unrecorded, part in the obscure lives of Victorian Englishwomen. The Mudies, by whatever name they might be called, were always the same. They were unfortunate; they were deserving; they must be helped. They came at inconvenient hours. They waited in the hall and sometimes had sandwiches and a glass of wine brought out to them on a tray. In this case the Mudies were two girls, Elizabeth and Juliet, 'flary, staring, and conceited, stolid-looking girls',[29] Carlyle called them, the daughters of a Dundee schoolmaster, who had written books on natural history and died, leaving a foolish widow and little or no provision for his family.[30] Somehow the Mudies arrived in Cheyne Row inconveniently, if one may hazard a guess, just as dinner was on the table. But the Victorian lady never minded that; she put herself to any inconvenience to help the Mudies. The question at once presented itself: what could be done for them? Who knew of a place? Who had influence with a rich man? Geraldine flashed into Mrs Carlyle's mind. Geraldine was always wishing she could be of use. Geraldine might fairly be asked if there were situations to be had for the Mudies in Manchester. Geraldine acted with a promptitude that was much to her credit. She placed Juliet at once. Soon she had heard of another place for Elizabeth. Mrs Carlyle, who was in the Isle of Wight, at once procured stays, gown and petticoat for Elizabeth, came up to London, took Elizabeth all the way across London to Euston Square at half-past seven in the evening, put her in charge of a benevolent-looking fat old man, saw that a letter to Geraldine was pinned to her stays and returned home, exhausted, triumphant, yet, as happens often to the devotees of Mudieism, with some secret misgivings. Would the Mudies be happy? Would they thank her for what she had done? A few days later the inevitable bugs appeared in Cheyne Row and were ascribed, with or without reason, to Elizabeth's shawl. What was far worse, Elizabeth herself appeared four months later, having proved herself 'wholly inapplicable to any practical purpose', having 'sewed a *black* apron with *white* thread' and, on being mildly scolded, having 'thrown herself on the kitchen floor and kicked and screamed'. 'Of course her immediate dismissal is the result.'[31] Elizabeth vanished – to sew more black aprons with white thread, to kick and scream and be dismissed – who knows what happened eventually to poor Elizabeth Mudie? She disappears from the world altogether.

Juliet, however, remained. Geraldine made Juliet her charge. She superintended and advised. The first place was unsatisfactory. Geraldine engaged herself to find another. She went off and sat in the hall of a 'very stiff old lady' who wanted a maid. The very stiff old lady said that she would want Juliet to clear-starch collars, to iron cuffs and to wash and iron petticoats. Juliet's heart failed her. All this clear-starching and ironing were beyond her. Off went Geraldine again, late in the evening, and saw the old lady's daughter. It was arranged that the petticoats should be 'put out' and only the collars and frills left for Juliet to iron. Off went Geraldine and arranged with her own milliner to give her lessons in quilling and trimming. And Mrs Carlyle wrote to cheer her up and sent her a packet. So it went on, with more places and more bothers and Juliet wrote a novel, which a gentleman praised very highly, and Juliet told Miss Jewsbury that she was annoyed by a gentleman who followed her home from church; but still she was a very nice girl and everybody spoke well of her until the year 1849, when suddenly, without any reason given, silence descends upon the last of the Mudies. It covers, one cannot doubt, another failure. The novel, the stiff old lady, the gentleman, the caps, the petticoats, the clear-starching – what was the cause of her downfall? Nothing is known. 'The wretched stalking blockheads,' wrote Carlyle, 'stalked fatefully, in spite of all that could be done and said, steadily downwards towards perdition and sank altogether out of view.'[32] For all her endeavours, Mrs Carlyle had to admit that Mudieism was always a failure.

But Mudieism had unexpected results. Mudieism brought Jane and Geraldine together again. Jane could not deny that 'the fluff of feathers'[33] whom she had served up, as her way was, in many a scornful phrase for Carlyle's amusement had 'taken up the matter with an enthusiasm even surpassing my own'.[34] She had grit in her as well as fluff. Thus when Geraldine sent her the manuscript of her first novel, Zoe,[35] Mrs Carlyle bestirred herself, and with surprising success, to find a publisher. ('For,' she wrote, 'what is to become of her when she is old without ties, without purposes?')[36] Chapman and Hall at once agreed to publish the book which, their reader reported, 'had taken hold of him with a grasp of iron'.[37] The book had been long on the way. Mrs Carlyle herself had been consulted at various stages of its career. She had read the first sketch 'with a feeling little short of *terror!* So much power of genius rushing so recklessly into unknown space'.[38] But she had also been deeply impressed. 'Geraldine in particular shows herself here a far more profound and daring speculator than ever I had fancied her. I do not believe there is a woman alive at the present day, not even George Sand herself, that could have written some of the best passages in this book . . . but they must not publish it . . . decency forbids!'[39] Mrs Carlyle complained that there was an indecency or 'want of reserve in the spiritual department'[40] which no respectable public could stand. Presumably Geraldine consented to make alterations, though she confessed that she 'had no vocation for propriety as such';[41] the book was re-written; and it appeared at last in February, 1845. The usual buzz and conflict of opinion at once arose. The least moral people, according to Mrs Carlyle, were the most shocked. The most moral, like Erasmus Darwin and Arthur Helps, either admired it or said nothing.[42] A prim Scotch Puritan like Miss Wilson owned that though '*avowedly* the book of an audacious *esprit forte* . . . I think it very clever and amusing' while 'old and young roués of the Reform Club almost go off into hysterics over – its *indecency*'.[43] The publisher was a little alarmed; but the scandal helped the sale and Geraldine became a lioness.

And now, of course, as one turns the pages of the three little yellowish volumes, one wonders what reason there was for approval or disapproval, what spasm of indignation or admiration scored that pencil mark or bent that leaf, what mysterious emotion pressed violets, now black as ink, between the pages of the love scene. Chapter after chapter glides amiably, fluently past. In a kind of haze we catch glimpses of an illegitimate girl called Zoe; of an enigmatic Roman Catholic priest called Everhard; of a castle in the country; of ladies lying on sky-blue sofas; of gentlemen reading aloud; of girls embroidering hearts in silk. There is a conflagration. There is an embrace in a wood.[44] There is incessant conversation. There is a moment of terrific emotion when the priest exclaims: 'Would that I had never been born!'[45] and proceeds to sweep a letter and a parcel into a drawer and all because Zoe has shaken his faith, for the letter had come from the Pope and had asked that he edit a translation of the principal works of the fathers of the first four centuries and the parcel contained a gold chain from the University of Göttingen. But what indecency there was pungent enough to shock the roués of the Reform Club, what genius there was brilliant enough to impress the shrewd intellect of Mrs Carlyle, it is impossible to guess. Colours that were fresh as roses eighty years ago have faded to a feeble pink; nothing remains of all those keen scents and savours but a faint perfume of faded violets or stale hair oil, we know not which. What miracles, we exclaim, are within the power of a few years to accomplish! But, even as one exclaims, one sees, far away, a trace perhaps of what they meant. The passion, in so far as it issues from the lips of live people, is completely spent. The Zoes, the Clothildes, the Everhards moulder on their perches; nevertheless, there is somebody in the room with them; an irresponsible spirit, a daring and agile woman, if one considers that she is cumbered with crinoline and stays; an absurd sentimental creature, languishing, expatiating, but, for all that, her opinions are still strangely alive. We catch a sentence now and then boldly rapped out, a thought subtly conceived. 'How much better to do right without religion!'[46] 'Oh! if they really believed all they preach, how would any priest or preacher be able to sleep in his bed!'[47] 'Insincerity has crept into the heart of the most sacred things.'[48] 'Weakness is the only state for which there is no hope.'[49] 'To love rightly is the highest morality of which mankind is capable.'[50] How she hated the 'compacted plausible theories of men'![51] Are women merely to cook, merely to sew? And what is life? For what end was it given us? Such questions, such convictions, still hurtle past the heads of the stuffed figures mouldering on their perches. They are dead but Geraldine Jewsbury herself still survives, independent, courageous, absurd, tripping about Manchester, seeing about a place, interviewing a milliner, chattering, writing page after page without stopping to correct and coming out with her views upon love, morality, religion and the relations of the sexes, whoever may be within hearing.

Some time before the publication of *Zoe*, Mrs Carlyle had forgotten or overcome her irritation towards Geraldine, partly because she had worked so zealously in the cause of the Mudies, partly also because by Geraldine's painstaking she was 'almost over-persuaded back into my old illusion that she has some sort of strange, passionate . . . incomprehensible *attraction* towards me'.[52] Not only was she drawn back into correspondence but, after all her vows to the contrary, she again stayed under the same roof with Geraldine, at Seaforth House near Liverpool in July, 1844. Not many days had passed before Mrs Carlyle's 'illusion' about the strength of Geraldine's affection for her was confirmed. One morning there was some slight tiff between them; Geraldine sulked all day; at night Geraldine came to Mrs Carlyle's bedroom and made a scene which was 'a revelation to me not only of Geraldine but of human nature! Such mad, *lover-like* jealousy on the part of one woman towards another it had never entered into my heart to conceive'.[53] Mrs Carlyle was angry and outraged and contemptuous. She saved up a full account of the scene to entertain her husband with. A few days later she turned upon Geraldine in public and set the whole company into fits of laughter by saying: 'I wondered she should expect me to behave decently to her after she had for a whole evening been making love before my very face to *another man!*'[54] The trouncing must have been severe, the humiliation painful. But Geraldine was incorrigible. A year later she was again sulking and raging and declaring that she had a right to rage because 'she loves me better than all the rest of the world';[55] and Mrs Carlyle was getting up and saying, 'Geraldine, until you can behave like a gentlewoman . . .',[56] and leaving the room. Again there were tears and apologies and promises of reform.

Yet, though Mrs Carlyle scolded and jeered, though they were estranged and though for a time they ceased to write to each other, still they always came together again. 'There was no quarrelling with the creature,'[57] said Mrs Carlyle. She sat on the floor and rubbed one's feet. She dried her eyes and smoked 'a cigarito'.[58] There was not an ounce of vanity in her composition. And Geraldine said, though Jane gave her pain 'to a degree you would hardly believe that one woman could inflict upon another',[59] though she was insensitive and had no consideration 'for the natural effects of things on others',[60] still it was beyond Jane's power to vex or estrange her permanently – 'as long as you are in this world the tie exists'.[61] So the letters always begin again – long, long letters written sometimes 'with a small kitten running up and down my dress',[62] letters full of gossip and stories such as Jane herself loved – how Mrs —— , whose husband used to put her at the top of the stairs and roll her to the bottom, was trying to keep herself from starvation by painting miniatures at two guineas apiece; how poor Mrs —— had been 'salivated in a mistake ! ! ! the surgery boy had made up the wrong prescription and given calomel instead of ipecacuanha! Did you ever? . . .'[63] The vacillations of Geraldine's susceptible heart are traced. The Egyptian had written to her. Q. had hinted but perhaps not altogether made a proposal. Mr —— had called again. She had bought a shawl. Through it all it is abundantly clear that Geraldine felt that Jane was in every way wiser, better, stronger than she was. She depended on her. She needed Jane to keep her out of scrapes; for Jane never got into scrapes herself. But though Jane was so much wiser and cleverer than anybody else, there were times when the foolish and irresponsible one of the two became the counsellor. Why, she asked, waste your time in mending old clothes? Why not work at something that will really employ your energies? Write, she advised her. Geraldine was convinced that Jane who was so profound, so far-seeing, could write something that would help women in 'their very complicated duties and difficulties'.[64] She owed a duty to her sex. But, the bold woman proceeded, 'Do not go to Mr Carlyle for sympathy, do not let him dash you with cold water. You must respect your own work and your own motives'[65] – a piece of advice that Jane would have done well to follow, but she was, as a matter of fact, afraid to accept the dedication of Geraldine's new novel, *The Half Sisters*, lest Mr Carlyle might object. The little creature was in some ways the bolder and the more independent of the two.

She had, moreover, a quality that Jane with all her brilliancy lacked – an element of poetry, a trace of the speculative imagination. She browsed upon old books and copied out romantic passages about the palm trees and cinnamon of Arabia and sent them to lie, incongruously enough, upon the breakfast table in Cheyne Row. Jane's genius, of course, was the very opposite; it was positive, direct and practical. Her imagination concentrated itself upon people. Her letters owe their brilliancy to the hawk-like swoop and descent of her mind upon facts. Nothing escapes her. She sees through clear water down to the rocks at the bottom. But the intangible eluded her; she dismissed the poetry of Keats[66] with a sneer; something of the narrowness and something of the prudery of a Scottish country doctor's daughter clung to her. Though infinitely the less masterly, Geraldine was sometimes the broader-minded.

Such sympathies and antipathies bound the two women together with an elasticity that made for permanence. The tie between them could stretch and stretch without breaking. Jane knew the extent of Geraldine's folly; Geraldine had felt the full lash of Jane's tongue. They had learned to tolerate each other. Then, if the 'cant of sensibility' raised Jane's fury, nobody rated the truth of feeling more highly than she did. Once, when she was ill and unhappy, she went to stay with Geraldine – Geraldine, the flighty, the gushing, the unpractical. To her surprise she found her house noiseless; she found her arrangements well ordered; she found Geraldine herself quiet and sensible. With her usual generosity she took back all she had ever said against Geraldine. 'People who are at ease in Zion – I myself when I have been so to a certain extent – may have found Geraldine very teazing and absurd – but let one be ill – suffering – especially *morbidly* suffering – and then one knows what Geraldine is! All the intelligent sympathy and real practical good that lies in her!'[67] She would be grateful to Geraldine as long as she lived, she said. Naturally they quarrelled again; but their quarrels were different now, as quarrels are that are bound to be made up. When, after her brother's marriage in 1854, Geraldine moved to London, it was to be near Mrs Carlyle at Mrs Carlyle's own wish. The woman who in 1843 would never be a friend of hers again was now the most intimate friend she had in the world. She was to lodge two streets off; and perhaps two streets was the right space to put between them. The emotional friendship was full of misunderstandings at a distance; it was intolerably exacting under the same roof. When they lived round the corner, however, their relationship broadened and simplified; and it became a natural intercourse whose ruffles and whose calms were based upon the depths of intimacy. They went about together. They went to hear the *Messiah*.[68] Characteristically, Geraldine wept at the beauty of the music and Jane had much ado to prevent herself from shaking Geraldine and from crying herself at the ugliness of the chorus women. They went to Norwood for a jaunt and Geraldine left a silk handkerchief and an aluminium brooch ('a love token from Mr Barlow')[69] in the hotel and a new silk parasol in the waiting-room. Also Jane noted with sardonic satisfaction that Geraldine, in an attempt at economy, bought two second class tickets, while the cost of a return ticket, first class, was precisely the same. They traipsed off to Dalston with the dog Nero to celebrate Geraldine's birthday by seeing 'a happy woman', Mrs Carlyle's old servant Eliza. They came home by omnibus and Jane gave Geraldine a 'pretty lace collar and a Bohemian glass vase, which is still unbroken'.[70] Mrs Carlyle would tell Geraldine story after story about her childhood – how the turkey-cock had frightened her; how she had made her father teach her Latin; how many men had loved her; how she had reverenced her father. At the mention of his name she would always fall silent. Then she would begin again about Craigenputtock and Carlyle and tell story after story about servant after servant. Nobody told stories as Mrs Carlyle did. Nobody was so witty, so dramatic or, when the mood took her, showed such penetration, such understanding.

Meanwhile Geraldine lay on the floor and generalised and speculated and tried to formulate some theory of life from her own experience. (Her language was always likely to be strong; she knew that she 'sinned against Jane's notions of good taste very often'.)[71] How loathsome the position of women was in many ways! How she herself had been crippled and stunted! How her blood boiled in her at the power that men had over women! She would like to kick certain gentlemen – 'the lying hypocritical beggars! Well, it's no good swearing – only, I am angry and it eases my mind'.[72] She had her own views about women. She did not agree with the ugly clever women who came to Manchester preaching the doctrines of women's rights. She did not hold with the professors and the essayists on female education. She thought that their theories and aims were wrong. She thought she could see far off another type of woman arising, a woman something like Jane and herself. 'I believe we are touching on better days,' she wrote, 'when women will have a genuine, normal life of their own to lead. There, perhaps, will not be so many marriages, and women will be taught not to feel their destiny *manqué* if they remain single. They will be able to be friends and companions in a way they cannot be now. . . . Instead of having appearances to attend to, they will be allowed to have their virtues, in any measure which it may please God to send, without being diluted down to the tepid "rectified spirit" of "feminine grace" and "womanly timidity" – in short they will be allowed to make themselves women as men are allowed to make themselves men.'[73]

And then her thoughts turned to Jane and herself and to the brilliant gifts – at any rate Jane had brilliant gifts – which had borne so little visible result. Nevertheless, except when she was ill, 'I do not think that either you or I are to be called failures. We are indications of a development of womanhood which as yet is not recognised. It has, so far, no ready-made channels to run in, but still we have looked and tried, and found that the present rules for women will not hold us – that something better and stronger is needed. . . . There are women to come after us, who will approach nearer the fullness of the measure of the stature of a woman's nature. I regard myself as a mere faint indication, a rudiment of the idea, of certain higher qualities and possibilities that lie in women, and all the eccentricities and mistakes and miseries and absurdities I have made are only the consequences of an imperfect formation, an immature growth'.[74] So she theorised, so she speculated and Mrs Carlyle listened and laughed and no doubt contradicted. She could have wished that Geraldine were more precise; she could have wished her to moderate her language. Carlyle might come in at any moment and, if there was one creature that Carlyle hated, it was a strong-minded woman of the George Sand species. Yet she could not deny that there was truth in what Geraldine said; she had always thought that Geraldine 'was born to spoil a horn or make a spoon'.[75] Geraldine was no fool in spite of appearances.

But what Geraldine thought and said, how she spent her mornings, what she did in the long evenings of the London winter – all, in fact, that constituted her life at Markham Square is completely unknown to us. Now, fittingly enough, the bright light of Jane extinguished the paler and more flickering fire of Geraldine. She had no need to write to Jane any more. She was in and out of the house – now writing a letter for Jane because Jane's fingers were swollen, now taking a letter to the post and forgetting, of course, to post it. We hear a crooning domestic sound now and again like the purring of a kitten or the humming of a tea kettle. So the years passed quickly away. On Saturday, the twenty-first of April, 1866, Geraldine was to help Jane with a tea party. She was dressing for the occasion when Mr Froude suddenly appeared at her house. He had had a message to say that 'something had happened to Mrs Carlyle'.[76] Geraldine flung on her cloak. They hastened together to St George's Hospital. They were taken to a little room. There they saw Mrs Carlyle beautifully dressed 'as if she had sate upon the bed after leaving the brougham, and had fallen back upon it asleep. . . . The brilliant mockery, the sad softness with which the mockery alternated, both were alike gone. The features lay composed in a stern majestic calm . . . (Geraldine) could not speak'.[77]

Nor, indeed, can we break that silence. Soon after Jane's death she went to live at Sevenoaks. She lived there alone for twenty-two years. It is said that she lost her vivacity. She wrote no more books. Cancer attacked her and she suffered much. On her death-bed she began tearing up Jane's letters, as Jane had wished, and she had destroyed all but one before she died. Thus, just as her life began in obscurity, so it ends in obscurity. We know her only for a few years in the middle. When we consider how little we know even of those we live with, how much we must guess of the feelings of those we see constantly, it is difficult to persuade ourselves that we can judge Geraldine Jewsbury and the true nature of her feeling for Jane Carlyle. Or, if we cherish such an illusion, it is soon destroyed by Geraldine herself. 'Oh, my dear,' she wrote, 'if you and I are drowned, or die, what would become of us if any superior person were to go and write our "life and errors"? What a precious mess a "truthful person" would go and make of us, and how very different to what we really are or were!'[78]

The echo of her mockery, ungrammatical, colloquial, reaches us from where she lies in Lady Morgan's vault in the Brompton Cemetery.

1 – An essay originally published (unsigned) as the leading article in the *TLS*, 28 February 1929, ostensibly as a review of the first two novels, *Zoe* (1845) and *The Half Sisters* (1848), by Geraldine Endsor Jewsbury (1812–80), and (signed, with variations) in the *Bookman* (NY), February 1929, (*Kp4* C309), and this is the version printed here. On the upper wrapper of the *Bookman* the essay was entitled 'A Friend of Jane Carlyle's'. In the issue of *Bookman* Raymond Mortimer wrote on 'Mrs. Woolf and Mr. Strachey' (partly reprinted in *M&M*), and there were also two poems by Katherine Mansfield, Dorothy Parker's 'Big Blonde' (a story), and the third instalment of Ford Madox Ford's 'The English Novel: From the Earliest Days to the Death of Joseph Conrad'. The issue of the *TLS* also contained: letters from Clive Bell about the review of his *Proust* (Hogarth Press, 1928) and from P. P. Howe about his edition of *The Complete Works of William Hazlitt* that would be published in 1930. It is clear that the *Bookman* version predates the *TLS*, which in turn was later revised and shortened for *CR2*. See p. 505 below, where the revised version, together with the *TLS* variants in the form of endnotes, is printed as part of *CR2*. VW wrote that she 'should be reading Miss Jewsbury' on 10 November 1928 (*III VW Diary*; see also 28 November). On about 9 January 1929 she wrote to Vita Sackville-West: 'I do nothing but try, vainly, to finish off a year's journalism in a week. If I can earn £400, by flights into the lives of Miss Burney and Miss Jewsbury, then I can pitch every book away, and sink back in my chair and give myself to the wings of the Moths [*The Waves*]. But I doubt it. There are dates to look up. One can't simply invent the whole of Chelsea and King George the 3rd and Johnson, and Mrs Thrale I suppose. Yet after all, thats the way to write; and if I had time to prove it, the truth of one's sensations is not in the fact,

but in the reverberation. When I have read three lines, I re-make them entirely, if they're prose, and not poetry; and it is this which is the truth' (*IV VW Letters*, no. 1981). On 23 February she had 'done a mild morning's work on Miss Jewsbury' (*ibid.*, no. 2006), which suggests that she was revising the article for the *TLS*. In response to a congratulatory letter from John Hayward, who had penetrated her anonymity in the *TLS*, VW wrote on 4 March: 'I daresay one could have found out more about Miss Jewsbury; I had only one volume of her letters to go upon. I could not read more than one of the novels [i.e. *Zoe*], and I expect that some old gentleman who has read all mid-Victorian memoirs will blast my theories completely. Her relation with Mrs Carlyle was interesting, and I had to be discreet' (*ibid.*, no. 2007). On 11 March she also replied to David ('Bunny') Garnett about the article: 'How angelic of you to write – one doesn't expect to be thanked for an anonymous article in The Lit Supt. This one was written in sheer idleness – you know my passion for pulling down all the memories in the house and lying on the floor surrounded by them. I was rather worried by the 72 volumes (or so) of Carlyle letters, and rather pleased to be so accurate in getting the bits together. I can't help thinking that "transitions" arrange themselves almost automatically with facts to deal with: fiction leads one a much worse dance. Your old George Moore conveyed his appreciation, much to my surprise' (*ibid.*, no. 2009). More is now known about Geraldine Jewsbury than when VW wrote her essay (but see the letters in the *TLS* of 7 March and 4 April 1929, written in response to VW's essay; and see the Introduction, p. xvi). Jewsbury wrote a number of other novels and children's books, and until her death she was a prolific reviewer of fiction for the *Athenaeum* from 1849 and as a reader of fiction for the publishing house of Richard Bentley from 1858. According to Joanne Wilkes: 'Long before she died in 1880, she had a secure position as a woman of letters, and was justifiably proud of what she had achieved. Her friends had come to include the Huxleys, the Kingsleys, the Rossettis, and Ruskin, while she had also met the Brownings, Tennyson, and Charlotte Brontë'; see the introduction to *The Half Sisters* (World's Classics, OUP, 1994), p. xxiv. See also 'The Letters of Jane Welsh Carlyle' and 'More Carlyle Letters', *I VW Essays*. Reading Notes (Berg, RN 1.13) (*VWRN XIII*).

2 – *Selections from the Letters of Geraldine Endsor Jewsbury to Jane Welsh Carlyle* [1801–66], ed. Mrs Alexander [Anne (Annie) Elizabeth, 1842–93] Ireland (Longmans, Green, 1892), p. viii. 'Jewsbury's posthumous reputation was damaged by the furore over Froude's writings on the Carlyles, which had drawn on her comments about their unhappy marriage; she was also trivialized by Annie Ireland's over-emphasis on her emotional volatility in her edition of Jewsbury's letters to Jane Carlyle' (*ODNB*).

3 – *Letters of G. E. Jewsbury*, pp. vii–viii.

4 – *Ibid.*, Letter 45, 14 July 1845, p. 166.

5 – *Ibid.*, Letter 115, 13 July 1851, p. 410.

6 – *Ibid.*, Letter 45, p. 166, which has: 'Struggling is of no use'.

7 – Ralph Cudworth (1617–88), divine, one of the Cambridge Platonists; see *Letters of G. E. Jewsbury*, Letter 27, 12 February 1844, p. 104: 'I fagged through Cudworth's folio before I finally abandoned myself to despair and hysterics'.

8 – *Ibid.*, Letter 27, 12 February 1844, p. 103: 'I took a fit of studying metaphysics before I was 16 . . . I was fired with a glorious ambition to say my say on the much-vexed question of "matter and spirit," and, save the mark! the nature of life . . .'

9 – *Ibid.*, Letter 26, 10 January 1844, p. 100.

10 – *Ibid.*, Letter 1, 15 April 1841, p. 5.

11 – *Ibid.*, pp. 6–7; VW has here conflated the comment of the 'man who has had *le plus grand succès*' with Geraldine's own opinions (cf. the *CR2* version).

12 – *Ibid.*, Letter 4, 15 June 1841, p. 16.

13 – *Ibid.*; VW has adapted the punctuation.

14 – *Ibid.*, Letter 7, 4 August 1841, p. 30.

15 – *Ibid.*, Letter 10, 29 October 1841, p. 39.

16 – *Jane Welsh Carlyle: Letters to her Family, 1839–1863*, ed. Leonard Huxley (John Murray, 1924), Letter 31, to Jeannie Welsh, 18 January 1843, p. 83.

17 – *Ibid.*

18 – *Ibid.*

19 – *Ibid.*, Letter 34, to the same, 24 February 1843, p. 89.

20 – *Ibid.*, Letter 37, to the same, 12 March 1843, p. 97.

21 – *Ibid.*, Letter 44, to the same, 18 April 1843, p. 120.

22 – *Ibid.*, Letter 147, to the same, 4 March 1850, p. 338, which has: 'To do Geraldine justice she is extremely *noble* in her *quarrels* . . .'

23 – *Ibid.*, Letter 63, to Helen Welsh, early December 1843, p. 165.

24 – *Letters of G. E. Jewsbury*, Letter 19, 17 October 1843, p. 75.

25 – *Ibid.*, p. 76.

26 – *Ibid.*, Letter 25, [1843–4], p. 93, which has: 'Carlyle is magnificent, and you are not wasted upon him, and that will be a consolation to feel some day. ¶ He is much too grand for everyday life. A sphinx does not fit in comfortably to our parlour-life arrangements . . .'

27 – *Ibid.*, p. 92.

28 – *Ibid.*, Letter 23, 11 June 1844, p. 128.

29 – *Letters and Memorials of Jane Welsh Carlyle* (3 vols, Longmans, Green, 1883), vol. i, Carlyle's note to Letter 60, to Mrs Aitken, October 1843, p. 263.

30 – Robert Mudie (b. 1777) 'died at Pentonville on 29 April 1842, leaving the widow of a second marriage in destitution, one son, and four daughters' (*DNB*).

31 – *Letters to her Family*, Letter 63, to Helen Welsh, early December 1843, p. 165.

32 – *Letters and Memorials*, vol. i, p. 263.

33 – *Letters to her Family*, Letter 34, to Jeannie Welsh, 24 February 1843, p. 89, quoting a description by her cousin: 'she is what [William] Dunlop described the Dumfries woman's hen – "nothing but just a fluff of feathers"'.

34 – *Ibid.*, Letter 51, to the same, 21 June 1843, p. 134, which has: '. . . that unwearied girl has fairly *conquered* me into a hot correspondence with her again after all – by taking up this matter I have so much at heart with enthusiasm – even surpassing my own!'

35 – Jewsbury, *Zoe. The History of Two Lives* (3 vols, Chapman & Hall, 1845).

36 – *Letters to her Family*, Letter 74, to Jeannie Welsh, 16 March 1844, p. 193, which continues: '. . . purposes, unless she apply herself to this *trade* [i.e. of writing books]?'

37 – Quoted *ibid.*, p. 194.

38 – *Ibid.*, Letter 27, to Jeannie Welsh, 25 December 1842, p. 66.

39 – *Ibid.*, which has: '. . . than even I had fancied her. . . . publish it – "decency forbids"!' George Sand, pseudonym of Amandine-Aurore Lucile Dupin, Baronne Dudevant (1804–76), French novelist and feminist.

40 – *Ibid.*, which has: 'there is an indecency or want of reserve (let us call it) in the spiritual department'.

41 – *Letters of G. E. Jewsbury*, Letter 40, [1844?], p. 145.

42 – Erasmus Alvey Darwin (1804–81), brother of Charles; Sir Arthur Helps (1813–75), public servant and author.

43 – *Letters to her Family*, Letter 95, to Jeannie Welsh, 26 February 1845, p. 236.

44 – For the meeting in the wood, see *Zoe*, vol. ii, ch. vi, pp. 96–9. The embraces take place during the conflagration: see vol. ii, ch. xi, pp. 202–4.

45 – *Ibid.*, vol. ii, ch. v, p. 79; cf. vol. i, ch. xv, p. 312: 'He wished in his heart that he had died as he lay sick upon his bed.'

46 – *Ibid.*, vol. ii, ch. iv, pp. 71–2, which has: 'How much better to teach people that whatever is really right to do, would have been equally right and equally imperative upon them, even though Moses never had delivered the ten commandments.'

47 – *Ibid.*, p. 68.

48 – *Ibid.*, p. 69.

49 – *Ibid.*, vol. iii, ch. i, p. 4, which continues: '. . . hope, either for this world or the world to come.'

50 – *Ibid.*, vol. ii, ch. xiv, p. 261, which continues: '. . . capable; no man can make an approach to true greatness till he can love – till he has loved.'

51 – *Ibid.*, vol. i, ch. xi, p. 220, which has: 'She brought to her recollection

all she had been taught, all she had read of the well compacted plausible theories by which men, living at ease, and in health, have complacently endeavoured to reconcile and account for every thing.'

52 – *Letters to her Family*, Letter 51, to Jeannie Welsh, 21 June 1843, p. 134.

53 – *New Letters and Memorials of Jane Welsh Carlyle*, annotated by Thomas Carlyle and ed. Alexander Carlyle with an intro. by Sir James Crichton-Browne (2 vols, John Lane, Bodley Head, 1903), Letter 52, to Thomas Carlyle, 12 July 1844, vol. i, p. 143.

54 – Quoting herself *ibid.*, Letter 53, to the same, 15 July 1844, vol. i, p. 146.

55 – *Ibid.*, Letter 59, to the same, 20 August 1845, vol. i, p. 163, which has: 'she "*loves* me better than all the rest of the world put together!"'

56 – Quoting herself *ibid.*

57 – *Letters to her Family*, Letter 99, to Jeannie Welsh, 10 June 1845, p. 243, which has: 'I received her very coldly but there is no quarrelling with that creature!'

58 – *New Letters and Memorials*, Letter 52, to Thomas Carlyle, 12 July 1844, vol. i, p. 144, which has: 'smoked a cigaretto!!' For Geraldine Jewsbury's expressions of enthusiasm for smoking, see *Letters of G. E. Jewsbury*, Letter 38, July 1844, p. 140, and Letter 58, 1846, pp. 220–1.

59 – *Letters of G. E. Jewsbury*, Letter 64, March 1848, p. 243.

60 – *Ibid.*, Letter 65, 13 July 1848, p. 246.

61 – *Ibid.*, Letter 64, March 1848, p. 243.

62 – *Ibid.*, Letter 78, 20 August 1849, p. 290, which has: 'A small kitten is running . . .'

63 – *Ibid.*, Letter 36, 24 June 1844, p. 135, which has: 'Her doctor . . . has salivated her in a mistake!!!'; the remainder of the quotation is from p. 136.

64 – *Ibid.*, Letter 121, 6 October 1851, p. 426.

65 – *Ibid.*

66 – John Keats (1795–1821).

67 – *Letters to her Family*, Letter 188, to Helen Walsh, probably 19 August 1846, pp. 280–1.

68 – Oratorio (1742) by George Frideric Handel (1685–1759).

69 – *New Letters and Memorials*, Letter 211, to Thomas Carlyle, 12 September 1860, vol. ii, p. 234.

70 – The origins of these two quotations have not been discovered. Eliza (d. 1850) lived in Deptford.

71 – *Letters of G. E. Jewsbury*, Letter 64, March 1848, p. 244, which has: 'I sin against your notions of good taste very often . . .'

72 – *Ibid.*, Letter 74, 12 January 1849, p. 279, which has: '– a set of lying, hypocritical beggars!'

73 – *Ibid.*, Letter 96, [1849?], p. 347, which has: 'in short, they will make themselves women,'.

74 – *Ibid.*, pp. 347–8.

75 – *Letters to her Family*, Letter 27, to Jeannie Welsh, 25 December 1842, p. 66, which has: 'One thing I feel no doubt about that this Geraldine will either "make a spoon or spoil a horn" . . .'

76 – James Anthony Froude (1818–94), *Thomas Carlyle: A History of his Life in London, 1834–1881* (2 vols, Longmans, Green, 1884), vol. ii, p. 312.

77 – *Ibid.*, p. 313.

78 – *Letters of G. E. Jewsbury*, Letter 92, [1849], p. 337.

Women and Fiction

The title of this article can be read in two ways: it may allude to women and the fiction that they write, or to women and the fiction that is written about them. The ambiguity is intentional, for, in dealing with women as writers, as much elasticity as possible is desirable; it is necessary to leave oneself room to deal with other things besides their work, so much has that work been influenced by conditions that have nothing whatever to do with art.

The most superficial inquiry into women's writing instantly raises a host of questions. Why, we ask at once, was there no continuous writing done by women before the eighteenth century? Why did they then write almost as habitually as men, and in the course of that writing produce, one after another, some of the classics of English fiction? And why did their art then, and why to some extent does their art still, take the form of fiction?

A little thought will show us that we are asking questions to which we shall get, as answer, only further fiction. The answer lies at present locked in old diaries, stuffed away in old drawers, half-obliterated in the memories of the aged. It is to be found in the lives of the obscure – in those almost unlit corridors of history where the figures of generations of women are so dimly, so fitfully perceived. For very little is known about women. The history of England is the history of the male line, not of the female. Of our fathers we know always some fact, some distinction. They were soldiers or they were sailors; they filled that office or they made that law. But of our mothers, our grandmothers, our great-grandmothers, what remains? Nothing but a tradition. One was beautiful; one was red-haired; one was kissed by a Queen. We know nothing of them except their names and the dates of their marriages and the number of children they bore.

Thus, if we wish to know why at any particular time women did this or that, why they wrote nothing, why on the other hand they wrote masterpieces, it is extremely difficult to tell. Anyone who should seek among those old papers, who should turn history wrong side out and so construct a faithful picture of the daily life of the ordinary woman in Shakespeare's time, in Milton's time, in Johnson's time,[2] would not only write a book of astonishing interest, but would furnish the critic with a weapon which he now lacks. The extraordinary woman depends on the ordinary woman. It is only when we know what were the conditions of the average woman's life – the number of her children, whether she had money of her own, if she had a room to herself, whether she had help in bringing up her family, if she had servants, whether part of the housework was her task – it is only when we can measure the way of life and the experience of life made possible to the ordinary woman that we can account for the success or failure of the extraordinary woman as a writer.

Strange spaces of silence seem to separate one period of activity from another. There was Sappho and a little group of women all writing poetry on a Greek island six hundred years before the birth of Christ. They fall silent. Then about the year 1000 we find a certain court lady, the Lady Murasaki, writing a very long and beautiful novel in Japan.[3] But in England in the sixteenth century, when the dramatists and poets were most active, the women were dumb. Elizabethan literature is exclusively masculine. Then, at the end of the eighteenth century and in the beginning of the nineteenth, we find women again writing – this time in England – with extraordinary frequency and success.

Law and custom were of course largely responsible for these strange intermissions of silence and speech. When a woman was liable, as she was in the fifteenth century, to be beaten and flung about the room if she did not marry the man of her parents' choice, the spiritual atmosphere was not favourable to the production of works of art. When she was married without her own consent to a man who thereupon became her lord and master, 'so far at least as law and custom could make him',[4] as she was in the time of the Stuarts, it is likely she had little time for writing, and less encouragement. The immense effect of environment and suggestion upon the mind, we in our psychoanalytical age are beginning to realise. Again, with memoirs and letters to help us, we are beginning to understand how abnormal is the effort needed to produce a work of art, and what shelter and what support the mind of the artist requires. Of those facts the lives and letters of men like Keats and Carlyle and Flaubert[5] assure us.

Thus it is clear that the extraordinary outburst of fiction in the beginning of the nineteenth century in England was heralded by innumerable slight changes in law and customs and manners. And women of the nineteenth century had some leisure; they had some education. It was no longer the exception for women of the middle and upper classes to choose their own husbands. And it is significant that of the four great women novelists – Jane Austen, Emily Brontë, Charlotte Brontë, and George Eliot – not one had a child, and two were unmarried.

Yet, though it is clear that the ban upon writing had been removed, there was still, it would seem, considerable pressure upon women to write novels. No four women can have been more unlike in genius and character than these four. Jane Austen can have had nothing in common with George Eliot; George Eliot was the direct opposite of Emily Brontë. Yet all were trained for the same profession; all, when they wrote, wrote novels.

Fiction was, as fiction still is, the easiest thing for a woman to write. Nor is it difficult to find the reason. A novel is the least concentrated form of art. A novel can be taken up or put down more easily than a play or a poem. George Eliot left her work to nurse her father. Charlotte Brontë put down her pen to pick the eyes out of the potatoes. And living as she did in the common sitting room, surrounded by people, a woman was trained to use her mind in observation and upon the analysis of character. She was trained to be a novelist and not to be a poet.

Even in the nineteenth century, a woman lived almost solely in her home and her emotions. And those nineteenth century novels, remarkable as they were, were profoundly influenced by the fact that the women who wrote them were excluded by their sex from certain kinds of experience. That experience has a great influence upon fiction is indisputable. The best part of Conrad's novels, for instance, would be destroyed if it had been impossible for him to be a sailor. Take away all that Tolstoi knew of war as a soldier, of life and society as a rich young man whose education admitted him to all sorts of experience, and *War and Peace*[6] would be incredibly impoverished.

Yet *Pride and Prejudice, Wuthering Heights, Villette,* and *Middlemarch*[7] were written by women from whom was forcibly withheld all experience save that which could be met with in a middle class drawing-room. No first-hand experience of war or seafaring or politics or business was possible for them. Even their emotional life was strictly regulated by law and custom. When George Eliot ventured to live with Mr Lewes without being his wife, public opinion was scandalised. Under its pressure she withdrew into a suburban seclusion which, inevitably, had the worst possible effects upon her work. She wrote that unless people asked of their own accord to come and see her, she never invited them.[8] At the same time, on the other side of Europe, Tolstoi was living a free life as a soldier, with men and women of all classes, for which nobody censured him and from which his novels drew much of their astonishing breadth and vigour.

But the novels of women were not affected only by the necessarily narrow range of the writer's experience. They showed, at least in the nineteenth century, another characteristic which may be traced to the writer's sex. In *Middlemarch* and in *Jane Eyre* we are conscious not merely of the writer's character, as we are conscious of the character of Charles Dickens,[9] but we are conscious of a woman's presence – of someone resenting the treatment of her sex and pleading for its rights. This brings into women's writing an element which is entirely absent from a man's, unless, indeed, he happens to be a working man, a Negro, or one who for some other reason is conscious of disability. It introduces a distortion and is frequently the cause of weakness. The desire to plead some personal cause or to make a character the mouthpiece of some personal discontent or grievance always has a distracting effect, as if the spot at which the reader's attention is directed were suddenly twofold instead of single.

The genius of Jane Austen and Emily Brontë is never more convincing than in their power to ignore such claims and solicitations and to hold on their way unperturbed by scorn or censure. But it needed a very serene or a very powerful mind to resist the temptation to anger. The ridicule, the censure, the assurance of inferiority in one form or another which were lavished upon women who practised an art, provoked such reactions naturally enough. One sees the effect in Charlotte Brontë's indignation, in George Eliot's resignation. Again and again one finds it in the work of the lesser women writers – in their choice of a subject, in their unnatural self-assertiveness, in their unnatural docility. Moreover, insincerity leaks in almost unconsciously. They adopt a view in deference to authority. The vision becomes too masculine or it becomes too feminine; it loses its perfect integrity and, with that, its most essential quality as a work of art.

The great change that has crept into women's writing is, it would seem, a change of attitude. The woman writer is no longer bitter. She is no longer angry. She is no longer pleading and protesting as she writes. We are approaching, if we have not yet reached, the time when her writing will have little or no foreign influence to disturb it. She will be able to concentrate upon her vision without distraction from outside. The aloofness that was once within the reach of genius and originality is only now coming within the reach of ordinary women. Therefore the average novel by a woman is far more genuine and far more interesting to-day than it was a hundred or even fifty years ago.

But it is still true that before a woman can write exactly as she wishes to write, she has many difficulties to face. To begin with, there is the technical difficulty – so simple, apparently; in reality, so baffling – that the very form of the sentence does not fit her. It is a sentence made by men; it is too loose, too heavy, too pompous for a woman's use. Yet in a novel, which covers so wide a stretch of ground, an ordinary and usual type of sentence has to be found to carry the reader on easily and naturally from one end of the book to the other. And this a woman must make for herself, altering and adapting the current sentence until she writes one that takes the natural shape of her thought without crushing or distorting it.

But that, after all, is only a means to an end, and the end is still to be reached only when a woman has the courage to surmount opposition and the determination to be true to herself. For a novel, after all, is a statement about a thousand different objects – human, natural, divine; it is an attempt to relate them to each other. In every novel of merit these different elements are held in place by the force of the writer's vision. But they have another order also, which is the order imposed upon them by convention. And as men are the arbiters of that convention, as they have established an order of values in life, so too, since fiction is largely based on life, these values prevail there also to a very great extent.

It is probable, however, that both in life and in art the values of a woman are not the values of a man. Thus, when a woman comes to write a novel, she will find that she is perpetually wishing to alter the established values – to make serious what appears insignificant to a man, and trivial what is to him important. And for that, of course, she will be criticised; for the critic of the opposite sex will be genuinely puzzled and surprised by an attempt to alter the current scale of values, and will see in it not merely a difference of view, but a view that is weak, or trivial, or sentimental, because it differs from his own.

But here, too, women are coming to be more independent of opinion. They are beginning to respect their own sense of values. And for this reason the subject matter of their novels begins to show certain changes. They are less interested, it would seem, in themselves; on the other hand, they are more interested in other women. In the early nineteenth century, women's novels were largely autobiographical. One of the motives that led them to write was the desire to expose their own suffering, to plead their own cause. Now that this desire is no longer so urgent, women are beginning to explore their own sex, to write of women as women have never been written of before; for of course, until very lately, women in literature were the creation of men.

Here again there are difficulties to overcome, for, if one may generalise, not only do women submit less readily to observation than men, but their lives are far less tested and examined by the ordinary processes of life. Often nothing tangible remains of a woman's day. The food that has been cooked is eaten; the children that have been nursed have gone out into the world. Where does the accent fall? What is the salient point for the novelist to seize upon? It is difficult to say. Her life has an anonymous character which is baffling and puzzling in the extreme. For the first time, this dark country is beginning to be explored in fiction; and at the same moment a woman has also to record the changes in women's minds and habits which the opening of the professions has introduced. She has to observe how their lives are ceasing to run underground; she has to discover what new colours and shadows are showing in them now that they are exposed to the outer world.

If, then, one should try to sum up the character of women's fiction at the present moment, one would say that it is courageous; it is sincere; it keeps closely to what women feel. It is not bitter. It does not insist upon its femininity. But at the same time, a woman's book is not written as a man would write it. These qualities are much commoner than they were, and they give even to second and third-rate work the value of truth and the interest of sincerity.

But in addition to these good qualities, there are two that call for a word more of discussion. The change which has turned the English woman from a nondescript influence, fluctuating and vague, to a voter, a wage earner, a responsible citizen, has given her both in her

33

life and in her art a turn toward the impersonal. Her relations now are not only emotional; they are intellectual, they are political. The old system which condemned her to squint askance at things through the eyes or through the interests of husband or brother, has given place to the direct and practical interests of one who must act for herself, and not merely influence the acts of others. Hence her attention is being directed away from the personal centre which engaged it exclusively in the past to the impersonal, and her novels naturally become more critical of society, and less analytical of individual lives.

We may expect that the office of gadfly to the state, which has been so far a male prerogative, will now be discharged by women also. Their novels will deal with social evils and remedies. Their men and women will not be observed wholly in relation to each other emotionally, but as they cohere and clash in groups and classes and races. That is one change of some importance. But there is another more interesting to those who prefer the butterfly to the gadfly – that is to say, the artist to the reformer. The greater impersonality of women's lives will encourage the poetic spirit, and it is in poetry that women's fiction is still weakest. It will lead them to be less absorbed in facts and no longer content to record with astonishing acuteness the minute details which fall under their own observation. They will look beyond the personal and political relationships to the wider questions which the poet tries to solve – of our destiny and the meaning of life.

The basis of the poetic attitude is of course largely founded upon material things. It depends upon leisure, and a little money, and the chance which money and leisure give to observe impersonally and dispassionately. With money and leisure at their service, women will naturally occupy themselves more than has hitherto been possible with the craft of letters. They will make a fuller and a more subtle use of the instrument of writing. Their technique will become bolder and richer.

In the past, the virtue of women's writing often lay in its divine spontaneity, like that of the blackbird's song or the thrush's. It was untaught; it was from the heart. But it was also, and much more often, chattering and garrulous – mere talk spilt over paper and left to dry in pools and blots. In future, granted time and books and a little space in the house for herself, literature will become for women, as for men, an art to be studied. Women's gift will be trained and strengthened. The novel will cease to be the dumping ground for the personal emotions. It will become, more than at present, a work of art like any other, and its resources and its limitations will be explored.

From this it is a short step to the practice of the sophisticated arts, hitherto so little practised by women – to the writing of essays and criticism, of history and biography. And that, too, if we are considering the novel, will be of advantage; for besides improving the quality of the novel itself, it will draw off the aliens who have been attracted to fiction by its accessibility while their hearts lay elsewhere. Thus will the novel be rid of those excrescences of history and fact which, in our time, have made it so shapeless.

So, if we may prophesy, women in time to come will write fewer novels, but better novels; and not novels only, but poetry and criticism and history. But in this, to be sure, one is looking ahead to that golden, that perhaps fabulous age when women will have what has so long been denied them – leisure, and money, and a room to themselves.

1 – A signed essay in the *Forum* (NY), March 1929, (*Kp4* C310). The essay was accompanied by small roundels by E. H. Suydam of Sappho, Jane Austen, George Sand (not mentioned in the essay) and Shikibu Murasaki, and at the end an essay on poetry by Paul Valéry was promised for the following month. The March issue also contained: an essay by Bertrand Russell, 'Your Child and the Fear of Death'; an instalment of *The School of Women*, a novel by André Gide; and a poem, 'Love Song', by Elinor Wylie. On 20 October 1928 VW spoke on 'Women and Fiction' at Newnham and on 26 October at Girton. According to *Room*, it was based upon the two papers which 'were too long to be read in full, and have since been altered and expanded' (p. 5, fn.). VW wrote on 28 November 1928: 'I am surprised & a little disquieted by the remorseless severity of my mind: that it never stops reading & writing; makes me write on Geraldine Jewsbury, on Hardy, on Women – is too professional, too little any longer a dreamy amateur' (*III VW Diary*). The original lectures have disappeared, but, according to S. P. Rosenbaum, this essay 'is probably as close as we can now come to what Virginia Woolf said at Cambridge' (*W&F*, p. xxi). See also 'Women and Leisure' and 'An Excerpt from *A Room of One's Own*'. Reprinted: *G&R, CE, W&W, W&F*.
2 – William Shakespeare (1564–1616); John Milton (1608–74); Samuel Johnson (1709–84).
3 – Sappho (b. c. 612 BC). Lady Shikibu Murasaki (c. 978–?1031), *The Tale of Genji*; VW reviewed vol. i, translated by Arthur Waley (George Allen and Unwin, 1925): see *IV VW Essays*.
4 – George Macaulay Trevelyan, *History of England* (Longmans, Green, 1926), p. 436.

5 – John Keats (1795–1821); Thomas Carlyle (1795–1881); Gustave Flaubert (1821–80).
6 – Joseph Conrad (1857–1924); Leo Tolstoy (1828–1910), *War and Peace* (1865–9).
7 – Jane Austen (1775–1817), *Pride and Prejudice* (1813); Emily Brontë (1818–48), *Wuthering Heights* (1847); Charlotte Brontë (1816–55), *Villette* (1853), *Jane Eyre* (1847); George Eliot (1819–80), *Middlemarch* (1871–2).
8 – See J. W. Cross, *George Eliot's Life as Related in her Letters and Journals* (3 vols, William Blackwood & Sons, 1885), vol. i, ch. vii, 'Richmond – "Scenes of Clerical Life"', George Eliot to Mrs Bray, 5 June 1857, p. 454: 'I wish it to be understood that I should never invite any one to come and see me who did not ask for the invitation.' This is quoted by VW in 'George Eliot', *CR1*: see *IV VW Essays*. George Henry Lewes (1817–78).
9 – Charles Dickens (1812–70).

The 'Censorship' of Books

As the law stands at present, a police magistrate has the right to destroy as obscene any book which he thinks likely to corrupt the mind of any reader who is liable to be corrupted. If it is advisable to entrust anyone with such power – of which I am doubtful – obviously the time has come when the nature of what is corrupting and thus destroyable must be more clearly defined. Nor is it difficult to suggest what lines that definition should follow. There can be no doubt that books fall, in respect of indecency, into two classes. There are books written, published and sold with the object of causing pleasure or corruption by means of their indecency. There is no difficulty in finding where they are to be bought, nor in buying them when found. There are others whose indecency is not the object of the book, but incidental to some other purpose – scientific, social, æsthetic – on the writer's part. The police magistrate's power should be definitely limited to the suppression of books which are sold as pornography to people who seek out and enjoy pornography. The others should be left alone. Any man or woman of average intelligence and culture knows the difference between the two kinds of book and has no difficulty in distinguishing one from the other.

Nor can any reasonable person doubt, after watching the law as it stands at work, that it causes more harm than it prevents. The average citizen is nowadays certainly a reader and quite frequently a writer. In both these capacities he is injured, annoyed, and possibly corrupted, by the censorship as exercised at present. Nothing can be more insulting to his intelligence and exciting to his curiosity than to be told that there is a book that he must not read because in the opinion of somebody else it would corrupt him to do so. As was amply proved last autumn, prohibition often serves only to stimulate the appetite. Discussion is roused where there would have been indifference; knowledge is sought where there would have been ignorance. The vice in question becomes a topic of conversation, and young people are made to think it attractive because it is fashionable and forbidden.

Even more serious is the effect upon the writer. The police magistrate's opinion is so incalculable – he lets pass so much that seems noxious and pounces upon so much that seems innocent – that even the writer whose record is hitherto unblemished is uncertain what may or may not be judged obscene, and hesitates in fear and suspicion. What he is about to write may seem to him perfectly innocent – it may be essential to his book; yet, he has to ask himself, what will the police magistrate say? And not only what will the police magistrate say, but what will the printer say and what will the publisher say? For both printer and publisher will be trying, uneasily and anxiously, to anticipate the verdict of the police magistrate and will naturally bring pressure to bear upon the writer to put them beyond the reach of the law. He will be asked to weaken, to soften, to omit. Such hesitation and suspense are fatal to freedom of mind, and freedom of mind is essential to good literature. Moreover, if modern books become so insipid, so blameless, so full of blank spaces and evasions that we cannot read them, we shall be driven to read the classics, where obscenity abounds.

For these reasons I think it desirable that the law should distinguish clearly between books that are written or sold for pornographic purposes and books whose obscenity is an incidental part of them – between Aristotle's works as they are sold in the rubber goods shops, that is to say, and Aristotle's works as they are sold in the shops of Messrs Hatchard and Bumpus.[2]

1 – A signed contribution to a symposium in the *Nineteenth Century and After*, April 1929, (*Kp4* C311). This was the fifth of six contributions. The others were by Lord Justice Darling (1849–1936); (Henry) Havelock Ellis (1859–1939), writer and sexologist; Stephen Foot, 'schoolmaster'; E. M. Forster (1879–1970); and Carrol Romer, editor of the *Nineteenth Century*.

VW wrote to her nephew Quentin Bell on 20 March 1929: 'I must implore you to write at length. You know my appetite for facts. Nothing is too small, remote, large, or obscene. I am so bothered by writing about the obscene. At this moment I ought to correct an article in a symposium of pundits upon that subject. If modern books are made pure, we shall read the classics I said; and then what happens? But all this is trivial worthless waste of time' (*IV VW Letters*, no. 2012).

The background to the symposium was the suppression in 1928 of *The Well of Loneliness* by Radclyffe Hall (1880–1943). The novel was published on 27 July, and LW reviewed it in his 'World of Books' column in the *N&A* on 4 August 1928: 'As a study of a psychology which is neither as uncommon nor as abnormal as many people imagine, the book is extremely interesting . . . And yet the book fails completely as a work of art.' On 24 August the book was withdrawn by its publisher, Jonathan Cape, on the advice of the Home Secretary. In the *N&A* on 1 September the situation was outlined in an unsigned editorial (by E. M. Forster), entitled 'The New Censorship': 'The point is that the book has never been put on its trial, it has never had a chance of justice . . . as the British Courts provide'. In the same issue a letter from J. R. A. Bradley asked: 'What is the test of indecency and obscenity? Surely it is not the theme of the book but the treatment of the theme?' VW wrote on 8 September 1928 to Vita Sackville-West who felt 'very violently about The Well of Loneliness': 'As for Radclyffe Hall, I agree: but what is one to do? She drew up a letter of her own, protesting her innocence and decency, which she asked us to sign, and would have no other sent out. So nothing could be done, except indeed one rather comic little letter written by Morgan Forster, which he asked me to sign: and now it appears that I, the mouthpiece of Sapphism, write letters from the Reform Club! Nothing else can be done' (*III VW Letters*, no. 1922). On the same day, that letter, entitled 'The New Censorship', (*Kp4* C302), appeared in the *N&A*:

'May we endorse Mr J. R. A. Bradley's letter from the point of view of novelists? We agree with him that "The Well of Loneliness" is restrained and perfectly decent, and that the treatment of its theme is unexceptionable. It has obviously been suppressed because of the theme itself. May we add a few words on this point? ¶ The subject-matter of the book exists as a fact among the many other facts of life. It is recognized by science and recognizable in history. It forms, of course, an extremely small fraction of the sum-total of human emotions, it enters personally into very few lives, and is uninteresting or repellent to the majority; nevertheless it exists, and novelists in England have now been forbidden to mention it by Sir W. Joynson-Hicks. May they mention it incidentally? Although it is forbidden as a main theme, may it be alluded to, or ascribed to subsidiary characters? Perhaps the Home Secretary will issue further orders on this point. And is it the only taboo, or are there others? What of the other subjects known to be more or less unpopular in Whitehall, such as birth-control, suicide, and pacifism? May we mention these? We await our instructions! ¶ The troubles of writers are, naturally enough, of little interest to the general public, and their protests are apt to raise a smile. Still, such as they are, writers produce literature, and they cannot produce great literature until they have free minds. The free mind has access to all the knowledge and speculation of its age, and nothing cramps it like a taboo. A novelist may not wish to treat any of the subjects above mentioned, but the sense that they are prohibited or prohibitable, that there is a taboo-list, will work on him and will make him alert and cautious instead of surrendering himself to his creative impulses. And he will tend to cling to subjects that are officially acceptable, such as murder and adultery, and to shun anything original lest it lead him into forbidden areas. ¶ That is why we feel that Miss Hall's fellow writers ought to protest vigorously against the action of the Home Office, an action which is apparently illegal and is in any case detrimental to the interests of litera-ture. Not only has a wrong been done to a seriously minded book, a blow has been struck at literature generally, and, as your editorial article points out, the blow will certainly be repeated unless public opinion can be aroused.'

In the *N&A* of 15 September, T. S. Eliot added 'a line in support of the admirable protest made by Mr. Forster and Mrs. Woolf'.

On 6 September Cape sent the moulds of the book to Paris, where it was published by the Pegasus Press and in due course copies were imported into the UK. (Meanwhile, the trade edition of *O* was published by the Hogarth Press on 11 October.) On 19 October two consignments of the book were seized under the search and seizure provisions of the Obscene Publications Act, 1857, and the two parties concerned, Leopold Hill (bookseller) and Jonathan Cape, 'were commanded to appear' at Bow Street Magistrates Court on 9 November to 'show cause why the said obscene books so found and seized as aforesaid should not be destroyed' (quoted in Diana Souhami, *The Trials of Radclyffe Hall* [Virago, 1999], p. 193). Harold Rubinstein, Hall's solicitor, 'compiled a mass of expert testimony to its virtues and gathered a glittering array of witnesses to give "good cause" why the book should freely circulate' (*ibid.*, p. 194). VW agreed to testify and her deposition states: 'In my opinion "The Well of Loneliness" treats a delicate subject with great decency and discretion.' In the event, the magistrate, Sir Chartres Biron, refused to admit expert testimony, and ruled that the book was obscene and that the copies be destroyed.

On 22 November, a letter drafted by George Bernard Shaw with 45 signa-tures, including those of VW and LW, (*Kp4* E17.2), appeared in at least four daily newspapers:

'The Magistrate at Bow Street has ordered the destruction as obscene of a book by a reputable author, published by a reputable publishing firm, and reviewed without protest in the leading critical journals. His definition of obscenity, quoted from Chief Justice Cockburn, was as follows: "I think the test of obscenity is whether the tendency of the matter charged is to deprave and corrupt those whose minds are open to immoral influences and into whose hands a publication of the sort may fall". ¶ The most serious part of the sentence is the outlawry of anything that can deprave and corrupt those whose minds are open to immoral influences. It was impossible to defend "The Well of Loneliness" against that charge. But it would have been equally impossible to defend many of the masterpieces of English literature, from Shakespeare's sonnets to "Tess of the D'Urbervilles". If such a test is to stand, then any magistrate can order the destruction of many of the most famous books or of photographs of some of the most famous pictures in our public galleries. ¶ We are not unmindful of the value to the police and the magistracy of a test which enables them to deal summarily with obscene photographs and the rest of the trash sold by dealers in vulgar pornography. As long as the authorities play the game scrupulously by not attacking literature and art with this bludgeon they need fear no protest from any reputable quarter. We do not claim impunity for literature; authors are and should be subject to the law like other people. But neither authors nor others should be subject to judicial defamation under cover, not of laws, but of ancient dicta which are too absurd to be discussed without a suspension of common sense.'

The appeal on 14 December was turned down. See also *III VW Diary*, pp. 201, 204, 206–7; *III VW Letters*, pp. 520, 525–6, 555–6, 559, 563; *IV VW Letters*, pp. 14–15, 29; *VI VW Letters*, 16 October [1928], no. 1942a; Desmond MacCarthy, *Experience* (Putnam, 1935), 'Obscenity and the Law', pp. 140–8.

2 – Hatchard's is still at 187 Piccadilly. John and Edward Bumpus's shop was at 350 Oxford St; there is an advertisement for it in *L&L*, October 1928, in which VW's 'The Niece of an Earl' appeared; and see *VWB*, no. 16 (May 2004), pp. 5–8.

Phases of Fiction

The following pages attempt to record the impressions made upon the mind by reading a certain number of novels in succession. In deciding which book to begin with and which book to go on with, the mind was not pressed to make a choice. It was allowed to read what it liked. It was not, that is to say, asked to read historically, nor was it asked to read critically. It was asked to read only for interest and pleasure and, at the same time, to comment as it read upon the nature of the interest and the pleasure that it found. It went its way, therefore, independent of time and reputation. It read Trollope before it read Jane Austen and skipped, by chance or negligence, some of the most celebrated books in English fiction. Thus, there is little reference or none to Fielding, Richardson or Thackeray.[2]

Yet, if nobody save the professed historian and critic reads to understand a period or to revise a reputation, nobody reads simply by chance or without a definite scale of values. There is, to speak metaphorically, some design that has been traced upon our minds which reading brings to light. Desires, appetites, however we may come by them, fill it in, scoring now in this direction, now in that. Hence, an ordinary reader can often trace his course through literature with great exactness and can even think himself, from time to time, in possession of a whole world as inhabitable as the real world. Such a world, it may be urged against it, is always in process of creation. Such a world, it may be added, likewise against it, is a personal world, a world limited and unhabitable perhaps by other people, a world created in obedience to tastes that may be peculiar to one temperament and distasteful to another – indeed, any such record of reading, it will be concluded, is bound to be limited, personal, erratic.

In its defence, however, it may be claimed that if the critic and the historian speak a more universal language, a more learned language, they are also likely to miss the centre and to lose their way for the simple reason that they know so many things about a writer that a writer does not know about himself. Writers are heard to complain that influences – education, heredity, theory – are given weight of which they themselves are unconscious in the act of creation. Is the author in question the son of an architect or a bricklayer? Was he educated at home or at the university? Does he come before or after Thomas Hardy?[3] Yet no one of these things is in his mind, perhaps, as he writes and the reader's ignorance, narrowing and limiting as it is, has at least the advantage that it leaves unhampered what the reader has in common with the writer, though much more feebly: the desire to create.

Here, then, very briefly and with inevitable simplifications, an attempt is made to show the mind at work upon a shelf full of novels and to watch it as it chooses and rejects, making itself a dwelling place in accordance with its own appetites. Of these appetites, perhaps, the simplest is the desire to believe wholly and entirely in something which is fictitious. That appetite leads on all the others in turn. There is no saying, for they change so much at different ages, that one appetite is better than another. The common reader is, moreover, suspicious of fixed labels and settled hierarchies. Still, since there must be an original impulse, let us give the lead to this one and start upon the shelf full of novels in order to gratify our wish to believe.

The Truth-Tellers

In English fiction there are a number of writers who gratify our sense of belief – Defoe, Swift, Trollope, Borrow, W. E. Norris, for example; among the French, one thinks instantly of Maupassant.[4] Each of them assures us that things are precisely as they say they are. What they describe happens actually before our eyes. We get from their novels the same sort of refreshment and delight that we get from seeing something actually happen in the street below. A dustman, for example, by an awkward movement of his arm knocks over a bottle apparently containing Condy's Fluid[5] which cracks upon the pavement. The dustman gets down; he picks up the jagged fragments of the broken bottle; he turns to a man who is passing in the street. We cannot take our eyes off him until we have feasted our powers of belief to the full. It is as if a channel were cut, into which suddenly and with great relief an emotion hitherto restrained rushes and pours. We forget whatever else we may be doing. This positive experience overpowers all the mixed and ambiguous feelings of which we may be possessed at the moment. The dustman has knocked over a bottle; the red stain is spreading on the pavement. It happens precisely so.

The novels of the great truth-tellers, of whom Defoe is easily the English chief, procure for us a refreshment of this kind. He tells us the story of Moll Flanders, of Robinson Crusoe, of Roxana,[6] and we feel our powers of belief rush into the channel, thus cut, instantly, fertilising and refreshing our entire being. To believe seems the greatest of all pleasures. It is impossible to glut our greed for truth, so rapacious is it. There is not a shadowy or insubstantial word in the whole book to startle our nervous sense of security. Three or four strong, direct strokes of the pen carve out Roxana's character. Her dinner is set indisputably on the table. It consists of veal and turnips. The day is fine or cloudy; the month is April or September. Persistently, naturally, with a curious, almost unconscious iteration, emphasis is laid upon the very facts that most reassure us of stability in real life, upon money, furniture, food, until we seem wedged among solid objects in a solid universe.

One element of our delight comes from the sense that this world, with all its circumstantiality, bright and round and hard as it is, is yet complete, so that in whatever direction we reach out for assurance we receive it. If we press on beyond the confines of each page, as it is our instinct to do, completing what the writer has left unsaid, we shall find that we can trace our way; that there are indications which let us realise them; there is an under side, a dark side to this world. Defoe presided over his universe with the omnipotence of a God, so that his world is perfectly in scale. Nothing is so large that it makes another thing too small; nothing so small that it makes another thing too large.

The name of God is often found on the lips of his people, but they invoke a deity only a little less substantial than they are themselves, a being seated solidly not so very far above them in the tree tops. A divinity more mystical, could Defoe have made us believe in him, would so have discredited the landscape and cast doubt upon the substance of the men and women that our belief in them would have perished at the heart. Or, suppose that he let himself dwell upon the green shades of the forest depths or upon the sliding glass of the summer stream. Again, however much we were delighted by the description, we should have been uneasy because this other reality would have wronged the massive and monumental reality of Crusoe and Moll Flanders. As it is, saturated with the truth of his own universe, no such discrepancy is allowed to intrude. God, man, nature are all real, and they are all real with the same kind of reality – an astonishing feat, since it implies complete and perpetual submission on the writer's part to his conviction, an obdurate deafness to all the voices which seduce and tempt him to gratify other moods. We have only to reflect how seldom a book is carried through on the same impulse of belief, so that its perspective is harmonious throughout, to realise how great a writer Defoe was. One could number on one's fingers half a dozen novels which set out to be masterpieces and yet have failed because the belief flags; the realities are mixed; the perspective shifts and, instead of a final clarity, we get a baffling, if only a momentary confusion.

Having, now, feasted our powers of belief to the full and so enjoyed the relief and rest of this positive world existing so palpably and completely outside of us, there begins to come over us that slackening of attention which means that the nerve in use is sated for the time being. We have absorbed as much of this literal truth as we can and we begin to crave for something to vary it that will yet be in harmony with it. We do not want, except in a flash or a hint, such truth as Roxana offers us when she tells us how her master, the Prince, would sit by their child and 'loved to look at it when it was asleep'.[7] For that truth is hidden truth; it makes us dive beneath the surface to realise it and so holds up the action. It is, then, action that we want. One desire having run its course, another leaps forward to take up the burden and no sooner have we formulated our desire than Defoe has given it to us. 'On with the story' – that cry is forever on his lips. No sooner has he got his facts assembled than the burden is floated. Perpetually springing up, fresh and effortless, action and event, quickly succeeding each other thus, set in motion this dense accumulation of facts and keep the breeze blowing in our faces. It becomes obvious, then, that if his people are sparely equipped and bereft of certain affections, such as love of husband and child, which we expect of people at leisure, it is that they may move quicker. They must travel light since it is for adventure that they are made. They will need quick wits, strong muscles and a rocky common sense on the road they are to travel rather than sentiment, reflection or the power of self-analysis.

Belief, then, is completely gratified by Defoe. Here, the reader can rest himself and enter into possession of a large part of his domain. He tests it; he tries it; he feels nothing give under him or fade before him. Still, belief seeks fresh sustenance as a sleeper seeks a fresh side of the pillow. He may turn, and this is likely, to someone closer to him in time than Defoe in order to gratify his desire for belief (for distance of time in a novel sets up picturesqueness, hence unfamiliarity). If he should take down, for example, some book of a prolific and once esteemed novelist, like W. E. Norris, he will find that the juxtaposition of the two books brings each out more clearly.

W. E. Norris was an industrious writer who is well worth singling out for inquiry if only because he represents that vast body of forgotten novelists by whose labours fiction is kept alive in the absence of the great masters. At first, we seem to be given all that we need: girls and boys, cricket, shooting, dancing, boating, love making, marriage; a park here; a London drawing room there; here, an English gentleman;

there, a cad; dinners, tea parties, canters in the Row; and, behind it all, green and grey, domestic and venerable, the fields and manor houses of England.[8] Then, as one scene succeeds another, half-way through the book, we seem to have a great deal more belief on our hands than we know what to do with. We have exhausted the vividness of slang; the modernity, the adroit turn of mood. We loiter on the threshold of the scene, asking to be allowed to press a little further; we take some phrase and look at it as if it ought to yield us more. Then, turning our eyes from the main figures, we try to sketch out something in the background, to pursue these feelings and relations away from the present moment; not, needless to say, with a view to discovering some overarching conception, something which we may call 'a reading of life'. No, our desire is otherwise: some shadow of depth appropriate to the bulk of the figures; some Providence such as Defoe provides or morality such as he suggests, so that we can go beyond the age itself without falling into inanity.

Then, we discover it is the mark of a second-rate writer that he cannot pause here or suggest there. All his powers are strained in keeping the scene before us, its brightness and its credibility. The surface is all; there is nothing beyond.

Our capacity for belief, however, is not in the least exhausted. It is only a question of finding something that will revive it for us. Not Shakespeare and not Shelley[9] and not Hardy; perhaps, Trollope, Swift, Maupassant. Above all, Maupassant is the most promising at the moment, for Maupassant enjoys the great advantage that he writes in French. Not from any merit of his own, he gives us that little fillip which we get from reading a language whose edges have not been smoothed for us by daily use. The very sentences shape themselves in a way that is definitely charming. The words tingle and sparkle. As for English, alas, it is *our* language – shop-worn, not so desirable, perhaps. Moreover, each of these compact little stories has its pinch of gunpowder, artfully placed so as to explode when we tread on its tail. The last words are always highly charged. Off they go, *bang*, in our faces and there is lit up for us in one uncompromising glare someone with his hand lifted, someone sneering, someone turning his back, someone catching an omnibus, as if this insignificant action, whatever it may be, summed up the whole situation forever.

The reality that Maupassant brings before us is always one of the body, of the senses – the ripe flesh of a servant girl, for example, or the succulence of food. 'Elle restait inerte, ne sentant plus son

45

corps, et l'esprit dispersé, comme si quelqu'un l'eût d'échiqueté avec un de ces instruments dont se servent les cardeurs pour effiloquer la laine des matelas.' Or her tears dried themselves upon her cheeks 'comme des gouttes d'eau sur du fer rouge'.[10] It is all concrete; it is all visualised. It is a world, then, in which one can believe with one's eyes and one's nose and one's senses; nevertheless, it is a world which secretes perpetually a little drop of bitterness. Is this all? And, if this is all, is it enough? Must we, then, believe this? So we ask. Now that we are given truth unadorned, a disagreeable sensation seems attached to it, which we must analyse before we go further.

Suppose that one of the conditions of things as they are is that they are unpleasant, have we strength enough to support that unpleasantness for the sake of the delight of believing in it? Are we not shocked somehow by *Gulliver's Travels*[11] and *Boule de Suif* and *La Maison Tellier*? Shall we not always be trying to get round the obstacle of ugliness by saying that Maupassant and his like are narrow, cynical and unimaginative when, in fact, it is their truthfulness that we resent – the fact that leeches suck the naked legs of servant girls, that there are brothels, that human nature is fundamentally cold, selfish, corrupt? This discomfort at the disagreeableness of truth is one of the first things that shakes very lightly our desire to believe. Our Anglo-Saxon blood, perhaps, has given us an instinct that truth is, if not exactly beautiful, at least pleasant or virtuous to behold. But let us look once more at truth and, this time, through the eyes of Anthony Trollope, 'a big, blustering, spectacled, loud voiced hunting man . . . whose language in male society was, I believe, so lurid that I was not admitted to breakfast with him . . . who rode about the country establishing penny posts, and wrote, as the story goes, so many thousand words before breakfast every day of his life'.[12]

Certainly, the Barchester Novels tell the truth, and the English truth, at first sight, is almost as plain of feature as the French truth, though with a difference. Mr Slope is a hypocrite, with a 'pawing, greasy way with him'.[13] Mrs Proudie is a domineering bully. The Archdeacon is well-meaning but coarse grained and thick cut. Thanks to the vigour of the author, the world of which these are the most prominent inhabitants goes through its daily rigmarole of feeding and begetting children and worshipping with a thoroughness, a gusto, which leave us no loophole of escape. We believe in Barchester as we believe in the reality of our own weekly bills. Nor, indeed, do we wish to escape from the consequences of our belief, for the truth of the Slopes and the Proudies, the truth of the evening party where Mrs Proudie has her dress torn off her back under the light of eleven gas jets, is entirely acceptable.

At the top of his bent Trollope is a big, if not first-rate novelist, and the top of his bent came when he drove his pen hard and fast after the humours of provincial life and scored, without cruelty but with hale and hearty common sense, the portraits of those well-fed, black-coated, unimaginative men and women of the 'fifties. In his manner with them, and his manner is marked, there is an admirable shrewdness, like that of a family doctor or solicitor, too well acquainted with human foibles to judge them other than tolerantly and not above the human weakness of liking one person a great deal better than another for no good reason. Indeed, though he does his best to be severe and is at his best when most so, he could not hold himself aloof, but let us know that he loved the pretty girl and hated the oily humbug so vehemently that it is only by a great pull on his reins that he keeps himself straight. It is a family party over which he presides and the reader who becomes, as time goes on, one of Trollope's most intimate cronies has a seat at his right hand. Their relation becomes confidential.

All this, of course, complicates what was simple enough in Defoe and Maupassant. There, we were plainly and straightforwardly asked to believe. Here, we are asked to believe, but to believe through the medium of Trollope's temperament and, thus, a second relationship is set up with Trollope himself which, if it diverts us, distracts us also. The truth is no longer quite so true. The clear, cold truth, which seems to lie before us unveiled in *Gulliver's Travels* and *Moll Flanders* and *La Maison Tellier*, is here garnished with a charming embroidery. But it is not from this attractive embellishment of Trollope's personality that the disease comes which in the end proves fatal to the huge, substantial, well buttressed, and authenticated truth of the Barchester Novels. Truth itself, however unpleasant, is interesting always. But, unfortunately, the conditions of storytelling are harsh; they demand that scene shall follow scene; that party shall be supported by another party, one parsonage by another parsonage; that all shall be of the same calibre; that the same values shall prevail. If we are told here that the palace was lit by gas, we must be told there that the manor house was faithful to the oil lamp. But what will happen if, in process of solidifying the entire body of his story, the novelist finds himself out of facts or flagging in his invention? Must he then go on? Yes, for the story has to be finished: the intrigue discovered, the guilty punished, the lovers married in the end. The record, therefore, becomes at times merely a chronicle. Truth peters out into a thin-blooded catalogue. Better would it be, we feel, to leave a blank or even to outrage our sense of probability than to stuff the crevices with this makeshift substance: the wrong side of truth is a worn, dull fabric, unsteeped in the waters of imagination and scorched. But the Novel has issued her orders; I consist, she says, of two and thirty chapters; and who am I, we seem to hear the sagacious and humble Trollope ask, with his usual good sense, that I should go disobeying the Novel? And he manfully provides us with makeshifts.

If, then, we reckon up what we have got from the truth-tellers, we find that it is a world where our attention is always being drawn to things which can be seen, touched and tasted, so that we get an acute sense of the reality of our physical existence. Having thus established our belief, the truth-tellers at once contrive that its solidity shall be broken before it becomes oppressive by action. Events happen; co-incidence complicates the plain story. But their actions are all in keeping one with another and they are extremely careful not to discredit them or alter the emphasis in any way by making their characters other than such people as naturally express themselves to the full in active and adventurous careers. Then, again, they hold the three great powers which dominate fiction – God, Nature, and Man – in stable relation so that we look at a world in proper perspective; where, moreover, things hold good not only here at the moment in front of us but, there, behind that tree or among those unknown people far away in the shadow behind those hills. At the same time, truth-telling implies disagreeableness. It is part of truth – the sting and edge of it. We cannot deny that Swift, Defoe and Maupassant all convince us that they reach a more profound depth in their ugliness than Trollope in his pleasantness. For this reason, truth-telling easily swerves a little to one side and becomes satiric. It walks beside the fact and apes it, like a shadow which is only a little more humped and angular than the object which casts it. Yet, in its perfect state, when we can believe absolutely, our satisfaction is complete. Then, we can say, though other states may exist which are better or more exalted, there is none that makes this unnecessary, none that supersedes it. But truth-telling carries in its breast a weakness which is apparent in the works of the lesser writers or in the masters themselves when they are exhausted. Truth-telling is liable to degenerate into perfunctory fact-recording,

48

the repetition of the statement that it was on Wednesday that the Vicar held his mother's meeting which was often attended by Mrs Brown and Miss Dobson in their pony carriage, a statement which, as the reader is quick to perceive, has nothing of truth in it but the respectable outside.

Summary

At length, then, taking into account the perfunctory fact-recording, the lack of metaphor, the plainness of the language and the fact that we believe most when the truth is most painful to us, it is not strange that we should become aware of another desire welling up spontaneously and making its way into those cracks which the great monuments of the truth-tellers wear inevitably upon their solid bases. A desire for distance, for music, for shadow, for space, takes hold of us. The dustman has picked up his broken bottle; he has crossed the road; he begins to lose solidity and detail over there in the evening dusk.

The Romantics

It was a November morning, and the cliffs which overlooked the ocean were hung with thick and heavy mist, when the portals of the ancient and half ruinous tower, in which Lord Ravenswood had spent the last and troubled years of his life, opened, that his mortal remains might pass forward to an abode yet more dreary and lonely.[14]

No change could be more complete. The dustman has become a lord; the present has become the past; homely Anglo-Saxon speech has become Latin and many syllabled; instead of pots and pans, gas jets and snug broughams, we have a half ruinous tower and cliffs, the ocean and November, heavy in mist. This past and this ruin, this lord and this autumn, this ocean and this cliff are as delightful to us as the change from a close room and voices to the night and the open air. The curious softness and remoteness of the *Bride of Lammermoor*, the atmosphere of rusty moorland and splashing waves, the dark and the distance actually seem to be adding themselves to that other more truthful scene which we still hold in mind, and to be giving it completeness. After that storm this peace, after that glare this coolness. The truth-tellers had very little love, it seems, of nature. They used nature almost entirely as an obstacle to overcome or as a background to complete, not æsthetically for contemplation or for any part it might play in the affairs of their characters. The town, after all, was their natural haunt. But let us compare them in more essential qualities: in their treatment of people. There comes towards us a girl tripping lightly and leaning on her father's arm:

... Lucy Ashton's exquisitely beautiful, yet somewhat girlish features, were formed to express peace of mind, serenity, and indifference to the tinsel of worldly pleasure. Her locks, which were of shadowy gold, divided on a brow of exquisite whiteness, like a gleam of broken and pallid sunshine upon a hill of snow. The expression of the countenance was in the last degree gentle, soft, timid and feminine, and seemed rather to shrink from the most casual look of a stranger than to court his admiration.[15]

Nobody could less resemble Moll Flanders or Mrs Proudie. Lucy Ashton is incapable of action or of self-control. The bull runs at her and she sinks to the ground; the thunder peals and she faints. She falters out the strangest little language of ceremony and politeness, 'O if you be a man, if you be a gentleman assist me to find my father'. One might say that she has no character except the traditional; to her father she is filial; to her lover, modest; to the poor, benevolent. Compared with Moll Flanders, she is a doll with sawdust in her veins and wax in her cheeks. Yet we have read ourselves into the book and grow familiar with its proportions. We come, at length, to see that anything more individual or eccentric or marked would lay emphasis where we want none. This tapering wraith hovers over the landscape and is part of it. She and Edgar Ravenswood are needed to support this romantic world with their bare forms, to clasp it round with that theme of unhappy love which is needed to hold the rest together. But the world that they clasp has its own laws. It leaves out and elimi-nates no less drastically than the other. On the one hand, we have feelings of the utmost exaltation – love, hate, jealousy, remorse; on the other hand, raciness and simplicity in the extreme. The rhetoric of the Ashtons and the Ravenswoods is completed by the humours of peasants and cackle of village women. The true romantic can swing us from earth to sky; and the great master of romantic fiction, who is undoubtedly Sir Walter Scott, uses his liberty to the full. At the same time, we retort upon this melancholy which he has called forth, as in the *Bride of Lammermoor*. We laugh at ourselves for having been so moved by machinery so absurd. However, before we impute this defect to romance itself, we must consider whether it is not Scott's fault. This lazy-minded man was quite capable when the cold fit was on him of filling a chapter or two currently, conventionally, from a fountain of empty, journalistic phrases which, for all that they have a charm of their own, let the slackened attention sag still further.

Carelessness has never been laid to the charge of Robert Louis Stevenson.[16] He was careful, careful to a fault – a man who combined most strangely a boy's psychology with the extreme sophistication of an artist. Yet, he obeyed no less implicitly than Walter Scott the laws of romance. He lays his scene in the past; he is always putting his characters to the sword's point with some desperate adventure; he caps his tragedy with homespun humour. Nor can there be any doubt that his conscience and his seriousness as a writer have stood him in good stead. Take any page of *The Master of Ballantrae* and it still stands wear and tear; but the fabric of the *Bride of Lammermoor* is full of holes and patches; it is scamped, botched, hastily flung together. Here, in Stevenson, romance is treated seriously and given all the advantages of the most refined literary art, with the result that we are never left to consider what an absurd situation this is or to reflect that we have no emotion left with which to meet the demand made upon us. We get, on the contrary, a firm, credible story, which never betrays us for a second but is corroborated, substantiated, made good in every detail. With what precision and cunning a scene will be made visible to us as if the pen were a knife which sliced away the covering and left the core bare!

It was as he said: there was no breath stirring; a windless stricture of frost had bound the air; and as we went forth in the shine of the candles, the blackness was like a roof over our heads.[17]

Or, again:

All the 27th that rigorous weather endured: a stifling cold; folk passing about like smoking chimneys; the wide hearth in the hall piled high with fuel; some of the spring birds that had already blundered north into our neighbourhood besieging the windows of the house or trotting on the frozen turf like things distracted.[18]

'A windless stricture of frost . . . folk passing about like smoking chimneys' – one may search the Waverley Novels in vain for such close writing as this. Separately, these descriptions are lovely and brilliant.

The fault lies elsewhere, in the whole of which they are a part. For in those critical minutes which decide a book's fate, when it is finished and the book swims up complete in the mind and lets us look at it, something seems lacking. Perhaps it is that the detail sticks out too prominently. The mind is caught up by this fine passage of description, by that curious exactitude of phrase; but the rhythm and sweep of emotion which the story has started in us are denied satisfaction. We are plucked back when we should be swinging free. Our attention is caught by some knot of ribbon or refinement of tracery when in fact we desire only a bare body against the sky.

Scott repels our taste in a thousand ways. But the crisis, that is the point where the accent falls and shapes the book under it, is right. Slouching, careless as he is, he will at the critical moment pull himself together and strike the one stroke needed, the stroke which gives the book its vividness in memory. Lucy sits gibbering 'couched like a hare upon its form'. 'So, you have ta'en up your bonnie bridegroom?'[19] she says, dropping her fine lady's mincing speech for the vernacular. Ravenswood sinks beneath the quicksands. 'One only vestige of his fate appeared. A large sable feather had been detached from his hat, and the rippling waves of the rising tide wafted it to Caleb's feet. The old man took it up, dried it, and placed it in his bosom.'[20] At both these points the writer's hand is on the book and it falls from him shaped. But in *The Master of Ballantrae*, though each detail is right and wrought so as separately to move our highest admiration, there is no such final consummation. What should have gone to help it seems, in retrospect, to stand apart from it. We remember the detail, but not the whole. Lord Dur[r]isdeer and the Master die together but we scarcely notice it. Our attention has been frittered away elsewhere.

It would seem that the romantic spirit is an exacting one; if it sees a man crossing the road in the lamplight and then lost in the gloom of the evening, it at once dictates what course the writer must pursue. We do not wish, it will say, to know much about him. We desire that he shall express our capacity for being noble and adventurous; that he shall dwell among wild places and suffer the extremes of fortune; that he be endowed with youth and distinction and allied with moors, winds and wild birds. He is, moreover, to be a lover, not in a minute, introspective way, but largely and in outline. His feelings must be part of the landscape; the shallow browns and blues of distant woods and harvest fields are to enter into them; a tower, perhaps, and a castle where the snapdragon flowers. Above all, the romantic spirit

7

demands here a crisis and there a crisis in which the wave that has swollen in the breast shall break. Such feelings Scott gratifies more completely than Stevenson, though with enough qualification to make us pursue the question of romance and its scope and its limitations a little further. Perhaps here it might be interesting to read *The Mysteries of Udolpho*.[21]

The Mysteries of Udolpho have been so much laughed at as the type of Gothic absurdity that it is difficult to come at the book with a fresh eye. We come, expecting to ridicule. Then, when we find beauty, as we do, we go to the other extreme and rhapsodise. But the beauty and the absurdity of romance are both present and the book is a good test of the romantic attitude, since Mrs Radcliffe pushes the liberties of romance to the extreme. Where Scott will go back a hundred years to get the effect of distance, Mrs Radcliffe will go back three hundred. With one stroke, she frees herself from a host of disagreeables and enjoys her freedom lavishly. As a novelist, it is her desire to describe scenery and it is there that her great gift lies. Like every true writer, she shoulders her way past every obstacle to her goal. She brings us into a huge, empty, airy world. A few ladies and gentlemen, who are purely Eighteenth Century in mind, manner, and speech, wander about in vast champaigns, listen to nightingales singing amorously in midnight woods; see the sun set over the lagoons of Venice; and watch the distant Alps turn pink and blue from the turrets of an Italian castle.

These people, when they are well born, are of the same blood as Scott's gentry; attenuated and formal silhouettes who have the same curious power of being in themselves negligible and insipid but of merging harmoniously in the design.

Again, we feel the force which the romantic acquires by obliterating facts. With the sinking of the lights, the solidity of the foreground disappears, other shapes become apparent and other senses are roused. We become aware of the danger and darkness of our existence; comfortable reality has proved itself a phantom too. Outside our little shelter we hear the wind raging and the waves breaking. In this mood our senses are strained and apprehensive. Noises are audible which we should not hear normally. Curtains rustle. Something in the semi-darkness seems to move. Is it alive? And what is it? And what is it seeking here? Mrs Radcliffe succeeds in making us feel all this, largely because she is able to make us aware of the landscape and, thus, induces a detached mood favourable to romance; but in her, more plainly than in Scott or Stevenson, the absurdity is evident, the wheels of the machine are visible and the grinding is heard. She lets us see clearly more than they do what demands the romantic writer makes upon us.

Both Scott and Stevenson, with the true instinct of the imagination, introduced rustic comedy and broad Scots dialect. It is in that direction, as they rightly divined, that the mind will unbend when it relaxes. Mrs Radcliffe, on the other hand, having climbed to the top of her pinnacle, finds it impossible to come down. She tries to solace us with comic passages, put naturally into the mouths of Annette and Ludovico who are servants. But the break is too steep for her limited and lady-like mind and she pieces out her high moments and her beautiful atmosphere with a pale reflection of romance which is more tedious than any ribaldry. Mysteries abound. Murdered bodies multiply; but she is incapable of creating the emotion to feel them by, with the result that they lie there, unbelieved in; hence, ridiculous. The veil is drawn; there is the concealed figure; there is the decayed face; there are the writhing worms – and we laugh.

Directly the power which lives in a book sinks, the whole fabric of the book, its sentences, the length and shape of them, its inflections, its mannerisms, all that it wore proudly and naturally under the impulse of a true emotion become stale, forced, unappetising. Mrs Radcliffe slips limply into the faded Scott manner and reels off page after page in a style illustrated by this example:

Emily, who had always endeavoured to regulate her conduct by the nicest laws, and whose mind was finely sensible, not only of what is just in morals, but of whatever is beautiful in the feminine character, was shocked by these words.[22]

And so it slips along and so we sink and drown in the pale tide. Nevertheless, *Udolpho* passes this test: it gives us an emotion which is both distinct and unique, however high or low we rate the emotion itself.

If we see now where the danger of romance lies: how difficult the mood is to sustain; how it needs the relief of comedy; how the very distance from common human experience and strangeness of its elements become ridiculous – if we see these things, we see also that these emotions are in themselves priceless jewels. The romantic novel realises for us an emotion which is deep and genuine. Scott, Stevenson,

Mrs Radcliffe, all in their different ways, unveil another country of the land of fiction; and it is not the least proof of their power that they breed in us a keen desire for something different.[23]

The Character-Mongers and Comedians

The novels which make us live imaginatively, with the whole of the body as well as the mind, produce in us the physical sensations of heat and cold, noise and silence, one reason perhaps why we desire change and why our reactions to them vary so much at different times. Only, of course, the change must not be violent. It is rather that we need a new scene; a return to human faces; a sense of walls and towns about us, with their lights and their characters after the silence of the wind-blown heath.

After reading the romances of Scott and Stevenson and Mrs Radcliffe, our eyes seem stretched, their sight a little blurred, as if they had been gazing into the distance and it would be a relief to turn for contrast to a strongly marked human face, to characters of extravagant force and character in keeping with our romantic mood. Such figures are most easily to be found in Dickens, of course, and particularly in *Bleak House* where, as Dickens said, 'I have purposely dwelt upon the romantic side of familiar things'.[24] They are found there with peculiar aptness – for if the characters satisfy us by their eccentricity and vigour, London and the landscape of the Dedlocks' place at Chesney Wold are in the mood of the moor, only more luridly lit up and more sharply dark and bright because in Dickens the character-making power is so prodigious that the very houses and streets and fields are strongly featured in sympathy with the people. The character-making power is so prodigious, indeed, that it has little need to make use of observation, and a great part of the delight of Dickens lies in the sense we have of wantoning with human beings twice or ten times their natural size or smallness who retain only enough human likeness to make us refer their feelings very broadly, not to our own, but to those of odd figures seen casually through the half-opened doors of public houses, lounging on quays, slinking mysteriously down little alleys which lie about Holborn and the Law Courts. We enter at once into the spirit of exaggeration.

Who, in the course of a long life, has met Mr Chadband or Mr Turveydrop or Miss Elite?[25] Who has met anybody who, whatever the day or the occasion, can be trusted to say the same phrase, to repeat the same action? This perpetual repetition has, of course, an enormous power to drive these characters home, to stabilise them. Mr Vholes, with his three dear girls at home and his father to support in the Vale of Taunton, Mrs Jellyby and the natives of Borrioboola-Gha, Mr Turveydrop and his deportment, all serve as stationary points in the flow and confusion of the narrative; they have a decorative effect as if they were gargoyles carved, motionless, at the corner of a composition. Wherever we may have wandered, we shall come back and find them there. They uphold the extraordinary intricacy of the plot in whose confusion we are often sunk up to our lips. For it is impossible to imagine that the Jellybys and the Turveydrops are ever affected by human emotions or that their habitual routine is disturbed by the astonishing events which blow through the pages of the book, from so many quarters at the same time. Thus they have a force, a sublimity, which the slighter and more idiosyncratic characters miss.

After all, is not life itself, with its coincidences and its convolutions, astonishingly queer? 'What connexion,' Dickens himself exclaims, 'can there have been between many people in the innumerable histories of this world, who, from opposite sides of great gulfs, have, nevertheless, been very curiously brought together!'[26] One after another his characters come into being, called into existence by an eye which has only to glance into a room to take in every object, human or inanimate, that is there; by an eye which sees once and for all; which snatches at a woman's steel hair curlers, a pair of red-rimmed eyes, a white scar and makes them somehow reveal the essence of a character; an eye gluttonous, restless, insatiable, creating more than it can use. Thus, the prevailing impression is one of movement, of the endless ebb and flow of life round one or two stationary points.

Often we cease to worry about the plot and wander off down some strange avenue of suggestion stirred in this vast and mobile world by a casual movement, a word, a glance. 'Still, very steadfastly and quietly walking towards it, a peaceful figure, too, in the landscape, went Mademoiselle Hortense, shoeless, through the wet grass.'[27] She goes and she leaves a strange wake of emotion behind her. Or, again, a door is flung open in the misty purlieus of London; there is Mr Tulkinghorn's friend, who appears once and once only – 'a man of the same mould and a lawyer too, who lived the same kind of life until he was seventy-five years old, and then, suddenly conceiving (as it is supposed) an impression that it was too monotonous, gave his gold watch to his hairdresser one summer evening, and walked leisurely home to the Temple, and hanged himself'.[28]

This sense that the meaning goes on after the words are spoken, that doors open and let us look through them, is full of romance. But romance in Dickens is impressed on us through characters, through extreme types of human beings, not through castles or banners, not through the violence of action, adventure or nature. Human faces, scowling, grinning, malignant, benevolent, are projected at us from every corner. Everything is unmitigated and extreme.

But at last, among all these characters who are so static and so extreme, we come upon one – Inspector Bucket, the detective – which is not, as the others are, of a piece, but made up of contrasts and discrepancies. The romantic power of the single-piece character is lost. For the character is no longer fixed and part of the design: it is in itself of interest. Its movements and changes compel us to watch it. We try to understand this many-sided man who has brushed his hair, which is thin, with a wet brush; who has breakfasted off chops and eggs; who has his bombastic, official side, yet with it combines, as we see when the mine is sprung, ability, conscience, even compassion – for all these qualities are displayed by turns in the astonishingly vivid account of the drive through the night and the storm, in pursuit of Esther's mother. If much more were added, so that Inspector Bucket drew more of our attention to him and diverted it from the story, we should begin with this new scale of values in our eyes to find the glaring opposites in use elsewhere too violent to be tolerable. But Dickens committed no such sin against his readers. He uses this clear-cut, many-faced figure to sharpen his final scenes and, then, letting Inspector Bucket of the detective force disappear, gathers the loose folds of the story into one prodigious armful and makes an end. But he has sharpened our curiosity and made us dissatisfied with the limitations and even with the exuberance of his genius. The scene becomes too elastic, too voluminous, too cloud-like in its contours. The very abundance of it tires us, as well as the impossibility of holding it all together. We are always straying down bypaths and into alleys where we lose our way and cannot remember where we were going.

Though the heart of Dickens burned with indignation for public wrongs, he lacked sensitiveness privately, so that his attempts at intimacy failed. His great figures are on too large a scale to fit nicely

into each other. They do not interlock. They need company to show
them off and action to bring out their humours. They are often out
of touch with each other. In Tolstoy, in the scenes between Princess
Marya and her father, the old Prince, the pressure of character upon
character is never relaxed.[29] The tension is perpetual, every nerve in
the character is alive. It may be for this reason that Tolstoy is the
greatest of novelists. In Dickens the characters are impressive in themselves but not in their personal relations. Often, indeed, when they
talk to each other they are vapid in the extreme or sentimental beyond
belief. One thinks of them as independent, existing forever, unchanged,
like monoliths looking up into the sky. So it is that we begin to want
something smaller, more intense, more intricate. Dickens has, himself,
given us a taste of the pleasure we derive from looking curiously and
intently into another character. He has made us instinctively reduce
the size of the scene in proportion to the figure of a normal man,
and now we seek this intensification, this reduction, carried out more
perfectly and more completely, we shall find, in the novels of Jane
Austen.

At once, when we open *Pride and Prejudice*,[30] we are aware that the
sentence has taken on a different character. Dickens, of course, at full
stride is as free-paced and far-stretched as possible. But in comparison
with this nervous style, how large-limbed and how loose. The sentence
here runs like a knife, in and out, cutting a shape clear. It is done in a
drawing-room. It is done by the use of dialogue. Half a dozen people
come together after dinner and begin, as they so well might, to discuss
letter-writing. Mr Darcy writes slowly and 'studies too much for words
of four syllables'.[31] Mr Bingley, on the other hand (for it is necessary
that we should get to know them both and they can be quickest shown
if they are opposed) 'leaves out half his words and blots the rest'.[32] But
such is only the first rough shaping that gives the outline of the face.
We go on to define and distinguish. Bingley, says Darcy, is really boasting,
when he calls himself a careless letter-writer because he thinks the defect
interesting. It was a boast when he told Mrs Bennet that if he left
Netherfield he would be gone in five minutes.[33] And this little passage
of analysis on Darcy's part, besides proving his astuteness and his cool
observant temper, rouses Bingley to show us a vivacious picture of Darcy
at home. 'I don't know a more awful object than Darcy, on particular
occasions, and in particular places; at his own house especially, and of
a Sunday evening, when he has nothing to do.'[34]

So, by means of perfectly natural question and answer, everyone is defined and, as they talk, they become not only more clearly seen, but each stroke of the dialogue brings them together or moves them apart, so that the group is no longer casual but interlocked. The talk is not mere talk; it has an emotional intensity which gives it more than brilliance. Light, landscape – everything that lies outside the drawing-room is arranged to illumine it. Distances are made exact; arrangements accurate. It is one mile from Meryton; it is Sunday and not Monday. We want all suspicions and questions laid at rest. It is necessary that the characters should lie before us in as clear and quiet a light as possible since every flicker and tremor is to be observed. Nothing happens, (as things so often happen in Dickens,) for its own oddity or curiosity but with relation to something else. No avenues of suggestion are opened up, no doors are suddenly flung wide; the ropes which tighten the structure, since they are all rooted in the heart, are so held firmly and tightly. For, in order to develop personal relations to the utmost, it is important to keep out of the range of the abstract, the impersonal; and to suggest that there is anything that lies outside men and women would be to cast the shadow of doubt upon the comedy of their relationships and its sufficiency. So with edged phrases where often one word, set against the current of the phrase, serves to fledge it (thus: 'and whenever any of the cottagers were disposed to be quarrelsome, discontented, or *too poor*')[35] we got down to the depths, for deep they are, for all their clarity.

But personal relations have limits, as Jane Austen seems to realise by stressing their comedy. Everything, she seems to say, has, if we could discover it, a reasonable summing up; and it is extremely amusing and interesting to see the efforts of people to upset the reasonable order, defeated as they invariably are. But if, complaining of the lack of poetry or the lack of tragedy, we are about to frame the familiar statement that this is a world which is too small to satisfy us, a prosaic world, a world of inches and blades of grass, we are brought to a pause by another impression which requires a moment further of analysis. Among all the elements which play upon us in reading fiction there has always been, though in different degrees, some voice, accent or temperament clearly heard, though behind the scenes of the book. 'Trollope, the novelist, a big, blustering, spectacled, loud-voiced, hunting man'; Scott, the ruined country gentleman, whose very pigs trotted after him, so gracious was the sound of his voice – both come to us with the gesture of hosts, welcoming us, and we fall under the spell of their charm or the interest of their characters.

We cannot say this of Jane Austen, and her absence has the effect of making us detached from her work and of giving it, for all its sparkle and animation, a certain aloofness and completeness. Her genius compelled her to absent herself. So truthful, so clear, so sane a vision would not tolerate distraction, even if it came from her own claims, nor allow the actual experience of a transitory woman to colour what should be unstained by personality. For this reason, then, though we may be less swayed by her, we are less dissatisfied. It may be the very idiosyncrasy of a writer that tires us of him. Jane Austen, who has so little that is peculiar, does not tire us, nor does she breed in us a desire for those writers whose method and style differ altogether from hers. Thus, instead of being urged as the last page is finished to start in search of something that contrasts and completes, we pause when we have read *Pride and Prejudice*.

The pause is the result of a satisfaction which turns our minds back upon what we have just read, rather than forward to something fresh. Satisfaction is, by its nature, removed from analysis, for the quality which satisfies us is the sum of many different parts, so that if we begin praising *Pride and Prejudice* for the qualities that compose it – its wit, its truth, its profound comic power – we shall still not praise it for the quality which is the sum of all these. At this point, then, the mind, brought to bay, escapes the dilemma and has recourse to images. We compare *Pride and Prejudice* to something else because, since satisfaction can be defined no further, all the mind can do is to make a likeness of the thing and, by giving it another shape, cherish the illusion that it is explaining it, whereas it is, in fact, only looking at it afresh. To say that *Pride and Prejudice* is like a shell, a gem, a crystal, whatever image we may choose, is to see the same thing under a different guise. Yet, perhaps, if we compare *Pride and Prejudice* to something concrete, it is because we are trying to express the sense we have in other novels imperfectly, here with distinctness, of a quality which is not in the story but above it, not in the things themselves but in their arrangement.

Pride and Prejudice, one says, has form; *Bleak House* has not. The eye (so active always in fiction) gives its own interpretation of impressions that the mind has been receiving in different terms. The mind has been conscious in *Pride and Prejudice* that things are said, for all their naturalness, with a purpose; one emotion has been contrasted with another; one scene has been short, the next long; so that all the time, instead of reading at random, without control, snatching at this and that, stressing one thing or another, as the mood takes us, we have been aware of check and stimulus, of spectral architecture built up behind the animation and variety of the scene. It is a quality so precise it is not to be found either in what is said or in what is done; that is, it escapes analysis. It is a quality, too, that is much at the mercy of fiction. Its control is invariably weak there, much weaker than in poetry or in drama because fiction runs so close to life the two are always coming into collision. That this architectural quality can be possessed by a novelist, Jane Austen proves. And she proves, too, that far from chilling the interest or withdrawing the attention from the characters, it seems on the contrary to focus it and add an extra pleasure to the book, a significance. It makes it seem that here is something good in itself, quite apart from our personal feelings.

Not to seek contrast but to start afresh – this is the impulse which urges us on after finishing *Pride and Prejudice*. We must make a fresh start altogether. Personal relations, we recall, have limits. In order to keep their edges sharp, the mysterious, the unknown, the accidental, the strange subside; their intervention would be confusing and distressing. The writer adopts an ironic attitude to her creatures, because she has denied them so many adventures and experiences. A suitable marriage is, after all, the upshot of all this coming together and drawing apart. A world which so often ends in a suitable marriage is not a world to wring one's hands over. On the contrary, it is a world about which we can be sarcastic; into which we can peer endlessly, as we fit the jagged pieces one into another. Thus, it is possible to ask not that her world shall be improved or altered (that our satisfaction forbids) but that another shall be struck off, whose constitution shall be different and shall allow of the other relations. People's relations shall be with God or nature. They shall think. They shall sit, like Dorothea Casaubon in *Middlemarch*, drawing plans for other people's houses; they shall suffer like Gissing's characters in solitude; they shall be alone.[36] *Pride and Prejudice*, because it has such integrity of its own, never for an instant encroaches on other provinces and, thus, leaves them more clearly defined.

Nothing could be more complete than the difference between *Pride and Prejudice* and *Silas Marner*.[37] Between us and the scene which was so near, so distinct, is now cast a shadow. Something intervenes. The character of Silas Marner is removed from us. It is held in relation to other men and his life compared with human life. This comparison is perpetually made and illustrated by some-body not implicit in the book but inside it, somebody who at once reveals herself as 'I', so that there can be no doubt from the first that we are not going to get the relations of people together, but the spectacle of life so far as 'I' can show it to us. 'I' will do my best to illumine these particular examples of men and women with all the knowledge, all the reflections that 'I' can offer you.

'I', we at once perceive, has access to many more experiences and reflections than can have come the way of the rustics themselves. She discovers what a simple weaver's emotions on leaving his native village are, by comparing them with those of other people. 'People whose lives have been made various by learning, sometimes find it hard to keep a fast hold on their habitual views of life, on their faith in the Invisible . . .'[38] It is the observer speaking and we are at once in communication with a grave mind – a mind which it is part of our business to understand. This, of course, darkens and thickens the atmosphere, for we see through so many temperaments; so many side lights from knowledge, from reflection, play upon what we see; often, even as we are watching the weaver, our minds circle round him and we observe him with an amusement, compassion or interest which it is impossible that he should feel himself.

Raveloe is not simply a town like Meryton now in existence with certain shops and assembly rooms; it has a past and therefore the present becomes fleeting, and we enjoy, among other things, the feeling that this is a world in process of change and decay, whose charm is due partly to the fact that it is past. Perhaps we compare it in our own minds with the England of today and the Napoleonic wars with those of our own time. All this, if it serves to enlarge the horizon, also makes the village and the people in it who are placed against so wide a view smaller and their impact on each other less sharp. The novelist who believes that personal relations are enough intensifies them and sharpens them and devotes his power to their investigation. But if the end of life is not to meet, to part, to love, to laugh, if we are at the mercy of other forces, some of them unknown, all of them beyond our power, the urgency of these meetings and partings is blurred and lessened. The edges of the coming together are blunted and the comedy tends to widen itself into a larger sphere and so to modulate into something melancholy, tolerant and perhaps resigned. George Eliot has removed herself too far from her characters to dissect them keenly or finely, but she has gained the use of her own mind

upon these same characters. Jane Austen went in and out of her people's minds like the blood in their veins.

George Eliot has kept the engine of her clumsy and powerful mind at her own disposal. She can use it, when she has created enough matter to use it upon, freely. She can stop at any moment to reason out the motives of the mind that has created it. When Silas Marner discovers that his gold has been stolen, he has recourse to 'that sort of refuge which always comes with the prostration of thought under an overpowering passion; it was that expectation of impossibilities, that belief in contradictory images, which is still distinct from madness, because it is capable of being dissipated by the external fact'.[39] Such analysis is unthinkable in Dickens or in Jane Austen. But it adds something to the character which the character lacked before. It makes us feel not only that the working of the mind is interesting but that we shall get a much truer and subtler understanding of what is actually said and done if we so observe it. We shall perceive that often an action has only a slight relation to a feeling and, thus, that the truth-tellers who are content to record accurately what is said and done are often ludicrously deceived and out in their estimate. In other directions there are changes. The use of dialogue is limited; for people can say very little directly. Much more can be said for them or about them by the writer himself. Then, the writer's mind, his knowledge, his skill, not merely the colour of his temperament, become means for bringing out the disposition of the character and also for relating it to other times and places. There is thus revealed underneath a state of mind which often runs counter to the action and the speech.

It is in this direction that George Eliot turns her characters and her scenes. Shadows checker them. All sorts of influences of history, of time, of reflection play upon them. If we consult our own difficult and mixed emotions as we read, it becomes clear that we are fast moving out of the range of pure character-mongering, of comedy, into a far more dubious region.

The Psychologists

Indeed, we have a strange sense of having left every world when we take up *What Maisie Knew*; of being without some support which, even if it impeded us in Dickens and George Eliot, upheld us and controlled us. The visual sense which has hitherto been so active, perpetually sketching fields and farmhouses and faces, seems now to fail or to use its powers to illumine the mind within, rather than the world without. Henry James has to find an equivalent for the processes of the mind, to make concrete a mental state. He says, she was 'a ready vessel for bitterness, a deep little porcelain cup in which biting acids could be mixed'.[40] He is forever using this intellectual imagery. The usual supports, the props and struts of the conventions, expressed or observed by the writer, are removed. Everything seems aloof from interference, thrown open to discussion and light, though resting on no visible support. For the minds of which this world is composed seem oddly freed from the pressure of the old encumbrances and raised above the stress of circumstances.

Crises cannot be precipitated by any of the old devices which Dickens and George Eliot used. Murders, rapes, seductions, sudden deaths have no power over this high, aloof world. Here the people are the sport only of delicate influences: of thoughts that people think, but hardly state, about each other; of judgments which people whose time is unoccupied have leisure to devise and apply. In consequence, these characters seem held in a vacuum at a great move from the substantial, lumbering worlds of Dickens and George Eliot or from the precise crisscross of convention which metes out the world of Jane Austen. They live in a cocoon, spun from the finest shades of meaning, which a society, completely unoccupied by the business of getting its living, has time to spin round and about itself. Hence, we are at once conscious of using faculties hitherto dormant, ingenuity and skill, a mental nimbleness and dexterity such as serve to solve a puzzle ingeniously; our pleasure becomes split up, refined, its substance infinitely divided instead of being served to us in one lump.

Maisie, the little girl who is the bone of contention between two parents, each of them claiming her for six months, each of them finally marrying a second husband or wife, lies sunk beneath the depths of suggestion, hint and conjecture, so that she can only affect us very indirectly, each feeling of hers being deflected and reaching us after glancing off the mind of some other person. Therefore she rouses in us no simple and direct emotion. We always have time to watch it coming and to calculate its pathway, now to the right, now to the left. Cool, amused, intrigued, at every second trying to refine our senses still further and to marshal all that we have of sophisticated intelligence into one section of ourselves, we hang suspended over this aloof little world and watch with intellectual curiosity for the event.

In spite of the fact that our pleasure is less direct, less the result of feeling strongly in sympathy with some pleasure or sorrow, it has a fineness, a sweetness, which the more direct writers fail to give us. This comes in part from the fact that a thousand emotional veins and streaks are perceptible in this twilight or dawn which are lost in the full light of midday. *for subtleties*

Besides this fineness and sweetness we get another pleasure which comes when the mind is freed from the perpetual demand of the novelist that we shall feel with his characters. By cutting off the responses which are called out in actual life, the novelist frees us to take delight, as we do when ill or travelling, in things in themselves. We can see the strangeness of them only when habit has ceased to immerse us in them, and we stand outside watching what has no power over us one way or the other. Then we see the mind at work; we are amused by its power to make patterns; by its power to bring out relations in things and disparities which are covered over when we are acting by habit or driven on by the ordinary impulses. It is a pleasure somewhat akin, perhaps, to the pleasure of mathematics or the pleasure of music. Only, of course, since the novelist is using men and women as his subjects, he is perpetually exciting feelings which are opposed to the impersonality of numbers and sound; he seems, in fact, to ignore and to repress their natural feelings, to be coercing them into a plan which we call with vague resentment 'artificial' though it is probable that we are not so foolish as to resent artifice in art. Either through a feeling of timidity or prudery or through a lack of imaginative audacity, Henry James diminishes the interest and importance of his subject in order to bring about a symmetry which is dear to him. This his readers resent. We feel him there, as the suave showman, skilfully manipulating his characters; nipping, repressing; dexterously evading and ignoring, where a writer of greater depth or natural spirits would have taken the risk which his material imposes, let his sails blow full and so, perhaps, achieved symmetry and pattern, in themselves so delightful, all the same.

But it is the measure of Henry James's greatness that he has given us so definite a world, so distinct and peculiar a beauty that we cannot rest satisfied but want to experiment further with these extraordinary perceptions, to understand more and more, but to be free from the perpetual tutelage of the author's presence, his arrangements, his anxieties. To gratify this desire, naturally, we turn to the work of Proust,[41] where we find at once an expansion of sympathy so great that it almost defeats its own object. If we are going to become conscious of everything, how shall we realise anything? Yet if Henry James's world, after the worlds of Dickens and George Eliot, seemed without material boundaries, if everything was pervious to thought and susceptible of twenty shades of meaning, here illumination and analysis are carried far beyond those bounds. For one thing, Henry James himself, the American, ill at ease for all his magnificent urbanity in a strange civilisation, was an obstacle never perfectly assimilated even by the juices of his own art. Proust, the product of the civilisation which he describes, is so porous, so pliable, so perfectly receptive that we realise him only as an envelope, thin but elastic, which stretches wider and wider and serves not to enforce a view but to enclose a world. His whole universe is steeped in the light of intelligence. The commonest object, such as the telephone, loses its simplicity, its solidity, and becomes a part of life and transparent. The commonest actions, such as going up in an elevator or eating cake, instead of being discharged automatically, rake up in their progress a whole series of thoughts, sensations, ideas, memories which were apparently sleeping on the walls of the mind.

What are we to do with it all? we cannot help asking, as these trophies are piled up round us. The mind cannot be content with holding sensation after sensation passively to itself; something must be done with them; their abundance must be shaped. Yet at first it would seem as if this vitalising power has become so fertile that it cumbers the way and trips us up, even when we have need to go quickest, by putting some curious object enticingly in our way. We have to stop and look even against our will.

Thus, when his mother calls him to come to his grandmother's deathbed, the author says, '"I was not asleep," I answered as I awoke'.[42] Then, even in this crisis, he pauses to explain carefully and subtly why at the moment of waking we so often think for a second that we have not been to sleep. The pause, which is all the more marked because the reflection is not made by 'I' himself but is supplied impersonally by the narrator and, therefore, from a different angle, lays a great strain upon the mind, stretched by the urgency of the situation to focus itself upon the dying woman in the next room.

Much of the difficulty of reading Proust comes from this content obliquity. In Proust, the accumulation of objects which surround any central point is so vast and they are often so remote, so difficult of approach and of apprehension that this drawing-together process is gradual, tortuous, and the final relation difficult in the extreme. There is so much more to think about them than one had supposed. One's relations are not only with another person but with the weather, food, clothes, smells, with art and religion and science and history and a thousand other influences.

If one begins to analyse consciousness, it will be found that it is stirred by thousands of small, irrelevant ideas stuffed with odds and ends of knowledge. When, therefore, we come to say something so usual as 'I kissed her', we may well have to explain also how a girl jumped over a man in a deck chair on the beach before we come tortuously and gradually to the difficult process of describing what a kiss means. In any crisis, such as the death of the grandmother or that moment when the Duchess learns as she steps into her carriage that her old friend Swann is fatally ill, the number of emotions that compose each of these scenes is immensely larger, and they are themselves much more incongruous and difficult of relation than in any other scene laid before us by a novelist.

Moreover, if we ask for help in finding our way, it does not come through any of the usual channels. We are never told, as the English novelists so frequently tell us, that one way is right and the other wrong. Every way is thrown open without reserve and without prejudice. Everything that can be felt can be said. The mind of Proust lies open with the sympathy of a poet and the detachment of a scientist to everything that it has the power to feel. Direction or emphasis, to be told that that is right, to be nudged and bidden to attend to that, would fall like a shadow on this profound luminosity and cut off some section of it from our view. The common stuff of the book is made of this deep reservoir of perception. It is from these depths that his characters rise, like waves forming, then break and sink again into the moving sea of thought and comment and analysis which gave them birth.

In retrospect, thus, though as dominant as any characters in fiction, the characters of Proust seem made of a different substance. Thoughts, dreams, knowledge are part of them. They have grown to their full stature, almost, indeed, beyond their full stature, and their actions have met with no rebuff. If we look for direction to help us put them in their places in the universe, we find it negatively in an absence of direction – perhaps sympathy is of more value than interference, understanding than judgment. As a consequence of the union of the thinker and the poet, often, on the heel of some fanatically precise observation, we come upon a flight of imagery – beautiful, coloured, visual, as if the mind, having carried its powers as far as possible in analysis, suddenly rose in the air and from a station high up gave us a different view of the same object in terms of metaphor. This dual vision makes the great characters in Proust and the whole world from which they spring more like a globe, of which one side is always hidden, than a scene laid flat before us, the whole of which we can take in at one glance.

To make this more precise, it might be well to choose another writer, of foreign birth also, who has the same power of illuminating the consciousness from its roots to the surface. Directly we step from the world of Proust to the world of Dostoevski, we are startled by differences which for a time absorb all our attention. How positive the Russian is, in comparison with the Frenchman. He strikes out a character or a scene by the use of glaring oppositions which are left unbridged. Extreme terms like 'love' and 'hate' are used so lavishly that we must race our imaginations to cover the ground between them. One feels that the mesh of civilisation here is made of a coarse netting and the holes are wide apart. Men and women have escaped, compared with the imprisonment that they suffer in Paris. They are free to throw themselves from side to side, to gesticulate, to hiss, to rant, to fall into paroxysms of rage and excitement. They are free, with the freedom that violent emotion gives, from hesitation, from scruple, from analysis. At first we are amazed by the emptiness and the crudity of this world compared with the other. But when we have arranged our perspective a little, it is clear that we are still in the same world – that it is the mind which entices us and the adventures of the mind that concern us. Other worlds, such as Scott's or Defoe's, are incredible. Of this we are assured when we begin to encounter those curious contradictions of which Dostoevski is so prolific. There is a simplicity in violence which we find nowhere in Proust, but violence also lays bare regions deep down in the mind where contradiction prevails. That contrast which marked Stavrogin's appearance, so that he was at once 'a paragon of beauty, yet at the same time there seemed something repellent about him',[43] is but the crude outer sign of the vice and virtue we meet, at full tilt, in the same breast. The simplification is only on the surface: when the bold and ruthless

68

process, which seems to punch out characters, then to group them together and then to set them all in violent motion, so energetically, so impatiently, is complete, we are shown how, beneath this crude surface, all is chaos and complication. We feel at first that we are in a savage society where the emotions are much simpler and stronger and more impressive than any we encounter in *A la Recherche du temps perdu*.

Since there are so few conventions, so few barriers (Stavrogin, for instance, passes easily from the depths to the heights of society) the complexity would appear to lie deeper, and these strange contradictions and anomalies which make a man at once divine and bestial would seem to be deep in the heart and not superimposed. Hence, the strange emotional effect of *The Possessed*. It appears to be written by a fanatic ready to sacrifice skill and artifice in order to reveal the soul's difficulties and confusions. The novels of Dostoevski are pervaded with mysticism; he speaks not as a writer but as a sage, sitting by the roadside in a blanket, with infinite knowledge and infinite patience.

'Yes,' she answered, 'the mother of God is the great mother – the damp earth, and therein lies great joy for men. And every earthly woe and every earthly fear is a joy for us; and when you water the earth with your tears a foot deep, you will rejoice at everything at once, and your sorrow will be no more, such is the prophecy.' That word sank into my heart at the time. Since then when I bow down to the ground at my prayers, I've taken to kissing the earth. I kiss it and weep.[44]

Such is a characteristic passage. But in a novel the voice of the teacher, however exalted, is not enough. We have too many interests to consider, too many problems to face. Consider a scene like that extraordinary party to which Varvara Petrovna has brought Marya, the lame idiot, whom Stavrogin has married 'from a passion for martyrdom, from a craving for remorse, through moral sensuality'.[45] We cannot read to the end without feeling as if a thumb were pressing on a button in us, when we have no emotion left to answer the call. It is a day of surprises, a day of startling revelations, a day of strange coincidences. For several of the people there (and they come flocking to the room from all quarters) the scene has the greater emotional importance. Everything is done to suggest the intensity of their emotions. They turn pale; they shake with terror; they go into hysterics.

They are thus brought before us in flashes of extreme brilliance – the mad woman with the paper rose in her hat; the young man whose words patter out 'like smooth big grains. . . . One somehow began to imagine that he must have a tongue of special shape, somehow exceptionally long and thin, and extremely red, with a very sharp everlastingly active little tip'.[46]

Yet though they stamp and scream, we hear the sound as if it went on next door. Perhaps the truth is that hate, surprise, anger, horror, are all too strong to be felt continuously. This emptiness and noise lead us to wonder whether the novel of psychology, which projects its drama in the mind, should not, as the truth-tellers showed us, vary and diversify its emotions, lest we shall become numb with exhaustion. To brush aside civilisation and plunge into the depths of the soul is not really to enrich. We have, if we turn to Proust, more emotion in a scene which is not supposed to be remarkable, like that in the restaurant in the fog. There we live along a thread of observation which is always going in and out of this mind and that mind; which gathers information from different social levels which makes us now feel with a prince, now with a restaurant keeper, and brings us into touch with different physical experiences such as light after darkness, safety after danger, so that the imagination is being stimulated on all sides to close slowly, gradually, without being goaded by screams or violence completely round the object. Proust is determined to bring before the reader every piece of evidence upon which any state of mind is founded; so convinced is Dostoevski of some point of truth that he sees before him, he will skip and leap to his conclusion with a spontaneity that is in itself stimulating.

By this distortion the psychologist reveals himself. The intellect, which analyses and discriminates, is always and almost at once overpowered by the rush to feeling; whether it is sympathy or anger. Hence, there is something illogical and contradictory often in the characters, perhaps because they are exposed to so much more than the usual current of emotional force. Why does he act like this? we ask again and again, and answer rather doubtfully, that so perhaps madmen act. In Proust, on the other hand, the approach is equally indirect, but it is through what people think and what is thought about them, through the knowledge and thoughts of the author himself, that we come to understand them very slowly and laboriously, but with the whole of our minds.

The books, however, with all these dissimilarities, are alike in this;

both are permeated with unhappiness. And this would seem to be inevitable when the mind is not given a direct grasp of whatever it may be. Dickens is in many ways like Dostoevski; he is prodigiously fertile and he has immense powers of caricature. But Micawber, David Copperfield and Mrs Gamp[47] are placed directly before us, as if the author saw them from the same angle, and had nothing to do, and no conclusion to draw, except direct amusement or interest. The mind of the author is nothing but a glass between us, or, at most, serves to put a frame round them. All the author's emotional power has gone into them. The surplus of thought and feeling which remained after the characters had been created in George Eliot, to cloud and darken her page, has been used up in the characters of Dickens. Nothing of importance remains over.

But in Proust and Dostoevski, in Henry James, too, and in all those who set themselves to follow feelings and thoughts, there is always an overflow of emotion from the author as if characters of such subtlety and complexity could be created only when the rest of the book is a deep reservoir of thought and emotion. Thus, though the author himself is not present, characters like Stephen Trofimovitch and Charlus can exist only in a world made of the same stuff as they are, though left unformulated. The effect of this brooding and analysing mind is always to produce an atmosphere of doubt, of questioning, of pain, perhaps of despair. At least, such would seem to be the result of reading *A la Recherche du temps perdu* and *The Possessed*.[48]

The Satirists and Fantastics

The confused feelings which the psychologists have roused in us, the strain they have put on us, the extraordinary intricacy which they have revealed to us, the network of fine and scarcely intelligible yet profoundly interesting emotions in which they have involved us, set up a craving for relief, at first so primitive that it is almost a physical sensation. The mind feels like a sponge saturated full with sympathy and understanding; it needs to dry itself, to contract upon something hard. Satire and the sense that the satirist gives us that he has the world well within his grasp, so that it is at the mercy of his pen, precisely fulfil our needs.

A further instinct will lead us to pass over such famous satirists as

Voltaire and Anatole France[49] in favour of someone writing in our own tongue, writing English. For without any disrespect to the translator, we have grown intolerably weary in reading Dostoevski, as if we were reading with the wrong spectacles or as if a mist had formed between us and the page. We come to feel that every idea is slipping about in a suit badly cut and many sizes too large for it. For a translation makes us understand more clearly than the lectures of any professor the difference between raw words and written words; the nature and importance of what we call style. Even an inferior writer, using his own tongue upon his own ideas, works a change at once which is agreeable and remarkable. Under his pen the sentence shrinks and wraps itself firmly round the meaning, if it be but a little one. The loose, the baggy, shrivels up. And while a writer of passable English will do this, a writer like Peacock does infinitely more.

When we open *Crotchet Castle*[50] and read that first very long sentence which begins 'In one of those beautiful valleys, through which the Thames (not yet polluted by the tide, the scouring of cities or even the minor defilement of the sandy streams of Surrey)' it would be difficult to describe the relief it gives us, except metaphorically. First there is the shape which recalls something visually delightful, like a flowing wave or the lash of a whip vigorously flung; then as phrase joins phrase and one parenthesis after another pours in its tributary, we have a sense of the whole swimming stream gliding beneath old walls with the shadows of ancient buildings and the glow of green lawns reflected in it. And what is even more delightful after the immensities and obscurities in which we have been living, we are in a world so manageable in scale that we can take its measure, tease it and ridicule it. It is like stepping out into the garden on a perfect September morning when every shadow is sharp and every colour bright after a night of storm and thunder. Nature has submitted to the direction of man. Man himself is dominated by his intelligence. Instead of being many-sided, complicated, elusive, people possess one idiosyncrasy apiece, which crystallises them into sharp separate characters, colliding briskly when they meet. They seem ridiculously and grotesquely simplified out of all knowledge. Dr Folliott, Mr Firedamp, Mr Skionar, Mr Chainmail and the rest seem after the tremendous thickness and bulk of the Guermantes and the Stavrogins nothing but agreeable caricatures which a clever old scholar has cut out of a sheet of black paper with a pair of scissors. But on looking closer we find that though it would be absurd to credit Peacock with any desire or perhaps capacity to explore the depths of the soul, his reticence is not empty but suggestive. The character of Dr Folliott is drawn in three strokes of the pen. What lies between is left out. But each stroke indicates the mass behind it, so that the reader can make it out for himself; while it has, because of this apparent simplicity, all the sharpness of a caricature. The world suffers the same simplification. A world so happily constituted that there is always trout for breakfast, wine in the cellar, and some amusing contretemps, such as the cook setting herself alight and being put out by the footman, to make us laugh – a world where there is nothing more pressing to do than to 'glide over the face of the waters, discussing everything and settling nothing',[51] is not the world as we know it. But it is not a dream world, a world of pure fantasy; it is close enough to be a parody of our world and to make our own follies and the solemnities of our institutions look a little silly.

The satirist does not, like the psychologist, labour under the oppression of omniscience. He has leisure to play with his mind freely, ironically. His sympathies are not deeply engaged. His sense of humour is not submerged.

But the prime distinction lies in the changed attitude towards reality. In the psychologists the huge burden of facts is based upon a firm foundation of dinner, luncheon, bed and breakfast. It is with surprise, yet with relief and a start of pleasure, that we accept Peacock's version of the world, which ignores so much, simplifies so much, gives the old globe a spin and shows another face of it on the other side. It is unnecessary to be quite so painstaking, it seems. And after all is not this quite as real, as true as the other? And perhaps all this pother about 'reality' is overdone. The great gain is perhaps that our relation with things is more distant. We reap the benefit of a more poetic point of view. A line like the charming 'At Godstow, they gathered hazel on the grave of Rosamond'[52] could be written only by a writer who was at a certain distance from his people, so that there need be no explanations. For certainly with Trollope's people explanations would have been necessary; we should have wanted to know what they had been doing, gathering hazel, and where they had gone for dinner afterwards and how the carriage had met them. 'They', however, being Chainmail, Skionar and the rest, are at liberty to gather hazel on the grave of Rosamond if they like; as they are free to sing a song if it so pleases them or to debate the march of mind.

The romantic took the same liberty but for another purpose. In the satirist we get not a sense of wildness and the soul's adventures, but that the mind is free and therefore sees through and dispenses with much that is taken seriously by writers of another calibre.

There are, of course, limitations, reminders, even in the midst of our pleasure, of boundaries that we must not pass. We cannot imagine in the first place that the writer of such exquisite sentences can cover many reams of paper; they cost too much to make. Then again a writer who gives us so keen a sense of his own personality by the shape of his phrase is limited. We are always being brought into touch, not with Peacock himself, as with Trollope himself (for there is no giving away of his own secrets: he does not conjure up the very shape of himself and the sound of his laughter as Trollope does), but all the time our thought is taking the colour of his thought, we are insensibly thinking in his measure. If we write, we try to write in his manner, and this brings us into far greater intimacy with him than with writers like Trollope again or Scott, who wrap their thought up quite adequately in a duffle grey blanket which wears well and suits everything. This may in the end of course lead to some restriction. Style may carry with it, especially in prose, so much personality that it keeps us within the range of that personality. Peacock pervades his book.

In order that we may consider this more fully let us turn from Peacock to Sterne, a much greater writer, yet sufficiently in the family of Peacock to let us carry on the same train of thought uninterruptedly.

At once we are aware that we are in the presence of a much subtler mind, a mind of far greater reach and intensity. Peacock's sentences, firmly shaped and beautifully polished as they are, cannot stretch as these can. Here our sense of elasticity is increased so much that we scarcely know where we are. We lose our sense of direction. We go backwards instead of forwards. A simple statement starts a digression; we circle; we soar; we turn round; and at last back we come again to Uncle Toby who has been sitting meanwhile in his black plush breeches with his pipe in his hand. Proust it may be said was as tortuous, but his indirectness was due to his immense powers of analysis, and to the fact that directly he had made a simple statement he perceived and must make us perceive all that it implied. Sterne is not an analyst of other people's sensations. Those remain simple, eccentric, erratic. It is his own mind that fascinates him, its oddities and its whims, its fancies and its sensibilities; and it is his own mind that colours the book and gives it walls and shape. Yet it is obvious that his claim is just when he says that however widely he may digress, to my Aunt Dinah and the coachman and then 'some millions of miles into the very heart of the planetary system' when he is by way of telling about Uncle Toby's character, still 'the drawing of my Uncle Toby's character went on gently all the time – not the great contours of it, – that was impossible – but some familiar strokes and faint designations of it . . . so that you are much better acquainted with my Uncle Toby now than you were before'.[53] It is true, for we are always alighting as we skim and circle to deposit some little grain of observation upon the figure of Uncle Toby sitting there with his pipe in his hand. There is thus built up intermittently, irregularly, an extraordinary portrait of a character – a character shown most often in a passive state, sitting still, through the quick glancing eyes of an erratic observer, who never lets his character speak more than a few words or take more than a few steps in his proper person, but is forever circling round and playing with the lapels of his coat and peering up into his face and teasing him affectionately, whimsically, as if he were the attendant sprite in charge of some unconscious mortal. Two such opposites were made to set each other off and draw each other out. One relishes the simplicity, the modesty, of Uncle Toby all the more for comparing them with the witty, indecent, disagreeable, yet highly sympathetic, character of the author.

All through *Tristram Shandy* we are aware of this blend and contrast. Laurence Sterne is the most important character in the book. It is true that at the critical moment the author obliterates himself and gives his characters that little extra push which frees them from his tutelage so that they are something more than the whims and fancies of a brilliant brain. But since character is largely made up of surroundings and circumstances, these people whose surroundings are so queer, who are often silent themselves but always so whimsically talked about, are a race apart among the people of fiction. There is nothing like them elsewhere, for in no other book are the characters so closely dependent on the author. In no other book are the writer and reader so involved together. So finally, we get a book in which all the usual conventions are consumed and yet no ruin or catastrophe comes to pass; the whole subsists complete by itself, like a house which is miraculously habitable without the help of walls, staircases or partitions. We live in the humours, contortions and oddities of the spirit, not in the slow unrolling of the long length of life. And the reflection comes, as we sun ourselves on one of these high pinnacles, can we not escape even further, so that we are not conscious of any author at all? Can we not find poetry in some novel or other? For Sterne by the beauty of his style has let us pass beyond the range of personality into a world which is not altogether the world of fiction. It is above.

The Poets

Certain phrases have brought about this change in us. They have raised us out of the atmosphere of fiction; they have made us pause to wonder. For instance:

I will not argue the matter; Time wastes too fast: every letter I trace tells me with what rapidity Life follows my pen; the days and hours of it more precious, – my dear Jenny – than the rubies about thy neck, are flying over our heads like light clouds of a windy day, never to return more; everything presses on, – whilst thou art twisting that lock; – see! it grows grey; and every time I kiss thy hand to bid adieu, and every absence which follows it, are preludes to that eternal separation which we are shortly to make.[54]

Phrases like this bring, by the curious rhythm of their phrasing, by a touch on the visual sense, an alteration in the movement of the mind which makes it pause and widen its gaze and slightly change its attention. We are looking out at life in general.

But though Sterne with his extraordinary elasticity could use this effect, too, without incongruity, that is only possible because his genius is rich enough to let him sacrifice some of the qualities that are native to the character of the novel without our feeling it. It is obvious that there is no massing together of the experiences of many lives and many minds as in *War and Peace*; and, too, that there is something of the essayist, something of the soliloquist in the quips and quirks of this brilliant mind with the nature of the novel. He is sometimes sentimental, as if after so great a display of singularity he must assert his interest in the normal lives and affections of his people. Tears are necessary; tears are pumped up. Be that as it may, exquisite and individual as his poetry is, there is another poetry which is more natural to the novel, because it uses the material which the novelist provides.

It is the poetry of situation rather than of language, the poetry which we perceive when Catherine in *Wuthering Heights* pulls the feathers from the pillow; when Oak[55] watches the sheep by night; when Natasha in *War and Peace* looks out of the window at the stars. And it is significant that we recall this poetry, not as we recall it in verse, by the words, but by the scene. The prose remains casual and quiet enough so that to quote it is to do little or nothing to explain its effect. Often we have to go far back and read a chapter or more before we can come by the impression of beauty or intensity that possessed us.

Yet it is not to be denied that two of the novelists who are most frequently poetical – Meredith and Hardy – are as novelists imperfect. Both *The Ordeal of Richard Feverel*[56] and *Far from the Madding Crowd* are books of great inequality. In both we feel a lack of control, an incoherence such as we never feel in *War and Peace* or in *A la Recherche du temps perdu* or in *Pride and Prejudice*. Both Hardy and Meredith are too fully charged, it would seem, with a sense of poetry and have too limited or too imperfect a sympathy with human beings to express it adequately through that channel. Hence, as we so often find in Hardy the impersonal element – Fate, the Gods, whatever name we choose to call it – dominates the people. They appear wooden, melodramatic, unreal. They cannot express the poetry with which the writer himself is charged through their own lips, for their psychology is inadequate, and thus the expression is left to the writer, who assumes a character apart from his people and cannot return to them with perfect ease when the time comes.

Again, in Meredith the writer's sense of the poetry of youth, of love, of nature is heard like a song to which the characters listen passively without moving a muscle; and then, when the song is done, on they move again with a jerk. This would seem to prove that a profound poetic sense is a dangerous gift for the novelist; for in Hardy and Meredith poetry seems to mean something impersonal, generalised, hostile to the idiosyncrasy of character, so that the two suffer if brought into touch. It may be that the perfect novelist expresses a different sort of poetry, or has the power of expressing it in a manner which is not harmful to the other qualities of the novel. If we recall the passages that have seemed to us, in retrospect at any rate, to be poetical in fiction we remember them as part of the novel. When Natasha in *War and Peace* looks out of the window at the stars, Tolstoy produces a feeling of deep and intense poetry without any disruption or that disquieting sense of song being sung to people who listen. He does this because his poetic sense finds expression in the poetry of the situation or because his characters express it in their own words, which are often of the simplest. We have been living in them and knowing them so that when Natasha leans on the window sill and thinks of her life to come our feelings of the poetry of the moment do not lie in what she says so much as in our sense of her who is saying it.

Wuthering Heights again is steeped in poetry. But here there is a difference, for one can hardly say that the profound poetry of the scene where Catherine pulls the feathers from the pillow has anything to do with our knowledge of her or adds to our understanding or our feeling about her future. Rather it deepens and controls the wild, stormy atmosphere of the whole book. By a master stroke of vision rarer in prose than in poetry people and scenery and atmosphere are all in keeping. And, what is still rarer and more impressive, through that atmosphere we seem to catch sight of larger men and women, of other symbols and significances. Yet the characters of Heathcliff and Catherine are perfectly natural; they contain all the poetry that Emily Brontë herself feels without effort. We never feel that this is a poetic moment, apart from the rest, or that here Emily Brontë is speaking to us through her characters. Her emotion has not overflowed and risen up independently, in some comment or attitude of her own. She is using her characters to express her conception, so that her people are active agents in the book's life, adding to its impetus and not impeding it. The same thing happens, more explicitly but with less concentration, in *Moby Dick*.[57] In both books we get a vision of presence outside the human beings, of a meaning that they stand for, without ceasing to be themselves. But it is notable that both Emily Brontë and Herman Melville ignore the greater part of those spoils of the modern spirit which Proust grasps so tenaciously and transforms so triumphantly. Both the earlier writers simplify their characters till only the great contours, the clefts and ridges of the face, are visible. Both seem to have been content with the novel as their form and with prose as their instrument provided that they could remove the scene far from towns, simplify the actors and allow nature at her wildest to take part in the scene. Thus we can say that there is poetry in novels both where the poetry is expressed through the characters and again where the poetry is expressed not so much by the particular character in a particular situation, like

Natasha in the window, but rather by the whole mood and temper of the book, like the mood and temper of *Wuthering Heights* or *Moby Dick* to which the characters of Catherine or Heathcliff or Captain Ahab give expression.

In *A la Recherche du temps perdu*, however, there is as much poetry as in any of these books; but it is poetry of a different kind. The analysis of emotion is carried further by Proust than by any other novelist; and the poetry comes, not in the situation, which is too fretted and voluminous for such an effect, but in those frequent passages of elaborate metaphor, which spring out of the rock of thought like fountains of sweet water and serve as translations from one language into another. It is as though there were two faces to every situation; one full in the light so that it can be described as accurately and examined as minutely as possible; the other half in shadow so that it can be described only in a moment of faith and vision by the use of metaphor. The longer the novelist pores over his analysis, the more he becomes conscious of something that forever escapes. And it is this double vision that makes the work of Proust to us in our generation so spherical, so comprehensive. Thus, while Emily Brontë and Herman Melville turn the novel away from shore out to sea, Proust on the other hand rivets his eyes on men.

And here we may pause, not, certainly, that there are no more books to read or no more changes of mood to satisfy, but for a reason which springs from the youth and vigour of the art itself. We can imagine so many different sorts of novels, we are conscious of so many relations and susceptibilities the novelist had not expressed that we break off in the middle with Emily Brontë or with Tolstoy without any pretence that the phases of fiction are complete or that our desires as a reader have received full satisfaction. On the contrary, reading excites them; they well up and make us inarticulately aware of a dozen different novels that wait just below the horizon unwritten. Hence the futility at present of any theory of 'the future of fiction'. The next ten years will certainly upset it; the next century will blow it to the winds. We have only to remember the comparative youth of the novel, that it is, roughly speaking, about the age of English poetry in the time of Shakespeare, to realise the folly of any summary, or theory of the future of the art. Moreover, prose itself is still in its infancy, and capable, no doubt, of infinite change and development.

But our rapid journey from book to book has left us with some notes made by the way and these we may sort out, not so much to seek a conclusion as to express the brooding, the meditative mood which follows the activity of reading. So then, in the first place, even though the time at our disposal has been short, we have travelled, in reading these few books, a great distance emotionally. We have plodded soberly along the high road talking plain sense and meeting many interesting adventures; turning romantic, we have lived in castles and been hunted on moors and fought gallantly and died; then tired of this, we have come into touch with humanity again, at first romantically, prodigiously, enjoying the society of giants and dwarfs, the huge and the deformed, and then again tiring of this extravagance, have reduced them by means of Jane Austen's microscope to perfectly proportioned and normal men and women and the chaotic world to English parsonage,[58] shrubberies and lawns.

But a shadow next falls upon that bright prospect, distorting the lovely harmony of its proportions. The shadow of our own minds has fallen upon it and gradually we have drawn within, and gone exploring with Henry James endless filaments of feeling and relationship in which men and women are enmeshed, and so we have been led on with Dostoevski to descend miles and miles into the deep and yeasty surges of the soul.

At last Proust brings the light of an immensely civilised and saturated intelligence to bear upon this chaos and reveals the infinite range and complexity of human sensibility. But in following him we lose the sense of outline, and to recover it seek out the satirists and the fantastics, who stand aloof and hold the world at a distance and eliminate and reduce so that we have the satisfaction of seeing round things after being immersed in them. And the satirists and the fantastics, like Peacock and Sterne, because of their detachment write often as poets write, for the sake of the beauty of the sentence and not for the sake of its use, and so stimulate us to wish for poetry in the novel. Poetry, it would seem, requires a different ordering of the scene; human beings are needed, but needed in their relation to love, or death, or nature rather than to each other. For this reason their psychology is simplified, as it is both in Meredith and Hardy, and instead of feeling the intricacy of life, we feel its passion, its tragedy. In *Wuthering Heights* and in *Moby Dick* this simplification, far from being empty, has greatness, and we feel that something beyond, which is not human yet does not destroy their humanity or the actions. So, briefly, we may sum up our impressions. Brief and fragmentary as they are, we have gained some sense of the vastness of fiction and the width of its range.

As we look back it seems that the novelist can do anything. There is room in a novel for story telling, for comedy, for tragedy, for criticism and information and philosophy and poetry. Something of its appeal lies in the width of its scope and the satisfaction it offers to so many different moods, desires and instincts on the part of the reader. But however the novelist may vary his scene and alter the relations of one thing to another – and as we look back we see the whole world in perpetual transformation – one element remains constant in all novels, and that is the human element; they are about *The Novel* people, they excite in us the feelings that people excite in us in real life. The novel is the only form of art which seeks to make us believe that it is giving a full and truthful record of the life of a real person. And in order to give that full record of life, not the climax and the crisis but the growth and development of feelings, which is the novelist's aim, he copies the order of the day, observes the sequence of ordinary things even if such fidelity entails chapters of description and hours of research. Thus we glide into the novel with far less effort and less break with our surroundings than into any other form of imaginative literature. We seem to be continuing to live, only in another house or country perhaps. Our most habitual and natural sympathies are roused with the first words; we feel them expand and contract, in liking or disliking, hope or fear on every page. We watch the character and behaviour of Becky Sharp[59] or Richard Feverel and instinctively come to an opinion about them as about real people, tacitly accepting this or that impression, judging each motive, and forming the opinion that they are charming but insincere, good or dull, secretive but interesting, as we make up our minds about the characters of the people we meet.

This engaging lack of artifice and the strength of the emotion that he is able to excite are great advantages to the novelist, but they are also great dangers. For it is inevitable that the reader who is invited to live in novels as in life should go on feeling as he feels in life. Novel and life are laid side by side. We want happiness for the character we like, punishment for those we dislike. We have secret sympathies for those who seem to resemble us. It is difficult to admit that the book may have merit if it outrages our sympathies, or describes a life which seems unreal to us. Again we are acutely aware of the novelist's character and speculate upon his life and adventures. These personal standards extend in every direction, for every sort of prejudice, every sort of vanity, can be snubbed or soothed by the novelist.

Indeed the enormous growth of the psychological novel in our time has been prompted largely by the mistaken belief, which the reader has imposed upon the novelist, that truth is always good; even when it is the truth of the psycho-analyst and not the truth of imagination.

Such vanities and emotions on the part of the reader are perpetually forcing the novelist to gratify them. And the result, though it may give the novel a short life of extreme vigour, is, as we know even while we are enjoying the tears and laughs and excitement of that life, fatal to its endurance. For the accuracy of representation, the looseness and simplicity of its method, its denial of artifice and convention, its immense power to imitate the surface reality – all the qualities that make a novel the most popular form of literature – also make it, even as we read it, turn stale and perish on our hands. Already some of the 'great novels' of the past, like *Robert Elsmere* or *Uncle Tom's Cabin*,[60] are perished except in patches because they were originally bolstered up with so much that had virtue and vividness only for those who lived at the moment that the books were written. Directly manners change, or the contemporary idiom alters, page after page, chapter after chapter, become obsolete and lifeless.

But the novelist is aware of this too and while he uses the power of exciting human sympathy which belongs to him he also attempts to control it. Indeed the first sign that we are reading a writer of merit is that we feel this control at work on us. The barrier between us and the book is raised higher. We do not slip so instinctively and so easily into a world that we know already. We feel that we are being compelled to accept an order and to arrange the elements of the novel – man, nature, God – in certain relations at the novelist's bidding. In looking back at the few novels that we have glanced at here we can see how astonishingly we lend ourselves to first one vision and then to another which is its opposite. We obliterate a whole universe at the command of Defoe; we see every blade of grass and snail shell at the command of Proust. From the first page we feel our minds trained upon a point which becomes more and more perceptible as the book proceeds and the writer brings his conception out of darkness. At last the whole is exposed to view. And then, when the book is finished, we seem to see (it is strange how visual the impression is) something girding it about like the firm road of Defoe's story telling; or we see it shaped and symmetrical with dome and column complete, like *Pride and Prejudice* and *Emma*.[61] A power which is not the power of accuracy or of humour or of pathos is also used by the great novelists to shape their work. As the pages are turned, something is built up which is not the story itself. And this power, if it accentuates and concentrates and gives the fluidity of the novel endurance and strength, so that no novel can survive even a few years without it, is also a danger. For the most characteristic qualities of the novel – that it registers the slow growth and development of feeling, that it follows many lives and traces their unions and fortunes over a long stretch of time – are the very qualities that are most incompatible with design and order. It is the gift of style, arrangement, construction, to put us at a distance from the special life and to obliterate its features; while it is the gift of the novel to bring us into close touch with life. The two powers fight if they are brought into combination. The most complete novelist must be the novelist who can balance the two powers so that the one enhances the other.

This would seem to prove that the novel is by its nature doomed to compromise, wedded to mediocrity. Its province, one may conclude, is to deal with the commoner but weaker emotions; to express the bulk and not the essence of life. But any such verdict must be based upon the supposition that 'the novel' has a certain character which is now fixed and cannot be altered, that 'life' has a certain limit which can be defined. And it is precisely this conclusion that the novels we have been reading tend to upset.

The process of discovery goes on perpetually. Always more of life is being reclaimed and recognised. Therefore, to fix the character of the novel, which is the youngest and most vigorous of the arts, at this moment would be like fixing the character of poetry in the Eighteenth Century and saying that because Gray's *Elegy* was 'poetry' *Don Juan* was impossible.[62] An art practised by hosts of people, sheltering diverse minds, is also bound to be simmering, volatile, unstable. And for some reason not here to be examined, fiction is the most hospitable of hosts; fiction today draws to itself writers who would even yesterday have been poets, dramatists, pamphleteers, historians. Thus 'the novel', as we still call it with such parsimony of language, is clearly splitting apart into books which have nothing in common but this one inadequate title. Already the novelists are so far apart that they scarcely communicate, and to one novelist the work of another is quite genuinely unintelligible or quite genuinely negligible.

The most significant proof of this fertility, however, is provided by our sense of feeling something that has not yet been said; of some desire still unsatisfied. A very general, a very elementary, view of this desire would seem to show that it points in two directions. Life – it is a commonplace – is growing more complex. Our self-consciousness is becoming far more alert and better trained. We are aware of relations and subtleties which have not yet been explored. Of this school Proust is the pioneer, and undoubtedly there are still to be born writers who will carry the analysis of Henry James still further, who will reveal and relate finer threads of feeling, stranger and more obscure imaginations.

But also we desire synthesis. The novel, it is agreed, can follow life; it can amass details. But can it also select? Can it symbolise? Can it give us an epitome as well as an inventory? It was some such function as this that poetry discharged in the past. But, whether for the moment or for some longer time, poetry with her rhythms, her poetic diction, her strong flavour of tradition, is too far from us today to do for us what she did for our parents. Prose perhaps is the instrument best fitted to the complexity and difficulty of modern life. And prose – we have to repeat it – is still so youthful that we scarcely know what powers it may not hold concealed within it. Thus it is possible that the novel will come to differ as widely from the novel of Tolstoy and Jane Austen as the poetry of Browning and Byron differs from the poetry of Lydgate and Spenser.[63] In time to come – but time to come lies far beyond our province.

1 – A signed essay published in three instalments in the *Bookman* (NY), April, May and June 1929, (*Kp4* C312). It was originally intended to appear in the *Hogarth Lectures on Literature* series, (*Kp4* E15), devised by George ('Dadie') Rylands and LW. It was announced as 'In Preparation' in the first volume, *A Lecture on Lectures* by Sir Arthur Quiller-Couch, published by the Hogarth Press in February 1928 (but dated 1927); however, it was called No. 7 *Phases in the Novel* on the dust-jacket. This note remained in subsequent vols until vol. xiv, *Some Religious Elements in English Literature* by Rose Macaulay, published in May 1931, when the list of volumes in preparation was omitted.

VW started to think about producing a critical book for the Hogarth Press when she wrote in her diary on 27 November 1925: 'I want to write "a book" by which I mean a book of criticism for the H.P. But on what? Letters? Psychology?'; and then on 7 December: 'This book for the H.P.: I think I will find some theory about fiction. I shall read six novels, & start some hares. The one I have in view, is about *perspective*. But I do not know. My brain may not last me out. I cannot think closely enough. But I can – if the C.R. is a test – beat up ideas, & express them now without too much confusion . . . I don't think it is a matter of "development" but something to do with prose & poetry, in novels. For instance Defoe at one end: E. Brontë at the other. Reality something they put at different distances. One would have to go into conventions; real life; & so on. It might last me – this theory – but I should have to support it with other things' (*III VW Diary*). However, she may have had a different book in mind, for *Poetry, Fiction & the Future* was announced on the dust-jacket of *I Speak of Africa* by William Plomer, published by the Hogarth Press in September 1927, as having already appeared in the *Hogarth Essays* series. For this Hogarth 'ghost', (*Kp4* E14), see 'Poetry, Fiction and the Future', *IV VW Essays*.

It will be seen from her diary and letters that VW undertook an enormous amount of work on 'Phases of Fiction' over several years, and she continued to work on the 'book' intermittently for a further five years following the *Bookman* publication. The following dates have been discovered in other sources:

11 August 1928: starts MS draft of 'The Character Mongers' (MHP B 6c).
20 August 1928: starts MS draft of 'The Psychologists' (*ibid.*).
1 September 1928: starts MS draft of '~~Stylists~~ Satirists' (*ibid.*).
9 September 1928: starts MS draft of 'The Poets. Conclusion' (*ibid.*).
26 February 1929: the instalments were posted to the *Bookman*.

Reading notes (Berg, RN 1.13, 1.14, 1.25, 1.26) and (MHP, B 2n) (*VWRN* XIII, XIV, XXV, XXVI and XLVI). Smith College holds reading notes on Trollope, Tolstoy, Peacock, Balzac and Richardson, which may have been made in connection with this essay. Drafts (MHP, B 6a–e, 7a–e [see Appendix II]). The April issue of the *Bookman* introduced the essay thus: 'Mrs. Woolf has been thinking about her craft of novelist, letting her eye and mind run over the great examples of the art in which, as the author of *Mrs. Dalloway*, *To the Lighthouse*, *Orlando*, etc., she has won such distinction. The result is a survey of fiction at once profound and charming.' The issue also contained: three poems by Stephen Crane and one by Edmund Wilson, and 'Thoreau: A Disparagement' by Llewellyn Powys, as well as Rebecca West's regular monthly contribution, 'A Commentary'. Reprinted (with errors and omissions): *G&R, CE*.

2 – Anthony Trollope (1815–82); Jane Austen (1775–1817); Henry Fielding (1707–54); Samuel Richardson (1689–1761); William Makepeace Thackeray (1811–63).

3 – Thomas Hardy (1840–1928).

4 – Daniel Defoe (1660?–1731); Jonathan Swift (1667–1745); George Henry Borrow (1803–81); W. E. (William Edward) Norris (1847–1925); Guy de Maupassant (1850–93).

5 – 'A strong solution of sodium manganate or permanganate, used as a disinfectant', named after 'Henry Bollmann *Condy*, 19th-c. English manufacturer of chemicals' (*OED*).

6 – Defoe, *Moll Flanders* (1722); for VW on *The . . . Adventures of Robinson Crusoe* (1719), see CR2; *Roxana* (1724).

7 – *Roxana*, ed. R. Brimley Johnson (Abbey Classics series, Simpson, Marshall, Hamilton, Kent, 1926), p. 76.

8 – VW reviewed six novels by W. E. Norris: see '*Barham of Beltana*' and '*Lone Marie*', I VW *Essays*; '*The Obstinate Lady*', '*Mr Norris's Method*' (*The Triumphs of Sara*) and '*Mr Norris's Standard*' (*Tony the Exceptional*), III VW *Essays*; '*The Square Peg*', VI VW *Essays*, Appendix. Here VW has in mind *The Triumphs of Sara* (Hutchinson, 1920), confirmed by her reading notes (Berg, RN 1.25); (*VWRN XXV*); cricket is mentioned on the first page and in VW's review. Rotten Row (ch. v, p. 62) is a 'road in Hyde Park, extending from Apsley Gate to Kensington Gardens, much used as a fashionable resort for horse or carriage exercise' (*OED*).

9 – Percy Bysshe Shelley (1792–1822).

10 – Guy de Maupassant, 'Histoire d'une fille de ferme', *Boule de suif et autres contes normands*, ed. M.-C. Bancquart (Éditions Garnier Frères, 1971), pp. 86 (which has 'déchiqueté') and 89. 'Boule de suif' (1880), the story that made his name, was first collected in Maupassant's *Oeuvres* (Havard, 1884). 'Histoire d'une fille de ferme' (1881) was first collected in *La Maison Tellier* (Havard, 1881); one story gave its name to the volume. The Woolfs owned at least two books by Maupassant: *Boule de suif*, Éditions de luxe, Oeuvres complètes illustrées de Guy de Maupassant, vol. xi (Société d'éditions littéraires et artistiques; Librairie P. Ollendorff, 1907); *La Maison Tellier* (P. Ollendorff, 1905).

11 – Jonathan Swift, *Gulliver's Travels* (1726).

12 – *Vignettes of Memory* by Lady Violet Greville (VW's fn.). (Hutchinson, n.d. [1927]), p. 100: the second quotation appears first; the third has not been discovered and, according to MHP, B 6e, is VW's own description of Trollope.

13 – Anthony Trollope, *Barchester Towers* (1857; J. M. Dent, 1906), ch. iv, 'The Bishop's Chaplain', p. 30; the second of the *Chronicles of Barsetshire*. For Mrs Proudie's discomfiture, see ch. xi, 'Mrs. Proudie's Reception – Concluded'. There were a *dozen* gas burners: see ch. x. 'Mrs. Proudie's Reception – Commenced', p. 76.

14 – Sir Walter Scott (1771–1832), *Tales of My Landlord, Third Series . . .* (4 vols, Archibald Constable, 1819), *The Bride of Lammermoor*, vol. i, ch. ii, p. 50. VW wrote on 12 September 1932 to Hugh Walpole: 'I cant read the Bride, because I know it almost by heart; also the Antiquary (I think those two, as a whole, are my favourites) . . . One of the things I want to write about one day is the Shakespearean talk in Scott: the dialogues: surely that is the last appearance in England of the blank verse of Falstaff and so on! We have lost the art of the poetic speech –' (V VW *Letters*, no. 2634; and see no. 2574 and fn. 3).

15 – *The Bride of Lammermoor*, vol. i, ch. iii, pp. 68–9.

16 – Robert Louis Stevenson (1850–94).

17 – Stevenson, *The Master of Ballantrae: A Winter's Tale* (Cassell, 1889), ch. v, p. 137; and *The Works of Robert Louis Stevenson* (Tusitala Edition, 35 vols, W. Heinemann, 1924), vol. x, *The Master of Ballantrae: A Winter's Tale*, ch. v, pp. 95–6. Both have: 'It was as he had said:'.

18 – *Ibid.*, p. 132 (Cassell) and p. 92 (Tusitala), which have: 'the folk'.

19 – *The Bride of Lammermoor*, vol. iii, ch. vii (ch. 34 in a 1-vol. ed.), pp. 105, 106.

20 – *Ibid.*, vol. iii, ch. viii (last ch. in a 1-vol. ed.), p. 128.

21 – Ann Radcliffe (1764–1823), *The Mysteries of Udolpho: A Romance* ... (1794; 3rd ed., 4 vols, G. G. & J. Robinson, 1795).

22 – *Ibid.*, vol. ii, ch. vi, p. 289.

23 – End of the April instalment in the *Bookman*. The May issue also contained: 'The Letters of Joseph Conrad to Stephen and Cora Crane' (concluded in the June issue) and 'A Letter to a Young Gentleman who Wishes to Enter Literature' by William McFee.

24 – Charles Dickens (1812–70), *Bleak House* (1852–3; Chapman & Hall, 1914), Preface to the First Edition, last sentence.

25 – I.e. Miss Flite.

26 – *Bleak House*, ch. xvi, 'Tom-all-Alone's', p. 185.

27 – *Ibid.*, ch. xviii, 'Lady Dedlock', p. 217; 'the maid wading through the long grass is a masterpiece that has always stuck in my mind' (*V VW Letters*, no. 2502, [4 January 1932], to Ethel Smyth).

28 – *Bleak House*, ch. xxii, 'Mr. Bucket', p. 257.

29 – Leo Tolstoy (1828–1910), *War and Peace* (1865–9).

30 – In the *Bookman*, a blank line precedes this paragraph. Jane Austen, *Pride and Prejudice* (3 vols, 1813; J. M. Dent, n.d. [1906]).

31 – *Pride and Prejudice*, ch. x, p. 47.

32 – *Ibid.*

33 – See *ibid.*, ch. ix, p. 41, and ch. x, p. 48.

34 – *Ibid.*, p. 50, which has: 'I do not know ...'

35 – *Ibid.*, ch. xxx, p. 172; VW's italics.

36 – George Eliot (1819–80), *Middlemarch: A Study of Provincial Life* (1871–2); for VW on George Gissing (1857–1903), see *CR2*.

37 – Eliot, *Silas Marner: The Weaver of Raveloe* (1861; *The Works of George Eliot*, William Blackwood, 1878).

38 – *Ibid.*, ch. ii, p. 20, which begins: 'Even people ...'

39 – *Ibid.*, ch. v., p. 64, which begins: 'Yes, there was a sort ...'

40 – Henry James (1843–1916), *What Maisie Knew* (1897; William Heinemann, 1898), p. 3.

41 – Marcel Proust (1871–1922).

42 – Proust, *Remembrance of Things Past* (*À la recherche du temps perdu;*

1913–27), part iv, *Le Côté de Guermantes*, as *The Guermantes Way*, trans. C. K. Scott Moncrieff (1920–1; Chatto & Windus, 1925), vol. ii, p. 34.

43 – Fyodor Dostoevsky (1821–81), *The Novels of Fyodor Dostoevsky*, vol. iii, *The Possessed: A Novel in Three Parts*, trans. Constance Garnett (1871; Heinemann, 1913), part i, ch. ii, 'Prince Harry. Matchmaking', sec. i, p. 36.

44 – *Ibid.*, ch. iv, 'The Cripple', sec. v, p. 133, which has 'earthly tear' (spoken by Marya Timofyevna).

45 – *Ibid.*, part ii, ch. i, 'Night', sec. vii, p. 237 (spoken by Shatov).

46 – *Ibid.*, part i, ch. v, 'The Subtle Serpent', sec. v, p. 166.

47 – Wilkins Micawber in *David Copperfield* (1849–50); Sarah Gamp in *The Life and Adventures of Martin Chuzzlewit* (1843–4).

48 – End of the May instalment in the *Bookman*. The June issue also contained: 'The Tales Dead Men Tell' by André Maurois, 'The Stationary Journey' by Edwin Muir (whose 'latest book . . . is *The Structure of the Novel*' [Hogarth Lectures on Literature, 1st Series, No. 6, Hogarth Press, 1928]) and 'Joseph Hergesheimer's Methods' by Sara Haardt.

49 – Voltaire (François-Marie Arouet, 1694–1778); Anatole France (Jacques Anatole François Thibault, 1844–1924).

50 – Thomas Love Peacock (1785–1866), *Crotchet Castle* (1831), in *'The Misfortunes of Elphin' and 'Crochet Castle'* (World's Classics, OUP, 1924).

51 – *Ibid.*, ch. x, 'The Voyage, continued', p. 219, which has: 'In this manner they glided, over the face of the waters, discussing every thing and settling nothing'.

52 – *Ibid.*, ch. ix, 'The Voyage', p. 212.

53 – Laurence Sterne (1713–68), *The Works of Laurence Sterne* (5 vols, s.p., 1769), *The Life and Opinions of Tristram Shandy, Gentleman* (9 vols, 1759–67), vol. i (1759), ch. xxii, p. 74.

54 – *Ibid.*, vol. ii (i.e. vol. ix [1767]), ch. viii, p. 294.

55 – Emily Brontë (1818–48), *Wuthering Heights* (1847); Gabriel Oak in Thomas Hardy (1840–1928), *Far from the Madding Crowd* (1874).

56 – George Meredith (1828–1909), *The Ordeal of Richard Feverel* (1859).

57 – Herman Melville (1819–91), *Moby-Dick* (1851).

58 – MHP, B 6e has: 'parsonages'.

59 – In Thackeray, *Vanity Fair* (1848).

60 – Mrs Humphry (Mary Augusta) Ward (1851–1920), *Robert Elsmere* (1888); Harriet Beecher Stowe (1811–96), *Uncle Tom's Cabin* (1851).

61 – Austen, *Emma* (1816).

62 – Thomas Gray (1716–71), *Elegy written in a Country Churchyard* (1751); George Gordon, Lord Byron (1788–1824), *Don Juan* (1819–24).

63 – Robert Browning (1812–89); John Lydgate (1370?–1451?); Edmund Spenser (1552?–99).

Dr Burney's Evening Party

Part I

The party was given either in 1777 or in 1778, on which day or month of the year is not known, but the night was cold. Fanny Burney, from whom we get much of our information, was accordingly either twenty-five or twenty-six, as we choose.[2] But in order to enjoy the party to the full it is necessary to go back some years and to scrape acquaintance with the guests.

Fanny, from the earliest days, had always been fond of writing. There was a cabin at the end of her stepmother's garden, at Kings Lynn, where she used to sit and write of an afternoon till the oaths of the seamen sailing up and down the river drove her in. But it was only in the afternoon, and in remote places, that her half suppressed, uneasy passion for writing had its way. Writing was held to be slightly ridiculous in a girl; rather unseemly in a woman. Besides, one never knew, if a girl kept a diary, whether she might not say something indiscreet – so Miss Dolly Young warned her,[3] and Miss Dolly Young, though exceedingly plain, was esteemed a woman of the highest character in Kings Lynn. Fanny's stepmother also disapproved of writing. Yet so keen was the joy – 'I cannot express the pleasure I have in writing down my thoughts at the very moment and my opinion of people when I first see them,'[4] she wrote – that scribble she must. Loose sheets of paper fell from her pocket and were picked up and read by her father to her agony and shame. Once she was forced to make a bonfire of all her papers in the back garden. At last some kind of compromise seems to have been arrived at. The morning was sacred to more serious tasks like sewing; it was only in the afternoon that she allowed herself to scribble letters, diaries, stories, verses, in the look-out place which overhung the river till the oaths of the sailors drove her in.

There was something strange in that, perhaps, for the eighteenth century was the age of oaths. Fanny's early diary is larded with them. 'God help me,' 'Split me,' 'Stap my vitals,' together with damneds and devilishes dropped daily and hourly from the lips of her adored father and her venerated Daddy Crisp.[5] Perhaps Fanny's attitude to language was altogether a little abnormal. She was immensely susceptible to the power of words, but not nervously, or acutely, as Jane Austen was. She adored fluency and the sound of language pouring warmly and copiously over the page. Directly she read *Rasselas* enlarged and swollen sentences formed on the end of her childish pen in the manner of Dr Johnson. Quite early in life she would go out of her way to avoid the plain name of Tomkins.[6] Thus, whatever she heard from her cabin at the end of the garden was sure to affect her more than most girls, and it is also clear that while her ears were sensitive to sound her soul was sensitive to meaning. There was something a little prudish in her nature. Just as she avoided the name of Tomkins, so she avoided the roughness, the asperity, the plainness of life. The chief fault that mars the extreme vivacity and vividness of the early diary is that the words tend in their smooth downpour to soften the edges, to smooth out the outlines. And thus, when she heard the sailors swearing, though Mary Allen, her half-sister would, one believes, have liked to stay and perhaps toss a kiss over the water – her future history allows us to take the liberty of thinking so – Fanny went indoors.

Fanny went indoors but not to solitary meditation. The house, whether it was in Lynn or in London – and by far the greater part of the year was spent in Poland Street – hummed with activity. There was the sound of the harpsichord, the sound of singing; there was the sound – for such concentration seems to pervade a whole house with its murmur – of Dr Burney writing furiously, surrounded by notebooks, in his study; and there were great bursts of chatter and laughter when, returning from their various occupations, the Burney children got together. Nobody enjoyed family life more than Fanny did. For there her shyness only served to fasten the nickname of 'Old Lady' upon her;[7] there she had a familiar audience for her humour; there she need not bother about her dress; there – perhaps the fact that their mother had died when they were all young was partly the cause of it – was that intimacy which expresses itself in jokes and legends and a private language ('The wig is wet,'[8] they would say, winking at each other); there were endless confabulations, confidences and criticisms between sisters and brothers and brothers and sisters. Nor could there be any doubt that the Burneys – Susan and James and Charles and Fanny and Hetty and Charlotte – were a gifted race. Charles was a scholar; James was a humorist; Fanny was a writer;

Susan was musical – each had some special gift or characteristic to add to the common stock. And besides their natural gifts they were happy in the fact that their father was a very popular man – a man, too, so admirably situated by his talents, which were social, and his birth, which was gentle, that they could mix without difficulty either with lords or with bookbinders, and had, in fact, as free a run of life as could be wished.

As for Dr Burney himself, there were some points about which, at this distance of time, one may feel dubious. It is difficult to be sure what, had one met him now, one would have felt for him. One thing is certain, one would have met him everywhere. Hostesses would be competing to catch him. Notes would wait for him. Telephone bells would interrupt him. For he was the most sought after, the most occupied of men. He was always dashing in and dashing off. Some times he dined off a box of sandwiches in his carriage; some times he went out at 7 and was not back from his round of music lessons till 11 at night. When he was not teaching he was writing. The 'habitual softness of his manners,'[9] his great social charm, his haphazard, untidy ways – everything, notes, money, manuscripts, was tossed into a drawer, and once he was robbed of his savings, but his friends were delighted to make it up for him; his odd adventures – did he not fall asleep after a bad crossing at Dover, and so return to France, and so have to cross the Channel again?[10] – endeared him to everybody. It is perhaps his diffuseness that makes him a trifle nebulous. He seems to be for ever writing, and then rewriting, and requiring his daughters to write for him endless books and articles, while over him, unchecked, unfiled, unread, pour down notes, letters, invitations to dinner which he cannot destroy and means some day to annotate and collect, until he melts away at last[11] in a cloud of words. When he died at the age of ninety-one[12] there was nothing to be done by the most devoted of daughters but to burn the whole accumulation. Even Fanny's love of language was suffocated. But if we fumble a little as to our feeling for Dr Burney, Fanny certainly did not. She adored her father. She never minded how many times she had to lay aside her own writing in order to copy his, and he returned her affection. Though his ambition for her success at court was foolish, perhaps, and almost cost her her life, she had only to cry, when a distasteful suitor was pressed on her, 'Oh, sir, I wish for nothing! Only let me live with you!' for the emotional doctor to reply, 'My life! Thou shalt live with me for ever if thou wilt. Thou canst not think I meant to get rid of thee?'[13] And not only were his eyes full of tears, but, what was more remarkable, he never mentioned Mr Barlow again. Indeed, the Burneys were a happy family – a mixed, composite, oddly assorted family, for there were the Allens, too, and little half-brothers and half-sisters being born and growing up.

So time passed and the passage of the years made it impossible for the family to continue in Poland Street any longer. First they moved to Queens Square and then in 1774 to the house where Newton had lived in St Martins Street, Leicester Fields,[14] where his observatory still stood and his room with the painted panels was still to be seen. Here in a mean street, but in the centre of the town, the Burneys set up their establishment. Here Fanny went on scribbling (the observatory was her favourite sitting place as the Cabin had been at Lynn) for she exclaimed 'I cannot any longer resist what I find to be irresistible, the pleasure of popping down my thoughts from time to time upon paper.'[15] Here come so many famous people either to be closeted with the doctor, or, like Garrick, to sit with him while his fine head of natural hair was brushed,[16] or to join the lively family dinner, or, more formally to gather together in a musical party where all the Burney children played and their father 'dashed away'[17] on the harpsichord and perhaps some foreign musician of distinction performed a solo – so many people came for one reason or another to the house in St Martins Street that it is only the eccentrics, the grotesques that catch the eye. One remembers for instance the Agujari, the astonishing soprano, because she had been 'mauled as an infant by a pig, in consequence of which she is reported to have a silver side.'[18] One remembers Bruce the traveller because he had a 'most extraordinary complaint . . . When he attempted to speak, his whole stomach suddenly seemed to heave like an organ bellows. He did not wish to make any secret about it, but spoke of it as having originated in Abyssinia. However, one evening, when he appeared rather agitated, it lasted much longer than usual, and was so violent that it alarmed the company.'[19] One seems to remember, for she paints herself while she paints the others, Fanny herself slipping eagerly and shyly in and out of all this company, with her rather prominent gnat-like eyes, her quick observant mind, that noted every gesture, remembered every word, so that as soon as the company had gone she stole to the observatory and wrote it all down in letters twelve pages long for her beloved Daddy Crisp at Chessington. For that old hermit – he had retired to a house in a field in dudgeon with society – though professing to be better pleased with a bottle of wine in his cellar and a horse in his stable, and a game of backgammon at night than with all the fine company in the world, was always agog for news.

Mr Crisp wanted to know in particular 'about Mr Greville and his notions.'[20] For, indeed, Mr Greville was a perpetual source of curiosity. It is a thousand pities that time with her poppy dust has covered Mr Greville, who was once so eminent, so that only his most prominent features – that is to say, his birth, his person and his pride – emerge. Mr Greville was the descendant – he must, one fancies, have emphasised the fact from the way in which it is repeated – of the friend of Sir Philip Sidney[21] – a coronet indeed 'hung almost suspended over his head.' In person he was tall and well proportioned. 'His face[,] features and complexion were striking for masculine beauty.' 'His air and carriage were noble with conscious dignity'; his bearing was 'lofty yet graceful.'[22] But all these gifts and qualities to which one must add that he rode and fenced and danced and played tennis to admiration were marred by prodigious faults. He was supercilious in the extreme, he was selfish, he was fickle. He was a man of violent temper. His introduction to Dr Burney, in the first place, was due to his doubt whether a musician could be fit company for a gentleman. When he found that young Burney not only played the harpsichord to perfection, but curved his finger and rounded his hand as he played; that he answered plain 'Yes, sir,' or 'No, sir,' being more interested in the music than in his patron;[23] that it was only, indeed, when Greville himself thrummed pertinaciously from memory that he could stand it no longer and broke into vivacious conversation – it was only when he found that young Burney was well bred and gifted that, being himself a very clever man, he no longer stood upon his dignity. Burney became his friend and equal. Burney, indeed, almost became his victim. For if there was one thing that the descendant of the friend of Sir Philip Sidney detested it was what he called 'fogrum.' By that expressive word he seems to have meant the middle-class virtues of discretion and respectability as opposed to the aristocratic virtues of what he called 'ton.'[24] Life must be lived dashingly, daringly, with perpetual display, even if the display was extremely expensive and, as seemed possible to those who trailed dismally round his grounds, as boring to the man who had made the improvements as to the unfortunate guests whose admiration he insisted upon extorting. But Greville could not endure fogrum in himself or in his friends. He threw the obscure young musician into the fast life of Whites[25] and Newmarket and watched with amusement to see if he sank or swam.[26] Burney, most adroit of men, swam as if born to the water, and the descendant of the friend of Sir Philip Sidney was pleased. From being his protégé Burney became his confidante. Indeed, the splendid gentleman, for all his high carriage, was in need of one, and in Burney, perhaps, he found a link between the world of ton and the world of fogrum. He was a man of the world who could dice and bet with the bloods; he was also a musician who could talk intellectual things and ask clever people to his house.

Thus Greville treated the Burneys as his equals and came to their house, though his visits were often interrupted by the violent quarrels which he managed to pick even with the amiable Dr Burney himself. Indeed, as time went on there was nobody with whom Greville did not quarrel. He had lost heavily at the gambling tables. His prestige in society was sunk. His habits were driving his family from him. Even his wife, by nature gentle and conciliatory, though excessive thinness made her seem fitted to sit for a portrait 'of a penetrating, puissant and sarcastic fairy queen,' was wearied by his infidelities. Inspired by them she had suddenly produced that famous 'Ode to Indifference' 'which has passed into every collection of fugitive pieces in the English language' and (it is Mme. D'Arblay who speaks) 'twined around her brow a garland of wide-spreading and unfading fragrance.'[27] Her fame, it may be, was another thorn in her husband's side; for he was, too, an author. He, himself, had produced a volume of 'Maxims and Characters'; and having 'waited for fame with dignity rather than anxiety because with expectation unclogged with doubt,'[28] was beginning perhaps to become a little impatient. Fame held aloof. Meanwhile, he was fond of the society of clever people, and it was largely at his desire that the famous party in St Martins Street met together that very cold night.

Part II

In those days when London was so small, it was easy, or easier than now, for people to stand out on an eminence which they scarcely struggled to keep but enjoyed by unanimous consent. Everybody knew and remembered when they saw her that Mrs Greville had written an 'Ode to Indifference;' everybody knew that Mr Bruce had travelled in Abyssinia; so, too, everybody knew that there was a house at Streatham presided over by a lady called Mrs Thrale. Without troubling to write an ode, without hazarding her life among savages, without possessing either high rank or vast wealth, Mrs Thrale was a celebrity. By the exercise of powers difficult to define, for to feel them one must have sat at table and noticed a thousand audacities and deftnesses and skilful combinations which die with the moment, Mrs Thrale had the reputation of a great hostess. Her fame spread far beyond her house. People who had never seen her discussed her. People wanted to know what she was like; whether she was really so witty and so well read; whether it was a pose; whether she had a heart; whether she loved her husband the brewer, who seemed a dull dog; why she had married him; whether Dr Johnson was in love with her – what in short was the secret of her power. For power she had – that was indisputable.

Even then perhaps it would have been difficult to say what it was. For she possessed the one quality which can never be named; she enjoyed the one gift which never ceases to excite discussion. Somehow or other she was a personality. The young Burneys, for instance, had never seen Mrs Thrale or been to Streatham, but the stir which she set going round her had reached them in St Martins Street. When their father came back from giving his first music lesson to Miss Thrale at Streatham, they flocked round him to ask for an account of her mother.

Dr Burney was in high good temper – in itself a proof of his hostess's power – and he replied, not we may be sure as Fanny rendered it, that she was a 'star of the first constellation of female wits; surpassing rather than equalising the reputation which her extraordinary endowments, and the splendid fortune which made them conspicuous, had blazoned abroad'[29] – that was written when Fanny's style was old and tarnished and its leaves were fluttering and falling profusely to the ground; the doctor, we may suppose, answered briskly that he had enjoyed himself hugely; that the lady was a very clever lady; that she had interrupted the lesson all the time; that she had a very sharp tongue, there was no doubt of that; but he would go to the stake that she was a good-hearted woman at bottom.

Many women might have possessed these qualities without being remembered for them. Mrs Thrale possessed besides one that has given her immortality – the power of being the friend of Dr Johnson. Without that addition her life might have fizzled and flamed to extinction, leaving nothing behind it. But the combination of Dr Johnson and Mrs Thrale created something as solid, as lasting, as remarkable as a work of art. And this was an achievement that called for much rarer powers on the part of Mrs Thrale than the qualities of a good hostess. When the Thrales first met Johnson he was in a state of profound gloom, crying out such lost and terrible words that Mr Thrale put his hand before his mouth to silence him. Physically, too, he was afflicted with asthma and dropsy; his manners were rough; his habits were gross; his clothes were dirty; his wig was singed; his linen was soiled, and he was the rudest of men. Yet Mrs Thrale carried this monster off with her to Brighton and then domesticated him in her house at Streatham, where he was given a room to himself and where he spent habitually some days in the middle of every week. This might have been, on her part, but the enthusiasm of a curiosity hunter ready to put up with a host of disagreeables for the sake of having at her house the original Dr Johnson whom everybody in England would gladly pay to see. But it is clear that her connoisseurship was of a finer type. She understood – her anecdotes prove it – that Dr Johnson was somehow a rare, an important, an impressive human being whose friendship was more of an honour than a burden. And it was not by any means so easy to know this then as it is now. What one knew then was that Dr Johnson was coming to dinner. Who would be there? One wondered with anxiety. For if it was a Cambridge man there might be an outburst. If it was a Whig there would certainly be a scene. If it was a Scotsman anything might happen. Such were his whims and prejudices. Next, one would have to bethink one, what had one got for dinner? For the food never went uncriticised; but one must not praise it. Were not the young peas charming, Mrs Thrale asked once. And he turned upon her, after gobbling down masses of pork and veal pie with lumps of sugar in it, and snapped, 'Perhaps they would be so – to a pig.'[30] And then what would the talk be about, one must have speculated. If it got upon painting or music he was likely to dismiss it with scorn and contempt. Then if a traveller told a tale he was sure to pooh-pooh it. Then if anyone were to express sorrow in his presence it might well draw down a rebuke. 'When one day I lamented the loss of a cousin killed in America – Prithee, my dear (said he), have done with canting: how would the world be the worse for it, I may ask, if all your relations were at once spitted like larks and roasted for Presto's supper?'[31] In short, the meal would be strewn with difficulties; the whole affair might run upon the rocks at any moment.

Had Mrs Thrale been a shallow curiosity hunter, she would have shown him for a season or so and then let him drop. But Mrs Thrale realised even at the moment that one must submit to be snubbed and bullied and irritated and offended by Dr Johnson because – well, what was the force that sent an impudent and arrogant young man like Boswell[32] slinking back to his chair like a beaten boy when Johnson bade him? Why did she herself sit up till 4 in the morning pouring out tea for him? There was a force in him that awed even a competent woman of the world, that subdued even a thick-skinned, conceited boy. He had a right to scold Mrs Thrale for inhumanity, when she knew that he spent only 70 pounds a year on himself and with the rest of his income supported a houseful of decrepit and ungrateful lodgers. If he gobbled at table and tore the peaches from the wall, he went back punctually to London to see that his wretched inmates had their three good meals over the week end. Moreover, he was a warehouse of knowledge. If the dancing master talked about dancing, Johnson could out-talk him[.] He could keep one amused by the hour with his tales of the underworld, of the topers and scallywags who haunted the Strand and the Temple. He said things casually that one never forgot. But what was perhaps more engaging than all his learning was his love of pleasure, his detestation of the solitary hermit, of the mere bookworm, his passion for life and society. And then, as a woman would, Mrs Thrale loved him for his courage – that he had separated two fierce dogs that were tearing each other to pieces in Mr Beaucler[k]'s sitting room; that he had thrown a man, chair and all, into the pit of a theatre; that, blind and twitching as he was, he rode out with the hounds on Bright[h]elmstone Downs and followed the hunt as if he had been a gay dog instead of a huge, melancholy, old man. Moreover, there was an affinity between them. She drew him out; she made him say what without her he would never have said; indeed, he had confessed to her some painful secret of his youth which she never revealed. Above all, they shared the same passion. Of talk they could neither of them ever have enough.

Thus, Mrs Thrale could always be counted on to produce Dr Johnson; and it was, of course, Dr Johnson whom Mr Greville most particularly wished to meet. At it happened, Dr Burney had renewed his acquaintance with Dr Johnson after many years, when he went to Streatham to give his first music lesson. Dr Johnson had been there 'wearing his mildest aspect,'[33] for he remembered Dr Burney with kindness. He remembered a letter that Dr Burney had written to him in praise of the dictionary. He remembered, too, that Dr Burney, having called upon him, years ago, and found him out, had dared to cut some bristles from the hearth broom to send to an admirer.[34] When he met Dr Burney again at Streatham he had instantly taken a liking to him; soon he was brought by Mrs Thrale to see Dr Burney's books; it was quite easy, therefore, for Dr Burney to arrange that on a certain night, which seems to have been in the early spring of 1777 or 1778, Mr Greville's great wish to meet Dr Johnson and Mrs Thrale should be gratified.

Nobody could fail to be aware that the meeting of so many marked and distinguished characters might be difficult. Dr Johnson was, of course, notoriously formidable. But the danger was not confined to him. Mr Greville himself was domineering and exacting; his temper had grown worse since his gambling losses had made him of less account in the world of 'ton.' Then Mrs Greville was a poetess; it was likely enough that she would prove her right to the laurel by some contest with a lady whose fame was at the moment brighter than her own. Mrs Thrale was good humour itself; still it was likely that she would try for a tilt with Mrs Greville; nor was she wholly dependable, for she had 'sudden flashes of wit which she left to their own consequences.'[35] Besides, it was an occasion; everybody felt it to be so; wits would be on the strain; expectation on tiptoe. Dr Burney, with the tact of a man of the world, foresaw these difficulties and took steps to avert them. But there was, one vaguely feels, something a little obtuse about Dr Burney. The eager, kind, busy man, with his head full of music, lacked discrimination. He had not noticed that Dr Johnson, when he visited them the other day and found them at the harpsichord, had withdrawn to the bookcase and browsed upon a volume of the British Encyclopedia till the music was done. He was not aware, in spite of the way in which Mrs Thrale interrupted his lessons, that she did not know 'a flat from a sharp.'[36] To his innocent mind music was the universal specific. If there was going to be difficulty, music would solve it. He therefore asked Signor Piozzi to be of the party.

The night arrived. The fire was lit. The chairs were placed. The company arrived. As Dr Burney had foreseen, the awkwardness was great. Things indeed seemed to go wrong from the start. Dr Johnson had come in his worsted wig prepared, evidently, for enjoyment. But after one look at him Mr Greville seemed to decide that there was something formidable about the old man; it would be better not to compete; it would be better to play the fine gentleman and leave it to literature to make the first advances. Murmuring, apparently, something about having the toothache, Mr Greville 'assumed his most supercilious air of distant superiority and planted himself, immovable as a noble statue, upon the hearth.'[37] He said nothing. Mrs Greville was longing to distinguish herself, but thought that it was proper for Dr Johnson to begin; she therefore said nothing. Mrs Thrale, who might have been expected to break up the solemnity, felt, it seemed, that the party was not her party and, waiting for the principals there to engage, resolved to say nothing. Mrs Crewe, the Grevilles' daughter, lovely and vivacious as she was, had come to be entertained and instructed, and therefore very naturally she, too, said nothing. Nobody said anything. Everybody waited. Here was the very moment for which Dr Burney, in his wisdom, had prepared. He spoke to Signor Piozzi and Signor Piozzi at once began to sing. Accompanying himself on the pianoforte, he sang an *aria parlante*. He sang beautifully. He sang his best. But far from breaking the awkwardness and loosing the tongues, the music increased the difficulty. Nobody spoke. Everybody waited for Dr Johnson to begin. But there was one thing that Dr Johnson never did; he never began. Somebody had always to start a topic before he consented to pursue it or to demolish it. Now he waited in silence to be challenged. Nobody dared. The roulades of Signor Piozzi continued uninterrupted. As he saw his chance of a pleasant evening of conversation diminish Dr Johnson sank into silent abstraction and sat with his back to the piano gazing at the fire. The *aria parlante* continued uninterrupted. At last the strain became unendurable. At last Mrs Thrale could stand it no longer. It was the attitude of Mr Greville, apparently, that roused her resentment. There he stood on the hearth in front of the fire 'staring around him at the whole company in curious silence sardonically.'[38] What right had he, even if he were the descendant of the friend of Sir Philip Sidney, to despise the company and absorb the fire? Her own pride of ancestry suddenly asserted itself. Did not the blood of Adam of Saltsburg[39] run in her veins? Was it not as blue as that of the Grevilles and far more sparkling? Giving rein to the spirit of recklessness which sometimes bubbled in her, she rose and stole on tiptoe to the pianoforte. Signor Piozzi was still singing and accompanying himself dramatically as he sang. She began a ludicrous mimicry of his gestures – she shrugged her shoulders, she cast up her eyes, she reclined her head on one side just as he did. At this singular display the company began to titter – indeed, it was a scene that was to be described 'from coterie to coterie throughout London, with comments and sarcasms of endless variety.'[40] People who saw Mrs Thrale at her mockery that night never forgot that this was the beginning of that criminal affair, the first scene of 'that most extraordinary drama'[41] which lost Mrs Thrale the respect of friends and children, which drove her in ignominy from England and scarcely allowed her to show herself in London again. This was the beginning of that most reprehensible, that most unnatural passion for one who was not only a foreigner, but a musician. All this still lay on the laps of the gods. Nobody yet knew of what iniquity the vivacious lady was capable. She was still the respected wife of a wealthy brewer. Happily, Dr Johnson was staring at the fire and saw nothing of the scene at the pianoforte. But Dr Burney put a stop to the laughter instantly. He was shocked that his guest, even if he were a foreigner and a musician, should be ridiculed behind his back, and stealing to Mrs Thrale he whispered kindly, but with authority, that if she had no taste for music herself she should consider the feelings of those who had. Mrs Thrale took the rebuke with admirable sweetness, nodded her acquiescence and returned to her chair. But she had done her part. After that nothing more could be expected from her.

If no one had dared to tackle Dr Johnson in the beginning it was scarcely likely that they would dare now. He had apparently decided that the evening was a failure so far as talk was concerned. If he had not come dressed in his best he might have had a book in his pocket which he could have pulled out and read. As it was, nothing but the resources of his own mind were left him, and these he explored as he sat with his back to the piano, looking the very image of gravity, dignity and composure.

Signor Piozzi had ceased to play. Signor Piozzi indeed, finding nobody to talk to, had fallen asleep. Even Dr Burney by this time must have been aware that music is not an infallible specific; but there was nothing for it now. Since people would not talk, the music must continue. He called upon his daughters to sing a duet. And when that was over, there was nothing to be done but that they must sing another. Signor Piozzi still slept, or still feigned sleep. Dr Johnson explored still further the magnificent resources of his own mind. Mr Greville still stood superciliously upon the hearth rug. And the night was cold.

But it was a grave mistake to suppose because Dr Johnson was apparently lost in thought and certainly almost blind that he was not aware of anything, particularly of anything reprehensible, that was taking place in the room. His 'starts of vision'[42] were always astonishing and almost always painful. So it was on the present occasion. He suddenly woke up. He suddenly roused himself. He suddenly uttered the words for which the company had been waiting all the evening.

'If it were not for depriving the ladies of the fire,' he said, looking fixedly at Mr Greville, 'I should like to stand upon the hearth myself!'[43] The effect of the outburst was prodigious. The Burney children said afterward that it was a comedy. The descendant of the friend of Sir Philip Sidney quailed before the Doctor's glance. All the blood of all the Brookes rallied itself to overcome the insult. The son of a bookseller should be taught his place. Greville did his best to smile – a faint, scoffing smile. He did his best to stand where he had stood the whole evening. He stood smiling, or trying to smile, for two or perhaps for three minutes more. But when he looked round the room and saw all eyes cast down, all faces twitching with amusement, all sympathies plainly on the side of the bookseller's son, he could stand there no longer. He glided away, sloping even his proud shoulders, to a chair. But as he went, he rang the bell 'with force.'[44] He demanded his carriage.

'The party then broke up; and no one from amongst it ever asked, or wished for its repetition.'[45]

1 – A signed essay in the *NYHT*, 21 (Part I) and 28 (Part II) July 1929, and (revised) in Desmond MacCarthy's *L&L*, September 1929, (Kp4 C313); it was later further revised for *CR2*. The reader is referred to p. 430 below, where the *CR2* version, together with the *L&L* variants in endnotes, is printed in its place as part of *CR2*. VW wrote on 31 May 1928: 'Now I want to write . . . an essay of some sort . . . Dr Burney's evening party I think for Desmond' (*III VW Diary*). The recorded history of the writing of this essay is largely contained in the abortive negotiations for its publication in the *Yale Review*. On 29 June 1928 VW wrote to Helen McAfee, managing editor of the *Yale Review*: 'I have just seen Desmond MacCarthy and have been arranging with him for a short story and an article called Dr Burneys Evening party – partly true, partly fictitious. This would appear in the December number. I could if you liked send you this for your Christmas number. ¶ But I wonder if you would think me very grasping if I asked what fee the Yale Review is able to pay for stories and articles? I ask because I have now made an arrangement with Curtis Brown for articles in various American papers. As I don't write many, I want of course to place my work as profitably as I can – but I shall of course quite understand if the Yale

Review is not able to offer more than the twenty pounds which I think it paid me before' (*III VW Letters*, no. 1907). On 12 August she wrote to Saxon Sydney-Turner: 'Leonard will drive me up to London, and I shall go to the London Library and ask for the Maxims and Characters of Fulke Greville – not *the* F.G. but his descendant who occurs in connection with Miss Burney's father's marriage and playing the harpsichord. Nothing pleases me more than to ferret out perfectly useless enquiries into the lives of completely valueless people; I see it might well usurp all other affections and employments, and is anyhow a refuge for old age, because employed at the British Museum one will scarcely notice deafness, blindness, the spring, the nightingale, or other infirmities or changes of season' (*ibid.*, no. 1913). She wrote to McAfee on 23 September: 'I should have written before but I have not been sure if I could get the article on Dr Burneys party ready for Oct. 1st as you suggest. I have been so busy that unfortunately I find that this is impossible. I should be able to let you have it early in November and go without seeing a proof if that suits you. I may, on getting to work, find it better to change the subject; but it would be an article of the same kind that I suggested to you. Unless I hear from you to the contrary, I will send you an article about the second week in November. It will appear here in December' (*ibid.*, no. 1925). Then on 7 October: 'I am so sorry you had the trouble of cabling. I am still more sorry to say that I dont see how I can possibly post the manuscript by October 25th. I have come back to find all sorts of things waiting to be done before I can start my Burney article. I think therefore I must hope that you will let me send it later and give up the idea of publishing it here in December. I will aim at sending it you early in December and if you will let me know when you will publish it, I will arrange about publication here. I am sorry to have been so changeable' (*ibid.*, no. 1937). And then on 15 October: 'I am so sorry that you had again the trouble of cabling to me. I hope by this time you have had my letter. I am afraid that I cannot commit myself to write the article for any definite date. I have had to postpone it here too. I cannot at present get the time that I need for reading the books I want to read for it; nor do I feel sure when I shall be more at leisure. ¶ Thus I fear I must leave it that I will let you know as soon as I can be certain. But I am extremely sorry that my half promise led you in any way to alter your plans. I am afraid that I must have been more optimistic than I had a right to be' (*ibid.*, no. 1940). VW wrote in her diary on 27 October 1928: 'When I have written here, I am going to open Fanny Burney's diaries, & work solidly at that article which poor Miss McKay [McAfee] cables about' (*III VW Diary*). A letter in reply ('we needn't press you for the manuscript immediately') from McAfee, dated 23 October 1928, is printed in *WSA*, vol. xii (2006), p. 52. By about 9 January 1929 VW was writing to Vita Sackville-West: 'I do nothing but try, vainly, to finish off a year's journalism in a week. If I can earn £400, by flights into the lives of Miss Burney and Miss Jewsbury, then I can pitch every book away, and sink back in my chair and give myself to the wings of the Moths [*The Waves*]. But I doubt it. There are dates to look up. One can't simply invent the whole of Chelsea and King George the 3rd and Johnson, and Mrs Thrale I suppose. Yet after all, thats the way to write; and if I had time to prove it, the truth of one's sensations is not in the fact, but in the reverberation. When I have read three lines, I re-make them entirely, if they're prose, and not poetry; and it is this which is the truth' (*IV VW Letters*, no. 1981). On 15 January she wrote to McAfee: 'I am afraid that there is no chance of my being able to send you the article on Dr Burney by the tenth of February. I am only now beginning to work at it, and as I have other work to do at the same time I shall certainly not have finished it by then. Also I think it will be a good deal longer than I supposed. Would it not be as well to give up the idea, and I will find a home for it elsewhere?' (*ibid.*, no. 1985). VW fell ill on her return from visiting the Nicolsons in Berlin, and wrote to Vita on 19 February: 'I wrote two pages yesterday; dull ones, but pages, with sentences and paragraphs; only about the Burneys, who attract me less than The Moths, though' (*ibid.*, no. 2005). LW wrote to McAfee on 25 February: 'My wife has been ill', and so she cannot complete the Burney article (letter summarised in Berg M 43, no. 90). The issue of *L&L* also contained: Desmond MacCarthy's short story, 'The Mark on the Shutter'. This version was translated into French by Jeanne Fournier-Pargoire and appeared in *Le Figaro*, (Kp4 D51) 19, 20, 22 and 24 August 1929; and it was included (with omissions) in *Prose Masterpieces of English and American Literature*, ed. Robert Silliman Hillyer *et al.* (Harcourt, Brace, 1931), for which VW was paid £4 (see Introduction, p. xvi). See also 'Fanny Burney's Half-Sister' below, and 'Mrs Thrale', *VI VW Essays*. Reading notes (Berg, RN 1.13) and (MHP, B 2n) (*VWRN* XIII and XLVI).

2 – Fanny Burney, later D'Arblay (13 June 1752–6 January 1840).

3 – For Miss Young's advice, see *The Early Diary of Frances Burney 1768–1778 . . .* , ed. Annie Raine Ellis (2 vols, George Bell, 1889), vol. i, pp. 18–20.

4 – *Ibid.*, p. 13.

5 – Samuel Crisp (1707–83), sometime dramatist and recluse, author of the play *Virginia* (1754) for which Garrick wrote prologue and epilogue. The appellation 'Daddy' had been given him by Dr Burney in his own youth.

6 – For Fanny's reaction to *The History of Rasselas, Prince of Abyssinia* (1759), by Samuel Johnson (1709–84), see *Early Diary*, vol. i, pp. 14–15 and 76, fn.: 'Perhaps (as she loved euphony) she did not care to write . . . Tomkin.'

7 – See *Memoirs of Doctor Burney . . .* , by his daughter Madame d'Arblay (3 vols, Edward Moxon, 1832), vol. ii, p. 168.

8 – In Burney family parlance: 'it can't be helped'; see *Early Diary*, vol. ii, p. 252 and fn. 2, and also *Memoirs*, vol. ii, pp. 170–1.

9 – *Anecdotes of the late Samuel Johnson* . . ., by Hester Lynch Piozzi (T. Cadell, 1786), p. 141, which has: 'of manners'. Hester Lynch Thrale, *née* Salusbury, later Piozzi (1741–1821).

10 – See *Memoirs*, vol. i, pp. 230–2.

11 – *NYHT* has: 'least'.

12 – Charles Burney (7 April 1726–12 April 1814).

13 – *Early Diary*, vol. ii, p. 70.

14 – Isaac Newton (1642–1727); St Martin's Street south of Leicester Fields (now Leicester Square).

15 – *Ibid.*, vol. i, p. 304.

16 – See *ibid.*, vol. ii, p. 28. David Garrick (1717–79).

17 – Cf. *ibid.*, vol. i, p. 59: 'He played with his usual successful velocity and his usual applause.'

18 – For Signora Lucrezia Agujari (known also as 'La Bastardini' or 'La Bastadella'), see *ibid.*, vol. ii, p. 2, and also *Memoirs*, vol. ii, pp. 31–2.

19 – James Bruce (1730–94) of Kinnaird, traveller and explorer who sought unsuccessfully the source of the Nile in Abyssinia. This account, by Joseph Cradock (1742–86), the friend of Dyer and of Garrick, from *Early Diary*, vol. ii, p. 14, fn. 3, which has (p. 15): '. . . complaint which could not well be accounted for; when . . .' For VW on George Dyer (1755–1841), see an uncollected letter of 28 January 1924, to Edmund Blunden, *VWB*, no. 26 (September 2007), p. 5, and *IV VW Essays*, p. 121.

20 – *Early Diary*, vol. i, p. 261, Mr Crisp in a letter to Fanny Burney, which has: 'I sadly want to know about Mr Greville and his motions [*sic*]; . . . have you seen him lately?'

21 – Sir Fulke Greville, 1st Baron Brooke (1554–1628), was a lifelong friend of Sir Philip Sidney (1554–86); his biography of Sidney was published in 1652.

22 – For this account of the absurd Richard Fulke Greville (c. 1717–c. 1806), see *Memoirs*, vol. i, pp. 25–6.

23 – *Ibid.*, p. 30.

24 – *Ibid.*, p. 46: '*fogrum*; a term which he [Greville] adopted for whatever speech, action, or mode of conduct, he disdainfully believed to be beneath the high *ton* to which he considered himself to be born and bred'.

25 – The 'oldest and grandest of London's gentlemen's clubs, White's is situated at 37–8 St James's Street. It was rebuilt in its present form in 1787–8, and its celebrated bow window was created in the middle of its façade in 1811': *Mrs Dalloway*, ed. David Bradshaw (Oxford World's Classics, OUP, 2000), p. 170.

26 – See *Memoirs*, vol. i, pp. 25 and 40.

27 – Frances Greville, *née* Macartney (1727?–89). 'A Prayer for Indifference', first published in the *Edinburgh Chronicle*, 19 April 1759, begins: 'Oft I've implor'd the Gods in vain, / And pray'd till I've been weary;' and continues for 16 stanzas: see *The Oxford Book of Eighteenth-Century Verse*, chosen

by David Nichol Smith (Clarendon Press, 1926), pp. 426–8, no. 276; *OBEV*, pp. 550–1, no. 475, prints stanzas 5–7. For the passage upon which this account is based, see *Memoirs*, vol. ii, p. 103. In a letter of 24 February 1933, Donald C. Brace informed VW: 'A woman writes us from Los Angeles, California, to complain that . . . the correct title of Mrs. Greville's poem is "A Prayer for Indifference." She says it is not an "Ode" at all' (LWP Ad. 18). The *ODNB*'s title is 'Ode to Indifference'.

28 – *Memoirs*, vol. i, p. 112, which has: '"Maxims, Characters, and Reflections, Moral, Serious, and Entertaining;" a title that seemed to announce that England, in its turn, was now to produce, in a man of family and fashion, a La Bruyère, or a La Rochefoucault. And Mr. Greville, in fact, waited for a similar fame with dignity . . .' It was published in 1756 by J. and R. Tonson; Greville also published *Reflection, a poem in four cantos* (1790).

29 – *Memoirs*, vol. ii, p. 75, which has: 'Mrs. Thrale, Dr. Burney had beheld as a star of the first magnitude in the constellation of female wits; surpassing . . .'

30 – *Anecdotes of the late Samuel Johnson*, p. 63.

31 – *Ibid.*, which has: 'a first cousin', and continues: '. . . supper? Presto was the dog that lay under the table while we talked.'

32 – James Boswell (1740–95).

33 – *Memoirs*, vol. ii, p. 74.

34 – See *Early Diary*, vol. i, p. 169, fn. 1.

35 – *Memoirs*, vol. ii, pp. 183–4, which has: 'sudden flashes of wit, which, carelessly, she left . . .'

36 – *Ibid.*, p. 89, letter from Fanny Burney to Samuel Crisp.

37 – *Ibid.*, pp. 106–7; adapted by VW.

38 – *Ibid.*, p. 109: 'When, however, she [Mrs Thrale] observed the sardonic disposition of Mr. Greville to stare around him at the whole company in curious silence, she felt a defiance against his aristocracy beat in every pulse; for, however grandly he might look back to the long ancestry of the Brookes and the Grevilles, she had a glowing consciousness that her own blood, rapid and fluent, flowed in her veins from Adam of Saltsberg . . .'

39 – The Salusbury family, 'gentry, were one of the most prominent families in north Wales in the sixteenth and seventeenth centuries. The origins of the family are obscure (they claimed descent from one Adam of Salzburg, who was alleged to have come to England in 1066)' (*ODNB*).

40 – *Memoirs*, vol. ii, p. 111.

41 – *Ibid.*, which has: '. . . this burlesque scene was but the first of a drama the most extraordinary of real life, of which these two persons were to be the hero and heroine . . .'

42 – *Ibid.*, p. 112.

43 – *Ibid.*

44 – *Ibid.*, p. 113.

45 – *Ibid.*

Cowper and Lady Austen

VW's essay in the *N&A*, 21 September, and the *NYHT*, 22 September 1929, (*Kp4* C314) was later revised for inclusion in *The Common Reader: Second Series* (1932). The reader is referred to p. 459 below, where the revised version, together with variants in the form of endnotes, is printed in its place as part of *CR2*.

Beau Brummell

When Cowper in the seclusion of Olney was roused to anger by the thought of the Duchess of Devonshire and predicted a time when 'instead of a girdle there will be a rent, and instead of beauty, baldness'[2] he was acknowledging the power of the lady whom he thought so despicable. Why otherwise should she haunt the damp solitude of Olney? Why should the rustle of her silken skirts trouble those gloomy meditations? Undoubtedly the Duchess was a good haunter. Long after those words were written when she was dead and buried beneath a tinsel coronet, her ghost mounted the stairs of a very different dwelling place. An old man was sitting in his arm chair at Caen. The door opened and the servant announced 'The Duchess of Devonshire.'[3] Beau Brummell at once rose, went to the door and made a bow that would have graced the Court of St James's. Only unfortunately there was no one there. The cold air blew up the staircase of the Inn. The Duchess was long dead, and Beau Brummell in his old age and imbecility was dreaming that he was back in London again giving a party. Cowper's curse had come true for both of them. The Duchess lay in her shroud, and Brummell whose clothes had been the envy of kings had now only one pair of much mended trousers, which he hid as best he could under a tattered cloak. As for his hair that had been shaven by order of the doctor.

But though Cowper's sour predictions had thus come to pass both the Duchess and the dandy might claim that they had had their day. They had been great figures in their time. Of the two perhaps Brummell might boast the more miraculous career. He had no advantage of birth and but little of fortune. His grandfather had let rooms in St James's Street. He had only a moderate capital of thirty thousand pounds to begin with and his beauty, of figure rather than of face, was marred by a broken nose. Yet without a single noble, important or valuable action to his credit he cuts a figure; he stands for a symbol; his ghost walks among us still.

The reason for this eminence is now a little difficult to determine. Skill of hand and nicety of judgment were his, of course, otherwise he would not have brought the art of tying neck cloths to perfection. The story is perhaps too well known – how drawing his head back he sunk his chin down so that the cloth wrinkled in perfect symmetry, or if one wrinkle went amiss the cloth was thrown into a basket and the attempt renewed while the Prince of Wales sat watching hour after hour. Yet skill of hand and nicety of judgment were not enough. Brummell owed his ascendency to some curious combination of wit, of taste, of insolence, of independence – for he was never a toady – which it were too heavy handed to call a philosophy of life but served the purpose. At any rate, ever since he was the most popular boy at Eton coolly jesting when they were for throwing a bargee into the river, 'My good fellows, don't send him into the river; the man is evidently in a high state of perspiration, and it almost amounts to a certainty that he will catch cold,'[4] he floated buoyantly and gaily and without apparent effort to the top of whatever society he found himself among. Even when he was a captain in the Tenth Hussars and so scandalously inattentive to duty that he only knew his troop by 'the very large blue nose'[5] of one of the men, he was liked and tolerated. When he resigned his commission, for the regiment was to be sent to Manchester – 'I really could not go – think, your Royal Highness, Manchester!'[6] – he had only to set up house in Chesterfield Street to become the head of the most jealous and exclusive society of his time. For example, he was at Almacks one night talking to Lord ——. The Duchess of —— was there, escorting her young daughter, Lady Louisa. The Duchess caught sight of Mr Brummell and at once warned her daughter that if that gentleman near the door came and spoke to them she was to be careful to impress him favourably, 'for,' and she sank her voice to a whisper, 'he is the celebrated Mr Brummell.'[7]

Lady Louisa might well have wondered why a Mr Brummell was celebrated, and why a Duke's daughter need take care to impress a Mr Brummell. And then directly he began to move towards them the reason of her mother's warning became apparent. The grace of his carriage was so astonishing; his bows were so exquisite. Everybody

looked overdressed or badly dressed, – some looked positively dirty
beside him. His clothes seemed to melt into each other with the perfection of their cut and the quiet harmony of their colour. Without a
single point of emphasis everything was distinguished – from his bow
to the way he opened his snuff box with his left hand invariably. He
was the personification of freshness and cleanliness and order. One
could well believe that he had his chair brought into his dressing
room and was deposited at Almacks without letting a puff of wind
disturb his curls or a spot of mud stain his shoes.

When he actually spoke to her Lady Louisa would be at first
enchanted – no one possessed the art of pleasing in a higher degree
– and then she would be puzzled. It was quite possible that before
the evening was out he would ask her to marry him, and yet his
manner of doing it was such that the most ingenuous debutante could
not believe that he meant it seriously. His odd grey eyes seemed to
contradict his lips; they had a look in them which made the sincerity
of his compliments very doubtful. And then he said very cutting things
about other people. They were not exactly witty; they were certainly
not profound but they had a turn in them which made them slip into
the mind and stay there inflicting fatal damage by their sarcasm or
a laugh that was even more destructive. 'Why, what could I do, my
good fellow, but cut the connection? I discovered that Lady Mary
actually ate cabbage!'[8] 'Yes, Madam, I once ate a pea,'[9] he said to a
lady who once asked him if he never ate vegetables. And again when
pestered about his tour in the north, 'Which of the lakes do I admire?'
he asked his valet, 'Windermere, sir.' 'Ah, yes – Windermere, so it is
– Windermere.'[10] That was his style, flickering, sneering, hovering on
the verge of insolence, skimming the edge of nonsense, but always
keeping within some curious mean, so that one knew the false
Brummell story from the true by its exaggeration. Brummell would
never have said 'Wales, ring the bell'[11] any more than he would have
worn a brightly coloured waistcoat or a glaring necktie. That 'certain
exquisite propriety' which Lord Byron[12] remarked in his dress stamped
his whole being and made him appear cool and refined and debonair
among the gentlemen who talked only of sport, which Brummell
detested, and smelt of the stable, which Brummell never visited. Lady
Louisa might well be on tenter-hooks to impress Mr Brummell
favourably. Mr Brummell's good opinion was of the utmost importance
in the world of Lady Louisa.

And unless that world fell into ruins his rule seemed assured.

Handsome and heartless and cynical, the Beau seemed invulnerable. His taste was impeccable, his health admirable; and his figure as fine as ever. His rule had lasted many years and survived many vicissitudes. The French Revolution had passed over his head without disordering a single hair. Empires had risen and fallen while [h]e experimented with neckcloths and criticised the cut of a coat. Now the battle of Waterloo had been fought and peace had come. It was the peace that undid him. For some time past he had been winning and losing at the gaming tables. Harriette Wilson[13] heard that he was ruined and then, rather to her regret, she heard that he was saved again. Now with the armies disbanded there were let loose upon London a horde of rough, ill-mannered men who had been fighting all these years and were determined to enjoy themselves. They flooded the gaming houses. They played very high. Brummell was forced into competition. He lost and he won and he vowed never to play again and then he did play again. At last his remaining ten thousand pounds was gone. He borrowed until he could borrow no more. And finally to crown the loss of so many thousands he lost the six-penny bit with a hole in it which had always brought him good luck. He gave it by mistake to a hackney-coachman, and then he said that rascal Rothschild got hold of it,[14] and that was the end of his luck. Such was his own account of the matter – other people put a less innocent interpretation on the matter. At any rate, there came a day, the sixteenth of May, 1816,[15] to be precise, and it was a day to be precise about everything, when he dined alone off a cold fowl and a bottle of claret at Watiers, and attended the opera, and then took coach for Dover. He drove rapidly all through the night and reached Calais the day after. He never set foot in England again.[16]

And now a curious process of disintegration set in. The peculiar and highly artificial society of London had acted as a preservative; it had kept him in being. Now that the pressure was removed the odds and ends, so trifling separately, so brilliant in combination which had made up the being of the Beau fell asunder and revealed what lay beneath. At first his lustre seemed undiminished. His old friends crossed the water to see him and made a point of standing him a dinner and leaving a little present behind them at his bankers. He held his usual levee at his lodgings; he spent the usual hours washing and dressing; he rubbed his teeth with a red root, tweezed out his hairs with a silver tweezer, tied his cravat to admiration and issued out at four precisely as perfectly equipped as if the Rue Royale had been St James's

Street and the Prince himself had hung upon his arm. But the Rue Royale was not St James's Street; the old French Countess who spat on the floor was not the Duchess of Devonshire; the good bourgeois who pressed him to dine off goose at four was not Lord Alvanley;[17] and though he soon won for himself the title of Roi de Calais, and was known to workmen as 'George ring the bell,'[18] the praise was gross, the society coarse, and the amusements of Calais very slender.

The Beau had to fall back upon the resources of his own mind. These might have been considerable. According to Lady Hester Stanhope[19] he might have been a very clever man had he chosen; and when she told him so, the Beau admitted that he had wasted his talents because a dandy's way of life was the only one 'which could place him in a prominent light and enable him to separate himself from the ordinary herd of men, whom he held in considerable contempt.'[20] That way of life allowed of verse-making – his verses called 'The Butterfly's Funeral'[21] were much admired – and of singing sentimental airs; and of some dexterity with the pencil. But now when the summer days were so long and empty he found that such accomplishments hardly served to while away the time. He tried to occupy himself with writing memoirs; he bought a screen and spent hours pasting it with pictures of great men and beautiful ladies whose virtues and frailties were symbolised by hyenas, and wasps, and profusions of cupids, fitted together with extraordinary skill; he collected Buhl furniture; he wrote letters in a curiously elegant and elaborate style to ladies. But these occupations palled. The resources of his mind had been whittled away in the course of years; now they soon gave out. And then the crumbling process went a little further, and another organ was laid bare – the heart. He who had played at love all these years and kept so adroitly beyond the range of passion now made violent advances to girls who were young enough to be his daughters. He wrote such violent love letters to Mademoiselle Ellen of Caen that she did not know whether to laugh or to be angry. She was angry, and the Beau who had tyrannised over the daughters of dukes prostrated himself before her in despair. But it was too late – the heart after all these years was not a very engaging object even to a simple country girl, and he seems at last to have lavished his affections upon animals. He mourned his terrier Vick for three weeks, and became the champion of all the neglected cats and starving dogs in Caen. Indeed, he said to a lady that if a man and a dog were drowning in the same pond he would prefer to save the dog if there were nobody looking. But happily he was still persuaded that everybody was looking; and his immense regard for appearances gave him a certain stoical endurance. Thus, when paralysis struck him he left the dinner table with the soup dribbling from his lips without a sign, he still picked his way over the cobbles on the points of his toes to keep his shoes clean, and when the terrible day came and he was thrown into prison for debt he won the admiration of murderers and thieves by appearing among them as cool and courteous as if about to pay a morning call.

But if he were to continue to act his part, it was essential that he should have a sufficiency of boot polish and gallons of eau de cologne and at least three changes of linen every day. His expenditure upon these items was enormous. Generous as his old friends were and persistently as he supplicated them there came a time when they could be squeezed no longer. It was decreed that he was to content himself with one change of linen daily and his allowance was to admit of necessaries only. Soon afterwards he mounted the black silk neckcloth which was the signal of the end. Black silk neckcloths had always been his aversion. After that everything that had made him and that had kept him in being dissolved. His self-respect vanished. He would dine with anyone who would pay the bill. His memory weakened and he told the same story over and over again till the burghers of Caen were bored. Then his manners degenerated. His extreme cleanliness lapsed into carelessness and then into positive filth. He was so dirty that people objected to his presence in the dining room of the hotel. Only one passion remained intact among the crumbled débris – an immense greed. To buy Rheims biscuits he sacrificed the greatest treasure that remained to him – he sold his snuff box. And then nothing was left but a heap of disagreeables, a mass of corruption, a senile and disgusting old man, who was fit only for the charity of nuns and the protection of an asylum. There the clergyman begged him to try to pray. 'I do try,' he said, 'but he added something which made me doubt if he understood me.'[22] He had no beliefs; he had no terrors[;] he had no desires, save for Rheims biscuits and a seat by a hot fire. Still, one must remember, Byron in his moments of dandyism 'always pronounced the name of Brummell with a mingled emotion of respect and jealousy.'[23]

1 – A signed essay in the *N&A*, 28 September, and (with variations) in the *NYHT*, 29 September 1929, (*Kp4* C315); it was later revised and published on 22 November 1930 in NY by Rimington & Hooper in a limited edition of 550 copies (*Kp4* A15), distributed by the Department of Limited Editions,

Doubleday, Doran and Company (see MHP, III, Box 78, for R. C. Rimington's enthusiastic proposal of 8 October 1929 to VW), for which VW received £30 (WSU). It was further revised for *CR2*. It is clear that the *NYHT* version predates the *N&A* version. The *NYHT* version was translated into French by Jeanne Fournier-Pargoire and appeared in *Le Figaro*, 14 and 15 October 1929 (*Kp4* D53). The series, called 'Four Figures' in *CR2*, was conceived as a set about eighteenth-century characters for the *NYHT* (see 'Cowper and Lady Austen' in *CR2* and Appendix VIII below). The reader is referred to p. 465 below, where the revised version, together with the *N&A* and Rimington & Hooper variants in the form of endnotes, is printed in its place as part of *CR2*. The issue of the *N&A* also contained: LW's 'World of Books' column, 'Ad Astra?', on *The Ascent of Humanity* by Gerald Heard; and 'New Novels', reviewed by Lyn Ll. Irvine. VW broadcast another version of the essay on 20 November 1929, which was published in the *Listener*, 27 November (*Kp4* C321): see *VI VW Essays*, Appendix. In February 1929 VW was 'reading Beau Brummell's life' (*IV VW Letters*, no. 1997; and see no. 2002). The essay is based on Captain [William] Jesse's *The Life of George Brummell, Esq., commonly called Beau Brummell* [1778–1840] (1844; revised ed., 2 vols, John C. Nimmo, 1886). Reading notes (Berg, RN 1.9, 1.20) (*VWRN IX, XX*).

2 – *The Correspondence of William Cowper* [1731–1800], ed. Thomas Wright (4 vols, Hodder & Stoughton, 1904), vol. ii, letter to the Rev. John Newton, 31 May 1783, p. 71. Georgiana, Duchess of Devonshire (1757–1806), of the famous Gainsborough portrait, author of the poem 'The Passage of the Mountain of St Gothard'.

3 – *Life*, vol. ii, ch. xxv, p. 293: '. . . at eight o'clock this man, to whom he had already given his instructions, opened wide the door of his sitting-room, and announced the "Duchess of Devonshire."'

4 – *Ibid.*, vol. i, ch. iii, p. 29.

5 – *Ibid.*, ch. iii, p. 40, which has: 'a very large, blue nose'.

6 – *Ibid.*, p. 45.

7 – *Ibid.*, ch. vii, p. 95.

8 – *Ibid.*, ch. ix, p. 119.

9 – *Ibid.*, ch. viii, p. 111.

10 – *Ibid.*

11 – *Ibid.*, ch. xix, p. 254.

12 – *Ibid.*, ch. v, p. 70: 'Mr Leigh Hunt, in a note in which he kindly referred me to some anecdotes of Brummell, says: "I remember that Lord Byron once described him to me, as having nothing remarkable in his style of dress, except a "certain exquisite propriety"'. George Gordon, Lord Byron (1788–1824).

13 – See *Harriet Wilson's Memoirs of Herself and Others*, ed. James Laver (Peter Davies, 1929), letter from Harriet's sister Fanny, p. 547: 'Brummell's sun, they say, is setting . . .' For VW on Harriette Wilson (1786–1845), courtesan, see 'Harriette Wilson', *IV VW Essays*, and p. 259, n. 1.

14 – Brummell quoted in *Life*, vol. i, ch. xxii, p. 305: '...no doubt that rascal Rothschild, or some of his set, got hold of it'.

15 – See *ibid.*, ch. xxiii, p. 307.

16 – But see VW's note appended to the *CR2* version, p. 471 below.

17 – Richard Pepper Arden (1744–1804), Lord Chief Justice and 1st Baron Alvanley from 1801.

18 – *Life*, vol. ii, ch. i, p. 13.

19 – For VW on Lady Hester Stanhope (1776–1839), traveller, see 'Lady Hester Stanhope', *I VW Essays*.

20 – *Life*, vol. i, ch. x, pp. 137–8, which has: 'from the society of the ordinary herd'.

21 – For 'The Butterfly's Funeral', see *ibid.*, ch. xvii, pp. 228–30.

22 – *Ibid.*, vol. ii, ch. xxviii, p. 323, which has: '"in reply to my repeated entreaties that he would try and pray, he said, 'I do try,' but ..."'; see also p. 324.

23 – Stendhal [i.e. Henri Beyle, 1783–1842], 'Lord Byron en Italie' (1830), trans. John Galt, in *The Works of Lord Byron. Letters and Journals*, ed. Rowland E. Prothero [later Lord Ernle], vol. iii (John Murray and Charles Scribner's Sons, 1899), Appendix viii, p. 440, which has: 'In his moments of dandyism, he always pronounced the name of Brummel ...'

Mary Wollstonecraft

VW's essay in the *N&A*, 5 October, and the *NYHT*, 20 October 1929, (*Kp4 C316*), was later revised for inclusion, under the same title, in *The Common Reader: Second Series* (1932). The reader is referred to p. 471 below, where the revised version, together with variants in the form of endnotes, is printed in its place as part of *CR2*.

Dorothy Wordsworth

Two very incongruous travellers, Mary Wollstonecraft and Dorothy Wordsworth, followed close upon each other's footsteps. Mary was in Altona on the Elbe in 1795 with her baby; three years later Dorothy came there with her brother and Coleridge.[2] Both kept a record of their travels; both saw the same places, but the eyes with which they saw them were very different. Whatever Mary saw served to start her mind upon some theory, upon the effect of government, upon the state of the people, upon the mystery of her own soul. The beat of the oars on the waves made her ask: 'Life, what are you? Where goes this breath – this *I* so much alive? In what element will it mix, giving and receiving fresh energy?'[3] The fields and the waves took the shape of her own agitated soul. Dorothy, on the other hand, noted what was before her accurately, literally and prosaically. 'The walk very pleasing between Hamburg and Altona. A large piece of ground planted with trees and intersected by gravel walks . . . The ground on the opposite side of the Elbe appears marshy.'[4] Dorothy never railed against 'the cloven hoof of despotism.'[5] Dorothy never asked 'men's questions' about exports and imports; Dorothy never confused her own soul with the sky. This '*I* so much alive' was ruthlessly subordinated to the trees and the grass.

So while Mary dashed her head against wall after wall and cried out: 'Surely something resides in this heart that is not perishable – and life is more than a dream'[6] – Dorothy went on methodically at Alfoxden noting the approach of spring. 'The sloe in blossom, the hawthorns green, the larches in the park changed from black to green, in two or three days.'[7] And next day, April 14, 1798, 'the evening very stormy, so we stayed indoors. Mary Wollstonecraft's life, &c., came.'[8] And the day after they walked in the squire's grounds and noticed that 'nature was very successfully striving to make beautiful what art had deformed – ruins, hermitages, &c.'[9] There is no reference to Mary Wollstonecraft; it seems as if her life and all its storms had been swept away in one of those compendious etceteras, and yet the next sentence reads like an unconscious commentary. 'Happily, we cannot shape the huge hills or carve out the valleys according to our fancy.'[10] No, we cannot reform, we must not rebel; we can only accept and try to understand. And so the notes go on.

Spring passed; summer came; summer turned to autumn; it was winter, and then again the sloes were in blossom and the hawthorns green and spring had come again. But it was spring in the North now, and Dorothy was living alone with her brother in a small cottage at Grasmere in the midst of the hills. Now after the hardships and separations of youth they were together under their own roof; now they could address themselves undisturbed to the absorbing occupation of living in the heart of nature and trying, day by day, to read her meaning. They had money enough at last to let them live together without the need of earning a penny. No family duties or professional tasks distracted them. Dorothy could walk all day on the hills and sit up talking to Coleridge all night without being scolded by her aunt for getting her feet wet or shocking the neighbours. The hours were theirs from sunrise to sunset and could be altered to suit the season.

If it was fine, there was no need to come in; if it was wet, there was no need to get up. One could go to bed at any hour. One could let the dinner cool if the cuckoo were shouting on the hill and William had not found the epithet he wanted. Sunday was not more holy than any other day. Everything was subordinated to the absorbing and exacting and exhausting task of living in the heart of nature and writing poetry. For exhausting it was. William would make his head ache in the effort to find the right word. He would go on hammering at a poem till Dorothy was afraid to suggest an alteration. A chance phrase of hers would run in his head and make it impossible for him to get back into the proper mood. He would come down to break-fast and sit 'with his shirt neck unbuttoned and his waistcoat open,' writing a poem on a butterfly[11] which some story of hers had suggested, and he would eat nothing, and then he would begin altering the poem and would be tired again.

It is strange how vividly all this is brought before us, considering that the diary is made up of brief notes, such as any quiet woman might make of her garden's changes and her brother's moods.

It is only gradually that the difference between this rough note-book and others discloses itself; only by degrees that the brief notes unfurl in the mind, and each terse description proves to be made of such sound material that we can rest our weight on it, and so direct that if we look exactly and closely along the line that she points we shall see precisely what she saw. 'The moonlight lay upon the hills like snow.'[12] 'The air was become still, the lake was of a bright slate colour, the hills darkening. The b[a]ys shot into the low fading shores. Sheep resting. All things quiet.'[13] 'There was no one waterfall above another – it was a sound of waters in the air – the voice of the air.[']'[14] Even in these brief notes one feels the suggestive power which is the gift of the poet rather than of the naturalist, the power that gives the flat statement its light and shadow, its completeness and coherency as a picture. Her first concern is to be truthful – grace and eloquence are subordinate to that.

But truth is sought because to falsify the look of the stir of the breeze on the lake is to tamper with the spirit which inspires appearances. And that truth is not mere truth of observation; it is something that lies further and is sunk deeper, so that when the phrase is found it has something of the intensity of an artistic triumph. The phrase was only to be found if all her faculties were on the stretch; and the landscape, with its vastness and its littleness, its sameness and its mutability, kept her faculties forever on the stretch. A sight or a sound would not let her be till she had traced her perception along its course and fixed it, in words however bald, in an image, however stark and angular. The exact prosaic detail must be rendered as well as the vast and visionary outline.

Indeed, she seemed scarcely to shut her eyes. They looked and they looked, urged on by the most indefatigable curiosity and reverence, as if some secret of the utmost importance lay beneath the surface. Her pen sometimes stammers with the intensity of the emotion that she controlled as De Quincey said that her tongue stammered with the conflict between her ardour and her shyness when she spoke. For controlled she was. Fiery and impulsive by nature, her eyes, 'wild and starting,'[15] tormented by feelings which she knew not how to order, she must control, she must repress or she would fail in her task – she would cease to see. But if one subdued one's self and submitted one's private agitations completely to nature, then as if in reward nature would bestow an exquisite satisfaction. 'Rydale was very beautiful, with spear-shaped streaks of polished steel. . . . It calls home the heart to quietness. I had been very melancholy,'[16] she wrote. She had been melancholy, for did not Coleridge walk over the hills and tap on the door late at night; did she not carry a letter from Coleridge safe hidden in her bosom?

Thus giving to nature and thus receiving back again from nature it seemed, as the arduous and ascetic days went by, that nature and Dorothy had grown together in perfect sympathy – a sympathy not cold or vegetable or inhuman because at the core of it burnt that other love for 'my beloved,' her brother, who was indeed its heart and inspiration. William and nature and Dorothy herself, were they not one being? Did they not compose a trinity, self-contained and self-sufficient and independent, whether indoors or out? They sit indoors. It was 'about 10 o'clock[,] a quiet night. The fire flickers and the watch ticks. I hear nothing but the breathing of my beloved as he now and then pushes his book forward, and turns over a leaf.'[17] And now it is an April day and they take the old cloak and lie in John's grove out of doors together. 'William heard me breathing, and rustling now and then, but we both lay still and unseen by one another.

He thought that it would be sweet thus to lie in the grave, to hear the peaceful sounds of the earth, and just to know that our dear friends were near. The lake was still; there was a boat out.'[18]

This love, in which nature played so great a part, was a strange love, profound, almost dumb, as if brother and sister had grown together and shared not the speech but the mood so that they hardly knew which felt, or which spoke, which saw the daffodils or the sleeping city; only Dorothy stored the mood in prose and later William came and bathed in it again and made it into poetry. But one could not act without the other. They must feel, they must think together. So now when they had lain out on the hillside they would rise and go home and make tea, and Dorothy would write to Coleridge, and they would sow the scarlet beans together, and William would work at the 'Leech Gatherer'[19] and Dorothy would copy the lines for him. Rapt but controlled, free yet strictly ordered, the homely narrative moves naturally from ecstasy on the hills to baking and ironing and fetching William his supper in the cottage.

For Dove Cottage, though its garden ran on to the fells, was on the highroad.[20] Through her cottage window Dorothy looked out and saw whoever might be passing – a tall beggar woman, perhaps, with her baby on her back; an old soldier, a coroneted landau with touring ladies prying inquisitively inside. The rich, the great she would let pass – they were sophisticated, they were no friends of hers – but she could never meet a beggar on the highroad without getting into talk with him and questioning him closely. Where had he been? What had he done? How old was he? She searched into the histories of the poor as if they held in them the same secret that the hills concealed. She made them come into the cottage. A beggar eating cold bacon over the kitchen fire might have been a starry night, so closely she observed how his old coat was patched 'with three bell-shaped patches of darker blue behind, where the buttons had been,'[21] how his beard of a fortnight's growth was like 'grey *plush*,'[22] and as they rambled on with their tales of seafaring and the press gang she never failed to capture the one phrase that sounds on in the mind long after the story is forgotten. 'What, you are stepping westward?'[23] 'To be sure there is great promise for virgins in Heaven.'[24] 'She could trip lightly by the graves of those who died when they were young.'[25] The poor had their poetry, as the hills had, crowned by the stars.

But it was out of doors, on the road or the hillside, that she was most at her ease. Her finest work was done tramping beside a jibbing horse on a wet Scotch moor without certainty of bed or supper. All she knew was that there was some sight ahead, some grove of trees to be noted, some waterfall to be inquired into. On they tramped hour after hour, in silence for the most part, though Coleridge, who was of the party, mused within himself, and sometimes debated aloud the different meanings of the words majestic, sublime and grand. They had to walk, because the horse had thrown the cart over a bank and the harness was mended with string and pocket handkerchiefs. And they were hungry, because Wordsworth had dropped the chicken and the bread into the lake and they were soaked through. They were uncertain of the way and did not know if they would find lodging; all they knew was that there was a sight of some kind ahead. At last Coleridge could stand it no longer. . . . He had rheumatism in the joints; the Irish jaunting car provided no shelter from the weather. The couple were silent and absorbed. He left them. But the Wordsworths tramped on. They looked like tramps themselves, for Dorothy's cheeks were as brown as an Egyptian's and her clothes were shabby and her gait was rapid and ungainly. But still her eye never failed; still she noticed everything. At last they came to the waterfall, to the grove of trees.

Then all Dorothy's powers of observation fell upon the sight, searching out its character, noting its resemblances and its differences and taking it to her heart with all the ardour of a discoverer, with all the rapture of a lover. She had seen it at last – she had laid it up in her mind for ever. It had become one of those 'inner visions' which she could call to mind at any time in their distinctness and in their particularity. It would come back to her long years afterward when she was old and her mind had failed her; it would come back stilled and heightened and mixed with all the happiest memories of her past – with Racedown and Alfoxden and Coleridge reading Christabel[26] and her beloved, her brother William. It would bring with it what no human being could give, consolation and peace. If then the passionate cry of Mary Wollstonecraft had reached her ears – 'Surely something resides in this heart that is not perishable – and life is more than a dream,' she would have no doubt whatever as to her answer. She would have said, quite simply, 'We looked about us, and we felt that we were happy.'[27]

1 – A signed essay in the *N&A*, 12 October, and (with variations) in the *NYHT*, 27 October 1929, (*Kp4* C317); it was later further revised for *CR2*. It is clear that the *NYHT* version predates the *N&A* version. The same issue of the *NYHT* contained a review by Mary Ross of *Room*, entitled 'Sunlight of the Mind', which began on the same page as VW's essay. The series, called

'Four Figures' in *CR2*, was conceived as a set about eighteenth-century characters for the *NYHT* (see 'Cowper and Lady Austen' in *CR2* and Appendix VIII below). The *N&A* version (or similar) was translated into French by Jeanne Fournier-Pargoire and appeared in *Le Figaro*, 5–6 May 1930 (*Kp4* D56). The same issue of the *N&A* also contained: LW's 'World of Books' column on the Autumn's new books; and 'New Novels', reviewed by Lyn Ll. Irvine. The reader is also referred to p. 477 below, where the revised version, together with the *N&A* variants in the form of endnotes, is printed in its place as part of *CR2*. Although VW was reading Dorothy Wordsworth in February 1921 and intending to write an article about her, this appears not to have eventuated (see *II VW Diary*, 16 February and 13 March; *Congenial Spirits: The Selected Letters of Virginia Woolf* [Hogarth Press, 1989], no. 1167a, 13 February to Katherine Mansfield). Brenda Silver deduces that VW was reading the *Journals of Dorothy Wordsworth* in May 1929 (*VWRN*, p. 111). VW wrote to Vita Sackville-West on 18 August 1929: 'I am recovered, and have, more or less, finished my articles. The last was Dorothy Wordsworth, and if the written word could cure rheumatism, I think her's might – like a dock leaf laid to a sting; yet rather astringent too. Have you ever read her diaries, the early ones, with the nightingale singing at Alfoxden, and Coleridge coming in swollen eyed – to eat a mutton chop? Wordsworth made his head ache, thinking of an epithet for cuckoo. I like them very much; but I cant say I enjoy writing about them, nine pages close pressed. How can one get it all in?' (*IV VW Letters*, no. 2057). See also 'Wordsworth Letters', *I VW Essays*. Reading notes (Berg, RN 1.20) (*VWRN XX*).

2 – Dorothy (1771–1855) and William (1770–1850) Wordsworth; Samuel Taylor Coleridge (1772–1834).

3 – Mary Wollstonecraft (1759–97), *Letters Written During a Short Residence in Sweden, Norway, and Denmark* (Cassell, 1889), Letter vii, p. 73, which begins: 'Life, what art thou?'

4 – *Journals of Dorothy Wordsworth*, ed. William Knight (2 vols, Macmillan, 1897), vol. i, 'Journal of days spent in Hamburgh in September and October 1798', entry headed 'Sunday', p. 24, which begins: 'The walks . . .'

5 – *Letters Written*, Letter xiii, p. 120: 'Here I saw the cloven foot of despotism. I boasted to you that they had no Viceroy in Norway, but these Grand Bailiffs, particularly the superior one, who resides at Christiana, are political monsters of the same species.'

6 – *Ibid.*, Letter viii, p. 78.

7 – *Journals*, vol. i, 'Journal written at Alfoxden [*sic*]', 9 April 1798, p. 16, which has: 'hawthorns'. VW and LW stayed near Alfoxton, at Holford in Somerset, on their honeymoon in August 1912: see Sheila M. Wilkinson, '"Who Lived at Alfoxton?"', *VWB*, no. 2 (July 1999), pp. 48–50.

8 – *Journals*, vol. i, p. 16; correctly dated by VW, but there are, however, brief entries for 10–13 April.

9 – *Ibid.*, 15 April 1798, p. 17.

10 – *Ibid.*

11 – *Ibid.*, 'Journal written at Grasmere', 14 March 1802, p. 100; the poem was 'To a Butterfly', which begins 'Stay near me – do not take thy flight!', and in stanza 2:

> Oh! pleasant, pleasant were the days,
> The time, when, in our childish plays,
> My sister Emmeline and I
> Together chased the butterfly!

12 – *Ibid.*, 2 October 1800, p. 50.

13 – *Ibid.*, 13 April 1802, p. 105. Cf. 'the sea running into the bays' in Greece (*V VW Letters*, no. 2575, 24 April [1932], to V. Sackville-West).

14 – *Journals*, vol. i, 29 April 1802, p. 114.

15 – Thomas De Quincey (1785–1859), *Works* (James Hogg & Sons, 1853), vol. ii, 'William Wordsworth' (originally published in *Tait's Edinburgh Magazine*, January, February and April 1839), p. 238, which has: 'startling'.

16 – *Journals*, vol. i, 'Journal written at Grasmere', 16 May 1800, p. 32; the ellipsis is in the original.

17 – *Ibid.*, 23 March 1802, pp. 103–4, which has: 'nothing save the breathing . . .' (The one-vol. reprint of 1924 has: 'The fire flutters, . . .', p. 103.)

18 – *Ibid.*, 29 April 1802, p. 114.

19 – 'Resolution and Independence' (or 'The Leech Gatherer'), written May–July 1802 at Grasmere.

20 – VW and LW visited Dove Cottage on 1 July 1938: see Sheila M. Wilkinson, 'Virginia in Westmoreland [*sic*]', *VWB*, no. 18 (January 2005), pp. 67–8.

21 – *Journals*, vol. i, 'Journal written at Grasmere', 22 December 1801, p. 72, which does not have 'with'.

22 – *Ibid.*, 30 June 1802, p. 135. These descriptions refer to two old men, not one.

23 – *Ibid.*, vol. ii, 'Recollections of a Tour Made in Scotland', Fifth Week, 11 September 1803, p. 105; the line was to be the *donnée* for Wordsworth's poem 'Stepping Westward' which Dorothy quotes (pp. 105–6): 'William wrote the following poem long after, in remembrance of his feelings and mine: –

> "What! you are stepping westward? Yea,
> 'Twould be a wildish destiny . . ."'

24 – Quoted *ibid.*, 13 September 1803, p. 121.

25 – Quoted *ibid.*, vol. i, 'Journal written at Grasmere', 3 June 1802, p. 127.

26 – In 1795, with the help of a legacy, the Wordsworths set up house together at Racedown Lodge, Dorset, and then moved to Alfoxden House two years later. Coleridge, 'Christabel' (1816).

27 – *Journals*, vol. i, 'Journal written at Grasmere', 23 January 1802, p. 81, which has: 'We talked about the Lake of Como, read the description, looked about us, and felt...' (The one-vol. reprint of 1924 has: '... read the *Descriptive Sketches*, ...', p. 81.)

Women and Leisure

I must thank Miss Irvine for her very intelligent and generous article on my book, *A Room of One's Own*. But perhaps you will allow me to dispute one or two of her contentions. 'The poorest community of men,' she says, 'would never sit down week in, week out, to such a diet' (*i.e.*, a diet of prunes and custard). And she infers that men are therefore endowed with some desirable power that women lack. But, after all, the majority of Englishmen are sitting down at this moment to such a diet. The working-class man does not possess either £500 a year or a room of his own. And if the majority of men, without the burden of child-bearing and with the professions open to them, yet find it impossible to earn a wage that admits of leisure and the production of works of art, it would seem to prove that both sexes, men as well as women, are forced to eat prunes and custard not because they like them, or are patient or can imagine nothing better, but because that is all that they can get. It is the middle-class man to whom we owe our art; but whether he would have enjoyed his very valuable degree of comfort and prosperity had the duty of childbirth been laid upon him in the flower of his youth, and had all the professions been closed to him by his sex, seems to me disputable.

Then again, Miss Irvine contends that if the Brontë sisters had lived now they would have become schoolmistresses, and would have travelled abroad under the auspices of Thomas Cook and Son;[2] but they would have lost their leisure, she says, and we should have lost *Jane Eyre* and *Wuthering Heights*.[3] What kind of 'leisure' the women of the nineteenth century enjoyed is, I think, made very plain by Florence Nightingale in *Cassandra*. 'Women never have half an hour in all their lives (excepting before or after anybody is up in the house) that they can call their own, without fear of offending or of hurting someone.'⁴ I submit that Charlotte Brontë would have enjoyed more true leisure as a schoolmistress now than she did as the daughter at home in close attendance upon a beloved, but it would seem somewhat exacting, parent in a vicarage in a graveyard. Nor can I stifle my suspicion that if Emily had travelled in the summer holidays even under the guidance of Mr Cook she might not have died of consumption at the age of twenty-nine. But, of course, in no circumstances could the Brontë sisters have been either typical schoolmistresses or typical globe-trotters. They remain rare and remarkable women. And my argument was that if we wish to increase the supply of rare and remarkable women like the Brontës we should give the Joneses and the Smiths rooms of their own and five hundred a year. One cannot grow fine flowers in a thin soil. And hitherto the soil – I mean no disrespect to Miss Smith and Miss Jones – has been very starved and very stony.

1 – A signed letter to the editor in the *N&A*, 16 November 1929, (*Kp4* C319), in response to a review of *Room*, by Lyn Ll. Irvine, on 9 November 1929. Irvine (1901–73), who graduated from Girton in 1927, joked in her review: 'Loyalty prompts me to observe here that Fernham cannot be Girton, for at Girton the staple sweet is dried apricots – the Students call them Dead Men's Ears.' A letter of introduction to LW had led to her reviewing in the *N&A*, and the Woolfs met her on a number of occasions: see especially *III VW Diary*, 2 September 1929. Irvine and VW corresponded 1929–37: see *VWB*, no. 25 (May 2007), pp. 4–13. The Hogarth Press published her *Ten Letter-Writers* in 1932. A rather whimsical letter from Frances M. Orr appeared in the *N&A*, 28 December 1929, ostensibly praising VW and criticising Irvine's review. This drew a response from Irvine in the *N&A* on 4 January 1930, in which she wrote: 'I was grateful to Mrs. Woolf for having written as she did. But I disagreed with her in her estimate of the extent to which improved conditions would affect the production of works of genius by women . . . Any general efforts that are made to encourage genius bring in a harvest of inferior and derivative work, and modern civilization on the whole is apparently unfavourable to the development of the supreme artist.' The 16 November 1929 issue also contained: LW's 'World of Books' column, 'The German Tribes'; and Ray Strachey's review of *Marriage and Morals* by Bertrand Russell. See also 'Women and Fiction' above, and 'An Excerpt from *A Room of One's Own*' below. Reprinted: *W&W*.

2 – Travel agents; Thomas Cook (1808–92).

3 – Charlotte Brontë (1816–55), *Jane Eyre* (1847); Emily Brontë (1818–48), *Wuthering Heights* (1847).

4 – Florence Nightingale (1820–1910), 'Cassandra' (1859), in Ray Strachey's

The Cause: A Short History of the Women's Movement in Great Britain
(G. Bell & Sons, 1928), p. 402, which has: 'an half-hour'. VW quotes part
of this in Room, ch. iv, p. 100: 'women never have an half hour . . . that
they can call their own' (VW's ellipsis).

An Excerpt from *A Room of One's Own*

As I leant against the wall the University indeed seemed a sanctuary
in which are preserved rare types which would soon be obsolete if
left to fight for existence on the pavement of the Strand. Old stories
of old deans and old dons came back to my mind,[a] but before I had
summoned up courage to whistle – it used to be said that at the sound
of a whistle old Professor —— instantly broke into a gallop[2] – the
venerable congregation had gone inside. The outside of the chapel
remained. As you know, its high domes and pinnacles can be seen,
like a sailing-ship always voyaging never arriving, lit up at night and
visible for miles, far away across the hills.[3] Once, presumably, this
quadrangle with its smooth lawns, its massive buildings and the chapel
itself, was marsh too, where the grasses waved and the swine rooted.
Teams of horses and oxen, I thought, must have hauled the stone in
wagons from far counties, and then with infinite labour the grey
blocks in whose shade I was now standing were poised in order one
on top of another, and then the painters brought their glass for the
windows, and the masons were busy for centuries up on that roof
with putty and cement, spade and trowel. Every Saturday somebody
must have poured gold and silver out of a leathern purse into their
ancient fists, for they had their beer and skittles presumably of an
evening. An unending stream of gold and silver, I thought, must have
flowed into this court perpetually to keep the stones coming and the
masons working; to level, to ditch, to dig and to drain. But it was
then the age of faith, and money was poured liberally to set these
stones on a deep foundation, and when the stones were raised, still
more money was poured in from the coffers of kings and queens and
great nobles to ensure that hymns should be sung here and scholars
taught. Lands were granted; tithes were paid. And when the age of
faith was over and the age of reason had come, still the same flow
of gold and silver went on; fellowships were founded; lectureships
endowed; only the gold and silver flowed now, not from the coffers

of the king, but from the chests of merchants and manufacturers, from the purses of men who had made, say, a fortune from industry, and returned, in their wills, a bounteous share of it to endow more chairs, more lectureships, more fellowships in the university where they had learnt their craft. Hence the libraries and laboratories; the observatories; the splendid equipment of costly and delicate instruments which now stands on glass shelves, where centuries ago the grasses waved and the swine rootled. Certainly, as I strolled round the court, the foundations[b] of gold and silver seemed deep enough; the pavement laid solidly over the wild grasses. Men with trays on their heads went busily from staircase to staircase. Gaudy blossoms flowered in window-boxes. The strains of the gramophone blared out from the rooms within. It was impossible not to reflect – the reflection whatever it may have be[e]n was cut short. The clock struck. It was time to find one's way to luncheon.

It is a curious fact that novelists have a way of making us believe that luncheon parties are invariably memorable for something very witty that was said, or for something very wise that was done. But they seldom spare a word for what was eaten. It is part of the novelist's convention not to mention soup and salmon and ducklings, as if soup and salmon and ducklings were of no importance whatsoever, as if nobody ever smoked a cigar or drank a glass of wine. Here, however, I shall take the liberty to defy that convention and to tell you that the lunch on this occasion[4] began with soles, sunk in a deep dish over which the college cook had spread a counterpane of the whitest cream, save that it was branded here and there with brown spots like the spots on the flanks of a doe. After that came the partridges, but if this suggests a couple of bald, brown birds on a plate you are mistaken. The partridges, many and various, came with all their retinue of sauces and salads, the sharp and the sweet, each in its order; their potatoes, thin as coins but not so hard; their sprouts, foliated as rosebuds but more succulent. And no sooner had the roast and its retinue been done with than the silent serving-man, the Beadle himself perhaps in a milder manifestation, set before us, wreathed in napkins, a confection which rose all sugar from the waves. To call it pudding and so relate it to rice and tapioca would be an insult. Meanwhile the wine-glasses had flushed yellow and flushed crimson; had been emptied; had been filled. And thus by degrees was lit, half-way down the spine, which is the seat of the soul, not that hard little electric light which we call brilliance, as it pops in and out upon our lips, but the more

profound, subtle and subterranean glow which is the rich yellow flame
of rational intercourse. No need to hurry. No need to sparkle. No
need to be anybody but oneself. We are all going to heaven and
Vandyck is of the company[5] – in other words, how good life seemed,
how sweet its rewards, how trivial this grudge or that grievance, how
admirable friendship and the society of one's kind, as, lighting a good
cigarette, one sunk among the cushions in the window-seat.

If by good luck there had been an ash-tray handy, if one had not
knocked the ash out of the window in default, if things had been a
little different from what they were, one would not have seen, presumably, a cat without a tail. The sight of that abrupt and truncated
animal padding softly across the quadrangle changed by some fluke
of the sub-conscious intelligence the emotional light for me. It was
as if someone had let fall a shade. Perhaps the excellent hock was
relinquishing its hold. Certainly, as I watched the Manx cat pause in
the middle of the lawn as if it too questioned the universe, something
seemed lacking, something seemed different.[6] But what was lacking,
what was different, I asked myself, listening to the talk? And to answer
that question I had to think myself out of the room, back into the
past, before the war indeed, and to set before my eyes the model of
another luncheon party held in rooms not very distant[c] from these;
but different. Everything was different. Meanwhile the talk went on
among the guests, who were many and young, some of this sex, some
of that; it went on swimmingly, it went on agreeably, freely, amus-
ingly. And as it went on I set it against the background of that other
talk, and as I matched the two together I had no doubt that one was
the descendant, the legitimate heir of the other. Nothing was changed;
nothing was different save only – here I listened with all my ears not
entirely to what was being said, but to the murmur or current behind
it. Yes, that was it – the change was there. Before the war at a luncheon
party like this people would have said precisely the same things but
they would have sounded different, because in those days they were
accompanied by a sort of humming noise, not articulate, but musical,
exciting, which changed the value of the words themselves. Could
one set that humming noise to words? Perhaps with the help of the
poets one could. A book lay beside me and, opening it, I turned casually enough to Tennyson. And here I found Tennyson was singing:

> There has fallen a splendid tear
> From the passion-flower at the gate.

She is coming, my dove, my dear;
　　She is coming, my life, my fate;
The red rose cries, 'She is near, she is near';
　　And the white rose weeps, 'She is late';
The larkspur listens, 'I hear, I hear';
　　And the lily whispers, 'I wait'.[7]

Was that what men hummed at luncheon parties before the war? And the women?

My heart is like a singing bird
　　Whose nest is in a water'd shoot;
My heart is like an apple tree
　　Whose boughs are bent with thick-set fruit;
My heart is like a rainbow shell
　　That paddles in a halcyon sea;
My heart is gladder than all these
　　Because my love is come to me.[8]

Was that what women hummed at luncheon parties before the war?
There was something so ludicrous in thinking of people humming such things even under their breath at luncheon parties before the war that I burst out laughing, and had to explain my laughter by pointing at the Manx cat, who did look a little absurd, poor beast, without a tail, in the middle of the lawn. Was he really born so, or had he lost his tail in an accident? The tailless cat, though some are said to exist in the Isle of Man, is rarer than one thinks. It is a queer animal, quaint rather than beautiful. It is strange what a difference a tail makes – you know the sort of things one says as a lunch party breaks up and people are finding their coats and hats.

This one, thanks to the hospitality of the host, had lasted far into the afternoon. The beautiful October day was fading and the leaves were falling from the trees in the avenues[d] as I walked through it. Gate after gate seemed to close with gentle finality behind me. Innumerable beadles were fitting innumerable keys into well-oiled locks; the treasure-house was being made secure for another night. After the avenue one comes out upon a road – I forget its name – which leads you, if you take the right turning, along to Fernham.[9] But there was plenty of time. Dinner was not till half-past seven. One could almost do without dinner after such a luncheon.[10]

The gardens of Fernham lay before me in the spring twilight, wild and open, and in the long grass, sprinkled and carelessly flung, were daffodils and bluebells, not orderly perhaps at the best of times, and now wind-blown and waving as they tugged at their roots. The windows of the building, curved like ships' windows among generous waves of red brick, changed from lemon to silver under the flight of the quick spring clouds. Somebody was in a hammock, somebody, but in this light they were phantoms only, half guessed, half seen, raced across the grass – would no one stop her? – and then on the terrace, as if popping out to breathe the air, to glance at the garden, came a bent figure, formidable yet humble, with her great forehead and her shabby dress – could it be the famous scholar, could it be J—— H—— herself?[11] All was dim, yet intense too, as if the scarf which the dusk had flung over the garden were torn asunder by star or sword – the flash of some terrible reality leaping, as its way is, out of the heart of the spring. For youth . . .

Here was my soup. Dinner was being served in the great dining-hall. Far from being spring it was in fact an evening in October. Everybody was assembled in the big dining-room. Dinner was ready. Here was the soup. It was a plain gravy soup. There was nothing to stir the fancy in that. One could have seen through the transparent liquid any pattern that there might have been on the plate itself. But there was no pattern. The plate was plain. Next came beef with its attendant greens and potatoes – a homely trinity, suggesting the rumps of cattle in a muddy market, and sprouts curled and yellowed at the edge, and bargaining and cheapening, and women with string bags on Monday morning. There was no reason to complain of human nature's daily food, seeing that the supply was sufficient and coal-miners doubtless were sitting down to less. Prunes and custard followed. And if any one complains that prunes, even when mitigated by custard, are an uncharitable vegetable (fruit they are not), stringy as a miser's heart and exuding a fluid such as might run in misers' veins who have denied themselves wine and warmth for eighty years and yet not given to the poor, he should reflect that there are people whose charity embraces even the prune. Biscuits and cheese came next, and here the water-jug was liberally passed round, for it is the nature of biscuits to be dry, and these were biscuits to the core. That was all. The meal was over. Everybody scraped their chairs back; the swing-doors swung violently to and fro; soon the hall was emptied of every sign of food and made ready no doubt for breakfast next morning. Down corridors and up staircases the youth of England went banging and singing. And was it for a guest, a stranger (for I had no more right here in Fernham than in Trinity or Somerville or Girton or Newnham or Christchurch),[12] to say, 'The dinner was not good,' or to say (we were now, Mary Seton and I,[13] in her sitting-room), 'Could we not have dined up here alone?' for if I had said anything of the kind I should have been prying and searching into the secret economies of a house which to the stranger wears so fine a front of gaiety and courage. No, one could say nothing of the sort. Indeed, conversation for a moment flagged. The human frame being what it is, heart, body and brain all mixed together, and not contained in separate compartments as they will be no doubt in another million years, a good dinner is of great importance to good talk. One cannot think well, love well, sleep well, if one has not dined well. The lamp in the spine does not light on beef and prunes. We are all *probably* going to heaven, and Vandyck is, we *hope*, to meet us round the next corner – that is the dubious and qualifying state of mind that beef and prunes at the end of the day's work breed between them. Happily my friend, who taught science, had a cupboard where there was a squat bottle and little glasses – (but there should have been sole and partridge to begin with) – so that we were able to draw up to the fire and repair some of the damages of the day's living. In a minute or so we were slipping freely in and out among all those objects of curiosity and interest which form in the mind in the absence of a particular person, and are naturally to be discussed on coming together again – how somebody has married, another has not; one thinks this, another that; one has improved out of all knowledge, the other most amazingly gone to the bad – with all those speculations upon human nature and the character of the amazing world we live in which spring naturally from such beginnings. While these things were being said, however, I became shamefacedly aware of a current setting in of its own accord and carrying everything forward to an end of its own. One might be talking of Spain or Portugal, of book or racehorse, but the real interest of whatever was said was none of those things, but a scene of masons on a high roof some five centuries ago. Kings and nobles brought treasure in huge sacks and poured it under the earth. This scene was for ever coming alive in my mind and placing itself by another of lean cows and a muddy market and withered greens and the stringy hearts of old men – these two pictures, disjointed and disconnected and nonsensical as they were, were for ever coming together and combating each other and had me entirely at their mercy. The best course, unless the whole talk was to be distorted, was to expose what was in my mind to the air, when with good luck it would fade and crumble like the head of the dead king when they opened the coffin at Windsor.[14] Briefly, then, I told Miss Seton about the masons who had been all those years on the roof of the chapel, and about the kings and queens and nobles bearing sacks of gold and silver on their shoulders, which they shovelled into the earth; and then how the great financial magnates of our own time came and laid cheques and bonds, I suppose, where the others had laid ingots and rough lumps of gold. All that lies beneath the colleges down there, I said: but this college, where we are now sitting, what lies beneath its gallant red brick and the wild unkempt grasses of the garden? What force is behind that plain china off which we dined, and (here it popped out of my mouth before I could stop it) the beef, the custard and the prunes?

Well, said Mary Seton, about the year 1860 – Oh, but you know the story, she said, bored, I suppose, by the recital. And she told me – rooms were hired. Committees met. Envelopes were addressed. Circulars were drawn up. Meetings were held; letters were read out; so-and-so has promised so much; on the contrary, Mr —— won't give a penny. The *Saturday Review* has been very rude. How can we raise a fund to pay for offices? Shall we hold a bazaar? Can't we find a pretty girl to sit in the front row? Let us look up what John Stuart Mill said on the subject.[15] Can any one persuade the editor of the —— to print a letter? Can we get Lady —— to sign it? Lady —— is out of town. That was the way it was done, presumably, sixty years ago, and it was a prodigious effort, and a great deal of time was spent on it. And it was only after a long struggle and with the utmost difficulty that they got thirty thousand pounds together.[16] So obviously we cannot have wine and partridges and servants carrying tin dishes on their heads, she said. We cannot have sofas and separate rooms. 'The amenities,' she said, quoting from some book or other, 'will have to wait.'[17]

At the thought of all those women working year after year and finding it hard to get two thousand pounds together, and as much as they could do to get thirty thousand pounds, we burst out in scorn at the reprehensible poverty of our sex. What had our mothers been doing then that they had no wealth to leave us? Powdering their noses? Looking in at shop windows? Flaunting in the sun at Monte

Carlo? There were some photographs on the mantelpiece. Mary's mother – if that was her picture – may have been a wastrel in her spare time (she had thirteen children by a minister of the church), but if so her gay and dissipated life had left too few traces of its pleasures on her face. She was a homely body; an old lady in a plaid shawl which was fastened by a large cameo; and she sat in a basket chair, encouraging a spaniel to look at the camera, with the amused, yet strained expression of one who is sure that the dog will move directly the bulb is pressed. Now if she had gone into business; had become a manufacturer of artificial silk or a magnate on the Stock Exchange; if she had left two or three hundred thousand pounds to Fernham, we could have been sitting at our ease to-night and the subject of our talk might have been archæology, botany, anthropology, physics, the nature of the atom, mathematics, astronomy, relativity, geography. If only Mrs Seton and her mother and her mother before her had learnt the great art of making money, and had left their money, like their fathers and their grandfathers before them, to found fellowships and lectureships and prizes and scholarships appropriated to the use of their own sex, we might have dined very tolerably up here alone off a bird and a bottle of wine; we might have looked forward without undue confidence to a pleasant and honourable life-time spent in the shelter of one of the liberally endowed professions. We might have been exploring or writing; mooning about the venerable places of the earth; sitting contemplative on the steps of the Parthenon, or going at ten to an office and coming home comfortably at half-past four to write a little poetry. Only, if Mrs Seton and her like had gone into business at the age of fifteen, there would have been – that was the snag in the argument – no Mary. What, I asked, did Mary think of that? There between the curtains was the October night, calm and lovely, with a star or two caught in the yellowing trees. Was she ready to resign her share of it and her memories (for they had been a happy family, though a large one) of games and quarrels up in Scotland, which she is never tired of praising for the fineness of its air and the quality of its cakes, in order that Fernham might have been endowed with fifty thousand pounds or so by a stroke of the pen? For, to endow a college would necessitate the suppression of families altogether. Making a fortune and bearing thirteen children – no human being could stand it. Consider the facts, we said. First there are nine months before the baby is born. Then the baby is born. Then there are three or four months spent in feeding the baby. After the baby is fed there are certainly five years spent in playing with the baby. You cannot, it seems, let children run about the streets. People who have seen them running wild in Russia say that the sight is not a pleasant one. People say, too, that human nature takes its shape in the years between one and five. If Mrs Seton, I said, had been making money, what sort of memories would you have had of games and quarrels? What would you have known of Scotland, and its fine air and cakes and all the rest of it? But it is useless to ask these questions, because you would never have come into existence at all. Moreover, it is equally useless to ask what might have happened if Mrs Seton and her mother and her mother before her had amassed great wealth and laid it under the foundations of college and library, because, in the first place, to earn money was impossible for them, and in the second, had it been possible, the law denied them the right to possess what money they earned. It is only for the last forty-eight years that Mrs Seton has had a penny of her own.[18] For all the centuries before that it would have been her husband's property – a thought, which, perhaps, may have had its share in keeping Mrs Seton and her mothers off the Stock Exchange. Every penny I earn, they may have said, will be taken from me and disposed of according to my husband's wisdom – perhaps to found a scholarship or to endow a fellowship in Balliol[19] or King's, so that to earn money, even if I could earn money, is not a matter that interests me very greatly. I had better leave it to my husband.

At any rate, whether or not the blame rested on the old lady who was looking at the spaniel, there could be no doubt that for some reason or other our mothers had mismanaged their affairs very gravely. Not a penny could be spared for 'amenities'; for partridges and wine, beadles and turf, books and cigars, libraries and leisure. To raise bare walls out of the bare earth was the utmost they could do.

So we talked standing at the window and looking, as so many thousands look every night, down on the domes and towers of the famous city beneath us. It was very beautiful, very mysterious in the autumn moonlight. The old stone looked very white and venerable. One thought of all the books that were assembled down there; of the pictures of old prelates and worthies hanging in the panelled rooms; of the painted windows that would be throwing strange globes and crescents on the pavement; of the tablets and memorials and inscriptions; of the fountains and the grass; of the quiet rooms looking across the quiet quadrangles. And (pardon me the thought) I thought too, of the admirable smoke and drink and the deep armchairs and the pleasant carpets; of the urbanity, the geniality, the dignity which are the offspring of luxury and privacy and space. Certainly our mothers had not provided us with anything comparable to all this – our mothers who found it difficult to scrape together thirty thousand pounds, our mothers who bore thirteen children to ministers of religion at St Andrews.

So I went back to the[e] inn, and as I walked through the dark streets I pondered this and that, as one does at the end of the day's work. I pondered why it was that Mrs Seton had no money to leave us; and what effect poverty has on the mind; and what effect wealth has on the mind; and I thought of the queer old gentlemen I had seen that morning with tufts of fur upon their shoulders;[20] and I remembered how if one whistled one of them ran; and I thought of the organ booming in the chapel and of the shut doors of the library; and I thought how unpleasant it is to be locked out; and I thought how it is worse perhaps to be locked in; and, thinking of the safety and prosperity of the one sex and of the poverty and insecurity of the other and of the effect of tradition and of the lack of tradition upon the mind of the[f] writer, I thought at last that it was time to roll up the crumpled skin of the day, with its arguments and its impressions and its anger and its laughter, and cast it into the hedge. A thousand stars were flashing across the blue wastes of the sky. One seemed alone with an inscrutable society. All human beings were laid asleep – prone, horizontal, dumb. Nobody seemed stirring in the streets of Oxbridge.[21] Even the door of the hotel sprang open at the touch of an invisible hand – not a boots was sitting up to light me to bed, it was so late.

a – Room: 'back to mind,'.
b – Room: 'foundation'.
c – Room: 'very far distant'.
d – Room: 'avenue'.
e – Room: 'my'.
f – Room: 'a'.

1 – An excerpt from *Room*, published in *Time and Tide*, 22 and 29 November 1929 (Kp4 C320). The Hogarth Press trade edition of *Room* had been published on 24 October, (Kp4 A12b), and the instalments are taken from ch. i, pp. 14–21 and 25–37. The first was introduced: '*Time and Tide* has secured from the Hogarth Press the right to publish two excerpts, of which this is the first, from Mrs. Woolf's book, "A Room of One's Own".' Theodora

Bosanquet had reviewed *Room* in *Time and Tide* on 15 November and called it an 'enchanting essay'. The 22 November issue of *Time and Tide* also contained: 'Autumn Near Tokio', a poem by William Plomer; reviews of 'New Fiction' by Vera Brittain; 'Nothing Over Much', a story by Naomi Mitchison; and, next to the opening of VW's excerpt, a paragraph in St John Ervine's column, 'Notes on the Way: Men, Women and Events', employed a favourite image of VW's: 'I wonder if women are really hardier than men. The other day a lady entered a railway carriage on a bitterly cold day and, without a "by your leave" to anybody, threw down all the windows. The men visibly shivered, but none of us had the courage to defy the female and shut the windows again. Why are women so passionately addicted to draughts?' See also 'Women and Fiction' and 'Women and Leisure' above.

2 – VW is probably remembering 'a singular old cousin, who trots if you whistle, and gallops if you sing', Albert Venn Dicey (1835–1922), Vinerian Professor of English Law at Oxford, 1882–1909: see *I VW Letters* (nos 635 and 637).

3 – Seemingly referring to King's College Chapel, Cambridge, which was built between 1446 and 1547.

4 – Susan Gubar (ed.), *Room* (Harvest Book, Harcourt, 2005): 'An imaginative rendering of a lunch at King's College, in George Rylands's rooms on October 21, 1928, the day after the first lecture version of *A Room* was delivered' (p. 118). 'Dadie' Rylands (1902–99) said in an interview: 'partridges *various*? I don't think there could be more than one kind of partridge. And I don't very much like the idea, except that it was very much like college cooking, of a counterpane of sauce with some brown flecks on it. Never mind. And I hope there were *two* wines. I think it unlikely and there was probably only one' (*Recollections of Virginia Woolf*, ed. Jean Russell Noble [Peter Owen, 1972], p. 144). See also 'Portrait of Virginia Woolf' in *Virginia Woolf: Critical Assessments*, ed. Eleanor McNees (4 vols, Helm Information, 1994), vol. i, p. 95.

5 – The reputed last words of Thomas Gainsborough (1727–88), painter of portraits and landscapes. The words refer to the Antwerp-born Sir Anthony Van Dyck (1599–1641), who painted portraits of the English Royal family.

6 – In Aldous Huxley's *Limbo* (1920), Mrs Cravister, who is based on Molly MacCarthy's mother, Blanche Warre-Cornish, comments on Manx cats: 'No tails, no tails. Like men. How symbolical everything is!' See 'Cleverness and Youth', *III VW Essays*, where VW quotes this remark. In *W&F* the narrator leaves this 'to Freud . . . to explain' (p. 14).

7 – 'Maud' (1855) by Alfred, Lord Tennyson (1809–92), *OBEV*, no. 708, p. 847. Tennyson reads 'Maud' throughout VW's play, *Freshwater* (Hogarth Press, 1976).

8 – 'A Birthday' by Christina Rossetti (1830–94), *OBEV*, no. 780, p. 948.

9 – Cambridge colleges for women, established in the late nineteenth century,

are outside the much older university area. VW has conflated Girton and Newnham.

10 – This is the end of the first instalment. The second was introduced: '*Time and Tide* has secured from the Hogarth Press the right to publish two excerpts from Mrs. Woolf's book, "A Room of One's Own". The first appeared last week and should be read before that which follows.' A poem, 'The Absence' by Sylvia Townsend Warner, followed the second extract. In the same issue, C. H. B. Kitchin's *Death of My Aunt* (Hogarth Press) was briefly reviewed; and there was a quarter-page Hogarth Press advertisement for the first four vols of VW's Uniform Edition 'just published', quoting most of the last paragraph of the review of *Jacob's Room* in the *Spectator*, 11 November 1922, p. 662.

11 – Jane Harrison (1850–1928), classical scholar and anthropologist. Her *Reminiscences of a Student's Life* had been published by the Hogarth Press in 1925. For VW's visit to Harrison on her deathbed, see *III VW Diary*, 18 February 1928 (and see *ibid.*, 17 and 21 April 1928).

12 – Trinity, Girton and Newnham are Cambridge colleges; Somerville and Christchurch are Oxford colleges.

13 – A reference to the 'Ballad of the Four Marys': Mary Beton, Mary Seton, Mary Carmichael and Mary Hamilton, all supposed to be companions to Mary Queen of Scots. The singer, Mary Hamilton, is to be executed as punishment for her relationship with the king and the murder of the child she bore him. The ballad is alluded to throughout *Room*. For further information, see *Room* (Harvest ed.), pp. 114–17, and see 'The Queen's Marie', *The Oxford Book of Ballads*, ed. Arthur Quiller-Couch (Clarendon Press, 1920), no. 83, pp. 369–73.

14 – See *Room* (Harvest ed.), pp. 120–1, editor's note: 'In 1813, as a consequence of excavations in St George's Chapel of Windsor, the vault containing King Charles I was found by workmen. When the coffin was opened and the cloth around the body unwrapped, according to an eyewitness, "'the left eye in the first moment of exposure was full and open, but vanished almost immediately'" (Charles Wheeler Coit, *The Royal Martyr* [London: Selwyn and Blount, 1924])'.

15 – John Stuart Mill (1806–73), philosopher, author of *The Subjection of Women* (1869).

16 – '"We are told that we ought to ask for £30,000 at least. . . . It is not a large sum, considering that there is to be but one college of this sort for Great Britain, Ireland and the Colonies, and considering how easy it is to raise immense sums for boys' schools. But considering how few people really wish women to be educated, it is a good deal." – Lady Stephen, *Life of Miss Emily Davies*.' (VW's fn. in *Room*.) The book title was corrected to *Emily Davies and Girton College*, from the fourth impression (December 1929) onwards of *Room*; see *Emily Davies and Girton College* (Constable, 1927),

Miss Davies to Madame Bodichon, 29 January 1867, pp. 150–1; VW had reviewed it: see 'Two Women', *IV VW Essays*.

17 – 'Every penny which could be scraped together was set aside for building, and the amenities had to be postponed. – R. Strachey, *The Cause*.' (VW's fn. in *Room*.) See *The Cause: A Short History of the Women's Movement in Great Britain* (G. Bell & Sons, 1928), p. 250.

18 – The Married Women's Property Act, allowing married women to keep £200 of their own earnings, was passed in 1870, and then amended by the Married Women's Property Act of 1882, giving married women the same property rights as unmarried women, and allowing both to carry on trades or businesses using their own property.

19 – Balliol College, Oxford.

20 – The Cambridge BA academic hood is fringed with white rabbit fur.

21 – A name coined by William Makepeace Thackeray (1811–63) in *Pendennis* (1849) for a fictional university, especially one regarded as a composite of Oxford and Cambridge. VW revived the expression in *Room*, but it did not gain popular currency until the 1950s.

1930

Foreword to *Recent Paintings by Vanessa Bell*

That a woman should hold a show of pictures in Bond Street, I said, pausing upon the threshold of Messrs Cooling's gallery, is not usual, nor, perhaps, altogether to be commended. For it implies, I fancy, some study of the nude,[2] and while for many ages it has been admitted that women are naked and bring nakedness to birth, it was held, until sixty years ago that for a woman to look upon nakedness with the eye of an artist, and not simply with the eye of mother, wife or mistress was corruptive of her innocency and destructive of her domesticity. Hence the extreme activity of women in philanthropy, society, religion and all pursuits requiring clothing.

Hence again the fact that every Victorian family has in its cupboard the skeleton of an aunt who was driven to convert the native because her father would have died rather than let her look upon a naked man. And so she went to Church; and so she went to China; and so she died unwed; and so there drop out of the cupboard with her bones half a dozen flower pieces done under the shade of a white umbrella in a Surrey garden when Queen Victoria was on the throne.

These reflections are only worth recording because they indicate the vacillations and prevarications (if one is not a painter or a critic of painting) with which one catches at any straw that will put off the evil moment when one must go into the gallery and make up one's mind about pictures. Were it not that Mrs Bell has

a certain reputation and is sometimes the theme of argument at
dinner tables, many no doubt would stroll up Bond Street, past
Messrs Cooling's, thinking about morality or politics, about grandfathers or great aunts, about anything but pictures as is the way
of the English.

But Mrs Bell has a certain reputation it cannot be denied. She is
a woman, it is said, yet she has looked on nakedness with a brush
in her hand. She is reported (one has read it in the newspapers) to
be 'the most considerable painter of her own sex now alive'.[3] Berthe
Morisot, Marie Laurencin,[4] Vanessa Bell – such is the stereotyped
phrase which comes to mind when her name is mentioned and makes
one's predicament in front of her pictures all the more exacting. For
whatever the phrase may mean, it must mean that her pictures stand
for something, are something and will be something which we shall
disregard at our peril. As soon not go to see them as shut the window
when the nightingale is singing.

But once inside and surrounded by canvases, this shillyshallying
on the threshold seems superfluous. What is there here to intimi-
date or perplex? Are we not suffused, lit up, caught in a sunny
glow? Does there not radiate from the walls a serene yet temperate
warmth, comfortable in the extreme after the rigours of the streets?
Are we not surrounded by vineyards and olive trees, by naked girls
couched on crimson cushions,[5] by naked boys ankle deep in the
pale green sea?[6] Even the puritans of the nineteenth century might
grant us a moment's respite from the February murk, a moment's
liberty in this serene and ordered world. But it is not the puritans
who move us on. It is Mrs Bell. It is Mrs Bell who is determined
that we shall not loll about juggling with pretty words or dallying
with delicious sensations. There is something uncompromising
about her art. Ninety-nine painters had nature given them her
susceptibility, her sense of the lustre of grass and flower, of the
glow of rock and tree, would have lured us on by one refinement
and felicity after another to stay and look for ever. Ninety-nine
painters again had they possessed that sense of satire which seems
to flash its laughter for a moment at those women in Dieppe in
the eighties,[7] would have caricatured and illustrated; would have
drawn our attention to the antics of parrots, the pathos of old
umbrellas, the archness of ankles, the eccentricities of noses.
Something would have been done to gratify the common, innocent and indeed very valuable gift which has produced in England

so rich a library of fiction. But look round the room: the approach to these pictures is not by that means. No stories are told; no insinuations are made. The hill side is bare; the group of women is silent; the little boy stands in the sea saying nothing. If portraits there are, they are pictures of flesh which happens from its texture or its modelling to be æsthetically on an equality with the China pot or the chrysanthemum.

Checked at that point in our approach (and the snub is none the less baffling for the beauty with which it is conveyed) one can perhaps draw close from another angle. Let us see if we can come at some idea of Mrs Bell herself and by thus trespassing, crack the kernel of her art. Certainly it would hardly be possible to read as many novels as there are pictures here without feeling our way psychologically over the features of the writer; and the method, if illicit, has its value. But here, for a second time, we are rebuffed. One says, Anyhow Mrs Bell is a woman; and then half way round the room one says, But she may be a man. One says, She is interested in children; one has to add, But she is equally interested in rocks. One asks, Does she show any special knowledge of clothes? One replies, Stark nakedness seems to please her as well. Is she dainty then, or austere? Does she like riding? Is she red haired or brown eyed? Was she ever at a University? Does she prefer herrings or Brussels sprouts? Is she – for our patience is becoming exhausted – not a woman at all, but a mixture of Goddess and peasant, treading the clouds with her feet and with her hands shelling peas? Any writer so ardently questioned would have yielded something to our curiosity. One defies a novelist to keep his life through twenty-seven volumes of fiction safe from our scrutiny. But Mrs Bell says nothing. Mrs Bell is as silent as the grave. Her pictures do not betray her. Their reticence is inviolable.[8] That is why they intrigue and draw us on; that is why, if it be true that they yield their full meaning only to those who can tunnel their way behind the canvas into masses and passages and relations and values of which we know nothing – if it be true that she is a painter's painter – still her pictures claim us and make us stop. They give us an emotion. They offer a puzzle.

And the puzzle is that while Mrs Bell's pictures are immensely expressive, their expressiveness has no truck with words. Her vision excites a strong emotion and yet when we have dramatised it or poetised it or translated it into all the blues and greens, and fines and exquisites and subtles of our vocabulary, the picture itself escapes. It goes on saying something of its own. A good example is to be found in the painting of the Foundling Hospital. Here one says, is the fine old building which has housed a million orphans; here Hogarth painted and kind-hearted Thackeray shed a tear, here Dickens, who lived down the street on the left-hand side, must often have paused in his walk to watch the children at play. And it is all gone, all perished.[9] Housebreakers have been at work, speculators have speculated. It is dust and ashes – but what has Mrs Bell got to say about it? Nothing. There is the picture, serene and sunny, and very still. It represents a fine eighteenth-century house and an equally fine London plane tree. But there are no orphans, no Thackeray, no Dickens, no housebreakers, no speculators, no tears, no sense that this sunny day is perhaps the last. Our emotion has been given the slip.

And yet somehow our emotion has been returned to us. For emotion there is. The room is charged with it. There is emotion in that white urn;[10] in that little girl painting a picture;[11] in the flowers and the bust; in the olive trees; in the provençal vineyard; in the English hills against the sky. Here, we cannot doubt as we look is somebody to whom the visible world has given a shock of emotion every day of the week. And she transmits it and makes us share it; but it is always by her means, in her language, with her susceptibility, and not ours. That is why she is so tantalising, so original, and so satisfying as a painter. One feels that if a canvas of hers hung on the wall it would never lose its lustre. It would never mix itself up with the loquacities and trivialities of daily life. It would go on saying something of its own imperturbably. And perhaps by degrees – who knows? – one would become an inmate of this strange painters' world, in which mortality does not enter, and psychology is held at bay, and there are no words. But is morality to be found there? That was the very question I was asking myself as I came in.

1 – A signed foreword, 4 February 1930, (*Kp4* B10), to a catalogue of twenty-seven paintings, priced between 18 and 50 guineas, by VW's sister Vanessa Bell (1879–1961), exhibited through the London Artists' Association at the Cooling Galleries, 92 New Bond St, from 4 February to 8 March 1930. John Maynard Keynes was instrumental in founding the Association in 1925, together with Samuel Courtauld, L. H. Myers and F. Hindley Smith. Angus Davidson was the Secretary from 1929. VW had been wanting to discuss Vanessa's paintings for some time. On 12 May [1928] she wrote to Vanessa: 'O and then I went to your show and spent

an hour making some extremely interesting theories: which I will condense into one paean of admiration for your Three Women . . . I had forgotten the extreme brilliancy and flow and wit and ardour of these works – I am greatly tempted to write "Variations on a Picture by Vanessa Bell" for Desmonds paper [L&L] – I should run the three women and the pot of flowers on a chair into one phantasmagoria. I think you are a most remarkable painter. But I maintain you are into the bargain, a satirist, a conveyer of impressions about human life: a short story writer of great wit and able to bring off a situation in a way that rouses my envy. I wonder if I could write the Three Women in prose' (III VW Letters, no. 1894). On 31 January 1930 Vanessa wrote to Clive Bell: 'I have been fearfully busy getting things finally ready for my show. Virginia suddenly offered to write a preface for it. I don't know what people will think but I daresay its a very good advertisement[.] Eddy [Sackville-West] came in to see a portrait of himself I am showing [no. 14] and nearly died of his proximity to a fat female nude' (Charleston Papers, University of Sussex). The day after the exhibition opened VW noted: 'Nessa sold 5 pictures I think the first day' (IV VW Letters, no. 2133); see also Bell's letter of 7 February [1930] to Duncan Grant in Selected Letters of Vanessa Bell, ed. Regina Marler (Bloomsbury, 1993), pp. 350–3. VW told her nephews (Vanessa's sons, Julian and Quentin) that the show was 'a great success and members of the aristocracy rend their gloves asunder competing for her pictures. My foreword has roused Mr Rory Mahoney [O'Mullen] as his name suggests to fury. He says I am indecent, and must be suppressed' (ibid., no. 2145, 17 February 1930; and see no. 2144). The Times, however, called the foreword 'enchanting' (7 February 1930, p. 12, col. b), and John Piper quoted from it approvingly in his review of the exhibition ('Vanessa Bell', N&A, 15 February 1930, p. 672). See also 'Foreword to Catalogue of Recent Paintings by Vanessa Bell' and 'Walter Sickert', VI VW Essays. Draft (Berg, M 1.3). Reprinted: CDML.

2 – There seem to have been three paintings of nudes: nos 7 'Sketch for a Composition' (see also n. 5), 15 'Wading' and 16 'Nude'.

3 – Quotation untraced; the draft of the foreword suggests that it may have been VW's invention. Roger Fry wrote in the New Statesman, 3 June 1922, p. 237: 'But, after all, it is as a colourist that Vanessa Bell stands out so markedly among contemporary artists. Indeed, I cannot think of any living English artist that is her equal in this respect' (reprinted in A Roger Fry Reader, ed. Christopher Reed [University of Chicago Press, 1996], p. 349). But Fry does not compare Vanessa's work with that of other women painters. Four years later, Fry was even more enthusiastic: 'Vanessa Bell takes her place . . . in the front rank of British painters to-day . . .' ('Vanessa Bell', Vogue, vol. lxvii, no. 3 [early February 1926], pp. 33–5, 78, at p. 33).

4 – Berthe Morisot (1841–95), the first woman French Impressionist, exhibited at all their exhibitions except the fourth. Marie Laurencin (1883–1956),
French painter, mainly of young girls, used a naive, decorative style usually
employing pastels. Fry refers to both in 'Vanessa Bell' (pp. 33, 34). In a
review of the 25th exhibition of the London Group, *The Times* 'ventured
that Miss Bell stands to the modern movement in England somewhat in
the relation of Berthe Morisot to French Impressionism, completing it by
a feminine turn' (4 June 1927, p. 8, col. c).

5 – No. 7 'Sketch for a Composition' (purchased by Keynes); it is illustrated
in Diane F. Gillespie's 'Godiva Still Rides: Virginia Woolf, Divestiture, and
Three Guineas', in *Virginia Woolf and the Art of Exploration: Selected Papers
from the Fifteenth Annual Conference on Virginia Woolf*, ed. Helen
Southworth and Elisa Kay Sparks (Clemson University Digital Press, 2006),
p. 14, fig. 6.

6 – No. 15 'Wading'.

7 – No. 26 'Dieppe in the Eighties'.

8 – Cf. Fry: 'Her great distinction lies in her reticence and her frankness.
Complete frankness of statement, but with never a hint of how she arrived
at her conviction. It is with her a point of honour to leave it at that, never
to explain herself, never to underline a word, never to exercise persuasion.
You are left with the completest statement she can contrive, to make what
you can of it or nothing at all, as the case may be' ('Vanessa Bell', p. 78).

9 – No. 22 'The Foundling Hospital'. The huge Foundling Hospital, which
provided a home for illegitimate children, stood between Brunswick and
Mecklenburgh Squares in the heart of Bloomsbury, and had been demolished in the late 1920s. The painter William Hogarth (1697–1764) had been
a strong supporter, painting it and its founder Thomas Coram. Charles
Dickens (1812–70) had lived close by at 48 Doughty Street, 1837–9. William
Makepeace Thackeray (1811–63) lived in Coram Street, 1837–43, and his
daughter Anne was born there in 1840; see 'The Ballad of Eliza Davis',
stanza 2, *Ballads and Tales* (The Works of William Makepeace Thackeray,
vol. xviii, Smith, Elder, 1869), p. 200: 'Praps you know the Fondling Chapel,
/ Vere the little children sings: / (Lor! I likes to hear on Sundies / Them
there pooty little things!)'. In a review of an exhibition by the London
Artists' Association, *The Times* commented that 'with all their excellences,
such works as ... "Foundling Hospital, Bloomsbury," by Miss Vanessa Bell
can only be described as "naice" pictures, produced in the "tin shoes and
tepid milk" spirit of Robert Louis Stevenson' (15 November 1929, p. 12,
col. d).

10 – No. 9 'The White Urn'.

11 – No. 24 'Child Drawing'.

Augustine Birrell

'But it is not bedtime,' a lady was heard to protest the other night. When assured that the clock had already struck twelve, she murmured that the clock might say what it liked, but that she must finish her book. And what was her book? It was a book by Mr Birrell, a new book, called *Et Cetera*.[2] And the new book, continuing as it did an old conversation, renewing an old charm, had led her to strew the floor with three robust red volumes containing the collected *Essays and Addresses* of Augustine Birrell so that she might get the flavour entire. It was the essays of Mr Birrell that she was engaged in sampling; it was these that kept her from her bed when the chimes of midnight were ringing and the voice of duty called.

Such being the truth and nothing more than the truth, it may be worth while to attempt to justify her defiance of discipline: to try to discover what are the qualities that make us slip from the end of one essay by Mr Birrell to the beginning of another and so on through page after page when not only is the hour late but when, to tell the truth, more serious and more learned volumes are shut with a snap on the stroke of eleven. In those words, perhaps, some glimpse of the reason sought for is to be found. One reads Mr Birrell for pleasure. Nobody has ever, in the mercantile sense of the term, read Mr Birrell for profit. It seems doubtful that tutors bent on steering young men into the safe pasturage of scholarships and fellowships have ever counselled them to commit his *Obiter Dicta* to memory. There is very little talk in Mr Birrell's pages of schools and influences and origins and developments and how one style grew out of another; no new theory of poetry is advanced; no key to aesthetics warranted to unlock all doors is forged. And since nature has so contrived it that we only feel highly virtuous when we are also feeling slightly uncomfortable, there has been a note of apology in the tones of Mr Birrell's admirers as if to be found reading *Obiter Dicta* or *Res Judicatae* or *Men, Women and Books*[3] was to be caught drinking champagne in the middle of the morning – a proceeding too pleasant to be right. If, on the other hand, one has muddled one's wits for an hour by the clock over some philosophical treatise and come to feel that all Shakespeare is a matter of mathematics, then very justly one bruits the fact abroad, claims the esteem of one's friends, and leaves the book lying about with a marker placed ostentatiously near the end.

So, then, Mr Birrell is no philosophical critic. But once that is said we have to explain why it is that one feels, nevertheless, no lack of substance in his pages – they are not airy flimsy gossip – they are not dainties made to serve up with the *soufflé* at luncheon parties. They have, on the contrary, a bluffness, a toughness, even a grittiness about them which makes one suspect that if it be true that Mr Birrell has not mined deeply in the darker galleries of thought he has, it may be, done a day's work in the open air.

There is something of the man of action in his style. He comes in with his hair slightly rumpled and a splash of mud on his boots. If we turn to the first pages of the collected essays, we shall find our surmise confirmed. 'I became an author,' he writes, 'quite by accident. I had never dreamt of such a thing. Some time in 1883, while pursuing in Lincoln's Inn, after a dimmish but not wholly unremunerative fashion, the now decayed profession of an equity draughtsman and conveyancer, it occurred to me'[4] – that he might perhaps print certain manuscripts which had been read aloud in friendly coteries and put back into the desk. This he did, and the little book – it was the famous *Obiter Dicta* – had an instant and remarkable success. But though when he had found his way into print he never lost it again, he yet went on, as everybody knows, to pursue the law, to fight cases, to win seats, to sit in Parliament, to enter the cabinet, to rule Ireland, and so to become, in course of time, the Right Honourable Augustine Birrell, after whose name there are many letters in distinguished combination.

Thus the life of letters and the life of action were lived simultaneously, and there can be no doubt that the politician influenced the author, and that the author influenced the politician. With the politician proper we have no concern; it is the author only who comes within our scope. Yet it is plain that the author gained something of great value from his partnership with the man of affairs. In the first place, he gained an unprofessional air, a holiday spirit. To sit down and write an essay was, it seemed, a treat that Mr Birrell had promised himself, not a duty that had to be accomplished. A zest clings to the performance. He would have been, one feels, as much put out at missing a day's writing as most people are annoyed at losing a day's sport.

But the advantage of the connection between the man of action and the man of letters goes deeper than that. The substance of Mr Birrell's essays, the point of view that collects them and makes them however disconnected in subject of one spiritual texture, is the result of knowing the world and of passing judgment upon human life. It is the moral sense, not the literary, that makes a unity of his scattered papers. We know, as we look back, what men Mr Birrell has liked, rather than what books he has admired. And since the moral sense has gone abroad and taken the air whether the sun shone or the rain poured, it is a healthy and active moral sense with blood in its cheeks and light in its eyes, and has none of that sour and leathery constitution which afflicts the moral sense of those who live indoors passing judgment upon their fellows from the sheltered library. There is not a trace of the pedagogue and scarcely a trace of the dictator about him.

It is this elastic and humane quality that has kept his essays, written as he reminds us by a contemporary of the Prince Consort,[5] so much fresher than the mass of their fellows. For it is not uncommon, though highly disagreeable, to be pulled up in the middle of one of the great Victorians by a perverse, provincial, and as it seems to us merely conventional judgment passed in a fit of the spleen upon the conduct of some great man. Thackeray's judgment on Sterne, Carlyle's upon Lamb, Matthew Arnold's upon Shelley,[6] reveal them in their Victorian setting far more certainly than their victims. We see the screens and the curtains that surround them, we peer about in the dark sad light, much that we talk of openly seems to be hidden away, and we feel like children in the presence of a schoolmaster. But when we read Mr Birrell, though he speaks like an elder, he does not speak as a superior. We are not reminded at every turn of his ineffable goodness, of his impeccable morality. We do not feel that he rates himself so much the superior of Sterne and Shelley and Lamb that he can afford to put them in their places. This is the more remarkable when we remember that, as was said, his chief concern is with character and not with art. Man after man, woman after woman, the big, the small, the wise, the foolish he summons before him, and yet in passing judgment his voice never loses its cordiality, his temper is almost consistently unruffled. If, as will happen, a pretentious fool comes his way, he buffets his victim so genially across the stage that even that great goose Hannah More[7] herself must have taken the process in good part.

For this again, credit must be given to politics. Life in the House of Commons, as Mr Birrell says, makes it difficult to maintain aloofness. 'You hob-nob at luncheon, you grumble together over your dinner, you lament the spread of football clubs and brass bands in your constituencies.'[8] And so what with lunching here and dining there, it has been very difficult for Mr Birrell to pull a long face over human failings, if at least they are such as proceed from good fellowship or hot-bloodedness or a warm appreciation of the pleasures of life. It is the prigs and the censors and the timid water drinkers whom he wholeheartedly despises, and them he can be trusted to trounce much to our delectation whenever they raise their voices to deplore Lamb's drunkenness or the sinful extravagance of Sir Walter Scott.

Yet, to be honest, it is somewhere about this point that we become aware of divergence. We begin to catch, now and again, a note of asperity in his voice, to hear some echoes of the sonorous Victorian trumpet. His love of charity, and good sense and good temper lead him on little by little to declaim not only against their opposites, but against speculation and introspection, and all those other vices of the new age which he suspects will lead to the clouding of the clear stream of English literature and to the paralysis of healthy human activity. Already early in the Eighties, he had scented the coming of change. He complained that 'The ruddy qualities of delightfulness, of pleasantness are all "sicklied o'er with the pale cast of thought." The varied elements of life . . . seem to be fading from literature.'[9] Indeed even in the Eighties, things had come to such a pass that he was about to make up his mind 'to look for no more Sir Walters, no more Thackerays, no more Dickenses. The stories have all been told. Plots are exploded. Incident is over'[10] – when, miraculously, *Treasure Island*[11] appeared and the honour of English literature was saved.

Thus for all his tolerance and catholicity Mr Birrell, it would seem, has his notion of what literature should be, and the fact that he eschews aesthetic criticism by no means implies that he has not a code of his own, and a will of his own, and a taste of his own, which exclude whole tracts of literature, and, we make bold to say, of very good literature into the bargain. He has nothing to say about the great Russians or the great Frenchmen. His essays, though they embrace the years from 1880 to 1930, make no mention of Meredith or Henry James or Hardy or Conrad. For

all he tells us to the contrary, one might suppose that English literature had fallen over a precipice about the year 1900 and lay in
shattered fragments not worth picking up and examining on the
stones beneath.

That perhaps is the weakness of treating books as if they might
at any moment turn into people. One detects in them what it is
that is antipathetic to one in real life – gloom, self-analysis,
morbidity, sexual aberration. And then, if one has let wither the
other sense which finds in literature something non-personal, like
beauty, or sound, or intellectual originality, and analyses it to feel
more keenly, one condemns the book because of the man, and has
nothing to say about a work, the fruit of a corrupt society and of
an introspective temperament, called *La Recherche du Temps
Perdu*.[12] About this Mr Birrell is perfectly decided. 'We want Lambs,'
he writes, 'not Coleridges. The verdict to be striven for is not "Well
guessed," but "Well done."'[13] And so with a great sweep of his
arm he throws into the waste-paper basket such trifles as *The Egoist*,
and *The Wings of the Dove*, *The Return of the Native*, *The Possessed*,
and *Lord Jim*.[14] That done, he heaves a sigh of relief and takes
down one of the many volumes, well worn and well loved, of his
Scott.

Thus we must accept the fact that Mr Birrell will neither illumine
the present nor acknowledge the future save as something disagreeable which it is the part of wise men not to anticipate. But once that
fact is faced – it is a fact that need not surprise us seeing that a politician is in partnership with the writer – there still remain the fine
volumes of witty, varied, and most entertaining reading, to which
others, we may hope, are still to be added.

Let us for a moment dwell upon the quality which kept our friend
so unrepentantly out of bed – the charm, the seductiveness of Mr
Birrell's writing. It is just and right so to pause, for it is perhaps by
this quality rather than any other that the books are destined to
endure. Yet how are we to define a word that is so easily and sometimes so condescendingly pronounced? 'It is not easy to define charm,
which is not a catalogue of qualities, but a mixture.'[15] So Mr Birrell
says himself; and there is much in the saying that applies to him.
Open Mr Birrell's books where you will and there is this mixture
in operation; this blending of many often mutually destructive gifts
into one effervescence – irony and feeling; sound sense and fantasy;
caustic humour and a sunny good temper. Hence the iridescence,

the sparkle, and the varied movement of his prose. It never forms into one great wave that comes crashing down upon our heads; it is forever rippling and dancing, giving and withholding, like a breeze-stirred lake.

And when this is said we have also said by implication that Mr Birrell is a born writer – not one of our great writers, certainly not one of our professional writers, but one of those writers who spring as naturally from our literature as the dog-rose from the hedge and scent it with as true a fragrance. How lightly and easily he casts the line of his sentence! How the images come flocking to his pen and how pleasant and sometimes more than pleasant they are to the ear! – 'gentle as is the breath with which a child disperses a dandelion-clock,'[16] he says in his preface; or – 'it must have been hard while still in the middle passage of life to scent the night-air'[17] – but to underline what is so natural is to spoil it. And then pervading the wit and the sparkle, there is something pungent as the smell of good tobacco – that profound love of books, which some good critics have lacked, but would have been better critics for possessing. 'No man of letters knew letters better than he. He knew literature in all its branches – he had read books, he had written books, he had sold books, he had bought books, and he had borrowed them. . . . He loved a catalogue; he delighted in an index.'[18] What he says of Johnson we might say of him. Everything about a book from the leather of the binding to the print on the page smells sweet in his nostrils.

So then if one seeks an excuse for reading Mr Birrell – and pleasure is still a little suspect – it is that he makes books seem lovable objects and reading an entrancing occupation. Literature when he writes of it ceases to be an art and a mystery and becomes an assembly of all sorts of interesting people. The books turn into people, and the people turn into books. There are the Waverley novels and *Tristram Shandy* and the *Essays of Elia*; there is also Miss Hannah More and Arthur Young and Arthur Young's little Bobbin.[19] Some of the books are very rare, and some of the people are very obscure. There are many theological volumes among them and a good many lawyers. Then suddenly Mr Browning or Mr Matthew Arnold appears in the flesh, or behold, there is Nathaniel Hawthorne walking along a street in Liverpool in the year 1856.[20]

In short, it is a splendid entertainment to which we are invited, call it what you will. And to have created so varied a prospect, to have brought together out of the dimness so many shapes, the queer and the hunchbacked as well as the stately and the splendid, to have led us up to the great writers in a mood of warmth and happy expectation, yet critically, too, and by no means ready to tolerate fustian or humbug – that is a great task to have accomplished. It tempts us to quote one of Mr Birrell's sentences, and, indeed, to alter one word without his permission. 'Even that most extraordinary compound, the rising generation of readers, whose taste in literature is as erratic as it is pronounced, read their Lamb,' says Mr Birrell – and here we interpose 'read their Birrell' – and then go on in concert 'with laughter and with love.'[21]

1 – A signed review in the *Yale Review*, June 1930, and revised (as 'The Essays of Augustine Birrell') in *L&L*, July 1930 (see Appendix III), (*Kp4* C323), of *The Collected Essays & Addresses of the Rt. Hon. Augustine Birrell, 1880–1920* (3 vols, J. M. Dent, 1922). In the same issue of the *Yale Review*, Katharine Fullerton Gerould wrote on 'Men, Women, and Thrillers' and commented on *Room* (pp. 692–3, 696–7); it also contained: Walter de la Mare's story 'The Orgy', Paul Valéry on 'Art and Progress', two poems by Helen MacAfee (*sic*), William Lyon Phelps's review of James Woodforde's *The Diary of a Country Parson*, and Marjorie Nicolson on 'Scholars and Ladies' ('how is it possible to be at once a scholar – and a lady?'). Essayist and Liberal statesman – Chief Secretary for Ireland, 1907–16 – Augustine Birrell (1850–1933) was born in Wavertree, near Liverpool, the younger son of Charles Morton Birrell, minister of the Pembroke Baptist Chapel. He was called to the Bar in 1875. VW met Birrell at Charleston early in July 1929, and wrote to thank him on 17 July for sending her his *Collected Essays*: 'I am more than glad that I plucked up courage at Charleston and tried to tell you how much I admire and enjoy your essays. Here they are in this splendid edition, and I have spent the evening foraging among them with a new delight now that they are mine and given me by you. I wish there were more I hadn't read. But I am going to re-read them, and then to put them where they belong – next my Hours in a Library [by Leslie Stephen]. It was very very good of you. Indeed I am almost precipitated by your goodness into the rashness of writing an essay upon Mr Birrell – making an attempt to find how [*sic*] what is the particular thing you do so much better than anybody else. That will be a pleasant occupation' (*IV VW Letters*, no. 2051). On 18 November 1929 she was 'having a holiday – reading old Birrell' (*III VW Diary*). On 15 April 1930 she wrote to Helen McAfee, managing editor of the *Yale Review*, who had been asking her for articles: 'I have cabled to you today to apply to the Bookman for an article of mine on Augustine Birrell, as I gather from your cable that you are counting on some thing from me for your

summer number. I sent them this article some time ago and as I have not heard from them, I should much prefer you to have it. I believe they meant to print it, but they have kept it so long that I do not think they can object to your having it. ¶ . . . I have been held up by an attack of influenza, and all my time is still used on a novel [*The Waves*] that I am trying to finish this summer. Thus I have not written any story or article since the autumn, and cannot yet say when I shall be free. The Birrell article is thus the only piece I have at present in a state ready for publication. ¶ Would you let me know as soon as you can when you intend to publish it? It is to appear here in Life and Letters' (*IV VW Letters*, no. 2166). On 29 April she wrote to McAfee: 'I just send a line to say that I have received your cable offering 250 dollars for the article on Mr Birrell on condition that it does not appear here before July 1st. ¶ I will accept the offer and see that the article does not appear until the time stated' (*ibid.*, no. 2171; see also nos 2079 and 2117). On 7 July she acknowledged receipt of the payment: see *VWB*, no. 9 (January 2002), p. 6. See also 'A Character Sketch', *III VW Essays*. Reading notes (Berg, RN 1.13, 1.20) (*VWRN* XIII, XX). Typescript draft (with holograph corrections) and galley proofs: *Yale Review* Papers, Beinecke Rare Book and Manuscript Library, Yale University.

2 – Birrell, *Et Cetera: A Collection* (Chatto and Windus, 1930); it includes essays published in the *N&A* while LW was literary editor.

3 – Birrell, *Obiter Dicta* (First Series, 1884; Second Series, 1887; *More Obiter Dicta*, 1924); *Res Judicatæ: Papers and Essays* (1892); *Essays about Men, Women, and Books* (1894).

4 – *Collected Essays & Addresses*, vol. i, 'Preface', p. vi, which has: 'whilst pursuing'.

5 – Prince Albert (1819–61).

6 – For these judgements, see William Makepeace Thackeray (1811–63), *The English Humourists of the Eighteenth Century* (1853); Thomas Carlyle (1795–1881), *Reminiscences*, ed. James Anthony Froude (1881); Matthew Arnold (1822–88), 'Shelley [1792–1822]', *Essays in Criticism. Second Series* (1888). Charles Lamb (1775–1834).

7 – See *Collected Essays & Addresses*, vol. i, 'Hannah More [1745–1833]' (1894), pp. 278–83, and vol. ii, 'Hannah More Once More' (1906), pp. 254–61.

8 – *Ibid.*, vol. iii, 'The House of Commons' (1896), p. 345, which has: 'hob-a-nob' and 'your respective constituencies'.

9 – *Ibid.*, vol. iii, 'The Muse of History' (1887), pp. 45–6, quoting *Hamlet*, III, i, 85.

10 – *Ibid.*, p. 46. Sir Walter Scott (1771–1832); Charles Dickens (1812–70).

11 – Robert Louis Stevenson (1850–94), *Treasure Island* (1883).

12 – Marcel Proust (1871–1922), *À la recherche du temps perdu* (1913–27).

13 – *Collected Essays & Addresses*, vol. iii, 'Truth-Hunting' (1884), p. 9; the reference is to Matthew 25: 21. Samuel Taylor Coleridge (1772–1834).

14 – George Meredith (1828–1909), *The Egoist* (1879); Henry James (1843–1916), *The Wings of the Dove* (1902); Thomas Hardy (1840–1928), *The Return of the Native* (1878); Fyodor Dostoevsky (1821–81), *The Possessed* (1872); Joseph Conrad (1857–1924), *Lord Jim* (1900).

15 – *Collected Essays & Addresses*, vol. i, 'John Wesley' (1902), p. 310.

16 – *Ibid.*, 'Preface', p. viii.

17 – *Ibid.*, vol. ii, 'Walter Bagehot' (1901), p. 233, which has: 'whilst still'.

18 – *Ibid.*, vol. i, 'Dr. Johnson' (1887), p. 125, which has: 'loved letters better'.

19 – Scott's Waverley novels began publication in 1814; Laurence Sterne (1713–68), *The Life and Opinions of Tristram Shandy* (1760, 1761–2, 1767); Charles Lamb, *Essays of Elia* (1823, 1833). For 'Arthur Young [1741–1820]' (1906), agriculturalist, see *Collected Essays & Addresses*, vol. i, pp. 284–91; his 'little Bobbin' was his beloved daughter Martha (1783–97); VW was reading his *Travels in France during 1787, 1788, and 1789* in January and February 1934 (see *IV VW Diary*); see also Leslie Stephen, *The English Utilitarians* (Duckworth, 1900), vol. i, ch. ii, sec. ii, pp. 69–86, and *Studies of a Biographer* (4 vols, Duckworth, 1898–1902), vol. i, pp. 188–226.

20 – Robert Browning (1812–89); for Nathaniel Hawthorne (1804–64), who was United States Consul in Liverpool, 1853–7, see 'Nathaniel Hawthorne' (1928), *Et Cetera*, p. 199.

21 – *Collected Essays & Addresses*, vol. ii, 'Charles Lamb' (1887), p. 9; there should be an ellipsis before 'read' which continues with: 'their Lamb, letters as well as essays, with laughter and with love'.

Fanny Burney's Half-Sister

Since a copy of *Evelina* was lately sold for the enormous sum of four thousand pounds;[2] since the Clarendon Press has lately bestowed the magnificent compliment of a new edition upon *Evelina*;[3] since Maria Allen was the half-sister[a] of the authoress of *Evelina*; since the story of Evelina owed much to the story of Maria Allen, it may not be impertinent to consider what is still to be collected of the history of that misguided and unfortunate girl.

As is well known, Dr Burney was twice married. He took for his second wife a Mrs Allen of Lynn, the widow of a substantial citizen who left her with a fortune which she promptly lost, and with three children, of whom one, Maria, was almost the same age as Fanny Burney when Dr Burney's second marriage made them half-sisters.[4] And half-sisters[b] they might have remained with none but a formal tie between them, had not the differences between the two families[c] brought about a much closer relationship. The Burneys were the gifted children of gifted parents. They had enjoyed all the stimulus that comes from running in and out of rooms where grown-up people are talking about books and music, where the piano is always open, and somebody – it may be David Garrick, it may be Mrs Thrale[5] – is always dropping in to dinner. Maria, on the other hand, had been bred in the provinces. The great figures of Lynn were well known to her, but the great figures of Lynn were merely Miss Dolly Young – who was so ugly – or Mr Richard Warren, who was so handsome. The talk she heard[d] was the talk of squires and merchants. Her greatest excitement was a[e] dance at the Assembly Rooms or a scandal in the town.

Thus she was rustic and unsophisticated where the Burneys were metropolitan and cultivated. But she was bold and dashing where they were timid and reserved. She was all agog for life and adventure where they were always running away in agonies of shyness to commit their innumerable observations to reams of paper. Unrefined, but generous and unaffected, she brought to Poland-street that whiff of fresh air, that contact with ordinary life and ease in the presence of ordinary things, which the precocious family lacked themselves and found most refreshing in others. Sometimes she visited them in London; sometimes they stayed with her at Lynn. Soon she came to feel for them all, but for Fanny in particular, a warm, a genuine, a surprised admiration. They were so learned and so innocent; they knew so many things; and yet they did not know half as much about life as she did. It was to them, naturally, that she confided her own peccadilloes and adventures, wishing perhaps for counsel, wishing perhaps to impress. Fanny was one of those shy people – 'I am not near so squeamish as you are,'[6] Maria observed – who draw out the confidences of their bolder friends and delight in accounts of actions which they could not possibly commit themselves. Thus in 1770 Fanny was imparting to her diary certain confidences that Maria had made her of such a nature that when she read the book later she judged it best to tear out twelve pages and burn them. Happily, a packet of letters survives which,[f] though rather meagrely doled out by an editor in the eighties, who thought them too full of dashes to be worthy of the dignity of print, allow us to guess pretty clearly what kind of secret Maria confided and Fanny recorded, and Fanny, grown mature, then tore up.

For example, there was an Assembly at Lynn some time in 1770 to which Maria did not want to go. Bet[g] Dickens, however, overcame her scruples, and she went. However, she was determined not to dance. However, she did dance. Martin was there. She broke her earring. She danced a minuet à quatre. She got into the chariot to come home. She came home. 'Was I alone? – guess – well, all is vanity and vexations of spirit.'[7] It needs little ingenuity to interpret these nods and winks and innuendoes. Maria danced with Martin. She came home with Martin. She sat alone with Martin, and she had been strictly forbidden by her mother to meet Martin. That is obvious. But what is not, after all these years, quite so clear is for what reason Mrs Allen disapproved. On the face of it Martin Rishton was a very good match for Maria Allen. He was well born, he had been educated at Oxford, he was the heir of his uncle Sir Richard Bettenson, and Sir Richard Bettenson had five thousand a year and no children.[h] Nevertheless, Maria's mother warmly opposed the match. She said rather vaguely that Martin 'had been extravagant at Oxford, and that she had heard some story that he had done something unworthy of a gentleman.'[8] But her ostensible objections were based perhaps upon[i] others which were less easy to state. There was her daughter's character for example. Maria was 'a droll girl with a very great love of sport and mirth'.[9] Her temper was lively and warm. She was extremely outspoken. 'If possible,' Fanny said, 'she is too sincere. She pays too little regard to the world; and indulges herself with too much freedom of raillery and pride of disdain towards those whose vices and follies offend her.'[10] When Mrs Allen looked from Maria to Martin she saw, there can be no doubt, something that made her uneasy. But what? Perhaps it was nothing more than that Martin was particular about appearances and Maria rather[j] slack; that Martin was conventional by nature and Maria the very opposite; that Martin liked dress and decorum and that Maria was one of those heedless girls who say the first thing that comes into their heads and never reflect, if they are amused themselves, what[k] people will say if they have holes in their stockings. Whatever the reason, Mrs Allen forbade the match; and Sir Richard Bettenson, whether to meet her views or for educational purposes, sent his nephew in the beginning of 1771 to travel for two years abroad. Maria remained at Lynn.

Five months, however, had not passed before Martin burst in unexpectedly at a dinner-party of relations in Welbeck-street. He looked very well, but when he was asked why he had come back in such a hurry, 'he smiled, but said nothing to the question.'[11] Maria, although still at Lynn, at once got wind of his arrival. Soon[l] she saw him at a dance, but she did not dance with him and the ban was evidently enforced, for her letters become plaintive and agitated and hint at secrets that she cannot reveal, even to her dear toads the Burneys. It was now her turn to be sent abroad, partly to be out of Martin's way, partly to finish her education. She was dispatched to Geneva. But the Burneys soon received a packet from her. In the first place, she had some little commissions that she must ask them to discharge. Would they send her a pianoforte, some music, Fordyce's sermons,[12] a tea cadet, an ebony inkstand with silver-plated tops, and a very pretty naked wax doll with blue eyes to be had in Fleet-street for half-a-crown – all of which, if well wrapped up, could travel safely in the case of the pianoforte. She had no money to pay with at the moment, for[m] she had been persuaded and indeed was sure that it was true economy if one passed through Paris to spend all one's money on clothes. But she could always sell her diamonds or she would give them 'a bill on somebody in London.'[13] These trifling matters dispatched, she turned to something of far greater importance. Indeed, what she had to say was so important that it must be burnt at once. Indeed, it was only her great distress and being alone in a foreign land that led her to tell them at all. But the truth was – so far as can now be ascertained among the fragments and the dashes – the truth was that she had gone much farther with Martin than anybody knew. She had in fact confessed her love to him. And he had proposed something which had made her very angry. She had refused to do it. She had written him a very angry letter. She had had indeed to write it three times over before she got it right. When he read it he was furious. 'Did my character,' he wrote, 'ever give you reason to imagine I should expose you because you loved me? 'Tis thoroughly unnatural – I defy the world to bring an instance of my behaving unworthy the Character of a Gentleman.'[14] These[n] were his very words. And, Maria wrote, 'I think such the sentiments of a Man of Honour, and such I hope to find him,'[15] she concluded; for although she knew very well that Hetty Burney and Mr Crisp disliked him, he was – here she came out with it – the man 'on whom all my happiness in this Life depends and in whom I *wish* to see no faults.'[16] The Burneys hid the letters, breathed not a word to their parents, and waited in suspense. Nor did they have to wait long.

Before the spring was over Maria was back again in Poland-street and in circumstances so romantic, so exciting, and above all so secret that 'I dare not,' Fanny exclaimed, 'commit particulars to paper.' This much (and one would have thought it enough) only could be said. 'Miss Allen – for the last time I shall call her so, – came home on Monday last . . . she – was married last Saturday!'[17] It was true. Martin Rishton had gone out secretly to join her abroad.[o] They had been married at Ypres on May 16, 1772. On the 18th Maria reached England and confided the grand secret to Fanny and Susan Burney, but she told no[p] one else. They were afraid to tell her mother. They were afraid to tell Dr Burney. In their dilemma they turned to the strange man who was always their confidant – to Samuel Crisp of Chesington.[18]

Many years before this Samuel Crisp had retired from the world. He had been a man of parts, a man of fashion, and a man of great social charm. But his fine friends had wasted his substance and his clever friends had damned his play. In disgust with the insincerity of fashionable life and the fickleness of fame he had withdrawn to a decayed manor house near London, which, however, was so far from the high road and so hidden from travellers in the waste of a common that no one could find it unless specially instructed. But Mr Crisp was careful to issue no instructions. The Burneys were almost the only friends who knew the way across the fields to his door. But the Burneys could never come often enough. He depended upon the Burneys for life and society and for news of the great world which he despised and yet could not forget.[q] The Burney children stood to him in the place of his own children. Upon them he lavished all the shrewdness and knowledge and disillusionment which he had won at such cost to himself and[r] now found so useless in an old manor house on a wild common with only old Mrs Hamilton and young Kitty Cook to bear him company.

It was, then, to Chesington and to Daddy Crisp that Maria Rishton and Susan Burney made their way on June 7 with their tremendous secret burning in their breasts. At first Maria was too nervous to tell him the plain truth. She tried[s] to enlighten him with hints and hums and ha[']s. But she succeeded only in rousing his wrath against Martin, which he expressed so strongly,[t] 'almost calling him a Mahoon,'[19] that Maria began to kindle and ran off in a huff to her bedroom. Here she resolved to take the bull by the horns. She summoned Kitty Cook and sent her to Mr Crisp with a saucy message: 'Mrs. Rishton sent compts. and hoped to see him at Stanhoe this summer.'[20] Upon receiving the message Mr Crisp came in haste to the girls' bedroom. An extraordinary scene then took place. Maria knelt on the floor and hid her face in the bedclothes. Mr Crisp commanded her to tell the truth – was she indeed Mrs Rishton? Maria could not speak. Kitty Cook 'claw'd hold of her left hand and shew'd him the ring.'[21] Then Susan[u] produced two letters from Martin which proved the fact beyond doubt. They had been married legally. They were man and wife. If that were so, there was only one thing to be done, Mr Crisp declared – Mrs Burney must be informed and the marriage must be made public at once. He behaved with all the sense and decision of a man of the world. He wrote to Maria's mother – he explained the whole situation. On getting the letter Mrs[v] Burney was extremely angry. She received the couple – she could do nothing else – but she never liked Martin and she never altogether forgave her daughter. However, the deed was done, and now the young couple had nothing to do but to settle down to enjoy the delights which they had snatched so impetuously.

All now depended, for those who loved Maria – and Fanny Burney loved her very dearly – upon the character of Martin Rishton. Was he, as Mr Crisp almost said, a Mahoon? Or was he, as his sister openly declared,[w] a Bashaw?[22] Would he make her happy or would he not? The discerning and affectionate eyes of Fanny were now turned observingly upon Martin to find out. And yet it was very difficult to find out anything for certain. He was a strange mixture. He[x] was high-spirited; he was 'prodigiously agreeable.'[23] But he was somehow, with his talk[y] of vulgarity and distinction, rather exacting – he liked his wife to do him credit. For example, the Rishtons went on to take the waters at Bath, and there were the usual gaieties in[z] progress. Fischer[24] was giving a concert, and the eldest Miss Linley[25] was singing, perhaps for the last time. All Bath would be there. But poor Maria sat alone in the lodgings writing to Fanny, and the reason she gave was a strange one. Martin, 'who is rather more exact about dress than I am, can't think of my appearing' unless she bought a 'suit of mignionet linen fringed for second mourning' to go in. She refused; the dress was too expensive; 'and as he was unwilling I should appear else, I gave up the dear Fischer – see what a cruel thing to have a sposo who is rather a p-p-y in those sort of things.'[26] So there she sat alone; and she hated Bath; and she found servants such a nuisance – she had had to dismiss the butler already. At the same time, she was head over heels in love with her Rishy, and one would like to suppose that the tiff about the dress was made up by the present of Romeo, the remarkably fine brown Pomeranian dog, which Martin bought for a large sum at this time and gave her. Martin himself had a passion for dogs.

It was no doubt in order to gratify his love of sport and Maria's dislike of towns that they moved on later[aa] that spring to Teignmouth, or as Maria calls it, to 'Tingmouth,' in Devon. The move was entirely to her liking. Her letters gushed and burbled, had fewer stops and more dashes than ever, as she endeavoured to describe the delights of Tingmouth to Fanny in London. Their cottage was 'one of the neatest Thatch'd cottages you ever saw.'[27] It belonged to a sea captain. It was full of china glass flowers that he had brought home from his voyages. It was hung with prints from the Prayer-book and the Bible. There were also two pictures, one said to be by Raphael, the other by Correggio. The Miss Minifies[28] might have described it as a retreat for a heroine. It looked on to a green. The fisher people were simple and happy. Their cottages were clean and their children were healthy. The sea was full of whiting, salmon and young mackerel. Martin had bought a brace of beautiful spaniels. It was a great diversion to make them go into the water. 'Indeed, we intend getting a very large Newfoundland dog before we leave this place.'[29] And they intended to go for expeditions[bb] and take their dinner with them. And Fanny must come. Nothing could serve them but that Fanny should come and stay. It was monstrous for her to say that she must stop at home and copy her father's manuscripts. She must come at once; and[cc] if she came she need not spend a penny, for Maria wore nothing but a common linen gown and had not had her hair dressed once since she came here.[dd] In short, Fanny must come.

Thus solicited, Fanny arrived some time in July, 1773, and for almost two months lodged in the boxroom – the other rooms were so littered with dogs and poultry that they had to put her in the boxroom – and observed the humours of Tingmouth society and the moods of the lovers. There could be no doubt that[ee] they were still very much in love, but the truth was that Tingmouth was very gay. A great many families made it their summer resort; there were the Phippses and the Hurrels and the Westerns and the Colbournes; there was Mr Crispen – perhaps the most distinguished man in Tingmouth – Mr Green who lodged with Mr Crispen and Miss Bowdler.[ff] Naturally, in so small a place, everybody knew everybody. The Phippses, the Hurrels, the Rishtons, the Colbournes, Mr Crispen, Mr Green and Miss Bowdler must meet incessantly. They must make up parties to go to the wrestling matches, and attend the races in their whiskeys,[30] and see the country people run after a pig whose tail had been cut off. Much coming and going was[gg] inevitable; but, as Fanny soon observed, it was not altogether to Martin's liking. 'They will soon make this as errant a public place as Bristol Hotwells or any other place,'[31] he grumbled. He had nothing whatever to say against the Phippses or the Westerns; he had the greatest respect for the Hurrels, which was odd, considering how very fat and greedy Mr Hurrel was; Mr[hh] Crispen, of course, who lived at Bath and spoke Italian perfectly, one must respect; but the fact was, Martin confided to Fanny, that he 'almost detested'[32] Miss Bowdler. Miss Bowdler came of a respectable family. Her brother was destined to edit Shakespeare.[33] Her family were old friends of the Allens. One could not forbid her the[ii] house; in fact she was always in and out of it; and yet, said Martin, 'he could not endure even the sight of her.' 'A woman,' said Martin, 'who despises the customs and manners of the country she lives in, must, consequently, conduct herself with impropriety.'[34] And, indeed, she did. For though she was only twenty-six she had come to Tingmouth alone; and then she made no secret of the fact, indeed she avowed it quite openly 'in the fair face of day,'[35] that she visited Mr Crispen in his lodgings, and not merely paid a call but stayed to supper. Nobody had 'the most distant shadow of doubt of Miss Bowdler's being equally innocent with those who have more worldly prudence,'[36] but at the same time nobody could doubt that Miss Bowdler found the society of gentlemen more entertaining than that of ladies – or could deny that though Mr Crispen was old, Mr Green who lodged with him was young. Then, of course, she[jj] came on to the Rishtons and encouraged Maria in her least desirable attribute – her levity, her love of chaff, her carelessness of dress and deportment. It was deplorable.

Fanny Burney liked Martin very much and listened to his complaints with sympathy; but for all her charm and distinction, indeed because of them, she was destined unfortunately to make matters worse. Among her gifts she had the art of being extremely attractive to elderly gentlemen. Soon Mr Crispen was paying her outrageous attentions. 'Little Burney'[37] he said was irresistible; the name of Burney would be found – with many others, Miss Bowdler interjected – cut upon his heart. Mr Crispen must implore one kiss. It was said of course in jest, but Miss Bowdler took it of course in[kk] earnest. Had she not nursed Mr Crispen through a dangerous illness? Had she not sacrificed her maidenly reputation by visiting him in his cottage? And then Martin, who had been perhaps already annoyed by Mr Crispen's social predominance, found it galling in the extreme to have that gentleman always in the house, always paying outrageous compliments to his guest. Anything that 'led towards flirtation'[38] he disliked; and soon Mr Crispen had become, Fanny observed, almost as odious[39] as Miss Bowdler. He threw himself into the study of Italian[ll] grammar; he read aloud to Maria and Fanny from the Faery Queen, 'omitting whatever, to the poet's great disgrace, has crept in that is improper for a woman's ear.'[40] But what with Miss Bowdler, Mr Crispen, the Tingmothians and the influence of undesirable acquaintances upon his wife, there can be no doubt that Martin was very uncomfortable at Tingmouth, and when the time came, on September 17, to say good-bye he appeared 'in monstrous spirits.'[41] Perhaps everybody was glad that the summer was at an end. They were glad to say good-bye and glad to be able to say it in civil terms. Mr Crispen left for Bath; and Miss Bowdler – there is no rashness in the assumption – left, for Bath also.

The Rishtons proceeded in their whiskey with all their dogs left to[mm] visit the Westerns, one of the few families with whom Martin cared to associate. But the journey was unfortunate. They began by taking the wrong turning, then they ran over Tingmouth, the Newfoundland dog, who was running under the body of the whiskey. Then at Oxford Maria longed to see the colleges, but feeling sure that Martin's pride would be hurt at showing himself in a whiskey with a wife where in the old days he had 'shone forth a gay bachelor with a phaeton and four bays,'[42] she refused his offer to take her, and had her hair dressed, very badly, instead. Off they went again, and again they ran over two more dogs. Worst of all, when they arrived at the Westerns' they[nn] found the whole house shut up and the Westerns gone to Buckinghamshire. Altogether it was an unfortunate expedition. And it is impossible, as one reads Maria's breathless volubility to Fanny, to resist the conviction that the journey with its accidents and mistakes, with its troop of dogs, and Martin's pride, and Maria's fears and her recourse to the hairdresser and the hairdresser's ill success, and Martin's memories of gay bachelor days and phaetons and bay horses and his respect for the Westerns and his love of servants was typical of the obscure years of married life that were now to succeed each other at Stanhoe, in Norfolk.

At Stanhoe they lived the lives[oo] of country gentry. They repaired the ancient house, though they had but the lease of it. They planted and cleaned and cut new walks in the garden. They bought a cow and started a dairy for Maria. Dog was added to dog – rare dogs, wonderful dogs, spaniels, lurchers, Portugal[pp] pointers from the banks of the Dowrow. To keep up the establishment as establishments should be kept up, nine servants, in Martin's opinion, were none too many. And so, though she had no children, Maria found that all her time was occupied with her household and the care of her establishment. But how far better, she wrote, to be active like this instead of leading 'the loitering life' she had led at Tingmouth! Surely, Maria continued, scribbling her heart out ungrammatically to Fanny Burney, 'there are pleasures for every station and employment,' and one cannot be bored if 'as I hope I am acting properly';[43] so that in sober truth she did not envy Fanny Lord Stanhope's *fête champêtre*, since she had her chickens and her dairy, and Tingmouth, who had had the distemper, must[qq] be led out on a string. Why, then, regret Miss Bowdler and Mr Crispen and the sport and gaiety of the old days at Tingmouth? Nevertheless, the old days kept[rr] coming back to her mind. At Tingmouth, she reflected, they had only kept a man and a maid. Here they had nine servants, and the more there are the more 'cabally and insolent'[44] they become. And then relations come over from Lynn and pried into her kitchen and made her more 'bashful,'[45] as Martin would say, than ever. And then if she sat down to her tambour for half an hour Martin, 'who is I believe the Most Active Creature alive,'[46] would burst in and say, 'Come Maria, you must go with me and see how charmingly Damon hunts' – or he would say 'I know of a pheasant's nest about two miles off, you shall go and see it.'[47]

Then away we trail broiling over Cornfields – and when we come to the pit some Unlucky boy has Stole the Eggs . . . then I spend Whole Mornings seeing him Shoot Rooks – grub up trees – and at night for we never come in now till Nine o'clock – when tea is over and I have settled my accounts or done some company business – bed-time Comes.[48]

Bedtime had come; and the day had been somehow disappointing.[ss]
How could she mend matters? How could she save money so that Martin could buy the phaeton upon which his heart had been set ever since they were married? She might save on dress, for she did not mind what she wore; but alas! Martin was very particular still; he did not like her to dress in linen. So she must manage better in the house, and she was not formed to manage servants. Thus she[tt] began to dwell upon those happy days before she had gone to Tingmouth, before she had married, before she had nine servants and a phaeton and ever so many dogs. She began to brood over that still more distant time when she had first known the Burneys and they had sat 'browsing over my little [fire] and eating good things out of the closet by the fire side.'[49] Her thoughts turned to all those friends whom she had lost, to that 'lovd society which I remember with the greatest pleasure';[50] and she could never forget in particular the paternal kindness of Dr Burney. Oh, she sighed as she sat alone in Norfolk among the pheasants and the fields, how she wished that 'none of my family had ever quitted his sheltering roof till placed under the protection of a worthy husband.'[51] For her own marriage – but enough; they had been very much in love; they had been very happy; she must go and do her hair; she must try to please her Rishy. And so the obscure history of the Rishtons fades away, save what is preserved by the sprightly pen of Maria's half-sister[uu] in the pages of *Evelina*. And yet – the reflection will occur – if Fanny had seen more of Maria, and more of Mr Crispen and even more of Miss Bowdler and the Tingmouth set, her later books, had they been less refined, might have been as amusing as her first.

a – *NYHT*: 'step sister'.
b – *NYHT*: 'step sisters. And step sisters'.
c – *NYHT*: 'the families'.
d – *NYHT*: 'she had heard'.
e – *NYHT*: 'was at a'.
f – *NYHT*: 'Happily a packet of letters survive, which'.
g – *NYHT*: 'But'.
h – *NYHT*: 'and was childless.'
i – *NYHT*: 'based upon'.
j – *NYHT*: 'Maria was rather'.

k – *NYHT*: 'reflect, in the height of their spirits, what'.

l – *NYHT*: 'Lynn, soon got wind of his arrival. She confided her ecstasies, with a great many dashes, to Fanny. "Rishton – my – yes – the very identical – Martin – Lucious – etc. – Rishton is come over – and now in England." Soon'. The quotation is from *Early Diary*, vol. i, p. 124, slightly adapted by VW. Lucius appears to have been one of Rishton's forenames: see *ibid.*, p. 103, n.

m – *NYHT*: 'with this time, for'.

n – *NYHT*: 'Those'.

o – *NYHT*: 'her.'

p – *NYHT*: 'but to no one'.

q – *NYHT*: 'upon them for . . . could never forget.'

r – *NYHT*: 'cost and'.

s – *NYHT*: 'She blushed, she stammered, she tried'.

t – *NYHT*: 'so vividly,'.

u – *NYHT*: 'There was then an explosion. Mr Crisp used expressions (it is Mrs Ellis in the eighties who speaks) "which, among cultivated gentlemen like himself were rather obsolete even in 1772, but were not *Oaths* and have to be omitted. He bade Susan explain the meaning of it all. 'You know all this affair – it is so?' – I had my cue before – 'Yes, sir – indeed,' 'She is really married,' said he, arching his eyebrows with such a stare of astonishment. 'She is, upon my honour.'" Here Maria, who was still hiding her face in the bed, tried to deny it. "No – No – No – Indeed – Nothing at all – it's all the lies of that impudent little toad," she cried. But then Susan'. The quotation is from *Early Diary*, vol. i, pp. 174–5, slightly adapted by VW.

v – *NYHT*: 'mother; he explained the whole situation. Mrs.'

w – *NYHT*: 'sister said openly,'.

x – *NYHT*: 'out. Against her step-mother's will she went with the Rishtons to Covent Garden Theatre to hear Miss Barsanti in Colman's play "An Occasional Prelude." They were to pick up Martin's rich uncle and aunt, the Bettensons, and go with them. But when they arrived in Queen Square, Mrs Bettenson was not ready. Martin refused to get out of the coach and sat there fuming. "How truly vulgar to make people wait!" he exclaimed, and it may have been while they waited that he regaled Fanny with a sketch of his aunt's character – how eccentric she was, how stingy, how, if there was any chance of a dinner party, she always excused her half-filled dishes by explaining that her cook had left that very day. Then, at the play, Fanny observed, the footmen wore the very same undress livery as Martin's own servants. At this, Maria looked at her husband and laughed. Fanny herself did not venture, for she observed "After all, his foible is certainly dress, and love of being *distinguished* from the *vulgar crew*." She noticed, too, that although Martin was only the presumptive, not the declared heir of his rich uncle, he treated both uncle and aunt independently. "Far from flattering, he even *trims* them for their foibles; and whenever they seem to exact any deference he treats them most cavalierly. . . . If he humbled himself to them he is convinced they would trample on him," and so, when they went back with the Bettensons to supper, and Mrs Bettenson excused her meagre fare by the fact that her cook had left her yesterday, Martin showed her no mercy but ate as if he had fasted for three days, though, in fact, he generally ate no supper. He'. The quotations are from *Early Diary*, vol. i, 1771, pp. 182, 184, 185.

y – NYHT: 'bulk'.

z – NYHT: 'Bath; and there the usual gayeties were in'.

aa – NYHT: 'moved later'.

bb – NYHT: 'go on expeditions'.

cc – NYHT: 'manuscripts. If she came, then Martin would not mind leaving Maria and could "go out oftener a-fishing and shooting." She must come at once; and she must bring two cricket bats of the best make, to cost four shillings or four shillings and sixpence; also, Martin said, would she "spring a tick" for him at the booksellers and order Hawksworth's Journal and an Italian grammar; and'. The quotations are from *Early Diary*, vol. i, 23 May and 6 June 1773, pp. 213, 215. John Hawkesworth (1720–73), *An Account of the Voyages Undertaken by the Order of His Present Majesty for making discoveries in the southern hemisphere . . . drawn up from the journals which were kept by the several commanders* (3 vols, T. Strahan & T. Cadell, 1773).

dd – NYHT: 'there.'

ee – NYHT: 'doubt that they suited each other very well; that'.

ff – NYHT: 'Tingmouth – and Mr Green who lodged with Mr Crispen, and Miss Bowdler. They were also families of less importance, indigenous, rather vulgar and inclined to divert themselves "in a very unmannerly *easy* and careless style."' The quotation is from *Early Diary*, vol. i, [July 1773], p. 227.

gg – NYHT: 'matches; they must attend the races in their whiskeys; they must see the country people run after a pig whose tail had been cut off. Society was'.

hh – NYHT: 'the Hurrels (which was odd, considering how very fat and greedy Mr Hurrel was, and how lustily, though he was a clergyman, he swore that dreadful day when they were almost drowned off Brixham, adding immediately, it is true, "God forgive me!"); Mr'. The quotation is from *Early Diary*, vol. i, [July 1773], p. 226.

ii – NYHT: 'a most respectable family. Her brother was destined, with what suc[c]ess the world was soon to know, to edit Shakespeare. Her family were old friends of the Allens. One could not forbid her in the'.

jj – NYHT: 'course, she mixed herself up with the vulgar party in the town, the Tingmothians as they were called, who danced about and diverted themselves so carelessly; and then she'.

kk – NYHT: 'took it in'.

ll – NYHT: 'his guest. Soon Mr. Crispen had become, Fanny observed, "almost as odious" as Miss Bowdler. To escape a home made intolerable by the chaff of Miss Bowdler and the compliments of Mr Crispen he took violently to sport. One day he beat Romeo so hard that he broke his leg. Next moment he was horror struck, and bore Mr Crispen's doubtless pointed advice as to the desirability of controlling one's passions with admirable good temper. He threw himself into the Italian'.

mm – NYHT: 'Rishtons went on, in their whiskeys, with their dogs, to'.

nn – NYHT: 'again and again, then ran over two more dogs. But when at last they arrived at the Westerns they'.

oo – NYHT: 'life'.

pp – NYHT: 'lurchers and Portugal'.

qq – NYHT: 'dairy and Tingmouth, the Newfoundland dog, had had the distemper and must'.

rr – NYHT: 'Nevertheless, Tingmouth kept'.

ss – NYHT: 'and they had been, somehow, disappointing.'

tt – NYHT: 'married? She did not mind what she wore; but, also, Martin was very particular still; he did not like her to dress in linen. So she must manage better in the house, and yet she was not formed to manage servants. And so she'.

uu – NYHT: 'step-sister'.

1 – An unsigned leading article in the *TLS*, 28 August 1930, and signed, with variations and entitled '"Evelina's" Step Sister', in the *NYHT*, 14 and 21 September, (*Kp4* C324). On 1 May 1930 VW wrote: 'we are going touring Devon & Cornwall on Sunday which means a week off; & then I shall perhaps make my critical brain do a months work, for exercise. What could it be set to? Or a story? – no, not another story now. Perhaps Miss Burney's half sister's story' (*III VW Diary*). She told Ethel Smyth on 6 July: 'Now I must do a little very dreary work – boiling 2 articles in to one and spreading one in to 3: that makes my years income; but I can assure you it is hardly earned. I have to wrench my head to the left when it's looking to the right' (*IV VW Letters*, no. 2201). Then on 21 July: 'Well, it is very wet, & I am rather discomposed, with making 2 articles into one & so on' (*III VW Diary*). These suggest that the *NYHT* version predates the *TLS*. On 2 August VW wrote to Ethel Smyth again about 'Dr Burney's Evening Party' in *L&L*: 'One thing I did thanks to you – I re-read my Burney article, which is a thing I never do (I have never read any of my books a second time, except when they were re-printed, I shudder past them on the shelf as if they might bite me) anyhow, I read this article again, thanks to you, and rather liked it. The truth is though, these articles, all architecture, a kind of cabinet work, fitting parts together, making one paragraph balance another; are such hard labour in the doing that one cant read them without remembering the drudgery. One starts full tilt; one sees a scene in a flash; but the working out is almost (with

me) unbelievably laborious. However, when I read it, I got more pleasure and less sense of backbreaking effort than usual – thanks to you again. Some of it needs emphasising though – some of it is too condensed. And I have just written another' (*IV VW Letters*, no. 2215). On 9 March 1931, Marguerite Scialtiel of the agents Curtis Brown, in Paris, sent VW 1500 francs, presumably payment for this article (*NYHT* version) which had appeared in *Le Figaro* on 16–18 February in a translation, entitled 'La Demi-Soeur de Fanny Burney', by Jeanne Fournier-Pargoire (*Kp4* D58). Scialtiel stated that *Le Figaro* was 'clamouring for more' (LWP Ad. 18). See also 'Dr Burney's Evening Party' above and in *CR2*. Reading notes (Berg, RN 1.13) (*VWRN* XIII). The same issue of the *TLS* contained: a letter from W. C. Northcott, the Mayor of Hampstead, about the Keats House. Reprinted (text from *TLS*): *G&R, CE*.

2 – Lot 386 on 15 April 1930 at Sotheby's, according to *Book Auction Records* (Henry Stevens Son & Stiles, 1930), vol. xxvii, p. 429: '*Evelina*, 3 vols., a few minor stains in each vol., small worm-holes in the fore-margins of the last four ll. of vol. 3, orig. bds., paper back-strips, entirely uncut (7 1/2 in. by 4 1/2 in.), 1778'. The sale was reported in the *TLS*, 24 April 1930, p. 356.

3 – Fanny Burney, *Evelina*, ed. Sir Frank D. Mackinnon (Clarendon Press, 1930), was advertised in the *N&A*, 6 December 1930, at 21s.: 'This edition is illustrated from 18th century sources, and is uniform in format and appearance with R. W. Chapman's five-volume Jane Austen'.

4 – Strictly speaking, Maria Allen and Fanny Burney were step-sisters.

5 – David Garrick (1717–79), actor, theatre manager and dramatist; Hester Lynch Thrale, *née* Salusbury, later Piozzi (1741–1821).

6 – *The Early Diary of Frances Burney 1768–1778, with a Selection from her Correspondence* . . . , ed. Annie Raine Ellis (2 vols, George Bell and Sons, 1889), vol. i, p. 100, which has: 'Maria most justly describes herself as not being "near so squeamish as you are"'.

7 – *Ibid.*, letter from Maria to Fanny, undated, c. 1770 or 1771, p. 102, which has: '. . . home – was I alone – guess – well all is vanity and vexation of spirit – did I pass a happy eve – guess . . .'

8 – *Ibid.*, p. 109.

9 – *Ibid.*, July 1771, p. 121, which has: 'That droll girl has so very great a love of sport and mirth, that there is nothing she will not do to contribute to it.'

10 – *Ibid.*, August 1771, p. 128, which has: 'But, if it is possible, she is too sincere; she pays too little regard to the world; and indulges . . .'

11 – According to Maria, *ibid.*, 1771, p. 125.

12 – James Fordyce (1720–96), *Sermons to Young Women* (1765, and often reprinted).

13 – According to Maria, *Early Diary*, vol. i, 21 November 1771, p. 136.

14 – Quoted by Maria, *ibid.*, 1772, p. 158, which has: 'room' instead of 'reason'.

15 – *Ibid.*, letter from Maria to Fanny, undated, 1772, which has: 'I think those the sentiments . . .'

16 – *Ibid.*

17 – *Ibid.*, letter from Maria to Fanny, 21 May 1772, p. 174.

18 – Samuel Crisp (1707–83), playwright.

19 – Maria in a joint letter to Fanny, undated, June 1772, *Early Diary*, vol. i, p. 174, which has: 'he almost made me mad – if he had been a Mahoon [i.e. a Turk] he could not have merited what Crisp said.'

20 – *Ibid.*

21 – *Ibid.*, Susan Burney in a joint letter to Fanny.

22 – According to Mrs Edgell, *ibid.*, p. 177. 'Bashaw' was an earlier form of 'Pasha', a haughty, imperious man.

23 – *Ibid.*, vol. i, January 1773, p. 184.

24 – Johann Christian Fischer (1733–1800), oboist and composer. Dr Burney wrote that 'Fischer was the most pleasing and perfect performer on the haut-bois, and the most ingenious composer for that instrument that has ever delighted our country during full sixty years' (quoted *ODNB*).

25 – Elizabeth Ann Linley (1754–92). Fanny commented that her voice was 'soft, sweet, clear, and affecting. She sings with good expression, and has great fancy and even taste in her cadences, though perhaps a finished singer would give less way to the former, and prefer few and select notes. She has an exceeding good shake, and the best and most critical judges all pronounce her to be infinitely superior to *all* other English singers' (*Early Diary*, vol. i, April 1773, p. 202).

26 – *Ibid.*, letter from Maria to Fanny, 22 February 1773, p. 193. Presumably 'p-p-y' stands for 'popinjay'.

27 – *Ibid.*, letter from Maria to Fanny, 25 April 1773, p. 204, which has: 'the very neatest *Thatchd* Cottages'.

28 – See *ibid.*, p. 204, fn. 2: 'The Misses Minifie, of Fairwater, Somersetshire, were novel writers of that day. One of them married General Gunning, brother of the beauties, Lady Coventry and the Duchess of Hamilton.' Raphael (Sanzio) (1483–1520); Antonio da Corregio (1489–1534).

29 – *Ibid.*, p. 204.

30 – See *ibid.*, p. 264, fn. 2: 'In 1824, Sir Walter Scott describes the whiskey of Mrs. Margaret Dods, of the Cleikum Inn, St Ronan's, as being "a vehicle, which, had it appeared in Piccadilly, would have furnished . . . laughter for a week. . . . It was a two-wheeled vehicle, sturdily and safely low upon its little old-fashioned wheels."'

31 – *Ibid.*, July 1773, p. 222.

32 – *Ibid.*, p. 221, which has: 'As to Mr. Rishton he almost *detests* her, but his wife is really attached to her, which is an unfortunate circumstance.'

33 – Frances Bowdler; Thomas Bowdler, MD (1754–1825).

34 – *Early Diary*, vol. i, July 1773, p. 221, which has: 'Mr. Rishton . . . cannot endure even the sight of her, a woman, he says, who despises . . .'
35 – *Ibid.*
36 – *Ibid.*
37 – *Ibid.*, 'Tingmouth Journal', pp. 230, 231, 232, *et passim*.
38 – *Ibid.*, August 1773, p. 242, which has: 'Mr. Rishton has an uncommon aversion to every thing that leads towards flirtation . . .'
39 – See *ibid.*, pp. 242–3: 'Mr. Crispen . . . is become almost odious. I fancy that his friendship for Miss Bowdler has much contributed to make Mr. Rishton dislike him.'
40 – *Ibid.*, p. 243. Edmund Spenser (1552?–99), *The Faerie Queen* (1590–6).
41 – *Ibid.*, 16 September 1773, p. 252.
42 – *Ibid.*, letter to Fanny from Maria, 2 October 1773, p. 265, which has: 'how coud we bear to be seen in Oxford, where we [sic] had once shone forth the gay, the extravagant Martin Rishton – whose only carriage was a phaeton . . .'
43 – *Ibid.*, 1773?, p. 266.
44 – *Ibid.*, which has: 'I am not formd to manage a set of caballing insolent servants.'
45 – *Ibid.*, which has: '. . . still so awkward and bashfull, (a favourite expression of Martin,) . . .'
46 – *Ibid.*, which has: 'Rishton, Who I believe is the Most Active Creature Alive . . .'
47 – *Ibid.*, which has: 'Come Maria you must go with me and see how charmingly Damon . . . hunts . . . I know of a pheasants Nest about two miles of you Shall go and see it'.
48 – *Ibid.*
49 – *Ibid.*, p. 268.
50 – *Ibid.*, which has: '. . . that I remember . . .'
51 – *Ibid.*, 1786, p. 268, fn. 1.

Wm. Hazlitt, the Man

Had one met Hazlitt no doubt one would have liked him on his own principle that 'We can scarcely hate anyone we know.'[2] But Hazlitt has been dead now a hundred years and it is perhaps a question how far we can know him well enough to overcome those feelings of dislike which his writings still so sharply arouse. For Hazlitt – it is one of his prime merits – was not one of those noncommittal writers who shuffle off in a mist and die of their own insignificance.

His essays are emphatically himself. He has no reticence and he has no shame. He tells us exactly what he thinks, and he tells us – the confidence is less seductive – exactly what he feels.

As of all men he had the most intense consciousness of his own existence, since never a day passed without inflicting on him some pang of hate or jealousy, some thrill of anger or pleasure, we cannot read him for long without coming in contact with a very singular character – ill-conditioned yet high-minded; mean yet noble; intensely egotistical yet inspired by the most genuine passion for the rights and liberties of mankind. Soon, so thin is the veil of the essay, his very person comes before us. We see him 'brow-hanging, shoe-contemplative, strange.'[3] He comes shuffling into the room, looking nobody straight in the face, shaking hands as with the fin of a fish.[4] 'His manners are 99 in 100 singularly repulsive,'[5] Coleridge said. Yet now and again his face lit up with intellectual beauty and his manner lost its asperity and became sympathetic and even tender.

Soon, too, as we read on we become familiar with the whole gamut of his grievances. He lived, one gathers, mostly at inns. No woman's form graced his board. He had quarrelled with all his old friends, save perhaps with Lamb.[6] Yet his only fault had been that he had stuck to his principles and 'not become a government tool.'[7] He was the object of malignant persecution – Blackwood's reviewers called him 'pimply Hazlitt,'[8] though it was a lie. These lies, however, got into print and then he was afraid to visit his friends because the footman had read the newspaper and the housemaid was tittering at him behind his back. He had – no one could deny it – one of the finest minds and he wrote indisputably the best prose of his times. But what did that avail with women? Fine ladies have no respect for scholars nor chambermaids either – so the growl and plaint of his own grievances keeps breaking through, and yet there is something so independent, subtle, fine and enthusiastic about him that dislike crumbles and turns to something much warmer and more complex. Hazlitt was right: 'It is the mask only that we dread and hate; the man may have something human about him! The notions, in short, which we entertain of people at a distance or from partial representation, or from guess-work, are simple, uncompounded ideas, which answer to nothing in reality; those which we derive from experience are mixed modes, the only true and, in general, the most favourable ones.'[9]

Certainly our ideas about Hazlitt are neither simple nor uncompounded. From the first he was a two-minded man – one of those
divided natures who are inclined almost equally to two quite opposite
careers.

His original impulse was not to essay writing but to painting
and philosophy. There was something in the remote and quiet art
of the painter that offered a refuge to his tormented spirit. He
noted enviously how happy the old age of painters was – 'their
minds keep alive to the last;'[10] he turned longingly to the calling
that takes one out of doors, among trees and woods, that deals
with bright pigments and has solid brush and canvas for its tools
and not immaterial ink and paper. Yet at the same time he was
bitten by an abstract curiosity that would not let him rest in the
contemplation of concrete beauty. When he was a boy of fourteen
he heard his father, the good Unitarian minister, dispute with an
old lady of the congregation as they were coming out of meeting
as to the limits of religious toleration, and 'it was this circumstance,' he said, 'that decided the fate of my future life.' It set him
off 'forming in my head ... the following system of political rights
and general jurisprudence.' He became aware that he must be
'satisfied for the reason of things.'[11]

The two ideals were ever after to clash. To be a thinker and to
express in the plainest and most accurate of terms 'the reason for
things,' and to be a painter gloating over blues and crimsons,
breathing fresh air and living sensually in the emotions – these were
two different, perhaps incompatible ideals, yet like all Hazlitt's
emotions both were tough and each strove for mastery. He yielded
now to one, now to the other. He spent months in Paris copying
pictures at the Louvre. He came home and toiled laboriously at the
portrait of an old woman in a bonnet day after day, seeking con-
scientiously to discover the secret of Rembrandt's[12] genius; but he
lacked some quality – perhaps it was invention – and in the end cut
the canvas to ribbons in a rage or turned it against the wall in
despair. At the same time he was writing that 'Essay Upon the
Principles of Human Actions'[13] which he preferred to all his other
works. For there he wrote plainly and truthfully, without glitter or
garishness, without any wish to please or to make money, but solely
to gratify the urgency of his own desire for truth. Naturally 'the
book dropped still-born from the press.'[14] At the same time his
political hopes, his belief that the age of freedom had come and

that the tyranny of kingship was over had proved vain. His friends went over to the government and he was left alone to uphold the doctrines of liberty, fraternity and revolution.

Thus he was a man of divided tastes and of thwarted ambition; a man whose happiness, even in early life, lay behind. His mind had set young and bore forever the stamp of first impressions. In his happiest moods he looked not forward but backward – to the garden where he played as a child, to the blue hills of Shropshire[15] and to all those landscapes which he had seen when hope was still his, and peace brooded upon him and he looked up from his painting or his book and saw the fields and woods as if they were the outward expression of his own inner quietude. It is to the books that he read then that he returns – to Rousseau and to Burke and to the Letters of Junius.[16] The impression that they made upon his youthful imagination was never effaced and scarcely overlaid, for after youth was over he ceased to read for pleasure, as in maturity he seldom read a book through; and writing was done generally at the last moment, against the grain.

But write he must. Very soon life became a matter of compromise – the pure and intense pleasures of youth had to undergo adulteration. He who was always so susceptible to the softer graces of the other sex, and at the same time so uncomfortably aware of his own lack of attraction, met Miss Sarah Stoddart[17] and was charmed, not by her face, which was plain, nor by her dress, which was garish, but by her ability and independence. She pleased him when he met her at the Lambs by the common sense with which she found the kettle and boiled it when Mary absent-mindedly delayed. But of domestic talents she had none.

They married. Children were born and children died, and it became necessary to give up country life and unprofitable brooding over abstract questions in order to earn a living. Instead of spending eight years in writing eight pages he must become a journalist and deliver up articles of the right length at the right moment. His ability and his success in his new calling were great. Soon the mantelpiece of the old house in York Street where Milton had lived was scribbled over with ideas for essays.[18] As the habit proves, the house was not a tidy house, nor did geniality and comfort excuse the lack of method. The Hazlitts were to be found eating breakfast at two in the afternoon without a fire in the grate or curtains in the window.

A stalwart walker, a clever and clear-sighted woman, Mrs Hazlitt had no delusions about her husband. He was unfaithful to her, and she knew it. But also 'He said I had always despised him and his abilities,'[19] she noted in her diary, and at length the prosaic marriage came lamely to an end. After that Hazlitt lived mainly in the parlours of the inns. There he made love to the innkeepers' daughters; there he suffered tortures of humiliation and deceit; but there, too, as he drank cup after cup of very strong tea, he wrote essay after essay, and Hazlitt's essays, of course, are among the best we have.

That they are not quite the best – that they do not haunt the mind as the essays of Montaigne, or Lamb or Bacon[20] haunt the mind is also true. He seldom reaches the perfection of those great writers or their unity. There is always something divided and discordant even in his finest work, as if two minds were in harness, who never succeed save for a few splendid moments in keeping in step together.

The two minds can be distinguished. In the first place there is the mind of the thinker. It is the thinker for the most part who is allowed the choice of the subject. He chooses some abstract idea, like envy, or egotism, or reason and imagination. He treats it with energy and independence. He explores its ramifications and scales its narrow paths as if it were a mountain road and the ascent both difficult and inspiring. Compared with this athletic progress, Lamb's seems to be the flight of a butterfly cruising capriciously among the flowers and perching for a second incongruously here upon a barn, there upon a wheelbarrow. Every sentence in Hazlitt carries us forward. He has his end in view and strides towards it with that straight and apparently effortless action in that 'pure conversational prose style,'[21] which is so much more difficult to learn than fine writing. There can be no question that Hazlitt the thinker is admirable. He is strong and fearless; he knows what he wants to say and he says it forcibly, yet brilliantly, too, for the readers of newspapers are a dull-eyed race who must be dazzled in order to make them see.

But besides Hazlitt the thinker, there is Hazlitt the artist. There is the sensuous and emotional man with his feeling for colour and touch, with his sensibility to all those emotions which disturb the reason and make it often seem futile enough to spend one's time slicing things up finer and finer with the intellect when the body of the world is so warm and demands so imperatively to be clasped to the heart. To know the reason of things is a poor substitute for being able to feel them. And Hazlitt felt with the intensity of a poet. The most abstract of his essays will suddenly glow red or white hot if something reminds him of his past. He will drop his fine analytic pen and paint a phrase or two with a full brush brilliantly and beautifully if some landscape stirs his imagination, or some book brings back the hour when he first read it. And it is this disparity and the sense of two forces in conflict that troubles the serenity and causes the inconclusiveness of some of Hazlitt's finest essays. They set out to give us a proof and they end by giving us a picture. We are about to plant our feet upon a solid rock of Q. E. D., and behold it turns to quagmire and we are knee deep in mud and water and flowers. 'Faces pale as the primrose with hyacinthine locks'[22] are in our eyes; the woods of Tuderly breathe their mystic voices in our ears. And suddenly we are recalled; and the thinker, austere, muscular, sardonic, leads us on to analyse, to dissect and to condemn.

It is easy to see where the limitations of Hazlitt's art lie. Compared with the other great masters in this line he is very narrow, very self-centred, very limited in his range. He has seen very little of the world. It was not his way to open the doors wide upon all experience, like Montaigne, and go urbanely among his fellow beings, rejecting nothing, tolerating everything, and watching the play of the soul with irony and detachment. On the contrary, his mind was made up; it had shut hard upon his first impressions with egotistic tenacity. Nor was it for him to play round the figures of his friends with sympathy and humour, like Lamb, creating them afresh in fantastic flights of imagination and reverie. His characters are seen with that quick sidelong glance, caustic, shrewd, suspicious, which he saw people in the flesh.

But on the other hand he has thought hard and suffered acutely. Convictions are his life blood: ideas are realities to him. They have formed in him like stalactites, drop by drop, year by year. He has added to them in a thousand solitary walks; he has tested them in many a midnight talk at the Southampton Inn. When he comes to write even upon the most threadbare abstraction – on Hot and Cold, on Envy, on Egotism[23] – he has something solid to write about. He never lets his brain slacken or trusts to the power of phrases to float him over a shallow stretch of thought. Wherever we open him, even when it is plain from the savagery and contempt with which he attacks his task that he is out of mood and only keeps his mind to the grindstone by sheer force of will we still find him mordant and searching and acute. His pages are full of fine sayings and unexpected turns of thought and independence and originality. Even in his most perfunctory criticism of books we feel that faculty for seizing on the important and indicating the main outline which learned critics often lose and timid critics never acquire. He is one of those rare critics who do not need to read – they have thought enough.

And sometimes when the mood was on him, at Winterslow, for example, with a bright fire burning and a partridge cooking for dinner, 'when he has warmed his mind,' as Coleridge put it, 'and the synovial juice has come out and spread over his joints, he will gallop for half an hour together with real eloquence.'[24] Then it was no effort to him to spread smooth his great white sheet and dip the pen in the ink. Then he wrote page after page without pause or correction in a mood of intense and spontaneous reverie. Footmen might laugh and chambermaids giggle – he was at peace as a top is at peace when it spins fastest. Then he described how he first met Coleridge; how he first read 'La Nouvelle Heloise'; how he had seen the famous fight between Neale and Hickman.[25] There is then no discord between thinker and artist. Sentence follows sentence with the healthy ring and chime of a blacksmith's hammer on the anvil; the words glow and the sparks fly; gently they fade and the essay is over. And as his writing has passage after passage of inspired description so his life had its seasons of intense enjoyment. Thus when he came to die, in lodgings, worn out, without book or furniture or anything of substance saved from the wreckage of his tempestuous career, his voice rang out with the old pugnacity and conviction: 'Well, I have had a happy life.'[26]

1 – A signed essay in the *NYHT*, 7 September 1930, and, unsigned with variations, and entitled 'William Hazlitt', as the leading article in the *TLS*, 18 September 1930, (*Kp4* C325), of *The Complete Works of William Hazlitt* [1778–1830], ed. P. P. Howe (J. M. Dent & Sons, 1930), vols i, iv, v; an advertisement for the 21-vol. edition appeared on p. 722 beside the *TLS* review; for VW's reading notes on vol. x of Howe's edition, see (Berg, RN 1.22) (*VWRN* XXII, B.14). The essay was further revised for CR2. The reader is referred to p. 494 below, where the revised version, together with the *TLS* variants in the form of endnotes, is printed in its place as part of CR2. The same issue of the *TLS* contained: a review of E. F. Benson's *As We Were: A Victorian Peep-Show*, a book VW 'moon[ed] torpidly through' (*III VW Diary*, 27 December 1930). On about 20 March

1928 VW wrote to Vita Sackville-West, informing her that she had finished the draft of O, and continued: 'I have been reading Hazlitt. For 5 minutes my mind runs on the same rails that the book runs on. I can only think in the same curves. Could you tell me where I began to read Hazlitt and where I left off?' (*III VW Letters*, no. 1873). On 29 April 1930 she wrote: 'I shall tire of Hazlitt & criticism after the first divine relief' of finishing the first draft of *The Waves* (*III VW Diary*). On 14 May: 'Shall I or shall I not read the three long MSS. on my table – or go on reading Hazlitt for an article that has to be begun tomorrow' (*IV VW Letters*, no. 2179). By 18 May she was 'thrusting through the mornings work (Hazlitt now)' (*III VW Diary*). On 6 July she seemed to be referring to 'Wm. Hazlitt, the Man' and 'Fanny Burney's Half-Sister' when she wrote: 'Now I must do a little very dreary work – boiling 2 articles in to one and spreading one in to 3: that makes my years income; but I can assure you it is hardly earned. I have to wrench my head to the left when it's looking to the right' (*IV VW Letters*, no. 2201). On 25 August she was 're-writing Hazlitt' (*III VW Diary*). On 28 August she 'must correct Hazlitt' (*IV VW Letters*, no. 2224). On 7 September she has been 'correcting a damnable article on Hazlitt' (*ibid.*, no. 2233). On 8 September she started a new volume of her diary: 'But the sentence with which this book was to open ran "Nobody has ever worked so hard as I do"– exclaimed in driving a paper fastener through the 14 pages of my Hazlitt just now. Time was when I dashed off these things all in the days work. Now, partly because I must do them for America & make arrangements far ahead, I spend I daresay a ridiculous amount of time, more of trouble on them. I began reading Hazlitt in January I think. And I am not sure that I have speared that little eel in the middle – that marrow – which is one's object in criticism. A very difficult business no doubt to find it, in all these essays; so many; so short; & on all subjects. Never mind; it shall go today; & my appetite for criticism is, oddly, whettened. I have some gift that way, were it not for the grind & the screw & the torture –' (*III VW Diary*). Reading notes (Berg, RN 1.22) (*VWRN XXII*).

2 – Hazlitt, *Table-Talk: Original Essays on Men and Manners* (1821–2), ed. by his son [William Hazlitt, 1811–93] (2 vols, C. Templeman, 1845–6), vol. ii, 'Why Distant Objects Please', p. 155, which has: '... any one that we'.

3 – *Unpublished Letters of Samuel Taylor Coleridge* [1772–1834] ..., ed. Earl Leslie Griggs (Constable, 1932), vol. i, Letter 126, to Tom Wedgwood, 16 September 1803, p. 278.

4 – On 4 January 1931 the *New York Times* included this in its 'A Sheaf of Similes for 1930'.

5 – *Unpublished Letters of Coleridge*, p. 278, which has: 'His manners are to 99 in 100 ...'

6 – Charles Lamb (1775–1834).

7 – Hazlitt, *The Plain Speaker: Opinions on Books, Men, and Things* (2 vols, Henry Colburn, 1826), vol. i, 'Whether Genius is Conscious of Its Powers?', p. 291, which has: 'not being a government-tool'.

8 – W. Carew Hazlitt [1834–1913, Hazlitt's grandson], *Memoirs of William Hazlitt* . . . (2 vols, Richard Bentley, 1867), vol. ii, p. 26, which has: '*pimpled*'. See also *Blackwood's Edinburgh Magazine*, vol. iii, no. xvii (August 1818), p. 599, col. b, in an unsigned review of *The Works of Charles Lamb*: 'to "pimpled Hazlitt," notwithstanding his "coxcomb lectures" on Poetry and Shakespeare, he [Lamb] does not condescend to say one syllable'.

9 – *Table-Talk*, vol. ii, 'Why Distant Objects Please', p. 157.

10 – Hazlitt, *Literary Remains of the Late William Hazlitt* (2 vols, Saunders and Otley, 1836), vol. ii, Essay xi, 'On the Conduct of Life; or, Advice to a School-boy', p. 108; also quoted in *Memoirs*, vol. ii, p. 19: 'Artists, I think, who have succeeded in their chief object, live to be old, and are agreeable old men. Their minds keep alive to the last.'

11 – *Memoirs*, vol. i, p. 25, for all three quotations. (In the version of 'Project for a new Theory of Civil and Criminal Legislation', collected in *Literary Remains*, vol. i, p. 3, the first and third quotes are omitted.)

12 – Rembrandt van Rijn (1606–69).

13 – Hazlitt, *Essay on the Principles of Human Action: Being an Argument in favour of the Natural Disinterestedness of the Human Mind. To which are added, Some Remarks on the Systems of Hartley and Helvetius* (J. Johnson, 1805).

14 – *Memoirs*, vol. i, p. 131, which has: 'The "Essay on Human Actions" dropped stillborn . . .'

15 – This seems to echo the 'blue remembered hills' in Poem xl, *A Shropshire Lad* (1896), although VW wrote two days after the death of A. E. Housman (1859–1936) that she found his poems 'too laden with a particular scent for [her] taste. May, death, lads, Shropshire' (*VI VW Letters*, no. 3126, 2 May 1936).

16 – Jean-Jacques Rousseau (1712–78); Edmund Burke (1729–97), statesman and political philosopher. The first of the letters of 'Junius', an anonymous (and still unidentified) Whig political correspondent, appeared in the *Public Advertiser* of October 1768. On 4 January 1928 VW wrote: 'there is a theory . . . that she [Orlando] was the author of the letters of Junius' (*O Holograph*, MS 179, and see Appendix A).

17 – On 1 May 1808 Hazlitt married Sarah Stoddart (1774–1840), the daughter of a retired naval lieutenant.

18 – In 1812–c. 1819, Hazlitt rented 19 York Street, Westminster, from Jeremy Bentham whose own house abutted the property.

19 – *Memoirs*, vol. ii, 'Mrs Hazlitt's Diary', Tuesday 30 April 1822, p. 40.

20 – For VW on Michel de Montaigne (1533–92), see 'Montaigne', *CR1* and *IV VW Essays*; Francis Bacon (1561–1626).

21 – Hazlitt, *Lectures on the English Poets* (Taylor and Hessey, 1818), 'On Swift, Young, Gray, Collins, &c', p. 208.
22 – *Table-Talk*, vol. i, 'On the Past and Future', pp. 6–7, which has: 'Without that face pale as . . .'
23 – For Hazlitt's 'Hot and Cold', 'On Envy (A Dialogue)' and 'On Egotism', see *The Plain Speaker*, vol. i, pp. 407–28, 231–53 and 377–403, respectively.
24 – *Unpublished Letters of Coleridge*, vol. i, Letter 126, p. 279.
25 – For the meeting with Coleridge, see 'My First Acquaintance with Poets', *Literary Remains*, vol. ii, pp. 361–96; for reading 'La Nouvelle Heloise', see 'On going a Journey', *Table-Talk*, vol. i, pp. 343–60, at p. 353; and for 'The Fight', on an encounter between Tom (the 'Gas-Man') Hickman and Bill Neate, see *Table-Talk*, vol. i, pp. 236–65 (and *Literary Remains*, vol. ii, pp. 195–226, and *Memoirs*, vol. ii, ch. vii and viii).
26 – *Memoirs*, vol. ii, p. 238, which has: 'I've'. Hazlitt died on 18 September 1830 at 6 Frith Street, Soho, *aetat* 52.

Memories of a Working Women's Guild

When you asked me to write a preface to a book which you had collected of papers by working women I replied that I would rather be drowned than write a preface to any book whatever. Books should stand on their own feet, my argument was (and I think it is a sound one). If they need shoring up by a preface here, an introduction there, they have no more right to exist than a table that needs a wad of paper under one leg in order to stand steady. But you left me the papers, and, turning them over, I saw that on this occasion the argument did not apply; this book is not a book. Turning the pages, I began to ask myself what is this book then, if it is not a book? What quality has it? What ideas does it suggest? What old arguments and memories does it rouse in me? and as all this had nothing to do with an introduction or a preface, but brought you to mind and certain pictures from the past, I stretched my hand for a sheet of notepaper and wrote you the following letter.

You have forgotten (I wrote) a hot June morning in Manchester[2] in the year 1913, or at least you will not remember what I remember, because you were otherwise engaged. Your attention was entirely absorbed by a green table, several sheets of paper, and a bell. Moreover, you were frequently interrupted. There was a woman wearing something like a Lord Mayor's chain round her shoulders; she took her seat perhaps at your right; there were other women without ornament save fountain pens and despatch boxes – they sat perhaps on your left. Soon a row had been formed up there on the platform, with tables and inkstands and tumblers of water; while we, many hundreds of us, scraped and shuffled and filled the entire body of some vast municipal building beneath. Perhaps an organ played. The proceedings somehow opened. The talking and laughing and shuffling suddenly subsided. A bell struck; a figure rose; she took her way from among us; she mounted a platform; she spoke for precisely five minutes; she descended. Directly she sat down another rose; mounted the platform; spoke for precisely five minutes and descended; then a third rose; then a fourth – and so it went on, speaker following speaker, one from the right, one from the left, one from the middle, one from the background – each took her way to the stand, said what she had to say and gave place to her successor. There was something military in the regularity of the proceeding. They were like marksmen, I thought, standing up in turn with rifle raised to aim at a target. Sometimes they missed, and there was a roar of laughter; sometimes they hit, and there was a roar of applause. But whether the particular shot hit or missed there was no doubt about the carefulness of the aim. There was no beating about the bush; there were no phrases of easy eloquence. The speaker made her way to the stand primed with her subject. Determination and resolution were stamped on her face. There was so much to be said between the strokes of the bell that she could not waste a second. The moment had come for which she had been waiting perhaps for many months. The moment had come for which she had stored hat, shoes, and dress – there was an air of discreet novelty about her clothing. But, above all, the moment had come when she was going to speak her mind, the mind of her constituency, the mind of the women who had sent her from Cornwall perhaps or Sussex, or some black mining village in Yorkshire, to speak their mind for them in Manchester.

It soon became obvious that the mind which lay spread over so wide a stretch of England was a vigorous mind working with great activity. It was thinking in June, 1913, of the reform of the divorce laws; of the taxation of land values; of the minimum wage. It was concerned with the care of maternity; with the Trades Board Act; with the education of children over fourteen; it was unanimously of opinion that adult suffrage should become a government measure – it was thinking, in short, about every sort of public question, and it was thinking constructively and pugnaciously. Accrington did not see eye to eye with Halifax, nor Middlesborough with Plymouth. There was argument and opposition; resolutions were lost and amendments won.

Meanwhile – let me try after seventeen years to sum up the thoughts that passed through the minds of your guests, middle-class people who had come from London and elsewhere not to take part, but to listen – meanwhile, what was it all about? What was the meaning of it? These women were demanding divorce, education, the vote – all good things. They were demanding higher wages and shorter hours – what could be more reasonable? And yet though it was all so reasonable, much of it so forcible, some of it so humorous, a weight of discomfort was settling and shifting itself uneasily from side to side in your visitors' minds. All those questions, I found myself thinking – and perhaps this was at the bottom of it – which matter so intensely to the people here, questions of sanitation and education and wages, this demand for an extra shilling, or another year at school, for eight hours instead of nine behind a counter or in a mill, leave me, in my own blood and bones, untouched. If every reform they demand was granted this very instant it would not matter to me a single jot. Hence my interest is merely altruistic. It is thin spread and moon-coloured. There is no life blood or urgency about it. However hard I clap my hands or stamp my feet, there is a hollowness in the sound which betrays me. I am a benevolent spectator. I am irretrievably cut off from the actors. I sit here hypocritically, clapping and stamping, an outcast from the flock.

On top of this too, my reason (it was in 1913, remember) could not help assuring me that even if the resolution, whatever it was, were carried unanimously, the stamping and the clapping was an empty noise. It would pass out of the open windows and become part of the clamour of the lorries and the striving of the hooves on the Manchester cobbles beneath – an inarticulate uproar. The mind might be active; the mind might be aggressive; but the mind was without a body; it had no legs and arms with which to enforce its will. In all that audience, among all those women who worked, women who had children, women who scrubbed and cooked and bargained and knew to a penny what they had to spend, there was not a single woman with a vote. Let them fire off their rifles if they liked, but they would hit no target; there were only blank cartridges inside. The thought was irritating and depressing.

The clock had now struck half past eleven; there were still then many hours to come. And if one had reached this stage of irritation and depression by half past eleven in the morning, into what depths of boredom would one not be plunged by half past five in the evening? How could one sit out another day of speechifying? How, above all, could one face you, our hostess, with the information that your Congress had proved so insupportably depressing that one was going back to London by the very first train? The only chance lay in some happy conjuring trick, some change of attitude by which the mist and blankness of the speeches could be turned to blood and bone. Otherwise they remained intolerable.

But suppose one played a childish game; suppose one said, as a child says, 'Let's pretend . . .'? 'Let's pretend,' one said to oneself, looking at the speaker, 'that I am Mrs Giles of Durham City.' A woman of that name had just turned to address us. "I am the wife of a miner. He comes back thick with coal grime. First he must have his bath. Then he must have his dinner. But there is only a wash tub. My range is filled with saucepans. There is no getting on with the work. All my crocks are covered with dust again. . . . Why in the Lord's name have I not hot water laid on and electric light when middle-class women . . .' So up I jump and demand passionately 'labour-saving appliances and housing reform.' Up I jump in the person of Mrs Giles of Durham; in the person of Mrs Phillips of Bacup; in the person of Mrs Edwards of Wolverton.[3] But, after all, the imagination is largely the child of the flesh. One could not be Mrs Giles because one's body had never stood at the wash tub; one's hands had never wrung and scrubbed and chopped up whatever the meat may be that makes a miner's dinner. The picture was always letting in irrelevancies. One sat in an armchair or read a book. One saw landscapes or seascapes, in Greece or perhaps in Italy, where Mrs Giles or Mrs Edwards must have seen slag heaps and row upon row of slate roofs in a mining village. Something at any rate was always creeping in from a world that was not their world and making the picture false and the game too much of a game to be worth playing.

It was true that one could always correct these fancy portraits by taking a look at the actual person – at Mrs Thomas, or Mrs Langrish, or Miss Bolt of Hebden Bridge. Certainly, there were no armchairs, electric light, or hot water laid on in their homes, no Greek hills or Mediterranean bays in their lives. They did not sign a cheque to pay the weekly bills, or order, over the telephone, a cheap but quite adequate seat at the Opera. If they travelled it was on excursion day, with paper bags and hot babies in their arms. They did not stroll through the house and say, that cover must go to the wash, or those sheets need changing. They plunged their arms in hot water and scrubbed the clothes themselves. In consequence they had thickset muscular bodies. They had large hands; they had the slow emphatic gestures of people who are often stiff and fall tired in a heap on hard-backed chairs. They touched nothing lightly. They gripped papers and pencils as if they were brooms. Their faces were firm, with heavy folds and deep lines. It seemed as if their muscles were always taut and on the stretch. Their eyes looked as if they were always set on something actual – on saucepans that were boiling over, on children who were getting into mischief. Their faces never expressed the lighter and more detached emotions that come into play when the mind is perfectly at ease about the present. They were not in the least detached and cosmopolitan. They were indigenous and rooted to one spot. Their very names were like the stones of the fields, common, grey, obscure, docked of all the splendours of association and romance. Of course they wanted baths and ovens and education and seventeen shillings instead of sixteen and freedom and air and . . . 'And,' said Mrs Winthrop of Spenny Moor, breaking into these thoughts with words that sounded like a refrain, 'we can wait.' 'Yes,' she repeated, at the conclusion of her speech – what demand she had been making I do not know – 'we can wait.'[4] And she got down rather stiffly from her perch and made her way back to her seat, an elderly woman dressed in her best clothes.

Then Mrs Potter spoke. Then Mrs Elphick. Then Mrs Holmes of Edgbaston. So it went on, and at last after innumerable speeches, after many communal meals at long tables and many arguments – after seeing jams bottled and biscuits made, after some song singing and ceremonies with banners – the new President received the chain of office with a kiss from the old President;[5] the Congress dispersed; and the separate members who had stood up and spoken out so boldly while the clock ticked its five minutes went back to Yorkshire and Wales and Sussex and Cornwall and hung their clothes in the wardrobe and plunged their hands in the wash tub again.

Later that summer the thoughts, here so inadequately described, were again discussed, but not in a public hall hung with banners and loud with voices. The head office of the Guild, the centre from which speakers, papers, inkstands, and tumblers, as I suppose, were issued, was then in Hampstead. There, if I may remind you again of what you may well have forgotten, you invited us to come; you asked us to tell you how the Congress had impressed us. But I must pause on the threshold of that very dignified old house with its eighteenth-century carvings and panelling, as we paused then in truth, for one could not enter and go upstairs without encountering Miss Wick.[6] Miss Wick sat at her typewriter in the outer office. Miss Wick, one felt, was set as a kind of watch-dog to ward off the meddlesome middle-class wasters of time who come prying into other people's business. Whether it was for this reason that she was dressed in a peculiar shade of deep purple I do not know. The colour seemed somehow symbolic. She was very short, but owing to the weight which sat on her brow and the gloom which seemed to issue from her dress she was also very weighty. An extra share of the world's grievances seemed to press upon her shoulders. When she clicked her typewriter, one felt that she was making that instrument transmit messages of foreboding and ill omen to an unheeding universe. But she relented and like all relentings after gloom hers came with a sudden charm. We went upstairs, and upstairs was a very different figure – there was Miss Janet Erskine[7] indeed, and Miss Erskine may have been smoking a pipe – there was one on the table. She may have been reading a detective story – there was a book of that kind on the table – at any rate, she seemed the image of detachment and equa-nimity. Had one not known that Miss Erskine was to the Congress what the heart is to the remoter veins – that the great engine at Manchester would not thump and throb without her – that she had collected and sorted and summoned and arranged that very intricate but orderly assembly of women – she would never have enlightened one. She had nothing whatever to do – she came to the office because an office is a good place in which to read detective stories – she licked a few stamps and addressed a few envelopes – it was a fad of hers – that was what her manner conveyed. It was Miss Erskine who moved the papers off the chairs and got the teacups out of the cupboard. It was she who answered questions about figures and put her hand on the right file of letters.

Again let me telescope into a few sentences and into one scene many random discussions at various places. We said then – for you now emerged from an inner room and if Miss Wick was purple and Miss Erskine was coffee-coloured, you, speaking pictorially (and I dare not speak more explicitly), were kingfisher blue[8] and as arrowy and decisive as that quick bird – we said then that the Congress had roused thoughts and ideas of the most diverse nature. It had been a revelation and a disillusionment. We had been humiliated and enraged. To begin with, all their talk, we said, or the greater part of it, was of matters of fact. They want baths and money. When people get together communally they always talk about baths and money; they always show the least desirable of their characteristics – their lust for conquest and their desire for possessions. To expect us, whose minds, such as they are, fly free at the end of a short length of capital to tie ourselves down again upon that narrow plot of acquisitiveness and desire is impossible. We have baths and money. Society has supplied us with all we need in that direction. Therefore however much we sympathised, our sympathy was largely fictitious. It was aesthetic sympathy, the sympathy of the eye and of the imagination, not of the heart and of the nerves; and such sympathy is always physically uncomfortable. Let us explain what we mean, we said.

The women are magnificent to look at. Ladies in evening dress are lovelier far, but they lack the sculpturesque quality that these working women have. Their arms are undeveloped. Fat has softened the lines of their muscles. And though the range of expression is narrower in working women, their expressions have a force and emphasis, of tragedy or humour, which the faces of ladies lack. But at the same time, it is much better to be a lady; ladies desire Mozart and Cézanne[9] and Shakespeare; and not merely money and hot water laid on. Therefore to deride ladies and to imitate, as some of the speakers did, their mincing speech and little knowledge of what it pleases them to call 'reality' is not merely bad manners, but it gives away the whole purpose of the Congress, for if it is better to be a working woman by all means let them remain so and not claim their right to undergo the contamination of wealth and comfort.

In spite of this, we went on, apart from prejudice and bandying compliments, undoubtedly the women at the Congress possess something which ladies have lost, something desirable, stimulating, and at the same time very difficult to define. One does not want to slip easily into fine phrases about 'contact with life,' about 'facing facts,' 'the teaching of experience,' for they invariably alienate the hearer, and moreover no working man or woman works harder with his hands or is in closer touch with reality than a painter with his brush or a writer with his pen. But the quality that they have – judging from a phrase caught here and there, a laugh, or a gesture seen in passing – is a quality that Shakespeare would have liked. One can fancy him slipping away from the brilliant salons of educated people to crack a joke in Mrs Robson's back kitchen. Indeed, we said, one of our most curious impressions at your Congress was that 'the poor,' 'the working classes,' or by whatever name you choose to call them are not down-trodden, envious, and exhausted; they are humorous and vigorous and thoroughly independent. Thus, if it were possible to meet them not as sympathisers, as masters or mistresses with counters between us or kitchen tables, but casually and congenially as fellow beings with the same ends and wishes even if the dress and body are different, a great liberation would follow. How many words, for example, must lurk in those women's vocabularies that have faded from ours! How many scenes must lie dormant in their eyes unseen by us! What images and saws and proverbial sayings must still be current with them that have never reached the surface of print; and very likely they still keep the power which we have lost of making new ones. There were many shrewd sayings in the speeches at the Congress which even the weight of a public meeting could not flatten out entirely.

But, we said, and here perhaps fiddled with a paper knife or poked the fire impatiently by way of expressing our discontent, what is the use of it all? Our sympathy is fictitious, not real. Because we pay our bills with cheques and our clothes are washed for us and we do not know the liver from the lights, we are condemned to remain forever shut up in the confines of the middle classes wearing tail coats and silk stockings and called Sir or Madam as the case may be, when we are all, in truth, simply Johns and Susans. And they remain equally deprived. For we have as much to give them as they us – wit and detachment, learning and poetry and all those good gifts which those who have never answered bells or touched their foreheads with their forefingers enjoy by right. But the barrier is impassable. And nothing perhaps exasperated us more at the Congress (you must have noticed at times a certain irritability) than the thought that this force of theirs, this smouldering heat which broke the crust now and then and licked the surface with a hot and fearless flame, is about to break through and melt us together so that life will be richer and books more complex and society will pool its possessions instead of segregating them – all this is bound to happen inevitably thanks to you, very largely, and to Miss Erskine and to Miss Wick – but only when we are dead.

It was thus that we tried in the Guild office that afternoon to explain the nature of fictitious sympathy and how it differs from real sympathy and how defective it is because it is not based upon sharing the same important emotions unconsciously. It was thus that we tried to describe the contradictory and complex feelings which beset the middle-class visitor forced to sit out a congress of working women in silence.

Perhaps it was at this point that you unlocked a drawer and took out a packet of papers. You did not at once untie the string that fastened them. Sometimes, you said, you got a letter which you could not bring yourself to burn; once or twice a Guildswoman at your suggestion had written a few pages about her life. It might be that we should find these papers interesting; it might be that if we read them the women would cease to be symbols and become instead individuals. But they were very fragmentary and ungrammatical; they had been jotted down in the intervals of housework. Indeed, you could not at once bring yourself to give them up, as if to expose their simplicity were a breach of confidence. It might be that their illiteracy would only perplex, you said; that the writing of people who do not know how to write – but at this point we burst in. In the first place, every English woman knows how to write, in the second, even if she does not she has only to take her own life for subject and write the truth and not fiction or poetry for our interest to be so keenly roused that – in short, we cannot wait but must read the packet at once.

Thus pressed you did by degrees and with many delays – there was the war for example, and Miss Wick died, and you and Janet Erskine retired from the Guild, and a testimonial was given you in a casket, and many thousand working women tried to say how you had changed their lives – tried to say what they will feel for you to their dying day – after all these interruptions, you did at last gather the papers together and finally put them in my hands. There they were, typed and docketed with a few snapshots and rather faded photographs stuck between the pages. And when, at last, I began to read, there started up in my mind's eye the figures that I had seen all those years ago at Manchester with such bewilderment and curiosity. But they were no longer addressing a large meeting in Manchester from a platform, dressed in their best clothes. The hot June day with its banners had vanished, and instead one looked back into the past of the women who had stood there; into the four-roomed houses of miners, into the homes of small shopkeepers and agricultural labourers, into the fields and factories of fifty or sixty years ago. Mrs Barrows for example

had worked in the Lincolnshire fens when she was eight with forty
or fifty other children, and an old man had followed the gang with
a long whip in his hand 'which he did not forget to use.'[10] That was
a strange reflection. Most of the women had started work at seven
or eight, earning a penny on Saturday for washing a doorstep, or
twopence a week for carrying suppers to the men at the iron foundry.
They had gone into factories when they were fourteen.

They had worked from seven in the morning till eight or nine at
night and had made thirteen or fifteen shillings a week. Out of this
money they had saved some pence with which to buy their mother
gin – she was often very tired in the evening and had borne perhaps
thirteen children in as many youthful years; or they fetched opium
to assuage some miserable old woman's ague in the fens. Betty
Potter[11] killed herself when she could get no more. They had seen
half-starved women standing in rows to be paid for their match
boxes while they snuffed the roast meat of their employers' dinner
cooking within.[12] The smallpox had raged in Bethnal Green, and
they had known that the boxes went on being made in the sick
room and sold to the public with the infection thick on them.[13]
They had been so cold working in the wintry fields that they could
not run when the ganger gave them leave. They had waded through
floods when the Wash overflowed its banks.[14] Kind old ladies had
given them parcels of food which turned out to contain only crusts
and rancid bacon rind.[15]

All this they had done and seen and known when other children
were still dabbling in seaside pools and spelling out fairy tales by the
nursery fire. Naturally their faces had a different look on them. But
they were also, one remembered, firm faces, faces with something
indomitable in their expression. And the reason can only be that
human nature is so tough that it will take such wounds, even at the
tenderest age, and survive them. Keep a child mewed up in Bethnal
Green and she will somehow snuff the country air from seeing the
yellow dust on her brother's boots, and nothing will serve her but
she must go there, and see the 'clean ground'[16] as she calls it for
herself. It was true that at first the 'bees were very frightening,'[17] but
all the same she got to the country and the blue smoke and the cows
came up to her expectations. Put girls after a childhood of minding
smaller brothers and sisters and washing doorsteps into a factory
when they are fourteen and their eyes will turn to the window and
they will be happy because, as the work room is six stories up, the

sun can be seen breaking over the hills 'and that was always such a comfort and a help.'[18]

Still stranger, if one needs additional proof of the strength of the human instinct to escape from bondage and attach itself to a country road or a sun rising over distant hills, is the fact that the highest ideals of duty flourish in an obscure hat factory as surely as on a battlefield. There were women in Christie's hat factory, for example, who worked for 'honour.' They gave their lives to the cause of putting straight stitches into the bindings of men's hat brims. Felt is hard and thick; it is difficult to push the needle through; there are no rewards or glory to be won; but such is the incorrigible idealism of the human mind that there were 'trimmers' in those obscure places who would never put a crooked stitch in their work and ruthlessly tore out the crooked stitches of others. And as they drove in their straight stitches they reverenced Queen Victoria and thanked God, drawing up to the fire, that they were all married to good Conservative working men.[19]

Certainly that story explained something of the force, of the obstinacy which one had seen in the faces of the speakers at the Congress in Manchester. And then if one went on reading these papers, one came upon other signs of the extraordinary vitality of the human spirit. The dauntless energy which no amount of childbirth and washing up can quench entirely had reached out, it seemed, and seized upon old copies of magazines; had attached itself to Dickens; had propped the poems of Burns against a dish-cover to read while cooking. They read at meals; they read before going to the mill. They read Dickens and Scott and Henry George and Bulwer-Lytton and Ella Wheeler Wilcox and Alice Meynell and would like 'to get hold of any good history of the French Revolution, not Carlyle's please,' and B. Russell on China, and William Morris and Shelley and Florence Barclay and Samuel Butler's Note Books[20] – they read with the indiscriminate greed of a hungry appetite that crams itself with toffee and beef and tarts and vinegar and champagne all in one gulp.

Naturally, such reading led to argument. The younger generation had the audacity to say that Queen Victoria was no better than an honest charwoman who had brought up her children respectably.[21] They had the temerity to doubt whether to sew straight stitches into men's hat brims should be the sole aim and end of a woman's life. They started arguments and even held rudimentary debating societies on the floor of the factory. In time the old trimmers even were shaken in their beliefs and came to think that there might be other ideals in the world besides straight stitches and Queen Victoria. Ideas, indeed, were seething in their brains. A girl, for instance, would reason, as she walked along the streets of a factory town, that she had no right to bring a child into the world if that child must earn its living in a mill. A chance saying in a book would fire her imagination and make her dream of future cities where there were to be baths and kitchens and wash houses and art galleries and museums and parks.

The minds of working women were humming and their imaginations were awake. But how were they to realise their ideals? How were they to express their needs? Of middle-class organisations there were many. Women were beginning to found colleges, and even here and there to enter the professions. But these were middle-class women with some amount of money and some degree of education behind them. How could women whose hands were full of work, whose kitchens were thick with steam, who had neither education nor encouragement nor leisure remodel the world according to the ideas of working women? It was then, I suppose, some time early in the Eighties, that the Women's Guild crept modestly and tentatively into existence, occupying for a time a certain space in the 'Co-operative News' which was called the 'Woman's Corner.' It was there that Mrs Acland asked, 'Why should we not hold our Co-operative Mothers' Meetings, when we may bring our work and sit together, one of us reading some co-operative work aloud, which may afterwards be discussed?'[22] And on April 18, 1883, she announced that there were seven members who had achieved this object.

This was the tiny magnet that drew to itself all that restless wishing and dreaming. This was the central meeting place where was formed and solidified what was else so scattered and incoherent. The Guild must have given the older women, with their husbands and children, what 'clean ground' had given the little girl in Bethnal Green, or the view of day breaking over the hills had given to the girls in the hat factory. It gave them in the first place a room where they could sit down and think remote from boiling saucepans and crying children; and then that room became a place where one could make, and share with others in making, the model of what a working woman's house should be. Then as the membership grew and twenty or thirty women made a practice of meeting weekly, that one house became a street of houses; and if you have a street of houses you must have stores and drains and post boxes; and at last the street becomes a town, and a town brings in questions of education and finance and the relation of one town to another town. And then the town becomes a country; it becomes England; it becomes Germany and America; and so from debating questions of butter and bacon, working women at their weekly meetings have to consider the relations of one great nation to another.

So it was that in the year 1913 Mrs Robson and Mrs Potter and Mrs Wright were getting up and asking not only for baths and wages and electric light but also for co-operative industry and adult suffrage and the taxation of land values and divorce law reform. It was thus that they were to ask, as the years went by, for peace and disarmament and the sisterhood of nations. And the force that lay behind their speeches was compact of many things – of men with whips, and sick rooms where match boxes are made, of hunger and cold, and many and difficult childbirths, of much scrubbing and washing up, of reading Shelley and William Morris and Samuel Butler, of meetings of the Women's Guild, and committees and congresses at Manchester and elsewhere. All this lay behind the speeches of Mrs Robson and Mrs Potter and Mrs Wright. The papers which you sent me certainly threw some light upon those old curiosities and bewilderments.

But it cannot be denied that, as I began by saying, they do not make a book; as literature they have many limitations. The writing lacks detachment and imaginative breadth, even as the women themselves lacked variety and play of feature. Here are no reflections; no view of life as a whole; no attempt to enter into the lives of other people. It is not from the ranks of working class women that the next great poet or novelist will be drawn. Indeed, we are reminded of those obscure writers before Shakespeare who had never been beyond the borders of their own parishes and found expression difficult and words few and awkward to fit together.

And yet since writing is an impure art much infected by life, the letters you gave me seem to possess some qualities even as literature that the literate and instructed might envy. Listen, for instance, to Mrs Scott the midwife: 'I have been over the hilltops when the snowdrifts were over three feet high, and six feet in some places. I was in a blizzard in Hayfield and thought I should never get round the corners. But it was life on the moors; I seemed to know every blade of grass and where the flowers grew and all the little streams were my companions.'[23] Could she have said that better if

Oxford had made her a doctor of letters? Or take Mrs Layton's description of a match box factory in Bethnal Green, and how she 'looked through the fence and saw three ladies sitting in the shade doing some kind of fancy work.'[24] It has something of the accuracy and clarity of a description by Defoe.[25] And when Mrs Burrows brings to mind that very bitter day when the children were about to eat their cold dinner and drink their cold tea under the hedge and the ugly woman asked them in to her parlour saying, 'Bring these children into my house and let them eat their dinner there,'[26] one must admit that she gets her effect, and brings the scene before us – the frozen children eating hot boiled potatoes in a ring on the floor – by whatever means she manages it. And then there is a fragment of a letter from Miss Wick, the sombre purple figure who typed as if the weight of the world rested on her shoulders. 'When I was a girl of seventeen,' she writes, 'my then employer, a gentleman of good position and high standing in the town, sent me to his home one night ostensibly to take a parcel of books, but really with a very different object. When I arrived at the house all the family were away, and before he would allow me to leave he forced me to yield to him. At eighteen I was a mother.'[27] The stiff words, which conceal all emotion conventionally enough, are yet illuminating. Such then was the burden that rested upon that squat and sombre figure – such were the memories that she stored as she sat typing your letters, guarding your door with such tremendous fidelity in her purple dress.

But I will quote no more. These letters are only fragments. These voices are beginning only now to emerge from silence into half articulate speech. These lives are still half-hidden in profound obscurity. To write even what is written has been a task of labour and difficulty. The writing has been done in kitchens, at odds and ends of time, in the midst of distractions and obstacles – but really there is no need for me, in a letter addressed to you, to lay stress upon the hardships of working women's lives. Have not you and Janet Erskine given your best years – but hush! you will not let me finish that sentence and therefore, with the old messages of friendship and admiration, I will make an end.

1 – A signed essay in the *Yale Review*, September 1930, (*Kp4* C326), which was revised as the introduction to *Life as We Have Known It* (*Kp4* B11): see 'Introductory Letter to Margaret Llewelyn Davies', p. 225 below.

At the invitation (LWP) of Margaret Llewelyn Davies (1861–1944), General Secretary of the Women's Co-operative Guild, 1889–1922, the Woolfs attended the Guild Congress in Newcastle, 9–11 June 1913. LW wrote to Davies on 13 June: 'I feel we must thank you for the Congress. I don't know when I've enjoyed anything so much & Virginia feels the same. It was simply absorbing from beginning to end, & everything about it was splendid. I only hope you'll allow us to come again another year. Virginia is so enthusiastic that she will not rest until she is sent some day as a delegate. [In VW's hand:] This is quite true about both of us. Being ignorant doesnt mean that one cant at least appreciate. (however, being ignorant only applies to me)' (*Letters of Leonard Woolf*, ed. Frederic Spotts [Weidenfeld & Nicolson, 1989], p. 381).

At least as far back as 1920 Davies was encouraging her members to write their recollections, for VW wrote to her in the middle of the year: 'I have read Mrs Layton with the greatest interest. I don't know how far I'm always biassed in favour of autobiographies, but I enjoyed it all. My only criticism would be that sometimes she writes too like a book. When she is natural she is very good. Now and then she drags in something rather shop-made. I'm keeping it, as Leonard wants to read it, but I'll send it back next week. You must make her go on, and go into every sort of detail, and try to make her say *everything*, but of course thats the difficulty. I feel she hushes things up a little. The description of the women sitting in front of the big house is so good – in fact I keep thinking of different scenes' (*II VW Letters*, no. 1134, and see no. 1536). In 1929 Davies invited VW to introduce the book of autobiographies that she was then editing. VW wrote to her from France on 6 June: 'I got your letters and the papers just as we were starting – I didn't like to risk bringing them here, but I will read them as soon as we get back, in about ten days or so. I'm rather doubtful about doing a preface – I'm too much of a picturesque amateur – and I daresay none would be needed. But we can see about this later' (*IV VW Letters*, no. 2036). At some point during 1930 she agreed to undertake the project: 'With great plodding I have managed to write about the Women's Guild' (*III VW Diary*, 18 May 1930); 'I have to write about working women all the morning' (*IV VW Letters*, no. 2188, 7 June [1930]). But even by 25 June LW had 'not yet read the papers' (*ibid.*, no. 2195, to Davies). VW must have sent a draft of the introduction to Davies, for on 6 July 1930 VW wrote: 'to tell the truth I am slightly annoyed, both with Margaret & with Mr Birrell. Those were two kind acts of mine: the Women's Guild article & the article on B. Neither has thanked me. M. sent a postcard. Yet I spent two or even 3 weeks on that Letter; & worked & worked. Never – this is the moral – do a kindness in writing. Never agree to use one's art as an act of friendship' (*III VW Diary*). VW offered the introduction to the *Yale Review*, writing to Helen McAfee, the managing editor, on 7 July: 'The only thing I have written that might interest you – as you ask about future work – is an introductory letter to a little book of working womens memoirs that we are publishing in the autumn. It is about 5,000 words in length, and consists really of my recollections of various co-operative congresses and reflections upon working women, in the form of a letter to Miss Llewellyn Davies who used to be the head of the Womens Guild. If you would care to see it I would send it, but of course it may not be at all in your line' (uncollected letter in *VWB*, no. 9 [January 2002], p. 6). She wrote to Davies on 25 July: 'I have not yet gone through your suggestions about my Guild paper. I am taking them to Rodmell, where we go on Tuesday, and hope in the quiet there to see what can be done to alter the paper as you and Lilian think desirable. I am much relieved that you like it in the main. Of course I was aware of great difficulties. And in spite of your kindness, I admit that I feel grave doubts whether the thing ought to be published as an introduction. I think it might be better for the book to stand on its own feet, or to have only a formal note of explanation. But I have not read my paper since I wrote it, and I will go through it again with Leonard. I have a strong feeling against introductions – and this one is full of difficulties. But I will see. ¶ Meanwhile an American editor, to whom I had promised an article, has read it; and wants to publish it in September as an article – or rather as fiction. What I want to know is whether you would object to my doing this, if I suppressed all real names, did not mention you or Lilian, and made it my personal view of congresses in general? I should put a note to say that it was based on some impressions received at a meeting of the Womens Guild and was intended as an introduction to a book by working women. The Americans, the editor said, are completely in the dark about co-operation and Guilds and it would be read as litera-ture simply. It has to be sent off on Tuesday, and thus I have no time to make the alterations in detail which you suggest. Can you trust me to make the thing blameless? I dont suppose any Guildswoman is likely to read the Yale Review. Leonard says that this would make no difference to our publishing it in England. Would you send me a card to say if you have any objection? ¶ Anyhow, I am awfully glad that you liked it – I felt it very imperfect. I dont think, by the way, that your swans, as you say, only provoked "a literary reaction" in me – or perhaps I include a good deal more in liter-ature than you would. My difficulty always was the political attitude to human beings – that some were always right, others always wrong. I did hate that. And do still. But as you say one gets more sensible . . . Yes of course I will send the final form of the letter for you to see, if we decide to keep it' (*IV VW Letters*, no. 2210). On 27 July she wrote again to Davies: 'Leonard has given on another page his oath that it will be quite all right about America – we are always printing there first and it makes no differ-ence. I feel it was my fault – I had promised to write an article and I never did and when the editor came down on me for it I excused myself by saying that I had been writing an introduction which would *not* do for them. This put their backs up and they demanded to see it, and now of course out of perversity say it is the very thing. I have scrapped all names and otherwise abolished traces of the book and have sent if off. But I always write things twice over, and let the Americans, who are in a hurry, have the first version. No doubt when I get to Rodmell I shall want to rewrite a good deal of this, so that it wont be the same thing. I have only glanced hastily at your notes, and it may be quite easy – if they dont involve a change of view entirely – to put them in. I've always meant to ask what the writers of the letters feel about a book? Did they write with a view to publication? Do they want their things to appear in print? Are they all alive? What was their motive in writing? It was stupid of me not to find out before I began' (*ibid.*, no. 2212). VW sent the article to McAfee the same day: 'I enclose the corrected copy of the paper. I think your suggestion of a title is very good and have adopted it. I have also put a note as you see, and have made various alterations which will I hope make it quite plain to your readers. But if any further alterations occur to you, would you very kindly note them in pencil on the proofs and I will add them when I make final corrections. As you see, I have altered the last words . . . On reading your letter again, I am not sure if you are going to send me proofs of the Womens Guild paper. If not, I will send you any alterations that may occur for you to add yourself' (*ibid.*, no. 2213).

The article in the *Yale Review* was footnoted: 'These pages relating to the English Women's Co-operative Guild are addressed to a former officer of this organization who had placed in Mrs. Woolf's hands a collection of letters written by its members. The Guild, which now has an enrolment of some 70,000 and is the largest association of its kind in England, was founded in 1883 to stimulate the ideas and activities of working women. It holds important annual Congresses, and it is one of these which met at Manchester, in 1913, that Mrs. Woolf gives her impressions in the early part of the article.' Facing the last page of the article was 'Take My Vows', a poem by Dorothy Parker; the issue also contained: John Galsworthy's 'The Buckles of Superior Dosset', Hugh Walpole's 'Spanish Dusk', Gordon Craig on 'Melodrama' and Wilbur Cross's review of two books on Thomas Hardy. See also Appendix IV below. Reading notes (Berg, RN 1.12) (*VWRN* XII). Reprinted: *CDB, CE.*

2 – I.e. Newcastle.

3 – There are several places called Wolverton in England, but the one meant here is probably what is now a constituent town of Milton Keynes; although it was a medieval settlement, the newer area was built for the railways in the nineteenth century.

4 – See an unsigned article by LW, 'Social Types. A Parliament of Women', *Nation*, 21 June 1913, p. 456: 'This Northern delegate, a typical working-class woman both in speech and appearance, spoke with passionate and yet restrained earnestness in favour of the resolution. She told with an eloquent

simplicity, which made her speech a work of art, how, as a child, she had learnt from her father to believe that the one hope for the working classes was to forget their differences and to work together loyally for the same ideals and the same ends. Then she paused, and told the delegates that she did not wish her words to influence their votes: if they had come prepared to vote against the resolution they should do so; but then they should go home and think over what she had said, and, if it convinced them, they should return to Congress next year and vote in favour of the resolution. "We can wait," she said, "we can wait. We women have waited years, thousands of years, even to be able to discuss things like this. We can wait."' This passage is quoted by LW in *Beginning Again: An Autobiography of the Years 1911–1918* (Hogarth Press, 1964), pp. 107–8. See also another unsigned article by LW on the Congress, 'A Democracy of Working Women', *New Statesman*, 21 June 1913, pp. 328–9. Although he states that one of his articles in the *Manchester Guardian* in June 1913 on the Congress was read by the Webbs (*Beginning Again*, p. 114), it was probably the Fabian *New Statesman* piece that impressed them. There were two anonymous detailed reports of the Congress in the *Manchester Guardian* on 11 and 12 June, and, while some 25 movers and seconders of motions were listed, none of the names and places of origin mentioned by VW appears.

5 – The National President for 1912–13 was Mrs Wimhurst and for 1913–14 Mrs Essery: see Jean Gaffin and David Thoms, *Caring & Sharing: The Centenary History of the Co-operative Women's Guild* (2nd ed., Holyoake Books, 1993), p. 275; and the *Manchester Guardian*, 11 and 12 June 1913, pp. 6 and 11, respectively.

6 – I.e. Kidd. See also n. 27.

7 – I.e. Lilian Harris (d. 1949 or 1950), Cashier of the Guild from 1893, Assistant Secretary, 1902–21, and Davies's lifelong companion. LW included her tract, 'The Position of Employees in the Co-operative Movement', in his collection *Fabian Essays on Co-operation* (Fabian Society, 1923).

8 – The Woolfs attended a meeting of the Guild in June 1922 in the Brighton Pavilion, at which Davies addressed the meeting as an honoured guest, 'all in grey, but with a dash of kingfisher blue about the bonnet' (*II VW Letters*, no. 1259, [7 June 1922], to Janet Case).

9 – Wolfgang Amadeus Mozart (1756–91); Paul Cézanne (1839–1906).

10 – *Life as We Have Known It* (Hogarth Press, 1931), 'A Childhood in the Fens about 1850–60' by the late Mrs Burrows, p. 109.

11 – See *ibid.*, p. 114, which has: 'Betty Rollet'.

12 – See *ibid.*, 'Memories of Seventy Years' by Mrs Layton, p. 14.

13 – See *ibid.*, p. 12.

14 – See *ibid.*, 'A Childhood in the Fens', pp. 111–12.

15 – See *ibid.*, 'Memories of Seventy Years', p. 9.

16 – *Ibid.*, p. 15.

17 – *Ibid.*, p. 18, which has: 'I was at first very frightened of the bees'.

18 – *Ibid.*, 'A Felt Hat Worker' by Mrs Scott, J.P., p. 87, which has: 'We had to be at work by 7 a.m., and you could see the day break over the hills, and they are always such a comfort and help.'

19 – See *ibid.*, pp. 87–8.

20 – See *ibid.*, 'Books Read by Various Guildswomen: Extracts from Letters Written in 1927', p. 115 (from Mrs Hood, J.P.), which has: 'can you tell me of any good history of the French Revolution, not Carlyle's, please'; cf. p. 123. Charles Dickens (1812–70); Robert Burns (1759–96); Sir Walter Scott (1771–1832); Henry George (1839–97), American writer on social questions whose most famous book is *Progress and Poverty* (1879; Hogarth Press published a condensed edition in 1953); Edward Bulwer-Lytton (1803–73); for VW on Ella Wheeler Wilcox (1850–1919), American poet, see 'Wilcoxiana', *III VW Essays*; for VW on Alice Meynell (1847–1922), poet and journalist, see 'Hearts of Controversy', *II VW Essays*; Thomas Carlyle (1795–1881), *History of the French Revolution* (1837), for VW on whom see specifically 'More Carlyle Letters', *I VW Essays*; Bertrand Russell (1872–1970), *The Problem of China* (G. Allen & Unwin, 1922); William Morris (1834–96); for VW on Percy Bysshe Shelley (1792–1822), see 'Shelley and Elizabeth Hitchener', *I VW Essays*, and 'Not One of Us', *IV VW Essays*; for VW on Florence L. Barclay (1862–1921), popular novelist, see 'A Letter to a Lady in Paraguay', *VI VW Essays*, Appendix; Samuel Butler (1835–1902), *The Notebooks of Samuel Butler* (1912), for VW on whom see 'A Man with a View', *II VW Essays*, 'The Way of All Flesh', *III VW Essays*, and 'The Two Samuel Butlers', *IV VW Essays*.

21 – See *Life as We Have Known It*, 'A Felt Hat Worker', p. 87.

22 – Quoted in Margaret Llewelyn Davies, *The Women's Co-operative Guild. 1883–1904* (Women's Co-operative Guild, 1904), p. 10; and see p. 9: 'April 15th. We now number seven.' Alice Sophia Acland, *née* Cunningham (1849–1935), Lady Acland from 1919; Guild Secretary, 1883–4; President, 1884–6.

23 – *Life as We Have Known It*, 'A Felt Hat Worker', p. 97; Hayfield, on the edge of the Derbyshire Peak District is near Whaley Bridge. Mrs Scott was not a midwife but, at this period, a 'sickness visitor for an Approved Society' (p. 96).

24 – *Ibid.*, 'Memories of Seventy Years', p. 13, which has: 'As we went past we saw three ladies . . . fancy work. We were rude enough to look through the fence to admire their pretty dresses, and were told to go about our business.'

25 – Daniel Defoe (1660?–1731).

26 – Quoted in *Life as We Have Known It*, 'A Childhood in the Fens', p. 111.

27 – Quoted *ibid.*, 'A Guild Office Clerk' contributed by the editor, p. 76, and see p. 73: 'An exceptional woman – Harriet A. Kidd – worked in the Guild Office from 1906 to 1917, when she died.'

On Being Ill

Considering how common illness is, how tremendous the spiritual change that it brings, how astonishing, when the lights of health go down, the undiscovered countries that are then disclosed, what wastes and deserts of the soul a slight attack of influenza brings to view, what precipices and lawns sprinkled with bright flowers a little rise of temperature reveals, what ancient and obdurate oaks are uprooted in us by the act of sickness, how we go down into the pit of death and feel the waters of annihilation close above our heads and wake thinking to find ourselves in the presence of the angels and the harpers when we have a tooth out and come to the surface in the dentist's arm-chair and confuse his 'Rinse the mouth – rinse the mouth' with the greeting of the Deity stooping from the floor of Heaven to welcome us[2] – when we think of this, as we are so frequently forced to think of it, it becomes strange indeed that illness has not taken its place with love and battle and jealousy among the prime themes of literature. Novels, one would have thought, would have been devoted to influenza; epic poems to typhoid; odes to pneumonia; lyrics to tooth-ache. But no; with a few exceptions – De Quincey attempted something of the sort in *The Opium Eater*; there must be a volume or two about disease scattered through the pages of Proust[3] – literature does its best to maintain that its concern is with the mind; that the body is a sheet of plain glass through which the soul looks straight and clear, and, save for one or two passions such as desire and greed, is null, and negligible and non-existent. On the contrary, the very opposite is true. All day, all night the body intervenes; blunts or sharpens, colours or discolours, turns to wax in the warmth of June, hardens to tallow in the murk of February. The creature within can only gaze through the pane – smudged or rosy; it cannot separate off from the body like the sheath of a knife or the pod of a pea for a single instant; it must go through the whole unending procession of changes, heat and cold, comfort and discomfort, hunger and satisfaction, health and illness, until there comes the inevitable catastrophe; the body smashes itself to smithereens, and the soul (it is said) escapes. But of all this daily drama of the body there is no record. People write always of the doings of the mind; the thoughts that come to it; its noble plans; how the mind has civilised the universe. They show it ignoring the body in the philosopher's turret; or kicking the body, like an old leather football, across leagues of snow and desert in the pursuit of conquest or discovery. Those great wars which the body wages with the mind a slave to it, in the solitude of the bedroom against the assault of fever or the oncome of melancholia, are neglected. Nor is the reason far to seek. To look these things squarely in the face would need the courage of a lion tamer; a robust philosophy; a reason rooted in the bowels of the earth. Short of these, this monster, the body, this miracle, its pain, will soon make us taper into mysticism, or rise, with rapid beats of the wings, into the raptures of transcendentalism. The public would say that a novel devoted to influenza lacked plot; they would complain that there was no love in it – wrongly however, for illness often takes on the disguise of love, and plays the same odd tricks. It invests certain faces with divinity, sets us to wait, hour after hour, with pricked ears for the creaking of a stair, and wreathes the faces of the absent (plain enough in health, Heaven knows) with a new significance, while the mind concocts a thousand legends and romances about them for which it has neither time nor taste in health. Finally, to hinder the description of illness in literature, there is the poverty of the language. English, which can express the thoughts of Hamlet and the tragedy of Lear, has no words for the shiver and the headache. It has all grown one way. The merest schoolgirl, when she falls in love, has Shakespeare or Keats to speak her mind for her; but let a sufferer try to describe a pain in his head to a doctor and language at once runs dry. There is nothing ready made for him. He is forced to coin words himself, and, taking his pain in one hand, and a lump of pure sound in the other (as perhaps the people of Babel did in the beginning), so to crush them together that a brand new word in the end drops out. Probably it will be something laughable. For who of English birth can take liberties with the language? To us it is a sacred thing and therefore doomed to die, unless the Americans, whose genius is so much happier in the making of new words than in the disposition of the old, will come to our help and set the springs aflow.[4] Yet it is not only a new language that we need, more primitive, more sensual, more obscene, but a new hierarchy of the passions; love must be deposed in favour of a temperature of 104;[5] jealousy give place to the pangs of sciatica; sleeplessness play the part of villain, and the hero become a white liquid with a sweet taste – that mighty Prince with the moths' eyes and the feathered feet, one of whose names is Chloral.

But to return to the invalid. 'I am in bed with influenza' – but what does that convey of the great experience; how the world has changed its shape; the tools of business grown remote; the sounds of festival become romantic like a merry-go-round heard across far fields; and friends have changed, some putting on a strange beauty, others deformed to the squatness of toads, while the whole landscape of life lies remote and fair, like the shore seen from a ship far out at sea, and he is now exalted on a peak and needs no help from man or God, and now grovels supine on the floor glad of a kick from a housemaid – the experience cannot be imparted and, as is always the way with these dumb things, his own suffering serves but to wake memories in his friends' minds of *their* influenzas, *their* aches and pains which went unwept last February, and now cry aloud, desperately, clamorously, for the divine relief of sympathy.

But sympathy we cannot have. Wisest Fate says no.[6] If her children, weighted as they already are with sorrow, were to take on them that burden too, adding in imagination other pains to their own, buildings would cease to rise; roads would peter out into grassy tracks; there would be an end of music and of paintings; one great sigh alone would rise to Heaven, and the only attitudes for men and women would be those of horror and despair. As it is, there is always some little distraction – an organ grinder at the corner of the hospital, a shop with book or trinket to decoy one past the prison or the workhouse, some absurdity of cat or dog to prevent one from turning the old beggar's hieroglyphic of misery into volumes of sordid suffering; and thus the vast effort of sympathy which those barracks of pain and discipline, those dried symbols of sorrow, ask us to exert on their behalf, is uneasily shuffled off for another time. Sympathy nowadays is dispensed chiefly by the laggards and failures, women for the most part (in whom the obsolete exists so strangely side by side with anarchy and newness), who, having dropped out of the race, have time to spend upon fantastic and unprofitable excursions; C. L. for example, who, sitting by the stale sickroom fire, builds up, with touches at once sober and imaginative, the nursery fender, the loaf, the lamp, barrel organs in the street, and all the simple old wives' tales of pinafores and escapades; A. R., the rash, the magnanimous, who, if you fancied a giant tortoise to solace you or a theorbo[7] to cheer you, would ransack the markets of London and procure them somehow, wrapped in paper, before the end of the day; the frivolous K. T.,[8] who, dressed in silks and feathers, powdered and painted (which takes time too) as if for a banquet of

Kings and Queens, spends her whole brightness in the gloom of the sick room, and makes the medicine bottles ring and the flames shoot up with her gossip and her mimicry. But such follies have had their day; civilisation points to a different goal; and then what place will there be for the tortoise and the theorbo?

There is, let us confess it (and illness is the great confessional), a[a] childish outspokenness in illness; things are said, truths blurted out, which the cautious respectability of health conceals. About sympathy for example – we can do without it. That illusion of a world so shaped that it echoes every groan, of human beings so tied together by common needs and fears that a twitch at one wrist jerks another, where however strange your experience other people have had it too, where however far you travel in your own mind someone has been there before you – is all an illusion. We do not know our own souls, let alone the souls of others. Human beings do not go hand in hand the whole stretch of the way. There is a virgin forest in each; a snowfield[b] where even the print of birds' feet is unknown. Here we go alone, and like it better so. Always to have sympathy, always to be accompanied, always to be understood would be intolerable. But in health the genial pretence must be kept up and the effort renewed – to communicate, to civilise, to share, to cultivate the desert, educate the native, to work together by day and by night to sport. In illness this make-believe ceases. Directly the bed is called for, or, sunk deep among pillows in one chair, we raise our feet even an inch above the ground on another, we cease to be soldiers in the army of the upright; we become deserters. They march to battle. We float with the sticks on the stream; helter-skelter with the dead leaves on the lawn, irresponsible and disinterested and able, perhaps for the first time for years, to look round, to look up – to look, for example, at the sky.

The first impression of that extraordinary spectacle is strangely overcoming. Ordinarily to look at the sky for any length of time is impossible. Pedestrians would be impeded and disconcerted by a public sky-gazer. What snatches we get of it are mutilated by chimneys and churches, serve as a background for man, signify wet weather or fine, daub windows gold, and, filling in the branches, complete the pathos of dishevelled autumnal plane trees in autumnal squares. Now, lying recumbent, staring straight up, the sky is discovered to be something so different from this that really it is a little shocking. This then has been going on all the time without our knowing it! – this incessant making up of shapes and casting them down, this buffeting of clouds together, and drawing vast trains of ships and waggons from North to South, this incessant ringing up and down of curtains of light and shade, this interminable experiment with gold shafts and blue shadows, with veiling the sun and unveiling it, with making rock ramparts and wafting them away – this endless activity, with the waste of Heaven knows how many million horse power of energy, has been left to work its will year in year out. The fact seems to call for comment and indeed for censure. Ought not some one to write to *The Times*? Use should be made of it. One should not let this gigantic cinema play perpetually to an empty house. But watch a little longer and another emotion drowns the stirrings of civic ardour. Divinely beautiful it is also divinely heartless. Immeasurable resources are used for some purpose which has nothing to do with human pleasure or human profit. If we were all laid prone, stiff, still the sky would be experimenting with its blues and its golds. Perhaps[c] then, if we look down at something very small and close and familiar, we shall find sympathy. Let us examine the rose. We have seen it so often flowering in bowls, connected it so often with beauty in its prime, that we have forgotten how it stands, still and steady, throughout an entire afternoon in the earth. It preserves a demeanour of perfect dignity and self-possession. The suffusion of its petals is of inimitable rightness. Now perhaps one deliberately falls; now all the flowers, the voluptuous purple, the creamy, in whose waxen flesh the spoon has left a swirl of cherry juice; gladioli; dahlias; lilies, sacerdotal, ecclesiastical; flowers with prim cardboard collars tinged apricot and amber, all gently incline their heads to the breeze – all, with the exception of the heavy sunflower, who proudly acknowledges the sun at midday and perhaps at midnight rebuffs the moon. There they stand; and it is of these, the stillest, the most self-sufficient of all things that human beings have made companions;[d] these that symbolise their passions, decorate their festivals, and lie (as if *they* knew sorrow) upon the pillows of the dead. Wonderful to relate,[9] poets have found religion in nature; people live in the country to learn virtue from plants. It is in their indifference that they are comforting. That snowfield of the mind, where man has not trodden, is visited by the cloud, kissed by the falling petal, as, in another sphere, it is the great artists, the Miltons and the Popes, who console not by their thought of us but by their forgetfulness.

Meanwhile, with the heroism of the ant or the bee, however indifferent the sky or disdainful the flowers, the army of the upright marches to battle. Mrs Jones catches her train. Mr Smith mends his motor. The cows are driven home to be milked. Men thatch the roof. The dogs bark. The rooks, rising in a net, fall in a net upon the elm trees.[10] The wave of life flings itself out indefatigably. It is only the recumbent who know what, after all, Nature is at no pains to conceal – that she in the end will conquer; heat will leave the world; stiff with frost we shall cease to drag ourselves about the fields; ice will lie thick upon factory and engine; the sun will go out. Even so, when the whole earth is sheeted and slippery, some undulation, some irregularity of surface will mark the boundary of an ancient garden, and there, thrusting its head up undaunted in the starlight, the rose will flower, the crocus will burn. But with the hook of life still in us still we must wriggle. We cannot stiffen[e] peaceably into glassy mounds. Even the recumbent spring up at the mere imagination of frost about the toes and stretch out to avail themselves of the universal hope – Heaven, Immortality. Surely, since men have been wishing all these ages, they will have wished something into existence; there will be some green isle for the mind to rest on even if the foot cannot plant itself there. The co-operative imagination of mankind must have drawn some firm outline. But no. One opens the *Morning Post* and reads the Bishop of Lichfield on Heaven.[11] One watches the church-goers file into those gallant temples where, on the bleakest day, in the wettest fields, lamps will be burning, bells will be ringing, and however the autumn leaves may shuffle and the winds sigh outside, hopes and desires will be changed to beliefs and certainties within. Do they look serene? Are their eyes filled with the light of their supreme conviction? Would one of them dare leap straight into Heaven off Beachy Head?[12] None but a simpleton would ask such questions; the little company of believers lags and drags and strays. The mother is worn; the father tired. As for imagining Heaven, they have no time. Heaven-making must be left to the imagination of the poets. Without their help we can but trifle – imagine Pepys[13] in Heaven, adumbrate little interviews with celebrated people on tufts of thyme, soon fall into gossip about such of our friends as have stayed in Hell, or, worse still, revert again to earth and choose, since there is no harm in choosing, to live over and over, now as man, now as woman, as sea-captain, or court lady, as Emperor or farmer's wife, in splendid cities and on remote moors, at the time of Pericles or Arthur, Charlemagne, or George the Fourth[14] – to live and live till we have lived out those embryo lives which attend about us in early youth until 'I' suppressed them. But 'I' shall not, if wishing can alter it, usurp Heaven too, and condemn us, who have played our parts here as William or Alice to remain William or Alice for ever. Left to ourselves we speculate thus carnally. We need the poets to imagine for us. The duty of Heaven-making should be attached to the office of the Poet Laureate.

Indeed it is to the poets that we turn. Illness makes us disinclined for the long campaigns that prose exacts. We cannot command all our faculties and keep our reason and our judgment and our memory at attention while chapter swings on top of chapter, and, as one settles into place, we must be on the watch for the coming of the next, until the whole structure – arches, towers, and battlements – stands firm on its foundations. *The Decline and Fall of the Roman Empire* is not the book for influenza, nor *The Golden Bowl* nor *Madame Bovary*.[15] On the other hand, with responsibility shelved and reason in the abeyance – for who is going to exact criticism from an invalid or sound sense from the bed-ridden? – other tastes assert themselves; sudden, fitful, intense. We rifle the poets of their flowers. We break off a line or two and let them open in the depths of the mind:

> and oft at eve
> Visits the herds along the twilight meadows[16]

> wandering in thick flocks along the mountains
> Shepherded by the slow unwilling wind.[17]

Or there is a whole three volume novel to be mused over in a verse of Hardy's or a sentence of La Bruyère.[18] We dip in Lamb's Letters – some prose writers are to be read as poets – and find 'I am a sanguinary murderer of time, and would kill him inchmeal just now. But the snake is vital,'[19] and who shall explain the delight? or open Rimbaud and read

> O saisons o châteaux
> Quelle âme est sans défauts?[20]

and who shall rationalise the charm? In illness words seem to possess a mystic quality. We grasp what is beyond their surface meaning, gather instinctively this, that, and the other – a sound, a colour, here a stress, there a pause – which the poet, knowing words to be meagre in comparison with ideas, has strewn about his page to evoke, when collected, a state of mind which neither words can express nor the reason explain. Incomprehensibility has an enormous power over us in illness, more legitimately perhaps than the upright will allow. In health meaning has encroached upon sound. Our intelligence domineers over our senses. But in illness, with the police off duty, we creep beneath some obscure poem by Mallarmé or Donne,[21] some phrase in Latin or Greek, and the words give out their scent and distil their flavour, and then, if at last we grasp the meaning, it is all the richer for having come to us sensually first, by way of the palate and the nostrils, like some queer odour. Foreigners, to whom the tongue is strange, have us at a disadvantage. The Chinese must know the sound of *Antony and Cleopatra* better than we do.

Rashness is one of the properties of illness – outlaws that we are – and it is rashness that we need in reading Shakespeare. It is not that we should doze in reading him, but that, fully conscious and aware, his fame intimidates and bores, and all the views of all the critics dull in us that thunder clap of conviction which, if an illusion, is still so helpful an illusion, so prodigious a pleasure, so keen a stimulus in reading the great. Shakespeare is getting flyblown; a paternal government might well forbid writing about him, as they put his monument at Stratford beyond the reach of scribbling fingers. With all this buzz of criticism about, one may hazard one's conjectures privately, make one's notes in the margin; but, knowing that someone has said it before, or said it better, the zest is gone. Illness, in its kingly sublimity, sweeps all that aside and leaves nothing but Shakespeare and oneself. What with his overweening power and our overweening arrogance, the barriers go down, the knots run smooth, the brain rings and resounds with *Lear* or *Macbeth*, and even Coleridge himself squeaks like a distant mouse.

But enough of Shakespeare – let us turn to Augustus Hare. There are people who say that even illness does not warrant these transitions; that the author of *The Story of Two Noble Lives* is not the peer of Boswell;[22] and if we assert that short of the best in literature we like the worst – it is mediocrity that is hateful – will have none of that either. So be it. The law is on the side of the normal. But for those who suffer a slight rise of temperature the names of Hare and Waterford and Canning[23] ray out as beams of benignant lustre. Not, it is true, for the first hundred pages or so. There, as so often in these fat volumes, we flounder and threaten to sink in a plethora of aunts and uncles. We have to remind ourselves that there is such a thing as atmosphere; that the masters themselves often keep us waiting intolerably while they prepare our minds for whatever it may be – the surprise, or the lack of surprise. So Hare, too, takes his time; the charm steals upon us imperceptibly; by degrees we become almost one of the family, yet not quite, for our sense of the oddity of it all remains, and share the family dismay when Lord Stuart[24] leaves the room – there was a ball going forward – and is next heard of in Iceland. Parties, he said, bored him – such were English aristocrats before marriage with intellect had adulterated the fine singularity of their minds. Parties bore them; they are off to Iceland. Then Beckford's[25] mania for castle building attacked him; he must lift a French *château* across the Channel,[g] and erect pinnacles and towers to use as servants' bedrooms at vast expense, upon the borders of a crumbling cliff, too, so that the housemaids saw their brooms swimming down the Solent, and Lady Stuart was much distressed, but made the best of it and began, like the high-born lady that she was, planting evergreens in the face of ruin. Meanwhile the daughters, Charlotte and Louisa, grew up in their incomparable loveliness, with pencils in their hands, for ever sketching, dancing, flirting, in a cloud of gauze. They are not very distinct it is true. For life then was not the life of Charlotte and Louisa. It was the life of families, of groups. It was a web, a net, spreading wide and enmeshing every sort of cousin, dependant, and old retainer. Aunts – Aunt Caledon, Aunt Mexborough – grandmothers – Granny Stuart, Granny Hardwicke[26] – cluster in chorus, and rejoice and sorrow and eat Christmas dinner together, and grow very old and remain very upright, and sit in hooded chairs cutting flowers it seems out of coloured paper. Charlotte married Canning and went to India; Louisa married Lord Waterford and went to Ireland. Then letters begin to cross vast spaces in slow sailing ships and communication becomes still more protracted and verbose, and there seems no end to the space and the leisure of those early Victorian days, and faiths are lost and the life of Hedley Vicars revives them; aunts catch cold but recover; cousins marry; there are the Irish famine and the Indian Mutiny,[27] and both sisters remain to their great, but silent, grief without children to come after them. Louisa, dumped down in Ireland with Lord Waterford at the hunt all day, was often very lonely; but she stuck to her post, visited the poor, spoke words of comfort ('I am sorry indeed to hear of Anthony Thompson's loss of mind, or rather of memory; if, however, he can understand sufficiently to trust solely in our Saviour, he has enough')[28] and sketched and sketched. Thousands of notebooks were filled with pen and ink drawings of an evening, and then the carpenter stretched sheets for her and she designed frescoes for schoolrooms, had live sheep into her bedroom, draped gamekeepers in blankets, painted Holy Families in abundance, until the great Watts exclaimed that here was Titian's peer and Raphael's master![29] At that Lady Waterford laughed (she had a generous, benignant sense of humour); and said that she was nothing but a sketcher; had scarcely had a lesson in her life – witness her angel's wings scandalously unfinished. Moreover, there was her father's house forever falling into the sea; she must shore it up; must entertain her friends; must fill her days with all sorts of charities, till her Lord came home from hunting, and then, at midnight often, she would sketch him with his knightly face half hidden in a bowl of soup, sitting with her sketchbook under a lamp beside him. Off he would ride again, stately as a crusader, to hunt the fox, and she would wave to him and think each time, what if this should be the last? And so it was, that winter's morning; his horse stumbled; he was killed. She knew it before they told her, and never could Sir John Leslie[30] forget, when he ran downstairs on the day of the burial, the beauty of the great lady standing to see the hearse depart, nor, when he came back, how[b] the curtain, heavy, mid-Victorian, plush perhaps, was all crushed together where she had grasped it in her agony.[31]

a – On Being Ill: '(confessional) a'.
b – On Being Ill: 'snow | field'.
c – On Being Ill: golds Perhaps'.
d – On Being Ill: 'compions;' (pace VW in n. 1).
e – On Being Ill: 'can- | notstiffen'.
f – On Being Ill: 'snall'.
g – On Being Ill: 'channel,'.
h – The last two sentences as amended by VW (see n. 31): '. . . it was, one winter's . . . downstairs the day they buried him, the . . . standing by the window to see . . . back again, how'.

1 – Originally published in the New Criterion, January 1926, (Kp4 C270), and then reprinted in a shorter version with revisions as 'Illness: An Unexploited Mine' in Forum, April 1926 (see IV VW Essays and Appendix I), this essay was published early in November 1930 in a slightly revised

form under its original title as a Hogarth Press book (*Kp4 A14*). For responses from VW's friends to the essay, see *IV VW Essays*, p. 328 n. 1. See in addition the introductory paragraph to 'Melodious Meditations', *II VW Essays*: 'The poets of the eighteenth century were fond of making their verses sound dignified by spelling certain qualities with a capital letter ... we sometimes fancy that these antiquated ghosts merely took ship to America, lodged with the best families, and now walk abroad in those essays which the Americans write so frequently upon Old Age, Old Maids, On Being Ill, and Sorrow.'

On Being Ill was one of the last of the Hogarth Press books to be hand-printed by VW and LW: 'I never print now' (*III VW Diary*, 13 April 1929); 'I must take up printing again' (*ibid.*, 13 May 1929). 'On 29 May [1930] the Hogarth Press installed a new printing machine; the old one was given to Vita Sackville-West, and is still at Sissinghurst Castle' (*ibid.*, p. 30, editor's note). On 16 June VW wrote: 'Ethel Smyth drops in; dropped in yesterday for instance, when I was so methodically devoting my morning to finishing the last page of type setting: On Being Ill' (*ibid.*). The Woolfs originally intended to produce only 125 copies, but the edition was heavily over-subscribed and they printed 250. It seems likely, however, that VW's exaggeration on 2 September that she was signing her name '600 times' on 'handmade paper' (*ibid.*) refers to the limited edition of 550 copies of *Beau Brummell*: see p. 111 above, n. 1. She wrote to an unidentified complainer on 10 December 1930: 'As one of the guilty parties I bow down to your strictures upon the printing of On Being Ill. I agree that the colour is uneven, the letters not always clear, the spacing inaccurate, and the word "campion" should read "companion". ¶ All I have to urge in excuse is that printing is a hobby carried on in the basement of a London house; that as amateurs all instruction in the art was denied us; that we have picked up what we know for ourselves; and that we practise printing in the intervals of lives that are otherwise engaged. In spite of all this, I believe that you can already sell your copy for more than the guinea you gave, as the edition is largely over subscribed, so that though we have not satisfied your taste, we hope that we have not robbed your purse. ¶ Yours, with apologies' (*IV VW Letters*, no. 2284). And on 5 January 1931 she wrote to Ethel Smyth: 'I swear I will go through the article and find the bad grammar this evening; I daresay all my own inaccuracy' (*ibid.*, no. 2306). Reprinted: *Mom, CE*.

Where the text printed above differs from the Hogarth Press edition, these divergences are given in the notes above.

2 – Cf. *I VW Diary*, 7 March 1919: 'Yesterday I had a tooth out, to which the bag of a large abscess had attached itself. Harrison showed it me, previous to putting it in the fire; a token of much pain he said. The queer little excursion into the dark world of gas always interests me. I

came home in the Tube wondering whether any of the people there suspected its existence. I wake from it, or seem rather to step out of it & leave it to go on hurtling through space while the world of Harrison & Dr Trueby engages my attention – "Open your mouth, Mrs Woolf – Now let me take out this little bit of wood." Suppose one woke instead to find the deity himself by one's side! The Christians believe it, I suppose.' See also 'Gas', *VI VW Essays*, Appendix.

3 – For VW on Thomas De Quincey (1785–1859) and his *Confessions of an English Opium Eater* (1822, 1856), see 'Impassioned Prose', *IV VW Essays*; Marcel Proust (1871–1922).

4 – Cf. 'On Not Knowing French' above, esp. n. 2.

5 – A normal body temperature is about 98.6°F or 37°C, so 104°F is equivalent to 40°C.

6 – 'But wisest Fate sayes no / This must not yet be so,' from 'Ode on the Morning of Christ's Nativity' (1629) by John Milton (1608–74), *OBEV*, no. 307, p. 315. This was one of Leslie Stephen's favourite poems: see 'Impressions of Sir Leslie Stephen', *I VW Essays*.

7 – A 'large kind of lute with a double neck . . . much in vogue in the 17th century' (*OED*).

8 – The identities of C. L., A. R. and K. T. remain undiscovered (conjecture suggests Charlotte Leaf, Anne [Thackeray] Ritchie and Katherine Thynne, as marginally possible candidates).

9 – The conventional translation of 'mirabile dictu': see, e.g., Virgil's *Aeneid*, i, l. 439.

10 – The image of flocking rooks rising and falling net-like is a favourite of VW's. See, e.g., *The Waves* (Hogarth Press, 1931), p. 158: 'the rooks rising and falling, and catching the elm-trees in their net'.

11 – The Bishop of Lichfield, 1913–37, was the Rt Rev. John Augustine Kempthorne (1864–1946). His views on heaven have regrettably not been discovered in the pages of the *Morning Post*.

12 – Chalk cliff 530 ft above sea level near Eastbourne, notorious for suicides. It is little more than 15 miles from the Woolfs' house in Rodmell.

13 – Samuel Pepys (1633–1703).

14 – Pericles (c. 500–429 BC), Athenian statesman; Arthur, mythical king of the Britons said to have been born in the fifth century; Charlemagne (742 or 747–814), king of the Franks; George IV (1762–1830), reigned from 1820.

15 – Edward Gibbon (1737–94), *The Decline and Fall of the Roman Empire* (1776, 1781, 1788); for VW on him, see 'The Historian and "The Gibbon"' and 'Reflections at Sheffield Place', *VI VW Essays*; for VW on Henry James (1843–1916), *The Golden Bowl* (1904), see 'Mr Henry James's Novel', *I VW Essays*; Gustave Flaubert (1821–80), *Madame Bovary* (1856).

16 – Milton, *A Mask (Comus)* (1637), ll. 843–4, spoken by the Attendant Spirit, concerning Sabrina.

17 – Percy Bysshe Shelley (1792–1822), *Prometheus Unbound; A Lyrical Drama, in Four Acts* (1820), II. i, spoken by Asia, in *The Poetical Works of Percy Bysshe Shelley*, ed. Mrs [Mary Wollstonecraft] Shelley (4 vols, Edward Moxon, 1839), vol. ii, p. 54.

18 – For VW on Thomas Hardy (1840–1928), see 'The Novels of Thomas Hardy' below, and 'Half of Thomas Hardy', *IV VW Essays*; Jean de La Bruyère (1645–96).

19 – *The Letters of Charles Lamb*, ed. Alfred Ainger (2 vols, Macmillan, 1904), vol. ii, Letter cccxcii, 25 July 1829, to Bernard Barton, p. 240.

20 – (Jean Nicholas) Arthur Rimbaud (1854–91), *Une Saison en enfer* (1873), which VW probably read in *Oeuvres de Arthur Rimbaud: Vers et proses*, ed. Paterne Berrichon, Préface de Paul Claudel [1868–1955] (*Mercure de France*, 1912), p. 295, which has: 'O saisons, ô chateaux!'

21 – Stéphane Mallarmé (1842–98) upon whose *Vers et Prose* (Perrin, 1893), probably in 1921, VW made reading notes (MHP, B 2d) (*VWRN XXXVIII*). Roger Fry lectured on Mallarmé at 37 Gordon Square on 1 May 1929, but VW did not attend (see *VI VW Letters*, no. 2026a and fn.). John Donne (1572–1631).

22 – Augustus J. C. Hare (1834–1903), *The Story of Two Noble Lives, Being Memorials of Charlotte, Countess Canning, and Louisa, Marchioness of Waterford* (3 vols, George Allen, 1893); James Boswell (1740–95), *Life of Samuel Johnson* (1791).

23 – Henry Beresford (1811–59), 3rd Marquis of Waterford, reformed reprobate and landowner; Charles John, Earl Canning (1812–62), governor-general and first viceroy of India.

24 – Sir Charles Stuart, later Baron Stuart of Rothesay (1779–1845), diplomat, and his wife Lady Elizabeth Margaret, *née* Yorke (1789–1867), were the parents of Charlotte (1817–61), wife of Earl Canning, and Louisa (1818–91), wife of the 3rd Marquis of Waterford. For Lord Stuart's sudden departure for Iceland, see *Story of Two Noble Lives*, vol. i, ch. iii, p. 196.

25 – William Beckford (1760–1844), creator of Fonthill Abbey and author of *Vathek* (1786). For Lord Stuart's folly, see *Story of Two Noble Lives*, vol. i, ch. ii, p. 170.

26 – Catherine, Countess of Caledon (1786–1863); Anne, Countess of Mexborough; Hon. Louisa, Lady Stuart; Elizabeth, Countess of Hardwicke.

27 – Hedley Shafto Johnstone Vicars (1826–55), an officer killed in the Crimea who underwent an extreme religious conversion in 1851, and whose story was told by Catherine M. Marsh in *The Memorials of Captain Hedley Vicars* (1855). The Irish Potato Famine, 1845–51; the Indian Mutiny began on 10 May 1857.

28 – *Story of Two Noble Lives*, vol. iii, ch. viii, Letter from Louisa, Lady Waterford to Canon T. F. Parker, 30 July 1859, p. 43, which has: 'I am sorry indeed to learn . . .'

29 – *Ibid.*, ch. x, p. 281: 'It was in this year that Mr. Watts and Mr. Burne Jones besought Lady Waterford to paint one of her designs on a sufficient scale and with a degree of completeness which should satisfy posterity that "in 1866 there lived an artist as great as Venice ever knew."' G. F. Watts (1817–1904); Edward Burne-Jones (1833–98). Titian (c. 1485–1576); Raphael (Sanzio) (1483–1520).

30 – Sir John (formerly Captain) Leslie, otherwise unidentified.

31 – See *Story of Two Noble Loves*, vol. iii, ch. viii, p. 24: 'This blind told me of her intense suffering, for there was the clutch of her fingers, as they wrinkled the surface in her anguish. There was writing in the folds caused by her squeeze that told more than words could of the heart's despair.'

On 26 October 1930, just before publication, VW sent a copy of *On Being Ill* to Geoffrey Keynes 'with corrections in the last sentence': 'I have only altered a few words near the end – though I know there's a whole sentence crumpled up some where. But if I begin, there will be no end, so I give you full liberty to re-write it for me!' (uncollected letter in *The Gates of Memory*, by Geoffrey Keynes [Oxford University Press, 1981], pp. 116–17). This correction was 'a sentence, which had to be crushed together, because of printing difficulties' (uncollected letter of 24 September [1930], to Geoffrey Keynes, in *Virginia Woolf, 1882–1941: An Exhibition, Organised by S. J. Hills, in Cambridge University Library and Opened on 2nd October 1991*, item 88). Keynes's copy (no. 5 of 250) is now held by the Rare Books Dept, Cambridge University Library.

I am Christina Rossetti

On the 5th of December Christina Rossetti celebrated her centenary, or, more properly speaking, we celebrated it for her, perhaps not a little to her distress, for she was one of the shyest of women, and to be spoken of, as we shall certainly speak of her, would have caused her acute discomfort. Nevertheless, it is inevitable; centenaries are inexorable; talk of her we must. We shall read her life; we shall read her letters; we shall study her portraits, speculate about her diseases of which she had a great variety; and rattle the drawers of her writing table, which are for the most part empty. Let us begin with the biography – for what could be more amusing? As everybody knows the fascination of reading biographies is irresistible. No sooner have we opened the pages of Miss Sandar's careful and competent book[2] than the old illusion returns. Here is the past and all its inhabitants miraculously sealed up as in a magic tank, and all we have to do is to look and to look and to listen and to listen and soon the little figures – for they are rather under life size – will begin to move and speak, and as they move we shall arrange them in all sorts of patterns of which they were ignorant,[3]

Here then is Hallam Street, Portland Place, about the year 1830; and here are the Rossettis, an Italian family consisting of father and mother and four small children.[4] The street was unfashionable and the home rather poverty stricken, but the poverty did not matter, for being foreigners the Rossettis did not care much about the customs and conventions of the usual middle class British family. They kept themselves to themselves, dressed as they liked, entertained Italian exiles, among them organ grinders and other distressed compatriots, and made ends meet by teaching and writing and other odd jobs. By degrees Christina detached herself from the family group. It is plain that she was a quiet and observant child, with her own way of life already fixed in her head – she was to write – but all the more did she admire the superior competence and energy of her elders. Soon we begin to surround her with a few friends and to endow her with a few characteristics. She detested parties. She dressed anyhow. She liked her brother's friends and little gatherings of young artists and poets, who were to reform the world, rather to her amusement, for although so sedate, she was also whimsical and freakish and liked making fun of people who took themselves too seriously. And though she meant to be a poet she had very little of the vanity and stress of young poets; her verses seemed to have formed themselves quickly in her mind and she did not worry very much what was said of them because in her own mind she knew that, on the whole, they were good. She had also immense powers of admiration – for her mother, for example, who was so quiet, so sagacious, so simple and so sincere; and for her elder sister Maria, who had no taste for painting and none for poetry, but was for that very reason perhaps more vigorous and energetic in daily life. For example Maria always refused to visit the Mummy Room at the British Museum because she said that the Day of Resurrection might suddenly dawn, and it would be very unseemly if the corpses had to put on immortality under the gaze of mere sightseers – a reflection which had not struck Christina, but seemed to her admirable.[5] Here, of course, we, who are outside the tank, enjoy a hearty laugh, but Christina, who is inside the tank and exposed to all its heats and currents, thought her sister's conduct admirable. Indeed, if we look at her a little more closely we shall see that something dark and hard, like a kernel, had already formed in the centre of Christina Rossetti's being.

It was religion, of course. Even when she was quite a girl her life-long absorption in the relation of the soul with God had taken possession of her. Her sixty-four years might seem outwardly spent in Hallam Street and Endsleigh Gardens and Torrington Square,[6] but in reality she dwelt in some curious region where the spirit strives toward an unseen God – in her case a dark God, a harsh God, a God who decreed that all the pleasures of the world were hateful to Him. The theatre was hateful, the opera was hateful, nakedness was hateful – so that when her friend, Miss Thompson, painted naked figures in her pictures she had to tell Christina that they were fairies,[7] but Christina saw through the imposture – everything in Christina's life radiated from that knot of agony and intensity in the centre. Her belief regulated her life in the smallest particulars. It taught her that chess was wrong, but that whist and cribbage did not matter. But also it interfered in the most tremendous questions of her heart. She loved James Collinson[8] and James Collinson loved her, but he was a Roman Catholic, and so she refused him; he became a member of the Church of England and she accepted him. Finally, however, for he was a slippery man, he wabbled back to Rome; and Christina, though it broke her heart and for ever shadowed her life, cancelled the engagement. Years afterward another and, it seems, better founded, prospect of happiness presented itself. Charles Cayley[9] proposed to her. But, alas, this abstract and erudite man who shuffled about the world in a state of absent-minded disha-bille and translated the gospel into Iroquois and asked smart ladies at a party 'whether they were interested in the Gulf Stream,'[10] and for a present gave Christina a sea mouse preserved in spirits,[11] was, not unnat-urally, a free thinker.[12] He, too, Christina put from her. Though 'no woman ever loved a man more deeply,'[13] she would not be the wife of a sceptic. She who loved the 'obtuse and furry'[14] – the wombats and toads and mice of the earth – and called Charles Cayley 'my blindest buzzard, my special mole,'[15] admitted no moles, wombats, buzzards or Cayleys to her heaven.

So one might go on looking into the tank and listening to its queer sound forever. There is no limit to the strangeness and terror and oddity of a world like this. But just as we are wondering which cranny of this extraordinary territory to explore next, the principal figure intervenes. It is as if a fish, whose unconscious gyrations we had been watching in and out of reeds round and round rocks, suddenly dashed at the glass and broke it. A tea party is the occasion. For some reason Christina went to a party given by Mrs Virtue Tebbs.[16] What happened there is unknown – perhaps something was said in a casual frivolous way about poetry. At any rate 'suddenly there uprose from a chair and paced forward into the centre of the room a little woman dressed in black who announced solemnly "I am Christina Rossetti!" and having so said returned to her chair.'[17] With those words the glass is broken. 'Yes,' she seems to say, 'I am a poet. You who pretend to honour my centenary are no better than those chattering women at Mrs Tebbs's tea party. Here you go rambling among unimportant trifles, rattling my writing table drawers, making fun of the Mummies and Maria and my love affairs, when all I care for you to know is here. Behold this green volume. It is a copy of my collected works. It costs four shillings and sixpence. Read that.' And so she returns to her chair.

How absolute and unaccommodating these poets are! Poetry, they say, has nothing to do with life. Mummies and wombats, Hallam Street and omnibuses, James Collinson and Charles Cayley, sea mice and Mrs Virtue Tebbs, Torrington Square and Endsleigh Gardens and even the vagaries of religious belief are irrelevant, extraneous, superfluous, unreal. It is poetry that matters. The only question of any interest is whether their poetry is good or bad. But this question of the goodness and badness of poetry, one might point out if only to gain time, is one of the greatest difficulty. Very little of value has been said about poetry since the world began. The judgment of contemporaries is almost always wrong. For example, most of the poems which figure in Christina Rossetti's complete works were rejected by editors. Her annual income from her poetry was for many years about £10. On the other hand, the works of Jean Ingelow, as she noted sardonically, went into eight editions.[18] There were of course among her contemporaries one or two poets and one or two critics whose judgment must be respectfully consulted. But what very different impressions they seem to gather from the same works! For instance, when Swinburne read her poetry he exclaimed: 'I have always thought that nothing more glorious in poetry has ever been written,'[19] and went on to say of her 'New Year Hymn' 'that it was touched as with the fire and bathed as in the light of sunbeams, tuned as to chords and cadences of a refluent sea of music beyond reach of harp and organ, large echoes of the serene and sonorous tides of heaven.'[20]

Then Professor Saintsbury comes with his vast learning and examines 'Goblin Market' and reports that 'The metre of the principal poem ("Goblin Market") may be best described as a dedoggerelised Skeltonic, with the gathered music of the various metrical progress since Spenser, utilised in the place of the wooden rattling of the followers of Chaucer. There may be discerned in it the same inclination toward line irregularity which has broken out at different times in the Pindaric of the late seventeenth and earlier eighteenth centuries and in the rhymelessness of Sayers earlier and of Mr. Arnold later.'[21]

And then there is Sir Walter Raleigh.

'I think she is the best poet alive. . . . The worst of it is you cannot lecture on really pure poetry any more than you can talk about the ingredients of pure water – it is adulterated, methylated, sanded poetry that makes the best lectures. The only thing that Christina makes me want to do, is cry, not lecture.'[22] It would appear then that there are many schools of criticism, the refluent sea of music school; the line irregularity school; the cry but do not criticise school, and that if we follow them all we shall only become confused. Better perhaps read for one's self, expose the mind bare to the poem, and transcribe in all its haste and imperfection whatever may be the result of the impact. Perhaps in that case it might run something like this: O Christina Rossetti, I have humbly to confess that though I know many of your poems by heart, I have not read your works from cover to cover. I have not followed your course and traced your development. I doubt indeed that you had a development; brain and senses were not unequally commingled. You were an instinctive poet. You saw the world from the same angle always. Years and the traffic of the mind with men and books did not affect you in the least. You carefully ignored any book that could shake your faith or any human being who could trouble your instincts. You were wise perhaps. Your instinct was so sure, so direct, so intense, that it produced poems that sing like music in one's ears – like a melody by Mozart or an air by Gluck.[23] Yet for all its symmetry, yours was a complex song. When you struck your harp many strings sounded together. Like all instinctives, you had a keen sense of the visual beauty of the world. Your poems are full of gold dust and poppies and 'sweet geraniums' varied brightness';[24] your eye noted incessantly how rushes are 'velvet-headed,'[25] and lizards have a 'strange metallic mail,'[26] and the 'scorpion jerked in the sand, black as black iron, or dusty pale'[27] – your eye observed with a precision and a joy that must have surprised Christina the Anglo-Catholic. But to her you owed perhaps the fixity and the sadness of your song. One feels the pressure of a tremendous faith circling and clamping together these little songs. Perhaps they owe to it their solidity, their unity. No sooner have you feasted on beauty with your eye, but your mind tells you that beauty is vain and beauty passes. Death and oblivion and rest lap about your songs like a dark wave. And then a sound of scurrying and laughter is heard. One hears the patter of animals' feet, and the odd guttural notes of rooks and the snufflings of obtuse furry animals grunting and nosing. For you were not a pure saint by any means. When Watts Dunton[28] heard your voice for the first time behind a door he realised that fact in a moment. You pulled legs; you tweaked noses. You were at war with all humbug and pretence. In one word you were an artist. Modest and demure you were though drastic, and sure of your gift. A firm hand pruned your lines; a sharp ear tested your sounds. Nothing soft, otiose, irrelevant cumbered your page. And thus was kept open, even when you wrote idly, tinkling bells for your own diversion, a pathway for the descent of that fiery visitant who came now and then and fused your lines into indissoluble connection. Here, at random: —

> But bring me poppies brimmed with sleepy death,
>   And ivy choking what it garlandeth,
>   And primroses that open to the moon.[29]

It is not for a prose writer to say how those lines came together; all he knows is that they will not be put asunder. Indeed, so strange is the constitution of things that some of the poems you wrote in your little back room will be found adhering in perfect symmetry when the proud pinnacles of the Albert memorial are dust; and our remote posterity will be singing

> When I am dead, my dearest,[30]
> Come to me in the silence of the night;
>   Come in the speaking silence of a dream[31]

when Torrington Square is a reef of coral perhaps and the fishes shoot in and out where your bedroom windows used to be; or perhaps the forest will have reclaimed those pavements and the wombat and the ratel will be shuffling on soft sagacious feet among the green undergrowth that will then tangle the area railings. In view of all this, and to return to your biography, had I been present when Mrs Virtue

Tebbs gave her party, and had a short elderly woman in black risen to her feet and advanced to the middle of the room, I should certainly have committed some indiscretion – have broken a paper knife or smashed a tea cup – from sheer gratitude and emotion when she said: 'I am Christina Rossetti.'

1 – A signed review in the *N&A*, 6 December 1930, and, with variations, including the title in quotation marks, in the *NYHT*, 14 December 1930, (*Kp4* C328), of *The Life of Christina Rossetti* by Mary F. Sandars (Hutchinson, n.d. [1930]) and of *Christina Rossetti & her Poetry* by Edith Birkhead (George G. Harrap, 1930). The latter book was published after the review was written: see letter of 3 December 1930 from Edmund Blunden, literary editor of the *N&A*, to VW, held in the Holland Library (MASC Cage 674), Washington State University. It is clear that the *NYHT* version predates the *N&A* version, which in turn was later revised and entitled '"I am Christina Rossetti"' for *CR2*. The reader is referred to p. 554 below, where the revised version, together with the *N&A* variants in the form of endnotes, is printed in its place as part of *CR2*. The issue of the *N&A* also contained: Edmund Blunden's 'World of Books' column, 'A Masterly Series', on the 'Oxford Poets' series published by OUP; a letter to the editor on a further proposal for the censorship of books; book reviews by Angus Davidson and Raymond Mortimer; and J. B. Sterndale Bennett on 'Bloomsbury Village' ('Lamb's Conduit Street . . . is the "Main Street" of Bloomsbury . . . there is still a pretty little statue of Rebecca at the well, facing the entrance to the Foundling gardens'). VW read and wanted to write about Christina Rossetti (1830–94) as far back as December 1906: see *I VW Letters*, nos 309, 317, 319, 320, 331. She got the opportunity two years later: see 'Letters of Christina Rossetti', *I VW Essays*. A stumbling block for VW was Rossetti's religion, and in 1918 she burst out: 'Christina has the great distinction of being a born poet, as she seems to have known very well herself. But if I were bringing a case against God she is one of the first witnesses I should call. It is melancholy reading. First she starved herself of love, which meant also life; then of poetry in deference to what she thought her religion demanded. There were two good suitors. The first indeed had his peculiarities. He had a conscience. She could only marry a particular shade of Christian. He could only stay that shade for a few months at a time. Finally he developed Roman Catholicism & was lost. Worse still was the case of Mr Collins [i.e. Cayley] – a really delightful scholar – an unwor[l]dly recluse – a single minded worshipper of Christina, who could never be brought into the fold at all. On this account she could only visit him affectionately in his lodgings, which she did to the end of her life [*his* life; he died in 1883]. Poetry was castrated too. She would set herself to do the psalms into verse; & to make all her poetry subservient to the Christian doctrines. Consequently, as I think, she starved into austere emaciation, a very fine original gift, which

only wanted licence to take to itself a far finer form than, shall we say, Mrs Browning's. She wrote very easily; in a spontaneous childlike kind of way one imagines, as is the case generally with a true gift; still undeveloped. She has the natural singing power. She thinks too. She has fancy. She could, one is profane enough to guess, have been ribald & witty. And, as a reward for all her sacrifices, she died in terror, uncertain of salvation. I confess though that I have only turned her poetry over, making my way inevitably to the ones I knew already' (*I VW Diary*, 4 [5?] August 1918). On 1 March 1927, Christina Rossetti is referred to several times in *O Holograph*, in a discussion on the changing nature of patronage (MS 247, 248); she was merely mentioned in passing in *O*, pp. 261-2. In October 1930, VW was writing her article: 'My brain is too energetic; it works; it throws off an article on Christina Rossetti; & girds itself up to deal with this & that' (*III VW Diary*, 15 October 1930; see also p. 323, editor's fn.: the 'page between the entries for 11 and 15 October is given up to part of a draft' of this essay 'which VW has crossed through, noting in the margin: "Written here by mistake"'). Reading Notes (Berg, RN 1.22) (*VWRN XXII*).

2 – Not referenced in the *NYHT*.

3 – *Sic*. Cf. *N&A* version, p. 554

4 – Gabriele Pasquale Giuseppe Rossetti (1783–1854) and Frances Mary Lavinia, *née* Polidori (1800–86), and their children, Maria Francesca (1827–76), Gabriel Charles Dante (later Dante Gabriel, 1828–82), William Michael (1829–1919), and Christina Georgina. They lived at 38 Charlotte Street, now rebuilt and renamed (there is a plaque for Dante Gabriel at 110 Hallam Street).

5 – See *Life*, p. 89.

6 – Christina lived at 30 Torrington Square from 1876 until her death; there is a plaque for her there. Before that, she lived with her mother and sister at 56 Euston Square; the south side of Euston Square was renamed Endsleigh Gardens in 1880.

7 – See *Life*, pp. 229–30.

8 – James Collinson (1825–81), 'an indifferent artist', for a time one of the Pre-Raphaelite Brotherhood (*Life*, pp. 59, 69, 72). See *Life*, p. 69: 'As Christina had only accepted Collinson's suit on the understanding of his being an English Churchman, so when he re-declared himself a Catholic she revoked her troth. This she did with deep sorrow and reluctance, and only at the bidding of a supposed duty', quoted from *Some Reminiscences of William Michael Rossetti* (2 vols, Brown Langham, 1906), vol. i, p. 73.

9 – Charles Bagot Cayley (d. 6 December 1883, *aetat* 60), an official in the Patent Office; see *Life*, pp. 93, 94.

10 – *Life*, p. 96.

11 – On 2 January 1877, *ibid.*, p. 208.

12 – See *ibid.*, p. 140: 'when questioned Charles Cayley allowed that he was not a Churchman, or orthodox in his beliefs'.

13 – Quoted *ibid.*, p. 141, from *Some Reminiscences*, vol. i, p. 315; in both places the comment concludes: 'or more constantly.'

14 – 'One like a wombat prowled obtuse and furry, / One like a ratel tumbled hurry scurry', 'Goblin Market', quoted in *Life*, p. 106; also in *The Poetical Works of Christina Georgina Rossetti*, with memoir and notes &c. by William Michael Rossetti (Macmillan, 1904), p. 2.

15 – 'My blindest buzzard that I know, / My special mole . . .', 'A Sketch', quoted in *Life*, p. 138; *Poetical Works*, p. 368. 'On August 15th, 1864, she wrote "A Sketch" which William Rossetti in his notes to her poems says he is sure refers to Charles Cayley' (*Life*, p. 137; see *Poetical Works*, p. 484).

16 – See A. M. W. Stirling, *Life's Little Day* (Thornton Butterworth, 1924), p. 215: Mrs Tebbs was 'the sister of [D. G.] Rossetti's friend, John Seddon, the architect, [who] married Mr. Virtue Tebbs'.

17 – *Life*, p. 130, where it is misquoted; *Life's Little Day*, p. 216, concludes: 'returned to her seat'.

18 – Jean Ingelow (1820–97), novelist and poet, whose most famous poem now is probably her popular ballad 'The High Tide on the Coast of Lincolnshire, 1571' (1863). See *Life*, p. 135: 'Christina Rossetti made the acquaintance of Jean Ingelow in 1864, but after that only met her a few times'; and, quoting Rossetti, 'I have just received a present of Jean Ingelow's 8th edition: imagine my feelings of envy and humiliation.'

19 – Quoted in *Life*, p. 123.

20 – Quoted *ibid.*; see A[lgernon] C[harles] Swinburne [1837–1909], *Essays and Studies* (Chatto & Windus, 1875), p. 175, fn. 1, where he quotes 'Passing away, saith the World, passing away:', the first line of 'Old and New Year Ditties', part 3, 'The Knell of the Year'; *Poetical Works*, p. 191.

21 – *Life*, p. 109, where it is misquoted; see George Saintsbury, *A History of English Prosody* (Macmillan, 1906–10), vol. iii (1910), p. 353: 'principal poem' should read 'title-poem'. *Goblin Market and Other Poems* (1862).

22 – Quoted in *Life*, pp. 111–12, from *The Letters of Sir Walter Raleigh (1879–1922)*, ed. Lady Raleigh (2 vols, Methuen, 1926), vol. i, Letter to his sister Alice, 11 January 1892, p. 164; for VW's review, see 'A Professor of Life', *IV VW Essays*.

23 – Wolfgang Amadeus Mozart (1756–91); Christoph Willibald (von) Gluck (1714–87).

24 – 'Summer' (dated 4 December 1845, and placed among the Juvenilia), *Poetical Works*, p. 86.

25 – 'From House to Home' (dated 19 November 1858), stanza 9, *ibid.*, p. 21: 'Where velvet-headed rushes rustling nod / And spill the morning dew.'

26 – *Ibid.*, stanza 8: 'My heath lay farther off, where lizards lived / In strange metallic mail, just spied and gone;'.
27 – 'The Prince's Progress' (dated 11 October 1861–March 1865), *ibid.*, p. 28:

> Only scorpions jerked in the sand,
> Black as black iron, or dusty pale;
> From point to point sheer rock was manned
> By scorpions in mail.

28 – Theodore Watts–Dunton (1832–1914).
29 – 'Looking Forward' (dated 8 June 1849), *Poetical Works*, concluding lines of stanza 2, p. 293.
30 – 'Song' (dated 12 December 1848), *ibid.*, p. 290, l.1.
31 – 'Echo' (dated 18 December 1854), *ibid.*, p. 314, ll. 1–2.

1931

All About Books

Your last letter ends with the following sentence: 'The cold profile of Mont Blanc; falling snow; peasants and pine trees; a string of stout fellows roped together with alpenstocks – such is the prospect from my window; so for pity's sake draw your chair to the fire, take your pen in your hand and write me a long, long letter all about books.' But you must realise that a long, long letter is apt to be exaggerated, inaccurate, and full of those irreticences and hyperboles which the voice of the speaker corrects in talk. A letter is not a review; it is not a considered judgment, but, on condition that you do not believe a word I say, I will scribble for an hour or two whatever comes into my head about books.

That it has been a very bad season goes without saying. The proof of it is that old Mr Baddeley[2] had read *Guy Mannering*[3] for the fifty-eighth time. Never was Jane Austen in greater demand. Trollope, Dickens, Carlyle and Macaulay[4] are all providing that solace, that security, that sense that the human heart does not change which our miserable age requires and our living authors so woefully fail to provide. When, therefore, the rumour spread that the diary of an old clergyman called Cole, who had gone to Paris in the autumn of 1765, was about to be published, and that Miss Waddell had put her brilliance and her erudition at our service, a purr of content and anticipation rose from half the arm-chairs of England. This Cole, moreover, was not anybody's Cole; he was Horace Walpole's Cole;[5] nor does it need any pedantic familiarity with history to be aware that the autumn of 1765 was for one old blind woman in Paris the most excruciating, the most humiliating, the most ecstatic of her life. At last Horace Walpole had come – after what snubs, what humiliations, what bitter disappointments! At last Madame du Deffand[6] would – not indeed see him in the flesh, but feel him with the spirit. He would be in the same room with her; he would talk his broken French; she would feel come over her that strange delight, that abasement, that ecstasy – call it not love, for love he would not have it called – which the presence of the elderly and elegant Horace never failed to inspire in a heart that had long out-lived any sensation but boredom, despair and[a] disgust. It was in that very autumn that Cole chose to visit Paris. Cole, it seemed probable since Walpole liked him, would have eyes in his head; certainly he had a diary in his portmanteau. What revelations might one not expect? What[b] confidences from one Englishman to another? And Horace Walpole was willing. Every day he sent his servant to ask Cole to dinner. And every day – it is incredible what the dead will do, but it is true – Cole preferred to go sightseeing. He went to Notre Dame; he went to the Sorbonne; he went to the Convent of that Virgin, to the Cathedral of this Saint. When he came home he sat down to digest and methodise[7] what he had seen. He was too tired to dine with Mr Walpole.[8] So instead of revelations we have information. 'On the right hand of the High Altar as one enters.[9] . . . The dome of this church is very beautiful.[10] . . . Over the door is a curious alto-relievo representing the Last Supper. . . .'[11] That is what he writes about, and, of course, about the habits of the natives. The habits of the natives are disgusting; the women hawk on the floor;[12] the forks are dirty;[13] the trees are poor;[14] the Pont Neuf is not a patch on London Bridge;[15] the cows are skinny;[16] morals are licentious; polish is good;[17] cabbages cost so much; bread is made of coarse flour; Mr Drumgold could not with patience mention the character of John James Rousseau;[18] the Coles are distantly related to the Herberts;[19] and a French turkey is about the size of an English hen. How natural it all is! How admirable Mr Cole would be at home in his own parish! How gladly we will read sixteen volumes about life in Bletchley if Miss Waddell will print them! But the present volume is nothing short of torture. 'Cole,' one is inclined to cry, 'if you don't give up sightseeing to-day, if you don't dine with Mr Walpole, if you don't report every word he says, leaving Drumgold out of it altogether, if you don't turn the talk somehow upon Madame du Deffand, if you don't somehow tell us more about one of the most curious affairs of the heart that was ever transacted, or failing that, rake up a few odds and ends of interest about that amazing society that was playing spillikins on the verge of revolution, we will –' But what can we do? The dead have no sense whatever of what is due to posterity. Mr Cole imperturbably pulls on his boots and proceeds to visit the Sorbonne.

Must one then read *Guy Mannering*, or take Jane Austen from the bookshelf? No, the advantage of belonging to a good library is that it is only upon very exceptional occasions that one need have recourse to the classics. New books, in fresh jackets, are delivered daily, and good books, too – *Things I Remember*, by the Grand Duchess Marie of Russia, for instance, a very terrible book; *The Diary of a Somersetshire Parson* – a very absorbing book; *By Guess and by God* – a very exciting yet infinitely childish book; and *Scrutinies*, a collection of critical essays by various writers.[20] But what kind of book is *Scrutinies*? That, indeed, I cannot tell you at the moment for the good reason that I have not read it; but you can guess from the title and a glance at the table of contents that it consists of articles by the tolerably young – Messrs Alec Brown, B. Higgins, Mary Butts, Jack Lindsay, P. Quennell, Sherard Vines, C. Saltmarshe, and so on, upon the tolerably old – Messrs Eliot, Huxley, Joyce, Lawrence, Sitwell, Strachey, and so on. And if I hesitate to read beyond the title page at present it is for the very sound and simple reason that it is so much pleasanter to look upon the young than upon the old, the young who are fresh and pliable, who have not stood out in the storm and stiff-ened[c] into attitudes and hardened into wrinkles. Beauty is theirs now, as soon the future will be theirs also. Let us, therefore, leave the figures of the elders where they stand and turn our bull's eye upon the advancing and victorious hordes of youth.

And what is our first impression as we look? A very strange one. How orderly they come! One could swear that they are all arrayed in troops, and all march in step, and all halt, charge and otherwise behave themselves under the command of officers mounted upon chargers. As far as one can see – a bull's eye, it must be admitted, is not a very steady or comprehensive weapon – there is not a single straggler or deserter among them; there is no dancing or disorder; no wild voice cries alone; no man or woman breaks the ranks and leaves the troop and takes to the wilderness stirring desire and unrest among the hearts of his companions. All is orderly, all is preconcerted.

If division there is, even that is regular. Camp is opposed to camp; the hostile parties separate, form, meet, fight, leave each other for dead upon the ground; rise, form and fight again. Classic is opposed to romantic; naturalist to metaphysic. Never was there such a sight since the world began. Never – as they come nearer this too becomes certain – were the young so well equipped as at present. No more respectable army has ever issued from the portals of the two great Universities – none more courageous, more instructed, more outspoken, more intolerant of humbug in all its forms, better fitted to deal pretence its death and falsity its finish – and yet (for all these flowers, of course, conceal a viper) there is a fatal defect; they do not lead, they follow. Where is the adventurous, the intolerant, the immensely foolish young man or woman who dares to be himself? He or she must, of course, be there. He or she will in time to come make himself known. But at present, since he always keeps the ranks, since if he fights he is careful, like Sir Walter Blunt in *Henry the Fourth*, to wear the armour of his king,[21] there is no knowing him at present from the seven hundred and fifty-five others who are similarly disguised.

If this is true, if there is now a uniformity and a drill and a discretion unknown before, what do you think can be the reason? In one word, and I have room for one only, and that is murmured in your private ear – education. Some years since, for reasons unknown, but presumably of value, it must have occurred to someone that the arts of reading and of writing can be taught. Degrees were given at the Universities to those who showed proficiency in their native tongue. And the teachers of the living language were not old and hoary; as fitted their subject they were young and supple. Persuasion sat on their tongues, and the taught, instead of mocking, loved their teachers. And the teachers took the manuscripts of the young and drew circles of blue chalk round this adjective and circles of red chalk round that adverb. They added in purple ink what Pope would have thought and what Wordsworth would have said.[22] And the young, since they loved their teachers, believed them. Hence it came about that, instead of knowing that the sun was in the sky and the bird on the branch, the young knew the whole course of English literature from one end to another; how one age follows another; and one influence cancels another; and one style is derived from another; and one phrase is better than another. They took service under their teachers instead of riding into battle alone. All their marriages – and what are the five years between twenty and twenty-five in the life of a writer but years of courtship and wedding, of falling in love with words and learning their nature, how[d] to mate them by one's own decree in sentences of one's own framing? – all their marriages were arranged in public; tutors introduced the couples; lecturers supervised the amours; and examiners finally pronounced whether the fruit of the union was blessed or the reverse. Such methods, of course, produce an erudite and eugenic offspring. But, one asks, turning over the honest, the admirable, the entirely sensible and unsentimental pages, where is love? Meaning by that, where is the sound of the sea and the red of the rose; where is music, imagery, and[e] a voice speaking from the heart?

That this is all great nonsense I am well aware. But what else can you expect in a letter? The time has come to open *Scrutinies* and begin to read – no, the time has come to rake out the cinders and go to bed.

a – NR: 'boredom and'.
b – NR: 'expect? What indiscretions? What'.
c – NR: '. . . old – the young who are fresh and pliable, who have not stiffened'.
d – NR: 'nature and how'.
e – NR: 'love? meaning by that where . . . rose, music, imagery and'.

1 – A signed review in the *NS&N*, 28 February 1931, and (with variations) in the *NR*, 15 April, (*Kp4* C329), of *A Journal of My Journey to Paris in the Year 1765* . . . by William Cole (1714–82), ed. Francis Griffin Stokes, with an introduction by Helen Waddell (Constable, 1931). The issue of the *NS&N* – the first amalgamation number of the *N&A* and the *New Statesman* – also contained: LW's review of D. S. Mirsky's *Russia: A Social History*; Dorothy Margaret Stuart on 'Milton and Prynne: Some New Light on the Secret History of the Commonwealth'; poems by Walter de la Mare and Edmund Blunden; and reviews of two novels published by the Hogarth Press: C. H. B. Kitchen's *The Sensitive One* and John Hampson's *Saturday Night at the Greyhound*. In the 'Special Literary Supplement' there was a one-page advertisement for the Hogarth Press (including VW's Uniform Edition), a review of Grand Duchess Marie of Russia's *Things I Remember* ('There is not a dull chapter in the book'), and an advertisement for *Scrutinies*, vol. ii. On 7 January 1931, VW wrote: 'I've stored a few ideas for articles: one on Gosse – the critic as talker; the armchair critic; one on Letters – one on Queens –' (*IV VW Diary*); editor's note 4: the '"armchair critic" [article] was probably that published as "All About Books"'. On 21 February VW wrote to Clive Bell who was in a Zurich eye hospital: 'Coles journey to France was a bitter disappointment however. I had promised to do it for the

first number of the New Statesman and Nation, but had to cry off and do an article, in the form of a letter to you instead' (*IV VW Letters*, no. 2330). There are no letters from Bell between 19 February 1930 and c. October 1931 in MHP, III. See also 'The Rev. William Cole: A Letter' below, and 'Two Antiquaries: Walpole and Cole', *VI VW Essays*. Reprinted (text from *NS&N*): *CDB, CE*.

2 – VW may have had in mind Welbore St Clair Baddeley (1856–1945), poet, dramatist, world traveller, amateur archaeologist and historian. The Stephens knew the family: see *PA*, 19 September 1897.

3 – Sir Walter Scott (1771–1832), *Guy Mannering* (1815).

4 – Jane Austen (1775–1817); Anthony Trollope (1815–82); Charles Dickens (1812–70); Thomas Carlyle (1795–1881); Thomas Babington Macaulay (1800–59).

5 – Horace Walpole (1717–97).

6 – Marie Anne de Vichy-Chamrond, marquise du Deffand (1697–1780). VW was reading her letters and discussing her with Lytton Strachey in January and February 1931: see *IV VW Letters*, nos 2304–5 and 2329, and see also *VWB*, no. 25 (May 2007), p. 8.

7 – See *Journal*, pp. 178–9: 'I was glad to get Home to sit down to my Dinner, & rest my Legs as well as to digest & methodize what I had seen in the Day.'

8 – See *ibid.*, 29 October 1765, p. 102. Cole dined with Walpole on 30 October (see p. 145), but on 31 October he wrote: 'I excused myself from dining with Mr Walpole this Day; & enjoyed myself by not stirring out anywhere' (p. 146). See also the introduction, pp. xx–xxi.

9 – See *ibid.*, p. 119: 'The Altar of the Chapel of the B. Virgin [in Notre Dame], on the right hand as you are going to enter the Choir, is really truly Magnificent . . .'

10 – See *ibid.*, p. 127: '. . . in the middle of the Church [at the Sorbonne] is a beautiful Dome'.

11 – *Ibid.*, p. 158, about the 'Abbey of St Germains des Prez'.

12 – See *ibid.*, p. 104, where women are not specifically mentioned, but see next note.

13 – See *ibid.*, pp. 270–1: 'having coarse ordinary Table Linen, & hardly clean, with dirty Spoons & Knives, was not so laudable: but what offended me more than all their Dirt, was the Beastliness of Madame [Eynhouts], who with all her affected Airs, was constantly hawking, & spitting upon the Floor, during the whole Time of Dinner.'

14 – See *ibid.*, pp. 37, 43–4.

15 – See *ibid.*, p. 48.

16 – See *ibid.*, p. 45.

17 – I.e. varnish; see *ibid.*, pp. 47–8.

18 – See *ibid.*, p. 67. Jean-Jacques Rousseau (1712–78).

19 – Including Lord Herbert of Cherbury (see 'The Poems [of] Lord Herbert of Cherbury', *III VW Essays*): see *Journal*, pp. 144–5.

20 – Grand Duchess Marie of Russia, *Things I Remember* (Cassell, 1930). John Skinner, *Journal of a Somerset Rector*, ed. Howard Coombs and Arthur N. Bax (John Murray, 1930); see 'The Rev. John Skinner', *CR2*. William Guy Carr, *By Guess and By God: The Story of the British Submarines in the War* (Hutchinson, 1930). *Scrutinies*, compiled by Edgell Rickword (2nd vol., Wishart, 1931; 1st vol., 1928); contributors included: Alex Brown on T. S. Eliot, Mary Butts on Aldous Huxley, Bertram Higgins on T. S. Eliot, Jack Lindsay on James Joyce, Peter Quennell on D. H. Lawrence, Christopher Saltmarshe on Lytton Strachey, Sherard Vines on Edith, Osbert and Sacheverell Sitwell. VW omits mention of William Empson (1906–84), who wrote about her (reprinted in *M&M*; and see Introduction). She would have had advance notice of the appearance of *Scrutinies*, for there were quarter-page advertisements for it in the *N&A* of 21 September (p. 801) and 12 October 1929 (p. 87, Literary Supplement), although VW was not among those listed as subjects.

21 – In *1Henry IV*, V, iii, Sir Walter Blunt, disguised as the king, is killed in battle by the Earl of Douglas.

22 – Alexander Pope (1688–1744); William Wordsworth (1770–1850).

Introductory Letter to Margaret Llewelyn Davies

When you asked me to write a preface to a book which you had collected of papers by working women I replied that I would be drowned rather than write a preface to any book whatsoever. Books should stand on their own feet, my argument was (and I think it is a sound one). If they need shoring up by a preface here, an introduction there, they have no more right to exist than a table that needs a wad of paper under one leg in order to stand steady. But you left me the papers, and, turning them over, I saw that on this occasion the argument did not apply; this book is not a book. Turning the pages, I began to ask myself what is this book then, if it is not a book? What quality has it? What ideas does it suggest? What old arguments and memories does it rouse in me? And as all this had nothing to do with an introduction or a preface, but brought you to mind and certain pictures from the past, I stretched my hand for a sheet of notepaper and wrote the following letter addressed not to the public but to you.

You have forgotten (I wrote) a hot June morning in Newcastle in the year 1913, or at least you will not remember what I remember, because you were otherwise engaged. Your attention was entirely absorbed by a green table, several sheets of paper, and a bell. Moreover you were frequently interrupted. There was a woman wearing something like a Lord Mayor's chain round her shoulders; she took her seat perhaps at your right; there were other women without ornament save fountain pens and despatch boxes – they sat perhaps at your left. Soon a row had been formed up there on the platform, with tables and inkstands and tumblers of water; while we, many hundreds of us, scraped and shuffled and filled the entire body of some vast municipal building beneath. The proceedings somehow opened. Perhaps an organ played. Perhaps songs were sung. Then the talking and the laughing suddenly subsided. A bell struck; a figure rose; a woman took her way from among us; she mounted a platform; she spoke for precisely five minutes; she descended. Directly she sat down another woman rose; mounted the platform; spoke for precisely five minutes and descended; then a third rose, then a fourth – and so it went on, speaker following speaker, one from the right, one from the left, one from the middle, one from the background – each took her way to the stand, said what she had to say, and gave place to her successor. There was something military in the regularity of the proceeding. They were like marksmen, I thought, standing up in turn with rifle raised to aim at a target. Sometimes they missed, and there was a roar of laughter; sometimes they hit, and there was a roar of applause. But whether the particular shot hit or missed there was no doubt about the carefulness of the aim. There was no beating the bush; there were no phrases of easy eloquence. The speaker made her way to the stand primed with her subject. Determination and resolution were stamped on her face. There was so much to be said between the strokes of the bell that she could not waste one second. The moment had come for which she had been waiting, perhaps for many months. The moment had come for which she had stored hat, shoes and dress – there was an air of discreet novelty about her clothing. But above all the moment had come when she was going to speak her mind, the mind of her constituency, the mind of the women who had sent her from Devonshire, perhaps, or Sussex, or some black mining village in Yorkshire to speak their mind for them in Newcastle.

It soon became obvious that the mind which lay spread over so wide a stretch of England was a vigorous mind working with great activity. It was thinking in June 1913 of the reform of the Divorce Laws; of the taxation of land values; of the Minimum Wage. It was concerned with the care of maternity; with the Trades Board Act; with the education of children over fourteen; it was unanimously of opinion that Adult Suffrage should become a Government measure – it was thinking in short about every sort of public question, and it was thinking constructively and pugnaciously. Accrington did not see eye to eye with Halifax, nor Middlesbrough with Plymouth. There was argument and opposition; resolutions were lost and amendments won. Hands shot up stiff as swords, or were pressed as stiffly to the side. Speaker followed speaker; the morning was cut up into precise lengths of five minutes by the bell.

Meanwhile – let me try after seventeen years to sum up the thoughts that passed through the minds of your guests, who had come from London and elsewhere, not to take part, but to listen – meanwhile what was it all about? What was the meaning of it? These women were demanding divorce, education, the vote – all good things. They were demanding higher wages and shorter hours – what could be more reasonable? And yet, though it was all so reasonable, much of it so forcible, some of it so humorous, a weight of discomfort was settling and shifting itself uneasily from side to side in your visitors' minds. All these questions – perhaps this was at the bottom of it – which matter so intensely to the people here, questions of sanitation and education and wages, this demand for an extra shilling, for another year at school, for eight hours instead of nine behind a counter or in a mill, leave me, in my own blood and bones, untouched. If every reform they demand was granted this very instant it would not touch one hair of my comfortable capitalistic head. Hence my interest is merely altruistic. It is thin spread and moon coloured. There is no life blood or urgency about it. However hard I clap my hands or stamp my feet there is a hollowness in the sound which betrays me. I am a benevolent spectator. I am irretrievably cut off from the actors. I sit here hypocritically clapping and stamping, an outcast from the flock. On top of this too, my reason (it was in 1913, remember) could not help assuring me that even if the resolution, whatever it was, were carried unanimously the stamping and the clapping was an empty noise. It would pass out of the open window and become part of the clamour of the lorries and the striving of the hooves on the cobbles of Newcastle beneath – an inarticulate uproar. The mind might be active; the mind might be aggressive; but the mind was without a body; it had no legs or arms with which to enforce its will. In all that audience, among all those women who worked, who bore children, who scrubbed and cooked and bargained, there was not a single woman with a vote. Let them fire off their rifles if they liked, but they would hit no target; there were only blank cartridges inside. The thought was irritating and depressing in the extreme.

The clock had now struck half-past eleven. Thus there were still then many hours to come. And if one had reached this stage of irritation and depression by half-past eleven in the morning, into what depths of boredom and despair would one not be plunged by half-past five in the evening? How could one sit out another day of speechifying? How could one, above all, face you, our hostess, with the information that your Congress had proved so insupportably exacerbating that one was going back to London by the very first train? The only chance lay in some happy conjuring trick, some change of attitude by which the mist and blankness of the speeches could be turned to blood and bone. Otherwise they remained intolerable. But suppose one played a childish game; suppose one said, as a child says, 'Let's pretend.' 'Let's pretend,' one said to oneself, looking at the speaker, 'that I am Mrs Giles of Durham City.' A woman of that name had just turned to address us. 'I am the wife of a miner. He comes back thick with grime. First he must have his bath. Then he must have his supper. But there is only a copper. My range is crowded with saucepans. There is no getting on with the work. All my crocks are covered with dust again. Why in the Lord's name have I not hot water and electric light laid on when middle-class women . . .' So up I jump and demand passionately 'labour saving appliances and housing reform.' Up I jump in the person of Mrs Giles of Durham; in the person of Mrs Phillips of Bacup; in the person of Mrs Edwards of Wolverton. But after all the imagination is largely the child of the flesh. One could not be Mrs Giles of Durham because one's body had never stood at the wash-tub; one's hands had never wrung and scrubbed and chopped up whatever the meat may be that makes a miner's supper. The picture therefore was always letting in irrelevancies. One sat in an armchair or read a book. One saw landscapes and seascapes, perhaps Greece or Italy, where Mrs Giles or Mrs Edwards must have seen slag heaps and rows upon rows of slate-roofed houses. Something was always creeping in from a world that was not their world and making the picture false and the game too much of a game to be worth playing.

It was true that one could always correct these fancy portraits by taking a look at the actual person – at Mrs Thomas, or Mrs Langrish, or Miss Bolt of Hebden Bridge. They were worth looking at. Certainly, there were no armchairs, or electric light, or hot water laid on in their lives; no Greek hills or Mediterranean bays in their dreams. Bakers and butchers did not call for orders. They did not sign a cheque to pay the weekly bills, or order, over the telephone, a cheap but quite adequate seat at the Opera. If they travelled it was on excursion day, with food in string bags and babies in their arms. They did not stroll through the house and say, that cover must go to the wash, or those sheets need changing. They plunged their arms in hot water and scrubbed the clothes themselves. In consequence their bodies were thick-set and muscular, their hands were large, and they had the slow emphatic gestures of people who are often stiff and fall tired in a heap on hard-backed chairs. They touched nothing lightly. They gripped papers and pencils as if they were brooms. Their faces were firm and heavily folded and lined with deep lines. It seemed as if their muscles were always taut and on the stretch. Their eyes looked as if they were always set on something actual – on saucepans that were boiling over, on children who were getting into mischief. Their lips never expressed the lighter and more detached emotions that come into play when the mind is perfectly at ease about the present. No, they were not in the least detached and easy and cosmopolitan. They were indigenous and rooted to one spot. Their very names were like the stones of the fields – common, grey, worn, obscure, docked of all splendours of association and romance. Of course they wanted baths and ovens and education and seventeen shillings instead of sixteen, and freedom and air and . . . 'And,' said Mrs Winthrop of Spennymoor, breaking into these thoughts with words that sounded like a refrain, 'we can wait.' . . . 'Yes,' she repeated, as if she had waited so long that the last lap of that immense vigil meant nothing for the end was in sight, 'we can wait.' And she got down rather stiffly from her perch and made her way back to her seat, an elderly woman dressed in her best clothes.

Then Mrs Potter spoke. Then Mrs Elphick. Then Mrs Holmes of Edgbaston. So it went on, and at last after innumerable speeches, after many communal meals at long tables and many arguments – the world was to be reformed, from top to bottom, in a variety of ways – after seeing Co-operative jams bottled and Co-operative biscuits made, after some song singing and ceremonies with banners, the new President received the chain of office with a kiss from the old President; the Congress dispersed; and the separate members who had stood up so valiantly and spoken out so boldly while the clock ticked its five minutes went back to Yorkshire and Wales and Sussex and Devonshire, and hung their clothes in the wardrobe and plunged their hands in the wash-tub again.

Later that summer the thoughts here so inadequately described, were again discussed, but not in a public hall hung with banners and loud with voices. The head office of the Guild, the centre from which speakers, papers, inkstands and tumblers, as I suppose, issued, was then in Hampstead. There, if I may remind you again of what you may well have forgotten, you invited us to come; you asked us to tell you how the Congress had impressed us. But I must pause on the threshold of that very dignified old house, with its eighteenth-century carvings and panelling, as we paused then in truth, for one could not enter and go upstairs without encountering Miss Kidd. Miss Kidd sat at her typewriter in the outer office. Miss Kidd, one felt, had set herself as a kind of watch-dog to ward off the meddlesome middle-class wasters of time who come prying into other people's business. Whether it was for this reason that she was dressed in a peculiar shade of deep purple I do not know. The colour seemed somehow symbolical. She was very short, but, owing to the weight which sat on her brow and the gloom which seemed to issue from her dress, she was also very heavy. An extra share of the world's grievances seemed to press upon her shoulders. When she clicked her typewriter one felt that she was making that instrument transmit messages of foreboding and ill-omen to an unheeding universe. But she relented, and like all relentings after gloom her's [sic] came with a sudden charm. Then we went upstairs, and upstairs we came upon a very different figure – upon Miss Lilian Harris, indeed, who, whether it was due to her dress which was coffee coloured, or to her smile which was serene, or to the ash-tray in which many cigarettes had come amiably to an end, seemed the image of detachment and equanimity. Had one not known that Miss Harris was to the Congress what the heart is to the remoter veins – that the great engine at Newcastle would not have thumped and throbbed without her – that she had collected and sorted and summoned and arranged that very intricate but orderly assembly of women – she would never have enlightened one. She had nothing whatever to do; she licked a few stamps and addressed a few envelopes – it was a fad of hers – that was what her manner conveyed. It was Miss Harris who moved the papers off the chairs and got the tea-cups out of the cupboard. It was she who answered questions about figures and put her hand on the right file of letters infallibly and sat listening, without saying very much, but with calm comprehension, to whatever was said.

Again let me telescope into a few sentences, and into one scene many random discussions on various occasions at various places. We said then – for you now emerged from an inner room, and if Miss Kidd was purple and Miss Harris was coffee coloured, you, speaking pictorially (and I dare not speak more explicitly) were kingfisher blue and as arrowy and decisive as that quick bird – we said then that the Congress had roused thoughts and ideas of the most diverse nature. It had been a revelation and a disillusionment. We had been humiliated and enraged. To begin with, all their talk, we said, or the greater part of it, was of matters of fact. They want baths and money. To expect us, whose minds, such as they are, fly free at the end of a short length of capital to tie ourselves down again to that narrow plot of acquisitiveness and desire is impossible. We have baths and we have money. Therefore, however much we had sympathised our sympathy was largely fictitious. It was æsthetic sympathy, the sympathy of the eye and of the imagination, not of the heart and of the nerves; and such sympathy is always physically uncomfortable. Let us explain what we mean, we said. The Guild's women are magnificent to look at. Ladies in evening dress are lovelier far, but they lack the sculpturesque quality that these working women have. And though the range of expression is narrower in working women, their few expressions have a force and an emphasis, of tragedy or humour, which the faces of ladies lack. But, at the same time, it is much better to be a lady; ladies desire Mozart and Einstein[2] – that is, they desire things that are ends, not things that are means. Therefore to deride ladies and to imitate, as some of the speakers did, their mincing speech and little knowledge of what it pleases them to call 'reality' is, so it seems to us, not merely foolish but gives away the whole purpose of the Congress, for if it is better to be working women by all means let them remain so and not undergo the contamination which wealth and comfort bring. In spite of this, we went on, apart from prejudice and bandying compliments, undoubtedly the women at the Congress possess something which ladies lack, and something which is desirable, which is stimulating, and yet very difficult to define. One does not want to slip easily into fine phrases about 'contact with life,' about 'facing facts' and 'the teaching of experience,' for they invariably alienate the hearer, and moreover no working man or woman works harder or is in closer touch with reality than a painter with his brush or a writer with his pen. But the quality that they have, judging from a phrase caught here and there, from a laugh, or a gesture seen in passing, is precisely the quality that Shakespeare would have enjoyed. One can fancy him slipping away from the brilliant salons of educated people to crack a joke in Mrs Robson's back kitchen. Indeed, we said, one of our most curious impressions at your Congress was that the 'poor,' 'the working classes,' or by whatever name you choose to call them, are not downtrodden, envious and exhausted; they are humorous and vigorous and thoroughly independent. Thus if it were possible to meet them not as masters or mistresses or customers with a counter between us, but over the washtub or in the parlour casually and congenially as fellow-beings with the same wishes and ends in view, a great liberation would follow, and perhaps friendship and sympathy would supervene. How many words must lurk in those women's vocabularies that have faded from ours! How many scenes must lie dormant in their eye which are unseen by ours! What images and saws and proverbial sayings must still be current with them that have never reached the surface of print, and very likely they still keep the power which we have lost of making new ones. There were many shrewd sayings in the speeches at Congress which even the weight of a public meeting could not flatten out entirely. But, we said, and here perhaps fiddled with a paper knife, or poked the fire impatiently by way of expressing our discontent, what is the use of it all? Our sympathy is fictitious, not real. Because the baker calls and we pay our bills with cheques, and our clothes are washed for us and we do not know the liver from the lights we are condemned to remain forever shut up in the confines of the middle classes, wearing tail coats and silk stockings, and called Sir or Madam as the case may be, when we are all, in truth, simply Johns and Susans. And they remain equally deprived. For we have as much to give them as they to give us – wit and detachment, learning and poetry, and all those good gifts which those who have never answered bells or minded machines enjoy by right. But the barrier is impassable. And nothing perhaps exacerbated us more at the Congress (you must have noticed at times a certain irritability) than the thought that this force of theirs, this smouldering heat which broke the crust now and then and licked the surface with a hot and fearless flame, is about to break through and melt us together so that life will be richer and books more complex and society will pool its possessions instead of segregating them – all this is going to happen inevitably, thanks to you, very largely, and to Miss Harris and to Miss Kidd – but only when we are dead.

It was thus that we tried in the Guild Office that afternoon to explain the nature of fictitious sympathy and how it differs from real sympathy and how defective it is because it is not based upon sharing the same important emotions unconsciously. It was thus that we tried to describe the contradictory and complex feelings which beset the middle-class visitor when forced to sit out a Congress of working women in silence.

Perhaps it was at this point that you unlocked a drawer and took out a packet of papers. You did not at once untie the string that fastened them. Sometimes, you said, you got a letter which you could not bring yourself to burn; once or twice a Guildswoman had at your suggestion written a few pages about her life. It might be that we should find these papers interesting; that if we read them the women would cease to be symbols and would become instead individuals. But they were very fragmentary and ungrammatical; they had been jotted down in the intervals of housework. Indeed you could not at once bring yourself to give them up, as if to expose them to other eyes were a breach of confidence. It might be that their crudity would only perplex, that the writing of people who do not know how to write – but at this point we burst in. In the first place, every Englishwoman knows how to write; in the second, even if she does not she has only to take her own life for subject and write the truth about that and not fiction or poetry for our interest to be so keenly roused that – that in short we cannot wait but must read the packet at once.

Thus pressed you did by degrees and with many delays – there was the war for example, and Miss Kidd died, and you and Lilian Harris retired from the Guild, and a testimonial was given you in a casket, and many thousands of working women tried to say how you had changed their lives – tried to say what they will feel for you to their dying day – after all these interruptions you did at last gather the papers together and finally put them in my hands early this May. There they were, typed and docketed with a few snapshots and rather faded photographs stuck between the pages. And when at last I began to read, there started up in my mind's eye the figures that I had seen all those years ago at Newcastle with such bewilderment and curiosity. But they were no longer addressing a large meeting in Newcastle from a platform, dressed in their best clothes. The hot June day with its banners and its ceremonies had vanished, and instead one looked back into the past of the women who had stood there; into the four-roomed houses of miners, into the homes of small shopkeepers and agricultural labourers, into the fields and factories of fifty or sixty years ago. Mrs Burrows, for example, had worked in the Lincolnshire fens when she was eight with forty or fifty other children, and an old man had followed the gang with a long whip in his hand 'which he did not forget to use.' That was a strange reflection. Most of the women had started work at seven or eight, earning a penny on Saturday for washing a doorstep, or twopence a week for carrying suppers to the men at the iron foundry. They had gone into factories when they were fourteen. They had worked from seven in the morning till eight or nine at night and had made thirteen or fifteen shillings a week. Out of this money they had saved some pence with which to buy their mother gin – she was often very tired in the evening and had borne perhaps thirteen children in as many years; or they fetched opium to assuage some miserable old woman's ague in the fens. Old Betty Rollett killed herself when she could get no more. They had seen half-starved women standing in rows to be paid for their match-boxes while they snuffed the roast meat of their employer's dinner cooking within. The smallpox had raged in Bethnal Green and they had known that the boxes went on being made in the sick-room and were sold to the public with the infection still thick on them. They had been so cold working in the wintry fields that they could not run when the ganger gave them leave. They had waded through floods when the Wash overflowed its banks. Kind old ladies had given them parcels of food which had turned out to contain only crusts of bread and rancid bacon rind. All this they had done and seen and known when other children were still dabbling in seaside pools and spelling out fairy tales by the nursery fire. Naturally their faces had a different look on them. But they were, one remembered, firm faces, faces with something indomitable in their expression. Astonishing though it seems, human nature is so tough that it will take such wounds, even at the tenderest age, and survive them. Keep a child mewed in Bethnal Green and she will somehow snuff the country air from seeing the yellow dust on her brother's boots, and nothing will serve her but she must go there and see the 'clean ground,' as she calls it, for herself. It was true that at first the 'bees were very frightening,' but all the same she got to the country and the blue smoke and the cows came up to her expectation. Put girls, after a childhood of minding smaller brothers and washing doorsteps, into a factory when they are fourteen and their eyes will turn to the window and they will be happy because, as the workroom is six storeys high, the sun can be seen breaking over the hills, 'and that was always such a comfort and help.' Still stranger, if one needs additional proof of the strength of the human instinct to escape from bondage and attach itself whether to a country road or to a sunrise over the hills, is the fact that the highest ideals of duty flourish in an obscure hat factory as surely as on a battlefield. There were women in Christies' felt hat factory, for example, who worked for 'honour.' They gave their lives to the cause of putting straight stitches into the bindings of men's hat brims. Felt is hard and thick; it is difficult to push the needle through; there are no rewards or glory to be won; but such is the incorrigible idealism of the human mind that there were 'trimmers' in those obscure places who would never put a crooked stitch in their work and ruthlessly tore out the crooked stitches of others. And as they drove in their straight stitches they reverenced Queen Victoria and thanked God, drawing up to the fire, that they were all married to good Conservative working men.

Certainly that story explained something of the force, of the obstinacy, which one had seen in the faces of the speakers at Newcastle. And then, if one went on reading these papers, one came upon other signs of the extraordinary vitality of the human spirit. That inborn energy which no amount of childbirth and washing up can quench had reached out, it seemed, and seized upon old copies of magazines; had attached itself to Dickens; had propped the poems of Burns against a dish cover to read while cooking. They read at meals; they read before going to the mill. They read Dickens and Scott and Henry George and Bulwer Lytton and Ella Wheeler Wilcox and Alice Meynell and would like 'to get hold of any good history of the French Revolution, not Carlyle's, please,' and B. Russell on China, and William Morris and Shelley and Florence Barclay and Samuel Butler's Note Books – they read with the indiscriminate greed of a hungry appetite, that crams itself with toffee and beef and tarts and vinegar and champagne all in one gulp. Naturally such reading led to argument. The younger generation had the audacity to say that Queen Victoria was no better than an honest charwoman who had brought up her children respectably. They had the temerity to doubt whether to sew straight stitches into men's hat brims should be the sole aim and end of a woman's life. They started arguments and even held rudimentary debating societies on the floor of the factory. In time the old trimmers even were shaken in their beliefs and came to think that there might be other ideals in the world besides straight stitches and Queen Victoria. Strange ideas indeed were seething in their brain. A girl, for instance, would reason, as she walked along the streets of a factory town, that she had no right to bring a child into the world if that child must earn its living in a mill. A chance saying in a book would fire her imagination to dream of future cities where there were to be baths and kitchens and washhouses and art galleries and museums and parks. The minds of working women were humming and their imaginations were awake. But how were they to realise their ideals? How were they to express their needs? It was hard enough for middle class women with some amount of money and some degree of education behind them. But how could women whose hands were full of work, whose kitchens were thick with steam, who had neither education nor encouragement nor leisure remodel the world according to the ideas of working women? It was then, I suppose, sometime in the eighties, that the Women's Guild crept modestly and tentatively into existence. For a time it occupied an inch or two of space in the *Co-operative News* which called itself The Women's Corner. It was there that Mrs Acland asked, 'Why should we not hold our Co-operative mothers' meetings, when we may bring our work and sit together, one of us reading some Co-operative work aloud, which may afterwards be discussed?' And on April 18th, 1883, she announced that the Women's Guild now numbered seven members. It was the Guild then that drew to itself all that restless wishing and dreaming. It was the Guild that made a central meeting place where formed and solidified all that was else so scattered and incoherent. The Guild must have given the older women, with their husbands and children, what 'clean ground' had given to the little girl in Bethnal Green, or the view of day breaking over the hills had given the girls in the hat factory. It gave them in the first place the rarest of all possessions – a room where they could sit down and think remote from boiling saucepans and crying children; and then that room became not merely a sitting-room and a meeting place, but a workshop where, laying their heads together, they could remodel their houses, could remodel their lives, could beat out this reform and that. And, as the membership grew, and twenty or thirty women made a practice of meeting weekly, so their ideas increased, and their interests widened. Instead of discussing merely their own taps and their own sinks and their own long hours and little pay, they began to discuss education and taxation and the conditions of work in the country at large. The women who had crept modestly in 1883 into Mrs Acland's sitting-room to sew and 'read some Co-operative work aloud,' learnt to speak out, boldly and authoritatively, about every question of civic life. Thus it came about that Mrs Robson and Mrs Potter and Mrs Wright at Newcastle in 1913 were asking not only for baths and wages and electric light, but also for adult suffrage and the taxation of land values and divorce law reform. Thus in a year or two they were to demand peace and disarmament and the spread of Co-operative principles, not only among the working people of Great Britain, but among the nations of the world. And the force that lay behind their speeches and drove them home beyond the reach of eloquence was compact of many things – of men with whips, of sick rooms where match-boxes were made, of hunger and cold, of many and difficult childbirths, of much scrubbing and washing up, of reading Shelley and William Morris and Samuel Butler over the kitchen table, of weekly meetings of the Women's Guild, of Committees and Congresses at Manchester and elsewhere. All this lay behind the speeches of Mrs Robson and Mrs Potter and Mrs Wright. The papers which you sent me certainly threw some light upon the old curiosities and bewilderments which had made that Congress so memorable, and so thick with unanswered questions.

But that the pages here printed should mean all this to those who cannot supplement the written word with the memory of faces and the sound of voices is perhaps unlikely. It cannot be denied that the chapters here put together do not make a book – that as literature they have many limitations. The writing, a literary critic might say, lacks detachment and imaginative breadth, even as the women themselves lacked variety and play of feature. Here are no reflections, he might object, no view of life as a whole, and no attempt to enter into the lives of other people. Poetry and fiction seem far beyond their horizon. Indeed, we are reminded of those obscure writers before the birth of Shakespeare who never travelled beyond the borders of their own parishes, who read no language but their own, and wrote with difficulty, finding few words and those awkwardly. And yet since writing is a complex art, much infected by life, these pages have some qualities even as literature that the literate and instructed might envy. Listen, for instance, to Mrs Scott, the felt hat worker: 'I have been over the hilltops when the snow drifts were over three feet high, and six feet in some places. I was in a blizzard in Hayfield and thought I should never get round the corners. But it was life on the moors; I seemed to know every blade of grass and where the flowers grew and all the little streams were my companions.' Could she have said that better if Oxford had made her a Doctor of Letters? Or take Mrs Layton's description of a match-box factory in Bethnal Green and how she looked through the fence and saw three ladies 'sitting in the shade doing some kind of fancy work.' It has something of the accuracy and clarity of a description by Defoe. And when Mrs Burrows brings to mind that bitter day when the children were about to eat their cold dinner and drink their cold tea under the hedge and the ugly woman asked them into her parlour saying, 'Bring these children into my house and let them eat their dinner there,' the words are simple, but it is difficult to see how they could say more. And then there is a fragment of a letter from Miss Kidd – the sombre purple figure who typed as if the weight of the world were on her shoulders. 'When I was a girl of seventeen,' she writes, 'my then employer, a gentleman of good position and high standing in the town, sent me to his home one night, ostensibly to take a parcel of books, but really with a very different object. When I arrived at the house all the family were away, and before he would allow me to leave he forced me to yield to him. At eighteen I was a mother.' Whether that is literature or not literature I do not presume to say, but that it explains much and reveals much is certain. Such then was the burden that rested on that sombre figure as she sat typing your letters, such were the memories she brooded as she guarded your door with her grim and indomitable fidelity.

But I will quote no more. These pages are only fragments. These voices are beginning only now to emerge from silence into half articulate speech. These lives are still half hidden in profound obscurity. To express even what is expressed here has been a work of labour and difficulty. The writing has been done in kitchens, at odds and ends of leisure, in the midst of distractions and obstacles – but really there is no need for me, in a letter addressed to you, to lay stress upon the hardship of working women's lives. Have not you and Lilian Harris given your best years – but hush! you will not let me finish that sentence and therefore, with the old messages of friendship and admiration, I will make an end.[3]

1 – Originally published as a signed essay, entitled 'Memories of a Working Women's Guild' (see p. 176 above; only material not in that version is annotated here), in the *Yale Review*, September 1930, (*Kp4* C326), it was revised as the introduction to *Life as We Have Known It* by Co-operative Working Women, ed. Margaret Llewelyn Davies, (*Kp4* B11), published by the Hogarth Press on 5 March 1931. Although the Yale University Press expressed an interest in the book, and VW drew it to the attention of her US publisher, Harcourt, Brace, it was not published in the USA until W. W. Norton & Company (NY) issued a reprint in 1975; see *IV VW Letters*, nos 2221, 2252, 2381. Indeed, even though the Hogarth Press had only 2000 copies printed, 350 sets of the sheets were still unbound in 1948 when the Guild agreed to buy them (bound) at 3s. per copy (see correspondence in Folder 62, Hogarth Press Archives, University of Reading).

Although Davies's letters to VW are not located, it is clear from VW's that Davies wanted a number of changes to the introduction before publication. On 25 August 1930 VW wrote: 'I told her [Ethel Smyth] about Margaret & my difficulties with the paper' (*III VW Diary*). On 28 August 1930 VW wrote to Smyth that she had 'to see about circumventing those intolerable hedgings that the Cooperative movement dictate' (*IV VW Letters*, no. 2224). On 14 September she wrote to Davies: 'I have at last gone through the Letter and your suggestions, and enclose it for your inspection. I have made some alterations, but I'm afraid by no means all. We both feel, for Leonard agrees, that if I made all the alterations you suggest, the point of view would be so much altered that it would no longer give my own meaning. And as the only merit of the letter is that it gives a particular persons impression we feel that it would be foolish to publish a modified version. One would simply fall between two stools. ¶ On the other hand we both think that you are very likely in the right, and that to publish my version would give pain and be misunderstood – and that of course is the last thing we want. Of this we think you and Lilian are the only judges, and therefore we suggest that you should look through the paper again and decide whether you think it can be printed with the alterations I have made. Honestly, I shall not mind in the very least (in fact in some ways I shall be rather relieved) if you say no. I have had my doubts from the first. Then, if you feel that it wont do, we suggest that we should send the papers to Barbara Stephen, unless you can think of anyone better, and ask her to write an introduction. We feel that there must be some introduction, other than a plain statement of facts, if the book is to make any appeal to the general public. I have always liked what Barbara Stephen has written, and I think that she would approach the subject from a much easier angle than mine. – I mean because she knows the thing from the inside and her account would therefore not be so dependent upon personal impressions. The difficulty with impressions is that if you once start altering from the best of motives everything gets blurred and out of proportion' (*ibid.*, no. 2236). On 27 September she told Violet Dickinson that the 'working women's book is held up and wont I think be out till the Spring' (*ibid.*, no. 2242). On 10 October she updated Davies: 'I am a wretch not to have written before but – there have been endless interruptions, and now of course our head clerk is ill, in the height of getting books out, and Leonard has to take on her work as well as his own. So I havent faced him with your questions about publication – partly indeed because I know he thinks the Press will be very glad indeed to do the book quite apart from my introduction (which is only a flourish.) But he will tell you about facts – date of publication and so on. I am very pleased that Mrs [Eleanor] Barton [General Secretary of the Guild, 1925–37] on the whole approves – at the same time I'm amused at the importance attached to the size of the Guilders. Vanity seems to be the same in all classes. But I swear that Mrs Barton shall say exactly what she thinks of the appearance of me and my friends and I wont think *her* unsympathetic. Indeed I wish she would – what fun to hand her a packet of our letters and let her introduce it! What rather appals me (I'm writing in a hurry, and cant spell, and dont please take my words altogether literally) is the terrific conventionality of the workers. Thats why – if you want explanations – I dont think they will be poets or novelists for another hundred years or so. If they cant face the fact that Lilian [Harris] smokes a pipe and reads detective novels, and cant be told that they weigh on an average 12 stone – which is largely because they scrub so hard and have so many children – and are shocked by the word "impure" how can you say that they face "reality"?, (I never know what "reality" means: but Lilian smoking a pipe to me is real, and Lilian merely coffee coloured and discreet is not nearly so real). What depresses me is that the workers seem to have taken on all the middle class respectabilities which we – at any rate if we are any good at writing or painting – have faced and thrown out. Or am I quite wrong? And how do you explain away these eccentricities on the part of your swans? It interests me very much. For you see, it is that to my thinking that now makes the chief barrier between us. One has to be "sympathetic" and polite and therefore one is uneasy and insincere. And why, with such a chance to get rid of conventionalities, do they cling to them? However, I must stop. And we must meet and go into the question by word of mouth – if you want me to make them sylphs I will' (*ibid.*, no. 2252). There were further delays, and VW wrote to Davies on 1 February 1931: 'Of course, of course, the introduction was a gift (though as a matter of fact I was handsomely paid by the Yale Review.) But about royalties [*sic*] – I'm afraid they wont amount to more than a pound or two, but whatever they do amount to, (my share I mean,) please let me hand that over to you to spend on any thing acceptable to the Guild. They must want money for something or other, and I should only feel I was paying my due for the immense interest their letters gave me. But that can wait. Leonard has explained to you the reason of this most irritating delay . . . I'm very anxious to see that the book looks attractive – has a good bright binding of some sort. I'm writing to tell my American publishers, Harcourt Brace, about it. ¶ By the way, when I came to read the proofs, I rather came round to your view that I made too much of the literary side of my interest; its partly a habit, through writing reviews for so many years. I tried to change the tone of some of the sentences, to suggest a more human outlook, and also, I brought in a few cigarettes in Lilians ash tray – do they matter? A little blue cloud of smoke seemed to me aesthetically desirable at that point. But the corrections were as usual done in a rush, and when I get my final proofs I will look at it carefully again. Perhaps we may meet and have a final revision' (*ibid.*, no. 2322). Following publication VW wrote to Davies: 'I have just read through the letters [written in response to the book], and feel greatly relieved. I somehow thought many of the women would dislike my butting in, and ask what business I had. They seem very generous on the contrary, and I am delighted they are so appreciative. But as a matter of fact I agree with your sister in law. I doubt that I was the right person to make people interested in the womens stories, because if one is a writer by profession, one cant help being one. It would be far worse to pretend not to be. And I think, as your sister in law says, that gets between and makes a distraction from what is the point of the book. However it cant be helped – old age makes one feel one cant change ones spots; much though I should like to . . . I have had some very enthusiastic comments on the book from very unlikely people – young intellectuals, who had never heard of working women or guilds or cooperation. They thought the letters amazing. I wish we could have had more' (*ibid.*, no. 2381).

Davies wrote to LW on 9 June 1941: 'How well I remember the letters about "Maternity" . . . and later how she encouraged the publication of the women's lives & wrote so beautifully her impressions in her Letter to me, making the book so specially dear to me. We should never have printed either book but for you both, & I cannot tell you what your support of "the Guild" has been to me' (LWP III). See also Appendix IV. Reprinted: *WE* (with the title 'Memories of a Working Women's Guild').

2 – Wolfgang Amadeus Mozart (1756–91); Albert Einstein (1879–1955).

3 – The introductory letter is here dated (misleadingly) May 1930.

Lockhart's Criticism

Lockhart was not an ambitious man, and, for all his powers, he was, save in one instance, rather careless in the use he made of them. As a young man he was content with the irresponsibilities of anonymous reviewing; and as an older man the same ephemeral occupation suited him well enough, though he pursued it more sedately, less anonymously and from the respectable comfort of an editor's chair. But he held no very exalted view of his mission. The business of reviewers, he said, was 'to think not of themselves, but of their author. . . . This excludes all chance of formal, original, or would-be original disquisition on the part of the journalist.'[2] Hence, though Lockhart must have filled volume upon volume with his reviews, very little of Lockhart is to be found embedded in them. When his editor comes – armed with an admirable introduction – to pick out from the lumber of old *Blackwoods* and *Quarterlies* the true Lockhart himself, she finds, for all her enthusiasm, that one slim volume holds all that can now be saved.

Yet the work was well worth doing, both because Lockhart had a bold, vivacious mind which leaked into his reviews in spite of his theories, and then again, though Miss Hildyard rates him too highly as a critic,[3] he is a fine sample of a reviewer and serves to show the nature and function of those curious creatures[a] whose lives, if they are as gay and giddy as a gnat's, are also as short. Here is one of them who has got himself, rather against his will, pinned down in a book; and it is highly amusing to look at him for a moment transfixed. His most necessary quality, it would seem, must be that which in other walks of life would be called, respectfully enough, courage. A new and unknown writer is a very dangerous person. Most of them die at a pinch without a gasp, but some survive and sting, and their sting can be fatal. When Lockhart, we have to remember, saw ranged on his table the usual new books, their names conveyed nothing to him. Keats, Hook, Godwin, Shelley, Brontë, Tennyson – who were they?[4] They might be somebodies, but they might, more probably, be nobodies. It was for him to make the trial and decide the question. Advancing alone with nothing but his own judgment to support him, the reviewer had need of all his courage, his acuteness, his education. He had to switch as adroitly as he could from one subject to another. Mr Shelley and Mr Keats, for example, were both poets, and wrote about Greek myths. Godwin and Brontë – Brontë might possibly be a woman – were both novelists; Jeffrey was a critic; Macaulay an historian; Beckford and Borrow were travellers; Coleridge was a poet again, but at the same time a very different poet from Crabbe;[5] somebody had written a book about heraldry, a Staff surgeon had published his memoirs, General Nott had written about Afghanistan, and there was also a valuable work about a new[b] method of treating dry rot.[6] All had to be read, sorted, placed, marked good or bad, and commended with a label tied round their necks to the attention or neglect of the public. The public who paid to be told what to read would be justly annoyed if they were told to read the wrong things.

Lockhart was well qualified for the business. He was a highly educated man. He had taken a first at Oxford, he had a considerable knowledge of Spanish literature, and he was more widely read than most young men of his age. All this was in his favour, but there were drawbacks. The Lockharts were an old Scottish family; and when you add an Oxford education to a young man of an old Scottish family you are making it very difficult for him to be just to apothecaries, for example, who think they can write poetry, or to Cockneys who have the temerity to talk about the Greeks. Moreover, Lockhart was one of those quick-witted, indolent people who, as Sir Walter complained, feel the attractions of 'the gown and slipper garb of life, and live with funny, easy companions'[7] gossiping and telling stories instead of attending to the serious business of life and making a name for themselves. The doors and windows of his study let in rumours, prejudices, odds and ends of unsubstantiated gossip. With it all, however, he had the makings of a prince of reviewers; and those who have a kindly feeling for the race might well feel forebodings when he and his cronies picked up for review one day in 1820 a new book of poems by John Keats. Keats, Lockhart knew, was a friend of Leigh Hunt,[8] and therefore presumably a Liberal, a Cockney. He knew vaguely that his father had kept livery stables. It was impossible, then, that he should be a gentleman and a[c] scholar. All Lockhart's prejudices were roused and he rushed to his doom – the worst that can befall a reviewer. He committed himself violently, he betrayed himself completely. He tried to snuff out between finger and thumb one of the immortal lights of English literature. For that failure he has been gibbeted ever since. No one who sees him swinging in the wind can help a shudder and a sigh lest the same fate may one of these days be his. After all, new books of poems still appear.

And it is plain, as we turn over the pages of Lockhart's resurrected reviews, that to write about a new book the moment it comes out is a very different matter from writing about it[d] fifty years afterwards. A new book is attached to life by a thousand minute filaments. Life goes on and the filaments break and disappear. But at the moment they ring and resound and set up all kinds of irrelevant responses.

Keats was an apothecary and lived in Hampstead, and consorted with Leigh Hunt and the Cockneys: Shelley was an atheist and had irregular views upon marriage: the author of *Jane Eyre* might be a woman, and, if so, was a very coarse one. It is easy to say that these were ephemeral accidents and that Lockhart should have brushed them aside; but they rang loud in his ears, and he could no more have disregarded them and the prejudices of his readers than he could have flung aside his blue dressing-gown and marched down Albemarle-street[9] in[e] a tweed cap and plus fours.

But even so, Lockhart was not so far out as might be expected; in other words, he was very often of the same opinion as we are. He saw the importance of Wordsworth[10] and Coleridge; he welcomed Borrow and Beckford; he placed *Jane Eyre*, in spite of its coarseness, very high.[11] It is true that he predicted a long life for *Zohrab the Hostage*,[12] who has had a short one. Probably because he was a novelist himself his criticism of fiction was erratic, and his enthusiasm for the novels of Godwin and Hook seems to show that they excited his own creative power and thus deflected his critical judgment. Tennyson he bullied with unchastened insolence, but, as Tennyson proved by accepting some of his criticism, not without acuteness.[13] In short, the case of Lockhart would seem to show that a good reviewer of contemporary work will get the proportions roughly right, but the detail wrong. He will single out from a number of unknown writers those who are going to prove men of substance, but he cannot be certain what qualities are theirs in particular, or how the importance of one compares with the importance of another.

One may regret, since this is so, that Lockhart fixed his mind so much upon contemporaries and did not give himself the benefit of a wider perspective. He might have written with far greater safety and perhaps with far greater authority upon the dead. But he was a diffident man and a fastidious; and he knew that criticism, to be worth anything, requires more effort and more austerity than he was able to command. All the brilliance of Jeffrey, as he perceived, was not enough 'to induce a man of research in the next century to turn over the volumes of his review.'[14] And Gifford, with his 'ill-natured abuse and cold rancorous raillery . . . is exquisitely formed for the purposes of political objurgation, but not at all for those of gentle and universal criticism.'[15] A reviewer can skim the surface, but there are 'matters of such moment, that it is absolutely impossible to be a great critic while the mind remains unsettled in regard to them.'[16] Because he was aware of this, Lockhart was a good reviewer, and content to remain one. But he was too sceptical, too diffident, too handsome and well bred perhaps; he lived too much under the shadow of Sir Walter Scott, he had too many worries and sorrows and dined out too often to push on into those calm and austere regions where the mind settles down to think things out and has its dwelling in a mood of gentle and universal contemplation. So he was content to go on knocking off articles, and cutting out quotations and leaving them to moulder where they lay. But if his reviews show by their power, their insolence, their very lack of ambition, that he had it in him to do better, they also remind us that there is a virtue in familiarity. We lose something when we have ceased to be able to talk naturally of Johnny Keats,[17] to regret the 'early death of this unfortunate and misguided gentleman' Mr Shelley.[18] A little of the irreverence with which Lockhart treated the living would do no harm to our more sober estimates of the dead.

a – *NR*: 'those creatures'.
b – *NR*: 'about some new'.
c – *NR*: 'and not a'.
d – *NR*: 'them'.
e – *NR*: 'Hampstead and . . . Cockneys. Shelley . . . views of marriage. The author of "Jane Eyre" . . . and if so, she was . . . say Lockhart should have brushed aside these ephemeral accidents and discussed the books pure and simple, but to him they were not nearly so ephemeral as to us, and, more-over, he was writing for a public that paid him to warn them of political or religious or moral abnormalities. Lockhart could no more have disregarded the prejudices of the subscribers to Blackwoods and The Quarterly than he could have sauntered down Albemarle Street dressed in'.

1 – An unsigned review in the *TLS*, 23 April 1931, and (signed, with a few variants, as 'The Pundit of the Quarterly') in the *NR*, 15 July, (*Kp4* C330), of *Lockhart's Literary Criticism*, with introduction and bibliography by M. Clive Hildyard (Basil Blackwell, 1931). John Gibson Lockhart (1794–1854) married (Charlotte) Sophia (1799–1837), the elder daughter of Sir Walter Scott (1771–1832). Lockhart's best-known work is his biography of Scott (7 vols, 1837–8; 2nd ed. revised, 10 vols, 1839; abridged and revised, 2 vols, 1848); VW was given the 1839 ed. by her father: see *PA*, 30 & 31 January 1897, and *I VW Letters*, nos 3, 4 and 42. On 7 April 1931 VW wrote to Ethel Smyth: 'I've written and written – so many articles – 8 to be exact. Five on London; one on Mrs Browning; one on Lockhart; one on Gosse; and all have to be sand papered, made to fit, smoothed, pressed, curled, and sent off' (*IV VW Letters*, no. 2343). See also 'Gas at Abbotsford', *VI VW*

Essays. This issue of the *TLS* also contained: 'The Enigma of Parnell', a review of *Parnell Vindicated: The Lifting of the Veil* by Henry Harrison. Draft (Berg, M 13). Reprinted (*TLS* version): *Mom, CE.*

2 – *Literary Criticism,* 'Editors and Reviewers', p. 60; review of *A Critical History of the Language and Literature of Ancient Greece*, 3 vols, by Col. William Mure of Caldwell (1799–1860), *Quarterly Review*, vol. lxxxvii, no. 174 (September 1850).

3 – See *Literary Criticism*, Introduction, p. 6: 'It can be claimed for Lockhart's reviews that they are, almost without exception, well worth re-reading to-day, and are not to be mistaken for ephemeral journalism.'

4 – John Keats (1795–1821); Theodore Hook (1788–1841); William Godwin (1756–1836); Percy Bysshe Shelley (1792–1822); Charlotte Brontë (1816–55), of whom Lockhart would have known by her pseudonym, Currer Bell; Alfred, Lord Tennyson (1809–92).

5 – Francis Jeffrey (1773–1850), writer and judge, editor of the *Edinburgh Review*; Thomas Babington Macaulay (1800–59); William Beckford (1759–1844); George Henry Borrow (1803–81); Samuel Taylor Coleridge (1772–1834); George Crabbe (1754–1832).

6 – See *Literary Criticism*, Bibliography, pp. 161–3: article on Heraldry, *Brewster's Edinburgh Encyclopædia* (1830), vol. x, pt 2, pp. 711–38; 'Recollections of a Staff Surgeon', *Quarterly Review*, vol. cxxxiv, no. 134 (March 1841); 'General Nott in Afghanistan', *ibid.*, vol. lxxviii, no. 156 (October 1846); 'Dry Rot – Kyan's Patent', *ibid.*, vol. xlix, no. 97 (April 1833).

7 – *Familiar Letters of Sir Walter Scott*, ed. David Douglas (David Douglas, 1894), vol. ii, Sir Walter Scott to Lockhart, 15 October 1825, p. 357.

8 – Leigh Hunt (1784–1859).

9 – In 1825 Lockhart moved to London to be editor of the *Quarterly Review*, a position that he held until 1853. The *Quarterly* had been established by John Murray in 1809 as a Tory voice to counter the Whig *Edinburgh Review*. Since 1812, 50 Albemarle Street has been the headquarters of John Murray, the publishers.

10 – William Wordsworth (1770–1850).

11 – See *Literary Criticism*, 'Brontë', p. 29, where *Jane Eyre* (1847) is analysed in a letter of 29 December 1847, from Lockhart to his daughter, Charlotte Hope-Scott.

12 – *Ibid.*, 'Morier', p. 100: 'This is the best novel that has appeared for several years past', review of *Zohrab the Hostage* by James Justinian Morier (1782–1849), *Quarterly Review*, vol. xlviii, no. 96 (December 1832). In 'Marryat', Lockhart describes Morier as 'the exquisite writer' (*Lockhart's*, p. 99); reprinted from the *Quarterly Review*, vol. xlix, no. 128 (October 1839).

13 – See *Literary Criticism*, 'Tennyson', pp. 132–44, review of *Poems of Alfred Tennyson* [1833, i.e. 1832], *Quarterly Review*, vol. xlix, no. 97 (April 1833) and Introduction, pp. 11–15. In a draft of *Reviewing* ([Berg, M 116]; see VI

VW *Essays*), VW quoted from Harold Nicolson's *Tennyson: Aspects of his Life, Character and Poetry* (Constable, 1923): this review 'was undoubtedly one of the main causes of the silent and morose decade that was to follow ... in that it kept Tennyson from publication at the most vital years of a poet's life ...the effect upon his literary development was all-important ... His first act was at once to withdraw from the press *The Lover's Tale*, which was then about to issue. We find him thinking of leaving England altogether, of living abroad' (pp. 117–18). See also *Three Guineas* (Hogarth Press, 1938), n. 10 to ch. iii, p. 311.

14 – *Literary Criticism*, 'Jeffrey', p. 84; 'Remarks on the Periodical Criticism of England', *Blackwood's Edinburgh Magazine*, vol. ii, no. 12 (March 1818), p. 676, col. a.

15 – *Literary Criticism*, 'Gifford', p. 62; 'Remarks on the Periodical Criticism of England', p. 672, col. b. William Gifford (1756–1826), satirist and editor.

16 – Quoted in Andrew Lang, *The Life and Letters of John Gibson Lockhart* (2 vols, John C. Nimmo, 1899), vol. i, ch. vi, 'Edinburgh, 1817–1819', pp. 170–1; 'Remarks on the Periodical Criticism of England', *Blackwood's Edinburgh Magazine*, p. 675, cols a–b: 'A lawyer is always a man of doubts; and the intellectual timidity of Jeffray's [*sic*] profession has clung to him in all his pursuits, and prevented him from coming manfully and decidedly to any firm opinion respecting matters ...' (Not included in *Literary Criticism*.)

17 – See *Literary Criticism*, 'Shelley', p. 125, review of Shelley's *Posthumous Poems* (1824), *Quarterly Review*, vol. xxxiv, no. 67 (June 1826); 'Letters of Timothy Tickler, Esq.', no. viii, *Blackwood's Edinburgh Magazine*, vol. xiv, no. 79 (August 1823).

18 – *Literary Criticism*, 'Shelley', p. 127.

George Eliot, 1819–1880

Sprung from country people but insatiably intellectual, George Eliot's early novels are the fruit of happy memory; her later of melancholy thought. Isolated by an ambiguous marriage, extravagantly praised, she early lost vitality and her novels suffered. But she stretched the capacity of fiction, and forced it not only to tell a story and reflect manners but to contain the comment and criticism of a large mind brooding over life.

1 – A signed caption on the verso of a picture postcard issued by the National Portrait Gallery, c. May 1931, (*Kp4* B12). The picture is a portrait of George Eliot from an 1865 chalk drawing by Sir Frederick William

Burton. On 12 June 1930 VW had written to Ernest Rhys, editor of Everyman's Library: 'I am . . . grateful that you should ask me to write an introduction to Middlemarch. But I have already written at length about George Eliot, and much though I admire her, I do not feel that I can begin again on that subject' (*IV VW Letters*, no. 2192). See 'George Eliot (1819–1880)', *III VW Essays*; 'George Eliot', *CR1* and *IV VW Essays*; and another essay entitled 'George Eliot', *IV VW Essays*. Draft (Berg, M 1.4).

For VW's relations with the gallery, see Charles Saumarez Smith, 'A Question of Fame: Virginia Woolf and the National Portrait Gallery', *Charleston Magazine*, no. 12 (Autumn/Winter 1995); *VWB*, no. 27 (January 2008), pp. 4–10; *IV VW Diary*, 14 February 1934; and *V VW Letters*, no. 2857, 15 February [1934]. For VW's support of the unsuccessful proposal that the gallery should acquire a painting of Katherine Mansfield, see her letter of 11 December 1932 to Theodora Bosanquet (*V VW Letters*, no. 2680); Houghton Library, Harvard University (bMS Eng 1213.3 [288]); and Claire Tomalin, 'Never Ending Stories', *Guardian*, 29 November 2003, Review section, pp. 5–9.

Edmund Gosse

When famous writers die it is remarkable how frequently they are credited with one particular virtue – the virtue of kindness to the young and obscure. Every newspaper has lately contained that eulogy upon Arnold Bennett.[2] And here is the same tribute paid to another writer who differed in every possible way from Arnold Bennett – Sir Edmund Gosse. He too, it is said, was generous to the young and obscure. Of Bennett it was certainly, although on some occasions rather obliquely, true. He might, that is to say, have formed a very low opinion of a book; he might have expressed that opinion as his habit was, bluntly and emphatically in print; and yet if he met the writer his sincerity, his concern, his assumption that both cared equally for the craft of letters made it perfectly easy for that unfortunate person to say, 'It is all true, and more than true, Mr Bennett; but if you hate my books, I can't tell you how completely I loathe yours'[3] – after which a frank discussion of fiction and its nature was possible; and a very obscure novelist was left with the feeling that a very famous one was indeed the kindest of men.

But what would have happened if, taking advantage of Sir Edmund's generosity, and assuming a common respect for letters, one had said 'But you can't hate my books, Sir Edmund, more than I hate yours'?

Instant annihilation would have been the only and the happiest solution of the situation. But nobody who had ever seen Sir Edmund in the flesh would have risked such folly. Bristling and brilliant, formal but uneasy, he radiated even from a distance all the susceptibilities that make young writers draw in their horns. Generous was not the adjective that sprang to the lips at the sight of him, nor is it one that frequently occurs on reading the life of him by Mr Charteris. He could be as touchy as a housemaid and as suspicious as a governess. He could smell out an offence where none was meant and hoard a grievance for years. He could quarrel permanently because a lamp wick was snuffed out too vigorously at a table under his nose.[4] Hostile reviews threw him into paroxysms of rage and despair. His letters are full of phrases like 'Mr. Clement Shorter, in terms of unexampled insolence, speaks of me as "the so-called critic".[5] . . . If that insolent notice in the *Times* is true . . . it is better I should know it . . . I feel I shall never have the heart to write another sentence.'[6] It seems possible that one severe review by Churton Collins[7] gave him more pain than he suffered from any private or public sorrow in the course of seventy-nine years. All this must have made him the most prickly of companions, and the young must have been possessed of greater tact than the young usually possess to reach the kindness that no doubt lay hid behind the thorns. For the great merit of the present biography is that it does not attempt to conceal the fact that Sir Edmund was a complex character composed of many different strains. Plain virtue was not a sure passport to his affection. He could disregard genius and ignore merit if they trod too clumsily upon his toes. On the other hand the House of Lords possessed a distinct glamour for him; the rigours of high society delighted him; and to see the words 'Marlborough Club'[8] at the head of his notepaper did, it seems, shed a certain lustre upon the page.

But these foibles, amusing and annoying as they are, become at once more interesting and less irritating when we learn that there lay behind them a very good cause – his education, his childhood. 'Far more than might be supposed of his conduct in life,' writes Mr Charteris, 'was due to unconscious protest against . . . the things which darkened his childhood.'[9] Readers of *Father and Son*[10] know well what those things were – the narrowness, the ugliness of his upbringing; the almost insane religious mania of his father; the absence from his home of culture, beauty, urbanity, graciousness – in fact, of all those elements in life to which Edmund Gosse turned as instinctively and needed as profoundly as a flower the sun. What could be more natural than that the flower, once transplanted, should turn, almost violently, the other way, should climb too high, should twine too lavishly, should – to drop these metaphors – order clothes in Savile Row[11] and emerge from behind the form of Dr Fog uttering what appear at this distance of time rather excessive praises of the now little known Danish poet, Paludin Müller? – a surly poet who objected to visitors. But young Edmund Gosse triumphed. 'Slowly, the poet murmured, "You flatter me too much, but thank you." The most stubborn of all the citadels had capitulated.'[12]

Few people can have been pitchforked, as Mr Charteris calls it,[13] into the world by a more violent propulsion than that which Gosse was given by the bleakness of his upbringing. It was no wonder that he overshot the mark, never quite got his equilibrium at parties which he loved, required to know the maiden names of married guests,[14] and observed formalities punctiliously which are taken as a matter of course by those who have never lived in dread of the instant coming of the Lord, and have ordered their clothes for generations in Savile Row. But the impulse itself was generous, and the tokens of kindling and expansion more admirable than ridiculous. The 'sensual sufficiency in life'[15] delighted one who had been starved of it. Happiness formed the staple of what he would certainly not have called his creed. 'To feel so saturated with the love of things,' to enjoy life and 'suck it as a wasp drains a peach,'[16] to 'roll the moments on one's tongue and keep the flavour of them';[17] above all, to cherish friendship and exalt the ideals of friendship – such were the enjoyments that his nature, long repressed, stretched out to, generously, naturally, spontaneously. And yet—

Those who are acquainted with Sir Edmund's lively portraits know what demure but devastating qualifications he was able to insinuate after those two small words. 'He possessed the truth and answered to the heavenly calling,' he wrote of Andrew Lang, 'and yet . . .'[18] Such expansion was natural, was right, was creditable, and yet, we echo, how much better Gosse would have been as a writer, how much more important he would have been as a man if only he had given freer rein to his impulses, if only his pagan and sensual joy had not been dashed by perpetual caution! The peculiarity which Mr Charteris notes in his walk – 'curiously suggestive at once of eagerness and caution'[19] – runs through his life and limits his intelligence. He hints, he qualifies, he insinuates, he suggests, but he never speaks out, for all the world as if some austere Plymouth Brother were lying in wait to make him do penance for his audacity. Yet it seems possible, given the nature of his gifts, that if only he had possessed greater boldness, if only he had pushed his curiosity further, had incurred wrath instead of irritation, and complete confusion instead of some petty social tribulation, he might have rivalled the great Boswell himself. When we read how young Edmund Gosse insinuated himself under cover of Dr Fog into the presence of an irascible poet and won the day by the adroitness of his flattery, we are reminded of the methods of Boswell in pursuit of Paoli or Voltaire or Johnson.[20] Both men were irresistibly attracted by genius. Both had 'a medium-like'[21] power of drawing other people's confidences into the open. Both were astonishingly adept at reporting the talk and describing the appearance of their friends. But where Boswell is drawn headlong by the momentum of his hero and his own veneration beyond discretion, beyond vanity, beyond his fear of what people will say, down into the depths, Gosse is kept by his respect for decorum, by his decency and his timidity dipping and ducking, fingering and faltering upon the surface. Thus where Boswell left us that profound and moving masterpiece, the *Life of Johnson*,[22] Gosse left us *Father and Son*, a classic doubtless, as Mr Charteris claims, certainly a most original and entertaining book, but how little and light, how dapper and superficial Gosse's portraits appear if we compare them with the portraits left by Boswell himself! Fear seems always to dog his footsteps. He dips his fingers with astonishing agility and speed into character, but if he finds something hot or gets hold of something large, he drops it and withdraws with the agility of a scalded cat. Thus we never know his sitters intimately; we never plunge into the depths of their minds or into the more profound regions of their hearts. But we know all that can be known by someone who is always a little afraid of being found out.

But if Gosse's masterpiece and his portraits suffer from his innate regard for caution, much of the fault must be laid upon his age. Even the most superficial student of letters must be aware that in the nineteenth century literature had become, for one reason or another, a profession rather than a vocation, a married woman rather than a lady of easy virtue. It had its organisation, its functions, its emoluments, and a host of people, not primarily writers, were attached to its service. Among them Gosse, of course, was one of the most eminent. '. . . no public dinner where literature was involved,' writes Mr Charteris, 'was complete without Gosse to propose or to return thanks for the cause.'[23] He welcomed strangers, addressed bodies, celebrated centenaries, presented prizes, and represented letters on all occasions and with the highest delight in the function. Then, again, some intellectual curiosity had risen in the 'nineties and ardent if uninstructed ladies wished to be enlightened. Here again Gosse was invaluable. By an odd irony, while Churton Collins, his deadly foe, was lecturing in St James's Square, Gosse was serving up Matthew Arnold to 'some of the smartest women in London' in Bruton Street. After this, says Mr Charteris, he became 'a much more frequent guest in Mayfair'[24] and his appetite for social life was whetted. Nothing would be more foolish than to sneer at a natural love of ceremony or a natural respect for the aristocracy, and yet it seems possible that this concern with the ritual of literature, this scrupulous observance of the rites of society encouraged Edmund Gosse in his growing decorum. Friendship had been his ideal; nobody can question the warmth of his youthful affection for Hamo Thornycroft;[25] and yet when one of his friends, Robert Ross, was involved in a famous scandal he could write 'I miss your charming company in which I have always delighted . . . I would say to you – be calm, be reasonable, turn for consolation to the infinite resources of literature . . . Write to me when you feel inclined, and however busy I am I will write in reply, and in a more happy season you must come back and be truly welcomed in this house.'[26] Is that the voice of friendship, disinterested, fearless, sincere, or the voice of an uneasy man of letters, who is terribly afraid that dear Lady C. will not ask him to dine, or that divine being the Countess of D.[27] will not invite him for the week-end if they suspect him of harbouring Robert Ross the friend of Oscar Wilde? And later his decorum seems to have drawn a film over his wonted perspicacity as a critic. M. Gide for example thought it well to mention certain facts openly in the third volume of his memoirs. 'Was it wise? Was it necessary? Is it useful?' Sir Edmund cried, in 'painful perplexity.'[28] And he was terribly shocked by an incident in E. M. Forster's *Howards End*. 'I should like to know,' he wrote to Mr Marsh, 'what you think of the new craze for introducing into fiction the high-born maiden who has had a baby? . . . I do not know how an Englishman can calmly write of such a disgusting thing, with such *sang-froid*. . . . I cannot help hoping that you may be induced to say something that will redeem him'.[29] But when Sir Edmund goes on to say that no high-bred maiden has ever had a baby illegitimately in a French novel one can only suppose that he was thinking, not unnaturally, of the House of Lords.

But if Gosse was no Boswell and still less a St Francis, he was able to fill a place and create a legend, and perhaps we have no right to demand more. To be oneself is after all an achievement of some rarity, and Gosse, as everybody must agree, achieved it, both in literature and in life. As a writer he expressed himself in book after book of history, of biography, of criticism. For over fifty years he was busily concerned, as he put it, with 'the literary character and the literary craft.'[30] There is scarcely a figure of any distinction, or a book of any importance in modern letters upon which we cannot have Gosse's opinion if we wish for it. For instance, one may have a curiosity about Disraeli's novels and hesitate which to begin upon. Let us consult Gosse. Gosse advises on the whole that we shall try *Coningsby*. He gives his reasons. He rouses us with a suggestive remark. He defines Disraeli's quality by comparing him with Bulwer, with Mrs Gore and Plumer Read. He tells an anecdote about Disraeli that was told him by his friend the Duke of Rutland.[31] He breaks off a phrase here and there for our amusement or admiration. All this he does with perfect suavity and precision, so that by the time he has done Disraeli is left glowing and mantling like an old picture lit up by a dozen bright candles. To illumine, to make visible and desirable was his aim as a critic. Literature to him was an incomparable mistress and it was his delight 'to dress her charms and make her more beloved.'[32] Lovers of course sometimes go further and a child is the result. Critics too sometimes love literature creatively and the fruit of their devotion has a toughness and a fibre that the smooth strains of Sir Edmund's platonic devotion are entirely without. Like all critics who persist in judging without creating he forgets the risk and agony of child-birth. His criticism becomes more and more a criticism of the finished article, and not of the article in the making. The smoothness, the craftsmanship of the work rouse his appreciation and he directs our attention only to its more superficial aspects. In other words, he is a critic for those who read rather than for those who write. But then no creator possesses Gosse's impartiality, or his width of reading, or his lightness and freedom of mind, so that if we want to hold a candle to some dark face in the long portrait gallery of literature there is no better illuminant than Edmund Gosse.

As for his own face, his own idiosyncrasy, only those who saw him at home among his books, or heard him, mimicking, remembering, in one of those club corners that he made, so characteristically, his own, can bring the odds and ends of this excitable but timid, this enthusiastic but worldly, this kindly but spiteful man into one complete synthesis. It was only in talk that he completely expressed himself. 'I was not born for solitude,' he wrote.[33] Neither was he born for old age and meditation. 'You speak of "the peace which the years bring," but they bring no peace for me', he wrote.[34] Thought and the ardours and agonies of life were not for him. 'I have no idea,' he said, 'how the spiritual world would look to me, for I have never glanced at it since I was a child and gorged with it.'[35] It is a cruel fate that makes those who only come into being when they talk fall silent. It is a harsh necessity that brings these warm and mobile characters into the narrow confines of the grave. Sir Edmund was not in the least anxious to depart and leave a world, which, with the solitary exception of Churton Collins, had showered upon him so many delightful gifts for seventy-nine years.

1 – A signed review in the *Fortnightly Review*, 1 June 1931, and revised, as 'As a Light to Letters', in the *NYHT*, 26 July 1931 (see Appendix VI), (*Kp4* C331), of *The Life and Letters of Sir Edmund Gosse* [1849–1928] by The Hon. Evan Charteris, K.C. (William Heinemann, 1931). The issue of the *Fortnightly Review* also contained: 'Rain in Bloomsbury', a poem by Margaret Brisbane, and V. S. Pritchett's 'Woolly Gloves', while in the 'Notes on Contributors' it was announced that VW, 'whose recent book *A Room of One's* was received with such enthusiasm by a discerning public, is now at work on another novel'. A French translation by Jeanne Fournier-Pargoire of this version, entitled 'Edmond Gosse', appeared in *Le Figaro* on 5 August 1931, (*Kp4* D59). VW thought of writing about Gosse in January 1931 (see *IV VW Diary*, 7 and 26 January 1931). On 7 April she wrote to Ethel Smyth: 'all tomorrow I must be toiling to finish an article on Gosse, whom I hope to hit off smartly, without malice, but without much love either – for he was a crafty, worldly, prim, astute little beast . . , I'm writing with the only pen, a gold one, slippery and false and fickle as Edmund Gosse –' (*IV VW Letters*, no. 2343). On 9 April she wrote to Vita Sackville-West: 'I've written so many articles and so bad – Gosse the last, about whom I've been candid and caustic. Lord what a letter to Robbie Ross . . . How cold cautious and clammy – like the writhing of a fat worm, red, shiny – disgusting . . .' (*ibid.*, no. 2345), and again on 9 April: 'how happy I was to finish Gosse (provisionally) this morning' (*ibid.*, no. 2346, to Smyth). On 15 April: 'There's Gosse got to catch the post: and I've written the last sentence I daresay 10 times and cant get the hang of it. One more shot, and so goodbye Ethel dear . . .' (*ibid.*, no. 2352, to Smyth). After publication Charteris sent VW a 'rectification . . . not that it alters my opinion one straw. No, it isnt "work" – I wish it were[,] my five hours only the deadliest of drudgery, copying, cutting out, putting in, re-reading and so finally sending to the typist; who then

leaves out and puts in on her own account, so that has to be altered too, twice, for America and here; a dismal business . . .' (*ibid.*, no. 2386, to Smyth). Charteris's letter appears not to have survived, probably because VW sent it to Sackville-West (see *ibid.*, no. 2403). See also 'Mr Gosse and his Friends' and 'Restoration Comedy', *III VW Essays*. Draft (Berg, M 13). Reprinted (*Fortnightly Review* version): *Mom, CE*.

2 – (Enoch) Arnold Bennett (1867–1931).

3 – See 'Am I a Snob?' (read to the Memoir Club on 1 December 1936), *MoB*, p. 212, for VW's own words to Bennett: 'You can't hate my books more than I hate yours, Mr Bennett'. Cf. *IV VW Diary*, 28 March 1931, for VW's reaction to his death on 27 March; and VW's letter of 12 April to Hugh Walpole: 'Yes, Arnold's death was queer. I never knew him, as you did, I suppose, but had two hours tête à tête at a party just before he drank the fatal tumbler; and we abused each other as usual, and as usual I liked him; and was bored; and yet found him impressive, as a presence' (*IV VW Letters*, no. 2350).

4 – See *Life*, p. 355.

5 – *Ibid.*, Letter to Thomas J. Wise (1859–1937), 4 April 1914, p. 364.

6 – *Ibid.*, Letter to Austin Dobson (1840–1921), 25 October 1894, p. 234, which has 'to-day's *Times*'.

7 – See the unsigned review by John Churton Collins [1848–1908], 'English Literature at the Universities', *Quarterly Review*, vol. clxiii, no. 326 (October 1886), pp. 289–329, in which he made a devastating attack on Gosse's Clark Lectures, *From Shakespeare to Pope: An Enquiry into the Causes and Phenomena of the Rise of Classical Poetry in England* ([Cambridge] University Press, 1885): 'a book so unworthy . . . of a great University has never before been given to the world . . .' (p. 295). In *Three Guineas* (Hogarth Press, 1938) VW refers to this controversy and quotes from *Life*, p. 196: 'His [Gosse's] self-confidence was undermined, his personality reduced . . . Was not everyone watching his struggles, and regarding him as doomed? . . . ¶ His own account of his sensations was that he went about feeling that he had been flayed alive' (n. 10 to ch. iii, p. 311).

8 – See *Life*, p. 373.

9 – *Ibid.*, p. 275; VW has rearranged the quotation.

10 – Gosse, *Father and Son: A Study of Two Temperaments* (William Heinemann, 1907), originally published anonymously.

11 – See *Life*, p. 26.

12 – *Ibid.*, p. 41; Dr Fog, 'distinguished Danish divine' (*ibid.*, p. 40); Frederik Paludan-Müller (1809–76), Danish romantic poet.

13 – See *ibid.*, p. 199: 'he was pitchforked into the world'.

14 – See *ibid.*, p. 22: 'He would require to know not only the names of individuals, but their vocations and almost their genealogies, even asking at times in tones of embarrassing audibility the maiden name of a married guest.'

15 – *Ibid.*, Letter to Robert Louis Stevenson (1850–94), 4 January 1886, p. 186.

16 – *Ibid.*, Letter to Evan Charteris (1864–1940), 27 August 1911, p. 330.

17 – *Ibid.*, Letter to Hamo Thornycroft, [early 1880?], p. 138.

18 – *Ibid.*, Letter to Henry James (1843–1916), 27 November 1912, p. 344. In response to the highly critical letter from James, Gosse continued: 'His [Lang's] puerility, as you say, was heart-rending'. However, Gosse had written only four months earlier that Andrew Lang (1844–1912) had been 'an old companion and friend of 35 years . . . There dies, with him, what was (no doubt) the most elegant mind that the English speaking race has brought forth in our time' (*ibid.*, Letter to Floris Delattre, 22 July 1912, p. 335).

19 – *Ibid.*, p. 25.

20 – James Boswell (1740–95); General Pasquale Paoli (1725–1807), leader of the insurgents seeking Corsica's independence from the Genoese; Voltaire (François Marie Arouet, 1694–1778); Samuel Johnson (1709–84).

21 – Not a quotation but a colloquial phrase (it is not between quotation marks in *NYHT*), but see *Life*, p. 172: 'Gosse was a born medium.'

22 – Boswell, *The Life of Samuel Johnson, LL.D.* (1791).

23 – *Life*, p. 245, which has: 'or return thanks'.

24 – *Ibid.*, Letter to James, 14 June 1896, p. 252, which has: 'smartest ladies in'; *ibid.*, p. 241; Matthew Arnold (1822–88).

25 – Sir (William) Hamo Thornycroft (1850–1925), sculptor.

26 – *Life*, Letter to Robert Baldwin Ross (1869–1918), 17 May 1895, p. 248; Ross was a close and loyal friend of Oscar Wilde (1856–1900), and became his literary executor.

27 – For Gosse's letters to Lady Charnwood, see *ibid.*, pp. 400, 427–8, 431; for letters to Lady Desborough, see pp. 397–9.

28 – *Ibid.*, Letter to André Gide (1869–1951), 7 January 1927, pp. 498–9, about *Si le grain ne meurt* (1924), objecting to the 'Deuxième Partie' in which Gide reveals his homosexual encounters, including those with Ali, an Arab boy, in Sousse, North Africa ('Sans doute mon aspect portait-il la marque de mon délire . . .'); with Mohammed, a street musician procured by Oscar Wilde in Algiers; and with a boatman on Lake Como. See *Si le grain ne meurt* (Librairie Gallimard, Éditions de la Nouvelle Revue française, 3rd ed., 1928), pp. 302, 345.

29 – *Life*, Letter to Edward Marsh (1872–1953), 27 December 1910, pp. 323–4. VW omits before the final sentence of her quotation: 'I hope you will not be vexed with me for speaking so plainly, because I know you have influence with the author of this unhappy book, and are genuinely interested in him.' In introducing the letter, Charteris wrote: 'In giving permission for the following letter to be used, Mr. E. M. Forster [1879–1970] took the opportunity to reproach Mr. Marsh for neglecting the injunction

"to use his influence" on the author of *Howards End* [Edward Arnold, 1910]' (p. 323).
30 – Gosse, *Some Diversions of a Man of Letters* (William Heinemann, 1919), p. 11.
31 – See *ibid.*, 'The Novels of Benjamin Disraeli [1804–81]', pp. 153–78, at p. 178: Disraeli 'found rivals in Bulwer and Mrs. Gore, and a master in Plumer Ward'; see also p. 155. The book was dedicated to Charteris, and reviewed by VW in 'Mr Gosse and his Friends', *III VW Essays. Coningsby* (1844), 'as a story, is the most attractive book of Disraeli's middle period, and one of the most brilliant studies of political character ever published' (*Some Diversions*, p. 165). Edward Bulwer-Lytton (1831–91); Catherine Gore (1799–1861); Robert Plumer Ward (1765–1846). For the Duke of Rutland's anecdote, see *ibid.*, p. 168.
32 – Quoted in *Life*, p. 438.
33 – *Ibid.*, Letter to Earl Spencer (1857–1922), 1 September 1917, p. 418.
34 – *Ibid.*, Letter to Viscount Haldane (1856–1928), 21 August 1917, p. 414, which has: 'no peace to me'.
35 – *Ibid.*, Letter to Stevenson, 4 January 1886, p. 186.

Aurora Leigh

By one of those ironies of fashion that might have amused the Brownings themselves, it seems likely that they are now far better known in the flesh than they have ever been in the spirit. Like so many other Victorian worthies they have been transformed in the past few years into figures of romance, passionate lovers with curls and side whiskers, peg-top trousers and sweeping skirts. In this guise thousands of people must know and love the Brownings who have never read a line of their poetry. They have become two of the most conspicuous figures in the bright and animated procession which, thanks to our modern habit of printing letters and writing memoirs and sitting to be photographed, keeps step with the paler, subtler, more obscure shades who, in times gone by, lived solely between the pages of their books. Henceforward the history of English literature will be accompanied by the pageant of English writers – Tennyson with his wideawake, Swinburne with his balloon of red hair, George Eliot, elongated and equine, Stevenson, romantic in tropical shirt sleeves, Meredith, Hardy, Oscar Wilde, Whistler[2] – we know them all by their clothes, by their habits, by their private tastes and vices even if we have never read their books. To such immortality – and we can hardly disparage it if we approve of telephone and aeroplane – the Brownings laid themselves particularly open. Their story, exploited in a popular current play,[3] appeals to all that is dramatic and romantic in our natures. He must be dull, blind, and no better than a bookworm who does not pore with delight over the picture of tiny Miss Barrett issuing one September morning in 1846 from Wimpole Street with the spaniel Flush under one arm and the maid Wilson following behind to meet Browning, Italy, health and freedom in the church round the corner.[4]

But it cannot be denied that the works of the Brownings have lost lustre even as much as their persons have gained it. 'Sordello,' 'The Ring and the Book,' and 'Men and Women,' 'Pippa Passes'[5] and the rest are said, if we interpret the ripples on the surface correctly, to have lost their vigour, their resonance, their significance. The modern verdict begins to hint that Robert Browning was a commonplace, hearty, middle-class poet who smothered a breezy and essentially shallow mind under a tangle of untidy verbiage, which it is no longer worth anybody's while to sort and part in order to find the rather dubious treasures concealed within. As for Elizabeth Barrett Browning her fate as a writer is even worse. Nobody reads her, nobody writes about her, nobody troubles to put her in her place. One has only to compare her reputation with Christina Rossetti's to trace her decline. Christina Rossetti mounts irresistibly to the first place among English women poets.[6] Elizabeth, so much more loudly applauded during her lifetime, falls further and further behind. That she was noble and passionate we allow; perhaps half one sonnet might pass muster if the preceding lines were expunged; but her grammar is slipshod, her style slovenly, and her mind confused, turbulent, and excessive. The primers dismiss her with contumely; her importance, they say, 'has now become merely historical. Neither education nor association with her husband ever succeeded in teaching her the value of words and a sense of form.'[7] In short, the only place in the mansion of literature that is assigned her is downstairs in the servants' quarters, where, in company with Mrs Hemans, Eliza Cook, Jean Ingelow, Alexander Smith, Edwin Arnold, and Robert Montgomery[8] she bangs the crockery about and eats vast handfuls of peas on the point of her knife.

If therefore we take *Aurora Leigh* from the shelf and open it, it is not so much in order to read it as to muse with kindly condescension over this token of bygone fashion: it is not a book but a dusty mantle with fringes and furbelows that our grandmothers actually wore; a cluster of wax fruit that they stood in a glass case on the drawing-room table among albums, views of Jerusalem, and handsome models of the Taj Mahal carved in alabaster. But to the Victorians, undoubtedly, the book was very dear as a book. Thirteen editions of *Aurora Leigh* had been demanded by the year 1873. And, to judge from the dedication, Mrs Browning herself was not afraid to say that she set great store by it – 'the most mature of my works,' she calls it, 'and the one into which my highest convictions upon Life and Art have entered.'[9]

From a glance at her letters we shall see that she had had the book in mind for many years. She was brooding over it when she first met Browning, and her intention with regard to its form was almost the first of those confidences about their work which the lovers delighted to share – 'my chief *intention*,' she wrote, 'just now is the writing of a sort of novel-poem . . . running into the midst of our conventions, and rushing into drawing rooms and the like, "where angels fear to tread"; and so, meeting face to face and without mask the Humanity of the age, and speaking the truth of it out plainly. That is my intention.'[10] But for reasons which later become clear, she hoarded her intention throughout the ten astonishing years of escape and happiness, and when at last the book appeared in 1856 she might well feel that she had poured into it the best that she had to give. Perhaps the hoarding and the saturation which resulted have something to do with the surprise that awaits us. At any rate, we cannot read the first twenty pages of *Aurora Leigh* without becoming aware that the Ancient Mariner who lingers, for unknown reasons, at the porch of one work and not of another has us by the hand, and makes us listen like a three years' child[11] while Mrs Browning pours out in nine Books of blank verse the story of Aurora Leigh. Speed and energy, forthrightness and complete self-confidence – these are the qualities that hold us enthralled. Floated off our feet by them we learn how Aurora was the child of an Italian mother 'whose rare blue eyes were shut from seeing' her when she was scarcely four years old.[12] Her father was 'an austere Englishman, / Who, after a dry life-time spent at home / In college-learning, law, and parish talk / Was flooded with a passion unaware,'[13] but died too, and the child was sent back to England to be brought up by an aunt. The aunt, of the well-known family of the Leighs, stood upon the hall step of her country house dressed in black to welcome her. Her somewhat narrow forehead was braided tight with brown hair pricked with grey; she had a close, mild mouth; eyes of no colour; and cheeks like roses pressed in books, 'Kept more for ruth than pleasure, – if past bloom / Past fading also.'[14] The lady had lived a quiet life, exercising her Christian gifts upon knitting stockings and stitching petticoats 'Because we are of one flesh, after all, / And need one flannel.'[15] At her hand Aurora suffered the education that was thought proper for women. She learnt a little French, a little algebra; the royal genealogies of Oviedo; the internal laws of the Burmese empire; by how many feet Mount Chimborazo outsoars Teneriffe; what navigable river joins itself to Lara; and what census of the year five was taken at Klagenfurt; also how to draw nereids neatly draped, to spin glass, to stuff birds, and model flowers in wax. For the aunt liked a woman to be womanly. Of an evening she did cross-stitch and embroidered a shepherdess with pink eyes owing to some mistake in her choice of silks. Under this torture of education, the passionate Aurora exclaimed, certain women have died; others pine; a few who have, as Aurora had, 'relations with the Unseen,'[16] survive, and walk demurely, and are civil to their cousins, and listen to the vicar, and pour out tea. But also they retire to their bedrooms. For Aurora was blessed with a little room papered in green, with a green carpet and green curtains to the bed. All the world outside was green, in the tame manner of the English countryside. There was a green lime tree, green turf, green elms. The sun set behind a distant ridge, and if you looked out at sunset you saw the sheep run along the outline, small as mice. And then her Cousin Romney called to walk with her, or the painter Vincent Carrington, 'Whom men judge hardly as bee-bonneted, / Because he holds that, paint a body well, / You paint a soul by implication.'[17] With them sometimes she talked; but her chief escape was provided by books, books, books! 'I had found the secret of a garret-room / Piled high with cases in my father's name, / Piled high, packed large, – where creeping in and out, . . . / Like some small nimble mouse between the ribs / Of a mastodon,'[18] she read and read. The mouse indeed took wings and plunged, for 'It is rather when / We gloriously forget ourselves and plunge / Soul-forward, headlong, into a book's profound, / Impassioned for its beauty and salt of truth – / 'Tis then we get the right good from a book.'[19] And so she read and read.

This hasty abstract of the first book of *Aurora Leigh* does it, of course, no sort of justice, but having gulped down the original much as Aurora herself advises soul-forward, headlong, we find ourselves in a state where some attempt at analysis and the ordering of our multitudinous impressions becomes imperative. The first of these impressions and the most pervasive is the sense of the writer's presence. Through the voice of Aurora, the character, the circumstances, the idiosyncrasies of Elizabeth Barrett Browning ring in our ears. Mrs Browning could no more conceal herself than she could control herself, a sign no doubt of imperfection in an artist, but a sign also that life has impinged upon art more than life should. Again and again in the pages we read, Aurora the fictitious seems to be throwing light upon Elizabeth the actual. The idea of the poem, we must remember, came to her in the early Forties, when the relation between a woman's art and a woman's life was at its closest, so that it is impossible for the most austere critic of that work not to take into account the circumstances under which it was done. And, as everybody knows, the life of Elizabeth Barrett was of a nature to affect the most authentic and individual of gifts. Her mother died when she was a child; she plunged, under the guidance of family friends, headlong into the classics and read privately and profusely; her favourite brother was drowned; her health broke down; she was immured by the mad tyranny of her father in a sick room in Wimpole Street; and after years of almost conventual seclusion she slipped out at the age of forty and married a poet. Such are the facts, and the effect of those facts upon her deserves close scrutiny by those who read *Aurora Leigh*. She herself has described it.

'I have lived only inwardly,' she wrote, 'or with *sorrow*, for a strong emotion. Before this seclusion of my illness, I was secluded still, and there are few of the youngest women in the world who have not seen more, heard more, known more, of society, than I, who am scarcely to be called young now. I grew up in the country – had no social opportunities, had my heart in books and poetry, and my experience in reveries. My sympathies drooped towards the ground like an untrained honeysuckle. . . . It was a lonely life, growing green like the grass around it. Books and dreams were what I lived in – and domestic life only seemed to buzz gently around, like the bees about the grass. And so time passed and passed – and afterwards, when my illness came . . . and no prospect (as appeared at one time) of ever passing the threshold of one room again; why then, I turned to thinking with some bitterness . . . that I had stood blind in this temple I was about to leave – that I had seen no Human nature, that my brothers and sisters of the earth were *names* to me, that I had beheld no great mountain or river, nothing in fact. . . . And do you also know what a disadvantage this ignorance is to my art? Why, if I live on and yet do not escape from this seclusion, do you not perceive that I labour under signal disadvantages, that I am, in a manner as a *blind poet?* Certainly, there is a compensation to a degree. I have had much of the inner life, and from the habit of self-consciousness and self-analysis, I make great guesses at Human nature in the main. But how willingly I would as a poet exchange some of this lumbering, ponderous, helpless knowledge of books, for some experience of life and man, for some . . .'[20] She breaks off, with three little dots, and we may take advantage of her pause, to turn once more to *Aurora Leigh.*

What damage had her life done her as a poet? A great one, we cannot deny. For it is clear, as we turn the pages whether of *Aurora Leigh* or her letters – one often echoes the other – that the mind which found its natural expression in this swift and chaotic poem about real men and women was not the mind to profit by solitude. A lyrical, a scholarly, a fastidious mind might have used seclusion and solitude to perfect its powers. Tennyson asked no better than to live with books in the heart of the country. But the mind of Elizabeth Barrett was lively and secular and satirical. She was no scholar. Books were to her not an end in themselves but a substitute for living. She raced through folios because she was forbidden to scamper on the grass. She wrestled with Aeschylus and Plato because it was out of the question that she should argue about politics with live men and women. Her favourite reading as an invalid was Balzac and George Sand and other 'immortal improprieties' because 'they kept the colour in my life to some degree.'[21] Nothing is more striking, when at last she broke the prison bars, than the fervour with which she flung herself into the life of the moment. She loved to sit in a café and watch people passing; she loved the arguments and politics and strife of the modern world. The past and its ruins, even the past of Italy and Italian ruins, interested her much less than the theories of Mr Hume the medium, or the politics of Napoleon, Emperor of the French.[22] Italian pictures, Greek poetry roused in her a clumsy and conventional enthusiasm in strange contrast to the original independence of her mind when it applied itself to the affairs of the moment.

Such being the natural temper of her mind, it is not surprising that even when she was triply imprisoned by sex, health, and her father in a bed room in Wimpole Street it was her intention to write a novel-poem. But her circumstances forbade. She was as she said 'a blind poet.' She had seen no human nature. She had lived entirely alone, guessing at what was outside and inevitably magnifying what was within. The loss of Flush the spaniel affected her as the loss of a child might have affected another woman. The tap of ivy on the pane became the thrash of trees in a gale. Every sound was enlarged, every incident exaggerated, for the silence of the sick room was profound and the monotony of Wimpole Street was intense. Wisely she waited until her escape gave her some measure of proportion and knowledge. But it cannot be doubted that the long years of seclusion had done her irreparable damage as an artist, so that when at last she was able to rush 'into drawing rooms and the like,' and meet 'face to face without mask the Humanity of the age,' and speak 'the truth of it out plainly,' she was too weak to stand the shock. Ordinary daylight, current gossip, the usual traffic of human beings left her exhausted, ecstatic, and dazzled into a state almost of intoxication.

Aurora Leigh, the novel-poem, is not therefore the masterpiece that it might have been. Rather it is a masterpiece in embryo: a work whose genius floats diffused and fluctuating in some prenatal stage waiting the final stroke of creative power to bring it into being. Stimulating and boring, ungainly and beautiful, monstrous and brilliant all by turns, it still nevertheless rouses our interest and respect. For it becomes clear as we read that, whatever Mrs Browning's faults, she was one of those rare people who risk themselves adventurously and disinterestedly in an imaginative life which is independent of their private lives and demands to be considered on its own account. Her 'intention' survives; the interest of her theory redeems much that is faulty in her practice. If we may abridge and simplify Aurora's own argument in the fifth Book of her poem, her reasons for attempting to write a novel-poem run something like this. The sole work of poets, she said, is to present their own age, not Charlemagne's. More passion takes place in drawing rooms than with Roland and his knights at Roncesvalles.[23] 'To flinch from modern varnish, coat or flounce, / Cry out for togas and the picturesque, / Is fatal, – foolish too.'[24] For living art presents and records true life, and the only life we can truly know is our own.

But what form, she asks, can a poem upon modern life take? The drama is impossible, for the standard of public taste has sunk so low that only servile and docile plays have any chance of success. Moreover, what we (in 1846)[25] have to say about life is not fit for 'boards, actors, prompters, gaslight and costume'; our stage is now the soul itself.[26] Therefore – but here Aurora had to confess that though she can see what she wishes to do, what she actually does falls short. All she can say is that she has wrung her life-blood on to every leaf of her book. As for the rest, 'Let me think / Of forms less, and the external. Trust the spirit, . . . / Keep up the fire / And leave the generous flames to shape themselves.'[27] And so the fire blazed, the flames shaped themselves.

The desire to deal with modern life in poetry was not confined to Miss Barrett. Robert Browning said that he had had the same ambition all his life. Coventry Patmore's *Angel in the House* and Clough's *Bothie*[28] were both to precede *Aurora Leigh* by some years. The novelists, after all, were dealing triumphantly with modern life in prose. *Jane Eyre, Vanity Fair, David Copperfield, Cranford, The Warden, Scenes of Clerical Life, Richard Feverel*,[29] all trod fast on each other's heels in the twelve years between 1847 and 1859. The poets may well have felt, with Aurora Leigh, that modern life had an intensity, a beauty, and an ugliness of its own. Why should all these spoils, they asked naturally, fall to the lot of the prose writers? Why should the poet be forced back to the remoteness of Charlemagne and Roland, the toga and the picturesque, when Jane Eyre and Lord Steyne and Peggotty and the battle of Waterloo and the humours and ironies of village life, drawing-room life, club life, and street life all cried aloud for celebration? It was true that the old form in which poetry had dealt with life – the drama – was obsolete; but was there none other that could take its place? Mrs Browning, convinced of the divinity of poetry, pondered, seized as much as she could of actual experience, and then at last threw down her challenge to the Brontës and the Thackerays in blank verse. It was in blank verse that she gave her proof that the poets need not trundle back five hundred years, 'past moat and drawbridge, into a castle court'[30] but can step out boldly into the streets of Shoreditch and Kensington; her testimony that they need not only sing of knights and dames but can also celebrate my aunt and the vicar, Romney Leigh and Vincent Carrington, Marian Erle, Lord Howe, and Aurora Leigh. But can they?

Let us see what happens to a poet when he poaches upon a novelist's preserves and tries to give us not merely a lyric about his own feelings, or an epic about men and women in togas, but the story of many lives that move and change and affect each other and are inspired by all the interests and passions which are ours at this precise moment in the middle of the age of Queen Victoria. In the first place, there is the story; the tale must be told; and how is the poet to convey to us the necessary information that the hero has been asked out to dinner? As quietly, a novelist would say, and prosaically as possible. For example, 'While I kissed her glove in a melancholy mood a note was brought saying that her father sent his regards and asked me to dine with them next day.' Emphasis is carefully avoided. But poetry with its raised voice and emphatic accent has to say:

> While thus I grieved, and kissed her glove,
>   My man brought in her note to say,
> Papa had bid her send his love,
>   And would I dine with them next day?[31]

– at which we laugh. The simple words have been made to strut and posture and take on an emphasis which they cannot bear without becoming ridiculous. Then, again, what will the poet do with dialogue? In modern life, as Mrs Browning indicated when she said that our stage is now the soul, the sword has been superseded by the tongue. It is in talk, slow or rapid, pointed with wit, or incoherent with passion, in dialogue or soliloquy, that character is expressed and defined. It is by what Becky Sharp or Richard Feverel said that we know them and their position of the moment. But poetry when set to report the speech that winds in and out of the intricacies of character, and gives accent to the crisis is terribly impeded. Listen to Romney talking to his old love Marian about the baby she has borne another man –

> 'May God so father me, as I do him,
> And so forsake me, as I let him feel,
> He's orphaned haply. Here I take the child
> To share my cup, to slumber on my knee,
> To play his loudest gambol at my foot,
> To hold my finger in the public ways'[32]

– in short Romney rants and reels like any orator on a tub or like any of those Elizabethan heroes whom Mrs Browning had so carefully warned off her modern drawing room. Blank verse has proved itself the most remorseless enemy of modern speech. Talk tossed up on the surge and swing of the verse becomes high, rhetorical, impassioned; and since the talk, for there is no action to stop it, goes on, the reader's mind stiffens and glazes under the monotony of the rhythm. Following the lilt of her rhythm rather than the emotions of her characters, Mrs Browning is swept on into generalisation and declamation. Forced by the nature of her medium she ignores the slighter, the subtler, the more hidden shades of emotion, by which a novelist builds up, touch by touch, a character in prose. Change and development, the effect of one character upon another – all this is abandoned. The poem becomes one long soliloquy, and the only character that is known to us, and the only story that is told us, are the character and story of Aurora Leigh herself.

Thus if Mrs Browning meant by a novel-poem a book in which character is closely and subtly revealed, in which the heart in its complexity is laid bare, in which the effect of one life upon another is displayed, in which a story unfalteringly unfolds itself, she failed completely. But if she meant rather to give us the sense of life in general, of people who are undoubtedly Victorians in substance wrestling with problems which are unmistakably Victorian in nature, all brightened and intensified and compacted by the fire of poetry, she succeeded. Aurora Leigh with her passionate interest in social questions, her ambitions as artist, her disabilities as woman, her longing for knowledge and freedom, is the true daughter of her age. Romney too, with his phalanstery and his earnest morality, is no less certainly a mid-Victorian gentleman who has thought about the social question and been converted, unhappily as it turned out, to the doctrines of Fourier.[33] The aunt, the antimacassars, and the country house from which Aurora escapes are real enough to fetch high prices in a second hand shop at this moment. The broad aspects of what it felt like to be a Victorian are seized as surely and stamped as vividly upon us as in any novel by Trollope or Mrs Gaskell.

Indeed, if we compare prose novel and the novel-poem, the triumphs are by no means all to the credit of prose. As we rush through page after page of narrative in which a dozen scenes that the novelist would smooth out separately are pressed into one, in which pages of deliberate description are fused into a single line, we cannot help feeling that the poet has outpaced the novelist. Her page is packed twice as full as his. Characters too, if they are not shown in conflict but snipped off and summed up with something of the audacity of a caricaturist have a vigour and completeness that prose with its gradual approach cannot rival. The general aspect of the world – here a scene in a church, here a flower market, here a London sunset, here a suburb – the look of things seen from a height by a bird as it flies, are all conveyed by the compressions and elision of poetry and the emotional current of metre with a brilliancy and with a continuity that mock the prose writer and his slow accumulations of careful detail.

For these reasons *Aurora Leigh* remains with all its imperfections a book that still lives and can still be read. And when, after all, we think how dead, for all their merits, the plays of Beddoes and Sir Henry Taylor are, how dead in our time are the classical dramas of Robert Bridges,[34] we may suspect that Elizabeth Barrett was right when she rushed into the streets and drawing rooms, armed so curiously with blank verse, and declared that here, where we live and work and have our being, is the true place for a poet. At any rate, her courage was justified in her own case. For her faults, both of nature and circumstance – her ignorance, her bad taste, her tortured ingenuity, her floundering and scrambling and confused impetuosity – have here space to spend themselves without inflicting a deadly wound; while her gifts of ardour and abundance, her brilliant descriptive powers, and her shrewd and caustic vein of humour when turned upon the life that she herself had seen and known, infect us with her own enthusiasm. We laugh, and we protest, and we find a thousand absurdities it may be, but we read to the end enthralled.

Yet perhaps the best tribute that we can pay to *Aurora Leigh* is that it makes us wonder why it has left no successors. Surely here, in the street and the drawing room, is a promising subject: modern life is worthy of the muse. And yet the rapid sketch that Elizabeth Barrett flung off when she leapt from her sofa and threw open the door upon her time, as if to tempt poets of greater skill and fortune to follow after, remains unfinished. The conservatism or the timidity of poets still leaves the chief spoils of modern life to the novelist. We have no novel-poem of the age of George the Fifth.[35]

1 – A signed essay in the *Yale Review*, June 1931, and unsigned, with revisions, as the leading article, entitled '"Aurora Leigh"', in the *TLS*, 2 July 1931, (*Kp4* C332), and then further revised for *CR2*. The reader is referred to p. 519 below, where the *CR2* version, together with the *TLS* variants in the form of endnotes, is printed in its place as part of *CR2*. VW was 'turning to ... Aurora Leigh' on 21 February 1931 (*IV VW Letters*, no. 2330). She wrote to Helen McAfee, managing editor of the *Yale Review*, on 25 March: 'Many thanks for your cable about my article on Mrs Browning. I have now arranged that it shall appear here after July 1st. I will therefore send you the copy so as to reach you by May 10th which I think you told me was the

date necessary for your summer number. I have not quite finished it, but think that it will run to about 4000 words. I hope this will be all right. It is really a study of Aurora Leigh, which I read by chance with great interest for the first time the other day' (*ibid*., no. 2340). She sent the essay to McAfee on 14 April, and on 7 May, having 'just got back from France', thanked McAfee for accepting it (see list of uncollected letters: [Berg, M 43], nos 104–5). On 2 July VW wrote again to McAfee: 'Many thanks for the cheque for 250 dollars for my essay on Aurora Leigh. I must also thank you for the very useful list of errata – I am ashamed that so many got past me in the typescript. I had already found some of the worst myself, but too late to send them on to you. They have been corrected in the English version, and I am very grateful for the help' (*IV VW Letters*, no. 2399). The issue of the *Yale Review* also contained: Julian S. Huxley on 'Human Power and its Control', Harold Nicolson on 'Hindenburg' and Conrad Aiken's poem 'Prelude'; among the reviews were O. W. Firkins's on *The Barretts of Wimpole Street* and F. O. Matthiessen's on Edmund Wilson's *Axel's Castle*. VW wrote to Ethel Smyth on [7 July 1931]: 'A furious old gentleman in Manchester, coeval with the Brownings has attacked me for what he's pleased to call iconoclasm. I'm replying, in my well-known style, something spicy about orgasm making a rhyme' (*IV VW Letters*, no. 2401). A French translation by Jeanne Fournier-Pargoire of the *TLS* version, entitled 'Un Roman-poème "Aurora Leigh"', appeared in *Le Figaro* on 5–7 January 1932 (*Kp4* D61). The issue of the *TLS* also contained: reviews of a biography of Hartley Coleridge, the poet's son, who would be referred to in 'The Man at the Gate' and 'Sara Coleridge' (see *VI VW Essays*), and of William Gerhardi's *Memoirs of a Polyglot*, from which VW would quote in *Three Guineas* (Hogarth Press, 1938), n. 18 to ch. iii., pp. 314–15. *Aurora Leigh* by Elizabeth Barrett Browning (1806–61) was first published in 1857; VW probably used the 13th ed. (Smith, Elder, 1873), a copy of which had been presented by Robert Browning (1812–89) to VW's half-sister Laura Stephen (1870–1945). The page references below are to this edition, while the line references to the edition by Cora Kaplan (Women's Press, 1978). See also 'Poets' Letters', *I VW Essays*. Typescript draft with holograph corrections: *Yale Review* Papers, Beinecke Rare Book and Manuscript Library, Yale University.

2 – Alfred, Lord Tennyson (1809–92); Algernon Charles Swinburne (1837–1909); George Eliot (1819–80); Robert Louis Stevenson (1850–94); George Meredith (1828–1909); Thomas Hardy (1840–1928); Oscar Wilde (1856–1900); James Abbott McNeill Whistler (1834–1903), painter.

3 – Rudolph Besier (1878–1942), *The Barretts of Wimpole Street* (1930). Together with Vita Sackville-West, the Woolfs saw the play at the Queen's Theatre on Monday 6 October 1930 (see *IV VW Letters*, no. 2245). VW thought it 'rather feeble' (*ibid*., no. 2393, [27 June 1931]), and commented to Helen McAfee on 2 July: 'The Barretts of Wimpole Street goes along here,

apparently without any slackening. I myself was rather disappointed, though amused by the astonishing story – which is not an exaggeration. But they might have made it hit harder I thought. However the Barretts themselves are furious, threatening libel actions as it is' (*ibid.*, no. 2399). The play had premiered at the Malvern Festival on 20 August 1930, but by the time it arrived in the West End Mr Barrett's incestuous impulses had been toned down. Three grandsons of Mr Barrett wrote to *The Times*, protesting about the play and regretting that 'the law provides no remedy against the gravest and most despicable libels on the dead'. This drew a disingenuous denial from the author and producer of the play. See *The Times*, 21 and 29 August, 24 September and 3 November 1930.

4 – For VW's retelling of the story, see *Flush: A Biography* (Hogarth Press, 1933). Robert Browning first wrote to Elizabeth Barrett on 10 January 1845; they were married clandestinely on 12 September 1846.

5 – See *The Poetical Works of Robert Browning, with Portraits* (2 vols, Smith, Elder, 1900): 'Sordello' (1840), vol. i, pp. 115–94; 'The Ring and the Book' (1868–9), vol. ii, pp. 1–291; 'Men and Women' (1840s–55), vol. i, pp. 508–49; 'Pippa Passes: A Drama' (1841), vol. i, pp. 195–220.

6 – For VW on Christina Rossetti (1830–94), see 'I am Christina Rossetti' above and '"I am Christina Rossetti"' in *CR2*.

7 – Stopford A. Brooke, MA, *English Literature from A.D. 670 to A.D. 1832*, with a chapter on Literature Since 1832 by George Sampson, MA (3rd ed., Macmillan, 1896; reprinted with additional ch., 1924), p. 173. See also 'Stopford Brooke', *II VW Essays*, esp. p. 187, n. 4.

8 – Felicia Dorothea Hemans (1793–1835), poet, author of 'The boy stood on the burning deck' and other popular pieces; Eliza Cook (1812–89), who ran a popular journal, 1849–54, and wrote such poems as 'The Old Arm-Chair' (1837); Jean Ingelow (1820–97), poet, author of 'The High Tide on the Coast of Lincolnshire, 1571' (1863) and 'A Story of Doom' (1867); Alexander Smith (1829–67), lace-pattern maker and author of 'A Life Drama' (1853) and *A Summer in Skye* (1865); Sir Edwin Arnold (1832–1904), author of a poem about Buddha, *The Light of Asia* (1879); Robert Montgomery (1807–55), whose verse enjoyed enormous popularity, especially in Low Church circles.

9 – *Aurora Leigh*, 'Dedication to [the author's cousin] John Kenyon, Esq.'

10 – *The Letters of Robert Browning and Elizabeth Barrett Barrett . . .*, ed. R. B. B. [Robert Barrett Browning] (2 vols in one, John Murray, 1930), vol. i, E. B. Barrett to Robert Browning, 27 February 1845, p. 32, which has: 'truth as I conceive of it out'.

11 – See Samuel Taylor Coleridge (1772–1834), 'The Rime of the Ancient Mariner' (1798), *OBEV*, no. 549, p. 628, 4th stanza.

12 – *Aurora Leigh*, First Book, p. 2 (1873), ll. 29–31 (1978):

> I write. My Mother was a Florentine,
> Whose rare blue eyes were shut from seeing me
> When scarcely I was four years old . . .

13 – *Ibid.*, p. 3 (1873), ll. 65–8 (1978).
14 – *Ibid.*, p. 11 (1873), ll. 286–7 (1978).
15 – *Ibid.*, p. 11 (1873), ll. 299–300 (1978). On 30 December 1931 VW wrote to Pernel Strachey: 'although the Stracheys and Stephen's may fight like cat and dog I cant help thinking we are of one flesh when it comes to a pinch' (*IV VW Letters*, no. 2500).
16 – *Ibid.*, p. 17 (1873), ll. 473–5 (1978):

> I had relations in the Unseen, and drew
> The elemental nutriment and heat
> From nature . . .

17 – *Ibid.*, p. 40 (1873), ll. 1096–8 (1978).
18 – *Ibid.*, p. 30 (1873), ll. 833–8 (1978).
19 – *Ibid.*, p. 26 (1873), ll. 705–9 (1978).
20 – *Letters*, vol. i, E. B. Barrett to Robert Browning, 20 March 1845, pp. 43–4, which has: 'drooped to the ground'.
21 – *The Letters of Elizabeth Barrett Browning*, ed. Frederic G. Kenyon (2 vols, Smith Elder, 1897), vol. i, 1 May 1848, to John Kenyon, p. 363. Aeschylus (525/4–456/5 BC); Plato (424/3–348/7 BC). Honoré de Balzac (1799–1850); George Sand, pseudonym of Armandine-Aurore Lucile Dupin, Baronne Dudevant (1804–76), French novelist and feminist.
22 – Daniel Dunglas Hume, later Home (1833–86), gave spiritualist displays in 1857 to Napoléon III (1808–73), Emperor of the French, 1852–70. Unlike Elizabeth, Robert Browning 'conceived a violent loathing of Home and later lampooned him viciously in "Mr Sludge the Medium" (1864)' (*ODNB*). The Brownings' views were debated in the *TLS*, 14 and 28 November, and 5 December 1902.
23 – Roncesvalles, a small village in northern Spain within five miles of the French frontier, is famous in history and legend for the defeat of Charlemagne and the death of Roland in 778 when Charlemagne's rearguard was destroyed by Basque tribes.
24 – *Aurora Leigh*, Fifth Book, p. 188 (1873), ll. 208–10 (1978).
25 – 1846 was the year of Elizabeth Barrett's marriage; *Aurora Leigh* was published in 1857; it is possible that VW intended to write '1856' (cf. p. 259), the year appended to the poem's dedication and presumably the year in which it was completed.
26 – *Aurora Leigh*, Fifth Book, p. 193 (1873), ll. 339–40 (1978):

Boards, actors, prompters, gaslight, and costume,
And take for a worthier stage the soul itself,

27 – *Ibid.*, p. 189 (1873), ll. 223–4, 235–6 (1978).
28 – Coventry Patmore (1823–96), *The Angel in the House* (the first part published anonymously in 1854; subsequent parts in 1856, 1860 and 1862); Arthur Hugh Clough (1819–61), *The Bothie of Toper-na-Fuosich* (1848; changed in later editions to *The Bothie of Tober-na-Vuolich*).
29 – Charlotte Brontë (1816–55), *Jane Eyre* (1847); William Makepeace Thackeray (1811–63), *Vanity Fair* (1847–8); Charles Dickens (1812–70), *David Copperfield* (1849–50); Elizabeth Gaskell (1810–65), *Cranford* (1851–3); Anthony Trollope (1815–82), *The Warden* (1855); George Eliot, *Scenes of Clerical Life* (1857); George Meredith, *The Ordeal of Richard Feverel* (1859).
30 – *Aurora Leigh*, Fifth Book, p. 188 (1873), l. 192 (1978).
31 – *The Angel in the House* (4th ed., Macmillan, 1866), Canto V, 'The Violets', pt 2, ll. 1–4, p. 33.
32 – *Aurora Leigh*, Ninth Book, p. 376 (1873), ll. 209–14 (1978).
33 – Charles Fourier (1772–1837), French social utopist.
34 – Thomas Lovell Beddoes (1803–49), poet and dramatist, notably of *Death's Jest-Book, or, The Fool's Tragedy*; Sir Henry Taylor (1800–86), author of many verse plays, the best-known being *Philip Van Artevelde* (1834); Robert Bridges (1844–1930), Poet Laureate from 1913.
35 – George V reigned 1910–36.

The Love of Reading

At this late hour of the world's history books are to be found in every room of the house – in the nursery, in the drawing room, in the dining room, in the kitchen. And in some houses they have collected so that they have to be accommodated with a room of their own. Novels, poems, histories, memoirs, valuable books in leather, cheap books in paper – one stops sometimes before them and asks in a transient amazement what is the pleasure I get, or the good I create, from passing my eyes up and down these innumerable lines of print?

Reading is a very complex art – the hastiest examination of our sensations as a reader will show us that much. And our duties as readers are many and various. But perhaps it may be said that our first duty to a book is that one should read it for the first time as if one were writing it. One should begin by sitting in the dock with the criminal not by mounting the bench to sit among the Judges. One should be an accomplice with the writer in his act, whether good or bad, of creation. For each of these books, however it may differ in kind and quality, is an attempt to make something. And our first duty as readers is to try and understand what the writer is making from the first word with which he builds his first sentence to the last with which he ends his book. We must not impose our design upon him; we must not try to make him conform his will to ours. We must allow Defoe to be Defoe and Jane Austen to be Jane Austen[2] as freely as we allow the tiger to have his fur and the tortoise to have his shell. And this is very difficult. For it is one of the qualities of greatness that it brings Heaven and earth and human nature into conformity with its own vision.

The great writers thus often require us to make heroic efforts in order to read them rightly. They bend us and break us. To go from Defoe to Jane Austen, from Hardy to Peacock, from Trollope to Meredith, from Richardson to Rudyard Kipling[3] is to be wrenched and distorted, to be thrown violently this way and that. And so, too, with the lesser writers. Each is singular; each has a view, a temperament, an experience of his own which may conflict with ours but must be allowed to express itself fully if we are to do him justice. And the writers who have most to give us often do most violence to our prejudices, particularly if they are our own contemporaries, so that we have need of all our imagination and understanding if we are to get the utmost that they can give us.

But reading, as we have suggested, is a complex art. It does not merely consist in sympathising and understanding. It consists, too, in criticising and in judging. The reader must leave the dock and mount the bench. He must cease to be the friend; he must become the judge. And this second process, which we may call the process of after-reading, for it is often done without the book before us, yields an even more solid pleasure than that which we receive when we are actually turning the pages. During the actual reading new impressions are always cancelling or completing the old. Delight, anger, boredom, laughter succeed each other incessantly as we read. Judgment is suspended, for we cannot know what may come next. But now the book is completed. It has taken a definite shape. And the book as a whole is different from the book received currently in several different parts. It has a shape, it has a being. And this shape, this being, can be held in the mind and compared with the shapes of other books and given its own size and smallness by comparison with theirs.

But if this process of judging and deciding is full of pleasure it is also full of difficulty. Not much help can be looked for from outside. Critics and criticism abound, but it does not help us greatly to read the views of another mind when our own is still hot from a book that we have just read. It is after one has made up one's own opinion that the opinions of others are most illuminating. It is when we can defend our own judgment that we get most from the judgment of the great critics – the Johnsons, the Drydens and the Arnolds.[4] To make up our own minds we can best help ourselves first by realising the impression that the book has left as fully and sharply as possible, and then by comparing this impression with the impressions that we have formulated in the past. There they hang in the wardrobe of the mind – the shapes of the books we have read, like clothes that we have taken off and hung up to wait their season. Thus, if we have just read say *Clarissa Harlowe* for the first time we take it and let it show itself against the shape that remains in our minds after reading *Anna Karenina*.[5] We place them side by side and at once the outlines of the two books are cut out against each other as the angle of a house (to change the figure) is cut out against the fullness of the harvest moon. We contrast Richardson's prominent qualities with Tolstoi's. We contrast his indirectness and verbosity with Tolstoi's brevity and directness. We ask ourselves why it is that each writer has chosen so different an angle of approach. We compare the emotion that we felt at different crises of their books. We speculate as to the difference between the eighteenth century in England and the nineteenth century in Russia – but there is no end to the questions that at once suggest themselves as we place the books together. Thus by degrees, by asking questions and answering them, we find that we have decided that the book we have just read is of this kind or that, has this degree of merit or that, takes its station at this point or at that in the literature as a whole. And if we are good readers we thus judge not only the classics and the masterpieces of the dead, but we pay the living writers the compliment of comparing them as they should be compared with the pattern of the great books of the past.

Thus, then, when the moralists ask us what good we do by running our eyes over these many printed pages, we can reply that we are doing our part as readers to help masterpieces into the world. We are fulfilling our share of the creative task – we are stimulating, encouraging, rejecting, making our approval and disapproval felt; and are thus acting as a check and a spur upon the writer. That is one reason for reading books – we are helping to bring good books into the world and to make bad books impossible. But it is not the true reason. The true reason remains the inscrutable one – we get pleasure from reading. It is a complex pleasure and a difficult pleasure; it varies from age to age and from book to book. But that pleasure is enough. Indeed that pleasure is so great that one cannot doubt that without it the world would be a far different and a far inferior place from what it is. Reading has changed the world and continues to change it. When the day of judgment comes therefore and all secrets are laid bare, we shall not be surprised to learn that the reason why we have grown from apes to men, and left our caves and dropped our bows and arrows and sat round the fire and talked and given to the poor and helped the sick – the reason why we have made shelter and society out of the wastes of the desert and the tangle of the jungle is simply this – we have loved reading.

1 – An adaptation by VW of her essay 'How Should One Read a Book?', used as a preface (pp. 3–5) to booklists entitled *Company of Books*, published November 1931, (*Kp4* B13), by the Hampshire Bookshop, Northampton, Massachusetts, and by the Walden Bookshop, Chicago. Nothing is known about the genesis of this version, except the statement at the end of the preface: 'Mrs. Woolf has prepared the above preface especially for Company of Books. It is abridged from a longer article from *The Yale Review*. (Copyright Yale University Press, New Haven, Conn.)'. On p. 2 is a full-page cropped photograph of VW in her mother's dress taken for *Vogue* in 1924. On p. 26 of the booklists, VW's books are advertised, with a description of *The Waves*, which had been published by Harcourt, Brace on 22 October: 'A book of great beauty, subtlety, and originality, in which the emotional responses to life, the innermost processes of thought, are Mrs. Woolf's chief concern as she traces the development from childhood to maturity of a group of six persons.' See 'How Should One Read a Book?', *IV VW Essays*, and *CR2*. See also 'Reading', 'On Re-reading Novels' and 'Byron and Mr Briggs', *III VW Essays*. Reprinted: *The Love of Reading* (Northampton, MA: Smith College Library, 1985).

2 – Daniel Defoe (1660?–1731); Jane Austen (1775–1817).

3 – Thomas Hardy (1840–1928); Thomas Love Peacock (1785–1866); Anthony Trollope (1815–82); George Meredith (1828–1909); Samuel Richardson (1689–1761); Rudyard Kipling (1865–1936).

4 – Samuel Johnson (1709–84); John Dryden (1631–1700); Matthew Arnold (1822–88).

5 – Samuel Richardson, *Clarissa* (1747–8); Leo Tolstoy (1828–1910), *Anna Karenina* (1875–7).

The Docks of London

'Whither, O splendid ship'[2] the poet asked as he lay on the shore and watched the great sailing ship pass away on the horizon. Perhaps, as he imagined, it was making for some port in the Pacific; but one day almost certainly it must have heard an irresistible call and come past the North Foreland and the Reculvers, and entered the narrow waters of the Port of London, sailed past the low banks of Gravesend and Northfleet and Tilbury, up Erith Reach and Barking Reach and Gallion's Reach, past the gas works and the sewage works till it found, for all the world like a car on a parking ground, a space reserved for it in the deep waters of the Docks.[3] There it furled its sails and dropped anchor.

However romantic and free and fitful they may seem, there is scarcely a ship on the seas that does not come to anchor in the Port of London in time. From a launch in midstream one can see them swimming up the river with all the marks of their voyage still on them. Liners come, high-decked, with their galleries and their awnings and their passengers grasping their bags and leaning over the rail, while the lascars tumble and scurry below – home they come, a thousand of these big ships every week of the year to anchor in the docks of London. They take their way majestically through a crowd of tramp steamers, and colliers and barges heaped with coal and swaying red sailed boats, which, amateurish though they look, are bringing bricks from Harwich or cement from Colchester – for all is business; there are no pleasure boats on this river. Drawn by some irresistible current, they come from the storms and calms of the sea, its silence and loneliness to their allotted anchorage. The engines stop; the sails are furled; and suddenly the gaudy funnels and the tall masts show up incongruously against a row of workmen's houses, against the black walls of huge warehouses. A curious change takes place. They have no longer the proper perspective of sea and sky behind them, and no longer the proper space in which to stretch their limbs. They lie captive, like soaring and winged creatures who have got themselves caught by the leg and lie tethered on dry land.

With the sea blowing its salt into our nostrils, nothing can be more stimulating than to watch the ships coming up the Thames – the big ships and the little ships, the battered and the splendid, ships from India, from Russia, from South America, ships from Australia coming from silence and danger and loneliness past us, home to harbour. But once they drop anchor, once the cranes begin their dipping and their swinging, it seems as if all romance were over. If we turn and go past the anchored ships towards London, we see surely the most dismal prospect in the world. The banks of the river are lined with dingy, decrepit-looking warehouses. They huddle on land that has become flat and slimy mud. The same air of decrepitude and of being run up provisionally stamps them all. If a window is broken, broken it remains. A fire that has lately blackened and blistered one of them seems to have left it no more forlorn and joyless than its neighbours. Behind the masts and funnels lies a sinister dwarf city of workmen's houses. In the foreground cranes and warehouses, scaffolding and gasometers line the banks with a skeleton architecture.

When, suddenly, after acres and acres of this desolation one floats past an old stone house standing in a real field, with real trees growing in clumps, the sight is disconcerting. Can it be possible that there is earth, that there once were fields and crops beneath this desolation and disorder? Trees and fields seem to survive incongruously like a sample of another civilisation among the wall-paper factories and soap factories that have stamped out old lawns and terraces. Still more incongruously one passes an old grey country church which still rings its bells, and keeps its churchyard green as if country people were still coming across the fields to service. Further down, an inn with swelling bow windows still wears a strange air of dissipation and pleasure making. In the middle years of the nineteenth century it was a favourite resort of pleasure makers, and figured in some of the most famous divorce cases of the time. Now pleasure has gone and labour has come; and it stands derelict like some beauty in her midnight finery looking out over mud flats and candle works, while malodorous mounds of earth, upon which trucks are perpetually tipping fresh heaps, have entirely consumed the fields where, a hundred years ago, lovers wandered and picked violets.

As we go on steaming up the river to London we meet its refuse coming down. Barges heaped with old buckets, razor blades, fish tails, newspapers and ashes – whatever we leave on our plates and throw into our dust bins – are discharging their cargoes upon the most desolate land in the world. The long mounds have been fuming and smoking and harbouring innumerable rats and growing a rank coarse grass and giving off a gritty, acrid air for fifty years. The dumps get higher and higher, and thicker and thicker, their sides more precipitous with tin cans, their pinnacles more angular with ashes year by year. But then, past all this sordidity, sweeps indifferently a great liner, bound for India. She takes her way through rubbish barges, and sewage barges, and dredgers out to sea. A little further, on the left hand, we are suddenly surprised – the sight upsets all our proportions once more – by what appear to be the stateliest buildings ever raised by the hand of man. Greenwich Hospital with all its columns and domes comes down in perfect symmetry to the water's edge, and makes the river again a stately waterway where the nobility of England once walked at their ease on green lawns, or descended stone steps to their pleasure barges.[4] As we come closer to the Tower Bridge the authority of the city begins to assert itself. The buildings thicken and heap themselves higher. The sky seems laden with heavier, purpler clouds. Domes swell; church spires, white with age, mingle with the tapering, pencil-shaped chimneys of factories. One hears the roar and the resonance of London itself. Here at last, we have landed at that thick and formidable circle of ancient stone, where so many drums have beaten and heads have fallen, the Tower of London itself. This is the knot, the clue, the hub of all those scattered miles of skeleton desolation and ant-like activity. Here growls and grumbles that rough city song that has called the ships from the sea and brought them to lie captive beneath its warehouses.[5]

Now from the dock side we look down into the heart of the ship that has been lured from its voyaging and tethered to the dry land. The passengers and their bags have disappeared; the sailors have gone too. Indefatigable cranes are now at work, dipping and swinging, swinging and dipping. Barrels, sacks, crates are being picked up out of the hold and swung regularly on shore. Rhythmically, dexterously, with an order that has some æsthetic delight in it, barrel is laid by barrel, case by case, cask by cask, one behind another, one on top of another, one beside another in endless array down the aisles and arcades of the immense low-ceiled, entirely plain and unornamented warehouses. Timber, iron, grain, wine, sugar, paper, tallow, fruit – whatever the ship has gathered from the plains, from the forests, from the pastures of the whole world is here lifted from its hold and set in its right place. A thousand ships with a thousand cargoes are being unladen every week. And not only is each package of this vast and varied merchandise picked up and set down accurately, but each is weighed and opened, sampled and recorded, and again stitched up and laid in its place, without haste, or waste, or hurry, or confusion by a very few men in shirt-sleeves, who, working with the utmost organisation in the common interest – for buyers will take their word and abide by their decision – are yet able to pause in their work and say to the casual visitor, 'Would you like to see what sort of thing we sometimes find in sacks of cinnamon? Look at this snake!'

A snake, a scorpion, a beetle, a lump of amber, the diseased tooth of an elephant, a basin of quicksilver – these are some of the rarities and oddities that have been picked out of this vast[a] merchandise and stood on a table. But with this one concession to curiosity, the temper of the Docks is severely utilitarian. Oddities, beauties, rarities may occur, but if so, they are instantly tested for their mercantile value. Laid on the floor among the circles of elephant tusks is a heap of larger and browner tusks than the rest. Brown they well may be, for these are the tusks of mammoths that have lain frozen in Siberian ice for fifty thousand years; but fifty thousand years are suspect in the eyes of the ivory expert. Mammoth ivory tends to warp; you cannot extract billiard balls from mammoths, but only umbrella handles and the backs of the cheaper kind of hand-glass. Thus if you buy an umbrella or a looking-glass not of the finest quality, it is likely that you are buying the tusk of a brute that roamed through Asian forests before England was an island.[6]

One tusk makes a billiard ball, another serves for a shoe-horn – every commodity in the world has been examined and graded according to its use and value. Trade is ingenious and indefatigable beyond the bounds of imagination. None of all the multitudinous products and waste products of the earth but has been tested and found some possible use for. The bales of wool that are being swung from the hold of an Australian ship are girt, to save space, with iron hoops; but the hoops do not litter the floor; they are sent to Germany and made into safety razors. The wool itself exudes a coarse greasiness. This grease, which is harmful to blankets, serves, when extracted, to make face cream. Even the burrs that stick in the wool of certain breeds of sheep have their use, for they prove that the sheep undoubtedly were fed on certain rich pastures. Not a burr, not a tuft of wool, not an iron hoop is unaccounted for. And the aptness of everything to its purpose, the forethought and readiness which have provided for every process, come, as if by the back door, to provide that element of beauty which nobody in the Docks has ever given half a second of thought to. The warehouse is perfectly fit to be a warehouse; the crane to be a crane. Hence beauty begins to steal in. The cranes dip and swing, and there is rhythm in their regularity. The warehouse walls are open wide to admit sacks and barrels; but through them one sees all the roofs of London, its masts and spires, and the unconscious, vigorous movements of men lifting and unloading. Because barrels of wine require to be laid on their sides in cool vaults all the mystery of dim lights, all the beauty of low arches is thrown in as an extra.

The wine vaults[7] present a scene of extraordinary solemnity. Waving long blades of wood to which lamps have been fixed, we peer about, in what seems to be a vast cathedral, at cask after cask lying in a dim sacerdotal atmosphere, gravely maturing, slowly ripening. We might be priests worshipping in the temple of some silent religion and not merely wine tasters and Customs' Officers as we wander, waving our lamps up this aisle, down that. A yellow cat precedes us; otherwise the vaults are empty of all human life. Here side by side the objects of our worship lie swollen with sweet liquor, spouting red wine if tapped. A winy sweetness fills the vaults like incense. Here and there a gas jet flares, not indeed to give light, or because of the beauty of the green and grey arches which it calls up in endless procession, down avenue after avenue, but simply because so much heat is required to mellow the wine. Use produces beauty as a bye-product. From the low arches a white cotton-wool-like growth depends. It is a fungus, but whether lovely or loathsome matters not; it is welcome because it proves that the air possesses the right degree of dampness for the health of the precious fluid.

Even the English language has adapted itself to the needs of commerce. Words have formed round objects and taken their exact outline. One may look in the dictionary in vain for the warehouse meaning of 'valinch,' 'shive,'[b] 'shirt,' and 'flogger,'[8] but in the warehouse they have formed naturally on the tip of the tongue. So too the light stroke on either side of the barrel which makes the bung start has been arrived at by years of trial and experiment. It is the quickest, the most effective of actions. Dexterity can go no further.

The only thing, one comes to feel, that can change the routine of the docks is a change in ourselves. Suppose, for instance, that we gave up drinking claret, or took to using rubber instead of wool for our blankets, the whole machinery of production and distribution would rock and reel and seek about to adapt itself afresh. It is we – our tastes, our fashions, our needs – that make the cranes dip and swing, that call the ships from the sea. Our body is their master. We demand shoes, furs, bags, stoves, oil, rice puddings, candles; and they are brought us. Trade watches us anxiously to see what new desires are beginning to grow in us, what new dislikes. One feels an important, a complex, a necessary animal as one stands on the quayside watching the cranes hoist this barrel, that crate, that other bale from the holds of the ships that have come to anchor. Because one chooses to light a cigarette, all those barrels of Virginian tobacco⁹ are swung on shore. Flocks upon flocks of Australian sheep have submitted to the shears because we demand woollen overcoats in winter. As for the umbrella that we swing idly to and fro, a mammoth who roared through the swamps fifty thousand years ago has yielded up its tusk to make the handle.

Meanwhile the ship flying the Blue Peter moves slowly out of the dock; it has turned its bows to India or Australia once more. But in the Port of London, lorries jostle each other in the little street that leads from the dock – for there has been a great sale, and the cart horses are struggling and striving to distribute the wool over England.

a – Typescript draft and *Good Housekeeping*: 'cast'.
b – Typescript draft and *Good Housekeeping*: 'shrive'.

1 – A signed essay in *Good Housekeeping*, December 1931, (*Kp4* C332.1); the first of six essays in 'The London Scene' (VW initially called the series 'Six Articles on London Life'). The essay was accompanied by pen-and-ink sketches by Robin Tanner and was introduced: 'To all who know or dream of the glamour of London we commend this finely etched word picture of London [*sic*] River, first in a gallery of scenes made vividly alive by the brilliant pen of Virginia Woolf'. When VW was negotiating through her agent, Curtis Brown, about writing for *Good Housekeeping*, she was conscious of the Huxleys visiting England to gather material for articles on industrial Britain: 'I feel us, compared with Aldous & Maria, unsuccessful. They're off today to do mines, factories . . . black country; did the docks when they were here; must see England . . . And I am to write 6 articles straight off about what? And a story. About what?' (*IV VW Diary*, 17 February 1931). She wrote to Clive Bell on 21 February: 'Aldous astounds me – his energy, his modernity. Is it that he can't see anything that he has to see so much? Not content with touring Europe with Sullivan to ask all great men of all countries what they think of God, science, the soul, the future and so on, he spends his week in London visiting docks, where with Maria's help he can just distinguish a tusk from frozen bullock: and now is off on a tour of the Black

Country, to visit works, to go down mines' (*IV VW Letters*, no. 2330). A month later she wrote: 'I am writing little articles of a morning, & should have been sketching the Houses of the Great this morning, but that I have not the material' (*IV VW Diary*, 16 March 1931). On 20 March she 'visited the docks in a Port of London Authority launch with a party which included LW, Vita Sackville-West and the Persian Ambassador; she returned with Harold Nicolson' (*ibid.*, p. 15, fn. 8); the 'launch went as far as Tilbury, and the party lunched with the P.L.A.' (*IV VW Letters*, p. 301, fn. 2). For Nicolson's broadcast on 27 March on 'The Port of London', see his *People and Things: Wireless Talks* (Constable, 1931), pp. 156–63. On 22 March VW wrote to Ethel Smyth: 'I'm being bored to death by my London articles – pure brilliant description – six of them – and not a thought for fear of clouding the brilliancy: and I have had to go all over the Thames, port of London, in a launch, with the Persian Ambassador – but that I liked – I dont like facts, though' (*ibid.*, no. 2339). On 11 April she wrote: 'Oh I am so tired of correcting my own writing ... I have however learnt I think to dash: & not to finick. I mean the writing is free enough: its the repulsiveness of correcting that nauseates me. And the cramming in & the cutting out. And articles & more articles are asked for. For ever I could write articles' (*IV VW Diary*). The same issue of *Good Housekeeping* also contained: the concluding chapters of John Galsworthy's *Maid-in-Waiting*. See Appendix VIII and also the other essays in the series: 'Oxford Street Tide', 'Great Men's Houses', 'Abbeys and Cathedrals', '"This is the House of Commons"' and 'Portrait of a Londoner'. A holograph draft, entitled 'The Port of London' (dated 13 March 1931), and a final typescript draft, entitled 'The Docks', together with the original layout and proofs (Berg, M 13, M 130). Reprinted: *LSc, CDML*.
2 – 'Whither, O splendid ship, thy white sails crowding / Leaning across the bosom of the urgent West, / That fearest nor sea rising, nor sky clouding, / Whither away, fair rover, and what thy quest?', from 'A Passer-by' by Robert Bridges (1844–1930), Poet Laureate, in *OBEV*, p. 1013, no. 835.
3 – *CDML*, pp. 203–4, n. 2: 'Woolf names the places passed by a ship sailing into the Port of London: North Foreland is the [east]ernmost point of Kent; Reculver is in north Kent; thereafter the ship sails into the mouth of the Thames, passing Tilbury on the north bank and Gravesend and Northfleet on the south. Stretches of the Thames as it passes Erith are known as Erith Reach, then Barking Reach (where the sewage works and power station are) and finally Gallion's Reach', where the entrance to the Royal Docks is located.
4 – Greenwich Hospital was founded in 1694 and begun by Christopher Wren; in 1931 it was occupied by the Royal Naval College. The vocabulary of VW's description is reminiscent of the opening of Coleridge's poem 'Kubla Khan' (1797): 'In Xanadu did Kubla Khan / A stately pleasure-dome decree: / Where Alph, the sacred river, ran ...' (*OBEV*, p. 650, no. 550).
5 – See *The Times*, 2 October 1928, 'Port of London Number': 'For the

purposes of this article London Docks and St. Katharine Dock may be taken together. They lie side by side, just below Tower Bridge, at the eastern end of the Pool. The name "London Docks" is not altogether a happy one; for the inference to be drawn from it is that it is the collective designation of all the docks on the Thames; whereas it denotes, in fact, a comparatively small part of these docks . . . Warehousing is here done on a scale more extensive than anywhere else in the Port of London . . . The variety of the goods handled is astonishing. Some of the more important of them are wine, ivory, wool, rubber, spices, canned fruits, seeds and skins. The floor space devoted to wool alone is nearly 30 acres; while about 27,000 pipes of wine can be stored in the vaults' ('The Docks of the Port of London', p. xi, cols b–c).

6 – See *The Times*, 2 October 1928: 'London is the ivory market of the world . . . the product is becoming scarce. Imports have shown a considerable decline in the past sixty years . . . As to the mammoth ivory of Siberia, few tusks of much commercial value reach London in these days . . . After the cargo has been unloaded at the Port it is weighed and classified and displayed ready for inspection on the ivory floor of warehouse no. 6 in the London Docks, where prospective buyers may investigate its density and whiteness previous to the quarterly auctions. Tusks 9ft. in length and 140lb. in weight are often to be seen on this floor . . . The small tusks are known as "scrivelloes" . . . the manufacturers of billiard balls buy the larger-sized scrivelloes' ('Ivory', p. xviii, col. g); see also 'Treasure Houses of London', p. xvii, photograph, p. xix, and advertisement, p. xxix.

7 – See *ibid.*: 'The storage of wines and spirits at the London Docks requires an area of more than 650,000 feet, as the bulk of imports into London are received by the Port Authority. The vaults here have been famous for more than 120 years, and some of the present stocks have been held since 1870. After having been unloaded from the ships . . . the wines and spirits are sampled and tested for strength at the Customs laboratory and the casks are gauged or measured . . . The rails in the gangways are 28 miles in length' ('Treasure Houses of London', p. xvii, cols e–f); see also 'Wines and Spirits', p. xix.

8 – See *CDML*, p. 204, n. 10: 'these are technical terms used in the storing of liquor. The "valinch" is a sampling tube, used for drawing wine from a cask through a bunghole; a 'shive' is a specially thin bung for sealing a cask; a "shirt" seems to be the term for an inner casing or lining, and a "flogger" is the instrument used to strike the cask in order to open the bung – as in the following sentence.'

9 – In a radio programme Lottie Hope, who worked for the Woolfs from 1916 to 1924 and then for other members of the Bloomsbury Group, described VW rolling her own cigarettes and using a brand of tobacco called 'Virginia'; see 'Portrait of Virginia Woolf', *Virginia Woolf: Critical Assessments*, ed. Eleanor McNees (4 vols, Helm Information, 1994), vol. i, p. 98.

1932

Oxford Street Tide

Down in the docks one sees things in their crudity, their bulk, their enormity. Here in Oxford Street they have been refined and transformed. The huge barrels of damp tobacco have been rolled into innumerable neat cigarettes laid in silver paper. The corpulent bales of wool have been spun into thin vests and soft stockings. The grease of sheep's thick wool has become scented cream for delicate skins. And those who buy and those who sell have suffered the same city change.[2] Tripping, mincing, in black coats, in satin dresses, the human form has adapted itself no less than the animal product. Instead of hauling and heaving, it deftly opens drawers, rolls out silk on counters, measures and snips with yard sticks and scissors.

Oxford Street, it goes without saying, is not London's most distinguished thoroughfare. Moralists have been known to point the finger of scorn at those who buy there, and they have the support of the dandies. Fashion has secret crannies off Hanover Square, round about Bond Street, to which it withdraws discreetly to perform its more sublime rites. In Oxford Street there are too many bargains, too many sales, too many goods marked down to one and eleven three that only last week cost two and six.[3] The buying and selling is too blatant and raucous. But as one saunters towards the sunset – and what with artificial light and mounds of silk and gleaming omnibuses, a perpetual sunset seems to brood over the Marble Arch – the garishness and gaudiness of the great rolling ribbon of Oxford Street has its fascination. It is like the pebbly bed of a river whose stones are for ever washed by a bright stream. Everything glitters and twinkles. The first spring day brings out barrows frilled with tulips, violets, daffodils in brilliant layers. The frail vessels eddy vaguely across the stream of the traffic. At one corner seedy magicians are making slips of coloured paper expand in magic tumblers into bristling forests of splendidly tinted flora – a subaqueous flower garden. At another, tortoises repose on litters of grass. The slowest and most contemplative of creatures display their mild activities on a foot or two of pavement, jealously guarded from passing feet. One infers that the desire of man for the tortoise, like the desire of the moth for the star,[4] is a constant element in human nature. Nevertheless, to see a woman stop and add a tortoise to her string of parcels is perhaps the rarest sight that human eyes can look upon.

Taking all this into account – the auctions, the barrows, the cheapness, the glitter – it cannot be said that the character of Oxford Street is refined. It is a breeding ground, a forcing house of sensation. The pavement seems to sprout horrid tragedies; the divorces of actresses, the suicides of millionaires occur here with a frequency that is unknown in the more austere pavements of the residential districts. News changes quicker than in any other part of London. The press of people passing seems to lick the ink off the placards and to consume more of them and to demand fresh supplies of later editions faster than elsewhere. The mind becomes a glutinous slab that takes impressions and Oxford Street rolls off upon it a perpetual ribbon of changing sights, sounds and movement. Parcels slap and hit; motor omnibuses graze the kerb; the blare of a whole brass band in full tongue dwindles to a thin reed of sound. Buses, vans, cars, barrows stream past like the fragments of a picture puzzle; a white arm rises; the puzzle runs thick, coagulates, stops; the white arm sinks, and away it streams again, streaked, twisted, higgledy-piggledy, in perpetual race and disorder. The puzzle never fits itself together, however long we look.

On the banks of this river of turning wheels our modern aristocrats have built palaces just as in ancient days the Dukes of Somerset and Northumberland, the Earls of Dorset and Salisbury lined the Strand with their stately mansions.[5] The different houses of the great firms testify to the courage, initiative, the audacity of their creators much as the great houses of Cavendish and Percy[6] testify to such qualities in some faraway shire. From the loins of our merchants will spring the Cavendishes and the Percys of the future. Indeed, the great Lords of Oxford Street are as magnanimous as any Duke or Earl who scattered gold or doled out loaves to the poor at his gates. Only their largesse takes a different form. It takes the form of excitement, of display, of entertainment, of windows lit up by night, of banners flaunting by day. They give us the latest news for nothing. Music streams from their banqueting rooms free. You need not spend more than one and eleven three to enjoy all the shelter that high and airy halls provide; and the soft pile of carpets, and the luxury of lifts, and the glow of fabrics, and carpets and silver. Percy and Cavendish could give no more. These gifts of course have an object – to entice the shilling and eleven pennies as freely from our pockets as possible; but the Percys and the Cavendishes were not munificent either without hope of some return, whether it was a dedication from a poet or a vote from a farmer. And both the old lords and the new added considerably to the decoration and entertainment of human life.

But it cannot be denied that these Oxford Street palaces are rather flimsy abodes – perching grounds rather than dwelling places. One is conscious that one is walking on a strip of wood laid upon steel girders, and that the outer wall, for all its florid stone ornamentation, is only thick enough to withstand the force of the wind. A vigorous prod with an umbrella point might well inflict irreparable damage upon the fabric. Many a country cottage built to house farmer or miller when Queen Elizabeth was on the throne will live to see these palaces fall into the dust. The old cottage walls, with their oak beams and their layers of honest brick soundly cemented together still put up a stout resistance to the drills and bores that attempt to introduce the modern blessing of electricity. But any day of the week one may see Oxford Street vanishing at the tap of a workman's pick as he stands perilously balanced on a dusty pinnacle knocking down walls and façades as lightly as if they were made of yellow cardboard and sugar icing.

And again the moralists point the finger of scorn. For such thinness, such papery stone and powdery brick reflect, they say, the levity, the ostentation, the haste and irresponsibility of our age. Yet perhaps they are as much out in their scorn as we should be if we asked of the lily that it should be cast in bronze, or of the daisy that it should have petals of imperishable enamel. The charm of modern London is that it is not built to last; it is built to pass. Its glassiness, its transparency, its surging waves of coloured plaster give a different pleasure and achieve a different end from that which was desired and attempted by the old builders and their patrons, the nobility of England. Their pride required the illusion of permanence. Ours, on the contrary, seems to delight in proving that we can make stone and brick as transitory as our own desires. We do not build for our descendants, who may live up in the clouds or down in the earth, but for ourselves and our own needs. We knock down and rebuild as we expect to be knocked down and rebuilt. It is an impulse that makes for creation and fertility. Discovery is stimulated and invention on the alert.

The palaces of Oxford Street ignore what seemed good to the Greeks, to the Elizabethan, to the eighteenth-century nobleman; they are overwhelmingly conscious that unless they can devise an architecture that shows off the dressing-case, the Paris frock, the cheap stockings, and the jar of bath salts to perfection, their palaces, their mansions and motor-cars and the little villas out at Croydon and Surbiton where their shop assistants live, not so badly after all, with a gramophone and wireless, and money to spend at the movies – all this will be swept to ruin. Hence they stretch stone fantastically; crush together in one wild confusion the styles of Greece, Egypt, Italy, America; and boldly attempt an air of lavishness, opulence, in their effort to persuade the multitude that here unending beauty, ever fresh, ever new, very cheap and within the reach of everybody, bubbles up every day of the week from an inexhaustible well. The mere thought of age, of solidity, of lasting for ever is abhorrent to Oxford Street.

Therefore if the moralist chooses to take his afternoon walk along this particular thoroughfare, he must tune his strain so that it receives into it some queer, incongruous voices. Above the racket of van and omnibus we can hear them crying. God knows, says the man who sells tortoises, that my arm aches; my chance of selling a tortoise is small; but courage! there may come along a buyer; my bed to-night depends on it; so on I must go, as slowly as the police allow, wheeling tortoises down Oxford Street from dawn till dusk. True, says the great merchant, I am not thinking of educating the mass to a higher standard of æsthetic sensibility. It taxes all my wits to think how I can display my goods with the minimum of waste and the maximum of effectiveness. Green dragons on the top of Corinthian columns may help; let us try. I grant, says the middle-class woman, that I linger and look and barter and cheapen and turn over basket after basket of remnants hour by hour. My eyes glisten unseemlily I know, and I grab and pounce with disgusting greed. But my husband is a small clerk in a bank; I have only fifteen pounds a year to dress on; so here I come, to linger and loiter and look, if I can, as well dressed as my neighbours. I am a thief, says a woman of that persuasion, and a lady of easy virtue into the bargain. But it takes a good deal of pluck to snatch a bag from a counter when a customer is not looking; and it may contain only spectacles and old bus tickets after all.[7] So here goes!

A thousand such voices are always crying aloud in Oxford Street. All are tense, all are real, all are urged out of their speakers by the pressure of making a living, finding a bed, somehow keeping afloat on the bounding, careless, remorseless tide of the street. And even a moralist, who is, one must suppose, since he can spend the afternoon dreaming, a man with a balance in the bank – even a moralist must allow that this gaudy, bustling, vulgar street reminds us that life is a struggle; that all building is perishable; that all display is vanity; from which we may conclude – but until some adroit shopkeeper has caught on to the idea and opened cells for solitary thinkers hung with green plush and provided with automatic glowworms and a sprinkling of genuine death's-head moths to induce thought and reflection, it is vain to try to come to a conclusion in Oxford Street.

1 – A signed essay in *Good Housekeeping*, January 1932, (*Kp4* C332.2); the second of six essays in 'The London Scene'. The essay was accompanied by black-and-white modernist illustrations by S. G. Hulme Beaman and was introduced: 'All the colour and fascination of London's most garish, rolling ribbon of a street are in this brilliant word picture: and in the beautiful precision of its language and thought it reveals the name of its distinguished author – Virginia Woolf.' On 28 March 1930 VW wrote: 'A fine spring day. I walked along Oxford St. The buses are strung on a chain. People fight & struggle. Knocking each other off the pavement. Old bareheaded men; a motor car accident; &c. To walk alone in London is the greatest rest' (*III VW Diary*). See also 'The Docks of London' above, and Appendix VIII. The same issue of *Good Housekeeping* also contained: St John Ervine's 'A Great Editor', on J. L. Garvin of the *Observer*. A holograph draft, entitled 'Streets and Shops', and a final typescript draft, entitled 'Oxford Street', together with the original layout and proofs (Berg, M 13, M 131). Reprinted: *LSc, CDML*.
2 – The phrase 'city change' adapts Shakespeare's 'a sea-change' from Ariel's song in *The Tempest*, I, ii, 400, but also suggests the Royal Exchange in the City, abbreviated to 'Change.
3 – I.e. goods costing 'two and six' (2s. 6d. or half a crown, one-eighth of £1, in pre-decimal currency) are marked down to 1s. 11 3/4d.
4 – See 'To ——' ('One word is too often profaned . . .'), by Percy Bysshe Shelley (1792–1822), in *OBEV*, p. 714, no. 615; the desire is defined as: 'The devotion to something afar / From the sphere of our sorrow'.

5 – The mid-sixteenth-century Somerset House was demolished in the late eighteenth century, and replaced by the present building. The early-seventeenth-century Northumberland House was demolished in 1874, and the Percy lion on the arch above the main gateway was removed to Syon House, the Duke's country house opposite Kew Gardens, where it is observed by Katherine Hilbery with 'incredulous laughter': see *Night and Day* (1919; Hogarth Press, 1930), ch. xxv, p. 348. The medieval Salisbury House (named after the Bishops of Salisbury) in Fleet Street was bought by Sir Richard Sackville in 1564; the Sackvilles were created Earls of Dorset in 1603; and the house was destroyed in the Great Fire of 1666. Robert Cecil, Earl of Salisbury, built Salisbury House on the south side of the Strand in the early seventeenth century.

6 – The family names of the Dukes of Northumberland and Devonshire.

7 – VW related in her diary: 'I will make this hasty note about being robbed. I put my bag under my coat at Marshall & Snelgrove's. I turned; & felt, before I looked "It is gone". So it was. Then began questions & futile messages. Then the detective came. He stopped a respectable elderly woman apparently shopping. They exchanged remarks about "the usual one – no she's not here today. Its a young woman in brown fur." Meanwhile I was ravaged, of course, with my own futile wishes – how I had thought, as I put down my bag, this is foolish. I was admitted to the underwor[l]d. I imagined the brown young woman peeping, pouncing. And it was gone my 6 pounds – my two brooches – all because of that moment. They throw the bags away, said the detective. These dreadful women come here – but not so much as to some of the Oxford St. shops. Fluster, regret, humiliation, curiosity, something frustrated, foolish, something jarred, by this underwor[l]d – a foggy evening – going home, penniless – thinking of my green bag – imagining the woman rifling it – her home – her husband . . .' (*III VW Diary*, 23 December 1930). VW wrote to Vanessa Bell on Christmas Day: 'I had a queer adventure by the way, the day I got your coat at Marshall and Snelgroves. I was given £6 to buy Xmas presents; I put my bag under my moleskin, and turned, for one moment, to try on your coat. Then I thought I ought not to leave the bag, so turned to get it – and behold – in that second a thief had snatched it! There was then a great hue and cry, and a detective appeared, and they said a woman in brown fur had been seen; but of course they could not catch her; so there I was, penniless, without key, spectacles, cigarette case or handkerchief. Marshall's refused to lend me a penny as they said I was not on their books; but the detective gave me 10/- of his own. Later that night the bag was found, thrown in a drain; and marvellously, though the £6 were gone, the thief had left my spectacles, keys, and one old earring. I had just bought two for a present. So didn't do as badly as I might' (*IV VW Letters*, no. 2291).

The Rev. William Cole: A Letter

My Dear William,

In my opinion you are keeping something back. Last year when you went to Paris and did not see Madame du Deffand but measured the exact length of every nose on every tombstone – I can assure you they have grown no longer or shorter since – I was annoyed, I admit.[2] But I had the sense to see that, after all, you were alive, and a clergyman, and from Bletchley – in fact, you were as much out of place in Paris as a cowslip impaled upon the diamond horns of a duchess's tiara. Put him back in Bletchley, I said, plant him in his own soil, let him burble on in his own fashion, and the miracle will happen. The cows will low; the church bells will ring; all Bletchley will come alive; and, reading over William's shoulder, we shall see deep, deep into the hearts of Mrs Willis and Mr Robinson.[3]

I regret to tell you that I was wrong. You are not a cowslip. You do not bloom. The hearts of Mrs Willis and Mr Robinson remain sealed books to us. You write Jan. 16th, 1766,[4] and it is precisely as if I had written Jan. 16th, 1932. In other words, you have rubbed all the bloom off two hundred years and that is so rare a feat – it implies something so queer in the writer – that I am intrigued and puzzled and cannot help asking you to enlighten me. Are you simply a bore, William? No, that is out of the question. In the first place, Horace Walpole[5] did not tolerate bores, or write to them, or go for country jaunts with them; in the second, Miss Waddell loves you. You shed all round you, in the eyes of Miss Waddell, that mysterious charm which those we love impart to their meanest belongings. She loves your parrot; she commiserates your cat. Every room in your house is familiar to her. She knows about your Gothic chamber and your neat arched bed; she knows how many steps led up to the pantry and down to the summer house; she knows, she approves, how you spent every hour of your day. She sees the neighbours through the light of your eyes. She laughs at some; she likes others; she knows who was fat and who was thin, and who told lies, who had a bad leg, and who was no better than she should have been. Mr and Mrs Barton, Thomas Tansley, Mr and Mrs Lord of Mursley, the Diceys, and Dr Pettingal,[6] are all real and alive to her; so are your roses, your horses, your nectarines and your knats.

Would that I could see through her eyes! Alas, wherever I look I see blight and mildew. The moss never grows upon your walls. Your nectarines never ripen.[7] The blackbird sings, but out of tune. The knats – and you say 'I hardly know a place so pestered with that vermin as Bletchley'[8] – bite, just like our gnats. As for the human beings they pass through the same disenchantment. Not that I have any fault to find with your friends or with Bletchley either. Nobody is very good, but then nobody is very bad. Tom sometimes hits a hare, oftener he misses,[9] the fish sometimes bite, but not always; if it freezes it also thaws, and though the harvest was not bad it might have been better. But now, William, confess. We know in our hearts, you and I, that England in the eighteenth century was not like this. We know from Woodforde, from Walpole, from Thomas Turner, from Skinner, from Gray, from Fielding, from Jane Austen,[10] from scores of memoirs and letters, from a thousand forgotten stone masons, bricklayers and cabinet makers, from a myriad sources, that I have not learning to name or space to quote, that England was a substantial, beautiful country in the eighteenth century; aristocratic and common; hand-made and horse-ploughed; an eating, drinking, bastard-begetting, laughing, cursing, humorous, eccentric, lovable land. If with your pen in your hand and the date facing you, Jan. 16th, 1766, you see none of all this, then the fault is yours. Some spite has drawn a veil across your eyes. Indeed, there are pouches under them I could swear. You slouch as you walk. You switch at thistles half-heartedly with your stick. You do not much enjoy your food. Gossip has no relish for you. You mention the 'scandalous story of Mr Felton Hervey, his two daughters and a favourite footman' and add, 'I hope it is not true.'[11] So do I, but I cannot put much life into my hoping when you withhold the facts. You stop Pettingal in the middle of his boasting – you cut him short with a sarcasm – just as he was proving that the Greeks liked toasted cheese and was deriving the word Bergamy from the Arabic.[12] As for Madame Geoffrin,[13] you never lose a chance of saying something disobliging about that lady; a coffee-pot[14] has only to be reputed French for you to defame it. Then look how touchy you are – you grumble, the servants are late with the papers,[15] you complain, Mr Pitt[16] never thanked you for the pigeons (yet Horace Walpole thought you a philosopher); then how you suspect people's motives; how you bid fathers thresh their little boys; how you are sure the servant steals the onions. All these are marks of a thin-blooded poverty-stricken disposition. And yet – you are a good man; you visit the poor; you bury the infected; you have been educated at Cambridge; you venerate antiquity. The truth is that you are concealing something, even from Miss Waddell.

Why, I ask, did you write this diary and lock it in a chest with iron hoops and insist that no one was to read it or publish it for twenty years after your death unless it were that you had something on your mind, something that you wished to confess and get rid of? You are not one of those people who love life so well that they cherish even the memory of roast mutton, like Woodforde; you did not hate life so much that you must shriek out your curse on it, like poor Skinner. You write and write, ramblingly, listlessly, like a person who is trying to bring himself to say the thing that will explain to himself what is wrong with himself. And you find it very hard. You would rather mention anything but that – Miss Chester, I mean, and the boat on the Avon. You cannot force yourself to admit that you have kept that lock of hair in your drawer these thirty years. When Mrs Robinson, her daughter, asked you for it (March 19th, 1766)[17] you said you could not find it. But you were not easy under that concealment. You did at length go to your private drawer (Nov. 26th, 1766)[18] and there it was, as you well knew. But even so, with the lock of hair in your hand, you still seek to put us off the scent. You ramble on about giving Mrs Robinson a barrel of oysters; about potted rabbits; about the weather, until suddenly out it comes, 'Gave Mrs Robinson a braided Lock of Lady Robinson's Mother's hair (and Sister to Mrs Robinson of Cransley), which I cut off in a Boat on the River Avon at Bath about 30 years ago when my Sister Jane and myself were much acquainted with her, then Miss Chester.'[19] There we have it. The poisoned tooth is out. You were once young and ardent and very much in love. Passion overcame you. You were alone. The wind blew a lock of Miss Chester's hair from beneath her hat. You reached forward. You cut it. And then? Nothing. That is your tragedy – you yourself failed yourself. You think of that scene twenty times a day, I believe, as you saunter, rather heavily, along the damp paths at Bletchley. That is the dreary little tune that you hum as you stoop over your parments[20] measuring noses, deciphering dates – 'I failed, failed, failed on the boat on the Avon.' That is why your nectarines are blighted; and the parrot dies; and the parlour cat is scalded; and you love nobody except, perhaps, your little dun-coloured horse.[21] That is why you 'always had a mind to live retired in Glamorganshire.'[22] That is why Mr Pitt never thanked you for the pigeons. That is why Mr Stonehewer became His Majesty's

Historiographer, while you visited paupers in Fenny Stratford. That is why he never came to see you, and why you observed so bitterly, that 'people suffer themselves to forget their old friends when they are surrounded by the great and are got above the world.'[23] You see, William, if you hoard a failure, if you come to grudge even the sun for shining – and that, I think, is what you did – fruit does not ripen; a blight falls upon parrots and cats; people would actually rather that you did not give them pigeons.

But enough. I may be wrong. Miss Chester's hair may have nothing to do with it. And Miss Waddell may be right – every good quality of heart and head may be yours. I am sure I hope so. But I beg, William, now that you are about to begin a fresh volume,[24] at Cambridge too, with men of character and learning, that you will pull yourself together. Speak out. Justify the faith that Miss Waddell has in you. For you are keeping one of the finest scholars of her time shut up in the British Museum among mummies and policemen and wet umbrellas. There must be a trifle of ninety-five volumes more of you in those iron-bound chests. Lighten her task; relieve our anxiety, and so add to the gratitude of your obliged obedient servant,

Virginia Woolf.

1 – A signed review in the NS&N, 6 February 1932, (Kp4 C333), of The Blecheley Diary of the Rev. William Cole, M.A. F.S.A., 1765–67, ed. Francis Griffin Stokes, with Introduction, 'A Description of the Principal Personages Mentioned in the Diary . . .' and Index by Helen Waddell (Constable, 1931). VW adopts the modern spelling of Bletchley. The issue of NS&N also contained: 'The Rev. William Cole: A Review' by Lord Ponsonby; letters from Julian Bell on animal cruelty and from Henry W. Nevinson on LW's article, 'Lytton Strachey', of 30 January; Desmond MacCarthy's review of Helen!, A. P. Herbert's adaptation of Offenbach's La Belle Hélène; and Augustine Birrell's review of Sir Alfred Pease's Elections and Recollections. See 'All About Books' above, and 'Two Antiquaries: Walpole and Cole', VI VW Essays. Reading notes (Berg, RN 1.8) (VWRN VIII). Reprinted: DoM, CE.

2 – See 'All About Books'. Opposite the title page of The Blecheley Diary, in an advertisement for Cole's Paris Journal 'uniform with this volume', and in between quotations from J. C. Squire in the Observer and Harold Nicolson in the Daily Express, the following quotation is taken from 'All About Books': 'When [. .] the rumour spread that the diary of an old clergyman called Cole, who had gone to Paris in the autumn of 1765, was about to be published, and that Miss Waddell had put her brilliance and her erudition at our service, a purr of content and anticipation rose from half the armchairs of England . . . How excellent [VW: admirable] Mr. Cole would be at

home in his own parish! How gladly we will read sixteen volumes about life in Blecheley if Miss Waddell will print them!'

3 – See *Blecheley Diary*, 'A Description of the Principal Personages', p. lix.

4 – *Ibid.*, pp. 8–9.

5 – Horace Walpole (1717–97).

6 – See *Blecheley Diary*, 'A Description', pp. xlix–lx.

7 – See *ibid.*, p. 129.

8 – *Ibid.*, p. 68; see also p. 181.

9 – See *ibid.*, p. 58: 'Tom went . . . to Master Watt's at Tatenhall in Quest of an Hare: but after all the Times he has been there & elsewhere in Persuit of one, he never brought me one in his Life.'

10 – For VW on James Woodforde (1740–1803), see *CR2*; Thomas Turner (1729–93), diarist and schoolmaster turned shopkeeper; for VW on John Skinner (1772–1839), see *CR2*; Thomas Gray (1716–71); Henry Fielding (1707–54); Jane Austen (1775–1817).

11 – *Blecheley Diary*, p. 164.

12 – See *ibid.*, p. 144.

13 – See *ibid.*, p. 141.

14 – See *ibid.*, pp. 96–7.

15 – See *ibid.*, p. 208.

16 – See *ibid.*, pp. 130–1; John Pitts, Rector of Great Brickhill.

17 – See *ibid.*, p. 26.

18 – See *ibid.*, p. 157.

19 – *Ibid.*

20 – A 'parment' is an obsolete word for a type of pear (see *OED*); presumably 'parchments' is meant.

21 – See *Blecheley Diary*, 'A Description', p. xlix: Cole's 'favourite little Dun fat Horse' was 'the only creature in Blecheley for whom Mr Cole felt something approaching passion'. For the parrot and the cat, see the Introduction, p. xxii; and p. 12 for the death of the parrot.

22 – *Ibid.*, p. 188, which has: 'I always had a Desire to live retired in that County'.

23 – *Ibid.*, p. 95.

24 – Lord Ponsonby concluded his review with: 'The Editor, we are glad to note, promises us another volume.' See *Blecheley Diary*, Editor's preface, p. xii: 'In the forthcoming volume, however, containing the Waterbeche and Milton journals, the diarist will be found in very different surroundings – the dons and combination-rooms of Cambridge to a great extent taking the place of rural clergy and parsonages'; and see also p. ix. This volume did not appear, but 'W. M. Palmer's *William Cole of Milton* (1935), which includes an edition of Cole's parochial notes and church drawings for Cambridgeshire, and two elaborate volumes of Walpole's correspondence with Cole issued by the University of Yale in 1937 were well received, and

Virginia Woolf took Cole and Walpole as the subject of an essay which has
been reprinted several times' (*ODNB*).

Great Men's Houses

London, happily, is becoming full of great men's houses, bought for
the nation and preserved entire with the chairs they sat on and the
cups they drank from, their umbrellas and their chests of drawers.
And it is no frivolous curiosity that sends us to Dickens's house and
Johnson's house[2] and Carlyle's house and Keats's house. We know
them from their houses – it would seem to be a fact that writers
stamp themselves upon their possessions more indelibly than other
people. Of artistic taste they may have none; but they seem always
to possess a much rarer and more interesting gift – a faculty for
housing themselves appropriately, for making the table, the chair, the
curtain, the carpet into their own image.

Take the Carlyles, for instance. One hour spent in 5 Cheyne Row[3]
will tell us more about them and their lives than we can learn from
all the biographies. Go down into the kitchen. There, in two seconds,
one is made acquainted with a fact that escaped the attention of
Froude,[4] and yet was of incalculable importance – they had no water
laid on. Every drop that the Carlyles used – and they were Scots,
fanatical in their cleanliness – had to be pumped by hand from a well
in the kitchen. There is the well at this moment and the pump and
the stone trough into which the cold water trickled. And here, too,
is the wide and wasteful old grate upon which all kettles had to be
boiled if they wanted a hot bath; and here is the cracked yellow tin
bath, so deep and so narrow, which had to be filled with the cans of
hot water that the maid first pumped and then boiled and then carried
up three flights of stairs from the basement.

The high old house without water, without electric light, without
gas fires, full of books and coal smoke and four-poster beds and
mahogany cupboards, where two of the most nervous and exacting
people of their time lived, year in year out, was served by one unfortunate maid. All through the mid-Victorian age the house was necessarily a battlefield where daily, summer and winter, mistress and maid
fought against dirt and cold for cleanliness and warmth.[5] The stairs,
carved as they are and wide and dignified, seem worn by the feet of

harassed women carrying tin cans. The high panelled rooms seem to echo with the sound of pumping and the swish of scrubbing. The voice of the house – and all houses have voices – is the voice of pumping and scrubbing, of coughing and groaning. Up in the attic under a skylight Carlyle groaned, as he wrestled with his history, on a horse-hair chair, while a yellow shaft of London light fell upon his papers and the rattle of a barrel organ and the raucous shouts of street hawkers came through walls whose double thickness distorted but by no means excluded the sound.[6] And the season of the house – for every house has its season – seems to be always the month of February, when cold and fog are in the street and torches flare and the rattle of wheels grows suddenly loud and dies away. February after February Mrs Carlyle lay coughing in the large four-poster hung with maroon curtains in which she was born, and as she coughed the many problems of the incessant battle, against dirt, against cold, came before her. The horse-hair couch needed recovering; the drawing-room paper with its small, dark pattern needed cleaning; the yellow varnish on the panels was cracked and peeling – all must be stitched, cleansed, scoured with her own hands; and had she, or had she not, demolished the bugs that bred and bred in the ancient wood panelling? So the long watches of the sleepless night passed, and then she heard Mr Carlyle stir above her, and held her breath and wondered if Helen[7] were up and had lit the fire and heated the water for his shaving. Another day had dawned and the pumping and the scrubbing must begin again.

Thus number 5 Cheyne Row is not so much a dwelling-place as a battlefield – the scene of labour, effort and perpetual struggle. Few of the spoils of life – its graces and its luxuries – survive to tell us that the battle was worth the effort. The relics of drawing-room and study are like the relics picked up on other battlefields. Here is a packet of old steel nibs; a broken clay pipe; a pen-holder such as schoolboys use; a few cups of white and gold china, much chipped; a horsehair sofa and a yellow tin bath. Here, too, is a cast of the thin worn hands that worked here; and of the excruciated and ravished face of Carlyle when his life was done and he lay dead here.[8] Even the garden at the back of the house seems to be not a place of rest and recreation, but another smaller battlefield marked with a tomb-stone beneath which a dog lies buried.[9] By pumping and by scrubbing, days of victory, evenings of peace and splendour were won, of course. Mrs Carlyle sat, as we see from the picture,[10] in a fine silk dress, in a chair pulled up to a blazing fire and had everything seemly and solid about her; but at what cost had she won it! Her cheeks are hollow; bitterness and suffering mingle in the half-tender, half-tortured expression of the eyes. Such is the effect of a pump in the basement and a yellow tin bath up three pairs of stairs. Both husband and wife had genius; they loved each other; but what can genius and love avail against bugs and tin baths and pumps in the basement?

It is impossible not to believe that half their quarrels might have been spared and their lives immeasurably sweetened if only number 5 Cheyne Row had possessed, as the house agents put it, bath, h. and c., gas fires in the bedrooms, all modern conveniences and indoor sanitation. But then, we reflect, as we cross the worn threshold, Carlyle with hot water laid on would not have been Carlyle; and Mrs Carlyle without bugs to kill would have been a different woman from the one we know.

An age seems to separate the house in Chelsea where the Carlyles lived from the house in Hampstead which was shared by Keats and Brown and the Brawnes.[11] If houses have their voices and places their seasons, it is always spring in Hampstead as it is always February in Cheyne Row. By some miracle, too, Hampstead has always remained not a suburb or a piece of antiquity engulfed in the modern world, but a place with a character peculiar to itself. It is not a place where one makes money, or goes when one has money to spend. The signs of discreet retirement are stamped on it. Its houses are neat boxes such as front the sea at Brighton with bow windows and balconies and deck chairs on verandahs. It has style and intention as if designed for people of modest income and some leisure who seek rest and recreation. Its prevailing colours are the pale pinks and blues that seem to harmonise with the blue sea and the white sand; and yet there is an urbanity in the style which proclaims the neighbourhood of a great city. Even in the twentieth century this serenity still pervades the suburb of Hampstead. Its bow windows still look out upon vales and trees and ponds and barking dogs and couples sauntering arm in arm and pausing, here on the hill-top, to look at the distant domes and pinnacles of London, as they sauntered and paused and looked when Keats lived here. For Keats lived up the lane in a little white house behind wooden palings. Nothing has been much changed since his day. But as we enter the house in which Keats lived some mournful shadow seems to fall across the garden. A tree has fallen and lies propped.[12] Waving branches cast their shadows up and down over the flat white walls of the house. Here, for all the gaiety and serenity of the neighbourhood, the nightingale sang; here, if anywhere, fever and anguish had their dwelling and paced this little green plot oppressed with the sense of quick-coming death and the shortness of life and the passion of love and its misery.[13]

Yet if Keats left any impress upon his house it is the impression not of fever, but of that clarity and dignity which come from order and self-control. The rooms are small but shapely; downstairs the long windows are so large that half the wall seems made of light. Two chairs turned together are close to the window as if someone had sat there reading and had just got up and left the room. The figure of the reader must have been splashed with shade and sun as the hanging leaves stirred in the breeze. Birds must have hopped close to his foot. The room is empty save for the two chairs, for Keats had few possessions, little furniture and not more, he said, than one hundred and fifty books.[14] And perhaps it is because the rooms are so empty and furnished rather with light and shadow than with chairs and tables that one does not think of people, here where so many people have lived. The imagination does not evoke scenes. It does not strike one that there must have been eating and drinking here; people must have come in and out; they must have put down bags, left parcels; they must have scrubbed and cleaned and done battle with dirt and disorder and carried cans of water from the basement to the bedrooms. All the traffic of life is silenced. The voice of the house is the voice of leaves brushing in the wind; of branches stirring in the garden. Only one presence – that of Keats himself – dwells here. And even he, though his picture is on every wall, seems to come silently, on the broad shafts of light, without body or footfall. Here he sat on the chair in the window and listened without moving, and saw without starting, and turned the page without haste though his time was so short.

There is an air of heroic equanimity about the house in spite of the death masks and the brittle yellow wreaths and the other grisly memorials which remind us that Keats died young and unknown and in exile. Life goes on outside the window. Behind this calm, this rustling of leaves, one hears the far-off rattle of wheels, the bark of dogs fetching and carrying sticks from the pond. Life goes on outside the wooden paling. When we shut the gate upon the grass and the tree where the nightingale sang we find, quite rightly, the butcher delivering his meat from a small red motor van at the house next door. If we cross the road, taking care not to be cut down by some rash driver – for they drive at a great pace down these wide streets – we shall find ourselves on top of the hill and beneath shall see the whole of London lying below us. It is a view of perpetual fascination at all hours and in all seasons. One sees London as a whole – London crowded and ribbed and compact, with its dominant domes, its guardian cathedrals; its chimneys and spires; its cranes and gasometers; and the perpetual smoke which no spring or autumn ever blows away. London has lain there time out of mind scarring that stretch of earth deeper and deeper, making it more uneasy, lumped and tumultuous, branding it for ever with an indelible scar. There it lies in layers, in strata, bristling and billowing with rolls of smoke always caught on its pinnacles. And yet from Parliament Hill one can see, too, the country beyond. There are hills on the further side in whose woods birds are singing, and some stoat or rabbit pauses, in dead silence, with paw lifted to listen intently to rustlings among the leaves. To look over London from this hill Keats came and Coleridge[15] and Shakespeare, perhaps. And here at this very moment the usual young man sits on an iron bench clasping to his arms the usual young woman.

1 – A signed essay in *Good Housekeeping*, March 1932, (*Kp4* C333.1); the third of six essays in 'The London Scene'. The essay was accompanied by four photographs with extracts from VW's essay as captions: two of Keats's House (one exterior and the other of his sitting room with 'two chairs turned together as if someone had sat there reading') and two of Carlyle's (the kitchen and an exterior of the house from the back garden). The essay was introduced: 'A visit to the homes of Carlyle and Keats takes us from the literary past into the world of "might-have-been," in company with Virginia Woolf'. On Monday, 16 March 1931, VW wrote: 'I am writing little articles of a morning, & should have been sketching the Houses of the Great this morning, but that I have not the material. This afternoon I shall try to see Carlyle's house & Keats' house' (*IV VW Diary*; fn. 2 adds that LW drove her to Keats's House that afternoon). The same issue of *Good Housekeeping* also contained: Mary Agnes Hamilton ('Labour ex-Member for Blackburn') on 'Mother Westminster', and 'The Sable Standard' by Winifred Holtby. See also 'The Docks of London' above, 'Geraldine and Jane' above, and *CR2*, and Appendix VIII; 'Haworth, November, 1904', 'Literary Geography', 'The Letters of Jane Welsh Carlyle' and 'More Carlyle Letters', *I VW Essays*; 'Flumina Amem Silvasque', *II VW Essays*; and 'Carlyle and the London Library', *VI VW Essays*, Appendix. A holograph draft and a final typescript draft, together with the original layout and proofs (Berg, M 13, M 132). Reprinted: *LSc, CDML*.

2 – Charles Dickens (1812–70), whose house, 48 Doughty St, WC1, was acquired by the Dickens Fellowship in 1925; Samuel Johnson (1709–84), whose house, 17 Gough Square, EC4, was restored and opened to the public in 1912.

3 – Now numbered 24, Thomas Carlyle (1795–1881) and his wife Jane

(1801–66) lived there from 1834. Leslie Stephen, who was friendly with Carlyle and had written his biography for the *DNB*, played a significant role as Chairman of the committee formed on 19 December 1894 to purchase Carlyle's house. In a letter published in *The Times* on 31 December, Stephen invited contributions to the fund. VW attended the meeting, presided over by the Lord Mayor of London, at the Mansion House on 22 February 1895 in support of the purchase fund, and she reported the proceedings in the *Hyde Park Gate News* on 25 February (ed. Gill Lowe [Hesperus Press, 2005], pp. 183–5); they were also reported at length in *The Times* on 23 February. The house was purchased on 15 May (Leslie Stephen contributed two guineas), and on 29 October 'The Carlyle's House Memorial Trust' was registered: see *Illustrated Memorial Volume of the Carlyle's House Purchase Fund Committee with Catalogue of Carlyle's Books, Manuscripts, Pictures and Furniture Exhibited Therein* (1895; facsimile ed., Saltire Society, 1995). VW described her father taking her to see the house on 29 January 1897 (*PA*, p. 24). According to the Visitors' Book, she visited again on 29 March 1898 together with Vanessa Bell and Hester Ritchie (Anne Thackeray Ritchie's daughter), who had contributed 10s. to the fund. VW visited yet again on 23 February 1909: see *Carlyle's House and Other Sketches*, ed. David Bradshaw (Hesperus Press, 2003). *CDML*: 'it may have been the house she imagined for the Hilberys in *Night and Day*' (p. 205, n. 1). VW wrote to Daphne Sanger on 11 June 1933 about raising money for the permanent preservation of the house: 'I enclose £1.1 for your Carlyle House fund. I feel much more sympathy with Mrs Carlyle than with Mr, anyhow where the house is concerned. I believe if your circular put more stress on her, you would wring more money from our purses. But anyhow I hope you'll get it' (*V VW Letters*, no. 2748); she probably wrote the wrong payee on the cheque (see an unpublished letter of 19 June, listed in [Berg, M 43], no. 133). The house was transferred to the National Trust in 1936. See also 'The Legacy of the Writing Desk: Jane Welsh Carlyle to Virginia Stephen Woolf' by Eleanor McNees, *Virginia Woolf Miscellany*, no. 68 (Fall 2005/Winter 2006), pp. 8–9, and '"*Night and Day* is Dead": Virginia Woolf in London "Literary and Historic"' by Andrea P. Zemgulys, *Twentieth Century Literature*, vol. xlvi, no. 1 (Spring 2000), pp. 56–77.

4 – As Carlyle's literary executor, J. A. Froude (1818–94) published Carlyle's *Reminiscences* (1881), a four-volume biography (1882–4), Jane Welsh Carlyle's *Letters and Memorials* (1883) and *My Relations with Carlyle* (1903).

5 – Cf. Mary Christie in 'Spring-Cleaning' (*Spectator*, 9 May 1896): 'It was given to Mrs. Carlyle to write the epic of house-cleaning . . . all the world revelled in Mrs. Carlyle's description of her gallant battle with the accumulated dirt of years . . .' (reprinted in *A Tardiness in Nature and Other Papers*, ed. Maud Withers [Manchester University Press, 1907], pp. 279–87, at p. 279; see 'Mary Christie', *VI VW Essays*, Appendix).

6 – Carlyle's attic study with its double walls, installed in 1853 in an unsuccessful attempt to shut out the noise, is a great feature of the house and the room that has changed least.

7 – The Carlyles' 'alcoholic servant Helen Mitchell, whom [Mrs Carlyle once] found lying on the kitchen floor "dead drunk – spread out like the three legs of Man – with a chair upset beside her and in the midst of a perfect chaos of dirty dishes and fragments of broken crockery" (27 Oct 1840)' (*ODNB*). For further information about Helen, see Carlyle's *Reminiscences: A New and Complete Edition*, ed. K. J. Fielding and Ian Campbell (World's Classics, OUP, 1997), pp. 62–5, and n., p. 438.

8 – All the items listed by VW can still be seen in the house.

9 – 'Mrs Carlyle's little dog Nero lies buried some five feet from the southeast corner of the garden. The headstone which originally marked the grave has unfortunately been removed' (*Carlyle's House, London* [National Trust, 1992], p. 38). See also *Flush*: 'It was common knowledge that Mrs. Carlyle's dog Nero had leapt from a top-storey window with the intention of committing suicide. He had found the strain of life in Cheyne Row intolerable, it was said' (Hogarth Press, 1933), ch. v, pp. 130–2; and see VW's note, pp. 160–2.

10 – *A Chelsea Interior* (1857), by Robert Tait, which hangs in the sitting room.

11 – John Keats (1795–1821) lived with Charles Armitage Brown (1786–1842), from 1818 to 1820, at Wentworth Place in what is now Keats Grove, Hampstead. Here he was to fall in love with Fanny Brawne (1800–65), when she and her mother moved into the other half of this semi-detached house in 1819. The two houses were converted into one in 1838–9 by the new owner Eliza Chester. The exterior remains very much as it was in Keats's time, except for an added drawing-room and conservatory. The house continued as a private dwelling until, threatened with demolition to make way for a new development, it was saved by public subscription from Europe and America. In 1925 it opened as a museum.

12 – There is a photograph of the propped-up mulberry tree, probably dating from Stuart times, in *The Keats House (Wentworth Place) Hampstead: An Historical and Descriptive Guide* [1926], facing p. 1. The house was open to the public on Mondays, Wednesdays and Saturdays from 10 a.m. to 6 p.m. (April–September), closing at 4 p.m. in winter (p. 12). The photograph of the 'two chairs turned together' (see n. 1 above), by J. Dixon Scott, is shown on p. 15.

13 – By an ancient plum tree (perished 1921; now replaced) in the garden of Wentworth Place, Keats heard the nightingale that inspired his ode (May 1819). See *OBEV*, pp. 726–9, no. 624.

14 – The source for this claim has not been traced. However, according to the list of Keats's books, compiled by Charles Armitage Brown in 1821, there were about 150 vols: see Sir Sidney Colvin's *John Keats, His Life and Poetry,*

His Friends, Critics and After-Fame (3rd ed., Macmillan, 1920), pp. 558–60.
15 – Samuel Taylor Coleridge (1772–1834) lived at nearby Highgate, from
1816 until his death.

Abbeys and Cathedrals

It is a commonplace, but we cannot help repeating it, that St Paul's
dominates London. It swells like a great grey bubble from a distance;
it looms over us, huge and menacing, as we approach. But suddenly St
Paul's vanishes. And behind St Paul's, beneath St Paul's, round St Paul's
when we cannot see St Paul's, how London has shrunk! Once there were
colleges and quadrangles and monasteries with fish ponds and cloisters;
and sheep grazing on the greensward; and inns where great poets stretched
their legs and talked at their ease. Now all this space has shrivelled. The
fields are gone and the fish ponds and the cloisters; even men and women
seem to have shrunk and become multitudinous and minute instead of
single and substantial. Where Shakespeare and Jonson[2] once fronted
each other and had their talk out, a million Mr Smiths and Miss Browns
scuttle and hurry, swing off omnibuses, dive into tubes. They seem too
many, too minute, too like each other to have each a name, a character,
a separate life of their own.

If we leave the street and step into a city church, the space that
the dead enjoy compared with what the living now enjoy, is brought
home to us. In the year 1737 a man called Howard died and was
buried in St Mary-le-Bow. A whole wall is covered with the list of
his virtues. 'He was blessed with a sound and intelligent mind which
shone forth conspicuously in the habitual exercise of great and godlike
virtues. . . . In the midst of a profligate age he was inviolably attached
to justice, sincerity and truth.'[3] He occupies space that might serve
almost for an office and demand a rent of many hundreds a year. In
our day a man of equal obscurity would be allotted one slice of white
stone of the regulation size among a thousand others and his great
and godlike virtues would have to go unrecorded. Again, in St Mary-
le-Bow all posterity is asked to pause and rejoice that Mrs Mary
Lloyd 'closed an exemplary and spotless life' without suffering and
indeed without regaining consciousness, aged 79 years.[4]

Pause, reflect, admire, take heed of your ways – so these ancient
tablets are always advising and exhorting us. One leaves the church

marvelling at the spacious days when unknown citizens could occupy so much room with their bones and confidently request so much attention for their virtues when we – behold how we jostle and skip and circumvent each other in the street, how sharply we cut corners, how nimbly we skip beneath motor cars. The mere process of keeping alive needs all our energy. We have no time, we were about to say, to think about life or death either, when suddenly we run against the enormous walls of St Paul's. Here it is again, looming over us, mountainous, immense, greyer, colder, quieter than before. And directly we enter we undergo that pause and expansion and release from hurry and effort which it is in the power of St Paul's, more than any other building in the world, to bestow.

Something of the splendour of St Paul's lies simply in its vast size, in its colourless serenity. Mind and body seem both to widen in this enclosure, to expand under this huge canopy where the light is neither daylight nor lamp-light, but an ambiguous element something between the two. One window shakes down a broad green shaft; another tinges the flagstones beneath a cool, pale purple. There is space for each broad band of light to fall smoothly. Very large, very square, hollow-sounding, echoing with a perpetual shuffling and booming, the Cathedral is august in the extreme; but not in the least mysterious. Tombs heaped like majestic beds lie between the pillars. Here is the dignified reposing room to which great statesmen and men of action retire, robed in all their splendour, to accept the thanks and applause of their fellow-citizens. They still wear their stars and garters, their emblems of civic pomp and military pride. Their tombs are clean and comely. No rust or stain has been allowed to spot them. Even Nelson looks a little smug. Even the contorted and agonised figure of John Donne, wrapped in the marble twists of his grave clothes, looks as if it had left the stonemason's yard but yesterday.[5] Yet it has stood here in its agony for three hundred years and has passed through the flames of the fire of London. But death and the corruption of death are forbidden to enter. Here civic virtue and civic greatness are ensconced securely. True, a heavy bossed door has above it the legend that through the gate of death we pass to our joyful resurrection;[6] but somehow the massive portals suggest that they open not upon fields of amaranth and moly where harps sound and heavenly choirs sing, but upon flights of marble steps that lead on to solemn council chambers and splendid halls, loud with trumpets and hung with banners. Effort and agony and ecstasy have no place in this majestic building.

No contrast could be greater than that between St Paul's and Westminster Abbey. Far from being spacious and serene, the Abbey is narrow and pointed, worn, restless and animated. One feels as if one had stepped from the democratic helter skelter, the hubbub and humdrum of the street, into a brilliant assembly, a select society of men and women of the highest distinction. The company seems to be in full conclave. Gladstone starts forward and then Disraeli.[7] From every corner, from every wall, somebody leans or listens or bends forward as if about to speak. The recumbent even seem to lie attentive, as if to rise next minute. Their hands nervously grasp their sceptres, their lips are compressed for a fleeting silence, their eyes lightly closed as if for a moment's thought. These dead, if dead they are, have lived to the full. Their faces are worn, their noses high, their cheeks hollowed. Even the stone of the old columns seems rubbed and chafed by the intensity of the life that has been fretting it all these centuries. Voice and organ vibrate wirily among the chasings and intricacies of the roof. The fine fans of stone that spread themselves to make a ceiling seem like bare boughs withered of all their leaves and about to toss in the wintry gale. But their austerity is beautifully softened. Lights and shadows are changing and conflicting every moment. Blue, gold and violet pass, dappling, quickening, fading. The grey stone, ancient as it is, changes like a live thing under the incessant ripple of changing light.

Thus the Abbey is no place of death and rest; no reposing-room where the virtuous lie in state to receive the rewards of virtue. Is it, indeed, through their virtues that these dead have come here? Often they have been violent; they have been vicious. Often it is only the greatness of their birth that has exalted them. The Abbey is full of Kings and Queens, Dukes and Princes. The light falls upon gold coronets, and gold still lingers in the folds of ceremonial robes. Reds and yellows still blazon coats of arms and lions and unicorns. But it is full also of another and even more potent royalty. Here are the dead poets, still musing, still pondering, still questioning the meaning of existence. 'Life is a jest and all things show it. I thought so once, and now I know it,' Gay laughs. Chaucer, Spenser, Dryden[8] and the rest still seem to listen with all their faculties on the alert as the clean-shaven clergyman in his spick-and-span red-and-white robes intones for the millionth time the commands of the Bible. His voice rings ripely, authoritatively through the building, and if it were not irreverent one might suppose that Gladstone and Disraeli were about to put the statement just propounded – that children should honour their parents – to the vote. Everybody in this brilliant assembly has a mind and a will of his own. The Abbey is shot with high-pitched voices; its peace is broken by emphatic gestures and characteristic attitudes. Not an inch of its walls but speaks and claims and illustrates. Kings and Queens, poets and statesmen still act their parts and are not suffered to turn quietly to dust. Still in animated debate they rise above the flood and waste of average human life, with their fists clenched and their lips parted, with an orb in one hand, a sceptre in another, as if we had forced them to rise on our behalf and testify that human nature can now and then exalt itself above the humdrum democratic disorder of the hurrying street. Arrested, transfixed, there they stand suffering a splendid crucifixion.

Where then can one go in London to find peace and the assurance that the dead sleep and are at rest? London, after all, is a city of tombs. But London nevertheless is a city in the full tide and race of human life. Even St Clement Danes[9] – that venerable pile planted in the midstream of the Strand – has been docked of all those peaceful perquisites – the weeping trees, the waving grasses that the humblest village church enjoys by right. Omnibuses and vans have long since shorn it of these dues. It stands, like an island, with only the narrowest rim of pavement to separate it from the sea. And moreover, St Clement Danes has its duties to the living. As likely as not it is participating vociferously, stridently, with almost frantic joy, but hoarsely as if its tongue were rough with the rust of centuries, in the happiness of two living mortals. A wedding is in progress. All down the Strand St Clement Danes roars its welcome to the bridegroom in tail coat and grey trousers; to the bridesmaids virginal in white; and finally to the bride herself whose car draws up to the porch, and out she steps and passes undulating with a flash of white finery into the inner gloom to make her marriage vows to the roar of omnibuses, while outside the pigeons, alarmed, sweep in circles, and Gladstone's statue is crowded, like a rock with gulls, with nodding, waving, enthusiastic sightseers.

The only peaceful places in the whole city are perhaps those old graveyards which have become gardens and playgrounds.[10] The tombstones no longer serve to mark the graves, but line the walls with their white tablets. Here and there a finely sculptured tomb plays the part of garden ornament. Flowers light up the turf, and there are benches under the trees for mothers and nursemaids to sit on, while the children bowl hoops and play hopscotch in safety. Here one might sit and read *Pamela*[11] from cover to cover. Here one might drowse away the first days of spring or the last days of autumn without feeling too keenly the stir of youth or the sadness of old age. For here the dead sleep in peace, proving nothing, testifying nothing, claiming nothing save that we shall enjoy the peace that their old bones provides for us. Unreluctantly they have given up their human rights to separate names or peculiar virtues. But they have no cause for grievance. When the gardener plants his bulbs or sows his grass they flower again and spread the ground with green and elastic turf. Here mothers and nursemaids gossip; children play; and the old beggar, after eating his dinner from a paper bag, scatters crumbs to the sparrows. These garden graveyards are the most peaceful of our London sanctuaries and their dead the quietest.

1 – A signed essay in *Good Housekeeping*, May 1932, (*Kp4* C333.2); the fourth of six essays in 'The London Scene'. The essay was accompanied by two large photographs of the interiors of St Paul's and Westminster Abbey, and a small one of a man sitting in a churchyard. VW returned the corrected proofs to her agent, Curtis Brown, on 18 March 1932, and they were sent on to *Good Housekeeping* the following day. The same issue also contained: 'Glimpses of America', book reviews by Clemence Dane. See also 'The Docks of London' above, and Appendix VIII. Two holograph drafts, entitled 'St. Paul's' (dated 13 March 1931) and 'Abbeys and Cathedrals', and a final typescript draft, together with the original layout and proofs (Berg, M 13, M133). Reprinted: *LSc*, *CDML*.

2 – The Mermaid Tavern, where Shakespeare and Ben Jonson (1572–1637) drank together, stood in Bread Street off Cheapside until it was destroyed in the Great Fire of 1666. Cheapside, one of the oldest streets in the city, runs west towards St Paul's Cathedral.

3 – St Mary-le-Bow, Cheapside, was rebuilt by Christopher Wren after the Great Fire. Only the tower survived the fire bombs of 1940, and the church was rebuilt 1956–62. There were a number of monuments on the south wall, including, 'with armorial bearings, and with an unusually full account of his children, the monument of Matthew Howard, of Thorpe, in the county of Norfolk, to whom the somewhat high-flown inscription attributes "great and God-like virtues in the midst of a profligate age." He died in 1737' (Arthur Wollaston Hutton, M.A., Rector, *A Short History and Description of Bow Church, Cheapside* [Elliott Stock, 1908], p. 27).

4 – No trace of such a memorial has been discovered, but a Mary Lloyd, widow, was buried on 10 October 1722: see *The Registers of St Mary le Bowe, Cheapside . . .*, ed. W. Bruce Bannerman, *Part I. – Baptisms and Burials*, vol. xliv (Publications of the Harleian Society, 1914), p. 224.

5 – The monument (1808–18) to Horatio, Viscount Nelson (1758–1805) by John Flaxman (1755–1826) is in the south transept. The sculpture

(1631–2) by Nicholas Stone (1585/8–1647) of John Donne (1572–1631), Dean of St Paul's from 1621, is in the south choir aisle and was virtually the only monument to survive intact the burning of the old cathedral in the Great Fire: 'It shows the famous poet and divine in his graveclothes, rising from an urn at the sound of the last trumpet. This was Donne's own idea and he posed for a painting which served as a model for the effigy' (ODNB).

6 – In the first recess west of the dome in the north nave aisle is a monument, by Marochetti (1805–67), representing two angels at the Gate of Death, in memory of Viscount Melbourne (1779–1848) and his brother, Frederick (1782–1853). Above the Gate – which indeed is a double-door – the inscription reads: 'Through the gate of death we pass to our joyful resurrection'.

7 – Visitors enter Westminster Abbey by the north transept where there are a series of monuments to eminent statesmen, including William Ewart Gladstone (1809–98) and Benjamin Disraeli (1804–81).

8 – Written by himself, this is the epitaph of John Gay (1685–1732), poet and playwright, buried in Poets' Corner in the south transept. Geoffrey Chaucer (c. 1340–1400) was the first poet to be buried there; Edmund Spenser (1552?–99) and John Dryden (1631–1700) were also buried there.

9 – St Clement Danes Church, designed and built by Christopher Wren, stands in the middle of the Strand. On 31 March 1931 Woolf attended a memorial service there for the novelist Arnold Bennett (see *IV VW Diary*, p. 16, editor's n.). The tradition of distributing oranges and lemons to the children of the parish was held on 27 March. There is a memorial (1900–05) by Sir (William) Hamo Thornycroft (1850–1925) to Gladstone outside the west front; it 'was praised by Gosse for showing "alertness and vigour and determination carried *just* over the verge of the normal"' (ODNB).

10 – VW is likely to have had in mind St George's Gardens behind Brunswick Square: see *I VW Letters*, no. 590; *Jacob's Room* (Hogarth Press, 1922), ch. x, first sentence; *III VW Diary*, 17 April 1928; and *V VW Diary*, 3 November 1936. She may also have remembered Paddington Street Gardens behind Violet Dickinson's house, 21 Manchester St: see *I VW Letters*, no. 324, and *III VW Letters*, no. 1452.

11 – Samuel Richardson (1689–1761), *Pamela, or, Virtue Triumphant* (1740–1).

A Letter to a Young Poet

My Dear John,

Did you ever meet, or was he before your day, that old gentleman – I forget his name – who used to enliven conversation, especially at breakfast when the post came in, by saying that the art of letter-writing is dead?[2] The penny post, the old gentleman used to say, has killed the art of letter-writing. Nobody, he continued, examining an envelope through his eye-glasses, has the time even to cross their t's. We rush, he went on, spreading his toast with marmalade, to the telephone. We commit our half-formed thoughts in ungrammatical phrases to the post card. Gray is dead, he continued; Horace Walpole is dead; Madame de Sévigné[3] – she is dead too, I suppose he was about to add, but a fit of choking cut him short, and he had to leave the room before he had time to condemn all the arts, as his pleasure was, to the cemetery. But when the post came in this morning and I opened your letter stuffed with little blue sheets written all over in a cramped but not illegible hand – I regret to say, however, that several t's were uncrossed and the grammar of one sentence seems to me dubious – I replied after all these years to that elderly nekrophilist – Nonsense. The art of letter-writing has only just come into existence. It is the child of the penny post. And there is some truth in that remark, I think. Naturally when a letter cost half a crown to send, it had to prove itself a document of some importance; it was read aloud; it was tied up with green silk; after a certain number of years it was published for the infinite delectation of posterity. But your letter, on the contrary, will have to be burnt. It only cost three-halfpence to send.[4] Therefore you could afford to be intimate, irreticent, indiscreet in the extreme. What you tell me about poor dear C. and his adventure on the Channel boat is deadly private; your ribald jests at the expense of M. would certainly ruin your friendship if they got about; I doubt, too, that posterity, unless it is much quicker in the wit than I expect, could follow the line of your thought from the roof which leaks ('splash, splash, splash into the soap dish') past Mrs Gape, the charwoman, whose retort to the greengrocer gives me the keenest pleasure, via Miss Curtis and her odd confidence on the steps of the omnibus; to Siamese cats ('Wrap their noses in an old stocking my Aunt says if they howl'); so to the value of criticism to a writer; so to Donne; so to Gerard Hopkins;[5] so to tombstones; so to gold-fish; and so with a sudden alarming swoop to 'Do write and tell me where poetry's going, or if it's dead?' No, your letter, because it is a true letter – one that can neither be read aloud now, nor printed in time to come – will have to be burnt. Posterity must live upon Walpole and Madame de Sévigné. The great age of letter-writing, which is, of course, the present, will leave no letters behind it. And in making my reply there is only one question that I can answer or attempt to answer in public; about poetry and its death.

But before I begin, I must own up to those defects, both natural and acquired, which, as you will find, distort and invalidate all that I have to say about poetry. The lack of a sound university training has always made it impossible for me to distinguish between an iambic and a dactyl, and if*a* this were not enough to condemn one for ever, the practice of prose has bred in me, as in most prose writers, a foolish jealousy, a righteous indignation – anyhow, an emotion which the critic should be without. For how, we despised prose writers ask when we get together, could one say what one meant and observe the rules of poetry? Conceive dragging in 'blade' because one had mentioned 'maid'; and pairing 'sorrow' with 'borrow'? Rhyme is not only childish, but dishonest, we prose writers say. Then we go on to say, And look at their rules! How easy to be a poet! How strait the path is for them, and how strict! This you must do; this you must not. I would rather be a child and walk in a crocodile down a suburban path than write poetry, I have heard prose writers say. It must be like taking the veil and entering a religious order – observing the rites and rigours of metre. That explains why they repeat the same thing over and over again. Whereas we prose writers (I am only telling you the sort of nonsense prose writers talk when they are alone) are masters of language, not its slaves; nobody can teach us; nobody can coerce us; we say what we mean; we have the whole of life for our province. We are the creators, we are the explorers. . . . So we run on – nonsensically enough, I must admit.

Now that I have made a clean breast of these deficiencies, let us proceed. From certain phrases in your letter I gather that you think that poetry is in a parlous way, and that your case as a poet in this particular autumn of 1931 is a great deal harder than Shakespeare's, Dryden's, Pope's, or Tennyson's.⁶ In fact it is the hardest case that has ever been known. Here you give me an opening, which I am prompt to seize, for a little lecture. Never think yourself singular, never think your own case much harder than other people's. I admit that the age we live in makes this difficult. For the first time in history there are readers – a large body of people, occupied in business, in sport, in nursing their grandfathers, in tying up parcels behind counters – they all read now; and they want to be told how to read and what to read; and*b* their teachers – the reviewers, the lecturers, the broadcasters – must in all humanity make reading easy for them; assure them that literature is violent and exciting, full of heroes and villains; of hostile forces perpetually in conflict; of fields strewn with bones; of solitary victors riding off on white horses wrapped in black cloaks to meet their death at the turn of the road. A pistol shot rings out. 'The age of romance was over. The age of realism had begun' – you know the sort of thing. Now of course writers themselves know very well that there is not a word of truth in all this – there are no battles, and no murders, and no defeats and no victories. But as it is of the utmost importance that readers should be amused, writers acquiesce. They dress themselves up. They act their parts. One leads; the other follows. One is romantic, the other realist. One is advanced,^{c} the other out of date. There is no harm in it, so long as you take it as a joke, but once you believe in it, once you begin to take yourself seriously as a leader, or as a follower, as a modern or as a conservative, then you become a self-conscious, biting, and scratching little animal whose work is not of the slightest value or importance to^d anybody. Think of yourself rather as something much humbler and less spectacular, but to my mind far more interesting – a poet in whom live all the poets of the past, from whom all poets in time to come will spring. You have a touch of Chaucer in you, and something of Shakespeare; Dryden, Pope, Tennyson – to mention only the respectable among your ancestors – stir in your blood and sometimes move your pen a little to the right or to the left. In short you are an immensely ancient, complex, and continuous character, for which reason please treat yourself with respect and think twice before you dress up as Guy Fawkes[7] and spring out upon timid old ladies at street corners, threatening death and demanding twopence-halfpenny.

However, as you say that you are in a fix ('it has never been so hard to write poetry as it is to-day') and that poetry may be, you think, at its last gasp in England ('the novelists are doing all the interesting things now'), let me while away the time before the post goes in imagining your state and in hazarding one or two guesses which, since this is a letter, need not be taken too seriously or pressed too far. Let me try to put myself in your place; let me try to imagine, with your letter to help me, what it feels like to be a young poet in the autumn of 1931. (And, taking my own advice, I shall treat you not as one poet in particular, but as several poets in one.) On the floor of your mind, then – is it not this that makes you a poet? – rhythm^e keeps up its perpetual beat. Sometimes it seems to die down to nothing; it lets you eat, sleep, talk like other people. Then again it swells and rises and attempts to sweep all the contents of your mind into one dominant dance. To-night is such an occasion. Although you are alone, and have taken one boot off and are about to undo the other, you cannot go on with the process of undressing,[8] but must instantly write at the bidding of the dance. You snatch pen and paper; you hardly trouble to hold the one or to straighten the other. And while you write, while the first stanzas of the dance are being fastened down, I will withdraw a little and look out of the window. A woman passes, then a man; a car glides to a stop and then – but there is no need to say what I see out of the window, nor indeed is there time, for I am suddenly recalled from my observations[f] by a cry of rage or despair. Your page is crumpled in a ball; your pen sticks upright by the nib in the carpet. If there were a cat to swing or a wife to murder now would be the time. So at least I infer from the ferocity of your expression. You are rasped, jarred, thoroughly out of temper. And if I am to guess the reason, it is, I should say, that the rhythm which was opening and shutting with a force that sent shocks of excitement from your head to your heels has encountered some hard and hostile object upon which it has smashed itself to pieces. Something has worked in which cannot be made into poetry; some foreign body, angular, sharp-edged, gritty, has refused to join in the dance. Obviously, suspicion attaches to Mrs Gape; she has asked you to make a poem of her; then to Miss Curtis and her confidences on the omnibus; then to C., who has infected you with a wish to tell his story – and a very amusing one it was – in verse. But for some reason you cannot do their bidding. Chaucer could; Shakespeare could; so could Crabbe, Byron, and perhaps Robert Browning.[9] But it is October 1931, and for a long time now poetry has shirked contact with – what shall we call it? – Shall we shortly and no doubt inaccurately call it life? And will you come to my help by guessing what I mean? Well then, it[g] has left all that to the novelist. Here you see how easy it would be for me to write two or three volumes in honour of prose and in mockery of verse; to say how wide and ample is the domain of the one, how starved and stunted the little grove of the other. But it would be simpler and perhaps fairer to check these theories by opening one of the thin books of modern verse that lie on your table. I open and I find myself instantly confuted. Here are the common objects of daily prose – the bicycle and the omnibus. Obviously the poet is making his muse face facts. Listen:

> Which of you waking early and watching daybreak
> Will not hasten in heart, handsome, aware of wonder
> At light unleashed, advancing, a leader of movement,

Breaking like surf on turf on road and roof,
Or chasing shadow on downs like whippet racing,
The stilled stone, halting at eyelash barrier,
Enforcing in face a profile, marks of misuse,
Beating impatient and importunate on boudoir shutters
Where the old life is not up yet, with rays
Exploring through rotting floor a dismantled mill –
The old life never to be born again?

Yes, but how will he get through with it? I read on and find:

Whistling as he shuts
His door behind him, travelling to work by tube
Or walking to the park to it to *ease the bowels*,

and read on and find again:

As a boy lately come up from country to town
Returns for the day to his village in *expensive shoes* –

and so on again to:

Seeking a heaven on earth he chases his shadow,
Loses his capital and his nerve in pursuing
What yachtsmen, explorers, climbers and *buggers are after*.[10]

These lines and the words I have emphasised are enough to confirm me in part of my guess at least. The poet is trying to include Mrs Gape. He is honestly of opinion that she can be brought into poetry and will do very well there. Poetry, he feels, will be improved by the actual, the colloquial. But though I honour him for the attempt, I doubt that it is wholly successful. I feel a jar. I feel a shock. I feel as if I had stubbed my toe on the corner of the wardrobe. Am I then, I go on to ask, shocked, prudishly and conventionally, by the words themselves? I think not. The shock is literally a shock. The poet as I guess has strained himself to include an emotion that is not domesticated and acclimatised to poetry; the effort has thrown him off his balance; he rights himself, as I am sure I shall find if I turn the page, by a violent recourse to the poetical – he invokes the moon or the nightingale.[11] Anyhow, the transition is sharp. The poem is cracked in the middle. Look, it comes apart in my hands: here is reality on one side, here is beauty on the other; and instead of acquiring a whole object rounded and entire, I am left with broken parts in[h] my hands which, since my reason has been roused and my imagination has not been allowed to take entire possession of me, I contemplate coldly, critically, and with distaste.

Such at least is the hasty analysis I make of my own sensations as a reader; but again I am interrupted. I see that you have overcome your difficulty, whatever it was; the pen is once more in action, and having torn up the first poem you are at work upon another. Now then if I want to understand your state of mind I must invent another explanation to account for this return of fluency. You have dismissed, as I suppose, all sorts of things that would come naturally to your pen if you had been writing prose – the charwoman, the omnibus, the incident on the Channel boat. Your range is restricted – I judge from your expression – concentrated and intensified. I hazard a guess that you are thinking now, not about things in general, but about yourself in particular. There is a fixity, a gloom, yet an inner glow that seem to hint that you are looking within and not without. But in order to consolidate these flimsy guesses about the meaning of an expression on a face, let me open another of the books on your table and check it by what I find there. Again I open at random and read this:

> To penetrate that room is my desire,
> The extreme attic of the mind, that lies
> Just beyond the last bend in the corridor.
> Writing I do it. Phrases, poems are keys.
> Loving's another way (but not so sure).
> A fire's in there, I think, there's truth at last
> Deep in a lumber chest. Sometimes I'm near,
> But draughts puff out the matches, and I'm lost.
> Sometimes I'm lucky, find a key to turn,
> Open an inch or two – but always then
> A bell rings, someone calls, or cries of 'fire'
> Arrest my hand when nothing's known or seen,
> And running down the stairs again I mourn.[12]

and then this:

> There is a dark room,
> The locked and shuttered womb,
> Where negative's made positive.
> Another dark room,
> The blind and bolted tomb,
> Where positives change to negative.
>
> We may not undo that or escape this, who
> Have birth and death coiled in our bones,
> Nothing we can do
> Will sweeten the real rue,
> That we begin, and end, with groans.[13]

And then this:

> Never being, but always at the edge of Being
> My head, like Death mask, is brought into the Sun.
> The shadow pointing finger across cheek,
> I move lips for tasting, I move hands for touching,
> But never am nearer than touching,
> Though the spirit leans outward for seeing.
> Observing rose, gold, eyes, an admired landscape,
> My senses record the act of wishing
> Wishing to be
> Rose, gold, landscape or another –
> Claiming fulfilment in the act of loving.[14]

Since these quotations are chosen at random and I have yet found three different poets writing about nothing, if not about the poet himself, I hold that the chances are that you too are engaged in the same occupation. I conclude that self offers no impediment; self joins in the dance; self lends itself to the rhythm; it is apparently easier to write a poem about oneself than about any other subject. But what does one mean by 'oneself'? Not the self that Wordsworth, Keats, and Shelley[15] have described – not the self that loves a woman, or that hates a tyrant, or that broods over the mystery of the world. No, the self that you are engaged in describing is shut out from all that. It is a self that sits alone in the room at night with the blinds drawn. In other words the poet is much less interested in what we have in common than in what he has apart. Hence[j] I suppose the extreme difficulty of these poems – and I have to confess that it would floor me completely to say from one reading or even from two or three what these poems mean. The poet is trying honestly and exactly, to describe a world that has perhaps no existence except for one particular person at one particular moment. And the more sincere he is in keeping to the precise outline of the roses and cabbages of his private universe, the more he puzzles us who have agreed in a lazy spirit of compromise to see roses and cabbages as they are seen, more or less, by the twenty-six passengers on the outside of an omnibus. He strains to describe; we strain to see; he flickers his torch; we catch a flying gleam. It is exciting; it is stimulating; but is that a tree, we ask, or is it perhaps an old woman tying up her shoe in the gutter?

Well, then, if there is any truth in what I am saying – if that is you cannot write about the actual, the colloquial, Mrs Gape or the Channel boat or Miss Curtis on the omnibus, without straining the machine of poetry, if, therefore, you are driven to contemplate landscapes and emotions within and must render visible to the world at large what you alone can see,[k] then indeed yours is a hard case, and poetry, though still breathing – witness these little books – is drawing her breath in short, sharp gasps. Still, consider the symptoms. They are not the symptoms of death in the least. Death in literature, and I need not tell you how often literature has died in this country or in that, comes gracefully, smoothly, quietly. Lines slip easily down the accustomed grooves. The old designs are copied so glibly that we are half inclined to think them original, save for that very glibness. But here the very opposite is happening: here in my first quotation the poet breaks his machine because he will clog it with raw fact. In my second, he is unintelligible because of his desperate determination to tell the truth about himself. Thus I cannot help thinking that though you may be right in talking of the difficulty of the time, you are wrong to despair.

Is there not, alas, good reason to hope? I say 'alas,' because then I must give my reasons, which are bound to be foolish and certain also to cause pain to the large and highly respectable society of nekrophils – Mr Peabody, and his like – who much prefer death to life and are even now intoning the sacred and comfortable words, Keats is dead, Shelley is dead, Byron is dead. But it is late: nekrophily induces slumber; the old gentlemen have fallen asleep over their classics, and if what I am about to say takes a sanguine tone – and for

my part I do not believe in poets dying; Keats, Shelley, Byron, are
alive here in this room in you and you and you – I can take comfort
from the thought that my hoping will not disturb their snoring. So
to continue – why should not poetry, now that it has so honestly
scraped itself free from certain falsities, the wreckage of the great
Victorian age, now that it has so sincerely gone down into the mind
of the poet and verified its outlines – a work of renovation that has
to be done from time to time and was certainly needed, for bad poetry
is almost always the result of forgetting oneself – all becomes distorted
and impure if you lose sight of that central reality – now, I say, that
poetry has done all this, why should it not once more open its eyes,
look out of the window and write about other people? Two or three
hundred years ago you were always writing about other people. Your
pages were crammed with characters of the most opposite and various
kinds – Hamlet, Cleopatra, Falstaff. Not only did we go to you for
drama, and for the subtleties of human character, but we also went
to you, incredible though this now seems, for laughter. You made us
roar with laughter. Then later, not more than a hundred years ago,
you were lashing our follies, trouncing our hypocrisies, and dashing
off the most brilliant of satires. You were Byron, remember; you wrote
Don Juan.[16] You were Crabbe also; you took the most sordid details
of the lives of peasants for your theme. Clearly therefore you have it
in you to deal with a vast variety of subjects; it is only a temporary
necessity that has shut you up in one room, alone, by yourself.

But how are you going to get out, into the world of other people?
That is your problem now, if I may hazard a guess – to find the right
relationship, now that you know yourself, between the self that you
know and the world outside. It[l] is a difficult problem. No living poet
has, I think, altogether solved it. And there[m] are a thousand voices proph-
esying despair. Science, they say, has made poetry impossible; there is
no poetry in motor cars and wireless. And we have no religion. All is
tumultuous and transitional. Therefore, so people say, there can be no
relation between the poet and the present age. But surely that is nonsense.
These accidents are superficial; they do not go nearly deep enough to
destroy the most profound and primitive of instincts, the instinct of
rhythm. All you need now is to stand at the window and let your rhythmical sense open and shut, open, and shut, boldly and freely, until one
thing melts in another, until the taxis are dancing with the daffodils,
until a whole has been made from all these separate fragments. I am
talking nonsense, I know. What I mean is, summon all your courage,

exert all your vigilance, invoke all the gifts that Nature has been induced to bestow. Then let your rhythmical sense wind itself in and out among men and women, omnibuses, sparrows – whatever comeⁿ along the street – until it has strung them together in one harmonious whole. That perhaps is your task – to find the relation between things that seem incompatible yet have a mysterious affinity, to absorb every experience that comes your way fearlessly and saturate it completely so that your poem is a whole, not a fragment; to re-think human life into poetry and so give us tragedy again and comedy by means of characters not spun out at length in the novelist's way, but condensed and synthesised in the poet's way – that is what we look to you to do now. But as I do not know what I mean by rhythm nor what I mean by life, and^o as most certainly I cannot tell you which objects can properly be combined together in a poem – that is entirely your affair – and as I cannot tell a dactyl from an iambic, and am therefore unable to say how you must modify and expand the rites and ceremonies of your ancient and mysterious art – I^p will move on to safer ground and turn again to these little books themselves.

When, then, I return to them I am, as I have admitted, filled, not with forebodings of death, but with hopes for the future. But one does not always want to be thinking of the future, if, as sometimes happens, one is living in the present. When I read these poems, now, at the present moment, I find myself – reading, you know, is rather like opening the door to a horde of rebels who swarm out attacking one in twenty places at once – hit, roused, scraped, bared, swung through the air, so that life seems to flash by; then again blinded, knocked on the head – all of which are agreeable sensations for a reader (since nothing is more dismal than to open the door and get no response), and all I believe certain proof that this poet is alive and kicking. And yet mingling with these cries of delight, of jubilation, I record also, as I read, the repetition in the bass of one word intoned over and over again by some malcontent. At last then, silencing the others, I say to this malcontent, 'Well, and what do *you* want?' Whereupon he bursts out, rather^q to my discomfort, 'Beauty.' Let me repeat, I take no responsibility for what my senses say when I read; I merely record the fact that there is a malcontent in me who complains that it seems to him odd, considering that English is a mixed language, a rich language; a language unmatched for its sound^r and colour, for its power of imagery and suggestion – it seems to him odd that these modern poets should write as if they had neither ears nor eyes, neither soles to their feet nor palms to their hands, but only honest enterprising book-fed brains, uni-sexual bodies and – but here I interrupted him. For when it comes to saying that a poet should be bi-sexual, and that I think is what he was about to say, even I, who have had no scientific training whatsoever, draw the line and tell that voice to be silent.

But how far, if we discount these obvious absurdities, do you think that there is truth in this complaint? For my own part now that I have stopped reading, and can see the poems more or less as a whole, I think it is true that the eye and the ear are starved of their rights. There is no sense of riches held in reserve behind the admirable exactitude of the lines I have quoted, as there is, for example, behind the exactitude of Mr Yeats.[17] The poet clings to his one word, his only word, as a drowning man to a spar. And[s] if this is so, I am ready to hazard a reason for it all[t] the more readily because I think it bears out what I have just been saying. The art of writing, and that is perhaps what my malcontent means by 'beauty,' the art of having at one's beck and call every word in the language, of knowing their weights, colours, sounds, associations, and thus making them, as is so necessary in English, suggest more than they can state, can be learnt of course to some extent by reading – it is impossible to read too much; but much more drastically and effectively by imagining that one is not oneself but somebody different. How can you learn to write if you write only about one single person? To[u] take the obvious example. Can you doubt that the reason why Shakespeare knew every sound and syllable in the language and could do precisely what he liked with grammar and syntax, was that Hamlet, Falstaff and Cleopatra rushed him into this knowledge; that the lords, officers, dependants, murderers and common soldiers of the plays insisted that he should say exactly what they felt in the words expressing their feelings? It[v] was they who taught him to write, not the begetter of the Sonnets. So that if you want to satisfy all those senses that rise in a swarm whenever we drop a poem among them – the reason, the imagination, the eyes, the ears, the palms of the hands and the soles of the feet, not to mention a million more that the psychologists have yet to name, you will do well to embark upon a long poem in which people as unlike yourself as possible talk at the tops of their voices. And for heaven's sake, publish nothing before you are thirty.

That, I am sure, is of very great importance. Most of the faults in the poems I have been reading can be explained, I think, by the fact that they have been exposed to the fierce light of publicity while they were still too young to stand the strain. It has shrivelled them into a skeleton austerity, both emotional and verbal, which should not be characteristic[w] of youth. The poet writes very well; he writes for the eye of a severe and intelligent public; but how much better he would have written if for ten years he had written for no eye but his own! After all, the years from twenty to thirty are years (let me refer to your letter again) of emotional excitement. The rain dripping, a wing flashing, someone passing – the commonest sounds and sights have power to fling one, as I seem to remember, from the heights of rapture to the depths of despair. And if the actual life is thus extreme, the visionary life should be free to follow. Write then, now that you are young, nonsense by the ream. Be silly, be sentimental, imitate Shelley, imitate Samuel Smiles;[18] give the rein to every impulse; commit every fault of style, grammar, taste, and syntax; pour out; tumble over; loose anger, love, satire, in whatever words you can catch, coerce or create, in whatever metre, prose, poetry, or gibberish that comes to hand. Thus you will learn to write. But if you publish, your freedom will be checked; you will be thinking what people will say; you will write for others when you ought only to be writing for yourself. And what point can there be in curbing the wild torrent of spontaneous nonsense which is now, for a few years only, your divine gift in order to publish prim little books of experimental verses? To make money? That, we both know, is out of the question. To get criticism? But your friends will pepper your manuscripts with far more serious and searching criticism than any you will get from the reviewers.[x] As for fame, look I implore you at famous people; see how the waters of dullness spread around them as they enter; observe their pomposity, their prophetic airs; reflect that the greatest poets were anonymous; think how Shakespeare cared nothing for fame; how Donne tossed his poems into the waste-paper basket; write an essay giving a single instance of any modern English writer who has survived the disciples and the admirers, the autograph hunters and the interviewers, the dinners and the luncheons, the celebrations and the commemorations with which English society so effectively stops the mouths of its singers and silences their songs.

But enough. I, at any rate, refuse to be nekrophilus.[y] So long as you and you and you, venerable and ancient representatives of Sappho,[19] Shakespeare, and Shelley are aged precisely twenty-three and propose – O enviable lot![z] – to spend the next fifty years of your lives in writing poetry, I refuse to think that the art is dead. And if ever the temptation to nekrophilise comes over you, be warned by the fate of that old gentleman whose name I forget, but I think that it was Peabody. In the very act of consigning all the arts to the grave he choked over a large piece of hot buttered toast and the consolation then offered him that he was about to join the elder Pliny[20] in the shades gave him, I am told, no sort of satisfaction whatsoever.

And now for the intimate, the indiscreet, and indeed, the only really interesting parts of this letter. . . .

a – *Yale Review*: 'and as if'.
b – *Yale Review*: 'and what; and'.
c – *Yale Review*: 'modern,'.
d – *Yale Review*: 'slightest importance or value to'.
e – *Yale Review*: 'then, for it is this that makes you a poet, rhythm'.
f – *Yale Review*: 'observation'.
g – *Yale Review*: 'it? – shall we shortly and no doubt inaccurately call it life? It'.
h – *Yale Review*: 'on'.
i – *Yale Review*: 'a'.
j – *Yale Review*: 'apart: in myself than in himself. Hence'.
k – *Yale Review*: 'alone see,'.
l – *Yale Review*: 'And it'.
m – *Yale Review*: 'Moreover, there'.
n – *Yale Review*: 'comes'.
o – *Yale Review*: 'by rhythm, and'.
p – *Yale Review*: 'your affair – nor can I tell you how metre can be modulated to do this business, I'.
q – *Yale Review*: 'he replies, rather'.
r – *Yale Review*: 'for sound'.
s – *Yale Review*: 'Yeats. And'.
t – *Yale Review*: 'reason all'.
u – *Yale Review*: 'about your self? To'.
v – *Yale Review*: 'words befitting them? It'.
w – *Yale Review*: 'be the characteristic'.
x – *Yale Review*: 'from reviewers.'
y – *Yale Review*: 'rate, will not be nekrophilous.'
z – *Yale Review*: 'fate!'

1 – A signed essay, entitled 'Letter to a Young Poet', in the *Yale Review*, June 1932, (*Kp4* C334), reprinted in a slightly revised form as a Hogarth Press pamphlet, (*Kp4* A17), No. 8 in the Hogarth Letters series, published on 7 July 1932 (see *IV VW Diary*, 6 July 1932) and for which she was paid £25 by the Press (WSU). John Lehmann (1907–87) is the 'John' of the Letter – the 'young poet': see, e.g., John Lehmann, *Thrown to the Woolfs* (Weidenfeld

and Nicolson, 1978), pp. 29–31. Lehmann started as manager at the Hogarth Press on 21 January 1931, and the series and contributors were devised by him and the Woolfs. Following Lehmann's enthusiastic letter in praise of *The Waves*, in which he also 'suggested that it was high time for her to define her views about modern poetry, which [they] had so often discussed together' (*The Whispering Gallery: Autobiography I* [Longmans, Green, 1955], p. 170), VW wrote on 17 September 1931: 'my brain is flushed & flooded & I'm at once inspired to write a Letter to a Young Poet' (*IV VW Diary*). She replied to Lehmann on the following day: 'I think your idea of a Letter most brilliant – To a Young Poet? because I'm seething with immature and ill considered and wild and annoying ideas about prose and poetry. So lend me your name – (and let me sketch a character of you by way of frontispiece) – and then I'll pour forth all I can think of about you young, and we old, and novels – how damned they are – and poetry, how dead. But I must take a look into the subject, and you must reply, "To an old novelist" – I must read Auden, whom I've not read, and Spender . . . The whole subject is crying out for letters – flocks, volleys, of them, from every side. Why not get Spender and Auden and Day Lewis to join in?' (*IV VW Letters*, no. 2437). On 30 September she wrote to him again: 'I am a wretch not to have thanked you for your book [*A Garden Revisited*, published that month by the Hogarth Press], which will not only stand on my shelf as you suggest but lie beneath the scrutiny of my aged eyes. I want to read it with some attention, and also Auden, and Day Lewis – I dont suppose there's anything for me to say about modern poetry, but I daresay I shall plunge, at your bidding. We must talk about it. I dont know what your difficulties are. Why should poetry be dead? etc. etc. But I wont run on, because then I shall spurt out my wild theories, and I've had not a moment to read for days and days' (*ibid.*, no. 2440). She was working on the essay on 5 October (see *IV VW Diary*). On 1 January 1932: 'My attempt to polish up John's letter in the lodge yesterday was a failure. Am I more severe, deeper, less of a flibbertigibbet now than of old, so that writing exacts a closer screw? – & my head is twisted with the effort? I think that possible' (*ibid.*). On 26 February she had '25 minutes in which . . . to correct my Letter to a Young Poet & give it to John' (*ibid.*). On 31 January she had 'just finished, as I say, the final version as I call it, of my Letter to a young poet' (*ibid.*). On 22 February she told William Plomer: 'There's not much to await in my letter to a young poet. I find one can hardly broach the subject in 4,000 words; and then some space has to go in the amenities of letter writing' (*V VW Letters*, no. 2532). Cf. *The Works of Jonathan Swift . . .*, ed. Sir Walter Scott (1814; 2nd ed., Archibald Constable, 1824), vol. ix, 'A Letter of Advice to a Young Poet . . .', dated December 1720, pp. 183–207.

On 12 March 1932 VW offered 'Letter to a Young Poet' to the *Yale Review* for the June number (*V VW Letters*, no. 2551), and stated that Harcourt, Brace would be publishing it some months later, but, in the event, it was not published in the US separately. Harcourt had taken the first three Hogarth Letters, but had only sold 125 copies by March 1932. Helen McAfee, the managing editor of the *Yale Review*, liked the essay (see *V VW Letters*, no. 2569), and VW corrected the proofs on 29 April in Athens while on holiday (see *VWB*, no. 9 [January 2002], p. 8, and no. 24 [January 2007], p. 65). The issue of the *Yale Review* also contained: an essay by Thomas Mann on Goethe, and Sidney L. Gulick, Jr's review of Bonamy Dobrée's six-volume edition of *The Letters of Lord Chesterfield*. VW acknowledged receipt of payment and copies of the *Yale Review* on 25 July (see *V VW Letters*, no. 2612).

After publication in the UK Lehmann wrote to VW about the essay, and she replied on 31 July 1932: 'Now for your points: of course dressing up may have some advantages; but not more than gin and bitter or evening dress or any other stimulant. Besides it becomes a habit, and freezes the elderly, like Wyndham Lewis, into ridiculous posings and posturing. But its not a matter of great importance. I admit your next point – that is that my quotations aren't good illustrations: but as usual, I couldn't find the ones I wanted when I was writing; and was too lazy to look. Anyhow my impression is that I could convince you by quotations: I do feel that the young poet is rather crudely jerked between realism and beauty, to put it roughly. I think he is all to be praised for attempting to swallow Mrs Gape; but he ought to assimilate her. What it seems to me is that he doesnt sufficiently believe in her: doesnt dig himself in deep enough; wakes up in the middle; his imagination goes off the boil; he doesnt reach the unconscious automated state – hence the spasmodic, jerky, self conscious effect of his realistic language. But I may be transferring to him some of the ill effects of my own struggles the other way round – writes poetry in prose. Tom Eliot I think succeeds; but then he is much more violent; and I think by being violent, limits himself so that he only attacks a minute province of his imagination; whereas you younger and happier spirits should, partly owing to him, have a greater range and be able to devise a less steep precipitous technique. But this is mere guesswork of course. As for publishing, I dont see your point that it is salutory because it wipes clean the slate: I think, on the contrary, it engraves the slate, what with reviewers and publicity. And if, as is quite likely, the best poems are written before 30, they wont spoil with keeping. ¶ But the fact is I'm not at all satisfied with the Letter, and would like to tear up, or entirely re-write. It is a bad form for criticism, because it seems to invite archness and playfulness, and when one has done being playful the times up and there's no room for more' (*V VW Letters*, no. 2615). Six years later VW wrote to Elizabeth E. Nielsen: 'I said thirty I suppose because thirty is a definite name for maturity and pamphlets require to be made very plain' ('Nineteen Letters to Eleven Recipients', ed. Joanne Trautmann Banks, *Modern Fiction Studies*, vol. xxx, no. 2 [Summer 1984], pp. 198–9, no. 3462a, 28 October 1938).

Although VW thought that her 'poet letter' had passed unnoticed (*IV VW*

Diary, 21 July 1932), a response was planned: 'I'm rather annoyed by the way that we've succumbed to ... Quennel,' she wrote to Lehmann, 'but Leonard thought we must have him if anyone: I'd much rather be answered and torn up and thrown in the waste paper basket by you or Day Lewis: but it cant be helped' (*V VW Letters*, no. 2615). The poet, biographer and critic Peter Quennell (1905–93) responded to VW on behalf of his generation in *A Letter to Mrs. Virginia Woolf* (Hogarth Letters, No. 12), published in October 1932. On 22 October 1935, VW wrote: 'I have a dull heavy hot mop inside my brain ... & am a prey to every flea, ant gnat (as for example that I let P. Quennel misrepresent me & never answered him)' (*IV VW Diary*). That may have been a reference to his *Letter*; in any case she was to continue her argument with the poets of the thirties in 'The Leaning Tower' (see *VI VW Essays*). Draft: Department of Manuscripts (MA 3333), Pierpont Morgan Library, New York. Typescript draft with holograph corrections: *Yale Review* Papers, Beinecke Rare Book and Manuscript Library, Yale University. Reprinted (from pamphlet): *DoM, CE*.

2 – Although later on VW suggests that the 'old gentleman' may have been called 'Peabody', she associates these sentiments with John Cann Bailey (1864–1931), essayist and critic: e.g. 'Really, if you go on writing, you will vitiate John Bailey's stock phrase "the art of letter writing is dying out –"' (*II VW Letters*, no. 653, 16 November [1912]; and see *VI VW Letters*, no. 3197, 6 December [1936]). See J. C. Bailey, *Studies in Some Famous Letters* (Thomas Burleigh, 1899), 'Cowper', p. 1: 'It is often said that the delightful art of letter-writing is dead ... the last century [was] the golden age of the letter-writer. It never does to have too much of a good thing, and so Rowland Hill, and Penny Posts, and hourly deliveries, have very nearly killed the old-fashioned letter ...' (reprinted from *Macmillan's Magazine*, November 1891). See also the first sentence of 'Real Letters', *III VW Essays*.

3 – Thomas Gray (1716–71); Horace Walpole (1717–97); Marie de Sévigné, marquise de Rabutin-Chantal (1626–96).

4 – For most of the inter-war years, inland letters not exceeding 2 oz. in weight cost 1 1/2 d. in postage.

5 – John Donne (1572–1631); Gerard Manley Hopkins (1844–89).

6 – John Dryden (1631–1700); Alexander Pope (1688–1744); Alfred, Lord Tennyson (1809–92).

7 – Guy Fawkes (1570–1606), conspirator whose failure to blow up Parliament has been celebrated annually since 5 November 1605.

8 – This image may be inspired by Hugh Walpole's reaction when he started reading Somerset Maugham's *Cakes and Ale* and recognised himself as Alroy Kear: see *V VW Letters*, no. 2274, 8 November 1930.

9 – Geoffrey Chaucer (c. 1340–1400); George Crabbe (1754–1832); George Gordon, Lord Byron (1788–1824); Robert Browning (1812–89).

10 – Poem II, in *Poems* by W. H. Auden (Faber & Faber, 1930), pp. 39, 40,

40–1; l.6 begins: 'Then stilled against stone,'. This poem was excluded from Auden's *Collected Shorter Poems, 1927-1957* (Faber & Faber, 1966) and from Edward Mendelson's edition of Auden's *Collected Poems* (Faber & Faber, 1994); see p. 901.

11 – In Poem IX, 'The crowing of the cock . . .', there is a reference to 'spidery moonlight' in the second stanza (*Poems* [1930], p. 48).

12 – 'To penetrate that room' by John Lehmann, in *New Signatures: Poems by Several Hands*, ed. Michael Roberts (Hogarth Living Poets No. 24, Hogarth Press, February 1932), p. 75.

13 – Poem XI, in *From Feathers to Iron* by Cecil Day Lewis (Hogarth Living Poets No. 22, Hogarth Press, 1931), p. 24.

14 – Poem I, 'At the Edge of Being' (written c. May 1930), in *Twenty Poems* by Stephen Spender (Basil Blackwell, n.d. [1930]), p. 2.

15 – William Wordsworth (1770–1850); John Keats (1795–1821); Percy Bysshe Shelley (1792–1822).

16 – *Don Juan* (1819–24). In *The Waves* (Hogarth Press, 1931), Bernard repeatedly thinks that he is, 'in some ways, like Byron' (p. 84) and reads *Don Juan* (p. 94). On 7 July 1931 VW was rereading *Don Juan* (see *IV VW Diary*); and see *IV VW Letters*, no. 2329, 16 February 1931 to Clive Bell – 'the Don Juan of Bloomsbury' (*III VW Diary*, 23 July 1927).

17 – William Butler Yeats (1865–1939).

18 – Samuel Smiles (1812–1904), biographer and didact, popularly remembered for *Self-Help, with Illustrations of Character and Conduct* (1859). 'Smiles became an almost burlesque figure in the early twentieth-century reaction against Victorianism' (*ODNB*).

19 – Sappho (b. c. 612 BC).

20 – Pliny the Elder (AD 23–79), author, natural philosopher, naval and military commander, died investigating the eruption of Mt Vesuvius.

'This is the House of Commons'

Outside the House of Commons stand the statues of great statesmen, black and sleek and shiny as sea lions that have just risen from the water. And inside the Houses of Parliament, in those windy, echoing halls, where people are for ever passing and repassing, taking green cards from policemen, asking questions, staring, accosting members, trooping at the heels of schoolmasters, nodding and laughing and running messages and hurrying through swing doors with papers and attaché cases and all the other emblems of business and haste – here, too, are statues – Gladstone, Granville, Lord John Russell[2] – white statues, gazing from white eyes at the old scenes of stir and bustle in which, not so very long ago, they played their part.

There is nothing venerable or time-worn, or musical, or ceremonious here. A raucous voice bawling 'The Speaker!' heralds the tramp of a plain democratic procession whose only pomp is provided by the mace and the Speaker's wig and gown and gold badges of the head waiters. The raucous voice bawls again, 'Hats off, Strangers!' upon which a number of dingy felt hats are flourished obediently and the head waiters bow from the middle downwards. That is all. And yet the bawling voice, the black gown, the tramp of feet on the stone, the mace and the dingy felt hats somehow suggest, better than scarlet and trumpets, that the Commons are taking their seats in their own House to proceed with the business of governing their own country. Vague though our history may be, we somehow feel that we common people won this right centuries ago, and have held it for centuries past, and the mace is our mace and the Speaker is our speaker and we have no need of trumpeters and gold and scarlet to usher our representative into our own House of Commons.

Certainly our own House of Commons from inside is not in the least noble or majestic or even dignified.[3] It is as shiny and as ugly as any other moderate-sized public hall. The oak, of course, is grained yellow. The windows, of course, are painted with ugly coats of arms. The floor, of course, is laid with strips of red matting. The benches, of course, are covered with serviceable leather. Wherever one looks one says, 'of course.' It is an untidy, informal-looking assembly. Sheets of white paper seem to be always fluttering to the floor. People are always coming in and out incessantly. Men are whispering and gossiping and cracking jokes over each other's shoulders. The swing doors are perpetually swinging. Even the central island of control and dignity where the Speaker sits under his canopy, is a perching ground for casual members who seem to be taking a peep at the proceedings at their ease. Legs rest on the edge of the table where the mace lies suspended; and the secrets which repose in the two brass-bound chests on either side of the table are not immune from the prod of an occasional toe. Dipping and rising, moving and settling, the Commons remind one of a flock of birds settling on a stretch of ploughed land. They never alight for more than a few minutes; some are always flying off, others are always settling again. And from the flock rises the gabbling, the cawing, the croaking of a flock of birds, disputing merrily and with occasional vivacity over some seed, worm, or buried grain.

One has to say to oneself severely, 'But this is the House of Commons. Here the destinies of the world are altered. Here Gladstone fought, and Palmerston and Disraeli.[4] It is by these men that we are governed. We obey their orders every day of the year. Our purses are at their mercy. They decide how fast we shall drive our cars in Hyde Park;[5] also whether we shall have war or peace.'[6] But we have to remind ourselves; for to look at they do not differ much from other people. The standard of dress is perhaps rather high. We look down upon some of the glossiest top hats still to be seen in England. A magnificent scarlet button-hole blazes here and there. Everybody has been well fed and given a good education doubtless. But what with their chatter and laughter, their high spirits, and impatience and irreverence, they are not a whit more judicious, or more dignified, or more respectable-looking than any other assembly of citizens met to debate parish business or to give prizes for fat oxen. This is true; but after a time some curious difference makes itself suspected. We feel that the Commons is a body of a certain character; it has been in existence for a long time; it has its own laws and licences. It is irreverent in a way of its own; and so, presumably, reverent too in its own way. It has somehow a code of its own. People who disregard this code will be unmercifully chastened; those who are in accord with it will be easily condoned. But what it condemns and what it condones, only those who are in the secret of the House can say. All we can be sure of is that a secret there is. Perched up high as we are, under the rule of an official who follows the prevailing informality by crossing his legs and scribbling notes on his knee, we feel sure that nothing could be easier than to say the wrong thing, either with the wrong levity or the wrong seriousness, and that no assurance of virtue, genius, valour is here sure of success if something else – some indefinable quality – is omitted.

But how, one asks, remembering Parliament Square, are any of these competent, well-groomed gentlemen going to turn into statues? For Gladstone, for Pitt, or for Palmerston even, the transition was perfectly easy.[7] But look at Mr Baldwin – he has all the look of a country gentleman poking pigs; how is he going to mount a plinth and wrap himself decorously in a towel of black marble? No statue that did not render the shine of Sir Austen's top hat could do justice to him. Mr Henderson seems constitutionally opposed to the pallor and severity of marble. As he stands there answering questions his fair complexion flushes scarlet, and his yellow hair seems to have been sleeked down with a wet brush ten minutes ago. Sir William Jowitt, it is true, might, if one took off his spruce bow tie, sit to some sculptor for a bust much in the style of the Prince Consort. Ramsay MacDonald has 'features,' as the photographers say, and could fill a marble chair in a public square without looking conspicuously ridiculous.[8] But for the rest, the transition into marble is unthinkable. Mobile, irreverent, commonplace, snub-nosed, red-jowled, squires, lawyers, men of business – their prime quality, their enormous virtue lies surely in the fact that no more normal, average, decent-looking set of human beings could be found in the four kingdoms. The flashing eye, the arched brow, the nervous, sensitive hand – these would be unseemly and out of place here. The abnormal man would be pecked to death by all these cheerful sparrows. Look how irreverently they treat the Prime Minister himself. He has to submit to being questioned and cross-examined by a youth who seems to have rolled out of a punt on the river; or again to be heckled by a stubby little man who, to judge by his accent, must have been shovelling sugar into little blue bags behind a counter before he came to Westminster. Neither shows the least trace of fear or reverence. If the Prime Minister should one of these days turn into a statue, this apotheosis will not be reached here among the irreverent Commons.

All this time the fire of question and answer had popped and cracked incessantly; at last it stopped. The Secretary for Foreign Affairs rose, raised some typewritten sheets and read, clearly and firmly, a statement about some difficulty with Germany.[9] He had seen the German Ambassador at the Foreign Office on Friday; he had said this, he had said that. He had crossed to Paris and seen M. Briand on Monday. They had agreed to this, they had suggested that. A plainer, a graver, a more business-like pronouncement could not be imagined. And as he spoke so directly, so firmly, a block of rough stone seemed to erect itself there on the Government benches. In other words, as one listened to the Secretary for Foreign Affairs endeavouring to guide our relations with Germany, it seemed clear that these ordinary-looking business-like men are responsible for acts which will remain when their red cheeks and top hats and check trousers are dust and ashes. Matters of great moment, which affect the happiness of people, the destinies of nations, are here at work chiselling and carving these very ordinary human beings. Down on this stuff of common humanity comes the stamp of a huge machine. And the machine itself and the man upon whom the stamp of the machine descends are both plain, featureless, impersonal.

Time was when the Foreign Secretary manipulated facts, toyed with them, elaborated them, and used all the resources of art and eloquence to make them appear what he chose that they should appear to the people who had to accept his will. He was no common hard-worked man of business, with a small car and a villa and a great longing to get an afternoon off and play golf with his sons and daughters on a Surrey common. The Minister was once dressed to fit his part. Fulminations, perorations shook the air. Men were persuaded, juggled with, played upon. Pitt thundered; Burke was sublime.[10] Individuality was allowed to unfold itself. Now no single human being can withstand the pressure of human affairs. They sweep over him and obliterate him; they leave him featureless, anonymous, their instrument merely. The conduct of affairs has passed from the hands of individuals to the hands of committees. Even committees can only guide them and hasten them and sweep them on to other committees. The intricacies and elegancies of personality are trappings that get in the way of business. The supreme need is despatch. A thousand ships come to anchor in the docks every week; how many thousand causes do not come daily to be decided in the House of Commons? Thus if statues are to be raised, they will become more and more monolithic, plain and featureless. They will cease to record Gladstone's collars, Dizzy's curl and Palmerston's wisp of straw. They will be like granite plinths set on the tops of moors to mark battles. The days of single men and personal power are over. Wit, invective, passion, are no longer called for. Mr MacDonald is addressing not the small separate ears of his audience in the House of Commons, but men and women in factories, in shops, in farms on the veldt, in Indian villages. He is speaking to all men everywhere, not to us sitting here. Hence the clarity, the gravity, the plain impersonality of his statement. But if the days of the small separate statue are over, why should not the age of architecture dawn? That question asks itself as we leave the House of Commons. Westminster Hall raises its immense dignity as we pass out. Little men and women are moving soundlessly about the floor. They appear minute, perhaps pitiable; but also venerable and beautiful under the curve of the vast dome, under the perspective of the huge columns. One would rather like to be a small nameless animal in a vast cathedral. Let us rebuild the world then as a splendid hall; let us give up making statues and inscribing them with impossible virtues.

Let us see whether democracy which makes halls cannot surpass the aristocracy which carved statues. But there are still innumerable policemen. A blue giant stands at every door to see that we do not hurry on with our democracy too fast. 'Admission is on Saturdays only between the hours of ten and twelve.'[11] That is the kind of notice that checks our dreaming progress. And must we not admit a distinct tendency in our corrupt mind soaked with habit to stop and think: 'Here stood King Charles when they sentenced him to death; here the Earl of Essex; and Guy Fawkes; and Sir Thomas More.'[12] The mind, it seems, likes to perch, in its flight through empty space, upon some remarkable nose, some trembling hand; it loves the flashing eye, the arched brow, the abnormal, the particular, the splendid human being. So let us hope that democracy will come, but only a hundred years hence, when we are beneath the grass; or that by some stupendous stroke of genius both will be combined, the vast hall and the small, the particular, the individual human being.

1 – A signed essay in *Good Housekeeping*, October 1932, (*Kp4* C334.1); the fifth of six essays in 'The London Scene'. The essay was accompanied by photographs of Big Ben and Parliament imposed on fainter photographs of statues of statesmen (including those of Gladstone and Pitt), each almost as tall as the Big Ben tower itself. The essay was introduced: 'Virginia Woolf looks down, in company with the shades of bygone statesmen, upon the Westminster scene'. On 29 March 1931 VW wrote to Ethel Smyth: 'Just back from the Webbs . . . I've got to get in House of Commons and Lords before Thursday' (*IV VW Letters*, no. 2339). Sidney (1859–1947) and Beatrice (1858–1943) Webb, old friends of the Woolfs, took them to the House of Commons as their guests on Monday 30 March 1931 (see *IV VW Diary*, p. 16, editor's note). Sidney had been created Baron Passfield in 1929, holding the post of Colonial Secretary in Ramsay MacDonald's second minority Labour government (8 June 1929–25 August 1931). The same issue of *Good Housekeeping* also contained: Dame Ethel Smyth on 'Women in Music'. See also 'The Docks of London' above, and Appendix VIII. A holograph draft and a final typescript draft, entitled 'The House of Commons' (the article is also given this title on the Contents page in *Good Housekeeping*), together with the proofs (Berg, M 13, M 134). Reprinted: *LSc, CDML*.

2 – William Ewart Gladstone (1809–98), Liberal statesman, Prime Minister 1868–74, 1880–5, 1886 and 1892–4; George Leveson-Gower, 2nd Earl Granville (1815–91), Whig–Liberal statesman, Foreign Secretary, 1851–2, 1870–4 and 1880–5; Lord John Russell, 1st Earl Russell (1792–1878), Whig–Liberal statesman, Prime Minister 1846–52 and 1865–6.

3 – Cf. Harold Nicolson, 'The Rebuilding of the Commons Chamber' (*Spectator*, 17 November 1944): 'After the fire of 1834', when all except Westminster Hall was destroyed, '[e]very morning Pugin would have another

bright idea, and would insist upon encrusting Barry's already overcharged surfaces with some new armorial motto or some fresh Norman or Angevin escutcheon . . . When on the night of May 10th, 1941, the Luftwaffe attacked the Palace of Westminster, they managed to destroy the Chamber without seriously damaging the remainder of the Palace, pulling out the House of Commons as neatly as a dentist extracts a tooth.' In the proposed reconstruction 'some innovations there will be: . . . That dim, that glaucous, air which rendered the old Chamber so reminiscent of an aquarium will give place to something more sprightly and less opaque' (reprinted in *Comments: 1944–1948* [Constable, 1948], pp. 56–60). See also his broadcast of 13 February 1931 on 'The House of Commons', in *People and Things: Wireless Talks* (Constable, 1931), pp. 123–6.

4 – Henry John Temple, 3rd Viscount Palmerston (1784–1865), Liberal statesman, Prime Minister 1855–8 and 1859–65; Benjamin Disraeli, Earl of Beaconsfield (1804–81), nicknamed 'Dizzy', Conservative statesman, Prime Minister 1868 and 1874–80.

5 – The speed limit of 20 mph was enforced in the London parks from early in 1931: see correspondence in *The Times*, 13 January and 17 February 1931. See also *III VW Diary*, 20 December 1930, and fn. 12.

6 – Closing quotation mark omitted from *Good Housekeeping*, but present in the final typescript draft.

7 – A statue of Gladstone is outside St Clement Danes (see 'Abbeys and Cathedrals' above), and one of William Pitt the Younger (1759–1806), Prime Minister, in Hanover Square; a statue of Viscount Palmerston by Thomas Woolner (1876) *is* in Parliament Square. VW may be thinking about the statues inside the Houses of Parliament.

8 – Stanley Baldwin (1867–1947), leader of the Conservative opposition, had been Prime Minister, 1924–9, and would be so again in 1935; Sir Austen Chamberlain (1863–1937), Conservative MP who, as Foreign Secretary, had pursued pro-French policies; Arthur Henderson (1863–1935), Foreign Secretary 1929–31, leader of the Labour Party, 1931–2; Sir William Jowitt (1885–1957), Attorney-General; Prince Albert (1819–61), consort of Queen Victoria; Ramsay MacDonald (1866–1937), Prime Minister until 1935, formed a National Government in August 1931 to deal with the economic crisis, thereby splitting the Labour Party. See *CDML*, p. 208, n. 4: 'In a similar passage in the last chapter of *Jacob's Room*, Woolf contrasts the modern statesmen who were taking the decision to declare war on Germany in 1914 with the busts of their greater predecessors (1922; Penguin Books, 1992, pp. 151–2).'

9 – This debate took place on 30 March 1931 on the projected Customs Union between Austria and Germany, and whether it violated Austria's economic independence, as established by the Geneva Protocol of 1922. Henderson took a prominent part. See the report in *The Times*, 31 March, p. 7. France's principal Foreign Minister, Aristide Briand (1862–1932), served

briefly as Prime Minister on ten occasions and was awarded the 1926 Nobel Peace Prize. His speech to the French Senate was reported in *The Times* on 30 March: he 'pointed out with great force [that] on the day that the loyal fulfilment of agreements could no longer be counted upon there would remain nothing, neither safeguard nor security' (p. 13).

10 – William Pitt, 1st Earl of Chatham (1708–78), Prime Minister, 1766–8; Edmund Burke (1729–97), statesman; both were famous for their eloquence.

11 – According to *A Pictorial and Descriptive Guide to London* (Ward, Lock, 51st ed. revised, n.d. [1934]), p. 97: 'The Houses are only shown on Saturdays . . . from 10 to 3.30 . . . When Parliament is sitting, persons of either sex desirous of listening to the debates can gain admission to the Members' Gallery . . . after 4.15 p.m. . . . . Applicants are required to give a Member's name as a reference, in case of necessity, before being admitted.' As for Westminster Hall, when 'Parliament is in session the Hall is open only from 10 to 2.45 p.m. Monday to Thursday . . . On Saturdays the Hall may be seen from 10 a.m. to 4.30 p.m.' (*ibid.*, p. 103).

12 – Westminster Hall (rebuilt 1397) housed the Law Courts until 1882, and there all these were sentenced to death: 'Charles I in 1649; the Earl of Essex during Elizabeth's reign, in 1601; Guy Fawkes in 1606, for his attempt to blow up James I and the Houses of Parliament; Sir Thomas More in 1535, for his refusal to acknowledge Henry VIII as supreme head of the English Church' (*CDML*, pp. 208–9, n. 13).

The Common Reader: Second Series

'...I rejoice to concur with the common reader; for by the common sense of readers, uncorrupted by literary prejudices, after all the refinements of subtilty and the dogmatism of learning, must be generally decided all claim to poetical honours' Dr Johnson, *Life of Gray*.[2]

1 – VW's first mention of what would become *The Common Reader: Second Series* was about 11 November 1930: 'Now what will happen next, when The Waves is done? I think some book of criticism' (*III VW Diary*). While her comments on the writing of specific essays are given in the first note to each essay, and further comments on the development of the book may be found in her diary and letters, the following have been discovered in other sources:

5 November 1931, letter (copy in LWP Ad. 18) to Donald C. Brace, of VW's American publisher, Harcourt, Brace:

In reply to your letter about another volume of the Common Reader – we hope to be able to bring this out in the spring. I do not want to commit myself for certain, because I have not yet gone through the material, and it may need more revision than I can manage by that time. But I suppose you would be able to say that the book was postponed till the autumn if necessary; and as I hope that I shall be able to do it, it would certainly be better to announce it in your spring list.

The title would be

The Common Reader.
Second Series

The table of contents would consist, as far as I can tell at the moment (but the alterations would not be serious) of the following articles:

Some Elizabethans.
The poems of Donne
Swift and Stella
Dorothy Osborne's Letters
Lord Chesterfields Letters
Defoe
Walter Scott [see '*The Antiquary*', *III VW Essays* and *VI VW Essays*, Appendix; see also *IV VW Diary*, 1 September, 1931]
De Quincey's Autobiography
Four Figures: Cowper; Dorothy Wordsworth. M. Wollstonecraft. Beau Brummell
Two Parsons: Woodforde and John Skinner
Hazlitt
Miss Geraldine Jewsbury
Dr. Burney's Evening Party
Fanny's Half Sister [see 'Fanny Burney's Half-Sister' above]
Aurora Leigh
David Copperfield [see *IV VW Essays*; see also *IV VW Diary*, 23 May 1932]

Jack Mytton
G Meredith
Hardy
C. Rossetti
Gosse [see 'Edmund Gosse' above]
Raleigh [see 'A Professor of Life', *IV VW Essays*]
Lawrence [see 'Notes on D. H. Lawrence', *VI VW Essays*, Appendix]

It would be about 80,000 words, I think. As you see the material is much the same as that of the first C.R. I think one might describe it as an unprofessional book of criticism, dealing with such lives and books as have chanced to come my way, rather from the point of view of a writer than of a student or critic. I have often no doubt been interested in a book as a novelist; but as often perhaps have read simply for amusement and without any wish to establish a theory.

I hope to get to work in a week or two, and will let you know as soon as I can be sure whether I can do it for the spring or must wait for the autumn.

Not included in VW's list above, but essays that appeared in *CR2*: 'The Countess of Pembroke's *Arcadia*', 'The *Sentimental Journey*', 'The Niece of an Earl', 'George Gissing' and 'How Should One Read a Book?'. Brace acknowledged this letter on 18 November 1931 and sent 'the usual agreement', which VW signed and returned on 28 November.

In March 1932 VW was revising the essays (Berg, M 23).

In the UK *CR2* was published by the Hogarth Press on 13 October 1932 in an edition of 3200 copies at 10s. 6d. There was a second impression of 1515 copies in November 1932. The third printing of 5124 copies was issued in the Uniform Edition on 25 October 1935. In the USA *CR2* was published by Harcourt, Brace on 27 October 1932 in an edition of 2000 copies at $2.50. There were second and third impressions of 1500 copies each in November and December 1932. The fourth impression of 2000 copies was issued as the Harbrace Edition on 2 February 1939.

The blurb on the inside front flap of the UK dust-jacket reads:

'This is the second volume of *The Common Reader*, and, like the first, it is a book of unprofessional criticism dealing with books and characters that have chanced to come the author's way. Its subjects include: – Some Elizabethans, Donne's Poems, Sidney's Arcadia, Swift and Stella, Dorothy Osborne's Letters, Lord Chesterfield's Letters, Defoe, Sterne, De Quincey's Autobiography, Four Figures, Cowper, Dorothy Wordsworth, Mary Wollstonecraft and Beau Brummell, Two Parsons: Woodforde and John Skinner, Hazlitt, Miss Geraldine Jewsbury, Dr. Burney's Evening Party, Jack Mytton, Meredith, Hardy, Christina Rossetti, and How Should One Read a Book.' This description is almost identical with that in *Books to be Published by The Hogarth Press: Autumn List 1932.* The blurb on the Penguin Books edition (Pelican, 1944) includes an extract from VW's letter of 5 November 1931. See also *VWB*, no. 8 (September 2001), pp. 26–7.

On 15 November 1932, Brace wrote to LW: 'The new volume of *The Common Reader* is being received here with general critical praise. I am enclosing a review from Sunday's *New York Times*, which you may not otherwise see. It is a delightful book and I hope that even in these times it will have a good sale.' See Introduction, p. xiv, for this and other reviews, and Appendix VII for textual emendations and variants.

2 – Samuel Johnson (1709–84), *Lives of the Most Eminent English Poets: With Critical Observations on their Works* . . . (1779–81; new ed. Chandos Classics, Frederick Warne and Scribner, Welford, n.d. [1872]), 'Gray', pp. 501–2, which has: 'uncorrupted with literary' and 'be finally decided'. The passage is quoted accurately in VW's reading notes (MHP, B 2d) (*VWRN* XXXVIII, B11).

The Strange Elizabethans

There are few greater delights than to go back three or four hundred years and become in fancy at least an Elizabethan. That such fancies are only fancies, that this 'becoming an Elizabethan', this reading sixteenth-century writing as currently and certainly as we read our own is an illusion, is no doubt true. Very likely the Elizabethans would find our pronunciation of their language unintelligible; our fancy picture of what it pleases us to call Elizabethan life would rouse their ribald merriment. Still, the instinct that drives us to them is so strong and the freshness and vigour that blow through their pages are so sweet that we willingly run the risk of being laughed at, of being ridiculous.

And if we ask why we go further astray in this particular region of English literature than in any other, the answer is no doubt that Elizabethan prose, for all its beauty and bounty, was a very imperfect medium. It was almost incapable of fulfilling one of the offices of prose which is to make people talk, simply and naturally, about ordinary things. In an age of utilitarian prose like our own, we know exactly how people spend the hours between breakfast and bed, how they behave when they are neither one thing nor the other, neither angry nor loving, neither happy nor miserable. Poetry ignores these slighter shades; the social student can pick up hardly any facts about daily life from Shakespeare's plays; and if prose refuses to enlighten us, then one avenue of approach to the men and women of another age is blocked. Elizabethan prose, still scarcely separated off from the body of its poetry, could speak magnificently, of course, about the great themes – how life is short, and death certain; how spring is lovely, and winter horrid – perhaps, indeed, the lavish and towering periods that it raises above these simple platitudes are due to the fact that it has not cheapened itself upon trifles. But the price it pays for this soaring splendour is to be found in its awkwardness when it comes to earth – when Lady Sidney, for example, finding herself cold at nights, has to solicit the Lord Chamberlain for a better bedroom at Court.[2] Then any housemaid of her own age could put her case more simply and with greater force. Thus, if we go to the Elizabethan prose-writers to solidify the splendid world of Elizabethan poetry as we should go now to our biographers, novelists, and journalists to

335

solidify the world of Pope, of Tennyson, of Conrad, we are perpetually baffled and driven from our quest. What, we ask, was the life
of an ordinary man or woman in the time of Shakespeare? Even the
familiar letters of the time give us little help. Sir Henry Wotton is
pompous and ornate and keeps us stiffly at arm's length.[3] Their histories resound with drums and trumpets. Their broadsheets reverberate
with meditations upon death and reflections upon the immortality of
the soul. Our best chance of finding them off their guard and so
becoming at ease with them is to seek one of those unambitious men
who haunt the outskirts of famous gatherings, listening, observing,
sometimes taking a note in a book. But they are difficult to find.
Gabriel Harvey perhaps, the friend of Spenser and of Sidney, might
have fulfilled that function. Unfortunately the values of the time
persuaded him that to write about rhetoric, to write about Thomas
Smith, to write about Queen Elizabeth in Latin, was better worth
doing than to record the table talk of Spenser and Sir Philip Sidney.[4]
But he possessed to some extent the modern instinct for preserving
trifles, for keeping copies of letters, and for making notes of ideas
that struck him in the margins of books. If we rummage among these
fragments we shall, at any rate, leave the highroad and perhaps hear
some roar of laughter from a tavern door, where poets are drinking;
or meet humble people going about their milking and their love-
making without a thought that this is the great Elizabethan age, or
that Shakespeare is at this moment strolling down the Strand and
might tell one, if one plucked him by the sleeve, to whom he wrote
the sonnets, and what he meant by Hamlet.

The first person whom we meet is indeed a milkmaid – Gabriel
Harvey's sister Mercy. In the winter of 1574 she was milking in the
fields near Saffron Walden accompanied by an old woman, when a
man approached her and offered her cakes and malmsey wine. When
they had eaten and drunk in a wood and the old woman had wandered
off to pick up sticks,[5] the man proceeded to explain his business. He
came from Lord Surrey, a youth of about Mercy's own age – seventeen or eighteen that is – and a married man. He had been bowling
one day and had seen the milkmaid; her hat had blown off and 'she
had somewhat changed her colour'.[6] In short, Lord Surrey had fallen
passionately in love with her; and sent her by the same man gloves,
a silk girdle, and an enamel posy ring which he had torn from his
own hat though his Aunt, Lady W ——, had given it him for a very
different purpose. Mercy at first stood her ground. She was a poor

milkmaid, and he was a noble gentleman. But at last she agreed to
meet him at her house in the village. Thus, one very misty, foggy
night just before Christmas, Lord Surrey and his servant came to
Saffron Walden. They peered in at the malthouse, but saw only her
mother and sisters; they peeped in at the parlour, but only her brothers
were there. Mercy herself was not to be seen; and 'well mired and
wearied for their labour',[7] there was nothing for it but to ride back
home again. Finally, after further parleys, Mercy agreed to meet Lord
Surrey in a neighbour's house alone at midnight. She found him in
the little parlour 'in his doublet and hose, his points untrust, and his
shirt lying round about him'.[8] He tried to force her on to the bed;
but she cried out, and the good wife, as had been agreed between
them, rapped on the door and said she was sent for. Thwarted, enraged,
Lord Surrey cursed and swore, 'God confound me, God confound
me',[9] and by way of lure emptied his pockets of all the money in
them – thirteen shillings in shillings and testers it came to – and made
her finger it. Still, however, Mercy made off, untouched, on condition that she would come again on Christmas eve. But when Christmas
eve dawned she was up betimes and had put seven miles between her
and Saffron Walden by six in the morning, though it snowed and
rained so that the floods were out, and P., the servant, coming later
to the place of assignation, had to pick his way through the water in
pattens. So Christmas passed. And a week later, in the very nick of
time to save her honour, the whole story very strangely was discovered
and brought to an end. On New Year's Eve her brother Gabriel, the
young fellow of Pembroke Hall, was riding back to Cambridge when
he came up with a simple countryman whom he had met at his father's
house. They rode on together, and after some country gossip, the man
said that he had a letter for Gabriel in his pocket. Indeed, it was
addressed 'To my loving brother Mr G. H.', but when Gabriel opened
it there on the road, he found that the address was a lie.[10] It was not
from his sister Mercy, but to his sister Mercy. 'Mine Own Sweet
Mercy', it began; and it was signed 'Thine more than ever his own
Phil'.[11] Gabriel could hardly control himself – 'could scarcely dissemble
my sudden fancies and comprimitt my inward passions' – as he read.[12]
For it was not merely a love-letter; it was more; it talked about
possessing Mercy according to promise. There was also a fair English
noble wrapped up in the paper. So Gabriel, doing his best to control
himself before the countryman, gave him back the letter and the coin
and told him to deliver them both to his sister at Saffron Walden

with this message: 'To look ere she leap. She may pick out the English of it herself.'[13] He rode on to Cambridge; he wrote a long letter to the young lord, informing him with ambiguous courtesy that the game was up. The sister of Gabriel Harvey was not to be the mistress of a married nobleman. Rather she was to be a maid, 'diligent, and trusty and tractable', in the house of Lady Smith at Audley End.[14] Thus Mercy's romance breaks off; the clouds descend again; and we no longer see the milkmaid, the old woman, the treacherous serving man who came with malmsey and cakes and rings and ribbons to tempt a poor girl's honour while she milked her cows.

This is probably no uncommon story; there must have been many milkmaids whose hats blew off as they milked their cows, and many lords whose hearts leapt at the sight so that they plucked the jewels from their hats and sent their servants to make treaty for them. But it is rare for the girl's own letters to be preserved or to read her own account of the story as she was made to deliver it at her brother's inquisition. Yet when we try to use her words to light up the Elizabethan field, the Elizabethan house and living-room, we are met by the usual perplexities. It is easy enough, in spite of the rain and the fog and the floods, to make a fancy piece out of the milkmaid and the meadows and the old woman wandering off to pick up sticks. Elizabethan song-writers have taught us too well the habit of that particular trick. But if we resist the impulse to make museum pieces out of our reading, Mercy herself gives us little help. She was a milkmaid, scribbling love-letters by the light of a farthing dip in an attic. Nevertheless, the sway of the Elizabethan convention was so strong, the accent of their speech was so masterful, that she bears herself with a grace and expresses herself with a resonance that would have done credit to a woman of birth and literary training. When Lord Surrey pressed her to yield she replied:

The thing you wot of, Milord, were a great trespass towards God, a great offence to the world, a great grief to my friends, a great shame to myself, and, as I think, a great dishonour to your lordship. I have heard my father say, Virginity is ye fairest flower in a maid's garden, and chastity ye richest dowry a poor wench can have. . . . Chastity, they say, is like unto time, which, being once lost, can no more be recovered.[15]

Words chime and ring in her ears, as if she positively enjoyed the act of writing. When she wishes him to know that she is only a poor country girl and no fine lady like his wife, she exclaims, 'Good Lord, that you should seek after so bare and country stuff abroad, that have so costly and courtly wares at home!'[16] She even breaks into a jog-trot of jingling rhyme, far less sonorous than her prose, but proof that to write was an art, not merely a means of conveying facts. And if she wants to be direct and forcible, the proverbs she has heard in her father's house come to her pen, the biblical imagery runs in her ears: 'And then were I, poor wench, cast up for hawk's meat, to mine utter undoing, and my friends' exceeding grief'.[17] In short, Mercy the milkmaid writes a natural and noble style, which is incapable of vulgarity, and equally incapable of intimacy. Nothing, one feels, would have been easier for Mercy than to read her lover a fine discourse upon the vanity of grandeur, the loveliness of chastity, the vicissitudes of fortune. But of emotion as between one particular Mercy and one particular Philip, there is no trace. And when it comes to dealing exactly in a few words with some mean object – when, for example, the wife of Sir Henry Sidney, the daughter of the Duke of Northumberland, has to state her claim to a better room to sleep in, she writes for all the world like an illiterate servant girl who can neither form her letters nor spell her words nor make one sentence follow smoothly after another. She haggles, she niggles, she wears our patience down with her repetitions and her prolixities. Hence it comes about that we know very little about Mercy Harvey, the milkmaid, who wrote so well, or Mary Sidney, daughter to the Duke of Northumberland, who wrote so badly. The background of Elizabethan life eludes us.

But let us follow Gabriel Harvey to Cambridge, in case we can there pick up something humble and colloquial that will make these strange Elizabethans more familiar to us. Gabriel, having discharged his duty as a brother, seems to have given himself up to the life of an intel-lectual young man with his way to make in the world. He worked so hard and he played so little that he made himself unpopular with his fellows. For it was obviously difficult to combine an intense interest in the future of English poetry and the capacity of the English language with card-playing, bear-baiting, and such diversions. Nor could he apparently accept everything that Aristotle[18] said as gospel truth. But with congenial spirits he argued, it is clear, hour by hour, night after night, about poetry, and metre, and the raising of the despised English speech and the meagre English literature to a station among the great tongues and literatures of the world. We are sometimes made to think, as we listen, of such arguments as might now be going forward in the new Universities of America. The young English poets speak with a bold yet uneasy arrogance – 'England, since it was England, never bred more honourable minds, more adventurous hearts, more valorous hands, or more excellent wits, than of late'.[19] Yet, to be English is accounted a kind of crime – 'nothing is reputed so contemptible and so basely and vilely accounted of as whatsoever is taken for English'.[20] And if, in their hopes for the future and their sensitiveness to the opinion of older civilisations, the Elizabethans show much the same susceptibility that sometimes puzzle us among the younger countries to-day, the sense that broods over them of what is about to happen, of an undiscovered land on which they are about to set foot, is much like the excitement that science stirs in the minds of imaginative English writers of our own time. Yet however stimulating it is to think that we hear the stir and strife of tongues in Cambridge rooms about the year 1570, it has to be admitted that to read Harvey's pages methodically is almost beyond the limits of human patience. The words seem to run red-hot, molten, hither and thither, until we cry out in anguish for the boon of some meaning to set its stamp on them. He takes the same idea and repeats it over and over again:

In the sovereign workmanship of Nature herself, what garden of flowers without weeds? what orchard of trees without worms? what field of corn without cockle? what pond of fishes without frogs? what sky of light without darkness? what mirror of knowledge without ignorance? what man of earth without frailty? what commodity of the world without discommodity?[21]

It is interminable. As we go round and round like a horse in a mill, we perceive that we are thus clogged with sound because we are reading what we should be hearing. The amplifications and the repetitions, the emphasis like that of a fist pounding the edge of a pulpit, are for the benefit of the slow and sensual ear which loves to dally over sense and luxuriate in sound – the ear which brings in, along with the spoken word, the look of the speaker and his gestures, which gives a dramatic value to what he says and adds to the crest of an extravagance some modulation which makes the word wing its way to the precise spot aimed at in the hearer's heart. Hence, when we lay Harvey's diatribes against Nash or his letters to Spenser upon poetry under the light of the eye alone, we can hardly make headway and lose our sense of any definite direction. We grasp any simple fact that floats to the surface as a drowning man grasps a plank – that the carrier was called Mrs Kerke, that Perne[22] kept a cub for his pleasure in his rooms at Peterhouse; that 'Your last letter . . . was delivered me at mine hostesses by the fireside, being fast hedged in round about on every side with a company of honest, good fellows, and at that time reasonable, honest quaffers';[23] that Greene died begging Mistress Isam 'for a penny pot of Malmsey',[24] had borrowed her husband's shirt when his own was awashing, and was buried yesterday in the new churchyard near Bedlam at a cost of six shillings and fourpence. Light seems to dawn upon the darkness. But no; just as we think to lay hands on Shakespeare's coat-tails, to hear the very words rapped out as Spenser spoke them, up rise the fumes of Harvey's eloquence and we are floated off again into disputation and eloquence, windy, wordy, voluminous, and obsolete. How, we ask, as we slither over the pages, can we ever hope to come to grips with these Elizabethans? And then, turning, skipping and glancing, something fitfully and doubtfully emerges from the violent pages, the voluminous arguments – the figure of a man, the outlines of a face, somebody who is not 'an Elizabethan' but an interesting, complex, and individual human being.

We know him, to begin with, from his dealings with his sister. We see him riding to Cambridge, a fellow of his college, when she was milking with poor old women in the fields. We observe with amusement his sense of the conduct that befits the sister of Gabriel Harvey, the Cambridge scholar. Education had put a great gulf between him and his family. He rode to Cambridge from a house in a village street where his father made ropes and his mother worked in the malthouse. Yet though his lowly birth and the consciousness that he had his way to make in the world made him severe with his sister, fawning to the great, uneasy and self-centred and ostentatious, it never made him ashamed of his family. The father who could send three sons to Cambridge and was so little ashamed of his craft that he had himself carved making ropes at his work and the carving let in above his fireplace, was no ordinary man. The brothers who followed Gabriel to Cambridge and were his best allies there, were brothers to be proud of. He could be proud of Mercy even, whose beauty could make a great nobleman pluck the jewel from his hat. He was undoubtedly proud of himself. It was the pride of a self-made man who must read when other people are playing cards, who owns no undue allegiance to authority and will contradict Aristotle himself, that made him unpopular at Cambridge and almost cost him his degree. But it was an unfortunate chance that led him thus early in life to defend his rights and insist upon his merits. Moreover, since it was true – since he was abler, quicker, and more learned than other people, handsome in person too, as even his enemies could not deny ('a smudge piece of a handsome fellow it hath been in his days' Nash admitted)[25] he had reason to think that he deserved success and was denied it only by the jealousies and conspiracies of his colleagues. For a time, by dint of much caballing and much dwelling upon his own deserts, he triumphed over his enemies in the matter of the degree. He delivered lectures. He was asked to dispute before the court when Queen Elizabeth came to Audley End. He even drew her favourable attention. 'He lookt something like an Italian',[26] she said when he was brought to her notice. But the seeds of his downfall were visible even in his moment of triumph. He had no self-respect, no self-control. He made himself ridiculous and his friends uneasy. When we read how he dressed himself up and 'came ruffling it out huffty tuffty in his suit of velvet'[27] how uneasy he was, at one moment cringing, at another 'making no bones to take the wall of Sir Phillip Sidney',[28] now flirting with the ladies, now 'putting bawdy riddles to them',[29] how when the Queen praised him he was beside himself with joy and talked the English of Saffron Walden with an Italian accent, we can imagine how his enemies jeered and his friends blushed. And so, for all his merits, his decline began. He was not taken into Lord Leicester's service; he was not made Public Orator; he was not given the Mastership of Trinity Hall. But there was one society in which he succeeded. In the small, smoky rooms where Spenser and other young men discussed poetry and language and the future of English literature, Harvey was not laughed at. Harvey, on the contrary, was taken very seriously. To friends like these he seemed as capable of greatness as any of them. He too might be one of those destined to make English Literature illustrious. His passion for poetry was disinterested. His learning was profound. When he held forth upon quantity and metre, upon what the Greeks had written and the Italians, and what the English might write, no doubt he created for Spenser that atmosphere of hope and ardent curiosity spiced with sound learning that serves to spur the imagination of a young writer and to make each fresh poem as it is written seem the common property of a little band of adventurers set upon the same quest. It was thus that Spenser saw him:

> Harvey, the happy above happiest men,
> I read: that, sitting like a looker-on
> Of this world's stage, doest note, with critic pen,
> The sharp dislikes of each condition.[30]

Poets need such 'lookers-on'; someone who discriminates from a watch-tower above the battle; who warns; who foresees. It must have been pleasant for Spenser to listen as Harvey talked; and then to cease to listen, to let the vehement, truculent voice run on, while he slipped from theory to practice and made up a few lines of his own poetry in his head. But the looker-on may sit too long and hold forth too curiously and domineeringly for his own health. He may make his theories fit too tight to accommodate the formlessness of life. Thus when Harvey ceased to theorise and tried to practise there issued nothing but a thin dribble of arid and unappetising verse or a copious flow of unctuous and servile eulogy. He failed to be a poet as he failed to be a statesman, as he failed to be a professor, as he failed to be a Master, as he failed, it might seem, in everything that he undertook, save that he had won the friendship of Spenser and Sir Philip Sidney.

But, happily, Harvey left behind him a commonplace book;[31] he had the habit of making notes in the margins of books as he read. Looking from one to the other, from his public self to his private, we see his face lit from both sides, and the expression changes as it changes so seldom upon the face of the Elizabethans. We detect another Harvey lurking behind the superficial Harvey, shading him with doubt and effort and despondency. For, luckily, the commonplace book was small; the margins even of an Elizabethan folio narrow; Harvey was forced to be brief, and because he wrote only for his own eye at the command of some sharp memory or experience he seems to write as if he were talking to himself. That is true, he seems to say; or that reminds me, or again: If only I had done this – . We thus become aware of a conflict between the Harvey who blundered among men and the Harvey who sat wisely at home among his books. The one who acts and suffers brings his case to the one who reads and thinks for advice and consolation.

Indeed, he had need of both. From the first his life was full of conflict and difficulty. Harvey the rope-maker's son might put a brave face on it, but still in the society of gentlemen the lowness of his birth galled him. Think, then, the sedentary Harvey counselled him, of all those unknown people who have nevertheless triumphed. Think of 'Alexander, an Unexpert Youth';[32] think of David, 'a forward stripling, but vanquished a huge Giant';[33] think of Judith and of Pope Joan and their exploits;[34] think, above all, of that 'gallant virago . . . Joan of Arc, a most worthy, valiant young wench . . . what may not an industrious and politic man do . . . when a lusty adventurous wench might thus prevail?'[35] And then it seems as if the smart young men at Cambridge twitted the rope-maker's son for his lack of skill in the gentlemanly arts. 'Leave writing', Gabriel counselled him, 'which consumeth unreasonable much time. . . . You have already plagued yourself this way'.[36] Make yourself master of the arts of eloquence and persuasion. Go into the world. Learn swordsmanship, riding, and shooting. All three may be learnt in a week. And then the ambitious but uneasy youth began to find the other sex attractive and asked advice of his wise and sedentary brother in the conduct of his love affairs. Manners, the other Harvey was of opinion, are of the utmost importance in dealing with women; one must be discreet, self-controlled. A gentleman, this counsellor continued, is known by his 'Good entertainment of Ladies and gentlewomen. No salutation, without much respect and ceremony'[37] – a reflection inspired no doubt by the memory of some snub received at Audley End. Health and the care of the body are of the utmost importance. 'We scholars make an Ass of our body and wit'.[38] One must 'leap out of bed lustily, every morning in ye whole year'.[39] One must be sparing in one's diet, and active, and take regular exercise, like brother H.,[40] 'who never failed to breathe his hound once a day at least'.[41] There must be no 'buzzing or musing'.[42] A learned man must also be a man of the world. Make it your 'daily charge' 'to exercise, to laugh; to proceed boldly'.[43] And if your tormentors brawl and rail and scoff and mock at you, the best answer is 'a witty and pleasant Ironie'.[44] In any case, do not complain, 'It is gross folly, and a vile Sign of a wayward and forward disposition, to be eftsoons complaining of this, or that, to small purpose'.[45] And if as time goes on without preferment, one cannot pay one's bills, one is thrust into prison, one has to bear the taunts and insults of landladies, still remember 'Glad poverty is no poverty';[46] and if, as time passes and the struggle increases, it seems as if 'Life is warfare',[47] if sometimes the beaten man has to own, 'But

344

for hope ye Hart would brust',[48] still his sage counsellor in the study will not let him throw up the sponge. 'He beareth his misery best, that hideth it most'[49] he told himself.

So runs the dialogue that we invent between the two Harveys – Harvey the active and Harvey the passive, Harvey the foolish and Harvey the wise. And it seems on the surface that the two halves, for all their counselling together, made but a sorry business of the whole. For the young man who had ridden off to Cambridge full of conceit and hope and good advice to his sister returned empty-handed to his native village in the end. He dwindled out his last long years in complete obscurity at Saffron Walden. He occupied himself superficially by practising his skill as a doctor among the poor of the neighbourhood. He lived in the utmost poverty off buttered roots and sheep's trotters. But even so he had his consolations, he cherished his dreams. As he pottered about his garden in the old black velvet suit, purloined, Nash says, from a saddle for which he had not paid, his thoughts were all of power and glory; of Stukeley and Drake;[50] of 'the winners of gold and the wearers of gold'.[51] Memories he had in abundance – 'The remembrance of best things will soon pass out of memory; if it be not often renewed and revived',[52] he wrote. But there was some eager stir in him, some lust for action and glory and life and adventure that forbade him to dwell in the past. 'The present tense only to be regarded'[53] is one of his notes. Nor did he drug himself with the dust of scholarship. Books he loved as a true reader loves them, not as trophies to be hung up for display, but as living beings that 'must be meditated, practised and incorporated into my body and soul'.[54] A singularly humane view of learning survived in the breast of the old and disappointed scholar. 'The only brave way to learn all things with no study and much pleasure',[55] he remarked. Dreams of the winners of gold and the wearers of gold, dreams of action and power, fantastic though they were in an old beggar who could not pay his reckoning, who pressed simples and lived off buttered roots in a cottage, kept life in him when his flesh had withered and his skin was 'riddled and crumpled like a piece of burnt parchment'.[56] He had his triumph in the end. He survived both his friends and his enemies – Spenser and Sidney, Nash and Perne. He lived to a very great age for an Elizabethan, to eighty-one or eighty-two; and when we say that Harvey lived we mean that he quarrelled and was tiresome and ridiculous and struggled and failed and had a face like ours – a changing, a variable, a human face.

1 – This essay was written specifically for *CR2*: 'I trotted out yesterday & laid in a stock of Elizabethans. I should like to write a chapter called Some Ethans as prelude to the 2nd Common Reader' (*IV VW Diary*, 20 October 1931). Two years earlier VW had written: 'Now ... I am free to begin reading Elizabethans – the little unknown writers, whom I, so ignorant am I, have never heard of, Puttenham, Webb, Harvey. This thought fills me with joy – no overstatement. To begin reading with a pen in my hand, discovering, pouncing, thinking of theories, when the ground is new, remains one of my great excitements ... I stopped writing, by which no great harm was done; & made out a list of Elizabethan poets ... I want to write criticism. Yes, & one might make out an obscure figure or two. It was the Elizabethan prose writers I loved first & most wildly, stirred by Hakluyt, which father lugged home for me – I think of it with some sentiment – father tramping over the Library with his little girl sitting at HPG [Hyde Park Gate] in mind. He must have been 65; I 15 or 16, then; & why I dont know, but I became enraptured, though not exactly interested, but the sight of the large yellow page entranced me. I used to read it & dream of those obscure adventurers, & no doubt practised their style in my copy books' (*III VW Diary*, 8 December 1929). Although not to her purpose, she may well have read G. M. Young's 'A Word for Gabriel Harvey', in *L&L* (June 1930). On 16 November 1931 she wrote: 'I am working very hard – in my way, to furbish up 2 long Elizabethan articles to front a new Common Reader' (*IV VW Diary*). Holograph draft (Berg, M 11). Reading notes (Berg, RN 1.11 and 1.12) (*VWRN* XI and XII). Reprinted: *CE*.

2 – See *Sir Philip Sidney* by Mona Wilson (Duckworth, 1931), pp. 78–9. Lady Mary Sidney, *née* Dudley (1530/5–86), wife of Sir Henry (1529–86), the Lord Deputy of Ireland, solicited the Lord Chamberlain (Thomas Radcliffe, 3rd Earl of Sussex) – without success – through the intermediary of her husband's secretary Edward Molyneux, to whom she wrote on the matter in October 1578.

3 – Sir Henry Wotton (1568–1639), diplomat and poet.

4 – Gabriel Harvey (1552/3–1631) wrote a series of Latin elegies, *Smithus, vel, Lachrymae Musarum* (1578), on the death of his patron, the statesman and scholar at Cambridge, Sir Thomas Smith (1513–77), who was also a native of Saffron Walden and to some unascertained degree a relation of the Harvey family. Edmund Spenser (1552?–99); Philip Sidney (1554–86).

5 – Cf. the 'old woman picking up sticks' in the background of Orlando and Sasha's love affair (*O*, ch. vi, p. 272; and see ch. i, pp. 43–4).

6 – *The Works of Gabriel Harvey, D.C.L.*, ed. Alexander B. Grosart (3 vols, Huth Library, 1884, 1885), vol. iii, 'The Story of Mercy Harvey, Sister of Dr. Gabriel Harvey – Love-Suit With a Nobleman. 1574–75.', pp. 75–97, which has: 'her hatt blue of, and she therewith sumwhat chaungid her colour' (p. 77). VW modernises the spelling in her quotations. The text of 'The

Story', but without the title, also appears in the *Letter-Book of Gabriel Harvey, A.D. 1573–1580*, ed. Edward John Long Scott (Camden Society, 1884), pp. 143–58. The nobleman was Philip Howard (1557–95), Earl of Surrey, later 13th Earl of Arundel.

7 – *Works*, vol. iii, p. 80.

8 – *Ibid.*, pp. 87–8, which has: 'and his hose, . . . lying out round'.

9 – *Ibid.*, p. 88.

10 – *Ibid.*, pp. 92 and 93.

11 – *Ibid.*, pp. 94–5, which has: 'more then his own, Phil'.

12 – *Ibid.*, p. 95, which has: 'full mutch adooe had I (God wot) to dissemble mie sudden fansies, and comprimitt mie jnward passions.' 'Comprimitt' is 'to settle, allay, appease' (*OED*).

13 – *Ibid.*, p. 96.

14 – For Harvey's letter from Pembroke Hall, 29 March [no year], to Philippa (1522–78), wife of Sir Thomas Smith, see *Letter-Book*, p. 171: 'thus mutch I dare assuredly prommis, that you shal have a diligent, and trusti, and tractable maiden of hir, besides sutch service as she is able to do in sowing, and the like qualities requisite in a maid'. VW has concluded that the sister concerned was Mercy; in fact, Harvey had two sisters and the letter does not name the girl.

15 – *Works*, vol. iii, pp. 81–2, up to the ellipsis. The final sentence occurs in a different letter, *ibid.*, p. 83.

16 – *Ibid.*, p. 85, which has: 'shuld thus seek . . . home.'

17 – *Ibid.*, which has: 'mine owne vtter'.

18 – Aristotle (384–322 BC).

19 – *Works*, vol. ii, 'Pierces Supererogation, or a New Prayse of the Old Asse' (1593), p. 95; also quoted in the introduction to *Gabriel Harvey's Marginalia*, ed. G. C. Moore Smith (Shakespeare Head Press, 1913), p. 66.

20 – *Letter-Book*, Harvey to Spenser, p. 66.

21 – *Works*, vol. ii, 'Pierces Supererogation', p. 288.

22 – Dr Andrew Perne (1519?–89), Dean of Ely and sometime Vice-Chancellor of Cambridge University, is the subject of an extended attack in 'Pierces Supererogation'.

23 – *Letter-Book*, Harvey to Spenser, p. 82, which begins: 'Your lastweekes letter, or rather bill of complaynte . . .'

24 – See *Works*, vol. i, 'Fovre Letters, and certaine Sonnets: Especially touching Robert Greene, and other parties, by him abused' (1592), pp. 170 (which has: 'would pittifully beg a penny-pott of Malmesie') and 171 (which has: 'his lamentable begging of a penny pott of Malmesy').

25 – Thomas Nashe's description of Harvey is quoted in the introduction to *Marginalia*, p. 69; for the original source, see *The Works of Thomas Nashe* [1567–1601], ed. R. B. McKerrow (5 vols, A. H. Bullen, 1904–), vol. iii, p. 94.

26 – See *Marginalia*, pp. 19–20, at p. 19; *Works of Nashe*, vol. iii, pp. 73–7, at p. 76.

27 – *Marginalia*, p. 19; *Works of Nashe*, vol. iii, p. 73.

28 – *Marginalia*, p. 19; *Works of Nashe*, vol. iii, p. 76; both have: 'make no'.

29 – *Marginalia*, p. 19; *Works of Nashe*, vol. iii, p. 75.

30 – 'To the right worshipfull, my singular good frend, M. Gabriell Harvey, Doctor of the Lawes' (dated Dublin, 18 July 1586), *The Works of Edmund Spenser*, ed. J. Payne Collier (5 vols, Bell and Daldy, 1862), vol. v, p. 264. Harvey was represented as Hobbinol in Spenser's 'The Shepheardes Calendar' (1579).

31 – This is now Add. MS. 32,494 in the British Library; see *Marginalia*, p. 87.

32 – *Marginalia*, p. 90, l. 18. Alexander the Great (356–323 BC), King of Macedon.

33 – *Ibid.*, p. 90, l. 21, which has: 'stripling, vanquisshed'. For David and Goliath, see 1 Samuel 17.

34 – See *Marginalia*, p. 92, ll. 29–31. For Judith, who cut off the head of Holofernes, see her book in the Apocrypha. Pope Joan supposedly reigned for fewer than two years in the 850s.

35 – *Marginalia*, p. 92, ll. 4–11, which has: 'Vnius Virginis Gallicæ', not 'Joan of Arc' (1412–31), the French national heroine.

36 – See *ibid.*, p. 89, ll. 25–7, which has: 'Auoyde all writing, but necessary: wch consumith . . . tyme, before you ar aware: you'.

37 – *Ibid.*, p. 99, ll. 1–3, which has: 'of Gentlewoomen and Ladyes . . . No'.

38 – *Ibid.*, p. 177, l. 8.

39 – *Ibid.*, p. 196, ll. 8–9, which has: 'of your bedd'.

40 – Dr Henry Harvey (d. 1585), Master of Trinity Hall, Cambridge, c. 1557/8–84/5.

41 – *Marginalia*, p. 90, l. 6, which has: 'he neuer'.

42 – *Ibid.*, p. 142, l. 33.

43 – *Ibid.*, p. 155, ll. 19–20.

44 – *Ibid.*, ll. 26–8, which has: 'No such confutation of Anger, rage, chiding, carving, brawling, rayling, threatening, scoffing, mocking, or such like: as witty, & pleasant Ironyes.'

45 – *Ibid.*, p. 88, ll. 3–5.

46 – *Ibid.*, p. 105, l. 7.

47 – See *ibid.*, p. 147: 'Vita, militia: uel Togata, uel Armata', against which is set in the margin at l. 31: 'Life is warfare.'

48 – *Ibid.*, p. 95, ll. 16–17.

49 – *Ibid.*, l. 22.

50 – Thomas Stukeley or Stucley (c. 1520–78), soldier and adventurer; Sir Francis Drake (1540–96).

51 – *Marginalia*, p. 198, l. 34, which has: 'winners of gowld, & wearers'.

52 – *Ibid.*, p. 101, ll. 11–12.
53 – *Ibid.*, p. 151, l. 25, which has: 'only in effect to'.
54 – *Ibid.*, p. 146, ll. 20–3, which has: 'This whole booke, written & printed, of continual & perpetual use: & therefore continually, and perpetually to be meditated, practised, and incorporated into my boddy, & sowle.'
55 – *Ibid.*, p. 151, ll. 4–5.
56 – Nashe quoted *ibid.*, p. 69; *Works of Nashe*, vol. iii, p. 93.

Donne After Three Centuries

When we think how many millions of words have been written and printed in England in the past three hundred years, and how the vast majority have died out without leaving any trace, it is tempting to wonder what quality the words of Donne possess that we should still hear them distinctly to-day. Far be it from us to suggest even in this year of celebration and pardonable adulation (1931) that the poems of Donne are popular reading or that the typist, if we look over her shoulder in the Tube, is to be discovered reading Donne as she returns from her office. But he is read; he is audible – to that fact new editions and frequent articles testify, and it is worth perhaps trying to analyse the meaning that his voice has for us as it strikes upon the ear after this long flight across the stormy seas that separate us from the age of Elizabeth.

But the first quality that attracts us is not his meaning, charged with meaning as his poetry is, but something much more unmixed and immediate; it is the explosion with which he bursts into speech. All preface, all parleying have been consumed; he leaps into poetry the shortest way. One phrase consumes all preparation:

> I long to talke with some old lover's ghost,[2]

or

> He is starke mad, whoever sayes,
> That he hath beene in love an houre.[3]

At once we are arrested. Stand still, he commands,

> Stand still, and I will read to thee
> A Lecture, Love, in love's philosophy.[4]

And stand still we must. With the first words a shock passes through us; perceptions, previously numb and torpid, quiver into being; the nerves of sight and hearing are quickened; the 'bracelet of bright hair'[5] burns in our eyes. But, more remarkably, we do not merely become aware of beautiful remembered lines; we feel ourselves compelled to a particular attitude of mind. Elements that were dispersed in the usual stream of life become, under the stroke of Donne's passion, one and entire. The world, a moment before, cheerful, humdrum, bursting with character and variety, is consumed. We are in Donne's world now. All other views are sharply cut off.

In this power of suddenly surprising and subjugating the reader, Donne excels most poets. It is his characteristic quality; it is thus that he lays hold upon us, summing up his essence in a word or two. But it is an essence that, as it works in us, separates into strange contraries at odds with one another. Soon we begin to ask ourselves of what this essence is composed, what elements have met together to cut so deep and complex an impression. Some obvious clues lie strewn on the surface of the poems. When we read the *Satyres*, for example, we need no external proof to tell us that these are the work of a boy. He has all the ruthlessness and definiteness of youth, its hatred of the follies of middle age and of convention. Bores, liars, courtiers – detestable humbugs and hypocrites as they are, why not sum them up and sweep them off the face of the earth with a few strokes of the pen? And so these foolish figures are drubbed with an ardour that proves how much hope and faith and delight in life inspire the savagery of youthful scorn. But, as we read on, we begin to suspect that the boy with the complex and curious face of the early portrait – bold yet subtle, sensual yet nerve drawn – possessed qualities that made him singular among the young. It is not simply that the huddle and pressure of youth which outthinks its words had urged him on too fast for grace or clarity. It may be that there is in this clipping and curtailing, this abrupt heaping of thought on thought, some deeper dissatisfaction than that of youth with age, of honesty with corruption. He is in rebellion, not merely against his elders, but against something antipathetic to him in the temper of his time. His verse has the deliberate bareness of those who refuse to avail themselves of the current usage. It has the extravagance of those who do not feel the pressure of opinion, so that sometimes judgment fails them, and they heap up strangeness for strangeness' sake. He is one of those nonconformists, like Browning and Meredith,[6] who cannot resist glorifying their nonconformity by a dash of wilful and gratuitous eccentricity. But to discover what Donne disliked in his own age, let us imagine some of the more obvious influences that must have told upon him when he wrote his early poems – let us ask what books he read. And by Donne's own testimony we find that his chosen books were the works of 'grave Divines';[7] of philosophers; of 'jolly Statesmen, which teach how to tie The sinewes of a cities mistique bodie';[8] and chroniclers. Clearly he liked facts and arguments. If there are also poets among his books, the epithets he applies to them, 'Giddie fantastique',[9] seem to disparage the art, or at least to show that Donne knew perfectly well what qualities were antipathetic to him in poetry. And yet he was living in the very spring of English poetry. Some of Spenser might have been on his shelves; and Sidney's *Arcadia*; and the *Paradise of Dainty Devices*, and Lyly's *Euphues*.[10] He had the chance, and apparently took it – 'I tell him of new playes'[11] – of going to the theatre; of seeing the plays of Marlowe[12] and Shakespeare acted. When he went abroad in London, he must have met all the writers of that time – Spenser and Sidney and Shakespeare and Jonson; he must have heard at this tavern or at that talk of new plays, of new fashions in verse, heated and learned discussion of the possibilities of the English language and the future of English poetry. And yet, if we turn to his biography, we find that he neither consorted with his contemporaries nor read what they wrote. He was one of those original beings who cannot draw profit, but are rather disturbed and distracted by what is being done round them at the moment. If we turn again to the *Satyres*, it is easy to see why this should be so. Here is a bold and active mind that loves to deal with actual things, which struggles to express each shock exactly as it impinges upon his tight-stretched senses. A bore stops him in the street. He sees him exactly, vividly.

His cloths were strange, though coarse; and black, though bare;
Sleevelesse his jerkin was, and it had beene
Velvet, but t'was now (so much ground was seene)
Become Tufftaffatie;[13]

Then he likes to give the actual words that people say:

> He, like to a high stretcht lute string squeakt, O Sir,
> 'Tis sweet to talke of Kings. At Westminster,
> Said I, The man that keepes the Abbey tombes,
> And for his price doth with who ever comes,
> Of all our Harries, and our Edwards talke,
> From King to King and all their kin can walke:
> Your eares shall heare nought, but Kings; your eyes meet
> Kings only; The way to it, is Kingstreet.[14]

His strength and his weakness are both to be found here. He selects one detail and stares at it until he has reduced it to the few words that express its oddity:

> And like a bunch of ragged carrets stand
> The short swolne fingers of thy gouty hand,[15]

but he cannot see in the round, as a whole. He cannot stand apart and survey the large outline so that the description is always of some momentary intensity, seldom of the broader aspect of things. Naturally, then, he found it difficult to use the drama with its conflict of other characters; he must always speak from his own centre in soliloquy, in satire, in self-analysis. Spenser, Sidney, and Marlowe provided no helpful models for a man who looked out from this angle of vision. The typical Elizabethan with his love of eloquence, with his longing for brave new words, tended to enlarge and generalise. He loved wide landscapes, heroic virtues, and figures seen sublimely in outline or in heroic conflict. Even the prose-writers have the same habit of aggrandisement. When Dekker sets out to tell us how Queen Elizabeth died in the spring, he cannot describe her death in particular or that spring in particular; he must dilate upon all deaths and all springs:

... the Cuckoo (like a single, sole Fiddler, that reels from Tavern to Tavern) plied it all the day long: Lambs frisked up and down in the vallies, kids and Goats leapt to and fro on the Mountains: Shepherds sat piping, country wenches singing: Lovers made Sonnets for their Lasses, whilst they made Garlands for their Lovers: And as the Country was frolic, so was the City merry ... no Scritch-Owl frighted the silly Countryman at midnight, nor any Drum the Citizen at noon-day; but all was more calm than a still water, all husht, as if the Spheres had been playing in Consort: In conclusion, heaven lookt like a Pallace, and the great hall of the earth, like a Paradise. But O the short-liv'd Felicity of man! O world, of what slight and thin stuff is thy happiness![16]

– in short, Queen Elizabeth died, and it is no use asking Dekker what the old woman who swept his room for him said, or what Cheapside looked like that night if one happened to be caught in the thick of the throng. He must enlarge; he must generalise; he must beautify.

Donne's genius was precisely the opposite of this. He diminished; he particularised. Not only did he see each spot and wrinkle which defaced the fair outline; but he noted with the utmost curiosity his own reaction to such contrasts and was eager to lay side by side the two conflicting views and to let them make their own dissonance. It is this desire for nakedness in an age that was florid, this determination to record not the likenesses which go to compose a rounded and seemly whole, but the inconsistencies that break up semblances, the power to make us feel the different emotions of love and hate and laughter at the same time, that separate Donne from his contemporaries. And if the usual traffic of the day – to be buttonholed by a bore, to be snared by a lawyer, to be snubbed by a courtier – made so sharp an impression on Donne, the effect of falling in love was bound to be incomparably greater. Falling in love meant, to Donne, a thousand things; it meant being tormented and disgusted, disillusioned and enraptured; but it also meant speaking the truth. The love poems, the elegies, and the letters thus reveal a figure of a very different calibre from the typical figure of Elizabethan love poetry. That great ideal, built up by a score of eloquent pens, still burns bright in our eyes. Her body was of alabaster, her legs of ivory; her hair was golden wire and her teeth pearls from the Orient.[17] Music was in her voice and stateliness in her walk. She could love and sport and be faithless and yielding and cruel and true; but her emotions were simple, as befitted her person. Donne's poems reveal a lady of a very different cast. She was brown but she was also fair; she was solitary but also sociable; she was rustic yet also fond of city life; she was sceptical yet devout, emotional but reserved – in short she was as various and complex as Donne himself. As for choosing one type of human perfection and restricting himself to love her and her only, how could Donne, or any man who allowed his senses full play and honestly recorded his own moods, so limit his nature and tell such lies to placate the conventional and the decorous? Was not 'love's sweetest part, Variety'?[18] 'Of music, joy, life and eternity Change is the nursery',[19] he sang. The timid fashion of the age might limit a lover to one woman. For his part he envied and admired the ancients, 'who held plurality of loves no crime':[20]

> But since this title honour hath been us'd,
> Our weak credulity hath been abus'd.[21]

We have fallen from our high estate; the golden laws of nature are repealed.

So through the glass of Donne's poetry now darkly clouded,[22] now brilliantly clear, we see pass in procession the many women whom he loved and hated – the common Julia whom he despised; the simpleton, to whom he taught the art of love; she who was married to an invalid husband, 'cag'd in a basket chair';[23] she could only be loved dangerously by strategy; she who dreamt of him and saw him murdered as he crossed the Alps; she whom he had to dissuade from the risk of loving him; and lastly, the autumnal, the aristocratic lady for whom he felt more of reverence than of love – so they pass, common and rare, simple and sophisticated, young and old, noble and plebeian, and each casts a different spell and brings out a different lover, although the man is the same man, and the women, perhaps, are also phases of womanhood rather than separate and distinct women. In later years the Dean of St Paul's would willingly have edited some of these poems and suppressed one of these lovers – the poet presumably of 'Going to Bed' and 'Love's Warr'. But the Dean would have been wrong. It is the union of so many different desires that gives Donne's love poetry not only its vitality but also a quality that is seldom found with such strength in the conventional and orthodox lover – its spirituality. If we do not love with the body, can we love with the mind? If we do not love variously, freely, admitting the lure first of this quality and then of that, can we at length choose out the one quality that is essential and adhere to it and so make peace among the warring elements and pass into a state of being which transcends the 'Hee and Shee'?[24] Even while he was at his most fickle and gave fullest scope to his youthful lusts, Donne could predict the season of maturity when he would love differently, with pain and difficulty, one and one only. Even while he scorned and railed and abused, he divined another relationship which transcended change and parting and might, even in the bodies' absence, lead to unity and communion:

> Rend us in sunder, though cans't not divide,
> Our bodies so, but that our souls are ty'd,

> And we can love by letters still and gifts,
> And thoughts and dreams;[25]

Again,

> They who one another keepe alive
> N'er parted be.[26]

And again,

> So to one neutrall thing both sexes fit,
> Wee dye and rise the same, and prove
> Mysterious by this love.[27]

Such hints and premonitions of a further and finer state urge him on and condemn him to perpetual unrest and dissatisfaction with the present. He is tantalised by the sense that there is a miracle beyond any of these transient delights and disgusts. Lovers can, if only for a short space, reach a state of unity beyond time, beyond sex, beyond the body. And at last, for one moment, they reach it. In the 'Extasie' they lie together on a bank,

> All day, the same our postures were,
> And wee said nothing, all the day....
>
> This Extasie doth unperplex
> (We said) and tell us what we love,
> Wee see by this, it was not sexe,
> Wee see, we saw not what did move: ...
>
> Wee then, who are this new soule, know,
> Of what we are compos'd, and made,
> For, th' Atomies of which we grow,
> Are soules, whom no change can invade.
> But O alas, so long, so farre
> Our bodies, why doe wee forbeare? ...[28]

But O alas, he breaks off, and the words remind us that however much we may wish to keep Donne in one posture – for it is in these Extasies that lines of pure poetry suddenly flow as if liquefied by a great heat – so to remain in one posture was against his nature. Perhaps it is against the nature of things also. Donne snatches the intensity because he is aware of the change that must alter, of the discord that must interrupt.

Circumstances, at any rate, put it beyond his power to maintain that ecstasy for long. He had married secretly; he was a father; he was, as we are soon reminded, a very poor yet a very ambitious man, living in a damp little house at Mitcham with a family of small children. The children were frequently ill. They cried, and their cries, cutting through the thin walls of the jerry-built house, disturbed him at his work. He sought sanctuary naturally enough elsewhere, and naturally had to pay rent for that relief. Great ladies – Lady Bedford, Lady Huntingdon, Mrs Herbert[29] – with well-spread tables and fair gardens, must be conciliated; rich men with the gift of rooms in their possession must be placated. Thus, after Donne the harsh satirist, and Donne the imperious lover, comes the servile and obsequious figure of Donne the devout servant of the great, the extravagant eulogist of little girls. And our relationship with him suddenly changes. In the satires and the love poems there was a quality – some psychological intensity and complexity – that brings him closer than his contemporaries, who often seem to be caught up in a different world from ours and to exist immune from our perplexities and swept by passions which we admire but cannot feel. Easy as it is to exaggerate affinities, still we may claim to be akin to Donne in our readiness to admit contrasts, in our desire for openness, in that psychological intricacy which the novelists have taught us with their slow, subtle, and analytic prose. But now, as we follow Donne in his progress, he leaves us in the lurch. He becomes more remote, inaccessible, and obsolete than any of the Elizabethans. It is as if the spirit of the age, which he had scorned and flouted, suddenly asserted itself and made this rebel its slave. And as we lose sight of the outspoken young man who hated society, and of the passionate lover, seeking some mysterious unity with his love and finding it miraculously, now here, now there, it is natural to abuse the system of patrons and patronage that thus seduced the most incorruptible of men. Yet it may be that we are too hasty. Every writer has an audience in view, and it may well be doubted if the Bedfords and the Drurys and the Herberts were worse influences than the libraries and the newspaper proprietors who fill the office of patron nowadays.

The comparison, it is true, presents great difficulties. The noble ladies who brought so strange an element into Donne's poetry, live only in the reflection, or in the distortion, that we find in the poems themselves. The age of memoirs and letter-writing was still to come. If they wrote themselves, and it is said that both Lady Pembroke[30] and Lady Bedford were poets of merit, they did not dare to put their names to what they wrote, and it has vanished. But a diary here and there survives from which we may see the patroness more closely and less romantically. Lady Ann Clifford, for example, the daughter of a Clifford and a Russell, though active and practical and little educated – she was not allowed 'to learn any language because her father would not permit it'[31] – felt, we can gather from the bald statements of her diary, a duty towards literature and to the makers of it as her mother, the patroness of the poet Daniel,[32] had done before her. A great heiress, infected with all the passion of her age for lands and houses, busied with all the cares of wealth and property, she still read good English books as naturally as she ate good beef and mutton. She read *The Faery Queen* and Sidney's *Arcadia*; she acted in Ben Jonson's Masques at Court; and it is proof of the respect in which reading was held that a girl of fashion should be able to read an old corrupt poet like Chaucer without feeling that she was making herself a target for ridicule as a blue-stocking. The habit was part of a normal and well-bred life. It persisted even when she was mistress of one estate and claimant to even vaster possession of her own. She had Montaigne read aloud to her as she sat stitching at Knole;[33] she sat absorbed in Chaucer while her husband worked. Later, when years of strife and loneliness had saddened her, she returned to her Chaucer with a deep sigh of content: '. . . if I had not excellent Chaucer's book here to comfort me', she wrote, 'I were in a pitiable case having as many troubles as I have here, but, when I read in that, I scorn and make light of them all, and a little part of his beauteous spirit infuses itself in me'.[34] The woman who said that, though she never attempted to set up a salon or to found a library, felt it incumbent on her to respect the men of low birth and no fortune who could write *The Canterbury Tales* or *The Faery Queen*. Donne preached before her at Knole. It was she who paid for the first monument to Spenser in Westminster Abbey, and if, when she raised a tomb to her old tutor, she dwelt largely upon her own virtues and titles, she still acknowledged that even so great a lady as herself owed gratitude to the makers of books. Words from great writers nailed to the walls of the room in which she sat, eternally transacting business, surrounded her as she worked, as they surrounded Montaigne in his tower in Burgundy.

Thus we may infer that Donne's relation to the Countess of Bedford was very different from any that could exist between a poet and a countess at the present time. There was something distant and ceremonious about it. To him she was 'as a vertuous Prince farre off'.[35] The greatness of her office inspired reverence apart from her personality, just as the rewards within her gift inspired humility. He was her Laureate, and his songs in her praise were rewarded by invitations to stay with her at Twickenham and by those friendly meetings with men in power which were so effective in furthering the career of an ambitious man – and Donne was highly ambitious, not indeed for the fame of a poet, but for the power of a statesman. Thus when we read that Lady Bedford was 'God's Masterpiece',[36] that she excelled all women in all ages, we realise that John Donne is not writing to Lucy Bedford; Poetry is saluting Rank. And this distance served to inspire reason rather than passion. Lady Bedford must have been a very clever woman, well versed in the finer shades of theology, to derive an instant or an intoxicating pleasure from the praises of her servant. Indeed, the extreme subtlety and erudition of Donne's poems to his patrons seems to show that one effect of writing for such an audience is to exaggerate the poet's ingenuity. What is not poetry but something tortured and difficult will prove to the patron that the poet is exerting his skill on her behalf. Then again, a learned poem can be handed round among statesmen and men of affairs to prove that the poet is no mere versifier, but capable of office and responsibility. But a change of inspiration that has killed many poets – witness Tennyson and the *Idylls of the King*[37] – only stimulated another side of Donne's many-sided nature and many-faceted brain. As we read the long poems written ostensibly in praise of Lady Bedford, or in celebration of Elizabeth Drury (*An Anatomie of the World* and the *Progresse of the Soul*),[38] we are made to reflect how much remains for a poet to write about when the season of love is over. When May and June are passed, most poets cease to write or sing the songs of their youth out of tune. But Donne survived the perils of middle age by virtue of the acuteness and ardour of his intellect. When 'the satyrique fires which urg'd me to have writt in skorne of all'[39] were quenched, when 'My muse (for I had one), because I'm cold, Divorced herself',[40] there still remained the power to turn upon the nature of things and dissect that. Even in the passionate days of youth Donne had been a thinking poet. He had dissected and analysed his own love. To turn from that to the anatomy of the world, from the personal to the impersonal, was the natural development of a complex nature. And the new angle to which his mind now pointed under the influence of middle age and traffic with the world, released powers that were held in check when they were directed against some particular courtier or some particular woman. Now his imagination, as if freed from impediment, goes rocketing up in flights of extravagant exaggeration. True, the rocket bursts; it scatters in a shower of minute, separate particles – curious speculations, wire-drawn comparisons, obsolete erudition; but, winged by the double pressure of mind and heart, of reason and imagination, it soars far and fast into a finer air. Working himself up by his own extravagant praise of the dead girl, he shoots on:

> We spur, we reine the starres, and in their race
> They're diversly content t'obey our pace.
> But keepes the earth her round proportion still?
> Doth not a Tenarif, or higher Hill
> Rise so high like a Rocke, that one might thinke
> The floating Moone would shipwracke there, and sinke?
> Seas are so deepe, that Whales being strooke to day,
> Perchance tomorrow, scarce at middle way
> Of their wish'd journies end, the bottome, die.
> And men, to sound depths, so much line untie,
> As one might justly thinke, that there would rise
> At end thereof, one of th'Antipodies:[41]

Or again, Elizabeth Drury is dead and her soul has escaped:

> she stayes not in the ayre,
> To looke what Meteors there themselves prepare;
> She carries no desire to know, nor sense,
> Whether th'ayres middle region be intense;
> For th'Element of fire, she doth not know,
> Whether she past by such a place or no;
> She baits not at the Moone, nor cares to trie
> Whether in that new world, men live, and die.
> *Venus* retards her not, to'enquire, how shee
> Can, (being one starre) *Hesper*, and *Vesper* bee;

> Hee that charm'd *Argus* eyes, sweet *Mercury*,
> Workes not on her, who now is growne all eye;[42]

So we penetrate into distant regions, and reach rare and remote speculations a million miles removed from the simple girl whose death fired the explosion. But to break off fragments from poems whose virtue lies in their close-knit sinews and their long-breathed strength is to diminish them. They need to be read currently rather to grasp the energy and power of the whole than to admire those separate lines which Donne suddenly strikes to illumine the stages of our long climb.

Thus, finally, we reach the last section of the book, the Holy Sonnets and Divine Poems. Again the poetry changes with the change of circumstances and of years. The patron has gone with the need of patronage. Lady Bedford has been replaced by a Prince still more virtuous and still more remote. To Him the prosperous, the important, the famous Dean of St Paul's now turns. But how different is the divine poetry of this great dignitary from the divine poetry of the Herberts and the Vaughans![43] The memory of his sins returns to him as he writes. He has been burnt with 'lust and envy';[44] he has followed profane loves; he has been scornful and fickle and passionate and servile and ambitious. He has attained his end; but he is weaker and worse than the horse or the bull. Now too he is lonely. 'Since she whom I lov'd' is dead 'My good is dead.'[45] Now at last his mind is 'wholly sett on heavenly things'. And yet how could Donne – that 'little world made cunningly of elements'[46] – be wholly set on any one thing?

> Oh, to vex me, contraryes meet in one:
> Inconstancy unnaturally hath begott
> A constant habit; that when I would not
> I change in vowes, and in devotione.[47]

It was impossible for the poet who had noted so curiously the flow and change of human life, and its contrasts, who was at once so inquisitive of knowledge and so sceptical –

> Doubt wisely; in strange way,
> To stand inquiring right, is not to stray;
> To sleep, or run wrong, is[48]

– who had owned allegiance to so many great Princes, the body, the King, the Church of England, to reach that state of wholeness and certainty which poets of purer life were able to maintain. His devotions themselves were feverish and fitful. 'My devout fitts come and goe away like a fantastique Ague.'[49] They are full of contraries and agonies. Just as his love poetry at its most sensual will suddenly reveal the desire for a transcendent unity 'beyond the Hee and Shee', and his most reverential letters to great ladies will suddenly become love poems addressed by an amorous man to a woman of flesh and blood, so these last divine poems are poems of climbing and falling, of incongruous clamours and solemnities, as if the church door opened on the uproar of the street. That perhaps is why they still excite interest and disgust, contempt and admiration. For the Dean still retained the incorrigible curiosity of his youth. The temptation to speak the truth in defiance of the world even when he had taken all that the world had to give, still worked in him. An obstinate interest in the nature of his own sensations still troubled his age and broke its repose as it had troubled his youth and made him the most vigorous of satirists and the most passionate of lovers. There was no rest, no end, no solution even at the height of fame and on the edge of the grave for a nature plaited together of such diverse strands. The famous preparations that he made, lying in his shroud, being carved for his tomb, when he felt death approach are poles asunder from the falling asleep of the tired and content. He must still cut a figure and still stand erect – a warning perhaps, a portent certainly, but always consciously and conspicuously himself. That, finally, is one of the reasons why we still seek out Donne; why after three hundred years and more we still hear the sound of his voice speaking across the ages so distinctly. It may be true that when from curiosity we come to cut up and 'survey each part', we are like the doctors and 'know not why'[50] – we cannot see how so many different qualities meet together in one man. But we have only to read him, to submit to the sound of that passionate and penetrating voice, and his figure rises again across the waste of the years more erect, more imperious, more inscrutable than any of his time. Even the elements seem to have respected that identity. When the fire of London destroyed almost every other monument in St Paul's,[51] it left Donne's figure untouched, as if the flames themselves found that knot too hard to undo, that riddle too difficult to read, and that figure too entirely itself to turn to common clay.

1 – This essay was written specifically for *CR2*. Although VW wrote on 10 August 1931 from Rodmell that she should be reading 'all Donne, all Sidney' (*IV VW Letters*, no. 2419), she seems actually to have begun the essay in September, when she made repeated notes in her diary. 'By the way, Elizabethan prose is magnificent: & all that I love most at the moment. I bathed myself in Dekker last night as in my natural element. Surely this is a nobler instrument than Scott or the 18th Century' (*IV VW Diary*, 3 September). 'But O – again – how happy I am: how calm, for the moment how sweet life is with L. here, in its regularity & order, & the garden & the room at night & music & my walks & writing easily & interestedly at Donne of a morning, & poems all about me' (*ibid.*, 19 September). 'Here am I writing about Donne, & we have "gone off the Gold Standard" this morning . . . Yes; & what could I do better, if we are ruined, & if everybody had spent their time writing about Donne we should not have gone off the Gold Standard – thats my version of the greatest crisis &c &c &c – gabble gabble go the geese, who cant lay golden eggs' (*ibid.*, 21 September). 'September improved. How happy I was writing about Donne' (*ibid.*, 30 September). The final version was begun about 1 February (Berg, M 23). On 3 February in London she was 'toiling at correcting Donne, who is to introduce the second volume of the Common Reader. I cant go on squeezing my sentences dry of water; & so write here for 20 minutes; then I think read Donne; then finish with a novel upon Hamlet, clever, oh yes – novels about Hamlet always are. Then lunch: then – Oh Ottoline this evening. Yet I am so much interested in Donne, or in my views that I cannot begin' (*IV VW Diary*). On 5 February she had 'been toiling over Donnes poetry all the morning – with antlike assiduity' (*V VW Letters*, no. 2522; and see no. 2523). On 8 February she was 'at the end of a long mornings work on Donne, which will have to be done again, & is it worth the doing?' (*IV VW Diary*). On 13 February: 'I break off from my plain duty which is to read the Anatomy of the World' (*ibid.*). Finally, on 16 February: 'I have just "finished" I use inverted commas ironically, my Donne, a great but I think well intentioned grind' (*ibid.*; and see [Berg, M 23]). Leslie Stephen confessed in his essay 'John Donne' (1899), that he found Donne's poems 'rather indigestible', but: 'How are we, . . . at a distance of some three centuries, to speak with any confidence?': see *Studies of a Biographer* (4 vols, Duckworth, 1898–1902), vol. iii, pp. 37, 40. Reading notes (Berg, RN 1.8, 1.11, 1.20) and (MHP, B 2p) (*VWRN* VIII, XI, XX and XLVIII). Holograph draft (MHP, B 2e). Reprinted: *CE*.

2 – *The Poems of John Donne* [1572–1631], ed. H. J. C. Grierson (OUP, Humphrey Milford, 1929), 'Loves Deitie', p. 48, l. 1.

3 – *Ibid.*, 'The broken heart', p. 43, ll. 1–2.

4 – *Ibid.*, 'A Lecture upon the Shadow', p. 63, ll. 1–2.

5 – *Ibid.*, 'The Relique', p. 56, l. 6.

6 – Robert Browning (1812–89); George Meredith (1828–1909).

7 – *Poems*, Satyre i, 'Away thou fondling motley humorist', p. 129, ll. 5–6: 'Here are Gods conduits, grave Divines; and here / Natures Secretary, the Philosopher;'.

8 – *Ibid.*, ll. 7–8.

9 – *Ibid.*, ll. 9–10: 'Here gathering Chroniclers, and by them stand / Giddie fantastique Poëts of each land.'

10 – For VW on *The Countess of Pembroke's Arcadia* (1593), by Sir Philip Sidney (1554–86), see the next essay; *The Paradyse of Daynty Devises* (1576), an anthology of poetry compiled by Richard Edwards (1523–66); *Euphues, or the Anatomy of Wit* (1578) and *Euphues and his England* (1580), a two-part prose romance by John Lyly (1554–1606).

11 – *Poems*, Satyre iiii, 'Well; I may now receive, and die; My sin', p. 144, ll. 92–3: 'He to another key, his stile doth addresse, / And askes, what newes? I tell him of new playes.'

12 – Christopher Marlowe (1564–93).

13 – *Poems*, Satyre iiii, pp. 141–2, ll. 30–3.

14 – *Ibid.*, p. 143, ll. 73–80.

15 – *Ibid.*, Elegy viii, 'The Comparison', p. 82, ll. 33–4.

16 – Thomas Dekker (1570?–1632), *The Wonderfull Yeare. 1603*, ed. G. B. Harrison (facsimile reprint, John Lane, Bodley Head, 1924), pp. 16–17; VW has modernised the spelling.

17 – Cf. Orlando in love with Sasha: he 'would try to tell her – plunging and splashing among a thousand images which had gone as stale as the women who inspired them – what she was like. Snow, cream, marble, cherries, alabaster, golden wire?' (O, ch. i, p. 45).

18 – *Poems*, 'The Indifferent', p. 12, ll. 19–21:

> *Venus* heard me sigh this song,
> And by Loves sweetest Part, Variety, she swore,
> She heard not this till now; and that it should be so no more.

19 – *Ibid.*, Elegy iii, 'Change', p. 75, last lines, which has: '. . . Change' is the nursery / Of musicke, joy, life, and eternity.'

20 – *Ibid.*, Elegy xvii, 'Variety', p. 102, l. 39.

21 – *Ibid.*, ll. 46–7.

22 – Cf. 1 Corinthians 13: 12.

23 – *Poems*, Elegy i, 'Jealosie', p. 71, l. 22, which has: 'in his basket'.

24 – *Ibid.*, 'The undertaking', p. 10, ll. 17–20:

> If, as I have, you also doe
> Vertue' attir'd in woman see,

> And dare love that, and say so too,
> And forget the Hee and Shee;

25 – *Ibid.*, Elegy xii, 'His parting from her', p. 92, ll. 69–72.

26 – *Ibid.*, 'Song', 'Sweetest love, I do not goe', p. 18, ll. 39–40, which has: 'keepe / Alive, ne'er'. VW quotes four lines from the third stanza of the same poem in an uncollected letter of [late March 1929?] to Christabel McLaren: see *VWB*, no. 15 (January 2004), p. 33.

27 – *Poems*, 'The Canonization', p. 14, ll. 25–7.

28 – *Ibid.*, 'The Extasy', pp. 46–7, ll. 19–20, 29–32, 45–50.

29 – Lucy Russell, Countess of Bedford (1580/1–1627) and Lady Elizabeth Hastings, *née* Stanley (1586/7–1633), Countess of Huntingdon, to both of whom Donne addressed poems; Mrs Magdalen(e) Herbert (d. 1627), mother of the poet George Herbert (1593–1633) and original recipient of Donne's Divine Poems and Holy Sonnets.

30 – Mary Herbert, *née* Sidney, Countess of Pembroke (1561–1621), whose translation of the Psalms, in part collaboration with her brother, Sir Philip Sidney, Donne commemorated in verse.

31 – Lady Anne Clifford (1590–1676), Countess of Dorset, Pembroke and Montgomery, quoted in *Lady Anne Clifford . . . Her Life, Letters and Work* by George C. Williamson (Titus Wilson and Son, 1922), p. 66. Williamson comments: 'It would have been an unusual thing for a girl of her position in life to have had no knowledge of French, and we are inclined to think that the statement respecting her knowledge of languages was only intended to apply to Latin and Greek, and she must surely have spoken and read the French tongue.'

32 – Samuel Daniel (1562/3–1619) acted somewhat reluctantly as Lady Anne's tutor; his epic, *The Civil Wars* (1609), was dedicated to her mother, Margaret Clifford, Countess of Cumberland (1560–1616).

33 – See *The Diary of the Lady Anne Clifford*, with an introduction by V. Sackville-West (William Heinemann, 1923), November 1616, p. 41: 'Upon the 9th I sat at my work and heard *Rivers* and *Marsh* read Montaigne's Essays which book they have read almost this fortnight.' Edmund Spenser (1552?–99), *The Faerie Queen* (1590–6); Ben Jonson (1572–1637); Geoffrey Chaucer (c. 1340–1400), *The Canterbury Tales* (begun in the late 1380s); for VW on Michel de Montaigne (1533–92), see *CR1* and *IV VW Essays*.

34 – Quoted in *Clifford . . . Her Life*, p. 197, which has: 'having so many'.

35 – *Poems*, 'To the Countess of Huntingdon' (c. 1614–15), p. 178, ll. 41–4:

> So you, as woman, one doth comprehend,
> And in the vaile of kindred others see;
> To some ye are reveal'd, as in a friend,
> And as a vertuous Prince farre off, to mee.

36 – *Ibid.*, 'To the Countess of Bedford' ('Madame, / Reason is our Soules left hand, Faith her right,'), p. 168, ll. 33–4:

> Since you are then Gods masterpeece, and so
> His Factor for our loves;

37 – Alfred, Lord Tennyson (1809–92), *Idylls of the King* (1859–72).

38 – Elizabeth Drury (d. 1610, *aetat* 14) is commemorated in Donne's meditative poems, 'The Anniversaries': 'An Anatomie of the World' (1611) and 'Of the Progresse of the Soule' (1612), *Poems*, pp. 205–42. See Drury Family, *ODNB*.

39 – *Poems*, 'To Mr R. W.' ('Kindly I envy thy songs perfection'), p. 186, ll. 5–8:

> In it is cherishing fyer which dryes in mee
> Griefe which did drowne me: and halfe quench'd by it
> Are satirique fyres which urg'd me to have writt
> In skorne of all: for now I admyre thee.

40 – *Ibid.*, 'To Mr B. B.' ('Is not thy sacred hunger of science'), p. 187, ll. 19–20.

41 – *Ibid.*, 'An Anatomie of the World', p. 216, ll. 283–94.

42 – *Ibid.*, 'Of the Progresse of the Soule', p. 232, ll. 189–200.

43 – Henry Vaughan (1621–95) and his brother Thomas (1621–66).

44 – *Ibid.*, 'Holy Sonnets', Sonnet v ('I am a little world made cunningly'), p. 295, l. 11.

45 – *Ibid.*, Sonnet xvii, p. 301, ll. 1–4:

> Since she whom I lov'd hath paid her last debt
> To Nature, and to hers, and my good is dead,
> And her Soule early into heaven ravished,
> Wholly on heavenly things my mind is sett.

46 – *Ibid.*, Sonnet v, p. 295, ll. 1–2:

> I am a little world made cunningly
> Of Elements, and an Angelike spright,

47 – *Ibid.*, Sonnet xix, p. 302, ll. 1–4.

48 – *Ibid.*, Satyre iii ('Kinde pitty chokes my spleene'), p. 139, ll. 76–9:

> To adore, or scorne an image, or protest,
> May all be bad; doubt wisely; in strange way
> To stand inquiring right, is not to stray;
> To sleep, or runne wrong is.

49 – *Ibid.*, 'Holy Sonnets', Sonnet xix, p. 302, ll. 12–14:

> So my devout fitts come and go away
> Like a fantastique Ague: save that here
> Those are my best dayes, when I shake with feare.

50 – *Ibid.*, 'The Dampe', p. 57, ll. 1–3:

> When I am dead, and Doctors know not why,
> And my friends' curiositie
> Will have me cut up to survay each part,

51 – Great Fire of London, 1666.

'The Countess of Pembroke's Arcadia'

If it is true that there are books written to escape from the present moment, and its meanness and its sordidity, it is certainly true that readers are familiar with a corresponding mood. To draw the blinds and shut the door, to muffle the noises of the street and shade the glare and flicker of its lights – that is our desire. There is then a charm even in the look of the great volumes that have sunk, like the 'Countess of Pembroke's Arcadia', as if by their own weight down to the very bottom of the shelf. We like to feel that the present is not all; that other hands have been before us, smoothing the leather until the corners are rounded and blunt, turning the pages until they are yellow and dog's-eared. We like to summon before us the ghosts of those old readers who have read their *Arcadia* from this very copy – Richard Porter, reading with the splendours of the Elizabethans in his eyes; Lucy Baxter, reading in the licentious days of the Restoration; Thos. Hake, still reading, though now the eighteenth century has dawned with a distinction that shows itself in the upright elegance of his signature. Each has read differently, with the insight and the blindness of his own generation. Our reading will be equally partial. In 1930 we shall miss a great deal that was obvious to 1655; we shall see some things that the eighteenth century ignored. But let us keep up the long succession of readers; let us in our turn bring the insight and the blindness of our own generation to bear upon the 'Countess of Pembroke's Arcadia', and so pass it on to our successors.

If we choose the *Arcadia* because we wish to escape, certainly the first impression of the book is that Sidney wrote it with very much the same intention: '. . . it is done only for you, only to you', he tells his 'dear lady and sister, the Countess of Pembroke'.[2] He is not looking at what is before him here at Wilton; he is not thinking of his own troubles or of the tempestuous mood of the great Queen in London. He is absenting himself from the present and its strife. He is writing merely to amuse his sister, not for 'severer eyes'. 'Your dear self can best witness the manner, being done in loose sheets of Paper, most of it in your presence, the rest, by sheets sent unto you, as fast as they were done.'[3] So, sitting at Wilton under the downs with Lady Pembroke, he gazes far away into a beautiful land which he calls Arcadia. It is a land of fair valleys and fertile pastures, where the houses are 'lodges of yellow stone built in the form of a star';[4] where the inhabitants are either great princes or humble shepherds; where the only business is to love and to adventure; where bears and lions surprise nymphs bathing in fields red with roses; where princesses are immured in the huts of shepherds; where disguise is perpetually necessary; where the shepherd is really a prince and the woman a man; where, in short, anything may be and happen except what actually is and happens here in England in the year 1580. It is easy to see why, as Sidney handed these dream pages to his sister, he smiled, entreating her indulgence. 'Read it then at your idle times, and the follies your good judgment will find in it, blame not, but laugh at.'[5] Even for the Sidneys and the Pembrokes life was not quite like that. And yet the life that we invent, the stories we tell, as we sink back with half-shut eyes and pour forth our irresponsible dreams, have perhaps some wild beauty; some eager energy; we often reveal in them the distorted and decorated image of what we soberly and secretly desire. Thus the *Arcadia*, by wilfully flouting all contact with the fact, gains another reality. When Sidney hinted that his friends would like the book for its writer's sake, he meant perhaps that they would find there something that he could say in no other form,

as the shepherds singing by the river's side will 'deliver out, sometimes joys, sometimes lamentations, sometimes challengings one of
the other, sometimes, under hidden forms, uttering such matters as
otherwise they durst not deal with'.[6] There may be under the disguise
of the *Arcadia* a real man trying to speak privately about something
that is close to his heart. But in the first freshness of the early pages
the disguise itself is enough to enchant us. We find ourselves with
shepherds in spring on those sands which 'lie against the Island of
Cithera'.[7] Then, behold, something floats on the waters. It is the
body of a man, and he grasps to his breast a small square coffer;
and he is young and beautiful – 'though he were naked, his nakedness was to him an apparel';[8] and his name is Musidorus; and he
has lost his friend. So, warbling melodiously, the shepherds revive
the youth, and row out in a bark from the haven in search of Pyrocles;
and a stain appears on the sea, with sparks and smoke issuing from
it. For the ship upon which the two princes Musidorus and Pyrocles
were voyaging has caught fire; it floats blazing on the water with a
great store of rich things round it, and many drowned bodies. 'In
sum, a defeat, where the conquered kept both field and spoil: a ship-
wrack without storm or ill footing: and a waste of fire in the midst of
the water.'[9]

There in a little space we have some of the elements that are woven
together to compose this vast tapestry. We have beauty of scene; a
pictorial stillness; and something floating towards us, not violently but
slowly and gently in time to the sweet warbling of the shepherds' voices.
Now and again this crystallises into a phrase that lingers and haunts
the ear – 'and a waste of fire in the midst of the waters'; 'having in
their faces a certain waiting sorrow'.[10] Now the murmur broadens and
expands into some more elaborate passage of description: 'each pasture
stored with sheep, feeding with sober security, while the pretty lambs
with bleating oratory crav'd the dam's comfort: here a shepherd's boy
piping, as though he should never be old: there a young shepherdess
knitting, and withal singing, and it seemed that her voice comforted her
hands to work, and her hands kept time to her voice-music'[11] – a passage
that reminds us of a famous description in Dorothy Osborne's *Letters*.[12]

Beauty of scene; stateliness of movement; sweetness of sound –
these are the graces that seem to reward the mind that seeks enjoyment
purely for its own sake. We are drawn on down the winding paths
of this impossible landscape because Sidney leads us without any end
in view but sheer delight in wandering. The syllabling of the words

even causes him the liveliest delight. Mere rhythm we feel as we sweep over the smooth backs of the undulating sentences intoxicates him. Words in themselves delight him. Look, he seems to cry, as he picks up the glittering handfuls, can it be true that there are such numbers of beautiful words lying about for the asking? Why not use them, lavishly and abundantly? And so he luxuriates. Lambs do not suck – 'with bleating oratory [they] craved the dam's comfort'; girls do not undress – they 'take away the eclipsing of their apparel';[13] a tree is not reflected in a river – 'it seemed she looked into it and dressed her green locks by that running river'.[14] It is absurd; and yet there is a world of difference between writing like this with zest and wonder at the images that form upon one's pen and the writing of later ages when the dew was off the language – witness the little tremor that stirs and agitates a sentence that a more formal age would have made coldly symmetrical:

And the boy fierce though beautiful; and beautiful, though dying, not able to keep his falling feet, fell down to the earth, which he bit for anger, repining at his fortune, and as long as he could, resisting death, which might seem unwilling too; so long he was in taking away his young struggling soul.[15]

It is this inequality and elasticity that lend their freshness to Sidney's vast pages. Often as we rush through them, half laughing, half in protest, the desire comes upon us to shut the ear of reason completely and lie back and listen to this unformed babble of sound; this chorus of intoxicated voices singing madly like birds round the house before anyone is up.[16]

But it is easy to lay too much stress upon qualities that delight us because they are lost. Sidney doubtless wrote the *Arcadia* partly to while away the time, partly to exercise his pen and experiment with the new instrument of the English language. But even so he remained young and a man; even in Arcadia the roads had ruts, and coaches were upset and ladies dislocated their shoulders; even the Princes Musidorus and Pyrocles have passions; Pamela and Philoclea, for all their sea-coloured satins and nets strung with pearls, are women and can love. Thus we stumble upon scenes that cannot be reeled off with a flowing pen; there are moments where Sidney stopped and thought, like any other novelist, what a real man or woman in this particular situation would say; where his own emotions come suddenly to the surface and light up the vague pastoral landscape with an incongruous glare. For a moment we get a surprising combination; crude daylight overpowers the silver lights of the tapers; shepherds and princesses suddenly stop their warbling and speak a few rapid words in their eager human voices.

... many times have I, leaning to yonder Palm, admired the blessedness of it, that it could bear love without sense of pain; many times, when my Master's cattle came hither to chew their cud in this fresh place, I might see the young Bull testify his love; but how? with proud looks and joyfulness. O wretched mankind (said I then to myself) in whom wit (which should be the governor of his welfare) become's the traitor to his blessedness: these beasts like children to nature, inherit her blessings quietly; we like bastards are laid abroad, even as foundlings, to be trained up by grief and sorrow. Their minds grudge not at their bodies comfort, nor their senses are letted from enjoying their objects; we have the impediments of honour, and the torments of conscience.[17]

The words ring strangely on the finicking, dandified lips of Musidorus. There is Sidney's own anger in them and his pain. And then the novelist Sidney suddenly opens his eyes. He watches Pamela as she takes the jewel in the figure of a crab-fish to signify 'because it looks one way and goes another'[18] that though he pretended to love Mopsa his heart was Pamela's. And she takes it, he notes,

with a calm carelessness letting each thing slide (just as we do by their speeches who neither in matter nor person do any way belong unto us) which kind of cold temper, mixt with that lightning of her natural majesty, is of all others most terrible unto me....[19]

Had she despised him, had she hated him, it would have been better.

But this cruel quietness, neither retiring to mislike, nor proceeding to favour; gracious, but gracious still after one manner; all her courtesies having this engraven in them, that what is done, is for virtue's sake, not for the parties.... This (I say) heavenliness of hers ... is so impossible to reach unto that I almost begin to submit myself unto the tyranny of despair, not knowing any way of persuasion....[20]

– surely an acute and subtle observation made by a man who had felt what he describes. For a moment the pale and legendary figures, Gynecia, Philoclea, and Zelmane, become alive; their featureless faces work with passion; Gynecia, realising that she loves her daughter's lover, foams into grandeur, 'crying vehemently Zelmane help me, O Zelmane have pity on me';[21] and the old King, in whom the beautiful strange Amazon has awakened a senile amorosity, shows himself old and foolish, looking 'very curiously upon himself, sometimes fetching a little skip, as if he had said his strength had not yet forsaken him'.[22]

But that moment of illumination, as it dies down and the princes once more resume their postures and the shepherds apply themselves to their lutes, throws a curious light upon the book as a whole. We realise more clearly the boundaries within which Sidney was working. For a moment he could note and observe and record as keenly and exactly as any modern novelist. And then, after this one glimpse in our direction, he turns aside, as if he heard other voices calling him and must obey their commands. In prose, he bethinks himself, one must not use the common words of daily speech. In a romance one must not make princes and princesses feel like ordinary men and women. Humour is the attribute of peasants. They can behave ridiculously; they can talk naturally; like Dametas they can come 'whistling, and counting upon his fingers, how many load of hay seventeen fat oxen eat up on a year';[23] but the language of great people must always be long-winded and abstract and full of metaphors. Further, they must either be heroes of stainless virtue, or villains untouched by humanity. Of human oddities and littleness they must show no trace. Prose also must be careful to turn away from what is actually before it. Sometimes for a moment in looking at Nature one may fit the word to the sight; note the heron 'wagling'[24] as it rises from the marsh, or observe the water-spaniel hunting the duck 'with a snuffling grace'.[25] But this realism is only to be applied to Nature and animals and peasants. Prose, it seems, is made for slow, noble, and generalised emotions; for the description of wide landscapes; for the conveyance of long, equable discourses uninterrupted for pages together by any other speaker. Verse, on the other hand, had quite a different office. It is curious to observe how, when Sidney wished to sum up, to strike hard, to register a single and definite impression, he turns to verse. Verse in the *Arcadia* performs something of the function of dialogue in the modern novel. It breaks up the monotony and strikes a high light. In those snatches of song that are scattered about the interminable adventures of Pyrocles and Musidorus our interest is once more fanned into flame. Often the realism and vigour of the verse comes with a shock after the drowsy languor of the prose:

> What needed so high spirits such mansions blind?
> Or wrapt in flesh what do they here obtain,
> But glorious name of wretched human kind?

> Balls to the stars, and thralls to fortune's reign;
>> Turn'd from themselves, infected with their cage,
>> Where death is fear'd, and life is held with pain.
> Like players plac't to fill a filthy stage. . . .[26]

– one wonders what the indolent princes and princesses will make of that vehement speaking? Or of this:

> A shop of shame, a Book where blots be rife,
>> This body is . . .
> This man, this talking beast, this walking tree.[27]

– thus the poet turns upon his languid company as if he loathed their self-complacent foppery; and yet must indulge them. For though it is clear that the poet Sidney had shrewd eyes – he talks of 'hives of wisely painful bees',[28] and knew like any other country-bred Englishman 'how shepherds spend their days. At blow-point, hot-cockles or else at keels',[29] – still he must drone on about Plangus and Erona, and Queen Andromana and the intrigues of Amphialus and his mother Cecropia in deference to his audience. Incongruously enough, violent as they were in their lives, with their plots and their poisonings, nothing can be too sweet, too vague, too long-winded for those Elizabethan listeners. Only the fact that Zelmane had received a blow from a lion's paw that morning can shorten the story and suggest to Basilius that it might be better to reserve the complaint of Klaius till another day.

Which she, perceiving the song had already worn out much time, and not knowing when Lamon would end, being even now stepping over to a new matter, though much delighted with what was spoken, willingly agreed unto. And so of all sides they went to recommend themselves to the elder brother of death.[30]

And as the story winds on its way, or rather as the succession of stories fall on each other like soft snowflakes, one obliterating the other, we are much tempted to follow their example. Sleep weighs down our eyes. Half dreaming, half yawning, we prepare to seek the elder brother of death. What, then, has become of that first intoxicating sense of freedom? We who wished to escape have been caught and enmeshed. Yet how easy it seemed in the beginning to tell a story to amuse a sister – how inspiriting to escape from here and now and wander wildly in a world of lutes and roses! But alas, softness has weighed down our steps; brambles have caught at our clothing. We have come to long for some plain statement, and the decoration of the style, at first so enchanting, has dulled and decayed. It is not difficult to find the reason. High spirited, flown with words, Sidney seized his pen too carelessly. He had no notion when he set out where he was going. Telling stories, he thought, was enough – one could follow another interminably. But where there is no end in view there is no sense of direction to draw us on. Nor, since it is part of his scheme to keep his characters simply bad and simply good without distinction, can he gain variety from the complexity of character. To supply change and movement he must have recourse to mystification. These changes of dress, these disguises of princes as peasants, of men as women, serve instead of psychological subtlety to relieve the stagnancy of people collected together with nothing to talk about. But when the charm of that childish device falls flat, there is no breath left to fill his sails. Who is talking, and to whom, and about what we no longer feel sure. So slack indeed becomes Sidney's grasp upon these ambling phantoms that in the middle he has forgotten what his relation to them is – is it 'I' the author who is speaking or is it 'I' the character? No reader can be kept in bondage, whatever the grace and the charm, when the ties between him and the writer are so irresponsibly doffed and assumed. So by degrees the book floats away into the thin air of limbo. It becomes one of those half-forgotten and deserted places where the grasses grow over fallen statues and the rain drips and the marble steps are green with moss and vast weeds flourish in the flower-beds. And yet it is a beautiful garden to wander in now and then; one stumbles over lovely broken faces, and here and there a flower blooms and the nightingale sings in the lilac-tree.

Thus when we come to the last page that Sidney wrote before he gave up the hopeless attempt to finish the *Arcadia*, we pause for a moment before we return the folio to its place on the bottom shelf. In the *Arcadia*, as in some luminous globe, all the seeds of English fiction lie latent. We can trace infinite possibilities: it may take any one of many different directions. Will it fix its gaze upon Greece and prince and princesses, and seek as it might so nobly, the statuesque, the impersonal? Will it keep to simple lines and great masses and the vast landscapes of the epic? Or will it look closely and carefully at what is actually before it? Will it take for its heroes Dametas and Mopsa, ordinary people of low birth and rough natural speech, and deal with the normal course of daily human life? Or will it brush through those barriers and penetrate within to the anguish and complexity of some unhappy woman loving where she may not love; to the senile absurdity of some old man tortured by an incongruous passion? Will it make its dwelling in their psychology and the adventures of the soul? All these possibilities are present in the *Arcadia* – romance and realism, poetry and psychology. But as if Sidney knew that he had broached a task too large for his youth to execute, had bequeathed a legacy for other ages to inherit, he put down his pen, midway, and left unfinished in all its beauty and absurdity this attempt to while away the long days at Wilton, telling a story to his sister.

1 – This essay was written specifically for *CR2*. Although VW was thinking of reading 'all Sidney' on 10 August 1931 (*IV VW Letters*, no. 2419), this essay was not listed when she sent details of her project to Donald Brace on 5 November (see n. 1 to *CR2*). However, on 16 November, although she 'cant get on with Philip Sidney', she was 'working very hard – in my way, to furbish up 2 long Elizabethan articles to front a new Common Reader' (*IV VW Diary*). On 29 December she suggested visiting the Sidney family home, Penshurst Place, near Tonbridge in Kent, to Vita Sackville-West: 'I'm so behindhand – I was going to write about Sidney, and cant get back into the mood' (*IV VW Letters*, no. 2497; see also no. 2477); but VW did not go until 1940 (see *V VW Diary*, 14 June). She had visited Wilton House (1649), the seat of the Earls of Pembroke, in 1903: see *PA*. On 26 February 1932 she wrote: 'I have "finished" the Arcadia' (*IV VW Diary*), while a note in Berg, M 23 states that it was begun on 22 and finished on 28 February. VW used the tenth edition of the *Arcadia*, printed by William Du-Gard in 1655, a version of the augmented text of 1593; it is divided into books (and the lines are usually numbered) but not into chapters; VW tended to keep Du-Gard's punctuation but modernise his spelling. The references below are to Du-Gard and to the edition by Maurice Evans (Penguin, 1977); quotations in the notes follow Du-Gard. Reading Notes (Berg, RN 1.8) and (MHP, B 2p) (*VWRN* VIII and XLVIII). Draft dated 22 February 1932 (Berg, M 13). See also 'The Strange Elizabethans' above; 'Philip Sidney', *I VW Essays*; 'The Elizabethan Lumber Room', *CR1* and *IV VW Essays*; and references in *Flush: A Biography* (Hogarth Press, 1933), pp. 10, 127.

2 – Sir Philip Sidney (1554–86), *The Countess of Pembroke's Arcadia*, from the dedicatory epistle: 'To My Dear Lady and Sister, The Countess of Pembroke', unnumbered (1655) and p. 57 (1977). The 'great Queen' is Elizabeth I (1533–1603), reigned from 1558.

3 – *Ibid.*

4 – *Ibid.*, bk i, p. 53, l. 5 (1655) and ch. xiii, p. 148 (1977), which has: 'The Lodg is of a yellow stone, built'.

5 – *Ibid.*, dedicatory epistle, unnumbered (1655) and p. 57 (1977).

6 – *Ibid.*, bk i, p. 15, ll. 13–15 (1655) and ch. iv, p. 84 (1977).

7 – *Ibid.*, bk i, p. 1, l. 6 (1655) and ch. i, opening paragraph, p. 61 (1977).

8 – *Ibid.*, bk i, p. 3, lines unnumbered (1655) and ch. i, p. 64 (1977); both have: 'naked, nakedness'.

9 – *Ibid.*, bk i, p. 4, lines unnumbered (1655) and ch. i, p. 66 (1977).

10 – *Ibid.*, bk i, p. 36, ll. 46–7 (1655) and ch. x, p. 120 (1977).

11 – *Ibid.*, bk i, p. 6, lines unnumbered (1655) and ch. ii, pp. 69–70 (1977).

12 – See *The Letters of Dorothy Osborne to William Temple*, ed. G. C. Moore Smith (Clarendon Press, 1928), Letter 24, 2–4 June 1653, pp. 51–2. See also *Room*, ch. iv, p. 94, where the passage concerned is quoted.

13 – *Arcadia*, bk ii, p. 138, ll. 8–9 (1655) and ch. xi, p. 285 (1977).

14 – *Ibid.*, bk ii, p. 137, ll. 45–6 (1655) and ch. xi, p. 285 (1977).

15 – *Ibid.*, bk iii, p. 253, ll. 27–31 (1655) and ch. viii, p. 472 (1977).

16 – Cf. the birds singing round the house in *The Waves* (Hogarth Press, 1931), pp. 6 and 29.

17 – *Arcadia*, bk ii, p. 100, ll. 35–44 (1655) and ch. ii, p. 222 (1977).

18 – *Ibid.*, bk ii, p. 107, ll. 18–19 (1655) and ch. iii, p. 233 (1977).

19 – *Ibid.*, bk ii, p. 107, ll. 27–31 (1655) and ch. iii, pp. 233–4 (1977).

20 – *Ibid.*, bk ii, p. 107, ll. 36–42 (1655) and ch. iii, p. 234 (1977).

21 – *Ibid.*, bk ii, p. 97, l. 18 (1655) and ch. i, p. 216 (1977).

22 – *Ibid.*, bk ii, p. 89 (i.e. 98), ll. 8–9 (1655) and ch. i, p. 217 (1977).

23 – *Ibid.*, bk ii, p. 108, ll. 1–3 (1655) and ch. iv, opening paragraph, p. 234 (1977).

24 – *Ibid.*, bk ii, p. 108, l. 40 (1655) and ch. iv, p. 236 (1977).

25 – *Ibid.*, bk ii, p. 138, l. 1 (1655) and ch. xi, p. 285 (1977).

26 – *Ibid.*, book ii, p. 145, ll. 1–7 (1655) and ch. xii, p. 296, ll. 10–16 (1977); these are Plangus's lines from the verse dialogue by Basilius recording his meeting with Plangus, read by Zelmane.

27 – *Ibid.*, bk ii, p. 145, ll. 13–15, 19–21 (1655) and ch. xii, pp. 296–7, ll. 22–4, 28–30 (1977):

> A shop of shame, a Book where blots bee rife,
>> This body is: this body so compos'd,
>> As in it self to nourish mortall strife: . . .
> Grief onely make's his wretched state to see
>> (Even like a top which nought but whipping move's)
>> This man, this talking beast, this walking tree,

28 – *Ibid.*, 'The Second Eclogues': *Geron. Philisides*, spoken by Geron, p. 223, ll. 22–4 (1655) and p. 423, last lines (1977):

> Cherish the hives of wisely painfull Bees,
> Let speciall care upon thy flock be staid,
> Such active minde but seldom passion see's.

29 – *Ibid.*, *Geron. Mastix*, spoken by Mastix, p. 224, ll. 41–2 (1655) and p. 425, ll. 22–3 (1977).
30 – *Ibid.*, bk i, p. 94, ll. 23–6 (1655) and p. 212, conclusion (1977).

'Robinson Crusoe'

There are many ways of approaching this classical volume; but which shall we choose? Shall we begin by saying that, since Sidney[2] died at Zutphen leaving the *Arcadia* unfinished, great changes had come over English life, and the novel had chosen, or had been forced to choose, its direction? A middle class had come into existence, able to read and anxious to read not only about the loves of princes and princesses, but about themselves and the details of their humdrum lives. Stretched upon a thousand pens, prose had accommodated itself to the demand; it had fitted itself to express the facts of life rather than the poetry. That is certainly one way of approaching *Robinson Crusoe* – through the development of the novel; but another immediately suggests itself – through the life of the author. Here too, in the heavenly pastures of biography,[3] we may spend many more hours than are needed to read the book itself from cover to cover. The date of Defoe's birth, to begin with, is doubtful – was it 1660 or 1661? Then again, did he spell his name in one word or in two? And who were his ancestors? He is said to have been a hosier; but what, after all, was a hosier in the seventeenth century? He became a pamphleteer, and enjoyed the confidence of William the Third; one of his pamphlets caused him to be stood in the pillory and imprisoned at Newgate;[4] he was employed by Harley and later by Godolphin; he was the first of the hireling journalists; he wrote innumerable pamphlets and articles; also *Moll Flanders*[5] and *Robinson Crusoe*; he had a wife and six children; was spare in figure, with a hooked nose, a sharp chin, grey eyes, and a large mole near his mouth. Nobody who has any slight acquaintance with English literature needs to be told how many hours can be spent and how many lives have been spent in tracing the development of the novel and in examining the chins of the novelists.

Only now and then, as we turn from theory to biography and from biography to theory, a doubt insinuates itself – if we knew the very moment of Defoe's birth and whom he loved and why, if we had by heart the history of the origin, rise, growth, decline, and fall of the English novel from its conception (say) in Egypt to its decease in the wilds (perhaps) of Paraguay, should we suck an ounce of additional pleasure from *Robinson Crusoe* or read it one whit more intelligently?

For the book itself remains. However we may wind and wriggle, loiter and dally in our approach to books, a lonely battle waits us at the end. There is a piece of business to be transacted between writer and reader before any further dealings are possible, and to be reminded in the middle of this private interview that Defoe sold stockings, had brown hair, and was stood in the pillory is a distraction and a worry. Our first task, and it is often formidable enough, is to master his perspective.[6] Until we know how the novelist orders his world, the ornaments of that world, which the critics press upon us, the adventures of the writer, to which biographers draw attention, are superfluous possessions of which we can make no use. All alone we must climb upon the novelist's shoulders and gaze through his eyes until we, too, understand in what order he ranges the large common objects upon which novelists are fated to gaze: man and men; behind them Nature; and above them that power which for convenience and brevity we may call God. And at once confusion, misjudgment, and difficulty begin. Simple as they appear to us, these objects can be made monstrous and indeed unrecognisable by the manner in which the novelist relates them to each other. It would seem to be true that people who live cheek by jowl and breathe the same air vary enormously in their sense of proportion; to one the human being is vast, the tree minute; to the other, trees are huge and human beings insignificant little objects in the background. So, in spite of the text-books, writers may live at the same time and yet see nothing the same size. Here is Scott, for example, with his mountains looming huge and his men therefore drawn to scale; Jane Austen picking out the roses on her tea-cups to match the wit of her dialogues; while Peacock bends over heaven and earth one fantastic distorting mirror in which a tea-cup may be Vesuvius or Vesuvius a tea-cup. Nevertheless Scott, Jane Austen, and Peacock lived through the same years;[7] they saw the same world; they are covered in the text-books by the same stretch of literary history. It is in their perspective that they are different. If, then, it were granted us to grasp this firmly, for ourselves, the battle would end in victory; and we could turn, secure in our intimacy, to enjoy the various delights with which the critics and biographers so generously supply us.

But here many difficulties arise. For we have our own vision of the world; we have made it from our own experience and prejudices, and it is therefore bound up with our own vanities and loves. It is impossible not to feel injured and insulted if tricks are played and our private harmony is upset. Thus when *Jude the Obscure* appears or a new volume of Proust, the newspapers are flooded with protests.[8] Major Gibbs of Cheltenham would put a bullet through his head tomorrow if life were as Hardy paints it; Miss Wiggs of Hampstead must protest that though Proust's art is wonderful, the real world, she thanks God, has nothing in common with the distortions of a perverted Frenchman. Both the gentleman and the lady are trying to control the novelist's perspective so that it shall resemble and reinforce their own. But the great writer – the Hardy or the Proust – goes on his way regardless of the rights of private property; by the sweat of his brow he brings order from chaos; he plants his tree there, and his man here; he makes the figure of his deity remote or present as he wills. In masterpieces – books, that is, where the vision is clear and order has been achieved – he inflicts his own perspective upon us so severely that as often as not we suffer agonies – our vanity is injured because our own order is upset; we are afraid because the old supports are being wrenched from us; and we are bored – for what pleasure or amusement can be plucked from a brand new idea? Yet from anger, fear, and boredom a rare and lasting delight is sometimes born.

Robinson Crusoe, it may be, is a case in point. It is a masterpiece, and it is a masterpiece largely because Defoe has throughout kept consistently to his own sense of perspective. For this reason he thwarts us and flouts us at every turn. Let us look at the theme largely and loosely, comparing it with our preconceptions. It is, we know, the story of a man who is thrown, after many perils and adventures, alone upon a desert island. The mere suggestion – peril and solitude and a desert island – is enough to rouse in us the expectation of some far land on the limits of the world; of the sun rising and the sun setting; of man, isolated from his kind, brooding alone upon the nature of society and the strange ways of men. Before we open the book we have perhaps vaguely sketched out the kind of pleasure we expect it to give us. We read; and we are rudely contradicted on every page. There are no sunsets and no sunrises; there is no solitude and no soul. There is, on the contrary, staring us full in the face nothing but a large earthenware pot. We are told, that is to say, that it was the 1st of September 1651; that the hero's name is Robinson Crusoe; and that his father has the gout. Obviously, then, we must alter our attitude. Reality, fact, substance is going to dominate all that follows. We must hastily alter our proportions throughout; Nature must furl her splendid purples; she is only the giver of drought and water; man must be reduced to a struggling, life-preserving animal; and God shrivel into a magistrate whose seat, substantial and somewhat hard, is only a little way above the horizon. Each sortie of ours in pursuit of information upon these cardinal points of perspective – God, man, Nature – is snubbed back with ruthless common sense. Robinson Crusoe thinks of God: 'sometimes I would expostulate with myself, why providence should thus completely ruin its creatures. . . . But something always return'd swift upon me to check these thoughts.'9 God does not exist. He thinks of Nature, the fields 'adorn'd with flowers and grass, and full of very fine woods',10 but the important thing about a wood is that it harbours an abundance of parrots who may be tamed and taught to speak. Nature does not exist. He considers the dead, whom he has killed himself. It is of the utmost importance that they should be buried at once, for 'they lay open to the sun and would presently be offensive'.11 Death does not exist. Nothing exists except an earthenware pot. Finally, that is to say, we are forced to drop our own preconceptions and to accept what Defoe himself wishes to give us.

Let us then go back to the beginning and repeat again, 'I was born in the year 1632 in the city of York of a good family'. Nothing could be plainer, more matter of fact, than that beginning. We are drawn on soberly to consider all the blessings of orderly, industrious middle-class life. There is no greater good fortune we are assured than to be born of the British middle class. The great are to be pitied and so are the poor; both are exposed to distempers and uneasiness; the middle station between the mean and the great is the best; and its virtues – temperance, moderation, quietness, and health – are the most desirable. It was a sorry thing, then, when by some evil fate a middle-class youth was bitten with the foolish love of adventure. So he proses on, drawing, little by little, his own portrait, so that we never forget it – imprinting upon us indelibly, for he never forgets it either, his shrewdness, his caution, his love of order and the comfort and respectability; until by whatever means, we find ourselves at sea, in a storm; and, peering out, everything is seen precisely as it appears to Robinson Crusoe. The waves, the seamen, the sky, the ship – all are seen through those shrewd, middle-class, unimaginative eyes. There is no escaping him. Everything appears as it would appear to that naturally cautious, apprehensive, conventional, and solidly matter-of-fact intelligence. He is incapable of enthusiasm. He has a natural slight distaste for the sublimities of Nature. He suspects even Providence of exaggeration. He is so busy and has such an eye to the main chance that he notices only a tenth part of what is going on round him. Everything is capable of a rational explanation, he is sure, if only he had time to attend to it. We are much more alarmed by the 'vast great creatures'[12] that swim out in the night and surround his boat than he is. He at once takes his gun and fires at them, and off they swim – whether they are lions or not he really cannot say. Thus before we know it we are opening our mouths wider and wider. We are swallowing monsters that we should have jibbed at if they had been offered us by an imaginative and flamboyant traveller. But anything that this sturdy middle-class man notices can be taken for a fact. He is for ever counting his barrels, and making sensible provisions for his water supply; nor do we ever find him tripping even in a matter of detail. Has he forgotten, we wonder, that he has a great lump of beeswax on board? Not at all. But as he had already made candles out of it, it is not nearly as great on page thirty-eight as it was on page twenty-three. When for a wonder he leaves some inconsistency hanging loose – why if the wild cats are so very tame are the goats so very shy? – we are not seriously perturbed, for we are sure that there was a reason, and a very good one, had he time to give it us. But the pressure of life when one is fending entirely for oneself alone on a desert island is really no laughing matter. It is no crying one either. A man must have an eye to everything; it is no time for raptures about Nature when the lightning may explode one's gunpowder – it is imperative to seek a safer lodging for it. And so by means of telling the truth undeviatingly as it appears to him – by being a great artist and forgoing this and daring that in order to give effect to his prime quality, a sense of reality – he comes in the end to make common actions dignified and common objects beautiful. To dig, to bake, to plant, to build – how serious these simple occupations are; hatchets, scissors, logs, axes – how beautiful these simple objects become. Unimpeded by comment, the story marches on with magnificent downright simplicity. Yet how could comment have made it more impressive? It is true that he takes the opposite way from the psychologist's – he describes the effect of emotion on the body, not on the mind. But when he says how, in a moment of anguish, he clinched his hands so that any soft thing would have been crushed; how 'my teeth in my head would strike together, and set against one another so strong, that for the time I could not part them again',[13] the effect is as deep as pages of analysis could have made it. His own instinct in the matter is right. 'Let the naturalists', he says, 'explain these things, and the reason and manner of them; all I can say to them is, to describe the fact. . . .'[14] If you are Defoe, certainly to describe the fact is enough; for the fact is the right fact. By means of this genius for fact Defoe achieves effects that are beyond any but the great masters of descriptive prose. He has only to say a word or two about 'the grey of the morning'[15] to paint vividly a windy dawn. A sense of desolation and of the deaths of many men is conveyed by remarking in the most prosaic way in the world, 'I never saw them afterwards, or any sign of them except three of their hats, one cap, and two shoes that were not fellows'.[16] When at last he exclaims, 'Then to see how like a king I din'd too all alone, attended by my servants'[17] – his parrot and his dog and his two cats, we cannot help but feel that all humanity is on a desert island alone – though Defoe at once informs us, for he has a way of snubbing off our enthusiasms, that the cats were not the same cats that had come in the ship. Both of those were dead; these cats were new cats, and as a matter of fact cats became very troublesome before long from their fecundity, whereas dogs, oddly enough, did not breed at all.

Thus Defoe, by reiterating that nothing but a plain earthenware pot stands in the foreground, persuades us to see remote islands and the solitudes of the human soul. By believing fixedly in the solidity of the pot and its earthiness, he has subdued every other element to his design; he has roped the whole universe into harmony. And is there any reason, we ask as we shut the book, why the perspective that a plain earthenware pot exacts should not satisfy us as completely, once we grasp it, as man himself in all his sublimity standing against a background of broken mountains and tumbling oceans with stars flaming in the sky?

1 – Originally published in the N&A, 6 February 1926, (Kp4 C271; see IV VW Essays), as a review of The Life and Strange Surprizing Adventures of Robinson Crusoe of York. Mariner. . . . Written by Himself [1719]; The

Farther Adventures of Robinson Crusoe...; Serious Reflections...of Robinson Crusoe, by Daniel Defoe (1660?–1731), with an introduction by Charles Whibley (3 vols, Constable, 1925); it was revised for *CR2*. Reading notes for this revision (MHP, B 2p) (*VWRN* XLVIII). Draft of this revision (Berg, M 14). Reprinted: *CE*.

2 – Sir Philip Sidney (1554–86); see 'The Countess of Pembroke's Arcadia' above.

3 – The reviewer of *CR2* in *The Times* called this 'an excellent phrase' in which 'we get a glimpse of one part of the secret of Mrs. Woolf's method' ('A Portrait Gallery', 28 October 1932, p. 17, col. e; and see Introduction, p. xii).

4 – The pamphlet for which Defoe was punished, in 1703, was his celebrated *The Shortest Way with Dissenters* (1702).

5 – *The Fortunes and the Misfortunes of the Famous Moll Flanders* (1722).

6 – VW's appeal to perspective recalls her diary entry for 7 December 1925 where she explored theories subsequently developed at length in 'Phases of Fiction' (see above): 'I don't think it is a matter of "development" but something to do with prose & poetry, in novels. For instance Defoe at one end: E. Brontë at the other. Reality is something they put at different distances' (*III VW Diary*).

7 – Sir Walter Scott (1771–1832); Jane Austen (1775–1817); Thomas Love Peacock (1785–1866) – all are discussed in 'Phases of Fiction'.

8 – Thomas Hardy (1840–1928), *Jude the Obscure* (1895), for VW on whom, see 'The Novels of Thomas Hardy' below. Marcel Proust (1871–1922) is discussed in 'Phases of Fiction' above.

9 – To the ellipsis, *Robinson Crusoe*, vol. i, pp. 71, and for the remainder, pp. 71–2.

10 – *Ibid.*, p. 126, which continues: 'I saw abundance of parrots, and fain I would have caught one, if possible, to have kept it to be tame, and taught it to speak to me.'

11 – *Ibid.*, p. 284, which has: 'which lay ... sun, and'.

12 – *Ibid.*, p. 27.

13 – *Ibid.*, p. 220.

14 – *Ibid.*

15 – *Ibid.*, p. 19.

16 – *Ibid.*, p. 53.

17 – *Ibid.*, p. 173.

Dorothy Osborne's 'Letters'

It must sometimes strike the casual reader of English literature that there is a bare season in it, sometimes like early spring in our country-side. The trees stand out; the hills are unmuffled in green; there is nothing to obscure the mass of the earth or the lines of the branches. But we miss the tremor and murmur of June, when the smallest wood seems full of movement, and one has only to stand still to hear the whispering and the pattering of nimble, inquisitive animals going about their affairs in the undergrowth. So in English literature we have to wait till the sixteenth century is over and the seventeenth well on its way before the bare landscape becomes full of stir and quiver and we can fill in the spaces between the great books with the voices of people talking.

Doubtless great changes in psychology were needed and great changes in material comfort – arm-chairs and carpets and good roads – before it was possible for human beings to watch each other curiously or to communicate their thoughts easily. And it may be that our early literature owes something of its magnificence to the fact that writing was an uncommon art, practised, rather for fame than for money, by those whose gifts compelled them. Perhaps the dissipation of our genius in biography, and journalism, and letter- and memoir-writing has weakened its strength in any one direction. However this may be, there is a bareness about an age that has neither letter-writers nor biographers. Lives and characters appear in stark outline. Donne, says Sir Edmund Gosse, is inscrutable;[2] and that is largely because, though we know what Donne thought of Lady Bedford, we have not the slightest inkling what Lady Bedford thought of Donne. She had no friend to whom she described the effect of that strange visitor; nor, had she had a confidante, could she have explained for what reasons Donne seemed to her strange.

And the conditions that made it impossible for Boswell or Horace Walpole[3] to be born in the sixteenth century were obviously likely to fall with far heavier force upon the other sex. Besides the material difficulty – Donne's small house at Mitcham with its thin walls and crying children typifies the discomfort in which the Elizabethans lived – the woman was impeded also by her belief that writing was an act unbefitting her sex. A great lady here and there whose rank secured her the toleration and it may be the adulation of a servile circle, might write and print her writings. But the act was offensive to a woman of lower rank. 'Sure the poore woman is a little distracted, she could never bee soe ridiculous else as to venture writeing book's and in verse too', Dorothy Osborne exclaimed when the Duchess of Newcastle published one of her books. For her own part, she added, 'If I could not sleep this fortnight I should not come to that'.[4] And the comment is the more illuminating in that it was made by a woman of great literary gift. Had she been born in 1827, Dorothy Osborne would have written novels;[5] had she been born in 1527, she would never have written at all. But she was born in 1627, and at that date though writing books was ridiculous for a woman there was nothing unseemly in writing a letter. And so by degrees the silence is broken; we begin to hear rustlings in the undergrowth; for the first time in English literature we hear men and women talking together over the fire.

But the art of letter-writing in its infancy was not the art that has since filled so many delightful volumes. Men and women were ceremoniously Sir and Madam; the language was still too rich and stiff to turn and twist quickly and freely upon half a sheet of notepaper. The art of letter-writing is often the art of essay-writing in disguise. But such as it was, it was an art that a woman could practise without unsexing herself. It was an art that could be carried on at odd moments, by a father's sick-bed, among a thousand interruptions, without exciting comment, anonymously as it were, and often with the pretence that it served some useful purpose. Yet into these innumerable letters, lost now for the most part, went powers of observation and of wit that were later to take rather a different shape in *Evelina* and in *Pride and Prejudice*.[6] They were only letters, yet some pride went to their making. Dorothy, without admitting it, took pains with her own writing and had views as to the nature of it: '. . . great Schollers are not the best writer's (of Letters I mean, of books perhaps they are) . . . all letters mee thinks should be free and easy as one's discourse'.[7] She was in agreement with an old uncle of hers who threw his standish at his secretary's head for saying 'put pen to paper'[8] instead of simply 'wrote'. Yet there were limits, she reflected, to free-and-easiness: '. . . many pritty things shuffled together'[9] do better spoken than in a letter. And so we come by a form of literature, if Dorothy Osborne will let us call it so, which is distinct from any other, and much to be regretted now that it has gone from us, as it seems, for ever.

For Dorothy Osborne, as she filled her great sheets by her father's bed or by the chimney-corner, gave a record of life, gravely yet playfully, formally yet with intimacy, to a public of one, but to a fastidious public, as the novelist can never give it, or the historian either. Since it is her business to keep her lover informed of what passes in her home, she must sketch the solemn Sir Justinian Isham – Sir Solomon Justinian, she calls him – the pompous widower with four daughters and a great gloomy house in Northamptonshire who wished to marry her. 'Lord what would I give that I had a Lattin letter of his for you', she exclaimed, in which he describes her to an Oxford friend and specially commended her that she was 'capable of being company and conversation for him';[10] she must sketch her valetudinarian Cousin Molle[11] waking one morning in fear of the dropsy and hurrying to the doctor at Cambridge; she must draw her own picture wandering in the garden at night and smelling the 'Jessomin', 'and yet I was not pleased'[12] because Temple was not with her. Any gossip that comes her way is sent on to amuse her lover. Lady Sunderland, for instance, has condescended to marry plain Mr Smith,[13] who treats her like a princess, which Sir Justinian thinks a bad precedent for wives. But Lady Sunderland tells everyone she married him out of pity, and that, Dorothy comments, 'was the pittyfull'st sayeing that ever I heard'.[14] Soon we have picked up enough about all her friends to snatch eagerly at any further addition to the picture which is forming in our mind's eye.

Indeed, our glimpse of the society of Bedfordshire in the seventeenth century is the more intriguing for its intermittency. In they come and out they go – Sir Justinian and Lady Diana,[15] Mr Smith and his countess – and we never know when or whether we shall hear of them again. But with all this haphazardry, the *Letters*, like the letters of all born letter-writers, provide their own continuity. They make us feel that we have our seat in the depths of Dorothy's mind, at the heart of the pageant which unfolds itself page by page as we read. For she possesses indisputably the gift which counts for more in letter-writing than wit or brilliance or traffic with great people. By being herself without effort or emphasis, she envelops all these odds and ends in the flow of her own personality. It was a character that was both attractive and a little obscure. Phrase by phrase we come closer into touch with it. Of the womanly virtues that befitted her age she shows little trace. She says nothing of sewing or baking. She was a little indolent by temperament. She browsed casually on vast French romances. She roams the commons, loitering to hear the milkmaids sing; she walks in the garden by the side of a small river, 'where I sitt downe and wish you were with mee'.[16] She was apt to fall silent in company and dream over the fire till some talk of flying, perhaps, roused her, and she made her brother laugh by asking what they were saying about flying, for the thought had struck her, if she could fly she could be with Temple. Gravity, melancholy were in her blood.

385

She looked, her mother used to say, as if all her friends were dead. She is oppressed by a sense of fortune and its tyranny and the vanity of things and the uselessness of effort. Her mother and sister were grave women too, the sister famed for her letters, but fonder of books than of company, the mother 'counted as wise a woman as most in England', but sardonic. 'I have lived to see that 'tis almost impossible to think People worse than they are and soe will you'[17] – Dorothy could remember her mother saying that. To assuage her spleen, Dorothy herself had to visit the wells at Epsom and to drink water that steel had stood in.

With such a temperament her humour naturally took the form of irony rather than of wit. She loved to mock her lover and to pour a fine raillery over the pomps and ceremonies of existence. Pride of birth she laughed at. Pompous old men were fine subjects for her satire. A dull sermon moved her to laughter. She saw through parties; she saw through ceremonies; she saw through worldliness and display. But with all this clearsightedness there was something that she did not see through. She dreaded with a shrinking that was scarcely sane the ridicule of the world. The meddling of aunts and the tyranny of brothers exasperated her. 'I would live in a hollow Tree', she said, 'to avoyde them.' A husband kissing his wife in public seemed to her as 'ill a sight as one would wish to see'. Though she cared no more whether people praised her beauty or her wit than whether 'they think my name Eliz: or Dor:',[18] a word of gossip about her own behaviour would set her in a quiver. Thus when it came to proving before the eyes of the world that she loved a poor man and was prepared to marry him, she could not do it. 'I confess that I have an humor that will not suffer mee to Expose myself to People's Scorne', she wrote. She could be 'sattisfyed within as narrow a compasse as that of any person liveing of my rank',[19] but ridicule was intolerable to her. She shrank from any extravagance that could draw the censure of the world upon her. It was a weakness for which Temple had sometimes to reprove her.

For Temple's character emerges more and more clearly as the letters go on – it is a proof of Dorothy's gift as a correspondent. A good letter-writer so takes the colour of the reader at the other end, that from reading the one we can imagine the other. As she argues, as she reasons, we hear Temple almost as clearly as we hear Dorothy herself. He was in many ways the opposite of her. He drew out her melancholy by rebutting it; he made her defend her dislike of marriage by

opposing it. Of the two Temple was by far the more robust and positive. Yet there was perhaps something – a little hardness, a little conceit
– that justified her brother's dislike of him. He called Temple the
'proudest imperious insulting ill-natured man that ever was'.[20] But, in
the eyes of Dorothy, Temple had qualities that none of her other suitors
possessed. He was not a mere country gentleman, nor a pompous
Justice of the Peace, nor a town gallant, making love to every woman
he met, nor a travelled Monsieur; for had he been any one of these
things, Dorothy, with her quick sense of the ridiculous, would have
had none of him. To her he had some charm, some sympathy, that
the others lacked; she could write to him whatever came into her head;
she was at her best with him; she loved him; she respected him. Yet
suddenly she declared that marry him she would not. She turned
violently against marriage indeed, and cited failure after failure. If
people knew each other before marriage, she thought, there would be
an end of it. Passion was the most brutish and tyrannical of all our
senses. Passion had made Lady Anne Blount the 'talk of all the footmen
and Boy's in the street'.[21] Passion had been the undoing of the lovely
Lady Izabella – what use was her beauty now married to 'that beast
with all his estate'?[22] Torn asunder by her brother's anger, by Temple's
jealousy, and by her own dread of ridicule, she wished for nothing but
to be left to find 'an early and a quiet grave'.[23] That Temple overcame
her scruples and overrode her brother's opposition is much to the credit
of his character. Yet it is an act that we can hardly help deploring.
Married to Temple, she wrote to him no longer. The letters almost
immediately cease. The whole world that Dorothy had brought into
existence is extinguished. It is then that we realise how round and
populous and stirring that world has become. Under the warmth of
her affection for Temple the stiffness had gone out of her pen. Writing
half asleep by her father's side, snatching the back of an old letter to
write upon, she had come to write easily though always with the
dignity proper to that age, of the Lady Dianas, and the Ishams, of the
aunts and the uncles – how they come, how they go; what they say;
whether she finds them dull, laughable, charming, or much as usual.
More than that, she has suggested, writing her mind out to Temple,
the deeper relationships, the more private moods, that gave her life its
conflict and its consolation – her brother's tyranny; her own moodi-
ness and melancholy; the sweetness of walking in the garden at night;
of sitting lost in thought by the river; of longing for a letter and finding
one. All this is around us; we are deep in this world, seizing its hints

and suggestions when, in the moment, the scene is blotted out. She married, and her husband was a rising diplomat. She had to follow his fortunes in Brussels, at The Hague, wherever they called him. Seven children were born and seven children died 'almost all in their cradle'.[24] Innumerable duties and responsibilities fell to the lot of the girl who had made fun of pomp and ceremony, who loved privacy and had wished to live secluded out of the world and 'grow old together in our little cottage'.[25] Now she was mistress of her husband's house at The Hague with its splendid buffet of plate. She was his confidante in the many troubles of his difficult career. She stayed behind in London to negotiate if possible the payment of his arrears of salary. When her yacht was fired on, she behaved, the King said, with greater courage than the captain himself. She was everything that the wife of an ambassador should be: she was everything, too, that the wife of a man retired from the public service should be. And troubles came upon them – a daughter died; a son, inheriting perhaps his mother's melancholy, filled his boots with stones and leapt into the Thames. So the years passed; very full, very active, very troubled. But Dorothy maintained her silence.

At last, however, a strange young man came to Moor Park as secretary to her husband. He was difficult, ill-mannered, and quick to take offence. But it is through Swift's eyes that we see Dorothy once more in the last years of her life. 'Mild Dorothea, peaceful, wise, and great', Swift called her;[26] but the light falls upon a ghost. We do not know that silent lady. We cannot connect her after all these years with the girl who poured her heart out to her lover. 'Peaceful, wise, and great' – she was none of those things when we last met her, and much though we honour the admirable ambassadress who made her husband's career her own, there are moments when we would exchange all the benefits of the Triple Alliance and all the glories of the Treaty of Nimuegen for the letters that Dorothy did not write.[27]

1 – Originally published in the NR (as 'Dorothy Osborne's Letters'), 24 October, and in the TLS (as 'Dorothy Osborne'), 25 October 1928, (Kp4 C304; see IV VW Essays), as a review of The Letters of Dorothy Osborne [1627–95] to William Temple [1628–99], ed. G. C. Moore Smith (Clarendon Press, 1928); it was revised for CR2. On 8 March 1932 VW noted: 'I am too tired to write this morning – cant finish my Dorothy Osborne' (IV VW Diary). Reading notes for this revision (MHP, B 2p) (VWRN XLVIII). Draft of this revision (Berg, M 14). Reprinted: CE, WE.
2 – See Edmund Gosse, The Life and Letters of John Donne (2 vols, William Heinemann, 1899), vol. i, p. 3, where inscrutability is given as one of several

characteristics said to belong superlatively to Donne. See Gosse, vol. i, p. 218: 'The verses sent by Lady Bedford to Donne have not been preserved.' See also 'Donne After Three Centuries' above, for Donne's relations with Lady Bedford.

3 – James Boswell (1740–95); Horace Walpole (1717–97).

4 – *Letters of D. Osborne*, Letter 17, 14 April 1653, p. 37, which has: 'I should not...' For VW on Margaret Cavendish, Duchess of Newcastle (1623?–73), see 'The Duchess of Newcastle', *CR1* and *IV VW Essays*; and see also *Room*, ch. iv, p. 93.

5 – Cf. 'Modern Letters' (written in June 1930): 'In our day, Dorothy Osborne would have been an admirable biographer'; see *VI VW Essays*, Appendix.

6 – Fanny Burney (1752–1840), *Evelina* (1778); Jane Austen (1775–1817), *Pride and Prejudice* (1813).

7 – *Letters of D. Osborne*, Letter 40, September 1653, p. 90.

8 – *Ibid.*, p. 91.

9 – *Ibid.*, Letter 60, 25 February 1653/4, p. 153.

10 – *Ibid.*, Letter 6, 29 January 1652/3, p. 15. Sir Justinian Isham (1611–75) of Lamport, MP for Northamptonshire after the Restoration; his first wife Jane, *née* Garrard, died in childbirth in 1639. The 'Emperour', as Dorothy Osborne also referred to him, was eventually remarried, in 1653, to Vere (d. 1704), daughter of Baron Leigh of Stoneleigh. See also Letter 9, 26 February 1652/3, p. 22.

11 – See *ibid.*, Letter 21, 14 May 1653, p. 43. Henry Molle (1597–1658), Fellow of King's College, Cambridge, author of light verse and prose 'characters', was distantly related to the Osborne family.

12 – *Ibid.*, Letter 30, 16 July 1653, p. 66.

13 – Lady Dorothy Spencer, *née* Sidney (1617–84; Edmund Waller's 'Sacharissa'), widow of the Earl of Sunderland (d. 1643), married in 1652 Robert Smythe or Smith (1613–64/7), Esq., of Boundes Park, Tonbridge, whose titular inadequacy was made good by the award of a baronetcy after the Restoration.

14 – *Letters of D. Osborne*, Letter 6, 29 January 1652/3, p. 16.

15 – Lady Diana Rich, youngest daughter of Henry, Earl of Holland, and Isabel, daughter of Sir Walter Cope.

16 – *Letters of D. Osborne*, Letter 24, 2–4 June 1653, p. 52. See *Room*, ch. iv, p. 94.

17 – *Letters of D. Osborne*, Letter 59, 19 February 1653/4, pp. 150, 151. Her mother, Dorothy, *née* Danvers (d. 1650 or 1651, *aetat* 60); the sister was Elizabeth, Lady Peyton (1610–42).

18 – *Ibid.*, Letter 21, 14 May 1653, p. 43; Letter 41, October 1653, p. 95; Letter 45, 23 October 1653, p. 110.

19 – *Ibid.*, Letter 53, 8 January 1653/4, p. 128.

20 – *Ibid.*, Letter 62, 2 April 1654, p. 158; it was 'J. B.' (James Beverley),

a suitor of Dorothy's – not Sir Henry Osborne (1619–75) – who made this observation; Temple had been at Emmanuel College with Beverley and called him 'a whelp' (see p. 270, n. 2).

21 – *Ibid.*, Letter 48, 16 December 1653, p. 118, which has: 'Blunt'. In April 1654 Lady Anne Blunt or Blount, daughter of the Earl of Newport, *aetat* 16, would petition the Protector, asserting that she had *not* in fact contracted marriage with one William Blount (no relation), a recusant Papist.

22 – *Ibid.*, Letter 43, October 1653, p. 100. Lady Isabella, *née* Rich, was married to Sir James Thynne.

23 – *Ibid.*, Letter 48, 16 December 1653, p. 119. The passage refers to Dorothy Osborne's cousin Elizabeth Franklin, *née* Cheke, and reads: '. . . but I doe not envy her, may she long injoy it, and I, an early, and a quiet grave, free from the trouble of this buissy world, where all with passion persue theire owne interests at theire Neighbours Charges, where nobody is pleased but sombody complain's ont, and where tis imposible to bee without giveing and receiveing injury's'.

24 – Thomas Peregrine Courtenay, *Memoirs of the Life, Works, and Correspondence of Sir William Temple, Bart.* (2 vols, Longman, Rees, Orme, Brown, Green & Longman, 1836), vol. ii, p. 114, quoting Temple's sister, Lady Gifford, who is referring to the period before Diana Temple's death. Six children died in infancy when the Temples were in Ireland, 1656–63; of the remaining two, Diana (1663–79) died of smallpox, and John (1664–89) became Secretary for War and committed suicide shortly thereafter.

25 – *Letters of D. Osborne*, Letter 54, 13–15 January 1653/4, p. 131.

26 – Jonathan Swift (1667–1745), 'Ode Occasioned by Sir William Temple's Late Illness and Recovery. Written December 1693', quoted by Thackeray in 'Swift', *The Four Georges. The English Humourists of the Eighteenth Century*, The Works of William Makepeace Thackeray (Smith, Elder, 1869), vol. xix, p. 148:

> Mild Dorothea, peaceful, wise, and great,
> Trembling beheld the doubtful hand of fate.

27 – Temple was a leading advocate of the Triple Alliance of 1668 between England, Sweden and the United Provinces (Holland), and was one of the English plenipotentiaries to draw up the Treaty of Nijmegen in 1678 that aimed (but failed) to put an end to the constant warfare that had ravaged the continent for years. See *The Life and Works of Lord Macaulay* (10 vols, Edinburgh Edition, Longmans, Green, 1897), vol. vi, 'Sir William Temple', pp. 246–325 (review of Courtenay, *Edinburgh Review*, October 1838).

Swift's 'Journal to Stella'

In any highly civilised society disguise plays so large a part, politeness is so essential, that to throw off the ceremonies and conventions and talk a 'little language'[2] for one or two to understand, is as much a necessity as a breath of air in a hot room. The reserved, the powerful, the admired, have the most need of such a refuge. Swift himself found it so. The proudest of men coming home from the company of great men who praised him, of lovely women who flattered him, from intrigue and politics, put all that aside, settled himself comfortably in bed, pursed his severe lips into baby language and prattled to his 'two monkies', his 'dear Sirrahs', his 'naughty rogues'[3] on the other side of the Irish Channel.

Well, let me see you now again. My wax candle's almost out, but however I'll begin. Well then don't be so tedious, Mr. Presto; what can you say to MD's letter? Make haste, have done with your preambles – why, I say, I am glad you are so often abroad.[4]

So long as Swift wrote to Stella[5] in that strain, carelessly, illegibly, for 'methinks when I write plain, I do not know how, but we are not alone, all the world can see us. A bad scrawl is so snug . . .',[6] Stella had no need to be jealous. It was true that she was wearing away the flower of her youth in Ireland with Rebecca Dingley, who wore hinged spectacles, consumed large quantities of Brazil tobacco, and stumbled over her petticoats as she walked. Further, the conditions in which the two ladies lived, for ever in Swift's company when he was at home, occupying his house when he was absent, gave rise to gossip; so that though Stella never saw him except in Mrs Dingley's presence, she was one of those ambiguous women who live chiefly in the society of the other sex. But surely it was well worth while. The packets kept coming from England, each sheet written to the rim in Swift's crabbed little hand, which she imitated to perfection, full of nonsense words, and capital letters, and hints which no one but Stella could understand, and secrets which Stella was to keep, and little commissions which Stella was to execute. Tobacco came for Dingley, and chocolate and silk aprons for Stella. Whatever people might say, surely it was well worth while.

Of this Presto, who was so different from that formidable character 't'other I',[7] the world knew nothing. The world knew only that Swift was over in England again, soliciting the new Tory government on behalf of the Irish Church for those First Fruits which he had begged the Whigs in vain to restore. The business was soon accomplished; nothing indeed could exceed the cordiality and affection with which Harley and St John greeted him;[8] and now the world saw what even in those days of small societies and individual pre-eminence must have been a sight to startle and amaze – the 'mad parson',[9] who had marched up and down the coffee-houses in silence and unknown a few years ago, admitted to the inmost councils of State; the penniless boy who was not allowed to sit down at table with Sir William Temple[10] dining with the highest Ministers of the Crown, making dukes do his bidding, and so run after for his good offices that his servant's chief duty was to know how to keep people out. Addison[11] himself forced his way up only by pretending that he was a gentleman come to pay a bill. For the time being Swift was omnipotent. Nobody could buy his services; everybody feared his pen. He went to Court, and 'am so proud I make all the lords come up to me'.[12] The Queen wished to hear him preach; Harley and St John added their entreaties; but he refused. When Mr Secretary one night dared show his temper, Swift called upon him and warned him

never to appear cold to me, for I would not be treated like a schoolboy. . . . He took all right; said I had reason . . . would have had me dine with him at Mrs. Masham's brother, to make up matters; but I would not. I don't know, but I would not.[13]

He scribbled all this down to Stella without exultation or vanity. That he should command and dictate, prove himself the peer of great men and make rank abase itself before him, called for no comment on his part or on hers. Had she not known him years ago at Moor Park and seen him lose his temper with Sir William Temple, and guessed his greatness and heard from his own lips what he planned and hoped? Did she not know better than anyone how strangely good and bad were blent in him and all his foibles and eccentricities of temper? He scandalised the lords with whom he dined by his stinginess, picked the coals off his fire, saved halfpence on coaches; and yet by the help of these very economies he practised, she knew, the most considerate and secret of charities – he gave poor Patty Rolt 'a pistole to help her a little forward against she goes to board in the country';[14] he took twenty guineas to young Harrison,[15] the sick poet, in his garret. She alone knew how he could be coarse in his speech and yet delicate in his behaviour; how he could be cynical superficially and yet cherish a depth of feeling which she had never met with in any other human being. They knew each other in and out; the good and the bad, the deep and the trivial; so that without effort or concealment he could use those precious moments late at night or the first thing on waking to pour out upon her the whole story of his day, with its charities and meannesses, its affections and ambitions and despairs, as though he were thinking aloud.

With such proof of his affection, admitted to intimacy with this Presto whom no one else in the world knew, Stella had no cause to be jealous. It was perhaps the opposite that happened. As she read the crowded pages, she could see him and hear him and imagine so exactly the impression that he must be making on all these fine people that she fell more deeply in love with him than ever. Not only was he courted and flattered by the great; everybody seemed to call upon him when they were in trouble. There was 'young Harrison'; he worried to find him ill and penniless; carried him off to Knightsbridge; took him a hundred pounds only to find that he was dead an hour before. 'Think what grief this is to me! . . . I could not dine with Lord Treasurer, nor anywhere else; but got a bit of meat toward evening.'[16] She could imagine the strange scene, that November morning, when the Duke of Hamilton was killed in Hyde Park, and Swift went at once to the Duchess and sat with her for two hours and heard her rage and storm and rail; and took her affairs, too, on his shoulders as if it were his natural office, and none could dispute his place in the house of mourning. 'She has moved my very soul',[17] he said. When young Lady Ashburnham died he burst out, 'I hate life when I think it exposed to such accidents; and to see so many thousand wretches burdening the earth, while such as her die, makes me think God did never intend life for a blessing'.[18] And then, with that instinct to rend and tear his own emotions which made him angry in the midst of his pity, he would round upon the mourners, even the mother and sister of the dead woman, and part them as they cried together and complain how 'people will pretend to grieve more than they really do, and that takes off from their true grief'.[19]

All this was poured forth freely to Stella; the gloom and the anger, the kindness and the coarseness and the genial love of little ordinary human things. To her he showed himself fatherly and brotherly; he laughed at her spelling; he scolded her about her health; he directed her business affairs. He gossiped and chatted with her. They had a fund of memories in common. They had spent many happy hours together. 'Do not you remember I used to come into your chamber and turn Stella out of her chair, and rake up the fire in a cold morning and cry *uth*, *uth*, *uth*!'[20] She was often in his mind; he wondered if she was out walking when he was; when Prior abused one of his puns he remembered Stella's puns and how vile they were;[21] he compared his life in London with hers in Ireland and wondered when they would be together again. And if this was the influence of Stella upon Swift in town among all the wits, the influence of Swift upon Stella marooned in an Irish village alone with Dingley was far greater. He had taught her all the little learning she had when she was a child and he a young man years ago at Moor Park. His influence was everywhere – upon her mind, upon her affections, upon the books she read and the hand she wrote, upon the friends she made and the suitors she rejected. Indeed, he was half responsible for her being.

But the woman he had chosen was no insipid slave. She had a character of her own. She was capable of thinking for herself. She was aloof, a severe critic for all her grace and sympathy, a little formidable perhaps with her love of plain speaking and her fiery temper and her fearlessness in saying what she thought. But with all her gifts she was little known. Her slender means and feeble health and dubious social standing made her way of life very modest. The society which gathered round her came for the simple pleasure of talking to a woman who listened and understood and said very little herself, but in the most agreeable of voices and generally 'the best thing that was said in the company'.[22] For the rest she was not learned. Her health had prevented her from serious study, and though she had run over a great variety of subjects and had a fine severe taste in letters, what she did read did not stick in her mind. She had been extravagant as a girl, and flung her money about until her good sense took control of her, and now she lived with the utmost frugality. 'Five nothings on five plates of delf'[23] made her supper. Attractive, if not beautiful, with her fine dark eyes and her raven black hair, she dressed very plainly, and thus contrived to lay by enough to help the poor and to bestow upon her friends (it was an extravagance that she could not resist) 'the most agreeable presents in the world'. Swift never knew her equal in that art, 'although it be an affair of as delicate a nature as most in the course of life'.[24] She had in addition that sincerity which Swift called 'honour',[25] and in spite of the weakness of her body 'the personal courage of a hero'.[26] Once when a robber came to her window, she had shot him through the body with her own hand. Such, then, was the influence which worked on Swift as he wrote; such the presence that mingled with the thought of his fruit trees and the willows and the trout stream at Laracor when he saw the trees budding in St James's Park and heard the politicians wrangle at Westminster. Unknown to all of them, he had his retreat; and if the Ministers again played him false, and once more, after making his friend's fortunes, he went empty-handed away, then after all he could retire to Ireland and to Stella and have 'no shuddering at all'[27] at the thought.

But Stella was the last woman in the world to press her claims. None knew better than she that Swift loved power and the company of men: that though he had his moods of tenderness and his fierce spasms of disgust at society, still for the most part he infinitely preferred the dust and bustle of London to all the trout streams and cherry trees in the world. Above all, he hated interference. If anyone laid a finger upon his liberty or hinted the least threat to his independence, were they men or women, queens or kitchen-maids, he turned upon them with a ferocity which made a savage of him on the spot. Harley once dared to offer him a bank-note; Miss Waring dared hint that the obstacles to their marriage were now removed.[28] Both were chastised, the woman brutally. But Stella knew better than to invite such treatment. Stella had learnt patience; Stella had learnt discretion. Even in a matter like this of staying in London or coming back to Ireland she allowed him every latitude. She asked nothing for herself and therefore got more than she asked. Swift was half annoyed:

... your generosity makes me mad; I know you repine inwardly at Presto's absence; you think he has broken his word, of coming in three months, and that this is always his trick: and now Stella says, she does not see possibly how I can come away in haste, and that MD is satisfied, etc. An't you a rogue to overpower me thus?[29]

But it was thus that she kept him. Again and again he burst into language of intense affection:

Farewell dear Sirrahs, dearest lives: there is peace and quiet with MD, and nowhere else.... Farewell again, dearest rogues: I am never happy, but when I write or think of MD.... You are as welcome as my blood to every farthing I have in the world: and all that grieves me is, I am not richer, for MD's sake.[30]

One thing alone dashed the pleasure that such words gave her. It was always in the plural that he spoke of her; it was always 'dearest Sirrahs, dearest lives'; MD stood for Stella and Mrs Dingley together. Swift and Stella were never alone. Grant that this was for form's sake merely, grant that the presence of Mrs Dingley, busy with her keys and her lap-dog and never listening to a word that was said to her, was a form too. But why should such forms be necessary? Why impose a strain that wasted her health and half spoilt her pleasure and kept 'perfect friends'[31] who were happy only in each other's company apart? Why indeed? There was a reason; a secret that Stella knew; a secret that Stella did not impart. Divided they had to be. Since, then, no bond bound them, since she was afraid to lay the least claim upon her friend, all the more jealously must she have searched into his words and analysed his conduct to ascertain the temper of his mood and acquaint herself instantly with the least change in it. So long as he told her frankly of his 'favourites' and showed himself the bluff tyrant who required every woman to make advances to him, who lectured fine ladies and let them tease him, all was well. There was nothing in that to rouse her suspicions. Lady Berkeley might steal his hat; the Duchess of Hamilton might lay bare her agony; and Stella, who was kind to her sex, laughed with the one and grieved with the other.

But were there traces in the *Journal* of a different sort of influence – something far more dangerous because more equal and more intimate? Suppose that there were some woman of Swift's own station, a girl, like the girl that Stella herself had been when Swift first knew her, dissatisfied with the ordinary way of life, eager, as Stella put it, to know right from wrong, gifted, witty, and untaught – she indeed, if she existed, might be a rival to be feared. But was there such a rival? If so, it was plain that there would be no mention of her in the *Journal*. Instead, there would be hesitations, excuses, an occasional uneasiness and embarrassment when, in the midst of writing freely and fully, Swift was brought to a stop by something that he could not say. Indeed, he had only been a month or two in England when some such silence roused Stella's suspicions. Who was it, she asked, that boarded near him, that he dined with now and then? 'I know no such person,' Swift replied; 'I do not dine with boarders. What the pox! You know whom I have dined with every day since I left you, better than I do. What do you mean, Sirrah?'[32] But he knew what she meant: she meant Mrs Vanhomrigh, the widow who lived near him; she meant her daughter Esther.[33] 'The Vans' kept coming again and again after that in the *Journal*. Swift was too proud to conceal the fact that he saw them, but he sought nine times out of ten to excuse it. When he was in Suffolk Street the Vanhomrighs were in St James's Street and thus saved him a walk. When he was in Chelsea they were in London, and it was convenient to keep his best gown and periwig there. Sometimes the heat kept him there and sometimes the rain; now they were playing cards, and young Lady Ashburnham reminded him so much of Stella that he stayed on to help her. Sometimes he stayed out of listlessness; again he stayed because he was very busy and they were simple people who did not stand on ceremony. At the same time Stella had only to hint that these Vanhomrighs were people of no consequence for him to retort, 'Why, they keep as good female company as I do male . . . I saw two lady Bettys there this afternoon.'[34] In short, to tell the whole truth, to write whatever came into his head in the old free way, was no longer easy.

Indeed, the whole situation was full of difficulty. No man detested falsehood more than Swift or loved truth more whole-heartedly. Yet here he was compelled to hedge, to hide, and to prevaricate. Again, it had become essential to him to have some 'sluttery'[35] or private chamber where he could relax and unbend and be Presto and not 't'other I'. Stella satisfied this need as no one else could. But then Stella was in Ireland; Vanessa was on the spot. She was younger and fresher; she too had her charms. She too could be taught and improved and scolded into maturity as Stella had been. Obviously Swift's influence upon her was all to the good. And so with Stella in Ireland and Vanessa in London, why should it not be possible to enjoy what each could give him, confer benefits on both and do no serious harm to either? It seemed possible; at any rate he allowed himself to make the experiment. Stella, after all, had contrived for many years to make shift with her portion; Stella had never complained of her lot.

But Vanessa was not Stella. She was younger, more vehement, less disciplined, less wise. She had no Mrs Dingley to restrain her. She had no memories of the past to solace her. She had no journals coming day by day to comfort her. She loved Swift and she knew no reason why she should not say so. Had he not himself taught her 'to act what was right, and not to mind what the world said'?[36] Thus when some obstacle impeded her, when some mysterious secret came between them, she had the unwisdom to question him. 'Pray what can be wrong

in seeing and advising an unhappy young woman? I can't imagine.'
'You have taught me to distinguish,' she burst out, 'and then you leave
me miserable.'[37] Finally in her anguish and her bewilderment she had
the temerity to force herself upon Stella. She wrote and demanded to
be told the truth – what was Stella's connexion with Swift? But it was
Swift himself who enlightened her. And when the full force of those
bright blue eyes blazed upon her, when he flung her letter on the table
and glared at her and said nothing and rode off, her life was ended.[38]
It was no figure of speech when she said that 'his killing, killing words'
were worse than the rack to her; when she cried out that there was
'something in your look so awful that it strikes me dumb'.[39] Within
a few weeks of that interview she was dead; she had vanished, to
become one of those uneasy ghosts who haunted the troubled background of Stella's life, peopling its solitude with fears.

Stella was left to enjoy her intimacy alone. She lived on to practise those sad arts by which she kept her friend at her side until,
worn out with the strain and the concealment, with Mrs Dingley
and her lap-dogs, with the perpetual fears and frustrations, she too
died. As they buried her, Swift sat in a back room away from the
lights in the churchyard and wrote an account of the character of
'the truest, most virtuous, and valuable friend, that I, or perhaps any
other person, was ever blessed with'.[40] Years passed; insanity overcame him; he exploded in violent outbursts of mad rage. Then by
degrees he fell silent. Once they caught him murmuring. 'I am what
I am',[41] they heard him say.

1 – Originally published (as 'Swift's Journal to Stella') in the *TLS*, 24 September
1925, (*Kp4* C268; see *IV VW Essays*); it was revised for *CR2*. Reading notes
for this revision (MHP, B 2p) (*VWRN* XLVIII). Reprinted: *CE*.
2 – *The Prose Works of Jonathan Swift* [1667–1745], ed. Temple Scott
(Bohn's Standard Library, George Bell and Sons 1897), vol. ii, *Journal to
Stella*, ed. Frederick Ryland, Letter xxii, 28 April 1711 (continuation written
on 4 May), p. 170: 'Do you know that every syllable I write I hold my lips
just for all the world as if I were talking in our own little language to MD.
Faith, I am very silly; but I can't help it for my life.' 'MD' seems to have
stood for 'My Dears': see p. xx. In *The Waves* (Hogarth Press, 1931), Bernard
needs a 'little language such as lovers use' (pp. 261 and 323); and see also
pp. 155 and 287.
3 – These expressions, in various formulations, are scattered throughout the
Journal: e.g. Letter viii, 31 October 1710 (2 November), p. 44: 'Well, little
monkies mine'; Letter xi, 9 December 1710 (23 December), p. 80: 'Good

morrow, dear sirrahs'; Letter viii, 3 November 1710, p. 45: 'a certain naughty rogue called MD'.

4 – *Ibid.*, Letter x, 25 November 1710 (30 November), p. 62, which begins 'Well, let me see now' and continues: '. . . abroad; your mother thinks it is want of exercise hurts you, and so do I'.

5 – Stella was Esther Johnson (1681–1728). At Swift's urging, in 1701 she had moved to Ireland with her companion Rebecca Dingley (c. 1665–1743).

6 – *Journal*, Letter viii, 3 November 1710, p. 44.

7 – *Ibid.*, Letter xxix, 25 August 1711, p. 231: 'But let me alone, sirrahs; for Presto is going to be very busy; not Presto, but t'other I.'

8 – Robert Harley, 1st Earl of Oxford and Mortimer (1661–1724), chancellor of the exchequer; Henry St John, 1st Viscount Bolingbroke (1678–1751), secretary of state.

9 – Leslie Stephen, *Swift* (1882; English Men of Letters series, Macmillan, 1889), ch. iv, p. 56: 'At one time, according to a story vague as to dates, he got the name of the "mad parson" from Addison and others, by his habit of taking half-an-hour's smart walk to and fro in the coffee-house, and then departing in silence.' See also Stephen on Swift in the *DNB*.

10 – Swift was secretary to Sir William Temple (1628–99), during 1689–94 and 1696–99, in whose household at Moor Park in Surrey he first met Esther Johnson; and see 'Dorothy Osborne's *Letters*' above.

11 – For VW on Joseph Addison (1672–1719), see *CR1* and *IV VW Essays*.

12 – *Journal*, Letter xxvii, 19 July 1711 (29 July), p. 215.

13 – *Ibid.*, Letter xix, 24 March 1710–11 (3 April), p. 148.

14 – *Ibid.*, Letter xxvii, 19 July 1711 (27 July), p. 214; Patty Rolt, afterwards Mrs Lancelot, was a cousin of Swift.

15 – William Harrison (1685–1713), poet, diplomatist and sometime 'Tatler', a protégé of Swift who generally refers to him in the *Journal* as 'little Harrison'.

16 – *Journal*, Letter lix, 25 January 1712–13 (14 February), p. 428.

17 – *Ibid.*, Letter lv, 15 November 1712, p. 393; James Douglas, 4th Duke of Hamilton (1658–1712) and Charles, 4th Baron Mohun (1675?–1712) died duelling on 15 November. The duke's (second) wife was Elizabeth, only daughter and heiress of Digby, Lord Gerard.

18 – *Ibid.*, Letter lvii, 18 December 1712 (3 January 1712–13), p. 410; Lady Mary Butler, daughter of the Duke of Ormond, had married Lord Ashburnham in 1710.

19 – *Ibid.*, Letter lviii, 4 January 1712–13 (14 January), p. 415.

20 – *Ibid.*, Letter xiv, 16 January 1710–11 (22 January), p. 106, which has: 'Don't you remember . . . *uth?*'

21 – See *ibid.*, Letter xxi, 14 April 1711 (23 April), p. 162: 'After dinner we had coarse Doiley napkins, fringed at each end . . . I told him I was glad to see there was such a *Fringeship* [Friendship] between Mr Prior and his lordship. Prior swore it was the worst he ever heard: I said I thought so too;

but at the same time I thought it was most like one of Stella's that I ever heard.' Matthew Prior (1664–1721), for whose puns see pp. 93 and 233. See also *The Works of Jonathan Swift...*, ed. Sir Walter Scott (1814; 2nd ed., Archibald Constable, 1824), vol. ix, 'Bon Mots de Stella', pp. 294–6.

22 – *Works*, vol. ix, 'On the Death of Mrs Johnson [Stella]', pp. 283–4; and see p. 286: 'She understood the Platonic and Epicurean philosophy, and judged very well of the defects of the latter. She made very judicious abstracts of the best books she had read. She understood the nature of government, and could point out all the errors of Hobbes, both in that and religion.'

23 – *Ibid.*, vol. xiv, 'Stella at Wood Park. / A House of Charles Ford, Esq. Near Dublin. 1723.', p. 525:

> Howe'er, to keep her spirits up,
> She sent for company to sup:
> When all the while you might remark,
> She strove in vain to ape Wood Park.
> Two bottles call'd for, (half her store,
> The cupboard could contain but four:)
> A supper worthy of herself,
> Five nothings in five plates of delf.

24 – *Ibid.*, vol. ix, 'On the Death of Mrs Johnson [Stella]', p. 289: 'But she had another quality that much delighted her ... I mean that of making agreeable presents; wherein I never knew her equal, although it be an affair of as delicate a nature as most in the course of life.'

25 – E.g. *ibid.*: 'Honour, truth, liberality, good nature, and modesty, were the virtues she chiefly possessed, and most valued in her acquaintance...'

26 – *Ibid.*, p. 284.

27 – *Journal*, Letter xxxii, 9 October 1711 (22 October), p. 265.

28 – For Harley's attempt to bribe Swift and its consequence, see Stephen, *Swift*, ch. v, p. 85; for the unfortunate Miss Waring, see *ibid.*, ch. iv, p. 52: 'Poor Varina [Waring] had resisted Swift's entreaties, on the ground of her own ill-health and Swift's want of fortune. She now, it seems, thought that the economical difficulty was removed by Swift's preferment, and wished the marriage to take place. Swift replied in a letter, which contains all our information: and to which I can apply no other epithet than brutal.'

29 – *Journal*, Letter xix, 24 March 1710–11 (5 April), p. 150.

30 – *Ibid.*, Letter xxviii, 11 August 1711 (25 August), p. 230; and, from the second ellipsis, Letter xxiii, 12 May 1711 (23 May), p. 181.

31 – *Works*, vol. xvii, Swift to Rev. Mr Worrall, p. 42 (in the famous letter of 15 July 1726 in which he says, p. 43: 'I am determined not to go to Ireland, to find her just dead, or dying.').

32 – *Journal*, Letter viii, 31 October 1710 (8 November), p. 48.

33 – Esther Vanhomrigh (1689/90–1723) whom Swift first met in 1708 and for whom he wrote the poem, 'Cadenus and Vanessa' (1713).

34 – *Journal*, Letter xvii, 24 February 1710–11 (26 February), p. 128, which has: 'You say they are of no consequence; why, they keep . . .'

35 – *Works*, vol. xix, Swift to Esther Vanhomrigh, n.d., pp. 318–19: 'I long to drink a dish of coffee in the sluttery, and hear you dun me for Secrete, and "Drink your coffee. – Why don't you drink your coffee?"'

36 – *Ibid.*, Esther Vanhomrigh to Swift, 1714, p. 344.

37 – *Ibid.*

38 – See Stephen, *Swift*, ch. vi, p. 136: 'He rode in a fury to Celbridge. His countenance, says Orrery, could be terribly expressive of the sterner passions. Prominent eyes –"azure as the heavens" (says Pope) . . . Vanessa had spoken of the "something awful in his looks," and of his killing words. He now entered her room, silent with rage, threw down her letter on the table and rode off. He had struck Vanessa's death-blow.' VW visited Celbridge on 7 May 1934: see *IV VW Diary*.

39 – *Works*, vol. xix, Esther Vanhomrigh to Swift, 1714, p. 345, which has: 'I am sure I could have born the rack much better than those killing, killing words of yours.'

40 – *Ibid.*, vol. ix, 'On the Death of Mrs Johnson [Stella]', p. 281.

41 – Stephen, *Swift*, ch. ix, p. 208: 'he was heard to mutter, "I am what I am; I am what I am."'

The 'Sentimental Journey'

Tristram Shandy, though it is Sterne's first novel, was written at a time when many have written their twentieth, that is, when he was forty-five years old. But it bears every sign of maturity. No young writer could have dared to take such liberties with grammar and syntax and sense and propriety and the long-standing tradition of how a novel should be written. It needed a strong dose of the assurance of middle age and its indifference to censure to run such risks of shocking the lettered by the unconventionality of one's style, and the respectable by the irregularity of one's morals. But the risk was run and the success was prodigious. All the great, all the fastidious, were enchanted. Sterne became the idol of the town. Only in the roar[a] of laughter and applause which greeted the book, the voice of the simple-minded public at large was to be heard protesting that it was a scandal coming from a clergyman and that the Archbishop of York ought to administer, to say the least of it, a scolding. The Archbishop, it seems, did nothing. But Sterne, however little he let it show on the surface, laid the criticism to heart. That heart too had been afflicted since the publication of *Tristram Shandy*.[2] Eliza Draper, the object of his passion, had[b] sailed to join her husband in Bombay.[3] In his next book Sterne was determined to give effect to the change that had come over him, and to prove, not only the brilliance of his wit, but the depths of his sensibility. In his own words, 'my design in it was to teach us to love the world and our fellow creatures better than we do'.[4] It was with such motives animating him that he sat down to write that narrative of a little tour in France which he called *A Sentimental Journey*.

But if it were possible for Sterne to correct his manners, it was impossible for him to correct his style. That had become as much a part of himself as his large[c] nose or his brilliant eyes. With the first words – They order, said I, this matter better in France – we are in the world of *Tristram Shandy*. It is a world in which anything may happen. We hardly know what jest, what jibe, what flash of poetry is not going to glance suddenly through the gap which this astonishingly agile pen has cut in the thick-set hedge of English prose. Is Sterne himself responsible? Does he know what he is going to say next for all his resolve to be on his best behaviour this time? The jerky, disconnected sentences are as rapid and it would seem as little under control as the phrases that fall from the lips of a brilliant talker. The very punctuation is that of speech, not writing, and brings the sound and associations[d] of the speaking voice in with it. The order of the ideas, their suddenness and irrelevancy, is more true to life than to literature. There is a privacy in this intercourse which allows things to slip out unreproved that[e] would have been in doubtful taste had they been spoken in public. Under the influence of this extraordinary style the book becomes semi-transparent. The usual ceremonies and conventions which keep reader and writer at arm's length disappear. We are as close to life as we can be.

That Sterne achieved this illusion only by the use of extreme art and extraordinary pains is obvious without going to his manuscript to prove it. For[f] though the writer is always haunted by the belief that somehow it must be possible to brush aside the ceremonies and conventions of writing and to speak to the reader as directly as by word of mouth, anyone who has tried the experiment has either been struck dumb by the difficulty, or waylaid into disorder and diffusity unutterable. Sterne somehow brought off the astonishing combination. No writing seems to flow more exactly into the very folds and creases of the individual mind, to express its changing moods, to answer its lightest whim and impulse, and yet the result is perfectly precise and composed. The utmost fluidity exists with the utmost permanence. It is as if the tide raced over the beach hither and thither and left every ripple and eddy cut on the sand in marble.

Nobody, of course, stood more in need of the liberty to be himself than Sterne. For[g] while there are writers whose gift is impersonal, so that a Tolstoy, for example, can create a character and leave us alone with it, Sterne must always be there in person to help us in our intercourse. Little[h] or nothing of *A Sentimental Journey* would be left if all that we call Sterne himself were extracted from it. He has no valuable information to give, no reasoned philosophy to impart. He left London, he tells us, 'with so much precipitation that it never enter'd my mind that we were at war with France'.[5] He has nothing to say of pictures or churches or the misery or well-being of the country-side. He was travelling in France indeed, but the road was often through his own mind, and his chief adventures were not with brigands and precipices but with the emotions of his own heart.

This change in the angle of vision was in itself a daring innovation. Hitherto, the traveller had observed certain laws of proportion and perspective. The Cathedral had always been a vast building in any book of travels and the man a little figure, properly diminutive, by its side. But Sterne was quite capable of omitting the Cathedral altogether. A girl with a green satin purse might be much more important than Notre-Dame. For[i] there is, he seems to hint, no universal scale of values. A girl may be more interesting than a cathedral; a dead donkey more instructive[j] than a living philosopher. It is all a question of one's point of view. Sterne's eyes were so adjusted that small things often bulked larger in them than big. The talk of a barber about the buckle of his wig told him more about the character of the French than the grandiloquence of her statesmen.

I think I can see the precise and distinguishing marks of national characters more in these nonsensical *minutiae*, than in the most important matters of state; where great men of all nations talk and stalk so much alike, that I would not give nine-pence to chuse amongst them.[6]

So too if one wishes to seize the essence of things as a sentimental traveller should, one should seek for it, not at broad noonday in large and open streets, but in an unobserved corner up a dark entry.[7] One should cultivate a kind of shorthand which renders the several turns of looks and limbs into plain words. It was an art that Sterne had long trained himself to practise.

For my own part, by long habitude, I do it so mechanically that when I walk the streets of London, I go translating all the way; and have more than once stood behind in the circle, where not three words have been said, and have brought off twenty different dialogues with me, which I could have fairly wrote down and swore to.[8]

It is thus that Sterne transfers our interest from the outer to the inner. It is no use going to the guide-book; we[k] must consult our own minds; only they can tell us what[l] is the comparative importance of a cathedral, of a donkey, and of a girl with a green satin purse. In this preference for the windings of his own mind to the guide-book and its hammered high road, Sterne is singularly of our own age. In this interest in silence rather than in speech Sterne is the forerunner of the moderns. And for these reasons he is on far more intimate terms with us to-day than his great contemporaries the Richardsons and the Fieldings.[9][m]

Yet there is a difference. For all his interest in psychology Sterne was far more nimble and less profound than[n] the masters of this somewhat sedentary school have since become. He is after all telling a story, pursuing a journey, however arbitrary and zigzag his methods. For all our divagations, we do make the distance between Calais and Modane[10][o] within the space of a very few pages. Interested as he was in the way[p] in which he saw things, the things themselves also interested him acutely. His choice is capricious and individual, but no realist could be more brilliantly successful in rendering the impression of the moment. A *Sentimental Journey* is a succession of portraits – the Monk, the lady, the Chevalier selling *pâtés*, the girl in the bookshop, La Fleur in his new breeches; – it is a succession of scenes. And though the flight of this erratic mind is as zigzag as a dragon-fly's, one cannot deny that this dragon-fly has some method in its flight, and chooses the flowers not at random but for some exquisite harmony or for some brilliant discord.[q] We laugh, cry, sneer, sympathise by turns. We change from one emotion to its opposite in the twinkling of an eye. This light attachment to the accepted reality,ʳ this neglect of the orderly sequence of narrative, allows Sterne almost the licence of a poet. He can express ideas which ordinary novelists would have to ignore in language which, even if the ordinary novelist could command it, would look intolerably outlandish upon his page.ˢ

I walked up gravely to the window in my dusty black coat, and looking through the glass saw all the world in yellow, blue, and green, running at the ring of pleasure. – The old with broken lances, and in helmets which had lost their vizards – the young in armour bright which shone like gold, beplumed with each gay feather of the east – all – all tilting at it like fascinated knights in tournaments of yore for fame and love.[11]

There are many passages of such pure poetry in Sterne. One can cut them out and read them apart from the text, and yet – for Sterne was a master of the art of contrast – they lie harmoniously side by side on the printed page. Hisᵗ freshness, his buoyancy, his perpetual power to surprise and startle are the result of these contrasts. He leads us to the very brink of some deep precipice of the soul; weᵘ snatch one short glance into its depths; next moment, we are whisked round to look at the green pastures glowing on the other side.

If Sterne distresses us, it is for another reason. And here the blame rests partly at least upon the public – the public which had been shocked, which had cried out after the publication of *Tristram Shandy* that the writer was a cynic who deserved to be unfrocked. Sterne, unfortunately, thought it necessary to reply.

The world has imagined [he told Lord Shelburne] because I wrote *Tristram Shandy*, that I was myself more Shandean than I really ever was. . . . If it (*A Sentimental Journey*) is not thought a chaste book, mercy on them that read it, for they must have warm imaginations, indeed![12]

Thus in *A Sentimental Journey* we are never allowed to forget that Sterne is above all things sensitive, sympathetic, humane; that above all things he prizes the decencies, the simplicities of the human heart. And directly a writer sets out to prove himself this or that our suspicions are aroused. For the little extra stress he lays on the quality he desires us to see in him, coarsens it and over-paintsᵛ it, so that instead of humour, we get farce, and instead of sentiment, sentimentality. Here, instead of being convinced of the tenderness of Sterne's heart – which in *Tristram Shandy* was never in question – we begin to doubt it. For we feel that Sterne is thinking not of the thing itself but of its effect upon our opinion of him. The[w] beggars gather round him and he gives the *pauvre honteux* more than he had meant to. But his mind is not solely and simply on the beggars; his mind is partly on[x] us, to see that we appreciate his goodness. Thus his conclusion, 'and I thought he thank'd me more than them all',[13] placed, for more emphasis, at the end of the chapter, sickens us with its sweetness like[y] the drop of pure sugar at the bottom of a cup. Indeed, the chief fault of *A Sentimental Journey* comes from Sterne's concern for our good opinion of his heart. It has a monotony about it, for all its brilliance, as if the author had reined in the natural variety and vivacity of his tastes, lest they should give offence. The mood is subdued to one that is too uniformly kind, tender, and compassionate to be quite natural. One misses the variety, the vigour, the ribaldry of *Tristram Shandy*. His concern for his sensibility has blunted his natural sharpness, and we are called upon to gaze rather too[z] long at modesty, simplicity, and virtue standing rather too still to be looked at.

But it is significant of the change of taste that has come over us that it is Sterne's sentimentality that offends us and not his immorality. In the eyes of the nineteenth century all that Sterne wrote was clouded[aa] by his conduct as husband and lover. Thackeray lashed him with his righteous indignation, and exclaimed that 'There is not a page of Sterne's writing but has something that were better away, a latent corruption – a hint as of an impure presence'.[14] To us at the present time, the arrogance of the Victorian novelist seems at least as culpable as the infidelities of the eighteenth-century parson. Where the Victorians deplored[bb] his lies and his levities, the courage which turned all the rubs of life to laughter and the brilliance of the expression are far more apparent now.[cc]

Indeed *A Sentimental Journey*, for all its levity and wit, is based upon something fundamentally philosophic. It is true that it is a philosophy that was much out of fashion in the Victorian age – the philosophy of pleasure; the philosophy which holds that it is as[dd] necessary to behave well in small things as in big, which makes the enjoyment, even of other people, seem more desirable than their suffering. The shameless man had the hardihood to confess to 'having been in love with one princess or another almost all my life', and to add, 'and I hope I shall go on so till I die, being firmly persuaded that if ever I do a mean action, it must be in some interval betwixt one passion and another'.[15] The wretch had the audacity to cry through the mouth of one of his characters, 'Mais vive la joie . . . Vive l'amour! et vive la bagatelle!'[16] Clergyman though he was, he had the irreverence to reflect, when he watched the French peasants dancing, that he could distinguish an elevation of spirit, different from that which is the cause or the effect of simple jollity. – 'In a word, I thought I beheld *Religion* mixing in the dance.'[17]

It was a daring thing for a clergyman to perceive a relationship[ee] between religion and pleasure. Yet it may, perhaps, excuse him that in his own case the religion of happiness had a[ff] great deal of difficulty to overcome. If you are no longer young, if you are deeply in debt, if your wife is disagreeable, if, as you racket about France in a post-chaise, you are dying of consumption all the time, then[gg] the pursuit of happiness is not so easy after all. Still, pursue it one must. One must pirouette about the world, peeping and peering, enjoying a flirtation here, bestowing a few coppers there, and sitting in whatever little patch of sunshine one can find. One must crack a joke, even if the joke is not altogether a decent one. Even in daily life one must not forget to cry 'Hail ye, small, sweet courtesies of life, for smooth do ye make the road of it!'[18] One must – but enough of must; it is not a word that Sterne was fond of using. It is only when one lays the book aside and recalls its symmetry, its fun, its whole-hearted joy in all the different aspects of life, and the brilliant ease and beauty with which they are conveyed to us, that one credits the writer with a backbone of conviction to support him. Was not Thackeray's coward[19] – the man who trifled so immorally with so many women and wrote love-letters on gilt-edged paper when he should have been lying on a sick-bed or writing sermons – was he not a stoic in his own way and a moralist, and a teacher? Most great writers are, after all. And that Sterne was[hh] a very great writer we cannot doubt.

a – NYHT and WC (World's Classics): 'babble'.
b – NYHT: 'little it showed on the surface laid . . . too, had been chastened after the publication of *Tristram Shandy* by a passionate love affair with Eliza Draper. The lady had'.
c – NYHT: 'long'.
d – NYHT and WC: 'sound, the associations,'.
e – NYHT: 'which'.
f – NYHT: 'it, for'.
g – NYHT: 'Sterne, for'.
h – NYHT and WC: 'character which has no shred of his own personality attached to it, Sterne's gift always includes a large part of himself. Little'.

i – *NYHT*: 'Notre Dame, for'.

j – *NYHT*: 'interesting'.

k – *NYHT*: 'guidebook he assures us; we'.

l – *NYHT* and *WC*: 'minds before we can say what'.

m – *NYHT*: 'And he is . . . contemporaries.'

n – *NYHT* and *WC*: 'nimble than'.

o – *NYHT*: 'Mondane'. *WC*: 'Madane'.

p – *NYHT*: 'ways'.

q – *NYHT*: 'is zigzag, like a dragonfly's, . . . dragonfly . . . flowers for their exquisite harmonies or for their brilliant discords.' *WC* follows *NYHT*, but has: 'flowers not haphazard but for'.

r – *NYHT*: 'eye. Moreover, this light attachment to reality,'. *WC*: 'eye. This light attachment to reality,'.

s – *NYHT*: 'page. For example:'. *WC*: 'page. For example,'.

t – *NYHT*: 'by side upon the page with the rest. His'.

u – *NYHT* and *WC*: 'of the precipice; we'.

v – *NYHT*: 'coarsens it and overpaints'. *WC*: 'coarsens, over-paints'.

w – *NYHT* and *WC*: 'is thinking of himself. The'.

x – *NYHT*: 'not on the beggars; his mind is on'.

y – *NYHT*: 'us like'.

z – *NYHT* and *WC*: 'gaze a moment too'.

aa – *NYHT* and *WC*: 'coloured'.

bb – *NYHT* and *WC*: 'the great Victorians seems . . . Where they deplored'.

cc – *NYHT*: 'laughter is more apparent to us.'

dd – *NYHT* and *WC*: 'which makes it seem as'.

ee – *NYHT*: 'perceive relationship'.

ff – *NYHT*: 'that the religion of happiness had in his own case a'.

gg – *NYHT*: 'young, if you have spent more than you should have done, if your wife is disagreeable, and though you like your daughter, she is parted from you, if as you racket . . . are fast dying of consumption, then'. *WC* follows *NYHT*, but has: 'you are dying of consumption all the time,'.

hh – *NYHT* and *WC*: 'lying in bed or . . . not something of a stoic in his own way? That he was'.

1 – A signed essay (entitled 'A Sentimental Journey') in the *NYHT*, 23 September 1928, (*Kp4* C303); revised as the Introduction to the Oxford University Press edition of the novel, which was published on 1 November 1928 as no. cccxxxiii in the World's Classics series, (*Kp4* B7); and further revised for *CR2*. Humphrey Milford, manager of OUP in London, wrote to VW on 6 January 1928, asking for a 'recommendatory introduction for the "common reader"' to be published in the World's Classics edition of Laurence Sterne's (1713–68) *A Sentimental Journey through France and Italy* (1768). VW agreed in principle on 11 January, with the intention of 'publishing it

in America before it came out in book form'. On 7 July 1928 she wanted 'to stay & write about Sterne' (*III VW Diary*). She submitted the typescript to OUP on 31 July. Milford agreed to VW's publishing the article in the *NYHT* on 9 September, with the proviso that the *NYHT* made it clear that it would shortly 'appear as an introduction to a reprint of the book in the World's Classics'. It was published with the requisite note. VW's uncollected letters to Milford are printed in *VWB*, no. 10 (May 2002), pp. 4–6. She received £15 for the Introduction and another £10 in January 1934 (WSU), possibly for the 1935 reprint. The *TLS*'s reviewer stated that the 'introducer was happily chosen' (10 January 1929, p. 25), while Augustine Birrell referred to the 'admirable introduction by Mrs. Virginia Woolf' (*N&A*, 2 March 1929, p. 754). See 'Sterne', *I VW Essays*, and its reading notes (Berg, M 22) (*VWRN XXIX*): *A Sentimental Journey* 'has some advantages over T. S. [*Tristram Shandy*] inasmuch as the story runs straight on. But there is [not?] nearly so much vigour or wit. The sensibility is insisted upon overmuch. However, it is perhaps more perfect in respect of style. The scenes are exquisitely finished – light yet perfectly distinct. There is some cause, I think, to dislike him occasionally: a kind of hypocrisy. But very gay on the whole, wonderfully sensitive.' See also 'Eliza and Sterne', *III VW Essays*; and 'Sterne's Ghost', *IV VW Essays*. Reading notes (Berg, RN 1.25) and (MHP, B 2n) (*VWRN XXV and XLVI*). Reprinted: *CE*.

2 – *The Life and Opinions of Tristram Shandy* (1759–67).

3 – Mrs Eliza Draper (1744–78), wife of Daniel Draper of the East India Company, of *Journal to Eliza* fame.

4 – *Letters of Laurence Sterne* (Basil Blackwell for the Shakespeare Head Press, 1927), Letter to Mr and Mrs William James, postscript, 12 November 1767, p. 174.

5 – *The Novels of Laurence Sterne: 'The Life and Opinions of Tristram Shandy, Gent.' and 'A Sentimental Journey through France and Italy'* (George Newnes; and Charles Scribner's Sons, 1905), *A Sentimental Journey*, vol. ii, 'The Passport, Paris', p. 668.

6 – *Ibid.*, vol. i, 'The Wig, Paris', p. 651.

7 – See *ibid.*, vol. ii, 'The Act of Charity, Paris', p. 707: 'The man who either disdains or fears to walk up a dark entry, may be an excellent good man, and fit for a hundred things; but he will not do to make a good sentimental traveller.'

8 – *Ibid.*, vol. i, 'The Translation, Paris', p. 658, which has: 'I do translating'.

9 – Samuel Richardson (1689–1761); Henry Fielding (1707–54).

10 – Modane (see n. 0 above), near the Italian border on the road from Lyons, is the modern name; Sterne calls it Madane in *A Sentimental Journey*, vol. ii, 'The Case of Delicacy', p. 721.

11 – *Ibid.*, vol. i, 'Paris', p. 650.

12 – *Letters*, Letter to the Earl of Shelburne, 28 November 1767, pp. 176–7.

13 – *A Sentimental Journey*, vol. i, 'Montriul', conclusion, p. 639. The same passage is quoted in 'Sterne', *I VW Essays*.

14 – William Makepeace Thackeray, 'Sterne and Goldsmith', *The Four Georges. The English Humourists of the Eighteenth Century*, The Works of William Makepeace Thackeray (Smith, Elder, 1869), vol. xix, p. 341.

15 – *A Sentimental Journey*, vol. i, 'Montriul', p. 636.

16 – *Ibid.*, 'The Letter' (to Madame de L***), p. 649.

17 – *Ibid.*, vol. ii, 'The Grace', p. 720.

18 – *Ibid.*, vol. i, 'The Pulse, Paris', p. 652.

19 – See 'Sterne and Goldsmith', p. 334.

Lord Chesterfield's Letters to his Son

When Lord Mahon edited the letters of Lord Chesterfield he thought it necessary to warn the intending reader that they are 'by no means fitted for early or indiscriminate perusal'. Only 'those people whose understandings are fixed and whose principles are matured' can, so his Lordship said, read them with impunity.[2] But that was in 1845. And 1845 looks a little distant now.[a] It seems to us now the age of enormous houses without any bathrooms. Men smoke in the kitchen after the cook has gone to bed. Albums lie upon drawing-room tables. The curtains are very thick and the women are very pure. But the eighteenth century also has undergone a change. To us in 1930 it looks less strange, less remote than those early Victorian years. Its civilisation seems more rational and more complete than the civilisation of Lord Mahon and his contemporaries. Then at any rate a small group of highly educated people lived up to their ideals. If the world was smaller it was also more compact; it knew its own mind; it had its own standards. Its poetry is affected by the same security. When we read the *Rape of the Lock*[3] we seem to find ourselves in an age so settled and so circumscribed that masterpieces were possible. Then, we say to ourselves, a poet could address himself whole-heartedly to his task and keep his mind upon it, so that the little boxes on a lady's dressing-table are fixed among the solid possessions of our imaginations. A game at cards or a summer's boating party upon the Thames has power to suggest the same beauty and the same sense of things vanishing that we receive from poems aimed directly at our deepest emotions. And just as the poet could spend all his powers upon a pair of scissors and a lock of hair, so too, secure in his world and its values, the aristocrat could lay down precise laws for the education of his son. In that world also there was a certainty, a security that we are now without. What with one thing and another times have changed. We can now read Lord Chesterfield's letters without blushing, or, if we do blush, we blush in the twentieth century at passages that caused Lord Mahon no discomfort whatever.

When the letters begin, Philip Stanhope, Lord Chesterfield's natural son by a Dutch governess, was a little boy of seven.[4] And if we are to make any complaint against the father's moral teaching, it is that the standard is too high for such tender years. 'Let us return to oratory, or the art of speaking well; which should never be entirely out of our thoughts', he writes to the boy of seven. 'A man can make no figure without it in Parliament, or the Church, or in the law',[5] he continues, as if the little boy were already considering his career. It seems, indeed, that the father's fault, if fault it be, is one common to distinguished men who have not themselves succeeded as they should have done and are determined to give their children – and Philip was an only child – the chances that they have lacked. Indeed, as the letters go on one may suppose that Lord Chesterfield wrote as much to amuse himself by turning over the stores of his experience, his reading, his knowledge of the world, as to instruct his son. The letters show an eagerness, an animation, which prove that to write to Philip was not a task, but a delight. Tired, perhaps, with the duties of office and disillusioned with its disappointments, he takes up his pen and, in the relief of free communication at last, forgets that his correspondent is, after all, only a schoolboy who cannot understand half the things that his father says to him. But, even so, there is nothing to repel us in Lord Chesterfield's preliminary sketch of the unknown world. He is all on the side of moderation, toleration, ratiocination. Never abuse whole bodies of people, he counsels; frequent all churches, laugh at none; inform yourself about all things. Devote your mornings to study, your evenings to good society. Dress as the best people dress, behave as they behave, never be eccentric, egotistical, or absent-minded. Observe the laws of proportion, and live every moment to the full.[b]

So, step by step, he builds up the figure of the perfect man – the man that Philip may become, he is persuaded, if he will only – and here Lord Chesterfield lets fall the words which are[c] to colour his teaching through and through – cultivate the Graces. These ladies are, at first, kept discreetly in the background. It is well that the boy should be indulged in fine sentiments about women and poets to begin with. Lord Chesterfield adjures him to respect them both. 'For my own part, I used to think myself in company as much above me when I was with Mr. Addison and Mr. Pope, as if I had been with all the Princes in Europe',[6] he writes. But as time goes on the Virtues are more and more taken for granted.[d] They can be left to take care of themselves. But the Graces assume tremendous proportions. The Graces dominate the life of man in this world. Their service[e] cannot for an instant be neglected. And the service is certainly exacting. For consider what it implies, this art of pleasing. To begin with, one must know how to come into a room and then how to go out again. As human arms and legs are notoriously perverse, this by itself is a matter needing[f] considerable dexterity. Then one must be dressed so that one's clothes seem perfectly fashionable without being new or striking; one's teeth must be perfect; one's wig beyond reproach; one's fingernails cut in the segment of a circle; one must be able to carve, able to dance, and, what is almost as great an art, able to sit gracefully in a chair. These things are the alphabet of the art of pleasing. We now come to speech. It is necessary to speak at least three languages to perfection. But before we open our lips we must take a further precaution – we must be[g] on our guard never to laugh. Lord Chesterfield himself never laughed. He always smiled. When at length the young man is pronounced capable of speech he[h] must avoid all proverbs and vulgar expressions; he must enunciate clearly and use perfect grammar; he must not argue; he must not tell stories; he must not talk about himself. Then, at last, the young man may begin to practise the finest of the arts of pleasing – the art of flattery. For every man and every woman has some prevailing vanity. Watch, wait, pry, seek out their weakness, 'and you will then know what to bait your hook with to catch them'.[7] For that is the secret of success in[i] the world.

It is at this point, such is the idiosyncrasy of our age, that we begin to feel uneasy. Lord Chesterfield's views upon success are far more questionable than his views upon love. For[j] what is to be the prize of this endless effort and self-abnegation? What do we gain when we have learnt to come into rooms and to go out again; to pry into people's secrets; to hold our tongues and to flatter, to[k] forsake the society of low-born people which corrupts and the society of clever people which perverts? What is the prize which is to reward us? It is simply that we shall rise in the world. Press for a further defin- ition, and it amounts perhaps to this: one will be popular with the best people. But if we are so exacting as to demand who the best people are we become involved in a labyrinth from which there is no returning. Nothing exists in itself. What is good society? It is the society that the best people believe to be good. What is wit? It is what the best people think to be witty. All value depends upon somebody else's[l] opinion. For it is the essence of this philosophy that things have no independent existence, but live only in the eyes of other people. It is a looking-glass world, this, to which we climb so slowly; and its prizes are all reflections. That may account for our baffled feeling as we shuffle, and shuffle vainly, among these urbane pages for something hard to lay our hands upon. Hardness is the last thing we shall find. But, granted the deficiency, how much that is ignored by sterner moralists is here seized upon, and who shall deny, at least while Lord Chesterfield's enchantment is upon him, that these imponderable qualities have their value and these shining Graces have their radiance? Consider for a moment what the Graces have done for their devoted servant, the Earl.

Here is a disillusioned politician, who is prematurely aged, who has lost his office, who is losing his teeth, who, worst fate of all, is growing deafer day by day. Yet he never allows a groan to escape him. He is never dull; he is never boring; he is never slovenly. His mind is as well groomed as his body. Never for a second does he 'welter in an easy-chair'.[8] Private though these letters are, and apparently spontaneous, they play with such ease in and about the single subject which absorbs them that it never becomes tedious or, what is still more remarkable, never becomes ridiculous. It may be that the art of pleasing has some connection with the art of writing. To be polite, considerate, controlled, to sink one's egotism,[m] to conceal rather than to obtrude one's personality, may profit the writer even as they profit the man of fashion.

Certainly there is much to be said in favour of the training, however we define it, which helped Lord Chesterfield to write his Characters. The little papers have the precision and formality of some old-fashioned minuet. Yet the symmetry is so natural to the artist that he can break it where he likes; it never becomes pinched and formal, as it would in the hands of an imitator. He can be sly; he can be witty; he can be sententious, but never for an instant does he lose his sense of time, and when the tune is over he calls a halt. 'Some succeeded, and others burst'[9] he says of George the First's mistresses: the King liked them fat. Again, 'He was fixed in the house of lords, that hospital of incurables.'[10] He smiles: he does not laugh. Here[n] the eighteenth century, of course, came to his help. Lord Chesterfield, though he was polite to everything, even to the stars and Bishop Berkeley's philosophy,[11] firmly refused, as became a son of his age, to dally with infinity or to suppose that things are not quite as solid as they seem. The world was good enough and the world was big enough as it was. This prosaic temper, while it keeps him within° the bounds of impeccable common sense, limits his outlook. No single phrase of his reverberates or penetrates as so many of La Bruyère's do.[12] But he would have been the first to deprecate any comparison with that great writer; besides, to write as La Bruyère wrote, one must perhaps believe in something, and then how difficult to observe the Graces! One might perhaps laugh; one might perhaps cry. Both are equally deplorable.

But° while we amuse ourselves with this brilliant nobleman and his views on life° we are aware, and the letters owe much of their fascination to this consciousness, of a dumb yet substantial figure on the farther° side of the page. Philip Stanhope is always there. It is true that he says nothing, but we feel his presence in Dresden, in Berlin, in Paris, opening the letters and poring over them and looking dolefully at the thick packets which have been accumulating year after year since he was a child of seven. He had grown into a rather serious, rather stout, rather short young man. He had a taste for foreign politics. A little serious reading was rather to his liking. And by every post the letters came – urbane,° polished, brilliant, imploring and commanding him to learn to dance, to learn to carve, to consider the management of his legs, and to seduce a lady of fashion. He did his best. He worked very hard in the school of the Graces,° but their service was too exacting. He sat down half-way up the steep stairs which lead to the glittering hall with all the mirrors. He could not do it. He failed in the House of Commons; he subsided into some small post in Ratisbon; he died untimely. He left it to his widow to break the news which he had lacked the heart or the courage° to tell his father – that he had been married all these years to a lady of low birth, who had borne him children.[13]

The Earl took the blow like a gentleman. His letter to his daughter-in-law is a model of urbanity. He began the education of his grandsons. But he seems to have become a little indifferent to what happened to himself after° that. He did not care greatly if he lived or died. But still to the very end he cared for the Graces. His last words were a tribute of respect to those goddesses. Someone° came into the room when he was dying; he roused himself: 'Give Dayrolles a chair,'[14] he said, and said no more.[x]

a – *TLS* concludes this paragraph: 'looks a little faded now. We envisage a house without a bathroom, where men smoke in the kitchen after the cook has gone to bed, and albums lie on the table, and curtains are very thick, and women are very pure. Naturally, in those days they could not read Lord Chesterfield's letters without blushing; but times are changed, and Mr Whibley induces us to try.' *NR* follows *TLS*, but has: 'times have changed'.

b – *NR*: 'full. There is even something Greek about it.'

c – *NR*: 'the word which is'.

d – *TLS* and *NR*: 'granted. One need say nothing about morality or religion.'

e – *NR*: 'services'.

f – *TLS*: 'out again, which, considering the perversity of human arms and legs is a matter of considerable'. *NR* follows *TLS*, but has: 'of the human'.

g – *TLS* and *NR*: 'lips we must be'.

h – *TLS* and *NR*: 'man speaks he'.

i – *NR*: 'them". And if you succeed, you will rise in'.

j – *TLS* and *NR*: 'At this point, if it were our part to warn the reader, we should add an expostulatory note as Lord Mahon does when the Earl airs his views on love. We should, at least, beg the reader to have his wits about him. For'.

k – *TLS* and *NR*: 'flatter and to'.

l – *NR*: 'upon the somebodies else's'.

m – *NR*: 'egotisms'.

n – *TLS* and *NR*: 'halt. Here'.

o – *NR*: 'keeps within'.

p – *TLS* and *NR*: 'Cry. ¶ But'.

q – *NR*: 'views of life,'.

r – *NR*: 'further'.

s – *NR*: 'letters come, urbane'.

t – *NR*: 'hard at the Graces;'.

u – *NR*: 'lacked heart or courage'.

v – *NR*: 'indifferent to what became of him after'.

w – *NR*: 'respect to them.'

x – *TLS* and *NR*: 'Some one came . . . dying, and with his last breath he roused himself to order a chair.'

1 – An unsigned essay (entitled 'An English Aristocrat') in the *TLS*, 8 March 1928, and (signed, with variants, as 'Lord Chesterfield and the Graces') in the *NR*, 21 March 1928, (*Kp4* C298), as a review of *The Characters of Lord Chesterfield* [1694–1773], ed. Charles Whibley (Little Books series, Peter Davies, 1927). It is likely that the *NR* version predates the *TLS* version. Herbert Croly,

the editor of the *NR*, wrote to VW on 29 February: 'You had in Lord Chesterfield's Letters a rare opportunity for a nicely balanced and nicely etched portrait, and, as we all think here, you have done it in a way that has delighted everybody in this office – that is, particularly, delighted us that we are to have the opportunity of publishing it' (MHP, III, Box 78). The essay was further revised for *CR2*. VW used Lord Mahon's five-volume edition of the *Letters* . . . (Lippincott, 1892), but the references below are to *The Letters of Philip Dormer Stanhope, Earl of Chesterfield* . . ., ed. Lord Mahon (Richard Bentley, 4 vols, 1845, vol. 5, 1853). On 20 December 1927 VW wrote: 'I should be reading . . . Lord Chesterfield's letters . . . I am still writing the 3rd Chap. of Orlando . . . I have just been thinking over the scene when O. meets a girl (Nell) in the Park' (*III VW Diary*; see *O Holograph*, 169, 173 *et seq.*). On 28 December 1927: 'I am trying to write about Lord Chesterfield and de Quincey' (*III VW Letters*, no. 1843). On 18 February 1928: 'I should be revising Lord Chesterfield at this moment, but I'm not' (*III VW Diary*). In *O* VW quotes Lord Chesterfield slightly inaccurately: 'Women are but children of a larger growth . . . A man of sense only trifles with them, plays with them, humours and flatters them' (*O*, p. 193, and see also pp. 198, 260; see *The Letters*, vol. i, 5 September OS [Old Style] 1748, p. 181). See also Leslie Stephen's essay, 'Lord Chesterfield' (*Cornhill Magazine*, vol. xxiv [1871], pp. 86–101), no. 2 in his series, 'Hours in a Library'. Reading notes (Berg, RN 1.14) and (MHP, B 2n and B 2p) (*VWRN XIV, XLVI* and *XLVIII*). Reprinted: *CE*.

2 – See Lord Mahon's Preface, *The Letters*, vol. i, p. xxx: 'they are yet by no means fitted for early or indiscriminate perusal. Only those persons whose principles are fixed, and whose understandings are matured, will be able to read them with advantage . . . without the danger of imbibing their laxity of morals . . .'

3 – Alexander Pope's (1688–1744) mock-heroic *Rape of the Lock* appeared in 1712 and in an enlarged form in 1714. VW's draft review, 'Tchekhov on Pope' (1925), of a new edition of the poem appears not to have been published: see *Kp4 Cb28* and *VI VW Essays*, Appendix.

4 – Philip Stanhope 1731–68.

5 – *The Letters*, vol. i, 1 November 1739, p. 4, which has: 'Oratory . . . your thoughts . . . Parliament, in the Church, or in the Law'.

6 – *Ibid.*, vol. i, 9 October OS 1747, p. 80.

7 – *Ibid.*, vol. i, 5 September OS 1748, p. 179.

8 – There are several references in *The Letters* to this sin, including one critical of those 'too negligent and easy' who *'se vautrent dans leur fauteuil'* (vol. ii, 10 June OS 1751, p. 158); see also 'welter in an easy chair', vol. ii, 13 June OS 1751, p. 162, and 25 December 1753, p. 345.

9 – 'The Mistresses of George the First' in 'Lord Chesterfield's Characters', *The Letters*, vol. iii, p. 439 (and *Characters*, p. 13): 'These standards of his Majesty's taste made all those ladies who aspired to his favour, and who were

near the Statutable size, strain and swell themselves, like the frogs in the fable, to rival the bulk and dignity of the ox. Some succeeded, and others burst.'
10 – Mr Pulteney in 'Lord Chesterfield's Characters', *The Letters*, vol. ii, p. 453 (*Characters*, p. 35).
11 – George Berkeley (1685–1753), Irish churchman and philosopher, who held that the reality of anything depended on its being perceived by a conscious mind. VW read him in 1920: see *II VW Diary*, pp. 32, 33, 36, 49. Shelmerdine 'has just read Bishop Berkeley's philosophy for the tenth time' (*O*, p. 233).
12 – Jean de La Bruyère (1645–96), satiric moralist, wrote *Les Caractères ou les moeurs de ce siècle* (1688). VW quotes him in *Room*, ch. ii, p. 44.
13 – Philip Stanhope left a widow, Eugenia, and two sons.
14 – These very famous last words were said to his Lordship's intimate friend and godson, Solomon Dayrolles (d. 1786) (*The Letters*, Preface, vol. i, p. xxiii).

Two Parsons

I

James Woodforde

One could wish that the psycho-analysts would go into the question of diary-keeping. For often it is the one mysterious fact in a life otherwise as clear as the sky and as candid as the dawn. Parson Woodforde is a case in point – his diary is the only mystery about him. For forty-three years he sat down almost daily to record what he did on Monday and what he had for dinner on Tuesday; but for whom he wrote or why he wrote it is impossible to say. He does not unburden his soul in his diary; yet it is no mere record of engagements and expenses. As for literary fame, there is no sign that he ever thought of it, and finally, though the man himself is peaceable above all things, there are little indiscretions and criticisms which would have got him into trouble and hurt the feelings of his friends had they read them. What purpose, then, did the sixty-eight little books fulfil? Perhaps it was the desire for intimacy. When James Woodforde opened one of his neat manuscript books he entered into conversation with a second

James Woodforde, who was not quite the same as the reverend gentleman who visited the poor and preached in the church. These two friends said much that all the world might hear; but they had a few secrets which they shared with each other only. It was a great comfort, for example, that Christmas when Nancy, Betsy, and Mr Walker seemed to be in conspiracy against him, to exclaim in the diary, 'The treatment I meet with for my Civility this Christmas is to me abominable'.[2] The second James Woodforde sympathised and agreed. Again, when a stranger abused his hospitality it was a relief to inform the other self who lived in the little book that he had put him to sleep in the attic story, 'and I treated him as one that would be too free if treated kindly'.[3] It is easy to understand why, in the quiet life of a country parish, these two bachelor friends became in time inseparable. An essential part of him would have died had he been forbidden to keep his diary. When indeed he thought himself in the grip of death he still wrote on and on. And as we read – if reading is the word for it – we seem to be listening to someone who is murmuring over the events of the day to himself in the quiet space which precedes sleep. It is not writing, and, to speak the truth, it is not reading. It is slipping through half a dozen pages and strolling to the window and looking out. It is going on thinking about the Woodfordes while we watch the people in the street below. It is taking a walk and making up the life and character of James Woodforde as we go. It is not reading any more than it is writing – what to call it we scarcely know.

James Woodforde, then, was one of those smooth-cheeked, steady-eyed men, demure to look at, whom we can never imagine except in the prime of life. He was of an equable temper, with only such acerbities and touchinesses as are generally to be found in those who have had a love affair in their youth and remained, as they fancy, unwed because of it. The Parson's love affair, however, was nothing very tremendous. Once when he was a young man in Somerset he liked to walk over to Shepton and to visit a certain 'sweet tempered' Betsy White who lived there. He had a great mind 'to make a bold stroke' and ask her to marry him. He went so far, indeed, as to propose marriage 'when opportunity served',[4] and Betsy was willing. But he delayed; time passed; four years passed indeed, and Betsy went to Devonshire, met a Mr Webster, who had five hundred pounds a year, and married him. When James Woodforde met them in the turnpike road he could say little, 'being shy', but to his diary he remarked –

and this no doubt was his private version of the affair ever after – 'she has proved herself to me a mere jilt'.[5]

But he was a young man then, and as time went on we cannot help suspecting that he was glad to consider the question of marriage shelved once and for all so that he might settle down with his niece Nancy at Weston Longueville, and give himself simply and solely, every day and all day, to the great business of living. Again, what else to call it we do not know.

For James Woodforde was nothing in particular. Life had it all her own way with him. He had no special gift; he had no oddity or infirmity. It is idle to pretend that he was a zealous priest. God in Heaven was much the same to him as King George upon the throne – a kindly Monarch, that is to say, whose festivals one kept by preaching a sermon on Sunday much as one kept the Royal birthday by firing a blunderbuss and drinking a toast at dinner. Should anything untoward happen, like the death of a boy who was dragged and killed by a horse, he would instantly, but rather perfunctorily, exclaim, 'I hope to God the Poor Boy is happy', and add, 'We all came home singing';[6] just as when Justice Creed's peacock spread its tail – 'and most noble it is' – he would exclaim, 'How wonderful are Thy Works O God in every Being'.[7] But there was no fanaticism, no enthusiasm, no lyric impulse about James Woodforde. In all these pages, indeed, each so neatly divided into compartments, and each of those again filled, as the days themselves were filled, quietly and fully in a hand steady as the pacing of a well-tempered nag, one can only call to mind a single poetic phrase about the transit of Venus. 'It appeared as a black patch upon a fair Lady's face',[8] he says. The words themselves are mild enough, but they hang over the undulating expanse of the Parson's prose with the resplendence of the star itself. So in the Fen country a barn or a tree appears twice its natural size against the surrounding flats. But what led him to this palpable excess that summer's night we cannot tell. It cannot have been that he was drunk. He spoke out too roundly against such failings in his brother Jack to be guilty himself. Temperamentally he was among the eaters of meat and not among the drinkers of wine. When we think of the Woodfordes, uncle and niece, we think of them as often as not waiting with some impatience for their dinner. Gravely they watch the joint as it is set upon the table; swiftly they get their knives to work upon the succulent leg or loin; without much comment, unless a word is passed about the gravy or the stuffing, they go on eating. So they munch, day after day, year in, year out, until between them they must have devoured herds of sheep and oxen, flocks of poultry, an odd dozen or so of swans and cygnets, bushels of apples and plums, while the pastries and the jellies crumble and squash beneath their spoons in mountains, in pyramids, in pagodas. Never was there a book so stuffed with food as this one is. To read the bill of fare respectfully and punctually set forth gives one a sense of repletion. Trout and chicken, mutton and peas, pork and apple sauce – so the joints succeed each other at dinner, and there is supper with more joints still to come, all, no doubt, home grown, and of the juiciest and sweetest; all cooked, often by the mistress herself, in the plainest English way, save when the dinner was at Weston Hall and Mrs Custance surprised them with a London dainty – a pyramid of jelly, that is to say, with a 'landscape appearing through it'.⁹ After dinner sometimes, Mrs Custance, for whom James Woodforde had a chivalrous devotion, would play the 'Sticcardo Pastorale', and make 'very soft music indeed';¹⁰ or would get out her work-box and show them how neatly contrived it was, unless indeed she were giving birth to another child upstairs. These infants the Parson would baptise and very frequently he would bury them. They died almost as frequently as they were born. The Parson had a deep respect for the Custances. They were all that country gentry should be – a little given to the habit of keeping mistresses, perhaps, but that peccadillo could be forgiven them in view of their generosity to the poor, the kindness they showed to Nancy, and their condescension in asking the Parson to dinner when they had great people staying with them. Yet great people were not much to James's liking. Deeply though he respected the nobility, 'one must confess', he said, 'that being with our equals is much more agreeable'.¹¹

Not only did Parson Woodforde know what was agreeable; that rare gift was by the bounty of Nature supplemented by another equally rare – he could have what he wanted. The age was propitious. Monday, Tuesday, Wednesday – they follow each other and each little compartment seems filled with content. The days were not crowded, but they were enviably varied. Fellow of New College though he was, he did things with his own hands, not merely with his own head. He lived in every room of the house – in the study he wrote sermons, in the dining-room he ate copiously; he cooked in the kitchen, he played cards in the parlour. And then he took his coat and stick and went coursing his greyhounds in the fields. Year in, year out, the provisioning of the house and its defence against the cold of winter and the drought of summer fell upon him. Like a general he surveyed the seasons and took steps to make his own little camp safe with coal and wood and beef and beer against the enemy. His day thus had to accommodate a jumble of incongruous occupations. There is religion to be served, and the pig to be killed; the sick to be visited and dinner to be eaten; the dead to be buried and beer to be brewed; Convocation to be attended and the cow to be bolused. Life and death, mortality and immortality, jostle in his pages and make a good mixed marriage of it: '. . . found the old gentleman almost at his last gasp. Totally senseless with rattlings in his Throat. Dinner to-day boiled beef and Rabbit rosted.'[12] All is as it should be; life is like that.

Surely, surely, then, here is one of the breathing-spaces in human affairs – here in Norfolk at the end of the eighteenth century at the Parsonage. For once man is content with his lot; harmony is achieved; his house fits him; a tree is a tree; a chair is a chair; each knows its office and fulfils it. Looking through the eyes of Parson Woodforde, the different lives of men seem orderly and settled. Far away guns roar; a King falls;[13] but the sound is not loud enough to scare the rooks here in Norfolk. The proportions of things are different. The Continent is so distant that it looks a mere blur; America scarcely exists; Australia is unknown. But a magnifying glass is laid upon the fields of Norfolk. Every blade of grass is visible there. We see every lane and every field; the ruts on the roads and the peasants' faces. Each house stands in its own breadth of meadow isolated and independent. No wires link village to village. No voices thread the air. The body also is more present and more real. It suffers more acutely. No anaesthetic deadens physical pain. The surgeon's knife hovers real and sharp above the limb. Cold strikes unmitigated upon the house. The milk freezes in the pans; the water is thick with ice in the basins. One can scarcely walk from one room to another in the Parsonage in winter. Poor men and women are frozen to death upon the roads.[14] Often no letters come and there are no visitors and no newspapers. The Parsonage stands alone in the midst of the frost-bound fields. At last, Heaven be praised, life circulates again; a man comes to the door with a Madagascar monkey; another brings a box containing a child with two distinct perfect heads; there is a rumour that a balloon is going to rise at Norwich. Every little incident stands out sharp and clear. The drive to Norwich even is something of an adventure. One must trundle every step of the way behind a horse. But look how distinct the trees stand in the hedges; how slowly the cattle move their heads as the carriage trots by; how gradually the spires of Norwich raise themselves above the hill. And then how clear-cut and familiar are the faces of the few people who are our friends – the Custances, Mr du Quesne. Friendship has time to solidify, to become a lasting, a valuable possession.

True, Nancy of the younger generation is visited now and then by a flighty notion that she is missing something, that she wants something. One day she complained to her uncle that life was very dull: she complained 'of the dismal situation of my house, nothing to be seen, and little or no visiting or being visited, &c.',[15] and made him very uneasy. We could read Nancy a little lecture upon the folly of wanting that 'et cetera'. Look what your 'et cetera' has brought to pass, we might say; half the countries of Europe are bankrupt; there is a red line of villas on every green hill-side; your Norfolk roads are black as tar; there is no end to 'visiting or being visited'. But Nancy has an answer to make us, to the effect that our past is her present. You, she says, think it a great privilege to be born in the eighteenth century, because one called cowslips pagles and rode in a curricle instead of driving in a car. But you are utterly wrong, you fanatical lovers of memoirs, she goes on. I can assure you, my life was often intolerably dull. I did not laugh at the things that make you laugh. It did not amuse me when my uncle dreamt of a hat or saw bubbles in the beer, and said that meant a death in the family; I thought so too. Betsy Davy mourned young Walker with all her heart in spite of dressing in sprigged paduasoy.[16] There is a great deal of humbug talked of the eighteenth century. Your delight in old times and old diaries is half impure. You make up something that never had any existence. Our sober reality is only a dream to you – so Nancy grieves and complains, living through the eighteenth century day by day, hour by hour.

Still, if it is a dream, let us indulge it a moment longer. Let us believe that some things last, and some places and some people are not touched by change. On a fine May morning, with the rooks rising and the hares scampering and the plover calling among the long grass, there is much to encourage the illusion. It is we who change and perish. Parson Woodforde lives on. It is the kings and queens who lie in prison. It is the great towns that are ravaged with anarchy and confusion. But the river Wensum still flows; Mrs Custance is brought to bed of yet another baby; there is the first swallow of the year. The spring comes, and summer with its hay and strawberries; then autumn, when the walnuts are exceptionally fine though the pears are poor; so we lapse into winter, which is indeed boisterous, but the house, thank God, withstands the storm; and then again there is the first swallow, and Parson Woodforde takes his greyhounds out a-coursing.

II

The Rev. John Skinner

A whole world separates Woodforde, who was born in 1740 and died in 1803, from Skinner, who was born in 1772 and died in 1839.

For the few years that separated the two parsons are those moment-ous years that separate the eighteenth century from the nineteenth. Camerton, it is true, lying in the heart of Somersetshire, was a village of the greatest antiquity; nevertheless, before five pages of the diary are turned we read of coal-works, and how there was a great shouting at the coal-works because a fresh vein of coal had been discovered, and the proprietors had given money to the workmen to celebrate an event which promised such prosperity to the village. Then, though the country gentlemen seemed set as firmly in their seats as ever, it happened that the manor house at Camerton, with all the rights and duties pertaining to it, was in the hands of the Jarretts, whose fortune was derived from the Jamaica trade. This novelty, this incursion of an element quite unknown to Woodforde in his day, had its disturbing influence no doubt upon the character of Skinner himself. Irritable, nervous, apprehensive, he seems to embody, even before the age itself had come into existence, all the strife and unrest of our distracted times. He stands, dressed in the prosaic and unbecoming stocks and pantaloons of the early nineteenth century, at the parting of the ways. Behind him lay order and discipline and all the virtues of the heroic past, but directly he left his study he was faced with drunkenness and immorality; with indiscipline and irreligion; with Methodism and Roman Catholicism; with the Reform Bill and the Catholic Emancipation Act, with a mob clamouring for freedom, with the overthrow of all that was decent and established and right. Tormented and querulous, at the same time conscientious and able, he stands at the parting of the ways, unwilling to yield an inch, unable to concede a point, harsh, peremptory, apprehensive, and without hope.

Private sorrow had increased the natural acerbity of his temper. His wife had died young, leaving him with four small children, and of these the best-loved, Laura, a child who shared his tastes and would have sweetened his life, for she already kept a diary and had arranged a cabinet of shells with the utmost neatness, died too. But these losses, though they served nominally to make him love God the better, in practice led him to hate men more. By the time the diary opens in 1822 he was fixed in his opinion that the mass of men are unjust and malicious, and that the people of Camerton are more corrupt even than the mass of men. But by that date he was also fixed in his profession. Fate had taken him from the lawyer's office, where he would have been in his element, dealing out justice, filling up forms, keeping strictly to the letter of the law, and had planted him at Camerton among church-wardens and farmers, the Gullicks and the Padfields, the old woman who had dropsy, the idiot boy, and the dwarf. Nevertheless, however sordid his tasks and disgusting his parishioners, he had his duty to them; and with them he would remain. Whatever insults he suffered, he would live up to his principles, uphold the right, protect the poor, and punish the wrongdoer. By the time the diary opens, this strenuous and unhappy career is in full swing.

Perhaps the village of Camerton in the year 1822, with its coal-mines and the disturbance they brought, was no fair sample of English village life. Certainly it is difficult, as one follows the Rector on his daily rounds, to indulge in pleasant dreams about the quaintness and amenity of old English rural life. Here, for instance, he was called to see Mrs Gooch – a woman of weak mind, who had been locked up alone in her cottage and fallen into the fire and was in agony. 'Why did you not help me, I say? Why do you not help me?'[2] she cried. And the Rector, as he heard her screams, knew that she had come to this through no fault of her own. Her efforts to keep a home together had led to drink, and so she had lost her reason, and what with the squabbles between the Poor Law officials and the family as to who should support her, what with her husband's extravagance and drunkenness, she had been left alone, had fallen into the fire, and so died. Who was to blame? Mr Purnell, the miserly magistrate, who was all for cutting down the allowance paid to the poor, or Hicks the Overseer, who was notoriously harsh, or the ale-houses, or the Methodists, or what? At any rate the Rector had done his duty. However he might be hated for it, he always stood up for the rights of the down-trodden; he always told people of their faults, and convicted them of evil. Then there was Mrs Somer, who kept a house of ill-fame and was bringing up her daughters to the same profession. Then there was Farmer Lippeatt, who, turned out of the Red Post at midnight, dead drunk, missed his way, fell into a quarry, and died of a broken breastbone. Wherever one turned there was suffering, wherever one looked one found cruelty behind that suffering. Mr and Mrs Hicks, for example, the Overseers, let an infirm pauper lie for ten days in the Poor House without care, 'so that maggots had bred in his flesh and eaten great holes in his body'.[3] His only attendant was an old woman, who was so failing that she was unable to lift him. Happily the pauper died. Happily poor Garratt, the miner, died too. For to add to the evils of drink and poverty and the cholera there was constant peril from the mine itself. Accidents were common and the means of treating them elementary. A fall of coal had broken Garratt's back, but he lingered on, though exposed to the crude methods of country surgeons, from January to November, when at last death released him. Both the stern Rector and the flippant Lady of the Manor, to do them justice, were ready with their half-crowns, with their soups and their medicines, and visited sick-beds without fail. But even allowing for the natural asperity of Mr Skinner's temper, it would need a very rosy pen and a very kindly eye to make a smiling picture of life in the village of Camerton a century ago. Half-crowns and soup went a very little way to remedy matters; sermons and denunciations made them perhaps even worse.

The Rector found refuge from Camerton neither in dissipation like some of his neighbours, nor in sport like others. Occasionally he drove over to dine with a brother cleric, but he noted acrimoniously that the entertainment was 'better suited to Grosvenor Square than a clergyman's home – French dishes and French wines in profusion',[4] and records with a note of exclamation that it was eleven o'clock before he drove home. When his children were young he sometimes walked with them in the fields, or amused himself by making them a boat, or rubbed up his Latin in an epitaph for the tomb of some pet dog or tame pigeon. And sometimes he leant back peacefully and listened to Mrs Fenwick as she sang the songs of Moore[5] to her husband's accompaniment on the flute. But even such harmless pleasures were poisoned with suspicion. A farmer stared insolently as he passed; someone threw a stone from a window; Mrs Jarrett clearly concealed some evil purpose behind her cordiality. No, the only refuge from

Camerton lay in Camalodunum. The more he thought of it the more certain he became that he had the singular good fortune to live on the identical spot where lived the father of Caractacus, where Ostorius established his colony, where Arthur had fought the traitor Modred, where Alfred very nearly came in his misfortunes. Camerton was undoubtedly the Camalodunum of Tacitus.[6] Shut up in his study alone with his documents, copying, comparing, proving indefatigably, he was safe, at rest, even happy. He was also, he became convinced, on the track of an important etymological discovery, by which it could be proved that there was a secret significance 'in every letter that entered into the composition of Celtic names'.[7] No archbishop was as content in his palace as Skinner the antiquary was content in his cell. To these pursuits he owed, too, those rare and delightful visits to Stourhead, the seat of Sir Richard Hoare, when at last he mixed with men of his own calibre, and met the gentlemen who were engaged in examining the antiquities of Wiltshire. However hard it froze, however high the snow lay heaped on the roads, Skinner rode over to Stourhead; and sat in the library, with a violent cold, but in perfect content, making extracts from Seneca, and extracts from Diodorus Siculus, and extracts from Ptolemy's *Geography*,[8] or scornfully disposed of some rash and ill-informed fellow-antiquary who had the temerity to assert that Camalodunum was really situated at Colchester. On he went with his extracts, with his theories, with his proofs, in spite of the malicious present of a rusty nail wrapped in paper from his parishioners, in spite of the laughing warning of his host: 'Oh, Skinner, you will bring everything at last to Camalodunum; be content with what you have already discovered; if you fancy too much you will weaken the authority of real facts'.[9] Skinner replied with a sixth letter thirty-four pages long; for Sir Richard did not know how necessary Camalodunum had become to an embittered man who had daily to encounter Hicks the Overseer and Purnell the magistrate, the brothels, the ale-houses, the Methodists, the dropsies and bad legs of Camerton. Even the floods were mitigated if one could reflect that thus Camalodunum must have looked in the time of the Britons.

So he filled three iron chests with ninety-eight volumes of manuscript. But by degrees the manuscripts ceased to be entirely concerned with Camalodunum; they began to be largely concerned with John Skinner. It was true that it was important to establish the truth about Camalodunum, but it was also important to establish the truth about John Skinner. In fifty years after his death, when the diaries were published, people would know not only that John Skinner was a great antiquary, but that he was a much wronged, much suffering man. His diary became his confidante, as it was to become his champion. For example, was he not the most affectionate of fathers, he asked the diary? He had spent endless time and trouble on his sons; he had sent them to Winchester and Cambridge, and yet now when the farmers were so insolent about paying him his tithes, and gave him a broken-backed lamb for his share, or fobbed him off with less than his due of cocks, his son Joseph refused to help him. His son said that the people of Camerton laughed at him; that he treated his children like servants; that he suspected evil where none was meant. And then he opened a letter by chance and found a bill for a broken gig; and then his sons lounged about smoking cigars when they might have helped him to mount his drawings. In short, he could not stand their presence in his house. He dismissed them in a fury to Bath. When they had gone he could not help admitting that perhaps he had been at fault. It was his querulous temper again – but then he had so much to make him querulous. Mrs Jarrett's peacock screamed under his window all night. They jangled the church bells on purpose to annoy him. Still, he would try; he would let them come back. So Joseph and Owen came back. And then the old irritation overcame him again. He 'could not help saying' something about being idle, or drinking too much cider, upon which there was a terrible scene and Joseph broke one of the parlour chairs.[10] Owen took Joseph's part. So did Anna. None of his children cared for him. Owen went further. Owen said 'I was a madman and ought to have a commission of lunacy to investigate my conduct'.[11] And, further, Owen cut him to the quick by pouring scorn on his verses, on his diaries and archaeological theories. He said 'No one would read the nonsense I had written. When I mentioned having gained a prize at Trinity College . . . his reply was that none but the most stupid fellows ever thought of writing for the college prize'.[12] Again there was a terrible scene; again they were dismissed to Bath, followed by their father's curses. And then Joseph fell ill with the family consumption. At once his father was all tenderness and remorse. He sent for doctors, he offered to take him for a sea trip to Ireland, he took him indeed to Weston and went sailing with him on the sea. Once more the family came together. And once more the querulous, exacting father could not help, for all his concern, exasperating the children whom, in his own crabbed way, he yet genuinely loved. The question of religion cropped up. Owen said his father was no better than a Deist or a Socinian. And Joseph, lying ill upstairs, said he was too tired for argument; he did not want his father to bring drawings to show him; he did not want his father to read prayers to him, 'he would rather have some other person to converse with than me'.[13] So in the crisis of their lives, when a father should have been closest to them, even his children turned away from him. There was nothing left to live for. Yet what had he done to make everyone hate him? Why did the farmers call him mad? Why did Joseph say that no one would read what he wrote? Why did the villagers tie tin cans to the tail of his dog? Why did the peacocks shriek and the bells ring? Why was there no mercy shown to him and no respect and no love? With agonising repetition the diary asks these questions; but there was no answer. At last, one morning in December 1839,[14] the Rector took his gun, walked into the beech wood near his home, and shot himself dead.

I James Woodforde

1 – Originally published as a signed review (entitled 'Life Itself') in the NR, 17 August 1927, and in the N&A, 20 August 1927, (Kp4 C285; see IV VW Essays), of vol. iii of The Diary of a Country Parson: The Reverend James Woodforde [1740–1803], ed. John Beresford (1927; 5 vols, OUP, 1924–31). This essay was revised and expanded for CR2. Reading notes for this revision: (MHP, B 2p) (VWRN XLVIII). One-page draft (MHP, B 2e). Reprinted: CDB ('Life Itself' version but with the title 'James Woodforde'), CE (CR2 version).
2 – Diary, vol. iii, 3 January 1789, p. 77. His niece, Anna Maria [Nancy] Woodforde (1757–1830), kept house for him from 1780. Robert George Walker was 'Betsy Davy's intended' (ibid., 18 July 1788, p. 37).
3 – Ibid., vol. ii, 4 August 1784, p. 146.
4 – Ibid., vol. i, 25 September 1771, p. 111, which has: 'She is a sweet tempered girl indeed, and I like her much, and I think would make a good wife, I do not know but I shall make a bold stroke that way'; 28 May 1774, p. 132, which has: 'when an opportunity offered'.
5 – Ibid., 16 September 1775, p. 168.
6 – Ibid., 11 July 1765, pp. 48–9: 'A terrible accident happened whilst we were at dinner, which many of us went to see the Body; viz. a Poor Boy was dragged and killed by a Horse about half a mile from us on the Ilchester Road. The boy was about fourteen years old. I hope to God the Poor Boy is happy. There was no bone broken, neither was his skull fractured, but he is dead. We all came home singing, and I thank God well.'
7 – Ibid., 9 May 1768, p. 75.
8 – Ibid., 3 June 1769, p. 86.

9 – *Ibid.*, vol. ii, 28 March 1782, p. 15, which has: 'a Landscape appearing thro' the Jelly'.

10 – *Ibid.*, vol. i, 9 September 1778, p. 235.

11 – *Ibid.*, vol. ii, 7 November 1783, p. 104.

12 – *Ibid.*, vol. iv, 5 April 1793, p. 20.

13 – See *ibid.*, vol. iii, 16 October 1789, p. 146: 'Sad news from France all anarchy and Confusion. The King, Queen and Royal Family confined at Paris. The Soldiers joined the people, many murdered.' See also *ibid.*, vol. iv, 26 January 1793, p. 4: 'The King of France Louis 16 inhumanly and unjustly beheaded on Monday last by his cruel blood-thirsty subjects.'

14 – Cf. O, ch. i, pp. 33–4.

15 – *Diary*, vol. iv, 19 January 1794, p. 90.

16 – In the eighteenth century Orlando wears 'flowered paduasoy' (*O*, ch. iv, pp. 141, 143, 148).

II The Rev. John Skinner

1 – First published in *CR2*. At Rodmell on 27 December 1930, VW was recovering from influenza: 'I moon torpidly through book after book ... The parson – Skinner [1772–1839] – who shot himself emerges like a bloody sun in a fog[;] a book worth perhaps looking at again in a clearer mood. He shot himself in the beech woods above his house; spent a life digging up stones & reducing all places to Camelodunum; quarrelled; bickered; yet loved his sons; yet turned them out of doors – a clear hard picture of one type of human life – the exasperated, unhappy, struggling, intolerably afflicted' (*III VW Diary*). On 29 December she wrote an extensive 'trial run' for this piece in her diary. The essay was turned down by the *Yale Review*: 'Miss McAfee has rejected my article on Skinner, & asks for one on Q. Elizabeth instead, which she shant get' (*IV VW Diary*, 16 February 1932), as she wrote to McAfee accordingly on 19 February 1932 (see *V VW Letters*, no. 2529). The essay is based on the *Journal of a Somerset Rector*, ed. Howard Coombs and Rev. Arthur N. Bax (John Murray, 1930), which was reprinted in a revised and enlarged edition, ed. Howard and Peter Coombs (Kingsmead Press, 1971). In the introduction to the 1971 edition, Peter Coombs wrote (p. 4): 'The Editors are of the opinion that the Camerton scene as Skinner found it, cannot be better described than in the essay by Virginia Woolf, and this is given in its entirety' (see pp. 4–9). Reprinted: *CE*.

2 – Quoted in *Journal*, 3 August 1822, pp. 26 (1930), 216 (1971), which begins: 'Why do . . .'

3 – For the infirm pauper, James Evans, see *ibid.*, 6 November 1823, pp. 67 (1930), 250 (1971).

4 – *Ibid.*, 18 November 1823, pp. 69 (1930), 252 (1971).

5 – Thomas Moore (1779–1852).

6 – For the senator and historian Tacitus (c. 56–c. 117) on the rebellion of the Iceni and the Tribantes in AD 61 and the fall of Camulodunum (usually identified as Colchester), see his *Annales*, bk xiv, sec. xxix–xxxix.

7 – *Journal*, (1930), Biographical Introduction, p. xviii (1930).

8 – Seneca the Younger (c. 4 BC – c. AD 65), philosopher, statesman and dramatist; for his suicide see Tacitus' *Annales*, bk xv, sec. 60–4. Diodorus Siculus (c. 90–c. 30 BC), Greek historian. Ptolemy (c. 90–c. 168 AD), Greek or Egyptian mathematician, geographer and astronomer.

9 – *Journal*, 21 August 1824, pp. 84 (1930), 267 (1971).

10 – It was Fitz Owen, not Joseph, who 'broke one of the parlour chairs': see *ibid.*, 20 September 1830, pp. 257 (1930), 417 (1971).

11 – *Ibid.*, 9 October 1831, pp. 278 (1930), 434 (1971).

12 – *Ibid.*, 17 November 1832, pp. 309 (1930), 460–1 (1971), which has: 'mentioned my having'.

13 – *Ibid.*, 18 November 1832, pp. 310 (1930), 462 (1971), which has: 'converse with on the subject of religion than me'.

14 – Although both the *DNB* and the *ODNB* give the rector's date of death as 12 October 1839, Coombs and Bax in the *Journal* (1930) state that it was in 'December 1839 . . . among the bare beech trees in the hanging wood hard by his home' (Preface, p. viii).

Dr Burney's Evening Party

I

The party was given either in 1777 or in 1778; on which day or month of the year is not known, but the night was cold. Fanny Burney, from whom we get much of our information, was accordingly either twenty-five or twenty-six, as we choose. But in order to enjoy the party to the full it is necessary to go back some years and to scrape acquaintance with the guests.

Fanny, from the earliest days, had always been fond of writing. There was a cabin at the end of her stepmother's garden at King's Lynn, where she used to sit and write of an afternoon till the oaths of the seamen sailing up and down the river drove her in. But it was only in the afternoon and in remote places that her half-suppressed, uneasy passion for writing had its way. Writing was held to be slightly ridiculous in a girl; rather unseemly in a woman. Besides, one never knew, if a girl kept a diary, whether she might not say something indiscreet – so Miss Dolly Young warned her; and Miss Dolly Young, though exceedingly plain, was esteemed a woman of the highest character in King's Lynn. Fanny's stepmother also disapproved of writing. Yet so keen was the joy – 'I cannot express the pleasure I have in writing down my thoughts at the very moment, and my opinion of people when I first see them'[a] – that scribble she must. Loose sheets of paper fell from her pocket and were picked up and read by her father to her agony and shame; once she was forced to make a bonfire of all her papers in the back garden. At last some kind of compromise seems to have been arrived at. The morning was sacred to serious tasks like sewing; it was only in the afternoon that she allowed herself to scribble – letters, diaries, stories, verses in the look-out place which overhung the river, till the oaths of the sailors drove her in.

There was something strange in that, perhaps, for the eighteenth century was the age of oaths. Fanny's early diary is larded with them. 'God help me', 'Split me', 'Stap my vitals', together with damneds and devilishes, dropped daily and hourly from the lips of her adored father and her venerated Daddy Crisp. Perhaps Fanny's attitude to language was altogether a little abnormal. She was immensely susceptible to the power of words, but not nervously or acutely as Jane Austen was. She adored fluency and the sound of language pouring warmly and copiously over the printed page. Directly she read *Rasselas*, enlarged and swollen sentences formed on the tip of her childish pen in the manner of Dr Johnson. Quite early in life she would go out of her way to avoid the plain name of Tomkins. Thus, whatever she heard from her cabin at the end of the garden was sure to affect her more than most girls, and it is also clear that while her ears were sensitive to sound, her soul was sensitive to meaning. There was something a little prudish in her nature. Just as she avoided the name of Tomkins, so she avoided the roughnesses, the asperities, the plainnesses of daily life. The chief fault that mars the extreme vivacity and vividness of the early diary is that the profusion of words tends to soften the edges of the sentences, and the sweetness of the sentiment to smooth out the outlines of the thought.[b] Thus, when she heard the sailors swearing, though Maria Allen, her half-sister, would, one believes, have liked to stay and toss a kiss over the water – her future history allows us to take the liberty of thinking so – Fanny went indoors.

Fanny went indoors, but not to solitary meditation. The house, whether it was in Lynn or in London – and by far the greater part of the year was spent in Poland Street – hummed with activity. There was the sound of the harpsichord; the sound of singing; there was the sound – for such concentration seems to pervade a whole house with its murmur – of Dr Burney writing furiously, surrounded by notebooks, in his study; and there were great bursts of chatter and laughter when, returning from their various occupations, the Burney children met together. Nobody enjoyed family life more than Fanny did. For there her shyness only served to fasten the nickname of Old Lady upon her; there she had a familiar audience for her humour; there she need not bother about her clothes; there – perhaps the fact that their mother had died when they were all young was partly the cause of it – was that intimacy which expresses itself in jokes and legends and a private language ('The wig is wet', they would say, winking at each other); there were endless confabulations, and confidences between sisters and brothers and brothers and sisters. Nor could there be any doubt that the Burneys – Susan and James and Charles and Fanny and Hetty and Charlotte – were a gifted race. Charles was a scholar; James was a humorist; Fanny was a writer; Susan was musical – each had some special gift or characteristic to add to the common stock. And besides their natural gifts they were happy in the fact that their father was a very popular man; a man, too, so admirably situated by his talents, which were social, and his birth, which was gentle, that they could mix without difficulty either with lords or with bookbinders, and had, in fact, as free a run of life as could be wished.

As for Dr Burney himself, there are some points about which, at this distance of time, one may feel dubious. It is difficult to be sure what, had one met him now, one would have felt for him. One thing is certain – one would have met him everywhere. Hostesses would be competing to catch him. Notes would wait for him. Telephone bells would interrupt him. For he was the most sought-after, the most occupied of men. He was always dashing in and dashing out.[c] Sometimes he dined off a box of sandwiches in his carriage. Sometimes he went out at seven in the morning, and was not back from his round of music lessons till eleven at night. The 'habitual softness of his manners', his great social charm, endeared him to everybody. His haphazard untidy ways – everything,[d] notes, money, manuscripts, was tossed into a drawer, and he was robbed of all his savings once, but his friends were delighted to make it up for him; his odd adventures – did he not fall asleep after a bad crossing at Dover, and so return to France and so have to cross the Channel again? – gave him a claim upon people's kindness and sympathy. It^e is, perhaps, his diffuseness that makes him a trifle nebulous. He seems to be for ever writing and then rewriting, and requiring his daughters to write for him, endless books and articles, while over him, unchecked, unfiled, unread perhaps, pour down notes, letters, invitations to dinner which he cannot destroy and means some day to annotate and collect, until he seems to melt away at last in a cloud of words. When he died at the age of eighty-eight, there was nothing to be done by the most devoted of daughters but to burn the whole accumulation entire. Even Fanny's love of language was suffocated. But if we fumble a little as to our feeling for Dr Burney, Fanny certainly did not. She adored her father. She never minded how many times she had to lay aside her own writing in order to copy out his. And he returned her affection. Though his ambition for her success at Court was foolish, perhaps, and almost cost her her life, she had only to cry when a distasteful suitor was pressed on her, 'Oh, Sir, I wish for nothing! Only let me live with you!' for the emotional doctor to reply, 'My Life! Thou shalt live with me for ever if thou wilt. Thou canst not think I meant to get rid of thee?' And not only were his eyes full of tears, but, what was more remarkable, he never mentioned Mr Barlow again. Indeed, the Burneys were a happy family; a mixed composite, oddly assorted family; for there were the Allens, too, and little half-brothers and half-sisters were being born and growing up.

So time passed, and the passage of the years made it impossible for the family to continue in Poland Street any longer. First they moved to Queen Square, and then, in 1774, to the house where Newton had lived, in St Martin's Street, Leicester Fields; where his Observatory still stood, and his room with the painted panels was still to be seen. Here in a mean street, but in the centre of the town, the Burneys set up their establishment. Here Fanny went on scribbling, stealing to the Observatory as she had stolen to the cabin at Lynn, for she exclaimed, 'I cannot any longer resist what I find to be irresistible, the pleasure of popping down my thoughts from time to time upon paper'. Here came so many famous people either to be closeted with the doctor, or, like Garrick, to sit with him while his fine head of natural hair was brushed, or to join the lively family dinner, or, more formally, to gather together in a musical party, where all the Burney children played and their father 'dashed away' on the harpsichord, and perhaps some foreign musician of distinction performed a solo – so many people came for one reason or another to the house in St Martin's Street that it is only the eccentrics, the grotesques, that catch the eye. One remembers, for instance, the Ajujari, the astonishing soprano, because she had been 'mauled as an infant by a pig, in consequence of which she is reported to have a silver side'. One remembers Bruce, the traveller, because he had a

most extraordinary complaint. When he attempted to speak, his whole stomach suddenly seemed to heave like an organ bellows. He did not wish to make any secret about it, but spoke of it as having originated in Abyssinia. However, one evening, when he appeared rather agitated, it lasted much longer than usual, and was so violent that it alarmed the company.

One seems to remember, for she paints herself while she paints the others, Fanny herself slipping eagerly and lightly in and out of all this company, with her rather prominent gnat-like eyes, and her shy, awkward manners. But the gnat-like eyes, the awkward manners, concealed the quickest observation, the most retentive memory. As soon[f] as the company had gone, she stole to the Observatory and wrote down every word, every scene, in letters twelve pages long, for her beloved Daddy Crisp at Chessington. That[g] old hermit – he had retired to a house in a field in dudgeon with society – though professing to be better pleased with a bottle of wine in his cellar and a horse in his stable, and a game of backgammon at night, than with all the fine company in the world, was always agog for news. He scolded his Fannikin if she did not tell him all about her fine goings-on. And he scolded her again if she did not write at full tilt exactly as the words came into her head.

Mr Crisp wanted to know in particular 'about Mr Greville and his notions'. For, indeed, Mr Greville was a perpetual source of curiosity. It is a thousand pities that time with her poppy dust has covered Mr Greville so[h] that only his most prominent features, his birth, his person, and his nose emerge. Fulke Greville was the descendant – he must, one fancies, have emphasised the fact from the way in which it is repeated – of the friend of Sir Philip Sidney. A coronet, indeed, 'hung almost suspended over his head'. In person he was tall and well proportioned. 'His face, features, and complexion were striking for masculine beauty.' 'His air and carriage were noble with conscious dignity'; his bearing was 'lofty, yet graceful'. But all these gifts and qualities, to which one must add that he rode and fenced and danced and played tennis to admiration, were marred by prodigious faults. He was supercilious in the extreme; he was selfish; he was fickle. He was a man of violent temper. His introduction to Dr Burney in the first place was due to his doubt whether a musician could be fit company for a gentleman. When he found that young Burney not only played the harpsichord to perfection, but curved his finger and rounded his hand as he played; that he answered plain 'Yes, Sir,' or 'No, Sir,' being more interested in the music than in his patron; that it was only indeed when Greville himself thrummed pertinaciously from memory that he could stand it no longer, and broke into vivacious conversation – it was only when he found that young Burney was both gifted and well bred that,*i* being himself a very clever man, he no longer stood upon his dignity. Burney became his friend and his equal.*j* Burney, indeed, almost became his victim. For if there was one thing that the descendant of the friend of Sir Philip Sidney detested it was what he called 'fogrum'. By that expressive word he seems to have meant the middle-class virtues of discretion and respectability, as opposed to the aristocratic virtues of what he called '*ton*'. Life must be lived dashingly, daringly, with perpetual display, even if the display was extremely expensive, and, as seemed possible to those who trailed dismally round his grounds praising the improvements, as boring to the man who made it as*k* to the unfortunate guests whose admiration he insisted upon extorting. But Greville could not endure fogrum in himself or in his friends. He threw the obscure young musician into the fast life of White's and Newmarket, and watched with amusement to see if he sank or swam. Burney, most adroit of men, swam as if born to the water, and the descendant of the friend of Sir Philip Sidney was pleased. From being his protégé, Burney became his confidant. Indeed, the splendid gentleman, for all his high carriage, was in need of one. For Greville, could one wipe away the poppy dust that covers him, was one of those tortured and unhappy souls who find themselves torn asunder by opposite desires. On the one hand he was consumed with the wish to be in the first flight of fashion and to do 'the thing', however costly or dreary 'the thing' might be.[2] On the other, he was secretly persuaded that 'the proper bent of his mind and understanding was for metaphysics'.[3] Burney, perhaps, was a link between the world of *ton* and the world of fogrum. He was a man of breeding who could dice and bet with the bloods; he was also a musician who could talk of intellectual things and ask clever people to his house.

Thus Greville treated the Burneys as his equals, and came to their house, though his visits were often interrupted by the violent quarrels which he managed to pick even with the amiable Dr Burney himself. Indeed, as time went on there was nobody with whom Greville did not quarrel. He had lost heavily at the gambling-tables. His prestige in society was sunk. His habits were driving his family from him. Even his wife, by nature gentle and conciliatory, though excessive thinness made her seem fitted to sit for a portrait 'of a penetrating, puissant and sarcastic fairy queen', was wearied by his infidelities. Inspired by them she had suddenly produced that famous Ode to Indifference, 'which had passed into every collection of fugitive pieces in the English language' and (it is Madam D'Arblay who speaks) 'twined around her brow a garland of wide-spreading and unfading fragrance'. Her fame, it may be, was another thorn in her husband's side; for he, too, was an author. He himself had produced a volume of Maxims and Characters; and having 'waited for fame with dignity rather than anxiety, because with expectation unclogged with doubt', was beginning perhaps to become a little impatient when fame delayed. Meanwhile[l] he was fond of the society of clever people, and it was largely at his desire that the famous party in St Martin's Street met together that very cold night.

II

In those days, when London was so small, it was easier than now for people to stand on[m] an eminence which they scarcely struggled to keep, but enjoyed by unanimous consent. Everybody knew and remembered when they saw her that Mrs Greville had written an Ode to Indifference; everybody knew that Mr Bruce had travelled in Abyssinia; so, too, everybody knew that there was a house at Streatham presided over by a lady called Mrs Thrale. Without troubling to write an Ode, without hazarding her life among savages, without possessing either high rank or vast wealth, Mrs Thrale was a celebrity. By the exercise of powers difficult to define – for to feel them one must have sat at table and noticed a thousand audacities and deftnesses and skilful combinations which die with the moment – Mrs Thrale had the reputation of a great hostess. Her fame spread far beyond her house. People who had never seen her discussed her. People wanted to know what she was like; whether she was really so witty and so well read; whether it was a pose; whether she had a heart; whether she loved her husband the brewer, who seemed a dull dog; why she had married him; whether Dr Johnson was in love with her – what, in short, was the truth of her story, the secret of[n] her power. For power she had – that was indisputable.

Even then, perhaps, it would have been difficult to say in what it consisted. For she possessed the one quality which can never be named; she enjoyed the one gift which never ceases to excite discussion. Somehow or other she was a personality. The young Burneys, for instance, had never seen Mrs Thrale or been to Streatham, but the stir which she set going round her had reached them in St Martin's Street. When their father came back from giving his first music lesson to Miss Thrale at Streatham they flocked about him to hear his account of her mother. Was she as brilliant as people made out? Was she kind? Was she cruel? Had he liked her? Dr Burney was in high good temper – in itself a proof of his hostess's power – and he replied, not, we may be sure, as Fanny rendered it, that she was a 'star of the first constellation of female wits: surpassing, rather than equalising the reputation which her extraordinary endowments, and the splendid fortune which made them conspicuous, had blazoned abroad' – that was written when Fanny's style was old and tarnished, and its leaves were fluttering and falling profusely to the ground; the doctor, we may suppose, answered briskly that he had enjoyed himself hugely; that the lady was a very clever lady; that she had interrupted the lesson all the time; that she had a very sharp tongue – there was no doubt of that; but he would go to the stake for it that she was a good-hearted woman at bottom. Then they must have pressed to know what she looked like. She looked younger than her age – which was about forty. She was rather plump, very small, fair with very blue eyes, and had a scar or cut on her lip. She painted her cheeks, which was unnecessary, because her complexion was rosy by nature. The whole impression she made was one of[o] bustle and gaiety and good temper. She was, he said, a woman 'full of sport',[4] whom nobody could have taken for a creature that the doctor could not bear, a learned lady. Less obviously, she was very observant, as her anecdotes were to prove; capable of passion, though that was not yet visible at Streatham; and, while curiously careless and good-tempered about

437

her dues as a wit or a blue-stocking, had an amusing pride in being descended from a long line of Welsh gentry (whereas the Thrales were obscure), and drew satisfaction now and then from the reflection that in her veins ran the blood, as the College of Heralds acknowledged, of Adam of Salzburg.

Many women might have possessed these qualities without being remembered for them. Mrs Thrale possessed besides one that has given her immortality: the power of being the friend of Dr Johnson. Without that addition, her life might have fizzled and flamed to extinction, leaving nothing behind it. But the combination of Dr Johnson and Mrs Thrale created something as solid, as lasting, as remarkable in its way as a work of art. And this was an achievement that called for much rarer powers on the part of Mrs Thrale than the qualities of a good hostess. When the Thrales first met Johnson he was in a state of profound gloom, crying out such lost and terrible words that Mr Thrale put his hand before his mouth to silence him. Physically, too, he was afflicted with asthma and dropsy; his manners were rough; his habits were gross; his clothes were dirty; his wig was singed; his linen was soiled; and he was the rudest of men. Yet Mrs Thrale carried this monster off with her to Brighton and then domesticated him in her house at Streatham, where he was given a room to himself, and where he spent habitually some days in the middle of every week. This might have been, it is true, but^p the enthusiasm of a curiosity hunter, ready to put up with a host of disagreeables for the sake of having at her house the original Dr Johnson, whom anybody in England would gladly pay to see. But it is clear that her connoisseurship was of a finer type. She understood – her anecdotes prove it – that Dr Johnson was somehow a rare, an important, an impressive human being whose friendship might be a burden but was certainly an honour. And it was not by any means so easy to know this then as it is now. What one knew then was that Dr Johnson was coming to dinner. And when Dr Johnson came to dinner one had to ask one's self who was coming too? For^q if it was a Cambridge man there might be an outburst. If it was a Whig there would certainly be a scene. If it was a Scotsman anything might happen. Such were his whims and prejudices. Next one would have to bethink one, what food had been ordered^r for dinner? For the food never went uncriticised; and even when one had provided him with young peas from the garden, one must not praise them. Were not the young peas charming, Mrs Thrale asked once? and he turned upon her, after gobbling down masses of pork and veal pie with lumps of sugar in it, and snapped, 'Perhaps they would be so – to a pig'. Then what would the talk be about – that was another cause for anxiety. If⁵ it got upon painting or music he was apt to dismiss it with scorn, for both arts were indifferent to him. Then if a traveller told a tale he was sure to pooh-pooh it, because he believed nothing that he had not seen himself. Then if anyone were to express sympathy inᵗ his presence it might well draw down upon one a rebuke for insincerity.

When, one day, I lamented the loss of a cousin killed in America: 'Prithee, my dear,' said he, 'have done with canting: how would the world be the worse for it, I may ask, if all your relations were at once spitted like larks, and roasted for Presto's supper?'⁵

In short, the meal would be strewn with difficulties; the whole affair might run upon the rocks at any moment.

Had Mrs Thrale been a shallow curiosity hunter she would have shown him for a season or so and then let him drop. But Mrs Thrale realised even at the moment that one must submit to be snubbed and bullied and irritated and offended by Dr Johnson because – well, what was the force that sent an impudent and arrogant young man like Boswell slinking back to his chair like a beaten boy when Johnson bade him? Why did she herself sit up till four in the morning pouring out tea for him? There was a force in him that awed even a competent woman of the world, that subdued even a thick-skinned, conceited boy. He had a right to scold Mrs Thrale for inhumanity, when she knew that he spent only seventy pounds a year on himself and with the rest of his income supported a houseful of decrepit and ungrateful lodgers. If he gobbled at table and tore the peaches from the wall, he went back punctually to London to see that his wretched inmates had their three good meals over the week-end. Moreover, he was a warehouse of knowledge. If the dancing-master talked about dancing, Johnson could out-talk him. He could keep one amused by the hour with his tales of the underworld, of the topers and scallywags who haunted his lodgings and claimed his bounty. He said things casually that one never forgot. But what was perhaps more engaging than all this learning and virtue, was his love of pleasure, his detestation of the mere bookworm,* his passion for life and society. And then, as a woman would, Mrs Thrale loved him for his courage – that he had separated two fierce dogs that were tearing each other to pieces in Mr Beauclerc's sitting-room; that he had thrown a man, chair and all, into the pit of a theatre; that, blind and twitching as he was, he rode to hounds on Brighthelmstone Downs, and followed the hunt as if he had been a gay dog instead of a huge and melancholy old man. Moreover, there was a natural affinity between them. She drew him out: she made him say what without her he would never have said; indeed, he had confessed to her some painful secret of his youth which she never revealed to anybody. Above all, they shared the same passion. Of talk they could neither of them ever have enough.

Thus Mrs Thrale could always be counted on to produce Dr Johnson; and it was, of course, Dr Johnson whom Mr Greville most particularly wished to meet. At it happened, Dr Burney had renewed his acquaintance with Dr Johnson after many years, when he went to Streatham to give his first music lesson, and Dr ^{v} Johnson had been there, 'wearing his mildest aspect'. For he remembered Dr Burney with kindness. He remembered a letter that Dr Burney had written to him in praise of the dictionary; he ^{w} remembered, too, that Dr Burney having called upon him, years ago, and found him out, had dared to cut some bristles from the hearth broom to send to an admirer. When he met Dr Burney again at Streatham, he had instantly taken a liking to him; soon he was brought by Mrs Thrale to see Dr Burney's books; it was quite easy, therefore, for Dr Burney to arrange that on a certain night in the early spring of 1777 or 1778, Mr Greville's great wish to meet Dr Johnson and Mrs Thrale should be gratified. A day was fixed and the engagement was made.

Whatever the day was it must have been marked in the host's calendar with a note of interrogation. Anything might happen. Any extreme of splendour or disaster might spring from the meeting of so many marked and distinguished characters. Dr Johnson was formidable. Mr Greville was domineering. Mrs Greville was a celebrity in one way; Mrs Thrale was a celebrity in another. Then it was an occasion. Everybody felt it to be so. Wits would be on the strain; expectation on tiptoe. Dr Burney foresaw these difficulties and took steps to avert them, but there was, one vaguely feels, something a little obtuse about Dr Burney. The eager, kind, busy man, with his head full of music and his desk stuffed with notes, lacked discrimination. The precise outline of people's characters was covered with a rambling pink haze. To his innocent mind music was the universal specific. Everybody must share his own enthusiasm for music. If there was going to be any difficulty, music could solve it. He therefore asked Signor Piozzi to be of the party.[x]

The night arrived and the fire was lit. The chairs were placed and the company[y] arrived. As Dr Burney had foreseen, the awkwardness was great. Things indeed seemed to go wrong from the start. Dr Johnson had come in his worsted wig, very clean and prepared evidently for enjoyment. But after one look at him, Mr Greville seemed to decide that there was something formidable about the old man; it would be better not to compete; it would be better to play the fine gentleman, and leave it to literature to make the first advances. Murmuring, apparently, something about having the toothache, Mr Greville 'assumed his most supercilious air of distant superiority and planted himself, immovable as a noble statue, upon the hearth'. He said nothing. Then Mrs Greville, though longing to distinguish herself, judged it proper for Dr Johnson to begin, so that she[z] said nothing. Mrs Thrale, who might have been expected to break up the solemnity, felt, it seemed, that the party was not her party and, waiting for the principals to engage, resolved to say nothing either.[aa] Mrs Crewe, the Grevilles' daughter, lovely and vivacious as she was, had come to be entertained and instructed and therefore very naturally she, too, said nothing. Nobody said anything. Complete silence reigned. Here[bb] was the very moment for which Dr Burney in his wisdom had prepared. He nodded to Signor Piozzi; and Signor Piozzi stepped to the instrument and began to sing. Accompanying himself on the pianoforte, he sang an *aria parlante*. He sang beautifully, he sang his best. But far from breaking the awkwardness and loosing the tongues, the music increased the constraint. Nobody spoke. Everybody waited for Dr Johnson to begin. There, indeed, they showed their fatal ignorance, for if there was one thing that Dr Johnson never did, it was to begin. Somebody had always to start a topic before he consented to pursue it or to demolish it. Now he waited in silence to be challenged. But he waited in vain. Nobody spoke. Nobody dared speak. The roulades of Signor Piozzi continued uninterrupted. As he saw his chance of a pleasant evening's talk drowned in the rattle of a piano, Dr[cc] Johnson sank into silent abstraction and sat with his back to the piano gazing at the fire. The *aria parlante* continued uninterrupted. At last the strain became unendurable. At last Mrs Thrale could stand it no longer. It was the attitude of Mr Greville, apparently, that roused her resentment. There he stood on the hearth in front of the fire 'staring around him at the whole company in curious silence sardonically'.

441

What right had he, even if he were the descendant of the friend of Sir Philip Sidney, to despise the company and absorb the fire? Her own pride of ancestry suddenly asserted itself. Did not the blood of Adam of Salzburg run in her veins? Was it not as blue as that of the Grevilles and far more sparkling? Giving rein to the spirit of recklessness which sometimes bubbled in her, she rose, and stole on tiptoe to the pianoforte. Signor Piozzi was still singing and accompanying himself dramatically as he sang. She began a ludicrous mimicry of his gestures: she shrugged her shoulders, she cast up her eyes, she reclined her head on one side just as he did. At this singular display the company began to titter – indeed, it was a scene that was to be described 'from coterie to coterie throughout London, with comments and sarcasms of endless variety'. People who saw Mrs Thrale at her mockery that night never forgot that this was the beginning of that criminal affair, the first scene of that 'most extraordinary drama' which lost Mrs Thrale the respect of friends and children, which drove her in ignominy from England, and scarcely allowed her to show herself in London again – this was the beginning of her most reprehensible, her most unnatural passion for one who was not only a musician but a foreigner. But all[dd] this still lay on the laps of the gods. Nobody yet knew of what iniquity the vivacious lady was capable. She was still the respected wife of a wealthy brewer. Happily, Dr Johnson was staring at the fire, and knew nothing of the scene at the piano. But Dr Burney put a stop to the laughter instantly. He was shocked that a guest, even if a[ee] foreigner and a musician, should be ridiculed behind his back, and stealing to Mrs Thrale he whispered kindly but with authority in her ear that if she had no taste for music herself she should consider the feelings of those who had. Mrs Thrale took the rebuke with admirable sweetness, nodded her acquiescence and returned to her chair. But she had done her part. After that nothing more could be expected from her. Let them now do what they chose – she washed her hands of it, and seated herself 'like a pretty little Miss', as she said afterwards, to endure what yet remained to be endured 'of one of the most humdrum evenings that she had ever passed'.[6]

If no one had dared to tackle Dr Johnson in the beginning, it was scarcely likely that they would dare now. He had apparently decided that the evening was a failure so far as talk was concerned. If he had not come dressed in his best clothes he might have had a book in his pocket which he could have pulled out and read. As it was, nothing but the resources of his own mind were left him; but these were huge; and these he explored as he sat with his back to the piano looking the very image of gravity, dignity, and composure.

At last the *aria parlante* came to an end. Signor Piozzi indeed, finding nobody to talk to, fell asleep in his solitude. Even Dr Burney by this time must have been aware that music is not an infallible specific; but there was nothing for it now. Since people would not talk, the music must continue. He called upon his daughters to sing a duet. And then, when that was over, there was nothing for it but that they must sing another. Signor Piozzi still slept, or still feigned sleep. Dr Johnson explored still further the magnificent resources of his own mind. Mr Greville still stood superciliously upon the hearth-rug. And the night was cold.

But it was a grave mistake to suppose that because Dr Johnson was apparently lost in thought, and certainly almost blind, he was not aware of anything, particularly of anything reprehensible, that was taking place in the room. His 'starts of vision' were always astonishing and almost always painful. So it was on the present occasion. He suddenly woke up. He suddenly roused himself. He suddenly uttered the words for which the company had been waiting all the evening.

'If it were not for depriving the ladies of the fire', he said, looking fixedly at Mr Greville, 'I should like to stand upon the hearth myself!' The effect of the outburst was prodigious. The Burney children said afterwards that it was as good as a comedy. The descendant of the friend of Sir Philip Sidney quailed before the Doctor's glance. All the blood of all the Brookes rallied itself to overcome the insult. The son of a bookseller should be taught his place. Greville did his best to smile – a faint, scoffing smile. He did his best to stand where he had stood the whole evening. He stood smiling, he stood trying[ff] to smile, for two or perhaps for three minutes more. But when he looked round the room and saw all eyes cast down, all faces twitching with amusement, all sympathies plainly on the side of the bookseller's son, he could stand there no longer. Fulke Greville slunk away, sloping even his proud shoulders, to a chair. But as he went, he rang the bell 'with force'. He demanded his carriage.

'The party then broke up; and no one from amongst it ever asked, or wished for its repetition.'

a – *L&L*: '"them", she wrote'.
b – *L&L*: 'the edges, and the sweetness of the sentiment to smooth out the outlines.'

c – *L&L*: 'off.'

d – *L&L*: 'night. And when he was not teaching he was writing. The 'habitual . . . charm, his haphazard untidy ways: everything,'.

e – *L&L*: 'again? – endeared him to everybody. It'.

f – *L&L*: 'eyes, her shy, awkward manners that concealed . . . memory, so that as soon'.

g – *L&L*: 'For that'.

h – *L&L*: 'Mr Greville, who was once so eminent so'.

i – *L&L*: 'was not only gifted but well bred into the bargain that,'.

j – *L&L*: 'and equal.'

k – *L&L*: 'who had made them as'.

l – *L&L*: 'impatient. Fame held aloof. Meanwhile'.

m – *L&L*: 'stand out on'.

n – *L&L*: 'short, was the secret of'.

o – *L&L*: 'made on one was of'.

p – *L&L*: 'been on her part but'.

q – *L&L*: 'dinner. Who would be there, one wondered with anxiety? For'.

r – *L&L*: 'what had one ordered'.

s – *L&L*: 'And then what . . . about, one must have speculated? If'.

t – *L&L*: 'not seen. Then if any one were to express sorrow in'.

u – *L&L*, 'all his learning . . . detestation of the hermit, the mere book-worm,'.

v – *L&L*, 'lesson. Dr'.

w – *L&L*, 'dictionary. He'.

x – Instead of this paragraph, *L&L* has: 'Nobody could fail to be aware that the meeting of so many marked and distinguished characters might be difficult. Dr Johnson was, of course, notoriously formidable. But the danger was not confined to Dr Johnson; Mr Greville himself was domineering and exacting; his temper had grown still more uncertain since his gambling losses had made him of less account in the world of *ton*. Then Mrs Greville was a poetess; it was likely enough that she would prove her right to the laurel by some contest with a lady whose fame was at the moment brighter than her own. Mrs Thrale was good humour itself; still, it was likely that she would try for a tilt with Mrs Greville; nor was she wholly dependable, for she had "sudden flashes of wit which she left to their own consequences". Besides, it was an occasion; everybody felt it to be so; wits would be on the strain; expectation on tiptoe. Dr Burney, with the tact of a man of the world, foresaw these difficulties, and took steps to avert them. But there was, one vaguely feels, something a little obtuse about Dr Burney. The eager, kind, busy man, with his head full of music and his desk stuffed with notes, lacked discrimination. He had not noticed that Dr Johnson, when he visited them the other day, and found them at the harpsichord, had withdrawn to the bookcase and browsed upon a volume of the *British Encyclopædia*, till the music was over. He was not aware, in spite of the way in which Mrs Thrale interrupted his lessons, that she did not know "a flat from a sharp". To his innocent mind, music was the universal specific. If there was going to be any difficulty music would solve it. He therefore asked Signor Piozzi to be of the party.'

y – L&L: 'arrived. The fire was lit. The chairs were placed. The company'.

z – L&L: 'nothing. Mrs Greville was longing . . . herself, but judging it . . . begin, she'.

aa – L&L: 'nothing.'

bb – L&L: 'anything. Everybody waited. Here'.

cc – L&L: 'vain. Nobody dared. The roulades . . . pleasant evening of conversation diminish,'.

dd – L&L: 'All'.

ee – L&L: 'that his guest, even if he were a'.

ff – L&L: 'smiling, or trying'.

1 – For periodical publication and composition, see 'Dr Burney's Evening Party', note 1 above; only material not in that version is annotated here. The essay was further revised for *CR2*. *L&L* variants in the form of endnotes are given here. For VW revising this essay in 1930, see 'Fanny Burney's Half-Sister', note 1 above. In March 1932 she was revising the essay for *CR2*: 'I'm so tired with correcting Dr Burney' (*IV VW Diary*, [29 March 1932]). See also 'Mrs Thrale', *VI VW Essays*. Reprinted: *CE*.

2 – See *Memoirs of Doctor Burney . . .*, by his daughter Madame d'Arblay (3 vols, Edward Moxon, 1832), vol. i, p. 44.

3 – *Ibid.*, p. 43, which has: 'metaphysics being, in his own conception and opinion, the proper bent of his mind and understanding.'

4 – *Ibid.*, vol. ii, p. 87, Fanny Burney writing to Mr Crisp.

5 – *Anecdotes of the late Samuel Johnson . . .*, by Hester Lynch Piozzi (T. Cadell, 1786), p. 63; adapted by VW. Mrs Thrale continues: 'Presto was the dog that lay under the table while we talked.'

6 – *Memoirs*, vol. ii, p. 111.

Jack Mytton

Are you curious to know what sort of person your neighbour is in a deck-chair on Brighton pier? Watch, then, which column of *The Times* – she has brought it, rolled like a French roll, and it lies on the top of her bag – she reads first. Politics, presumably, or an article upon a temple in Jerusalem? Not a bit of it – she reads the sporting news. Yet one could have sworn, to look at her – boots, stockings, and all – that she was a public servant of some sort; with an Act of Parliament, a blue-book or two, and a frugal lunch of biscuits and bananas in her bag.[a] If for a moment she basks on Brighton pier while Madame Rosalba,[2] poised high on a platform above the sea, dives for coins or soup-plates it is only to refresh herself before renewing her attack upon the iniquities of our social system. Yet she begins by reading the sporting news.

Perhaps there is nothing so strange in it after all. The great English sports are pursued almost as fiercely by sedentary men who cannot sit a donkey, and by[b] quiet women who cannot drown a mouse, as by the booted and spurred. They hunt in imagination. They follow the fortunes of the Berkeley, the Cattistock, the Quorn, and the Belvoir upon phantom hunters. They roll upon their lips the odd-sounding, beautifully crabbed English place-names – Humblebee, Doddles Hill, Caroline Bog, Winniats Brake. They imagine as they read (hanging to a strap in the Underground or propping the paper against a suburban teapot) now a 'slow, twisting hunt', now a 'brilliant gallop'. The rolling meadows are in their eyes; they hear the thunder and the whimper of horses and hounds; the shapely slopes of Leicestershire unfold before them, and in imagination they ride home again, when evening falls, soothed and satisfied, and watch the lights coming out in farmhouse windows. Indeed the English sporting writers, Beckford, St John, Surtees, Nimrod,[3] make no mean reading. In their slapdash, gentlemanly way they have ridden their pens as boldly as they have ridden their horses. They have had their effect upon the language. This riding and tumbling, this being blown upon and rained upon and splashed from head to heels with mud, have worked themselves into the very texture of English prose and given it that leap and dash, that stripping of images from flying hedge and tossing tree which distinguish it not indeed above the French but so emphatically from it. How much English poetry depends upon English hunting this is not the place to enquire. That Shakespeare was a bold if erratic horseman scarcely needs proving. Therefore that an Englishwoman should choose to read the sporting news rather than the political gossip need cause us no surprise; nor need we condemn her if, when she has folded up her paper, she takes from her bag not a blue-book but a red book and proceeds, while Madame Rosalba dives and the band blares and the green waters of the English Channel sparkle and sway between the chinks of the pier, to read the Life of Jack Mytton.[c]

Jack Mytton was by no means an estimable character. Of an old

Shropshire family (the name was Mutton once;[4] so Brontë was Prunty), he[d] had inherited a fine property and a large income. The little boy who was born in the year 1796 should have carried on the tradition of politics and sport which his ancestors had pursued respectably for five centuries before him.[5] But families have their seasons, like the year. After months of damp and drizzle, growth and prosperity, there come the wild equinoctial gales, a roaring in the trees all day, fruit destroyed and blossom wasted. Lightning strikes the house and its roof-tree goes up in fire. Indeed, Nature and society between them had imposed upon the Mytton of 1796 a burden which might have crushed a finer spirit – a body hewn from the solid rock, a fortune of almost indestructible immensity. Nature and society dared him, almost, to defy them. He accepted the challenge. He went shooting in the thinnest silk stockings,[6] he let the rain pelt on his bare skin, he swam rivers, charged gates, crouched naked on the snow, but still his body remained obdurate and upright. He had his breeches made without pockets; wads of bank-notes were picked up in the woods, but still his fortune survived. He begot children[e] and tossed them in the air and pelted them with oranges; he married wives whom he tormented and imprisoned until one died and the other snatched her chance and ran away.[7] While he shaved, a glass of port stood by his side, and as the day wore on he worked through five or six bottles of wine and sopped them up with pound upon pound of filberts.[8] There[f] was an extremity about his behaviour which raises it from the particular to the general. The shaggy body of primeval man, with all his appetites and aptitudes, seemed[g] to have risen from his grave under the barrows, where the great stones were piled on top of him, where once he sacrificed rams and did homage to the rising sun, to carouse with tippling fox-hunters of the time of George the Fourth. His limbs themselves seemed carved from more primitive materials than modern men's. He had neither beauty of countenance nor grace of manner, yet he bore himself, for all his violence of body and mind, with an air of natural breeding which one can imagine in a savage stepping on his native turf. When he talked, says Nimrod,[9] which he did sparely, he said, in a very few words, things which made everybody laugh; but, unequally gifted as he was, acute in some senses, dull in others, he had a deafness which made him unwieldy in general society.

What, then, could a primeval man do, who was born in England in the reign of George the Fourth?[10] He[h] could take bets and make them. Was it a watery winter's night? He would drive his gig across country under the moon. Was it freezing? He would make his stable-boys hunt rats upon skates. Did some moderately cautious guest admit that he had never been upset in a gig? Mytton at once ran the wheel up the bank and flung them both into the road.[11] Put any obstacle in his way and he leapt it, swam it, smashed it, somehow surmounted it, at the cost of a broken bone or a broken carriage. To yield to danger or to own to pain were both unthinkable. And so the Shropshire peasantry were amazed (as we see them in Alken's and Rawlins's pictures)[12] by the apparition of a gentleman setting his tandem at a gate, riding a bear round his drawing-room, beating a bulldog with naked fists, lying between the hoofs of a nervous horse, riding with broken ribs unmurmuring when every jar was agony. They were amazed; they were scandalised; his eccentricities and infidelities and generosities were the talk of every inn and farmhouse for miles; yet somehow no bailiff in the four counties would arrest him. They looked up at him as one looks at something removed from ordinary duties and joys – a monument, a menace – with contempt and pity and some awe.[i]

But Jack Mytton himself – what was he feeling meanwhile? The thrill of perfect satisfaction, the delight of joys snatched unhesitatingly without compunction? The barbarian surely should have been satisfied. But the by no means introspective mind of Nimrod was puzzled. 'Did[j] the late Mr. Mytton really enjoy life amidst all this profusion of expenditure?'[13] No; Nimrod was of opinion that he did not. He had everything that the human heart could desire, but he lacked 'the art of enjoyment'.[14] He was bored. He was unhappy. 'There was that about him which resembled the restlessness of the hyena.'[15] He hurried from thing to thing, determined to taste and enjoy, but somehow blunted and bruised his pleasures as he touched them. Two hours before his own exquisite dinner he devoured fat bacon and strong ale at a farmhouse, and then blamed his cook.[16] Still, without an appetite, he would eat; still he would drink, only instead of port it must be brandy to lash his flagging palate into sensation. A 'sort of destroying spirit egged him on'.[17] He was magnificent, wasteful, extravagant in every detail. '. . . it was his largeness of heart that ruined Mr. Mytton', said Nimrod, 'added to the lofty pride which disdained the littleness of prudence.'[18]

By the time he was thirty, at any rate, Jack Mytton had done two things that to most men would have been impossible: he[k] had almost ruined his health; he had almost spent his money. He had to leave the ancestral home of the Myttons. But it was no primeval man, glowing with health, bristling with energy, but a 'round-shouldered, tottering old-young man bloated by drink'[19] who joined the company of shady adventurers whose necessities obliged them to live at Calais. Even in that society his burden was upon him; still he must shine; still he must excel. No one should call him Johnny Mytton with impunity. Four horses must draw Mr Mytton the three hundred yards to his rooms or he preferred to walk. And then the hiccough attacked him. Seizing his bedroom candle, he set a light to his shirt and staggered, burning and blazing, to show his friends how Jack Mytton cured the hiccough. What' more could human beings ask of him? To what further frenzies would the gods dare their victim? Now that he had burnt himself alive, it seemed as if he had discharged his obligation to society and could lay the primeval man to rest. He might perhaps allow that other spirit, the civilised gentleman who was so incongruously coupled with the barbarian, to come to the surface. He had once learnt Greek. Now as he lay burnt and bloated in bed he quoted Sophocles – 'the beautiful'[m] passage . . . wherein Oedipus recommends his children to the care of Creon'.[20] He remembered the Greek anthology. When they moved him to the seaside he began to pick up shells, and could hardly sit out dinner in his eagerness to be at the work of brushing them 'with a nail brush dipped in vinegar'. 'He to whom the whole world had appeared insufficient to afford pleasure . . . was now completely happy.'[21] But alas, shells and Sophocles, peace and happiness, were whelmed in the general dissolution which could not be delayed. The King's Bench prison seized him, and there, corrupt in body, ruined in fortune, worn out in mind, he died at the age of thirty-eight. And his wife cried that she could not 'help loving him with all his faults',[22] and four horses drew him to the grave, and three thousand poor people sobbed for the loss of one who had somehow acted out for the benefit of the crowd an odious, monstrous part, laid on him by the gods, for the edification of mankind and their pleasure too, but for his own unutterable misery.[n]

For the truth is we like these exhibitions of human nature. We like to see exalted above us some fox-hunter, like Jack Mytton, burning himself alive to cure the hiccough, some diver like Madame Rosalba, who, mounting higher and higher, wraps herself about in sacking, and then, with a look of indifference and satiety as if she had renounced and suffered and dedicated herself to some insane act of defiance for no pleasure of her own, dives into the Channel and brings up a twopenny-halfpenny soup-plate between her teeth. The lady on the pier feels gratified. It is because of this, she says, that I love my kind.[23][o]

a – Vogue: 'with Acts of Parliament in her bag, findings of Commissions, and a frugal lunch of biscuits and bananas.'

b – Vogue: 'donkey, by'.

c – Vogue: 'gallop"; the rolling meadows; the thunder . . . hounds; the beautiful fields of Leicestershire unfolding; and then the ride home again, stretched, soothed, and satisfied, with the lights coming out in the farmhouses in the dark. The sporting . . . slapdash gentlemanly way, without any special respect for pen and ink, they have written far better than the professionals. This riding and tumbling, being blown . . . to heel with mud have . . . very marrow of English prose and given it that leaping quality, that glow of imagery stripped from hedge and hillside which distinguishes it, not, indeed, above the French, but . . . it. In short, why should she not, in spite of boots and stockings, biscuits and bananas, read the sporting news? Why should she not, having folded up her paper, take from her bag a square red book and proceed, while . . . the life of Jack Mytton?'

d – Vogue: 'Yet Jack . . .' once), he'.

e – Vogue: 'defy them. He went . . . stockings, let . . . skin, swam . . . snow, and still . . . woods, and still . . . He had children'.

f – Vogue: 'filberts. It was as if among all his bets was one with the gods that he would waste their gifts. There'.

g – Vogue: 'aptitudes (Jack Mytton never wore a watch, for he knew the time by instinct), seemed'.

h – Vogue: 'could primeval man do, having cracked his jokes, devoured his filberts, swilled his wine? He'.

i – Vogue: 'and awe.'

j – Vogue: 'compunction? That was a question which occurred to the by . . . of Nimrod. "Did'.

k – Vogue: 'Mytton had gone farther than most men thought possible; he'.

l – Vogue: 'how he cured it. What'.

m – Vogue: 'rest whose antics had dazzled the world, and revive for a few seconds the scholar, the peaceful English Squire, who, if fate had been kinder, might also have had his day. He quoted Sophocles, as he lay burnt and bloated in bed. . . . "the beautiful'.

n – Vogue: 'thirty-eight, and his . . . horses drew his hearse, and three . . . unutterable boredom.'

o – Vogue does not have this sentence.

1 – Originally published as a signed review, entitled 'The Life of John Mytton' (1796–1834) and sub-titled 'A Sporting Writer's History of an Extraordinary | Character of the Early Nineteenth Century', in *Vogue*, early March 1926, (Kp4 C272), of *Memoirs of the Life of the Late John Mytton, Esq. . . .* by Nimrod (Edward Arnold, 1925). This essay was revised for *CR2*. The *Memoirs*

were first published in 1837 (the Preface is dated 1835). Reading Notes (MHP, B 3a) (*VWRN L*). Reprinted: *CE.*

2 – Almost certainly a fictional character. As a child, VW told 'wild stories of the Dilke family and Miss Rosalba the governess' (*MoB*, p. 79). The name is probably derived from a character in William Makepeace Thackeray's story *The Rose and the Ring* (1855) that was well known to the Stephen children. It was adapted for the stage by Harris Deans and put on at Wyndham's in December 1923. VW's niece, Angelica Garnett, was 'named after the Princess Angelica' in that story: see Angelica Garnett, *The Eternal Moment: Essays and a Short Story* (Puckerbrush Press, 1998), p. 33.

3 – Peter Beckford (1739/40–1811), sportsman, master of hounds, and author noted for his great urbanity and wit; his *Thoughts upon Hare and Fox Hunting . . .* and *Essays on Hunting . . .* 'with an introduction describing the method of Hare-hunting among the Greeks' were published in 1781; VW owned a copy of his *Thoughts on Hunting*, intro. by Charles Richardson (Abbey Classics, Chapman & Donn, n.d. [1923]). Charles George William St John (1809–56), sportsman and naturalist, author of *Short Sketches of the Wild Sports and Natural History of the Highlands* (1846). Robert Smith Surtees (1805–64), novelist, creator of the inimitable Jorrocks and Soapy Sponge. Clarissa Dalloway thinks of buying *Jorrocks's Jaunts and Jollities* (1838; Methuen reprinted in September 1923) or *Mr. Sponge's Sporting Tour* (1853) from Hatchard's in Piccadilly: see *Mrs. Dalloway* (Hogarth Press, 1925), p. 17. 'Nimrod', pseudonym of Charles James Apperley (1778–1843), huntsman and sporting writer, author of several books and celebrated contributor to the *Sporting Magazine*, *Sporting Review* and, most beneficially to his reputation, the *Quarterly Review*. He was an early champion of the work of Surtees.

4 – See *Memoirs*, p. 2.

5 – Mytton did follow briefly in the footsteps of his ancestors, serving as Tory MP for Shrewsbury, May 1819–February 1820.

6 – See *Memoirs*, p. 13.

7 – Mytton married in 1818 Harriet Emma (d. 1820), eldest daughter of Sir Thomas Tyrwhitt Jones; and in 1821, Caroline Mallett, *née* Giffard.

8 – See *Memoirs*, p. 14.

9 – See *ibid.*, p. 59.

10 – George IV (1762–1830), reigned from 1820.

11 – See *Memoirs*, p. 16.

12 – Henry (Thomas) Alken (1785–1851), sporting artist, and T. J. Rawlins, collaborated in the illustration of Nimrod's work on Mytton.

13 – *Memoirs*, pp. 34–5.

14 – *Ibid.*, p. 35, which has: 'It is true he had most of the requisites for a man of a noble fortune . . . but one thing was wanting . . . *the art of enjoying it*, to which he, Mytton, was a stranger.'

15 – *Ibid.*, p. 35.

16 – See *ibid.*

17 – *Ibid.*, p. 131.

18 – *Ibid.*, p. 30, which has: 'It was that "largeness of heart, even as is the sand that is on the sea shore," which Solomon possessed [1 Kings 4: 29], but unaccompanied by his means as well as his wisdom, which ruined Mr. Mytton; added to a lofty pride which disdained the littleness of prudence, and a sort of destroying spirit that appeared to run amuck at fortune.'

19 – *Ibid.*, p. 92, which has: 'round-shouldered, decrepid, tottering *old-young* man . . . bloated by drink'.

20 – *Ibid.*, p. 106. See *The Oedipus Tyrannus of Sophocles* [c. 496–406 BC], trans. J. T. Sheppard (Cambridge University Press, 1922), pp. 46–8.

21 – *Memoirs*, p. 110.

22 – Quoted *ibid.*, p. 87.

23 – Cf. 'The Man who Loved his Kind', *CSF*. The short story was probably drafted no earlier than 22 May 1925.

De Quincey's Autobiography

It must often strike the reader that very little criticism worthy of being called so has been written in English of prose – our great critics have given the best of their minds to poetry. And the reason perhaps why prose so seldom calls out the higher faculties of the critic, but invites him to argue a case or to discuss the personality of the writer – to take a theme from the book and make his criticism an air played in variation on it – is to be sought in the prose-writer's attitude to his own work. Even if he writes as an artist, without a practical end in view, still he treats prose as a humble beast of burden which must accommodate all sorts of odds and ends; as an impure substance in which dust and twigs and flies find lodgment. But more often than not the prose-writer has a practical aim in view, a theory to argue, or a cause to plead, and with it adopts the moralist's view that the remote, the difficult, and the complex are to be abjured. His duty is to the present and the living. He is proud to call himself a journalist. He must use the simplest words and express himself as clearly as possible in order to reach the greatest number in the plainest way. Therefore he cannot complain of the critics if his writing, like the irritation in the oyster, serves only to breed other art; nor be surprised if his pages, once they have delivered their message, are thrown on the rubbish heap like other objects that have served their turn.

But sometimes we meet even in prose with writing that seems inspired by other aims. It does not wish to argue or to convert or even to tell a story. We can draw all our pleasure from the words themselves; we have not to enhance it by reading between the lines or by making a voyage of discovery into the psychology of the writer. De Quincey, of course, is one of these rare beings. When we bring his work to mind we recall it by some passage of stillness and completeness, like the following:

'Life is Finished!' was the secret misgiving of my heart; for the heart of infancy is as apprehensive as that of maturest wisdom in relation to any capital wound inflicted on the happiness. *'Life is Finished! Finished it is!'* was the hidden meaning that, half-unconsciously to myself, lurked within my sighs; and, as bells heard from a distance on a summer evening seem charged at times with an articulate form of words, some monitory message, that rolls round unceasingly, even so for me some noiseless and subterraneous voice seemed to chant continually a secret word, made audible only to my own heart – that 'now is the blossoming of life withered for ever'.[2]

Such passages occur naturally, for they consist of visions and dreams, not of actions or of dramatic scenes, in his autobiographic sketches. And yet we are not made to think of him, De Quincey, as we read. If we try to analyse our sensations we shall find that we are worked upon as if by music – the senses are stirred rather than the brain. The rise and fall of the sentence immediately soothes us to a mood and removes us to a distance in which the near fades and detail is extinguished. Our minds, thus widened and lulled to a width of apprehension, stand open to receive one by one in slow and stately procession the ideas which De Quincey wishes us to receive; the golden fullness of life; the pomps of the heaven above; the glory of the flowers below, as he stands 'between an open window and a dead body on a summer's day'.[3] The theme is supported and amplified and varied. The idea of hurry and trepidation, of reaching towards something that for ever flies, intensifies the impression of stillness and eternity. Bells heard on summer evenings, palm-trees waving, sad winds that blow for ever, keep us by successive waves of emotion in the same mood. The emotion is never stated; it is suggested and brought slowly by repeated images before us until it stays, in all its complexity, complete.

The effect is one that is very rarely attempted in prose and is rarely appropriate to it because of this very quality of finality. It does not lead anywhere. We do not add to our sense of high summer and death and immortality any consciousness of who is hearing, seeing, and feeling. De Quincey wished to shut out from us everything save the picture 'of a solitary infant, and its solitary combat with grief – a mighty darkness, and a sorrow without a voice',[4] to make us fathom and explore the depths of that single emotion. It is a state which is general and not particular. Therefore De Quincey was at odds with the aims of the prose-writer and his morality. His reader was to be put in possession of a meaning of that complex kind which is largely a sensation. He had to become fully aware not merely of the fact that a child was standing by a bed, but of stillness, sunlight, flowers, the passage of time and the presence of death. None of this could be conveyed by simple words in their logical order; clarity and simplicity would merely travesty and deform such a meaning. De Quincey, of course, was fully aware of the gulf that lay between him as a writer who wished to convey such ideas and his contemporaries. He turned from the neat, precise speech of his time to Milton and Jeremy Taylor and Sir Thomas Browne;[5] from them he learnt the roll of the long sentence that sweeps its coils in and out, that piles its summit higher and higher. Then followed a discipline exacted, most drastically, by the fineness of his own ear – the weighing of cadences, the consideration of pauses; the effect of repetitions and consonances and assonances – all this was part of the duty of a writer who wishes to put a complex meaning fully and completely before his reader.

When, therefore, we come to consider critically one of the passages that has made so deep an impression we find that it has been produced much as a poet like Tennyson would produce it. There is the same care in the use of sound; the same variety of measure; the length of the sentence is varied and its weight shifted. But all these measures are diluted to a lower degree of strength and their force is spread over a much greater space, so that the transition from the lowest compass to the highest is by a gradation of shallow steps and we reach the utmost heights without violence. Hence the difficulty of stressing the particular quality of any single line as in a poem and the futility of taking one passage apart from the context, since its effect is compound of suggestions that have been received sometimes several pages earlier. Moreover, De Quincey, unlike some of his masters, was not at his best in sudden majesty of phrase; his power lay in suggesting large and generalised visions; landscapes in which nothing is seen in detail; faces without features; the stillness of midnight or summer; the tumult and trepidation of flying multitudes; anguish that for ever falls and rises and casts its arms upwards in despair.

But De Quincey was not merely the master of separate passages of beautiful prose; if that had been so his achievement would have been far less than it is. He was also a writer of narrative, an autobiographer, and one, if we consider that he wrote in the year 1833, with very peculiar views of the art of autobiography. In the first place he was convinced of the enormous value of candour.

If he were really able to pierce the haze which so often envelops, even to himself, his own secret springs of action and reserve, there cannot be a life moving at all under intellectual impulses that would not, through that single force of absolute frankness, fall within the reach of a deep, solemn, and sometimes even of a thrilling interest.[6]

He understood by autobiography the history not only of the external life but of the deeper and more hidden emotions. And he realised the difficulty of making such a confession: '. . . vast numbers of people, though liberated from all reasonable motives of self-restraint, *cannot* be confidential – have it not in their power to lay aside reserve'.[7] Aerial chains, invisible spells, bind and freeze the free spirit of communication. 'It is because a man cannot see and measure these mystical forces which palsy him that he cannot deal with them effectually.'[8] With such perceptions and intentions it is strange that De Quincey failed to be among the great autobiographers of our literature. Certainly he was not tongue-tied or spellbound. Perhaps one of the reasons that led him to fail in his task of self-delineation was not the lack of expressive power, but the superfluity. He was profusely and indiscriminately loquacious. Discursiveness – the disease that attacked so many of the nineteenth-century English writers[9] – had him in her coils. But while it is easy to see why the works of Ruskin or Carlyle are huge and formless – every kind of heterogeneous object had to be found room for somehow, somewhere – De Quincey had not their excuse. The burden of the prophet was not laid upon him. He was, moreover, the most careful of artists. Nobody tunes the sound and modulates the cadence of a sentence more carefully and more exquisitely. But strangely enough, the sensibility which was on the alert to warn him instantly if a sound clashed or a rhythm flagged failed him completely when it came to the architecture of the whole. Then he could tolerate a disproportion and profusion that make his book as dropsical and shapeless as each sentence is symmetrical and smooth. He is indeed, to use the expressive word coined by his brother to describe De Quincey's tendency as a small boy 'to plead some distinction or verbal demur',[10] the prince of Pettifogulisers. Not only did he find 'in everybody's words an unintentional opening left for double interpretations';[11] he could not tell the simplest story without qualifying and illustrating and introducing additional information until the point that was to be cleared up has long since become extinct in the dim mists of the distance.

Together with this fatal verbosity and weakness of architectural power, De Quincey suffered too as an autobiographer from a tendency to meditative abstraction. 'It was my disease', he said, 'to meditate too much and to observe too little.'[12] A curious formality diffuses his vision to a general vagueness, lapsing into a colourless monotony. He shed over everything the lustre and the amenity of his own dreaming, pondering absent-mindedness. He approached even the two disgusting idiots with their red eyes with the elaboration of a great gentleman who has by mistake wandered into a slum. So too he slipped mellifluously across all the fissures of the social scale – talking on equal terms with the young aristocrats at Eton or with the working-class family as they chose a joint of meat for their Sunday dinner. De Quincey indeed prided himself upon the ease with which he passed from one sphere to another: '. . . from my very earliest youth', he observed, 'it has been my pride to converse familiarly, *more Socratico*, with all human beings, man, woman, and child, that chance might fling in my way'.[13] But as we read his descriptions of these men, women, and children we are led to think that he talked to them so easily because to him they differed so little. The same manner served equally for them all. His relations even with those with whom he was most intimate, whether it was Lord Altamont, his schoolboy friend,[14] or Ann the prostitute, were equally ceremonial and gracious. His portraits have the flowing contours, the statuesque poses, the undifferentiated features of Scott's heroes and heroines. Nor is his own face exempted from the general ambiguity. When it came to telling the truth about himself he shrank from the task with all the horror of a well-bred English gentleman. The candour which fascinates us in the confessions of Rousseau[15] – the determination to reveal the ridiculous, the mean, the sordid in himself – was abhorrent to him. 'Nothing indeed is more revolting to English feelings', he wrote, 'than the spectacle of a human being obtruding on our notice his moral ulcers and scars.'[16]

Clearly, therefore, De Quincey as an autobiographer labours under great defects. He is diffuse and redundant; he is aloof and dreamy and in bondage to the old pruderies and conventions. At the same time he was capable of being transfixed by the mysterious solemnity of certain emotions; of realising how one moment may transcend in value fifty years. He was able to devote to their analysis a skill which the professed analysts of the human heart – the Scotts, the Jane Austens, the Byrons[17] – did not then possess. We find him writing passages which, in their self-consciousness, are scarcely to be matched in the fiction of the nineteenth century:

And, recollecting it, I am struck with the truth, that far more of our deepest thoughts and feelings pass to us through perplexed combinations of *concrete* objects, pass to us as *involutes* (if I may coin that word) in compound experiences incapable of being disentangled, than ever reach us *directly* and in their own abstract shapes. . . . Man is doubtless *one* by some subtle *nexus*, some system of links, that we cannot perceive, extending from the new-born infant to the superannuated dotard: but, as regards many affections and passions incident to his nature at different stages, he is *not* one, but an intermitting creature, ending and beginning anew; the unity of man, in this respect, is coextensive only with the particular stage to which the passion belongs. Some passions, as that of sexual love, are celestial by one-half of their origin, animal and earthly by the other half. These will not survive their own appropriate stage. But love which is *altogether* holy, like that between two children, is privileged to revisit by glimpses the silence and the darkness of declining years. . . .[18]

When we read such passages of analysis, when such states of mind seem in retrospect to be an important element in life and so to deserve scrutiny and record, the art of autobiography as the eighteenth century knew it is changing its character. The art of biography also is being transformed. Nobody after that could maintain that the whole truth of life can be told without 'piercing the haze'; without revealing 'his own secret springs of action and reserve'. Yet external events also have their importance. To tell the whole story of a life the autobiographer must devise some means by which the two levels of existence can be recorded – the rapid passage of events and actions; the slow opening up of single and solemn moments of concentrated emotion.[19] It is the fascination of De Quincey's pages that the two levels are beautifully, if unequally, combined. For page after page we are in company with a cultivated gentleman who describes with charm and eloquence what he has seen and known – the stage coaches, the Irish rebellion, the appearance and conversation of George the Third. Then suddenly the smooth narrative parts asunder, arch opens beyond arch, the vision of something for ever flying, for ever escaping, is revealed, and time stands still.

1 – This essay was written specifically for *CR2*, for which VW primarily used the first volume of Thomas De Quincey's *Works* (James Hogg & Sons, 1853). In December 1927 VW had been thinking about De Quincey (1785–1859): 'I am trying to write about Lord Chesterfield and de Quincey. But the moment I start writing, I think I should like to write a story. Then I begin a story: then I think about de Quincey' (*III VW Letters*, no. 1843). However, it seems that it was only in 1932 that she drafted this essay. On 25 March she wrote: 'I think I'll go into the house & fetch my de Quincey who comes next'; then on 11 April: 'This perpetual criticism tires my brain. I've almost done de Quincey though, & am well on with the book'; and finally on 28 June: 'Just "finished De Quincey". Thus am I trying to keep pace with the days & deliver the 2nd C.R. done on the last of June – which I see with dismay is Thursday' (*IV VW Diary*). See also 'The English Mail Coach', *I VW Essays*, Appendix I; '"Impassioned Prose"', *IV VW Essays*. Reading notes (MHP, B 2p) (*VWRN XLVIII*). Draft (MHP, B 2e). Reprinted: *CE*.
2 – 'The Affliction of Childhood', ch. i, opening paragraph, in *Autobiographic Sketches*; *Works*, vol. i, p. 1.
3 – *Ibid.*, pp. 16–17.
4 – Preface, *Autobiographic Sketches*; *Works*, vol. i, p. xi, which does not have: 'of'.
5 – John Milton (1608–74); Jeremy Taylor (1613–67); Sir Thomas Browne (1605–82).
6 – Preface, *Autobiographic Sketches*; *Works*, vol. i, p. xii, which has: 'able really'.
7 – *Ibid.*, p. xi, which has: 'motives to self-restraint'.
8 – *Ibid.*, p. xii.
9 – Cf. O, ch. v, p. 207: in the nineteenth century 'sentences swelled, adjectives multiplied, lyrics became epics, and little trifles that had been essays a column long were now encyclopaedias in ten or twenty volumes. But Eusebius Chubb shall be our witness to the effect this all had upon the mind of a sensitive man who could do nothing to stop it. There is a passage towards the end of his memoirs where he describes how, after writing thirty-five folio pages one morning "all about nothing" he screwed the lid on his inkpot and went for a turn in his garden.'
10 – 'Introduction to the World of Strife', ch. ii, *Autobiographic Sketches*; *Works*, vol. i, p. 60.
11 – *Ibid.*, p. 61, which has: 'in almost everybody's words,'.
12 – De Quincey, *Confessions of an English Opium-Eater*, ed. Richard Garnett

(1821; Kegan Paul, Trench, 1885), pt ii, 'The Pleasures of Opium', p. 92, which begins: 'I, whose disease it was . . .'
13 – *Ibid.*, pt i, 'Preliminary Confessions', p. 40.
14 – Peter Howe Brown (1788–1845), Lord Westport, son of the Earl of Altamont.
15 – Jean-Jacques Rousseau (1712–78).
16 – *Confessions*, 'To the Reader', p. 3.
17 – Sir Walter Scott (1771–1832); Jane Austen (1775–1817); George Gordon, Lord Byron (1788–1824).
18 – 'The Affliction of Childhood', ch. i, *Autobiographic Sketches; Works*, vol. i, pp. 13, 18–19.
19 – Cf. the last paragraph of 'The New Biography', *IV VW Essays*.

Four Figures

I

Cowper and Lady Austen

It happened, of course, many years ago, but there must have been something remarkable about the meeting, since people still like to bring it before their eyes. An elderly gentleman was looking out of his window in a village street in the summer of 1781 when he saw two ladies go into a draper's shop opposite. The look of one of them interested him very much, and he seems to have said so, for soon a meeting was arranged.

A quiet and solitary life that must have been, in which a gentleman stood in the morning looking out of the window, in which the sight of an attractive face was an event. Yet perhaps it was an event partly because it revived some half-forgotten but still pungent memories. For Cowper had not always looked at the world from the windows of a house in a village street. Time was when the sight of ladies of fashion had been familiar enough. In his younger days he had been very foolish. He had flirted and giggled; he had gone smartly dressed to Vauxhall and Marylebone Gardens. He had taken his work at the Law Courts with a levity that alarmed his friends – for he had nothing whatever to live upon. He had fallen in*a* love with his cousin Theodora

Cowper.[2] Indeed, he had been a thoughtless, wild young man. But suddenly in the heyday of his youth, in the midst of his gaiety, something[b] terrible had happened. There lurked beneath that levity and perhaps inspired it a morbidity that sprang from some defect of person, a dread which made action, which made marriage, which made any public exhibition of himself insupportable. If goaded[c] to it, and he was now committed to a public career in the House of Lords, he must fly, even into the jaws of death. Rather than take up his appointment he would drown himself. But a man sat on[d] the quay when he came to the water's edge; some invisible hand mysteriously forced the laudanum from his lips when he tried to drink it; the knife which he pressed to his heart broke; and the garter with which he tried to hang himself from the bed-post let him fall. Cowper was condemned to live.

When, therefore, that July morning he looked out of the window at the ladies shopping, he had come through gulfs of despair, but he had reached at last not only the haven of a quiet country town, but a settled state of mind, a settled way[e] of life. He was domesticated with Mrs Unwin, a widow six years his elder.[3] By letting him talk, and listening to his terrors and understanding them, she had brought him very wisely, like a mother, to[f] something like peace of mind. They had lived side by side for many years in methodical monotony. They began the day by reading the Scriptures together; they then went to church; they parted to read or walk; they met after dinner to converse on religious topics or to sing hymns together; then again they walked if it were fine, or read and talked if it were wet, and at last the day ended with more hymns and more prayers. Such for many years had been the routine of Cowper's life with Mary Unwin. When his fingers found their way to a pen they traced the lines of a hymn, or if they wrote a letter it was to urge some misguided mortal, his brother John,[4] for instance, at Cambridge, to seek salvation before it was too late. Yet this urgency was akin perhaps to the old levity; it, too, was an attempt to ward off some terror, to propitiate some deep unrest[g] that lurked at the bottom of his soul. Suddenly the peace was broken. One night in February 1773 the enemy rose; it smote once and for ever. An awful voice called out to Cowper in a dream. It proclaimed that he was damned, that he was outcast, and he[h] fell prostrate before it. After that he could not pray. When the others said grace at table, he took up his knife and fork as a sign that he had no right to join their prayers. Nobody, not even Mrs Unwin, understood the terrific import of the dream. Nobody realised why he was unique; why he[i] was singled out from all mankind and stood alone in his damnation. But that loneliness had a strange effect – since he was no longer capable of help or direction he was free. The Rev. John Newton[5] could no longer guide his pen or inspire his muse. Since doom had been pronounced and damnation was inevitable, he might sport with hares, cultivate cucumbers, listen to village gossip, weave nets, make tables; all[j] that could be hoped was to while away the dreadful years without the ability to enlighten others or to be helped himself.[k] Never had Cowper written more enchantingly, more gaily, to his[l] friends than now that he knew himself condemned. It was only at moments, when[m] he wrote to Newton or to Unwin, that the terror raised its horrid head above the surface and that he cried aloud: 'My days are spent in vanity. . . . Nature revives again; but a soul once slain lives no more.'[6] For the most part, as he idled his time away in pleasant pastimes, as he looked with[n] amusement at what passed in the street below, one might think him the happiest of men. There was Geary Ball[7] going to the 'Royal Oak' to drink his dram – that happened as regularly as Cowper brushed his teeth; but behold – two[o] ladies were going into the draper's shop opposite. That was an event.

One of the ladies he knew already – she was Mrs Jones, the wife of a neighbouring clergyman. But the other was a stranger. She was arch and sprightly, with dark hair and round dark eyes. Though a widow – she had been the wife of a Sir[p] Robert Austen[8] – she was far from old and not at all solemn. When she talked, for she and Cowper were soon drinking tea together, 'she laughs and makes laugh, and keeps up a conversation without seeming to labour at it'.[9] She was a lively, well-bred woman who had lived much in France, and, having seen much of the world, 'accounts it a great simpleton as it is'.[10] Such were Cowper's first impressions of Ann Austen. Ann's first impressions of the queer couple who lived in the large house in the village street were even more enthusiastic. But that was natural – Ann was an enthusiast by nature. Moreover, though she had seen a great deal of the world and had a town house in Queen Anne Street, she had no friends or relations in that world much[q] to her liking. Clifton Reynes, where her sister lived, was a rude, rough English village where the inhabitants broke into the house if a lady were left unprotected. Lady Austen was[r] dissatisfied; she wanted society, but she also wanted to be settled and to[s] be serious. Neither Clifton Reynes nor Queen Anne Street gave her altogether what she wanted. And then in the

461

most opportune way – quite by chance – she met a refined, well-bred couple who were ready to appreciate what she had to give and ready to invite her to share the quiet pleasures of the countryside which were so dear to them. She*t* could heighten those pleasures deliciously. She made the days seem full of movement and laughter. She organised picnics – they went to the Spinnie and ate their dinner in the root-house and drank their tea on the top of a wheelbarrow. And when autumn came and the evenings drew in, Ann Austen enlivened them too; she it was who stirred William to write a poem about a sofa, and told him, just as he was sinking into one of his fits of melancholy, the story of John Gilpin,[11] so that he leapt out of bed, shaking with laughter. But beneath her sprightliness they were*u* glad to find that she was seriously inclined. She longed for peace and quietude, 'for with all that gaiety', Cowper wrote, 'she is a great thinker'.[12]

And with all that melancholy, to paraphrase*v* his words, Cowper was a man of the world. As he said himself, he was not by nature a recluse. He was no lean and solitary hermit. His limbs were sturdy; his cheeks were ruddy; he was growing plump. In his younger days he, too, had known the world, and provided, of course, that you have seen through it, there is something to be said for having known it. Cowper, at any rate, was a little proud of his gentle birth. Even at Olney he kept certain standards of gentility. He must have an elegant box for his snuff and silver buckles for his shoes; if he wanted a hat it must be 'not a round slouch, which I abhor, but a smart, well-cocked, fashionable affair'.[13] His letters preserve this serenity, this good sense, this sidelong, arch humour embalmed in page after page of beautiful*w* clear prose. As the post went only three times a week he had plenty of time to smooth out every little crease in daily life to perfection. He had time to tell how a farmer was thrown from his cart and one of the pet hares had escaped; Mr Grenville had called; they had been caught in a shower and Mrs Throckmorton had asked*x* them to come into the house – some little*y* thing of the kind happened every week very aptly for his purpose. Or if nothing happened and it was true that the days went by at Olney 'shod with felt',[14] then he was able to let his mind play with rumours*z* that reached him from the outer world. There was talk of flying. He would write a few pages on the subject of flying and its impiety; he would express his opinion of the wickedness, for Englishwomen at any rate, of painting*aa* the cheeks. He would discourse upon Homer and Virgil[15] and perhaps attempt a few translations himself. And when the days were dark and even he could no longer trudge through the mud, he would open one of his favourite travellers and dream that he was voyaging with Cook or with Anson,[16] for he travelled widely in imagination, though in body he moved no further than from Buckingham to Sussex and from Sussex back to Buckingham again.[bb]

His letters preserve what must have made the charm of his company. It is easy to see that his wit, his stories, his sedate, considerate ways, must have made his morning visits – and he had got into the habit of visiting Lady Austen at eleven every morning – delightful. But there was more in his society than that – there was some charm, some peculiar fascination, that made it indispensable. His cousin Theodora had loved him – she still loved[cc] him anonymously; Mrs Unwin loved him; and now Ann Austen was beginning to feel something stronger than friendship rise[dd] within her. That strain of intense and perhaps inhuman passion which rested with tremulous ecstasy like that of a hawk-moth over a flower, upon some tree, some hill-side – did that not tensify[ee] the quiet of the country morning, and give to intercourse with him some keener interest than belonged to the society of other men? 'The very stones in the garden walls are my intimate acquaintance',[17] he wrote. 'Everything I see in the fields is to me an object, and I can look at the same rivulet, or at a handsome tree, every day of my life with new pleasure.'[18] It is this intensity of vision that gives his poetry, with all its moralising and didacticism, its unforgettable qualities. It is this that makes passages[ff] in *The Task* like clear windows let into the prosaic fabric of the rest. It was this that gave the edge and zest to his talk. Some finer vision suddenly seized and possessed him. It[gg] must have given to the long winter evenings, to the early morning visits, an indescribable combination of pathos and charm. Only, as Theodora could have warned Ann Austen, his passion was not for men and women; it[hh] was an abstract ardour; he was a man singularly without thought of sex.

Already early in their friendship Ann Austen had been warned. She adored her friends, and she expressed her adoration with the enthusiasm that was natural to her. At[ii] once Cowper wrote to her kindly but firmly admonishing her of the folly of her ways. 'When we embellish a creature with colours taken from our fancy,' he wrote, 'we make it an idol . . . and shall derive nothing from it but a painful conviction of our error.'[19] Ann read the letter, flew into a rage, and left the country in a huff. But the breach was soon healed; she worked him ruffles; he acknowledged them with a present of his book. Soon she had embraced Mary Unwin and was back again on more intimate terms than ever. In another month indeed, with such rapidity did her plans take effect, she had sold the lease of her town house, taken part of the vicarage next door to Cowper, and declared that she had now no home but Olney and no friends but Cowper and Mary Unwin. The door between the gardens was opened; the two families dined together on alternate nights; William called Ann sister; and Ann called William brother. What arrangement could have been more idyllic? 'Lady Austen and we pass our days alternately at each other's chateau. In the morning I walk with one or other of the ladies, and in the afternoon wind thread',[20] wrote Cowper, playfully comparing himself to Hercules and Samson.[21] And then the evening came, the winter evening which he loved best, and he dreamt in the firelight and watched the shadows dance uncouthly and the sooty films play upon[jj] the bars until the lamp was brought, and in that level light he had out his netting, or wound silk, and then, perhaps, Ann sang to the harpsichord and Mary and William played battledore and shuttlecock together. Secure, innocent, peaceful, where then was that 'thistly sorrow'[22] that grows inevitably, so Cowper said, beside human happiness? Where would discord come, if come it must? The danger lay perhaps with the women. It might be that Mary would notice one evening that[kk] Ann wore a lock of William's hair set in diamonds. She might find a poem to Ann in which he expressed more than a brotherly affection. She would grow jealous. For Mary Unwin was[ll] no country simpleton, she was a well-read woman with 'the manners of a Duchess';[23] she[mm] had nursed and consoled William for years before Ann came to flutter the 'still life'[24] which they both loved best. Thus the two ladies would compete; discord would enter at that point. Cowper would be forced to choose between them.

But we are forgetting another presence at that innocent evening's entertainment. Ann might sing; Mary might play; the fire might burn brightly and the frost and the wind[nn] outside make the fireside calm all the sweeter. But there was a shadow among them. In that tranquil room a gulf opened. Cowper trod on the verge of an abyss. Whispers mingled with the singing, voices hissed in his ear words of doom and damnation. He was haled by a terrible voice to perdition. And then Ann Austen expected him to make love to her! Then Ann[oo] Austen wanted him to marry her! The thought was odious; it was indecent; it was intolerable. He wrote her another letter, a letter to which there could be no reply. In her bitterness Ann burnt it. She left

Olney and no word ever passed between them again. The friendship was over.

And Cowper did not mind very much. Everybody was extremely kind to him. The Throckmortons gave him the key of their garden. An anonymous friend – he never guessed her name – gave[pp] him fifty pounds a year. A cedar desk with silver handles was sent him by another friend who wished also to[qq] remain unknown. The kind people at Olney supplied him with almost too many tame hares. But if you are damned, if you are solitary, if you are cut off from God and man, what does human kindness avail? 'It is all vanity. . . . Nature revives again; but a soul once slain lives no more.' He sank from gloom to gloom, and died in misery.

As for Lady Austen, she married a Frenchman. She was happy – so people said.[25]

II

Beau Brummell

When Cowper, in the seclusion of Olney, was roused to anger by the thought of the Duchess of Devonshire and predicted a time when 'instead of a girdle there will be a rent, and instead of beauty, baldness', he was acknowledging the power of the lady whom he thought so despicable. Why, otherwise, should she haunt the damp solitudes of Olney? Why should the rustle of her silken skirts disturb those gloomy meditations? Undoubtedly the Duchess was a good haunter. Long after those words were written, when she was dead and buried beneath a tinsel coronet, her ghost mounted the stairs of a very different dwelling-place. An old man was sitting in his arm-chair at Caen. The door opened, and the servant announced, 'The Duchess of Devonshire'. Beau Brummell at once rose, went to the door and made a bow that would have graced the Court of St James's. Only, unfortunately, there was nobody there. The cold air blew up the staircase of an Inn. The Duchess was long dead, and Beau Brummell, in his old age and imbecility, was dreaming that he was back in London again giving a party. Cowper's curse had come true for both of them. The Duchess lay in her shroud, and Brummell, whose clothes had been the envy of kings, had now only one pair of much-mended trousers, which he hid as best he could under a tattered cloak. As for his hair, that had been shaved by order of the doctor.

But though Cowper's sour predictions had thus come to pass, both the Duchess and the dandy might claim that they had had their day. They had been great figures in their time. Of the two, perhaps Brummell might boast the more miraculous career. He had no advantage of birth, and but little of fortune. His grandfather had let rooms in St James's Street. He had only a moderate capital of thirty thousand pounds to begin with, and his beauty, of figure rather than of face, was marred by a broken nose. Yet without a single noble, important, or valuable action to his credit he cuts a figure; he stands for a symbol; his ghost walks among us still. The reason for this eminence is now a little difficult to determine. Skill of hand and nicety of judgment were his, of course, otherwise he would not have brought the art of tying neck-cloths to perfection. The story is, perhaps, too well known – how he drew his head far back and sunk his chin slowly down so that the cloth wrinkled in perfect symmetry, or if one wrinkle were[a] too deep or too shallow, the cloth was thrown into a basket and the attempt renewed, while the Prince of Wales sat, hour after hour, watching. Yet skill of hand and nicety of judgment were not enough. Brummell owed his ascendency to some curious combination of wit, of taste, of insolence, of independence – for he was never a toady – which it were too heavy-handed to call a philosophy of life, but served the purpose. At any rate, ever since he was the most popular boy at Eton, coolly jesting when they were for throwing a bargee into the river, 'My good fellows, don't send him into the river; the man is evidently in a high state of perspiration, and it almost amounts to a certainty that he will catch cold', he floated buoyantly and gaily and without apparent effort to the top of whatever society he found himself among.[b] Even when he was a captain in the Tenth Hussars and so scandalously inattentive to duty that he only knew his troop by 'the very large blue nose' of one of the men, he was liked and tolerated. When he resigned his commission, for the regiment was to be sent to Manchester – and 'I really could not go – think, your Royal Highness, Manchester!' – he had only to set up house in Chesterfield Street to become the head of the most jealous and exclusive society of his time. For example, he was at Almack's one night talking to Lord ——. The Duchess of —— was there, escorting her young daughter, Lady Louisa. The Duchess caught sight of Mr Brummell, and at once warned her daughter that if that gentleman near the door came and spoke to them she was to be careful to impress him favourably, 'for', and she sank her voice to a whisper, 'he is the celebrated Mr Brummell'. Lady Louisa might well have wondered why a Mr Brummell was celebrated, and why a Duke's daughter need take care to impress a Mr Brummell. And then, directly he began to move towards them, the reason of her mother's warning became apparent. The grace of his carriage was so astonishing; his bows were so exquisite. Everybody looked overdressed or badly dressed – some, indeed, looked positively dirty – beside^c him. His clothes seemed to melt into each other with the perfection of their cut and the quiet harmony of their colour. Without a single point of emphasis everything was distinguished – from his bow to the way he opened his snuff-box, with his left hand invariably. He was the personification of freshness and cleanliness and order. One could well believe that he had his chair brought into his dressing-room and was deposited at Almack's without letting a puff of wind disturb his curls or a spot of mud stain his shoes. When he actually spoke to her, Lady Louisa would be at first enchanted – no one was more agreeable, more amusing, had a manner that was more flattering and enticing – and then she would be puzzled. It was quite possible that before the evening was out he would ask her to marry him, and yet his manner of doing it was such that the most ingenuous débutante could not believe that he meant it seriously. His odd grey eyes seemed to contradict his lips; they had a look in them which made the sincerity of his compliments very doubtful. And then he said very cutting things about other people. They were not exactly witty; they were certainly not profound; but they were so skilful, so adroit – they had a twist in them^d which made them slip into the mind and stay there when more important phrases were forgotten. He had downed the Regent himself with his dexterous 'Who's your fat friend?'[2] and his method was the same with humbler people who snubbed him or bored him. 'Why, what could I do, my good fellow, but cut the connection? I discovered that Lady Mary actually ate cabbage!' – so he explained to a friend his failure to marry a lady.^e And, again, when some dull citizen pestered him about his tour to the North, 'Which of the lakes do I admire?' he asked his valet. 'Windermere, sir.' 'Ah, yes – Windermere, so it is – Windermere.' That was his style, flickering, sneering, hovering on the verge of insolence, skimming the edge of nonsense, but always keeping within some curious mean, so that one knew the false Brummell story from the true by its exaggeration.

(corrected markers: beside[c], them[d], friend?'[2], lady.[e])

Brummell could never have said, 'Wales, ring the bell', any more than he could have^f worn a brightly coloured waistcoat or a glaring necktie. That 'certain exquisite propriety' which Lord Byron remarked in his dress stamped his whole^g being, and made him appear cool, refined, and debonair among the gentlemen who talked only of sport, which Brummell detested, and smelt of the stable, which Brummell never visited. Lady Louisa might well be on tenter-hooks to impress Mr Brummell favourably. Mr Brummell's good opinion was of the utmost importance in the world of Lady Louisa.

And unless that world fell into ruins his rule seemed assured. Handsome, heartless, and cynical, the Beau seemed invulnerable. His taste was impeccable, his health admirable,^{h} and his figure as fine as ever. His rule had lasted many years and survived many vicissitudes. The French Revolution had passed over his head without disordering a single hair. Empires had risen and fallen while he experimented with the crease of a neck-cloth and criticised the cut of a coat. Now the battle of Waterloo had been fought and peace had come. The battle left him untouched; it^i was the peace that undid him. For some time past he had been winning and losing at the gaming-tables. Harriette Wilson had heard that he was ruined, and then, not without disappointment, that he was safe again. Now, with the armies disbanded, there was let loose upon London a horde of rough, ill-mannered men who had been fighting all those^j years and were determined to enjoy themselves. They flooded the gaming-houses. They played very high. Brummell was forced into competition. He lost and won and vowed^k never to play again, and then he did play again. At last his remaining ten thousand pounds was gone. He borrowed until he could borrow no more. And finally, to crown the loss of so many thousands, he lost the sixpenny-bit with a hole in it which had always brought him good luck. He gave it by mistake to a hackney coachman: that rascal Rothschild got hold of it, he said, and that was the end of his luck. Such was his own account of the affair – other people put a less innocent interpretation on the matter. At any rate there came a day, 16th May 1816, to be precise – it was a day upon which everything was precise – when he dined alone off a cold fowl and a bottle of claret at Watier's, attended the opera, and then took coach for Dover. He drove rapidly all through the night and reached Calais the day after. He never set foot in England again.

And now a curious process of disintegration set in. The peculiar and highly artificial society of London had acted as a preservative; it had kept him in being; it had concentrated him into one single gem.

Now that the pressure was removed, the odds and ends, so trifling separately, so brilliant in combination, which had made up the being of the Beau, fell asunder and revealed what lay beneath. At first his lustre seemed undiminished. His old friends crossed the water to see him and made a point of standing him a dinner and leaving a little present behind them at his bankers. He held his usual levee at his lodgings; he spent the usual hours washing and dressing; he rubbed his teeth with a red root, tweezed out hairs with a silver tweezer, tied his cravat to admiration, and issued at[l] four precisely as perfectly equipped as if the Rue Royale had been St James's Street and the Prince himself had hung upon his arm. But the Rue Royale was not St James's Street; the old French Countess who spat on the floor was not the Duchess of Devonshire; the good bourgeois who pressed him to dine off goose at four was not Lord Alvanley; and though he soon won for himself the title of Roi de Calais, and was known to workmen as 'George, ring the bell', the praise was gross, the society coarse, and the amusements of Calais very slender. The Beau had to fall back upon the resources of his own mind. These might[m] have been considerable. According to Lady Hester Stanhope, he might have been, had he chosen, a very clever man; and when she told him so, the Beau admitted that he had wasted his talents because a dandy's way of life was the only one 'which could place him in a prominent light, and enable him to separate himself from the ordinary herd of men, whom he held in considerable contempt'. That way of life allowed of verse-making – his verses, called 'The Butterfly's Funeral', were much admired; and of singing, and of some dexterity with the pencil. But now, when the summer days were so long and so empty,[n] he found that such accomplishments hardly served to while away the time. He tried to occupy himself with writing his memoirs; he bought a screen and spent hours pasting it with pictures of great men and beautiful ladies whose virtues and frailties were symbolised by hyenas, by wasps, by profusions of cupids, fitted[o] together with extraordinary skill; he collected Buhl furniture; he wrote letters in a curiously elegant and elaborate style to ladies. But these occupations palled. The resources of his mind had been whittled away in the course of years; now they failed him.[p] And then the crumbling process went a little farther,[q] and another organ was laid bare – the heart. He who had played at love all these years and kept so adroitly beyond the range of passion, now made violent advances to girls who were young enough to be his daughters. He wrote such passionate letters to Mademoiselle Ellen of Caen that she did not know whether to laugh or to be angry. She was angry, and the Beau, who had tyrannised over the daughters of Dukes, prostrated himself before her in despair. But it was too late – the heart after all these years was not a very engaging object even to a simple country girl, and he seems at last to have lavished his affections upon animals. He mourned his terrier Vick for three weeks; he had a friendship with a mouse; he became the champion of all the neglected cats and starving dogs in Caen. Indeed, he said to a lady that if a man and a dog were drowning in the same pond he would prefer to save the dog – if, that is, there were nobody looking. But he was still persuaded that everybody was looking; and his immense regard for appearances gave him a certain stoical endurance. Thus, when paralysis struck him at dinner he left the table without a sign; sunk deep in debt as he was, he still picked his way over the cobbles on the points of his toes to preserve his shoes, and when the terrible day came and he was thrown into prison he won the admiration of murderers and thieves by appearing among them as cool and courteous as if about to pay a morning call. But if he were to continue to act his part, it was essential that he should be supported – he must have a sufficiency of boot polish, gallons of eau-de-Cologne, and three changes of linen every day. His expenditure upon these items was enormous. Generous as his old friends were, and persistently as he supplicated them, there came a time when they could be squeezed no longer. It was decreed that he was to content himself with one change of linen daily, and his allowance was to admit of necessaries only. But how could a Brummell exist upon necessaries only? The demand was absurd. Soon afterwards he showed his sense of the gravity of the situation by mounting a black silk neck-cloth. Black silk neck-cloths had always been his aversion. It was a signal of despair, a sign that the end was in sight. After that everything that had supported him and kept him in being dissolved. His self-respect vanished. He would dine with anyone who would pay the bill. His memory weakened and he told the same story over and over again till even the burghers of Caen were bored. Then his manners degenerated. His extreme cleanliness lapsed into carelessness, and then into positive filth. People objected to his presence in the dining-room of the hotel. Then his mind went – he thought that the Duchess of Devonshire was coming up the stairs when it was only the wind.[3] At last but one passion remained intact among the crumbled debris of so many – an immense greed. To buy Rheims biscuits he sacrificed the greatest treasure that remained to him – he sold his snuff-box. And then nothing was left but a heap of disagreeables, a mass of corruption, a senile and disgusting old man fit only for the charity of nuns and the protection of an asylum. There the clergyman begged him to pray. '"I do try", he said, but he added something which made me doubt whether he understood me.' Certainly, he would try; for the clergyman wished it and he had always been polite. He had been polite to thieves and to duchesses and to God Himself. But it was no use trying any longer. He[x] could believe in nothing now except a hot fire, sweet biscuits, and another cup of coffee if he asked for it. And so there was nothing for it but that the Beau who had been compact of grace and sweetness should be shuffled into the grave like any other ill-dressed, ill-bred, unneeded old man. Still, one must remember that Byron, in his moments of dandyism, 'always pronounced the name of Brummell with a mingled emotion of respect and jealousy'.

[NOTE. – Mr Berry of St James's Street has courteously drawn my attention to the fact that Beau Brummell certainly visited England in 1822. He came to the famous wine-shop on 26th July 1822 and was weighed as usual. His weight was then 10 stones 13 pounds. On the previous occasion, 6th July 1815, his weight was 12 stones 10 pounds. Mr Berry adds that there is no record of his coming after 1822.][4y]

III

Mary Wollstonecraft

Great wars are strangely intermittent in their effects. The French Revolution took some people and tore them asunder; others it passed over without disturbing a hair of their[a] heads. Jane Austen, it is said, never mentioned it; Charles Lamb ignored it; Beau Brummell[2] never gave the matter a thought. But to Wordsworth and to Godwin it was the dawn; unmistakably they saw[b]

> France standing on the top of golden hours,
> And human nature seeming born again.[3]

Thus it would be easy for a picturesque historian to lay side by side the most glaring contrasts – here in Chesterfield Street was Beau

Brummell letting his chin fall carefully upon his cravat and discussing in a tone studiously free from vulgar emphasis the proper cut of the lapel of a coat; and here in Somers Town was a party of ill-dressed, excited young men, one with a head too big for his body and a nose too long for his face, holding forth day by day over the tea-cups upon human perfectibility, ideal unity, and the rights of man. There was also a woman present with very bright eyes and a very eager tongue, and the young men, who had middle-class names, like Barlow and Holcroft and Godwin,[4] called her simply 'Wollstonecraft', as if it did not matter whether she were[c] married or unmarried, as if she were a young man like themselves.

Such glaring[d] discords among intelligent people – for Charles Lamb and Godwin, Jane Austen and Mary Wollstonecraft were all highly intelligent – suggest how much influence circumstances have upon opinions. If Godwin had been brought up in the precincts of the Temple and had drunk deep of antiquity and old letters at Christ's Hospital,[5] he might never have cared a straw for the future of man and his rights in general. If Jane Austen had lain as a child on the landing to prevent her father from thrashing her mother, her soul might have burnt with such a passion against tyranny that all her novels might have been consumed in one[e] cry for justice.

Such had been Mary Wollstonecraft's first experience of the joys of married life. And then her sister Everina had been married miserably and had bitten her wedding ring to pieces in the coach. Her brother[f] had been a burden on her; her father's farm had failed, and in order to start that disreputable man with the red face and the violent temper and the dirty hair in life again she had gone into bondage among the aristocracy as a governess – in short, she had never known what happiness was, and, in its default, had[g] fabricated a creed fitted to meet the sordid misery of real human[h] life. The staple of her doctrine was that nothing mattered save independence. 'Every obligation we receive from our fellow-creatures is a new shackle, takes from our native freedom, and debases the mind.'[6] Independence was the first necessity for a woman; not grace or charm, but energy and courage and the power to put her will into effect, were her necessary qualities.[i] It was her highest boast to be able to say, 'I never yet resolved to do anything of consequence that I did not adhere readily to it'.[7] Certainly Mary could say this with truth. When she was a little more than thirty[j] she could look back upon a series of actions which she had carried out in the teeth of opposition. She had taken a house by prodigious efforts for her friend Fanny, only to find that Fanny's mind was changed and she did not want a house after all. She had started a school. She had persuaded[k] Fanny into marrying Mr Skeys. She had thrown up her school and gone to Lisbon alone to nurse Fanny when she died. On the voyage back she had forced the captain of the ship to rescue a wrecked French vessel by threatening to expose him if he refused. And when, overcome by a passion for Fuseli,[8] she declared[l] her wish to live with him and been refused flatly by his wife, she had put her principle of decisive action instantly into effect, and had gone to Paris determined to make her living by her pen.

The Revolution thus was not merely an event that[m] had happened outside her; it was an active agent in her own blood.[n] She had been in revolt all her life – against tyranny, against law, against convention. The reformer's love[o] of humanity, which has so much of hatred in it as well as love,[p] fermented within her. The outbreak of revolution in France expressed some of her deepest theories and convictions, and she dashed off in the heat of that extraordinary moment those two eloquent and daring books – the *Reply to Burke* and the *Vindication of the Rights of Woman*,[9q] which are so true that they seem now to contain nothing new in them – their originality has become our commonplace. But when she was in Paris lodging by herself in a great house, and saw with her own eyes the King whom she despised driving past surrounded by National Guards and holding himself with greater dignity than she expected, then, 'I can scarcely tell you why', the tears came to her eyes. 'I am going to bed,' the letter ended, 'and, for the first time in my life, I cannot put out the candle.'[10] Things were not so simple after all. She could not understand even her[r] own feelings. She saw the most cherished of her convictions put into practice – and her eyes filled with tears. She had won fame and independence and the right to live her own life – and she wanted something different.[s] 'I do not want to be loved like a goddess,' she wrote, 'but I wish to be necessary to you.'[11] For Imlay, the fascinating American to whom her[t] letter was addressed, had been very good to her. Indeed, she had fallen passionately in love with him. But it was one of her theories that love should be free – 'that mutual affection was marriage and that the marriage tie should not bind after the death of love, if love should die'.[12] And yet at the same time that she wanted freedom she[u] wanted certainty. 'I like the word affection,' she wrote, 'because it signifies something habitual.'[13]

The conflict of all these contradictions shows itself in her face, at once so resolute and so dreamy, so sensual and so intelligent, and beautiful into the bargain with its great coils of hair and the large bright eyes that Southey thought the most expressive he had ever seen.[14] The life of such a woman was bound to be tempestuous. Every^v day she made theories by which life should be lived; and every day she came smack against the rock of other people's prejudices. Every day too – for she was no pedant, no cold-blooded theorist – something^w was born in her that thrust aside her theories and forced her to model them afresh. She acted upon her theory that she had no legal claim upon Imlay; she refused to marry him; but when he left her alone week after week with the child she had borne him her agony was unendurable.

Thus distracted, thus puzzling even to herself, the plausible and treacherous Imlay cannot be^x altogether blamed for failing to follow the rapidity of her changes and the alternate reason and unreason of her moods. Even friends whose liking was impartial were disturbed by her discrepancies. Mary had a passionate, an exuberant, love of Nature, and yet one night when the colours in the sky were so exquisite that Madeleine Schweizer could not help saying to her, 'Come, Mary – come, nature-lover – and enjoy this wonderful spectacle – this constant transition from colour to colour', Mary never took her eyes off the Baron de Wolzogen. 'I must confess,' wrote Madame Schweizer, 'that this erotic absorption made such a disagreeable impression on me, that all my pleasure vanished.'[15] But if the sentimental Swiss was disconcerted by Mary's sensuality, Imlay, the shrewd man of business, was exasperated by her intelligence. Whenever he saw her he yielded to her charm, but then her quickness, her penetration, her^y uncompromising idealism harassed him. She saw through his excuses; she met all his reasons; she was even capable of managing his business. There was no peace with her – he must be off again. And then her letters followed him, torturing him with their sincerity and their insight. They were so outspoken; they pleaded so passionately to be told the truth; they showed such a contempt for soap and alum and wealth^z and comfort; they repeated, as he suspected, so truthfully that he had only to say the word, 'and you shall never hear of me more',[16] that he could not endure it. Tickling minnows he had hooked a dolphin, and the creature rushed him through the waters till he was dizzy and only wanted to escape.[17] After all, though he had played at theory-making too, he was a business man, he depended upon soap and alum; 'the*aa* secondary pleasures of life', he had to admit, 'are very necessary to my comfort'.[18] And among them was one that for ever evaded*bb* Mary's jealous scrutiny. Was it business, was it politics, was it a woman, that perpetually took him away from her? He shillied and shallied; he was very charming when they met; then he disappeared again. Exasperated at last, and half insane with suspicion, she forced the truth from the cook. A little actress in a strolling company was his mistress, she learnt. True*cc* to her own creed of decisive action, Mary at once soaked her skirts so that she might sink unfailingly, and threw herself from Putney Bridge.*dd* But she was rescued; after unspeakable agony she recovered, and then her 'unconquerable greatness of mind',[19] her girlish creed of independence, asserted itself again, and she determined to make another bid for happiness and to earn her living without taking a penny from Imlay for herself or their child.

It was in this crisis that she again saw Godwin,*ee* the little man with the big head, whom she had met when the French Revolution was making the young men in Somers Town think that a new world was being born.*ff* She met him – but that is a euphemism, for in fact Mary Wollstonecraft actually visited him in his own house. Was it the effect of the French Revolution? Was it the blood she had seen spilt on the pavement and the cries of the furious crowd that had rung in her ears that made it seem a matter of no importance whether*gg* she put on her cloak and went to visit Godwin in Somers Town, or waited in Judd Street West for Godwin to come to her?*hh* And what strange upheaval of human life was it that inspired that curious man, who was so queer a mixture of meanness and magnanimity, of coldness and deep feeling – for the memoir of his wife could not have been written without unusual depth of heart – to hold the view that she did right – that he respected Mary for trampling upon the idiotic convention by which women's lives were tied down?*ii* He held the most extraordinary views on many subjects, and upon the relations of the sexes in particular. He thought that reason should influence even the love between men and women. He thought that there*jj* was something spiritual in their relationship. He had written that 'marriage is a law, and the worst of all laws . . . marriage is an affair of property, and the worst of all properties'.[20] He held the belief that if two people of the opposite sex like each other, they should live together without any ceremony, or, for living together is*kk* apt to blunt love, twenty doors off, say, in*ll* the same street. And he went further; he said that if another man liked your wife 'this will create no difficulty. We may all enjoy her conversation, and we shall all be wise enough to consider the sensual intercourse a very trivial object.'[21] True, when he wrote those words he had never been in love; now for the first time he was to experience that sensation.[mm] It came very quietly and naturally, growing 'with equal advances in the mind of each'[22] from those talks in Somers Town, from those discussions upon everything under the sun which they held so improperly alone in his rooms. 'It was friendship melting into love . . .', he wrote. 'When, in the course of things, the disclosure came, there was nothing in a manner for either party to disclose to the other.'[23] Certainly they were in agreement upon the most essential points; they were both of opinion,[nn] for instance, that marriage was unnecessary. They would continue to live apart. Only when Nature again intervened, and Mary found herself with child, was it worth while to lose valued friends, she asked, for the sake of a theory? She thought not, and they were married. And then that other theory – that it is best for husband and wife to live apart – was not that also incompatible with other feelings that were coming to birth in her? 'A husband is a convenient part of the furniture of the house',[24] she wrote. Indeed, she discovered that she was passionately domestic. Why not, then, revise that theory too, and share the same roof? Godwin[oo] should have a room some doors off to work in; and they should dine out separately if they liked – their work, their friends, should be separate. Thus they settled it, and the plan worked admirably. The arrangement combined 'the novelty and lively sensation of a visit with the more delicious and heart-felt pleasures of domestic life'.[25] Mary admitted that she was happy; Godwin confessed that, after all one's philosophy, it was 'extremely gratifying' to find that 'there is someone who takes[pp] an interest in one's happiness'.[26] All sorts of powers and emotions were liberated in Mary by her new satisfaction. Trifles gave her an exquisite pleasure – the sight of Godwin and Imlay's child playing together; the thought of their own child who was to be born; a day's jaunt into[qq] the country. One day, meeting Imlay in the New Road, she greeted him without bitterness. But, as Godwin wrote, 'Ours is[rr] not an idle happiness, a paradise of selfish and transitory pleasures'.[27] No, it too was an experiment, as Mary's life had been an experiment from the start, an attempt to make human conventions[ss] conform more closely to human needs. And their marriage was only a beginning; all sorts of things were to follow after. Mary[tt] was going to have a child. She was going to write a book to be called *The^uu Wrongs of Women*.[28] She was going to reform education. She was going to come down to dinner the day after her child was born. She was going to employ^vv a midwife and not a doctor at her confinement – but that experiment was her last. She died in child-birth. She whose sense of her own existence was so intense, who had cried out even in her misery, 'I cannot bear to think of being no more – of losing myself – nay, it appears to me impossible that I should cease to exist',[29] died at the age of thirty-six. But she has her revenge. Many millions have died and been forgotten in the hundred and thirty years that have passed since she was buried; and yet as we read her letters and listen to her arguments and consider her experiments, above all, that most fruitful experiment, her relation with Godwin, and realise the high-handed^ww and hot-blooded manner in which she cut her way to the quick of life, one form of immortality is hers undoubtedly: she is alive and active, she argues and experiments, we hear her voice and trace her influence even now among the living.^xx

IV

Dorothy Wordsworth

Two highly incongruous travellers, Mary Wollstonecraft and Dorothy Wordsworth, followed close upon each other's footsteps. Mary was in Altona on the Elbe in 1795 with her baby; three years later Dorothy came there with her brother and Coleridge. Both kept a record of their travels; both saw the same places, but the eyes with which they saw them were very different. Whatever Mary saw served to start her mind upon some theory, upon the effect of government, upon the state of the people, upon the mystery of her own soul. The beat of the oars on the waves made her ask, 'Life, what are you? Where goes this breath? This *I* so much alive? In what element will it mix, giving and receiving fresh energy?' And sometimes she forgot to look at the sunset and looked instead at the Baron Wolzogen. Dorothy, on the other hand, noted what was before her accurately, literally, and with prosaic precision.^a 'The walk very pleasing between Hamburgh and Altona. A large piece of ground planted with trees, and intersected by gravel walks. . . . The ground on the opposite side of the Elbe appears marshy.' Dorothy never railed against 'the cloven hoof of despotism'. Dorothy never asked 'men's questions' about exports and imports; Dorothy never confused her own soul with the sky. This 'I so much alive' was ruthlessly subordinated to the trees and the grass. For if she let 'I' and its rights and its wrongs and its passions and its suffering get between her and the object, she would be calling the moon 'the Queen of the Night';[2] she would be talking of dawn's 'orient beams';[3] she would be[b] soaring into reveries and rhapsodies and forgetting to find the exact phrase for the ripple of moonlight upon the lake. It was like 'herrings in the water'[4] – she could not have said that if she had been thinking about herself.[c] So while Mary dashed her head against wall after wall, and cried out, 'Surely something resides in this heart that is not perishable – and life is more than a dream',[5] Dorothy went on methodically at Alfoxden noting the approach of spring. 'The sloe in blossom, the hawthorn[d] green, the larches in the park changed from black to green, in two or three days.' And next day, 14th April 1798, 'the evening very stormy, so we staid indoors. Mary Wollstonecraft's life, &c., came.' And the day after they walked in the squire's grounds and noticed that 'Nature was very successfully striving to make beautiful what art had deformed – ruins, hermitages, &c., &c.'. There is no reference to Mary Wollstonecraft; it seems as if her life and all its storms had been swept away in one of those compendious et ceteras, and yet the next sentence reads like an unconscious comment. 'Happily we cannot shape the huge hills, or carve out the valleys according to our fancy.' No, we cannot re-form, we must not rebel; we can only accept and try to understand the message of Nature.[e] And so the notes go on.

Spring passed; summer came; summer turned to autumn; it was winter, and then again the sloes were in blossom and the hawthorns green and spring had come. But it was spring in the North now, and Dorothy was living alone with her brother in a small cottage at Grasmere in the midst of the hills. Now after the hardships and separations of youth they were together under their own roof; now they could address themselves undisturbed to the absorbing occupation of living in the heart of Nature and trying, day by day, to read her meaning. They had money enough at last to let them live together without the need of earning a penny. No family duties or professional tasks distracted them. Dorothy could ramble all day on the hills and sit up talking to Coleridge all night without being scolded by her aunt for unwomanly behaviour. The hours were theirs from sunrise to sunset, and could be altered to suit the season. If it was fine, there was no need to come in; if it was wet, there was no need to get up. One could go to bed at any hour. One could let the dinner cool if the cuckoo were shouting on the hill and William had not found the exact epithet[f] he wanted. Sunday was a day like any other. Custom, convention, everything was subordinated to the absorbing, exacting, exhausting[g] task of living in the heart of Nature and writing poetry. For exhausting it was. William would make his head ache in the effort to find the right word. He would go on hammering at a poem until[h] Dorothy was afraid to suggest an alteration. A chance phrase of hers would run in his head and make it impossible for him to get back into the proper mood. He would come down to breakfast and sit 'with his shirt neck unbuttoned, and his waistcoat open', writing a poem on a Butterfly which some story of hers had suggested, and he would eat nothing, and then he would begin altering the poem and again would be exhausted.[i]

It is strange how vividly all this is brought before us, considering that the diary is made up of brief notes such as any quiet woman might make of her garden's changes and her brother's moods and the progress of the seasons. It was warm and mild, she notes, after a day of rain. She met a cow in a field. 'The cow looked at me, and I looked at the cow, and whenever I stirred the cow gave over eating.'[6] She met an old man who walked with two sticks – for days on end she met nothing more out of the way than a cow eating and an old man walking. And[j] her motives for writing are common enough – 'because I will not quarrel with myself, and because I shall give William pleasure by it when he comes home again'.[7] It is only gradually that the difference between this rough notebook and others discloses itself; only by degrees that the brief notes unfurl in the mind and open a whole landscape before us, that the plain statement proves to be aimed so directly at the object that if we look exactly along the line that it points we shall see precisely what she saw. 'The moonlight lay upon the hills like snow.' 'The air was become still, the lake of a bright slate colour, the hills darkening. The bays shot into the low fading shores. Sheep resting. All things quiet.'[8] 'There was no one waterfall above another – it was the[k] sound of waters in the air – the voice of the air.'[9] Even in such brief notes one feels the suggestive power which is the gift of the poet rather than of the naturalist, the power which, taking only the simplest facts, so orders them that the whole scene comes before us, heightened and composed, the lake in its quiet, the hills in their splendour. Yet she was no descriptive writer in the usual sense. Her first concern was to be truthful – grace and symmetry must be made subordinate to truth. But[l] then truth is sought because to falsify the look of the stir of the breeze on the lake is to tamper with the spirit which inspires appearances. It is that spirit which[m] goads her and urges her and keeps her faculties for ever on the stretch. A sight or a sound would not let her be till she had traced her perception along its course and fixed it in words, though they might be bald, or in an image, though it might be angular. Nature was a stern taskmistress. The exact prosaic detail must be rendered as well as the vast and visionary outline. Even when the distant hills trembled before her in the glory of a dream she must note with literal accuracy 'the glittering silver line on the ridge of the backs of the sheep',[10] or remark how 'the crows at a little distance from us became white as silver as they flew in the sunshine, and when they went still further, they looked like shapes of water passing over the green fields'.[11] Always trained and in use, her powers of observation became in time so expert and so acute that a day's walk stored her mind's eye with a vast assembly of[n] curious objects to be sorted at leisure. How strange the sheep looked mixed with the soldiers at Dumbarton Castle! For some reason the sheep looked their real size, but the soldiers looked like puppets. And then the movements of the sheep were so natural and fearless, and the motion of the dwarf soldiers was so restless and apparently without meaning. It was extremely queer. Or lying in bed she would look up at the ceiling and think how the varnished beams were 'as glossy as black rocks on a sunny day cased in ice'.[12] Yes, they

crossed each other in almost as intricate and fantastic a manner as I have seen the underboughs of a large beech-tree withered by the depth of the shade above. . . . It was like what I should suppose an underground cave or temple to be, with a dripping or moist roof, and the moonlight entering in upon it by some means or other, and yet the colours were more like melted gems. I lay looking up till the light of the fire faded away. . . . I did not sleep much.[13]

Indeed, she scarcely seemed to shut her eyes. They looked and they looked, urged on not only by an indefatigable curiosity but also by reverence,[o] as if some secret of the utmost importance lay hidden beneath the surface. Her pen sometimes stammers with the intensity of the emotion that she controlled, as De Quincey said that her tongue stammered with the conflict between her ardour and her shyness when she spoke. But controlled she was. Emotional and impulsive by nature, her eyes 'wild and starting', tormented by feelings which almost mastered her, still she must control, still she[p] must repress, or she would fail in her task – she would cease to see. But if one subdued oneself, and resigned one's private agitations, then, as if in reward, Nature would bestow an exquisite satisfaction. 'Rydale was very beautiful, with spear-shaped streaks of polished steel. . . . It calls home the heart to quietness. I had been very melancholy', she wrote. For did not Coleridge come walking over the hills and tap at the cottage door late at night – did she not carry a letter from Coleridge hidden safe in her bosom?

Thus giving to Nature, thus[q] receiving from Nature, it seemed, as the arduous and ascetic days went by, that Nature and Dorothy had grown together in perfect sympathy – a sympathy not cold or vegetable or inhuman because at the core of it burnt that other love for 'my beloved', her brother, who was indeed its heart and inspiration. William and Nature and Dorothy herself, were they not one being? Did they not compose a trinity, self-contained and self-sufficient and independent whether indoors or out? They sit indoors. It was

about ten o'clock and a quiet night. The fire flickers and the watch ticks. I hear nothing but the breathing of my Beloved as he now and then pushes his book forward, and turns over a leaf.[14]

And now it is an April day, and they take the old cloak and lie in John's grove out of doors together.

William heard me breathing, and rustling now and then, but we both lay still and unseen by one another. He thought that it would be sweet thus to lie in the grave, to hear the peaceful sounds of the earth, and just to know that our dear friends were near. The lake was still; there was a boat out.

It was a strange love, profound, almost dumb, as if brother and sister had grown together and shared not the speech but the mood, so that they hardly knew which felt, which spoke, which saw the daffodils or the sleeping city; only Dorothy stored the mood in prose, and later William came and bathed in it and[r] made it into poetry. But one could not act without the other. They must feel, they must think, they must be together. So now, when they had lain out on the hill-side they would rise and go home and make tea, and Dorothy would write to Coleridge, and they would sow the scarlet beans together, and William would work at his[s] 'Leech Gatherer', and Dorothy would copy the lines for him. Rapt but controlled, free yet strictly ordered, the homely narrative moves naturally from ecstasy on the hills to baking bread and ironing linen and fetching William his supper in the cottage.

The cottage,[t] though its garden ran up into the fells, was on the highroad. Through her parlour[u] window Dorothy looked out and saw whoever might be passing – a tall beggar woman perhaps with her baby on her back; an old soldier; a coroneted landau with touring ladies peering inquisitively inside. The rich and the great she would let pass – they interested her no more than cathedrals or picture galleries or great cities; but she could never see a beggar at the door without asking him in and questioning him closely. Where had he been? What had he seen? How many children had he? She searched into the lives of the poor as if they held in them the same secret as the hills.[v] A tramp eating cold bacon over the kitchen fire might have been a starry night, so closely she watched him; so clearly she noted how his old coat was patched 'with three bell-shaped patches of darker blue behind, where the buttons had been', how his[w] beard of a fortnight's growth was like 'grey *plush*'. And then as they rambled on with their tales of seafaring and the press-gang and the Marquis of Granby,[15] she never failed to capture the one phrase that sounds on in the mind after[x] the story is forgotten, 'What, you are stepping westward?' 'To be sure there is great promise for virgins in Heaven.' 'She could trip lightly by the graves of those who died when they were young.' The poor had their poetry as the hills had theirs. But it was out of doors, on the road or on the moor, not in the cottage parlour, that her imagination had freest play. Her happiest moments were passed tramping beside a jibbing horse on a wet Scottish road[y] without certainty of bed or supper. All she knew was that there was some[z] sight ahead, some grove of trees to be noted, some waterfall to be inquired into. On they tramped hour after hour in silence for the most part, though Coleridge, who was of the party, would suddenly begin to debate aloud the true meaning of[aa] the words majestic, sublime, and grand. They had to trudge on foot because the horse had thrown the cart over a bank and the harness was only mended[bb] with string and pocket-handkerchiefs. They were hungry, too, because[cc] Wordsworth had dropped the chicken and the bread into the lake, and they had nothing else for dinner. They were uncertain of the way, and did not know where[dd] they would find lodging: all they knew was that there was a waterfall[ee] ahead. At last Coleridge could stand it no longer. He had rheumatism in the^{ff} joints; the Irish jaunting car provided no shelter from the weather; his companions were silent and absorbed. He left them. But William and Dorothy tramped on. They looked like tramps themselves. Dorothy's cheeks were brown as a gipsy's, her clothes were shabby, her gait was rapid and ungainly. But still she was indefatigable; her eye never failed her; she noticed everything. At last they reached the waterfall. And then all Dorothy's powers fell upon it. She searched out its character, she noted its resemblances, she defined its differences, with all the ardour of a discoverer, with all the exactness of a naturalist, with all the rapture of a lover. She possessed it^{gg} at last[16] – she had laid it up in her mind for ever. It had become one of those 'inner visions'[17] which she could call to mind at any time in their distinctness and in their particularity. It would come back to her long years afterwards when she was old and her mind had failed her; it would come back stilled and heightened and mixed with all the happiest memories of her past – with the thought of Racedown^{hh} and Alfoxden and Coleridge reading 'Christabel', and her beloved, her brother William. It would bring with it what no human being could give, what no human relation could offer – consolation and quiet.^{ii} If, then, the passionate cry of Mary Wollstonecraft had reached her ears – 'Surely something resides in this heart that is not perishable – and life is more than a dream' – she would have had no doubt whatever as to her answer. She would have said quite simply, 'We looked about us, and we felt^{ij} that we were happy'.

I Cowper and Lady Austen

a – *NYHT*: 'had been in'.

b – *NYHT*: 'youth something'.

c – *NYHT*: 'action, which made any public . . . insupportable. Indeed, if goaded'.

d – *N&A* and *NYHT*: 'appointment, he would drown himself; but there was a man sitting on'.

e – *N&A* and *NYHT*: 'But when that July . . . despair, not only into the haven . . . but into a settled state of mind, into a settled way'.

f – *NYHT*: 'elder. She had brought him very wisely, like a mother, by letting him talk, and listening to his terrors and understanding them, to'.

g – *N&A* and *NYHT*: 'some profound unrest'.

h – *N&A* and *NYHT*: 'outcast. He'.

i – *N&A* and *NYHT*: 'realised in what way he was unique; how it was that he'.

j – *N&A* and *NYHT*: 'tables, for all'.

k – N&A and *NYHT*: 'oneself.'

l – NYHT: 'enchantingly friends'.

m – N&A: 'moments, chiefly when'.

n – N&A and *NYHT*: 'part idling his . . . pastimes, looking with'.

o – N&A and *NYHT*: 'Now it was Geary . . . teeth; now it was two'.

p – NYHT: 'of Sir'.

q – N&A: 'relations in England much'. *NYHT*: 'relations in England who were much'.

r – NYHT: 'lady was left unprotected. She was'.

s – N&A and *NYHT*: 'wanted to settle, to'.

t – NYHT: 'share the pleasures of the country side. She'.

u – NYHT: 'sprightliness William and Mary were'.

v – N&A and *NYHT*: 'melancholy, one might paraphrase'.

w – NYHT: 'this sense, this sidelong arch humor, embalmed in a beautiful'.

x – NYHT: 'hares escaped . . . they were caught . . . Throckmorton asked'.

y – N&A: 'house; the greenhouse had been lined with mats – some little'. *NYHT*: 'house; the greenhouse had been lined with mats. Some little'.

z – NYHT: 'humors'.

aa – NYHT: 'opinion on the wickedness of painting'.

bb – N&A and *NYHT*: 'for he was in imagination a great traveller, though . . . than from Buckingham to Sussex.'

cc – NYHT: 'she loved'.

dd – NYHT: 'rising'.

ee – N&A and *NYHT*: 'break'.

ff – N&A and *NYHT*: 'that gave his . . . It was this that made passages'.

gg – NYHT: 'talk. It'.

hh – NYHT: 'not for mortal beings; it'.

ii – NYHT: 'warned. Enthusiast as she was, she adored her friends and expressed her adoration openly. It'.

jj – N&A: 'dreamt in the firelight watching . . . films playing upon'. *NYHT*: 'dreamed in the firelight, watching the . . . films playing upon'.

kk – NYHT: 'women. Mary one evening would notice that'.

ll – NYHT: 'For she was'.

mm – N&A and *NYHT*: 'with the . . . Duchess; she'. See n. 23.

nn – N&A and *NYHT*: 'and wind'.

oo – N&A: 'abyss. He was haled by a terrible voice to perdition. Whispers mingled with the singing, voices hissed in his ear words of doom and damnation. And then . . . her! Then Ann'. *NYHT*: 'abyss. He was haled by a terrible voice to perdition. Whispers mingled with the singing. Voices reminded him that he was damned. And then . . . to her! Ann'.

pp – NYHT: 'friend gave'.

qq – N&A and *NYHT*: 'wished to'.

1 – Originally published as a signed essay, based on *The Correspondence of William Cowper* [1731–1800] . . . , ed. Thomas Wright (4 vols, Hodder and Stoughton, 1904), in the *N&A*, 21 September, and (with variants) in the *NYHT*, 22 September 1929, (*Kp4* C314); it was revised for *CR2*. It is clear that the *NYHT* version predates the *N&A* version. A version close to that in the *N&A* was translated into French by Jeanne Fournier-Pargoire and appeared in *Le Figaro*, 22–23 September 1929 (*Kp4* D52). The *N&A* also contained: LW's 'World of Books' column, 'Born Writers', on *Alice Meynell, a Memoir* by Viola Meynell and on *A Book about Myself* by Theodore Dreiser; and 'The Oyster' by V. Sackville-West, a review of *The Glorious Oyster* by Hector Bolitho.

This series, called 'Four Figures' in *CR2*, was conceived as a group of articles about eighteenth-century figures for the *NYHT* (see Appendix VIII below), and VW's reading notebook containing notes on Cowper and Mary Wollstonecraft has a heading 'Possible articles for Herald'. VW wrote to Vita Sackville-West on 15 August 1929: 'I am quite well again, and spent the morning writing. It wasn't you; as you were only the tailend – I had been badgered by people in London, and then this writing of four articles, all pressed as tight as hay in a stack (an image that comes you see from [Vita's] The Land) – that was what did it – not that it [a headache] was bad . . . But what about next week – towards the end, say Friday, when I shall have written the last word of these excruciating little biographies' (*IV VW Letters*, no. 2056). But then on 27 August: 'I have now no excuse for not correcting my articles – I shall do that tomorrow instead of coming to you' (*ibid.*, no. 2064). The articles were published in the *N&A* on consecutive weeks. VW wrote to Desmond MacCarthy, as editor of *L&L*, on 19 September 1929: 'Thanks for the cheque [for 'Dr Burney's Evening Party']. I will write you a better article one day. I have had to send the American articles to the Nation as they all hang together – four figures living at the same time – but I have others in my mind' (*IV VW Letters*, no. 2070).

Although VW was reading Cowper in February and March 1927, and had him on her mind in 1928 – 'The Singer [car] I know for a fact to be hermaphrodite, like the poet Cowper' (*III VW Letters*, no. 1864, to Vanessa Bell); 'Cowper, whom I suspect of hidden divinities unnumbered' (*ibid.*, no. 1976) – she 'wrote a little article on Cowper' at Cassis in the first half of June 1929, 'but lifting the words with difficulty in the heat, surrounded by black & white butterflies' (*III VW Diary*, 15 June 1929). Years later she protested that she had read Cowper when she was 15 (see *IV VW Diary*, 7 September 1935). See also 'Swinburne Letters', *II VW Essays*, esp. p. 232, n. 2. Reading notes (Berg, RN 1.9) (*VWRN* IX). Reprinted: *CE*.

2 – Theodora Jane Cowper (1734?–1824) was the youngest daughter of Ashley Cowper (1701–88) who forbade the match that seemed imminent between his daughter and nephew. She died unmarried; the poems Cowper had addressed to her were published in 1825.

3 – From 1765 Cowper lodged with Mary Unwin, *née* Cawthorne (1723–96), and her husband Morley and continued to reside with her after she was widowed in 1767.

4 – John Cowper (1737–70), Fellow of Corpus Christi College, Cambridge.

5 – Rev. John Newton (1725–1806), evangelical divine, curate and Cowper's neighbour and close friend at Olney. He published the sixty-six *Olney Hymns* in 1779, most of which were written by Cowper.

6 – *Correspondence*, vol. ii, Letter to the Rev. John Newton, 20 April 1783, p. 60; 13 January 1784, p. 147.

7 – See *ibid.*, 19 February 1785, p. 299: 'He [Ball] is now languishing in a dropsy . . . So long as he was able to crawl into the street, his journey was to the Royal Oak and home again; and so punctual were we both, I in cleaning my teeth at my window, and he in drinking his dram at the same time, that I seldom failed to observe him.'

8 – See *ibid.*, vol. i, p. 325. Lady Austen (d. 1802), *née* Ann Richardson, was the widow of Sir Robert Austen and the sister of Mrs Jones, the wife of the Rev. Thomas Jones, the curate of Clifton Reynes.

9 – *Ibid.*, Letter to the Rev. John Newton, 7 July 1781, p. 326.

10 – *Ibid.*

11 – *The Task* (1785), of which the first part (bk i) is entitled 'The Sofa', is in a volume also containing *The Diverting History of John Gilpin* (1782).

12 – *Correspondence*, vol. i, Letter to the Rev. William Unwin, 9 February 1782, p. 443.

13 – *Ibid.*, vol. ii, Letter to the Rev. John Newton, 21 March 1784, p. 181.

14 – *Ibid.*, vol. i, Letter to Mrs Maria Frances Cowper, 20 July 1780, p. 217: 'My days steal away silently, and march on (as poor mad King Lear would have made his soldiers march) as if they were shod with felt; not so silently but that I hear them . . .'

15 – Homer, legendary Greek poet, author of the *Iliad* and the *Odyssey*; Virgil (70–19 BC), classical Roman poet.

16 – James Cook (1728–79), explorer; George Anson (1697–1762), naval officer and politician.

17 – *Correspondence*, vol. ii, Letter to the Rev. John Newton, 27 July 1783, pp. 85–6.

18 – *Ibid.*, Letter to the Rev. William Unwin, 10 November 1783, p. 121.

19 – *Ibid.*, vol. i, 9 February 1782, p. 443; slightly adapted by VW.

20 – *Ibid.*, vol. ii, 19 February 1783, p. 36.

21 – For Hercules, see Thomas Bulfinch, *The Golden Age of Myth & Legend* (George G. Harrap, 1905), pp. 181–2: 'Hercules in a fit of madness killed his friend Iphitus, and was condemned for this offence to become the slave of Queen Omphale for three years. While in this service the hero's nature seemed changed. He lived effeminately, wearing at times the dress of a woman, and spinning wool with the handmaidens of Omphale,

while the queen wore his lion's skin.' For the binding of Samson, see Judges 16: 6–14.

22 – *The Task* (John Sharpe, 1817), bk iv, 'The Winter Evening', p. 102:

> In such a world, so thorny, and where none
> Finds happiness unblighted, or, if found,
> Without some thistly sorrow at its side;

23 – Cf. *Correspondence*, vol. i, Letter to Joseph Hill, 25 October 1765, p. 53, about Mrs Unwin who 'has a very uncommon understanding, has read much to excellent purpose, and is more polite than a duchess.'

24 – *ibid.*, vol. i, Letter to the Rev. William Unwin, 24 February 1782, p. 448: 'Retirement is our passion and our delight; it is in still life alone that we look for that measure of happiness we can rationally expect below.'

25 – See *ibid.*, vol. ii, p. 198, editor's note: 'Subsequently Lady Austen married a French gentleman named Tardiff, with whom she lived happily. She died in Paris in 1802.'

II Beau Brummell

a – *N&A* and *BB* (*Beau Brummell* [Rimington & Hooper, 1930]): 'was'.

b – *BB*: 'himself.'

c – *N&A* and *BB*: 'dirty beside'.

d – *N&A* and *BB*: 'a turn to them'.

e – *BB*: 'lady of title.'

f – *N&A* and *BB*: 'Brummell would never . . . he would have'.

g – *N&A*: 'dress, stamped his manner, his whole'. *BB*: 'dress, stamped his manner, permeated his whole'.

h – *N&A*: 'health admirable;'. *BB*: 'health was admirable;'.

i – *N&A* and *BB*: 'come. And it'.

j – *BB*: 'these'.

k – *BB*: 'won; he vowed'.

l – *N&A* and *BB*: 'out his hairs . . . issued out at'.

m – *BB*: 'These indeed might'.

n – *N&A*: 'and empty,'.

o – *BB*: 'cupids, cut out and fitted'.

p – *N&A* and *BB*: 'now they soon gave out.'

q – *N&A* and *BB*: 'further,'.

r – *BB*: 'a sentimental friendship'.

s – *N&A* and *BB*: 'dog if there'.

t – *BB*: 'he got up and left'.

u – *N&A* and *BB*: 'It was the signal of the end. After'.

v – *N&A*: 'till the'.

w – *N&A* and *BB*: 'débris – an'.

x – *N&A* and *BB*: 'try; for he had always . . . duchesses and to religion itself. But . . . longer; indeed there was nothing to try for. He'.

y – *N&A* and *BB* do not have the Note.

1 – For periodical publication and composition, see 'Beau Brummell' above; only material not in that version is annotated here. The essay was further revised for *CR2*. On this series in *CR2*, see 'Cowper and Lady Austen' above. The essay is based on Captain Jesse's *The Life of George Brummell, Esq., commonly called Beau Brummell* (1844; revised ed., 2 vols, John C. Nimmo, 1886). Reprinted: *CE*.

2 – *Life of . . . Beau Brummell*, vol. i, ch. xix, p. 258.

3 – Cf. *ibid.*, vol. ii, ch. xxv, p. 293: '. . . at eight o'clock this man, to whom he had already given his instructions, opened wide the door of his sitting-room, and announced the "Duchess of Devonshire."'

4 – This note derives from a letter to the BBC, printed in the *Listener*, 27 November 1929, in response to VW's broadcast: see *VI VW Essays*, Appendix.

III Mary Wollstonecraft

a – *NYHT*: 'hair on their'.

b – *NYHT*: 'dawn; without doubt they saw –'.

c – *N&A* and *NYHT*: 'was'.

d – *N&A* and *NYHT*: 'And these glaring'.

e – *N&A* and *NYHT*: 'a'.

f – *NYHT*: 'brothers'.

g – *N&A* and *NYHT*: 'she had'.

h – *N&A* and *NYHT*: 'of human'.

i – *N&A*: 'mind." Independence . . . grace and charm . . . her essential qualities.' *NYHT*: 'mind." Grace and charm were not what a young woman needed, but energy and courage and the power to put her will into effect.'

j – *N&A*: 'truth. When she was little more than thirty'. *NYHT*: 'truth. Even at the age of thirty'.

k – *NYHT*: 'forced'.

l – *N&A* and *NYHT*: 'she had declared'.

m – *N&A* and *NYHT*: 'merely a thing that'.

n – *N&A* and *NYHT*: 'her blood.'

o – *NYHT*: 'reformer's complex love'.

p – *N&A* and *NYHT*: 'as of love,'.

q – *N&A*: '"Vindication of the Right of Women",'. *NYHT*: '"Vindication of the Rights of Women" –'.

r – *NYHT*: 'not even understand her'.

s – *N&A* and *NYHT*: 'something more, something different.'

t – *NYHT*: 'the'.

u – *N&A* and *NYHT*: 'time, for all her love of experiment, she'.

v – *NYHT*: 'bargain, with its lustrous coils of hair and its large bright eyes. Every'.

w – *NYHT*: 'too – and it was this that puzzled her most – something'.

x – *N&A*: 'And if she was puzzled herself by the conflict within her, not even the plausible and treacherous Imlay himself can be'. *NYHT* follows *N&A*, but has: 'puzzled by'.

y – *NYHT*: 'penetration and her'.

z – *NYHT*: 'alum and for wealth'.

aa – *N&A* and *NYHT*: 'business man; "the'.

bb – *NYHT*: 'that perpetually evaded'.

cc – *N&A*: 'cook. A . . . mistress. True'. *NYHT*: 'cook. True'.

dd – *N&A* and *NYHT*: 'once threw herself from Putney Bridge, having soaked her skirts so that she might sink unfailingly.'

ee – *NYHT*: 'she met Godwin,'.

ff – *NYHT*: 'that the world was being born anew.'

gg – *N&A* and *NYHT*: 'of indifference to Mary whether'.

hh – *NYHT*: 'waited for Godwin to come and visit her in Judd Street West?'

ii – *NYHT*: 'were fettered?'

jj – *N&A*: 'particular. He . . . love of men and women. He thought that there'. *NYHT*: 'particular. He thought that there'.

kk – *NYHT*: 'for cohabitation is'.

ll – *N&A* and *NYHT*: 'love, say, twenty doors off in'.

mm – *N&A* and *NYHT*: 'wrote that he had never been in love, but now . . . experience the sensation.'

nn – *N&A* and *NYHT*: 'of the opinion,'.

oo – *N&A* and *NYHT*: 'Why, then, not revise that theory, too, and . . . roof, only Godwin'.

pp – *NYHT*: 'that "some one takes'.

qq – *N&A* and *NYHT*: 'born; a little ride into'.

rr – *NYHT*: 'was'.

ss – *NYHT*: 'convention'.

tt – *N&A*: 'beginning. All sorts of things were to follow after. Mary'. *NYHT*: 'beginning. Mary'.

uu – *N&A* and *NYHT*: 'book called the'.

vv – *NYHT*: 'education. She was going to employ'.

ww – *N&A*: 'Godwin and realize the intimacy and freedom which she achieved in that age of formality and convention – the high-handed'.

xx – *NYHT*: 'But she has her revenge; many people have died . . . the 130 years . . . buried, and . . . letters and follow her arguments and listen to her theories – above all as we study her relation with Godwin and realize its intimacy, its freedom, its assumption of values, we could swear that she is not dead. Surely we have met her only a night or two ago.'

1 – Originally published as a signed essay in the *N&A*, 5 October, and (with variants) in the *NYHT*, 20 October 1929, (*Kp4* C316); it was revised for *CR2*. It is clear that the *NYHT* version predates the *N&A* version. A version close to that in the *NYHT* was translated into French by Jeanne Fournier-Pargoire and appeared in *Le Figaro*, 26–27 December 1929. On this series in *CR2*, see 'Cowper and Lady Austen' above. On 5 August 1929 VW wrote that she 'should be tackling Mary Wollstonecraft' (*III VW Diary*). The *N&A* also contained: LW's 'World of Books' column on *The Letters of Disraeli to Lady Bradford and Lady Chesterfield*, ed. the Marquis of Zetland; and Ray Strachey on 'Monogamy', a review of *Halcyon, or the Future of Monogamy* by Vera Brittain. Reading notes (Berg, RN 1.9) (*VWRN* IX). Reprinted: *CE*.

2 – Jane Austen (1775–1817); Charles Lamb (1775–1834); George Bryan Brummell (1778–1840). On 12 October 1929 a letter from Augustine Birrell appeared in the *N&A*: 'May I be permitted to make a small criticism upon Mrs. Woolf's paper on Mary Wollstonecraft, which to praise would be super-fluous. ¶ It has reference to a remark made in passing on the supposed indifference displayed by Charles Lamb to the political and moral questions of his time . . .' VW responded in the issue of 19 October (*Kp4* C318):

'Needless to say, I would accept any judgment of Mr Birrell's on any subject with unhesitating acquiescence. That his view of Charles Lamb's character is the right one I do not doubt. But, whatever inference maybe drawn from it, my remark that Lamb did not mention the French Revolution, and that it passed him over without disturbing a hair of his head, has, I think, some foundation in fact. For example, one may search his letters from 1796 to 1800 without finding a single reference to politics in general or to the French Revolution in particular. And though in 1800 he does mention public affairs and the French Revolution in a letter to Manning, it is in these terms: "Public affairs – except as they touch upon me, and so turn into private – I cannot whip up my mind to find any interest in. I grieve, indeed, that War, and Nature, and Mr. Pitt, that hangs up in Lloyd's best parlour, should have conspired to call up three neces-saries, simple commoners as our fathers knew them, into the upper house of luxuries; bread, and beer, and coals, Manning. But as to France and Frenchmen, and the Abbé Sieyès and his constitutions, I cannot make these present times present to me. I read histories of the past, and I live in them. . . . Burnet's good old prattle I can bring present to my mind: I can make the revolution present to me; the French Revolution, by a converse perversity in my nature, I fling as far *from me*." And I do not think that it is mentioned again.'

VW quotes *The Letters of Charles Lamb, Newly Arranged, with Additions*, ed. Alfred Ainger (2 vols, 2nd ed., Macmillan, 1904), vol. i, Letter lv, to Thomas Manning, 1 March 1800, p. 125, which has: 'Sieyes'.

3 – William Wordsworth (1770–1850), *The Prelude* (Edward Moxon, 1850), bk vi, 'Cambridge and the Alps', p. 149. On 22 August 1929 VW quoted from bk vii in *III VW Diary*.

4 – Joel Barlow (1754–1812), American poet and diplomatist, friend of Tom Paine (1737–1809); settled in Paris in 1788, retreating to London in 1790. Mary Wollstonecraft (1759–97) met him in Paris and their acquaintance was renewed in London. Thomas Holcroft (1745–1809), dramatist and author of memoirs and novels. The man with the big head, William Godwin (1756–1836), considered Holcroft to be among his 'four principal oral instructors, to whom I feel my mind indebted for improvement': see *William Godwin. His Friends and Contemporaries* by C. Kegan Paul (2 vols, Henry S. King, 1876), vol. i, p. 17.
5 – As was Charles Lamb.
6 – *Memoirs of Mary Wollstonecraft* by William Godwin, ed. W. Clark Durant (1798; Constable and Greenberg, 1927), Wollstonecraft's letter to Joseph Johnson, 13 September 1787, pp. 172–3, continues: '. . . debases the mind, makes us mere earthworms – I am not fond of grovelling!'
7 – *Ibid.*, p. 172, which has: 'adhere resolutely to'.
8 – Henry Fuseli, formerly Johann Heinrich Füssli (1741–1825), painter and writer.
9 – *A Vindication of the Rights of Men, in a Letter to . . . Edmund Burke* (1790); *A Vindication of the Rights of Woman . . .* (1792).
10 – *Mary Wollstonecraft. Letters to Imlay*, with Prefatory Memoir by C. Kegan Paul (Kegan Paul, 1879), pp. xxxiv–xxxv; also in *Memoirs*, p. 223, Letter to Joseph Johnson, 26 December 1792.
11 – *Letters to Imlay*, Letter x, from Paris, 1–2 January 1794, p. 26. Gilbert Imlay (1754–1828), land speculator and author.
12 – *William Godwin*, vol. i, p. 214: 'On the question alone of the relation of the sexes, there is no indication of any approximation to her theories. Her view had now become that mutual affection was marriage . . . It must be remembered that her own experience of family life was not likely to ennoble it in her eyes.'
13 – *Letters to Imlay*, Letter ii, from Paris, August 1793, p. 3.
14 – See *William Godwin*, vol. i, p. 234, Letter from Robert Southey to J. Cottle, 13 March 1797: 'Her eyes are light brown, and although the lid of one of them is affected by a little paralysis, they are the most meaning I ever saw.' See also *Letters to Imlay*, 'Memoir', p. xxxiii.
15 – Mary Wollstonecraft was an occasional guest of Madeleine, *née* Hess (1751–1814), and Jean Caspard Schweizer (1754–1811), both of them Swiss, at their luxurious home in Paris. For an account of this outing to the countryside during 1794, see *Memoirs*, p. 247. Madeleine's journal entry is transcribed as: 'B(aron) de W(olzogen?)', who is not otherwise identified.
16 – *Letters to Imlay*, Letter xxxi, from Paris, 30 December 1794, p. 86.
17 – Cf. Orlando in love with Sasha: 'he felt as if he had been hooked by a great fish through the nose and rushed through the waters unwillingly, yet with his own consent' (*O*, ch. i, p. 50).
18 – Quoted in *Letters to Imlay*, Letter xxxiv, from Paris, 30 January 1795, p. 95: '"The secondary pleasures of life," you say, "are very necessary to my

comfort:" it may be so; but I have ever considered them as secondary.'

19 – See *Memoirs*, p. 30: 'there were some essential characteristics of genius, which she possessed . . . The principal of these was a firmness of mind, an unconquerable greatness of soul, by which, after a short internal struggle, she was (for the most part) accustomed to rise above difficulties and suffering.'

20 – See *William Godwin*, vol. i, p. 113; the extract is from in Godwin's *An Enquiry Concerning Political Justice* . . . (G. G. J. & J. Robinson, 1793), vol. ii, pp. 849–51.

21 – *William Godwin*, vol. i, p. 114, quoting from Godwin's *An Enquiry*, vol. ii, pp. 849–51.

22 – *Letters to Imlay*, quoted in 'Memoir', p. liv.

23 – *Ibid.*

24 – *William Godwin*, vol. i, p. 251, Letter from Mary Wollstonecraft Godwin to William Godwin, 6 June 1797; VW omits: 'unless he be a clumsy fixture'.

25 – *Memoirs*, p. 110.

26 – *William Godwin*, vol. i, p. 255, Letter from William Godwin to Mary Wollstonecraft Godwin, 10 June 1797: 'after all one's philosophy, it must be confessed that the knowledge that there is some one that takes an interest in one's happiness, something like that which each man feels in his own, is extremely gratifying.'

27 – *Memoirs*, p. 109, which has: 'Ours was not . . .'

28 – *The Wrongs of Woman; or, Maria; A Fragment* (1798).

29 – Wollstonecraft, *Letters Written During a Short Residence in Sweden, Norway, and Denmark* (Cassell, 1889), Letter viii, p. 78, which has: 'I cannot bear to think of being no more – of losing myself – though existence is often but a painful consciousness of misery; nay, it appears to me impossible that I should cease to exist, or that this active, restless spirit, equally alive to joy and sorrow, should only be organised dust – ready to fly abroad the moment the spring snaps, or the spark goes out which kept it together.' Mary Wollstonecraft was born in April 1759 and died in September 1797, so she was thirty-eight when she died.

IV Dorothy Wordsworth

a – *N&A*: 'and prosaically.'

b – *N&A*: 'For if one lets "I" . . . between one and the object, one will be . . . Night"; one will be . . . beams"; one will be'.

c – *N&A*: '– one could . . . if one had . . . about oneself.'

d – *N&A*: 'hawthorns'.

e – *N&A*: 'understand.'

f – *N&A*: 'cuckoo was shouting . . . the epithet'.

g – *N&A*: 'other. Everything was . . . absorbing and exacting and exhausting'.

h – *N&A*: 'till'.

i – *N&A*: 'and would be tired again.'

j – *N&A*: 'sticks – nothing happens more out of the way than that. And'.

k – *N&A*: 'a'.

l – *N&A*: 'symmetry are subordinate to that. But'.

m – *N&A*: 'that which'.

n – *N&A*: 'with a variety of'.

o – *N&A*: 'urged on by an indefatigable curiosity and reverence,'.

p – *N&A*: 'which she knew not how to master, still she must control, she'.

q – *N&A*: 'to nature and thus'.

r – *N&A*: 'it again and'.

s – *N&A*: 'the'.

t – *N&A*: 'For Dove Cottage,'.

u – *N&A*: 'cottage'.

v – *N&A*: 'into the histories of . . . secret that the hills concealed.'

w – *N&A*: 'so closely she observed how . . . been", and his'.

x – *N&A*: 'mind long after'.

y – *N&A*: 'or the moor, that she was most at her ease. Her finest work was done tramping . . . wet Scots road'.

z – *N&A*: 'a'.

aa – *N&A*: 'party, mused within himself, and sometimes debated aloud, the different meanings of'.

bb – *N&A*: 'had to walk, because . . . was mended'.

cc – *N&A*: 'And they were hungry because'.

dd – *N&A*: 'if'.

ee – *N&A*: 'sight'.

ff – *N&A*: 'his'.

gg – *N&A*: 'But the brother and sister tramped . . . themselves, for Dorothy's . . . as an Egyptian's and her clothes were shabby and her . . . they came to the waterfall. And . . . powers of observation fell upon it, searching out its character, noting its resemblances, defining its differences with all the ardour of a discoverer, with all the rapture of a lover. She had seen it'.

hh – *N&A*: 'with Racedown'.

ii – *N&A*: 'peace.'

jj – *N&A*: 'and felt'.

1 – For periodical publication and composition, see 'Dorothy Wordsworth' above; only material not in that version is annotated here. The essay was further revised for *CR2*. On this series in *CR2*, see 'Cowper and Lady Austen' above. See also 'Wordsworth Letters', *I VW Essays*. Reprinted: *CE*.

2 – Mary Wollstonecraft, *Letters Written During a Short Residence in Sweden, Norway, and Denmark* (Cassell, 1889), Letter v, pp. 53–4: 'But it is not the Queen of the Night alone who reigns here in all her splendour, though

the sun, loitering just below the horizon, decks her with a golden tinge from his car, illuminating the cliffs that hide him . . .'

3 – *Ibid.*, p. 54: 'The grey morn, streaked with silvery rays, ushered in the orient beams (how beautifully varying into purple!).'

4 – *Journals of Dorothy Wordsworth,* ed. William Knight (2 vols, Macmillan, 1897), vol. i, 'Journal written at Grasmere', 31 October 1800, p. 56.

5 – *Letters Written,* Letter viii, p. 78 (this sentence concludes the passage from which the quotation in n. 29 in 'Mary Wollstonecraft' above is extracted).

6 – *Journals,* vol. i, 18 March 1802, p. 102.

7 – *Ibid.,* 14 May 1800, p. 32.

8 – *Ibid.,* 13 April 1802, p. 105, which has: 'the lake was of'.

9 – *Ibid.,* 29 April 1802, p. 114, which has: 'it was a sound'.

10 – *Ibid.*

11 – *Ibid.,* 16 April 1802, pp. 108–9, which has: 'us become white'.

12 – *Ibid.,* 'Recollections of a Tour Made in Scotland', Second Week, 27 August 1803, pp. 253–4.

13 – *Ibid.,* final paragraph, pp. 254–5.

14 – *Ibid.,* 23 March 1802, pp. 103–4, which begins: 'It is about 10 o'clock, a quiet night . . . nothing save the breathing'.

15 – John Manners (1721–70), Marquess of Granby, army officer and politician.

16 – Cf. the variant penultimate paragraphs of 'Moments of Being: "Slater's Pins Have No Points"' (1927), *CSF,* p. 10.

17 – See William Wordsworth, 'The Inner Vision' (1833), which begins: 'Most sweet it is with unuplifted eyes'.

William Hazlitt

Had one met Hazlitt no doubt one would have liked him on his own principle that 'We can scarcely hate anyone we know'. But Hazlitt has been dead now a hundred years, and it is perhaps a question how far we can know him well enough to overcome those feelings of dislike, both personal and intellectual, which his[a] writings still so sharply arouse. For Hazlitt – it is one of his prime merits – was not one of those non-committal writers who shuffle off in a mist and die of their own insignificance. His essays are emphatically himself. He has no reticence and he has no shame. He tells us exactly what he thinks, and he tells us – the confidence is less seductive – exactly what he feels. As of all men he had the most intense consciousness of his own existence, since never a day passed without inflicting on him some pang of hate or of jealousy, some thrill of anger or of pleasure,[b] we cannot read him for long without coming in contact with a very singular character – ill-conditioned yet high-minded; mean yet noble; intensely egotistical yet inspired by the most genuine passion for the rights and liberties of mankind.

Soon, so thin is the veil of the essay as Hazlitt wore it, his very look comes before us. We see him as Coleridge saw him, 'browhanging, shoe-contemplative, strange'. He comes shuffling into the room, he looks nobody straight in the face, he shakes hands^c with the fin of a fish; occasionally he darts a malignant glance from his corner. 'His manners are 99 in 100 singularly repulsive', Coleridge said. Yet now and again his face lit up with intellectual beauty, and his manner became radiant with sympathy and understanding. Soon, too, as we read on, we become familiar with the whole gamut of his grudges and his grievances.^d He lived, one gathers, mostly at inns. No woman's form graced his board. He had quarrelled with all his old friends, save perhaps with Lamb. Yet his only fault had been that he had stuck to his principles and 'not become a government tool'. He was the object of malignant persecution – Blackwood's reviewers called him 'pimply Hazlitt', though his cheek was pale as alabaster. These lies, however, got into print, and then he was afraid to visit his friends because the footman had read the newspaper and the housemaid tittered behind his back. He had – no one could deny it – one of the finest minds, and he wrote indisputably the best prose style of his time. But what did that avail with women? Fine ladies have no respect for scholars, nor chambermaids either – so the growl and plaint of his grievances^e keeps breaking through, disturbing us, irritating us; and yet there is something so independent, subtle, fine, and enthusiastic about him – when he can forget himself he is so rapt in ardent speculation about other things – that dislike crumbles and turns to something much warmer and more complex. Hazlitt was right:

It is the mask only that we dread and hate; the man may have something human about him! The notions in short which we entertain of people at a distance, or from partial representation, or from guess-work, are simple, uncompounded ideas, which answer to nothing in reality; those which we derive from experience are mixed modes, the only true and, in general, the most favourable ones.

Certainly no one could read Hazlitt and maintain a simple and uncompounded idea of him. From the first he was a twy-minded[2] man – one of those divided natures which are inclined almost equally to two quite opposite careers. It is significant that his^f first impulse was not to essay-writing but to painting and philosophy. There was something in the remote and silent art[g] of the painter that offered a refuge to his tormented spirit. He noted enviously how happy the old age of painters was – 'their minds keep alive to the last'; he turned longingly to the calling that takes one out of doors, among fields and woods, that deals with bright pigments, and has solid brush and canvas for its tools and not merely black ink and white paper. Yet at the same time he was bitten by an abstract curiosity that would not let him rest in the contemplation of concrete beauty. When he was a boy of fourteen he heard his father, the good Unitarian minister, dispute with an old lady of the congregation as they were coming out of Meeting as to the limits of religious toleration, and, he said, 'it was this circumstance that decided the fate of my future life'. It set him off 'forming in my head . . . the following system of political rights and general jurisprudence'. He wished 'to be satisfied of the reason of things'. The two ideals were ever after to clash. To be a thinker and to express in the plainest and most accurate of terms 'the reason of things', and to be a painter gloating over blues and crimsons, breathing fresh air and living sensually in the emotions – these were two different, perhaps incompatible ideals, yet like all Hazlitt's emotions both were tough and each strove for mastery. He yielded now to one, now to the other. He spent months in Paris copying pictures at the Louvre. He came home and toiled laboriously at the portrait of an old woman in a bonnet day after day, seeking by industry and pains to discover the secret of Rembrandt's genius; but he lacked some quality – perhaps it was invention – and in the end cut the canvas to ribbons in a rage or turned it against the wall in despair. At the same time he was writing the 'Essay on the Principles of Human Action' which he preferred to all his other works. For there he wrote plainly and truthfully, without glitter or garishness, without any wish to please or to make money, but solely to gratify the urgency of his own desire for truth. Naturally, 'the book dropped still-born from the press'. Then, too, his political hopes, his belief that the age of freedom had come and that the tyranny of kingship was over, proved vain. His friends deserted to the Government, and he was left to uphold the doctrines of liberty, fraternity, and revolution in that perpetual minority which requires so much self-approval to support it.[h]

Thus he was a man of divided tastes and of thwarted ambition; a man whose happiness, even in early life, lay behind. His mind had set early and bore for ever the stamp of first impressions. In his happiest moods he looked not forwards but backwards – to the garden where he had played as a child, to the blue hills of Shropshire and to all those landscapes which he had seen when hope was still his, and peace brooded upon him and he looked up from his painting or his book and saw the fields and woods as if they were the outward expression of his own inner quietude. It is to the books that he read then that he returns – to Rousseau and to Burke and to the *Letters of Junius*. The impression that they made upon his youthful imagination was never effaced and scarcely overlaid; for after youth was over he ceased to read for pleasure, and youth and the pure and intense pleasures of youth were soon left behind.

Naturally, given his susceptibility to the charms of the other sex, he married; and naturally, given his consciousness of his own 'misshapen form made to be mocked',[3] he married unhappily.[i] Miss Sarah Stoddart pleased him when he met her at the Lambs' by the commonsense with which she found the kettle and boiled it when Mary absent-mindedly delayed. But of domestic talents she had none. Her little income was insufficient to meet the burden of married life, and Hazlitt soon found that instead of spending eight years in writing eight pages he must turn journalist and write articles upon politics and plays and pictures and books of the right length, at the right moment. Soon the mantelpiece of the old house at York Street where Milton had lived was scribbled over with ideas for essays. As the habit proves, the house was not a tidy house, nor did geniality and comfort excuse the lack of order. The Hazlitts were to be found eating breakfast at two in the afternoon, without a fire in the grate or a curtain to the window. A valiant walker and a clear-sighted woman, Mrs Hazlitt had no delusions about her husband. He was not faithful to her, and she faced the fact with admirable commonsense. But 'he said that I had always despised him and his abilities', she noted in her diary, and that was carrying commonsense too far. The prosaic marriage came lamely to an end. Free at last from the encumbrance of home and husband, Sarah Hazlitt pulled on her boots and set off on a walking tour through Scotland, while Hazlitt, incapable of attachment or comfort, wandered from inn to inn, suffered tortures of humiliation and disillusionment, but, as he drank cup after cup of very strong tea and made love to the innkeeper's daughter, he wrote those essays that are of course among the very best that we[j] have.

That they are not quite the best – that they do not haunt the mind and remain entire in the memory as the essays of Montaigne or Lamb haunt the mind – is also true. He seldom reaches the perfection of these great writers or their unity. Perhaps it is the nature of these short pieces that they need unity and a mind at harmony with itself. A little jar there makes the whole composition tremble. The essays of Montaigne, Lamb, even Addison,[4] have the reticence which springs from composure, for with all their familiarity they never tell us what they wish to keep hidden. But with Hazlitt it is different. There is always something divided and discordant even in his finest essays, as if two minds were at work who never succeed save for a few moments in making a match of it. In the first place there is the mind of the inquiring boy who wishes to be satisfied of the reason of things – the mind of the thinker. It is the thinker for the most part who is allowed the choice of the subject. He chooses some abstract idea, like Envy, or Egotism, or Reason and Imagination. He treats it with energy and independence. He explores its ramifications and scales its narrow paths as if it were a mountain road and the ascent both difficult and inspiring. Compared with this athletic progress, Lamb's seems the flight of a butterfly cruising capriciously among the flowers and perching for a second incongruously here upon a barn, there upon a wheelbarrow. But every[k] sentence in Hazlitt carries us forward. He has his end in view and, unless some accident intervenes, he strides towards it in that 'pure conversational prose style' which, as he points out, is so much more difficult to practise[l] than fine writing.

There can be no question that Hazlitt the thinker is an admirable companion. He is strong and fearless; he knows his mind and he speaks his mind forcibly yet brilliantly too, for the readers of newspapers are a dull-eyed race who must be dazzled in order to make them see. But besides Hazlitt the thinker there is Hazlitt the artist. There is the sensuous and emotional man, with his feeling for colour and touch, with his passion for prize-fighting and Sarah Walker,[5] with his sensibility to all those emotions which disturb the reason and make it often seem futile enough to spend one's time slicing things up finer and finer with the intellect when the body of the world is so firm and so warm and demands so imperatively to be pressed[m] to the heart. To know the reason of things is a poor substitute for being able to feel them. And Hazlitt felt with the intensity of a poet. The most abstract of his essays will suddenly glow red-hot or white-hot[n] if something reminds him of his past. He will drop his fine analytic pen and paint a phrase or two with a full brush brilliantly and beautifully if some landscape stirs his imagination or some book brings back the hour when he first read it. The famous passages about reading

Love for Love and drinking coffee from a silver pot, and reading *La Nouvelle Héloïse* and eating a cold chicken, are known to all,[6] and yet how oddly they often break into the context, how violently we are switched from reason to rhapsody – how embarrassingly our austere thinker falls upon our shoulders and demands our sympathy! It is this disparity and the sense of two forces in conflict that trouble the serenity and cause the inconclusiveness of some of Hazlitt's finest essays. They set out to give us a proof and they end by giving us a picture. We are about to plant our feet upon the solid rock of Q.E.D., and behold the rock turns[o] to quagmire and we are knee-deep in mud and water and flowers. 'Faces pale as the primrose with hyacinthine locks' are in our eyes; the woods of Tuderly breathe their mystic voices in our ears. Then suddenly we are recalled, and the thinker, austere, muscular, and sardonic,[p] leads us on to analyse, to dissect, and to condemn.

Thus if we compare Hazlitt with the other great masters in his line it is easy to see where his limitations lie. His range is narrow and his sympathies few if intense.[q] He does not open the doors wide upon all experience like Montaigne, rejecting nothing, tolerating everything, and watching the play of the soul with irony and detachment. On the contrary, his mind shut hard with egotistic tenacity upon his first impressions and froze them to unalterable convictions. Nor was it for him to make play, like Lamb, with the figures of his friends, creating[r] them afresh in fantastic flights of imagination and reverie. His characters are seen with the same quick[s] sidelong glance full of shrewdness and suspicion which he darted upon people in the flesh. He does not use the essayist's licence to circle and meander. He is tethered by his egotism and by his convictions to one time and one place and one being. We never forget that this is England in the early days of the nineteenth century; indeed, we feel ourselves in the Southampton Buildings or in the inn parlour that looks over the downs and on to the high road at Winterslow. He has an extraordinary power of making us contemporary with himself. But as we read on through the many volumes which he filled with so much energy and yet with so little love of his task, the comparison with the other essayists drops from us. These are not essays, it seems independent[t] and self-sufficient, but fragments broken off from some larger book – some searching enquiry into the reason for human actions or into the nature of human institutions. It is only accident that has cut them short, and only deference to the public taste that has decked them out with gaudy images and[u] bright colours. The phrase which occurs in one form or another so frequently and indicates the structure which if he were free he would follow[v] – 'I will here try to go more at large into the subject and then give such instances and illustrations of it as occur to me'[7] – could by no possibility occur[w] in the *Essays of Elia* or *Sir Roger de Coverley*.[8] He loves to grope among the curious depths of human psychology and to track down the reason of things. He excels in hunting out the obscure causes that lie behind some common saying or sensation, and the drawers of his mind are well stocked with illustrations and arguments. We can believe him when he says that for twenty years he had thought hard and suffered acutely. He is speaking of what he knows from experience when he exclaims, 'How many ideas and trains of sentiment, long and deep and intense, often pass through the mind in only one day's thinking or reading!'[9] Convictions are his life-blood; ideas have formed in him like stalactites, drop by drop, year by year. He has sharpened them in a thousand solitary walks; he has tested them[x] in argument after argument, sitting in his corner, sardonically observant, over a late supper at the Southampton Inn. But he has not changed them. His mind is his own and it is made up.

Thus[y] however threadbare the abstraction – *Hot and Cold*, or *Envy*, or *The Conduct of Life*, or *The Picturesque and the Ideal*[10] – he has something solid to write about. He never lets his brain slacken or trusts to his great gift of picturesque phrasing to float him over a stretch of shallow thought.[z] Even when it is plain from the savagery and contempt with which he attacks his task that he is out of the mood and only keeps his mind to the grindstone by strong tea and sheer[aa] force of will, we still find him mordant and searching and acute. There is a stir and trouble, a vivacity[bb] and conflict in his essays as if the very contrariety of his gifts kept him on the stretch. He is always hating, loving, thinking, and suffering. He could never come to terms with authority or doff his own idiosyncrasy in deference to opinion. Thus chafed and goaded the level of his essays is extraordinarily high. Often dry, garish in their bright imagery, monotonous in the undeviating energy of their rhythm – for Hazlitt believed too implicitly in his own saying, 'mediocrity, insipidity, want of character, is the great fault',[11] to be an easy writer to read for long at a stretch – there is scarcely an essay without[cc] its stress of thought, its thrust of insight, its moment of penetration. His pages are full of fine sayings and unexpected turns and[dd] independence and originality. 'All that is worth remembering of life is the poetry of it.'[12] 'If the truth were known, the most disagreeable people are the most amiable.'[13] 'You will hear more good things on the outside of a stage-coach from London to Oxford, than if you were to pass a twelve-month with the undergraduates or heads of colleges of that famous University.'[14] We are constantly plucked at by sayings that we would like to put by to examine[ee] later.

But besides the volumes of Hazlitt's essays there are the volumes of Hazlitt's criticism. In one way or another, either as lecturer or reviewer, Hazlitt strode through the greater part of English literature and delivered his opinion of the majority of famous books. His criticism has the rapidity and the daring, if it has also[ff] the looseness and the roughness, which arise from the circumstances in which it was written. He must cover a great deal of ground, make his points clear to an audience not of readers but of listeners, and has time only to point to the tallest towers and the brightest[gg] pinnacles in the landscape. But even in his most perfunctory criticism of books we feel that faculty for seizing on the important and indicating the main outline which learned critics often lose and timid critics never acquire. He is one of those rare critics who have thought so much that they can dispense with reading. It matters very little that Hazlitt had read only one poem by Donne;[15] that he found Shakespeare's sonnets unintelligible; that he never read a book through after he was thirty; that he came indeed to dislike reading altogether. What he had read he had read with fervour. And since in his view it was the duty of a critic to 'reflect the colours, the light and shade, the soul and body of a work',[16] appetite, gusto, enjoyment were far more important than analytic subtlety or prolonged and extensive study. To communicate his own fervour was his aim. Thus he first cuts out with vigorous and direct strokes the figure of one author and contrasts it with another, and next builds up with the freest use of imagery and colour the brilliant ghost that the book has left[hh] glimmering in his mind. The poem is re-created in glowing phrases – 'A rich distilled perfume emanates from it like the breath of genius; a golden cloud envelops it; a honeyed paste of poetic diction encrusts it, like the candied coat of the auricula'.[17] But since the analyst in Hazlitt is never far from the surface, this painter's imagery is kept in check by a nervous sense of the hard and lasting in literature, of what a book means and where it should be placed, which models his enthusiasm and gives it angle and outline. He singles out the peculiar quality of his author and stamps it vigorously. There is the 'deep, internal, sustained sentiment'[18] of Chaucer; 'Crabbe is the only poet who has attempted and succeeded in the *still life* of tragedy'.[19] There is nothing flabby, weak, or[ii] merely ornamental in his criticism of Scott – sense and enthusiasm run hand in hand. And if such criticism is the reverse of final, if it is initiatory and inspiring rather than conclusive and complete, there is something to be said for the critic who starts the reader on a journey and fires him with a phrase to shoot off on adventures of his own.[jj] If one needs an incentive to read Burke, what is better than 'Burke's style was forked and playful like the lightning, crested like the serpent'?[20] Or again, should one be trembling on the brink of a dusty folio, the following passage is enough to plunge one in midstream:

It is delightful to repose on the wisdom of the ancients; to have some great name at hand, besides one's own initials always staring one in the face; to travel out of one's self into the Chaldee, Hebrew, and Egyptian characters; to have the palm-trees waving mystically in the margin of the page, and the camels moving slowly on in the distance of three thousand years. In that dry desert of learning, we gather strength and patience, and a strange and insatiable thirst of know-ledge. The ruined monuments of antiquity are also there, and the fragments of buried cities (under which the adder lurks) and cool springs, and green sunny spots, and the whirlwind and the lion's roar, and the shadow of angelic wings.[21]

Needless to say that is not criticism. It is sitting in an arm-chair and gazing into the fire, and building up image after image of what one has seen in a book. It is loving and taking the liberties of a lover. It is being[kk] Hazlitt.

But it is likely that Hazlitt will survive not in his lectures, nor in his travels, nor in his *Life of Napoleon*, nor in his *Conversations of Northcote*,[22] full as they are of energy and integrity, of broken and fitful splendour and shadowed with the shape of some vast unwritten book that looms on the horizon. He will live in a volume of essays in which is distilled all those powers that are dissipated and distracted elsewhere, where the parts of his complex and tortured spirit come together in a truce of amity and concord. Perhaps a fine day was needed, or a game of fives or a long walk in the country, to bring about this consummation. The body has a large share in everything that Hazlitt writes. Then a mood of intense and spontaneous reverie came over him; he soared into what Patmore called 'a calm so pure and serene that one did not like to interrupt it'.[23] His brain worked smoothly and swiftly and without consciousness of its own operations; the pages dropped without an erasure from his pen. Then his mind ranged in a rhapsody of well-being over books and love, over the past and its beauty, the present and its comfort, and the future that would bring a partridge hot from the oven or a dish of sausages sizzling in the pan.

I look out of my window and see that a shower has just fallen: the fields look green after it, and a rosy cloud hangs over the brow of the hill; a lily expands its petals in the moisture, dressed in its lovely green and white; a shepherd-boy has just brought some pieces of turf with daisies and grass for his young mistress to make a bed for her skylark, not doomed to dip his wings in the dappled dawn – my cloudy thoughts draw off, the storm of angry politics has blown over – Mr. Blackwood, I am yours – Mr. Croker, my service to you – Mr. T. Moore, I am alive and well.[24]

There is then no division, no discord, no bitterness. The different faculties work in harmony and unity. Sentence follows sentence with the healthy ring and chime of a blacksmith's hammer on the anvil; the words glow and the sparks fly; gently they fade and the essay is over. And as his writing had such passages of inspired description, so, too, his life had its seasons of intense enjoyment. When he lay dying a hundred years ago in a lodging in Soho his voice rang out with the old pugnacity and conviction: 'Well, I have had a happy life'. One has only to read him to believe it.[ll]

a – *TLS*: 'dislike which, among many others, his'.
b – *TLS*: 'or jealousy, . . . or pleasure,'.
c – *TLS*: 'room, looking nobody . . . face, shaking hands'.
d – *TLS*: 'gamut of his grievances.'
e – *TLS*: 'his own grievances'.
f – *TLS*: 'careers. His'.
g – *TLS*: 'and quiet art'.
h – *TLS*: 'over, had proved vain. His friends went over to the Government and he was left alone in a perpetual minority to uphold the doctrines of liberty, fraternity and revolution.'
i – *TLS*: 'He who was so susceptible to . . . sex and so uneasily aware of his own . . . mocked," married and, unfortunately, for reason rather than for love.'
j – *TLS*: 'to inn making love to the innkeeper's daughter, suffering tortures of humiliation and deceit, but, as . . . tea, writing those essays which are, of course, among the best we'.
k – *TLS*: 'wheelbarrow. Every'.
l – *TLS*: 'learn'.
m – *TLS*: 'taken'.
n – *TLS*: 'glow red or white hot'.
o – *TLS*: 'behold it turns'.

p – *TLS*: 'muscular, sardonic,'.
q – *TLS*: 'few and intense.'
r – *TLS*: 'play with the figures of his friends, like Lamb, creating'.
s – *TLS*: 'with that quick'.
t – *TLS*: 'seems, not little worlds governed by a law of their own, independent'.
u – *TLS*: 'It is only an accident . . . gaudy phrases and'.
v – *TLS*: 'the structure which he follows'.
w – *TLS*: 'fit'.
x – *TLS*: 'tested them and proved them rather than changed them'.
y – *TLS*: 'Inn. ¶ Thus'.
z – *TLS*: 'a shallow stretch of thought.'
aa – *TLS*: 'grindstone by sheer'.
bb – *TLS*: 'trouble and vivacity'.
cc – *TLS*: 'scarcely a page without'.
dd – *TLS*: 'His essays are . . . sayings, and unexpected turns of thought and'.
ee – *TLS*: 'by and examine'.
ff – *TLS*: 'if also'.
gg – *TLS*: 'and brightest'.
hh – *TLS*: 'aim. First cutting out . . . author against another, he next . . . book left'.
ii – *TLS*: 'flabby or weak or'.
jj – *TLS*: 'phrase to find out what lies beneath it.'
kk – *TLS*: 'It is lying in an arm-chair and looking into the fire and being'.
ll – *TLS* does not have this sentence.

1 – For periodical publication and composition, see 'Wm. Hazlitt, the Man' above; only material not in that version is annotated here. The essay was revised for *CR2*. Reprinted: *CE*.
2 – Prefix ('twy-') with the sense of 'having two' (*OED*).
3 – Hazlitt, *Liber Amoris or the New Pygmalion, with additional matter . . .*, introduced by Richard le Gallienne (privately printed, 1894), 'Text of the 1823 Edition', part ii, Letter vi, p. 105.
4 – For VW on Joseph Addison (1672–1719), see 'Addison', *CR1* and *IV VW Essays*.
5 – For Hazlitt's passion for Sarah Walker (b. 1800), see W. Carew Hazlitt, *Memoirs of William Hazlitt . . .* (2 vols, Richard Bentley, 1867), and, more particularly, *Liber Amoris*.
6 – William Congreve (1670–1729), *Love for Love* (1695); Jean-Jacques Rousseau, *La Nouvelle Héloïse* (1761). The second passage is recalled by Leslie Stephen in his essay 'William Hazlitt' (1875), reprinted in *Hours in a Library* (1892), vol. ii.
7 – Hazlitt, *Table-Talk: Original Essays on Men and Manners* (1821–2), ed. by his son (2 vols, C. Templeman, 1845–6), vol. i, 'On Genius and Common Sense', p. 26, which has: 'I shall try here . . . subject, and to give such instances . . .'

8 – Lamb, *Essays of Elia* (1823, 1833); Sir Roger de Coverley, a fictional character invented by Sir Richard Steele (1672–1729) for the pages of the *Spectator* and developed by his colleague, Joseph Addison.

9 – *Table-Talk*, vol. i, 'On the Past and Future', p. 14, which has: 'reading, for instance!'

10 – For Hazlitt's 'Hot and Cold' and 'On Envy (A Dialogue)', see *The Plain Speaker: Opinions on Books, Men, and Things* (2 vols, Henry Colburn, 1826), vol. i, pp. 407–28 and 231–53, respectively; for 'On the Conduct of Life', see *Literary Remains of the Late William Hazlitt* (2 vols, Saunders and Otley, 1836), vol. ii, pp. 73–109; and for 'On the Picturesque and Ideal', see *Table-Talk*, vol. ii, pp. 272–80.

11 – *Table-Talk*, vol. i, 'On Genius and Common Sense', p. 57.

12 – Hazlitt, *Lectures on the English Poets* (Taylor and Hessey, 1818), 'On Poetry in General', p. 3, which has: 'remembering in life, is'.

13 – Hazlitt, *The Round Table* (Samson Low, Son, and Marston, 1869), 'On Good-Nature', p. 130.

14 – *Table-Talk*, vol. i, 'On the Ignorance of the Learned', p. 93.

15 – John Donne (1572–1631).

16 – *Table-Talk*, vol. ii, 'On Criticism', p. 60.

17 – *Lectures on the English Poets*, 'On Swift', p. 232.

18 – *Ibid.*, 'On Chaucer and Spenser', p. 57.

19 – *Ibid.*, 'On Thomson and Cowper', pp. 192–3. Geoffrey Chaucer (c. 1340–1400); George Crabbe (1754–1832).

20 – *The Plain Speaker*, vol. ii, 'On Reading Old Books', p. 80. Leslie Stephen also quotes this in 'William Hazlitt'.

21 – *The Plain Speaker*, vol. ii, 'On Old English Writers and Speakers', pp. 292–3; the first sentence is quoted in *Memoirs*, vol. ii, p. 297.

22 – Hazlitt, *The Life of Napoleon Buonaparte* (vols i and ii, 1828; iii and iv, 1830); *Conversations of James Northcote, Esq., RA* (1830).

23 – P. G. Patmore, *My Friends and Acquaintances* (3 vols, Saunders and Otley, 1854), vol. ii, p. 344, which has: 'he would sometimes subside into an entire self-absorption, an utter abstraction from all but his own thoughts ... a calm, so pure and serene, that it seemed like a sin to call him from it to that actual reality which had, for him, so little to compensate for the change'.

24 – *The Plain Speaker*, vol. i, 'Whether Genius is Conscious of Its Powers?', pp. 295–6.

Geraldine and Jane

Geraldine Jewsbury would certainly not have expected anybody at this time of day to bother themselves about her novels. If she had caught one pulling them down from the shelf in some library she would have expostulated. 'They're such nonsense, my dear', she would have said. And then one likes to fancy that she would have burst out in that irresponsible, unconventional way of hers against libraries and literature and love and life and all the rest of it with a 'Damn it all!' or a 'Confound it!' for Geraldine was fond of swearing.

The odd thing about Geraldine Jewsbury, indeed, was the way in which she combined oaths and endearments, sense and effervescence, daring and gush: '... defenceless and tender on the one hand, and strong enough to cleave the very rocks on the other' – that is how Mrs Ireland, her biographer, puts it; or again: 'Intellectually she was a man, but the heart within her was as womanly as ever daughter of Eve could boast'. Even to look at there was, it would seem, something incongruous, queer, provocative about her. She was very small and yet boyish; very ugly yet attractive. She dressed very well, wore her reddish hair in a net, and ear-rings made in the form of miniature parrots swung in her ears as she talked. There, in the only portrait we have of her, she*a* sits reading, with her face half-turned away, defenceless and tender at the moment rather than cleaving the very rocks.

But what had happened to her before she sat at the photographer's table reading her book it is impossible to say. Until she was twenty-nine we know nothing of her except that she was born in the year 1812, was the daughter of a merchant, and lived in Manchester, or near it. In the first part of the nineteenth century a woman of twenty-nine was no longer young; she had lived her life or she had missed it. And though Geraldine, with her unconventional ways, was an exception, still it cannot be doubted that something very tremendous had happened in those dim years before we know her. Something had happened in Manchester. An obscure male figure looms in the background – a faithless but fascinating creature who had taught her that life is treacherous, life is hard, life is the very devil for a woman. A dark pool of experience had formed in the back of her mind into which she would dip for the consolation or for the instruction of others. 'Oh! it is too frightful to talk about. For two years I lived only in short respites from this blackness of darkness', she exclaimed from time to time. There had been seasons 'like dreary, calm November days when there is but one cloud, but that one covers the whole heaven'. She had struggled, 'but struggling is no use'. She had read Cudworth through. She had written an essay upon materialism before giving way. For, though the prey to so many emotions, she was also oddly detached and speculative. She liked to puzzle her head with questions about 'matter and spirit and the nature of life' even while her heart was bleeding. Upstairs there was a box full of extracts, abstracts, and conclusions. Yet what conclusion could a woman come to? Did anything avail a woman when love had deserted her, when her lover had played her false? No. It was useless to struggle; one had better let the wave engulf one, the cloud close over one's head. So she meditated, lying often on a sofa with a piece of knitting in her hands and a green shade over her eyes. For she suffered from a variety of ailments – sore eyes, colds, nameless exhaustion; and Greenheys, the suburb outside Manchester, where she kept house for her brother, was very damp. 'Dirty, half-melted snow and fog, a swampy meadow, set off by a creeping cold damp' – that was the view from her window. Often she could hardly drag herself across the room. And then there were incessant interruptions: somebody had come unexpectedly for dinner; she had to jump up and run into the kitchen and cook a fowl with her own hands. That done, she would put on her green shade and peer at her book again, for she was a great reader. She read metaphysics, she read travels, she read old books and new books – and especially the wonderful books of Mr Carlyle.[b]

Early in the year 1841 she came to London and secured an introduction to the great man whose works she so[c] much admired. She met Mrs Carlyle. They must have become intimate with great rapidity. In a few weeks Mrs Carlyle was 'dearest Jane'. They must have discussed everything. They must have talked about life and the past and the present, and certain 'individuals' who were sentimentally interested or were not sentimentally interested in Geraldine. Mrs Carlyle, so metropolitan, so brilliant, so deeply versed in life and scornful of its humbugs, must have captivated the young woman from Manchester completely, for[d] directly Geraldine returned to Manchester she began writing long letters to Jane which echo and continue the intimate conversations of Cheyne Row. 'A man who has had *le plus grand succès* among women, and who was the most passionate and poetically refined lover in his manners and conversation you would wish to find, once said to me . . . So she would begin. Or she would reflect:

It may be that we women are made as we are in order that they may in some sort fertilise the world. We shall go on loving, they [the men] will go on struggling and toiling, and we are all alike mercifully allowed to die – after a while. I don't know whether you will agree to this, and I cannot see to argue, for my eyes are very bad and painful.[2]

Probably Jane agreed to very little of all this. For Jane was eleven years the elder. Jane was not given to abstract reflections upon the nature of life. Jane was the most caustic, the most concrete, the most clear-sighted of women. But it is perhaps worth noting that when she first fell in with Geraldine she was beginning to feel those premonitions of jealousy, that uneasy sense that old relationships had shifted and that new ones were forming themselves, which had come to pass with the establishment of her husband's fame. No doubt, in the course of those long talks in Cheyne Row, Geraldine had received certain confidences, heard certain complaints, had drawn[e] certain conclusions. For besides being a mass of emotion and sensibility, Geraldine was a clever, witty woman who thought for herself and hated what she called 'respectability' as much as Mrs Carlyle hated what she called 'humbug'. In addition, Geraldine had from the first the strangest feelings about Mrs Carlyle. She felt 'vague undefined yearnings to be yours in some way'. 'You will let me be yours and think of me as such, will you not?' she urged again and again. 'I think of you as Catholics think of their saints', she said: '. . . you will laugh, but I feel towards you much more like a lover than a female friend!' No doubt Mrs Carlyle did laugh, but also she could scarcely fail to be touched by the little creature's adoration.

Thus when Carlyle himself early in 1843 suggested unexpectedly that they should ask Geraldine to stay with them, Mrs Carlyle, after debating the question with her usual candour, agreed. She reflected that a little of Geraldine would be 'very enlivening', but, on the other hand, much of Geraldine would be very exhausting. Geraldine dropped hot tears on to one's hands; she watched one; she fussed one; she was always in a state of emotion. Then 'with all her good and great qualities' Geraldine had in her 'a born spirit of intrigue' which might make mischief between husband and wife, though not in the usual way, for, Mrs Carlyle reflected, her husband 'had the habit' of preferring her to other women, 'and habits are much stronger in him than passions'. On the other hand, she herself was getting lazy intellectually; Geraldine loved talk and clever talk; with all her aspirations and enthusiasms it would be a kindness to let the young woman marooned in Manchester come to Chelsea; and so she came.

She came on the 1st or 2nd of February, and she stayed till the Saturday, the 11th of March. Such were visits in the year 1843. And the house was very small, and the servant was inefficient. Geraldine was always there. All the morning she scribbled letters. All the afternoon she lay fast asleep on the sofa in the drawing-room. She dressed herself in a low-necked dress to receive visitors on Sunday. She talked too much. As for her reputed intellect, 'she is sharp as a meat axe, but as narrow'. She flattered. She wheedled. She was insincere. She flirted. She swore. Nothing would make her go. The charges against her rose in a crescendo of irritation. Mrs Carlyle almost had to turn her out of the house. At last they parted; and Geraldine, as she got into the cab, was in floods of tears, but Mrs Carlyle's eyes were dry. Indeed, she was immensely relieved to see the last of her visitor. Yet when Geraldine had driven off and she found herself alone she was not altogether easy in her mind. She knew that her behaviour to a guest whom she herself had invited had been far from perfect. She had been 'cold, cross, ironical, disobliging'. Above all, she was angry with herself for having taken Geraldine for a *confidante*. 'Heaven grant that the consequences may be only *boring* – not *fatal*', she wrote. But it is clear that she was very much out of temper; and with herself as much as with Geraldine.

Geraldine, returned to Manchester, was well aware that something was wrong. Estrangement and silence fell between them. People repeated malicious stories which she half believed. But Geraldine was the least vindictive of women – 'very noble in her quarrels', as Mrs Carlyle herself admitted – and, if foolish and sentimental, neither conceited nor proud. Above all, her love for Jane was sincere. Soon she was writing to Mrs Carlyle again 'with an assiduity and disinterestedness that verge on the superhuman', as Jane commented with a little exasperation. She was worrying about Jane's health and saying that she did not want witty letters, but only dull letters telling the truth about Jane's state. For – it may have been one of those things that made her so trying as a visitor – Geraldine had not stayed for four weeks in Cheyne Row without coming to conclusions which it is not likely that she kept entirely to herself. 'You have no one who has any sort of consideration for you', she wrote. 'You have had patience and endurance till I am sick of the virtues, and what have they done for you? Half-killed you.' 'Carlyle', she burst out, 'is much too grand for everyday life. A sphinx does not fit in comfortably to our parlour life arrangements.' But she could do nothing. 'The more one loves, the more helpless one feels', she moralised. She could only watch from Manchester the bright kaleidoscope of her friend's existence and compare it with her own prosaic life, all made up of little odds and ends; but somehow, obscure though her own life was,*f* she no longer envied Jane the brilliance of her lot.

So they might have gone on corresponding in a desultory way at a distance – and 'I am tired to death of writing letters into space', Geraldine exclaimed; 'one only writes after a long separation, to oneself, instead of one's friend' – had it not been for the Mudies. The Mudies and Mudieism, as Geraldine called it, played a vast, if almost unrecorded, part in the obscure lives of Victorian gentlewomen. In this case the Mudies were two girls, Elizabeth and Juliet: 'flary, staring, and conceited, stolid-looking girls', Carlyle called them, the daughters of a Dundee schoolmaster, a respectable man who had written books on natural history and died, leaving a foolish widow and little or no provision for his family. Somehow the Mudies arrived in Cheyne Row inconveniently, if one may hazard a guess, just as dinner was on the table. But the Victorian lady never minded that – she put herself to any inconvenience to help the Mudies. The question at once presented itself to Mrs Carlyle, what could be done for them? Who knew of a place? who had influence with a rich man? Geraldine flashed into her mind. Geraldine was always wishing she could be of use. Geraldine might fairly be asked if there were situations to be had for the Mudies in Manchester. Geraldine acted with a promptitude that was much to her credit. She 'placed' Juliet at once. Soon she had heard of another place for Elizabeth. Mrs Carlyle, who was in the Isle of Wight, at once procured stays, gown, and petticoat for Elizabeth, came up to London, took Elizabeth all the way across London to Euston Square at half past seven in the evening, put her in charge of a benevolent-looking, fat old man, saw that a letter to Geraldine was pinned to her stays, and returned home, exhausted, triumphant, yet, as happens often with the devotees of Mudieism, a prey to secret misgivings. Would the Mudies be happy? Would they thank her for what she had done? A few days later the inevitable bugs appeared in Cheyne Row, and were ascribed, with or without reason, to Elizabeth's shawl. What was far worse, Elizabeth herself appeared four months later, having proved herself 'wholly inapplicable to any practical purpose', having 'sewed a *black* apron with *white* thread', and, on being mildly scolded, having 'thrown herself on the kitchen floor and kicked and screamed'. 'Of course, her immediate dismissal is the result.' Elizabeth vanished – to sew more black aprons with white thread, to kick and scream and be dismissed – who knows what happened eventually to poor Elizabeth Mudie? She disappears from the world altogether, swallowed up in⁸ the dark shades of her sisterhood. Juliet, however, remained. Geraldine made Juliet her charge. She superintended and advised. The first place was unsatisfactory. Geraldine engaged herself to find another. She went off and sat in the hall of a 'very stiff old lady' who wanted a maid. The very stiff old lady said she would want Juliet to clear-starch collars, to iron cuffs, and to wash and iron petticoats. Juliet's heart failed her. All this clear-starching and ironing, she exclaimed, were beyond her. Off went Geraldine again, late in the evening, and saw the old lady's daughter. It was arranged that the petticoats should be 'put out' and only the collars and frills left for Juliet to iron. Off went Geraldine and arranged with her own milliner to give her lessons in quilling and trimming. And Mrs Carlyle wrote kindly to Juliet and*ʰ* sent her a packet. So it went on with more places and more bothers, and more old ladies, and more interviews till Juliet wrote a novel, which a gentleman praised very highly, and Juliet told Miss Jewsbury that she was annoyed by another gentleman who followed her home from church; but still she was a very nice girl, and everybody spoke well of her until the year 1849, when suddenly, without any reason given, silence descends upon the last of the Mudies. It covers, one cannot doubt, another failure. The novel, the stiff old lady, the gentleman, the caps, the petticoats, the clear-starching – what was the cause of her downfall? Nothing is known. 'The wretched stalking blockheads', wrote Carlyle, 'stalked fatefully, in spite of all that could be done and said, steadily downwards towards perdition and sank altogether out of view.' For all her endeavours, Mrs Carlyle had to admit that Mudieism was always a failure.

But Mudieism had unexpected results. Mudieism brought Jane and Geraldine together again. Jane could not deny that 'the fluff of feathers' whom she had served up, as her way was, in so many a scornful phrase for Carlyle's amusement, had 'taken up the matter with an enthusiasm even surpassing my own'. She had grit in her as well as fluff. Thus when Geraldine sent her the manuscript of her first novel, *Zoe*, Mrs Carlyle bestirred herself to find a publisher ('for', she wrote, 'what is to become of her when she is old without ties, without purposes?') and with surprising success. Chapman & Hall at once agreed to publish the book, which, their reader reported, 'had taken

hold of him with a grasp of iron'. The book had been long on the
way. Mrs Carlyle herself had been consulted at various stages of its
career. She had read the first sketch 'with a feeling little short of
terror! So much power of genius rushing so recklessly into unknown
space.' But she had also been deeply impressed.

Geraldine in particular shows herself here a far more profound and daring
speculator than ever I had fancied her. I do not believe there is a woman
alive at the present day, not even Georges Sand herself, that could have
written some of the best passages in this book . . . but they must not publish
it – decency forbids!

There was, Mrs Carlyle complained, an indecency or 'want of reserve
in the spiritual department', which no respectable public would stand.
Presumably Geraldine consented to make alterations, though she
confessed that she 'had no vocation for propriety as such'; the book
was rewritten, and it appeared at last in February 1845. The usual
buzz and conflict of opinion at once arose. Some were enthusiastic,
others were shocked. The 'old and young roués' of the Reform Club
almost go off into hysterics over – its *indecency*'. The publisher was
a little alarmed; but the scandal helped the sale, and Geraldine became
a lioness.

   And now, of course, as one turns the pages of the three little
yellowish volumes, one wonders what reason there was for approval
or disapproval, what spasm of indignation or admiration scored that
pencil mark, what mysterious emotion pressed violets, now black as
ink, between the pages of the love scenes. Chapter after chapter glides
amiably, fluently past. In a kind of haze we catch glimpses of an illegitimate girl called Zoe; of an enigmatic Roman Catholic priest called
Everhard; of a castle in the country; of ladies lying on sky-blue sofas;
of gentlemen reading aloud; of girls embroidering hearts in silk. There
is a conflagration. There is an embrace in a wood. There is incessant
conversation. There is a moment of terrific emotion when the priest
exclaims, 'Would that I had never been born!' and proceeds to sweep
a letter from the Pope asking him to edit a translation of the principal works of the Fathers of the first four centuries and a parcel
containing a gold chain from the University of Göttingen into a drawer
because Zoe has shaken his faith. But what indecency there was
pungent enough to shock the roués of the Reform Club, what genius
there was brilliant enough to impress the shrewd intellect of Mrs

Carlyle, it is impossible to guess. Colours that were fresh as roses eighty years ago have faded to a feeble pink; nothing remains of all those scents and savours but a faint perfume of faded violets, of stale hair-oil, we know not which. What miracles, we exclaim, are within the power of a few years to accomplish! But even as we exclaim, we see, far^k away, a trace perhaps of what they meant. The passion, in so far as it issues from the lips of living people, is completely spent. The Zoes, the Clothildes, the Everhards moulder on their perches; but, nevertheless, there is somebody in the room with them; an irresponsible spirit, a daring and agile woman, if one considers that she is cumbered with crinoline and stays; an absurd sentimental creature, languishing, expatiating, but for all that still strangely alive. We catch a sentence now and then rapped out boldly, a^l thought subtly conceived. 'How much better to do right without religion!' 'Oh!^{m} if they really believed all they preach, how would any priest or preacher be able to sleep in his bed!' 'Weakness is the only state for which there is no hope.' 'To love rightly is the highest morality of which mankind is capable.' Then how she hated the 'compacted, plausible theories of men'! And^n what is life? For what end was it given us? Such questions, such convictions, still hurtle past the heads of the stuffed figures mouldering on their perches. They are dead, but Geraldine Jewsbury herself still survives, independent, courageous, absurd, writing^o page after page without stopping to correct, and coming out with her views upon love, morality, religion,^{p} and the relations of the sexes, whoever may be within hearing, with a cigar between her lips.

  Some time before the publication of *Zoe*, Mrs Carlyle had forgotten, or overcome, her irritation with Geraldine, partly because she had worked so zealously in the cause of the Mudies, partly also because by Geraldine's painstaking she was 'almost over-persuaded back into my old illusion that she has some sort of strange, passionate... incomprehensible *attraction* towards me'. Not only was she drawn back into correspondence – after all her vows to the contrary she again stayed under the same roof with Geraldine, at Seaforth House near Liverpool, in July 1844. Not many days had passed before Mrs Carlyle's 'illusion' about the strength of Geraldine's affection for her proved to be no illusion but a monstrous fact. One morning there was some slight tiff between them: Geraldine sulked all day; at night Geraldine came to Mrs Carlyle's bedroom and made a scene which was 'a revelation to me, not only of Geraldine, but of human nature! Such mad, lover-like jealously on the part of one woman towards another it had never entered into my heart to conceive.' Mrs Carlyle was angry and outraged and contemptuous. She saved up a full account of the scene to entertain her husband with. A few days later she turned upon Geraldine in public and sent the whole company into fits of laughter by saying, 'I wondered she should expect me to behave decently to her after she had for a whole evening been making love before my very face to *another man*!' The trouncing must have been severe, the humiliation painful. But Geraldine was incorrigible. A year later she was again sulking and raging and declaring that she had a right to rage because 'she loves me better than all the rest of the world'; and Mrs Carlyle was getting up and saying, 'Geraldine, until you can behave like a gentlewoman . . .' and leaving the room. And again there were tears and apologies and promises to reform.

Yet though Mrs Carlyle scolded and jeered, though they were estranged, and though for a time they ceased to write to each other, still they always came together again. Geraldine, it is abundantly clear, felt^q that Jane was in every way wiser, better, stronger than she was. She depended on Jane. She needed Jane to keep her out of scrapes; for Jane never got into scrapes herself. But though Jane was so much wiser and cleverer than Geraldine, there were times when the foolish and irresponsible one of the two became the counsellor. Why, she asked, waste your time in mending old clothes? Why not work at something that will really employ your energies? Write, she advised her. For Jane, who was so profound, so far-seeing, could, Geraldine was convinced, write something that would help women in 'their very complicated duties and difficulties'. She owed a duty to her sex. But, the bold woman proceeded, 'do not go to Mr. Carlyle for sympathy, do not let him dash you with cold water. You must respect your own work, and your own motives' – a piece of advice that Jane, who was afraid to accept the dedication of Geraldine's new novel *The Half Sisters*, lest Mr Carlyle might object, would have done well to follow. The little creature was in some ways the bolder and the more independent of the two.

She had, moreover, a quality that Jane with all her brilliancy lacked – an element of poetry, a trace of the speculative imagination. She browsed upon old books and copied out romantic passages about the palm trees and cinnamon of Arabia and sent them to lie, incongruously enough, upon the breakfast table in Cheyne Row. Jane's genius, of course, was the very opposite; it was positive, direct, and practical. Her imagination concentrated itself upon people. Her letters owe their incomparable brilliancy to the hawk-like swoop and descent of her mind upon facts. Nothing escapes her. She sees through clear water down to the rocks at the bottom. But the intangible eluded her; she dismissed the poetry of Keats with a sneer; something of the narrowness and something of the prudery of a Scottish country doctor's daughter clung to her. Though infinitely the less masterly, Geraldine was sometimes the broader minded.

Such sympathies and antipathies bound the two women together with an elasticity that made for permanence. The tie between them could stretch and stretch indefinitely without breaking. Jane knew the extent of Geraldine's folly; Geraldine had felt the full lash of Jane's tongue. They had learnt to tolerate each other. Naturally, they quarrelled again; but their quarrels were different now; they were quarrels that were bound to be made up. And when after her brother's marriage in 1854 Geraldine moved to London, it was to be near Mrs Carlyle at Mrs Carlyle's own wish. The woman who in 1843 would never be a friend of hers again was now the most intimate friend she had in the world. She was to lodge two streets off; and perhaps two streets off was the right space to put between them. The emotional friendship was full of misunderstandings at a distance; it was intolerably exacting under the same roof. But when they lived round the corner their relationship broadened and simplified; it became a natural intercourse whose ruffles and whose calms were based upon the depths of intimacy. They went about together. They went to hear *The Messiah*; and, characteristically, Geraldine wept at the beauty of the music and Jane had much ado to prevent herself from shaking Geraldine for crying and from crying herself at the ugliness of the chorus women. They went to Norwood for a jaunt, and Geraldine left a silk handkerchief and an aluminium brooch ('a love token from Mr Barlow') in the hotel and a new silk parasol in the waiting-room. Also Jane noted with sardonic satisfaction that Geraldine, in an attempt at economy, bought two second-class tickets, while the cost of a return ticket first class was precisely the same.

Meanwhile Geraldine lay on the floor and generalised and speculated and tried to formulate some theory of life from her own tumultuous experience. 'How loathsome' (her language was always apt to be strong – she knew that she 'sinned against Jane's notions of good taste' very often), how loathsome the position of women was in many ways! How she herself had been crippled and stunted! How her blood boiled in her at the power that men had over women! She would like to kick certain gentlemen – 'the lying hypocritical beggars! Well, it's no good swearing – only, I am angry and it eases my mind.'

And[r] then her thoughts turned to Jane and herself and to the brilliant gifts – at any rate, Jane had brilliant gifts – which had borne so little visible result. Nevertheless, except when she was ill,

I do not think that either you or I are to be called failures. We are indications of a development of womanhood which as yet is not recognised. It has, so far, no ready-made channels to run in, but still we have looked and tried, and found that the present rules for women will not hold us – that something better and stronger is needed. . . . There are women to come after us, who will approach nearer the fullness of the measure of the stature of a woman's nature. I regard myself as a mere faint indication, a rudiment of the idea, of certain higher qualities and possibilities that lie in women, and all the eccentricities and mistakes and miseries and absurdities I have made are only the consequences of an imperfect formation, an immature growth.

So she theorised, so she speculated; and Mrs Carlyle listened, and laughed, and contradicted, no doubt, but with more of sympathy than of derision: she[s] could have wished that Geraldine were more precise; she could have wished her to moderate her language. Carlyle might come in at any moment; and if there was one creature that Carlyle hated, it was a strong-minded woman of the George Sand species. Yet she could not deny that there was an element of truth in what Geraldine said; she had always thought that Geraldine 'was born to spoil a horn or make a spoon'. Geraldine was no fool in spite of appearances.

But what Geraldine thought and said; how she spent her mornings; what she did in the long evenings of the London winter – all, in fact, that constituted her life at Markham Square – is but slightly and doubtfully known to us. For, fittingly enough, the bright light of Jane extinguished the paler and more flickering fire of Geraldine. She had no need to write to Jane any more. She was in and out of the house – now writing a letter for Jane because Jane's fingers were swollen, now taking a letter to the post and forgetting, like[t] the scatter-brained romantic creature she was, to post it. A crooning domestic sound like the purring of a kitten or the humming of a tea-kettle seems to rise, as we turn the pages of Mrs Carlyle's letters, from the intercourse of the two incompatible but deeply attached women. So the years passed. At length, on Saturday, 21st April 1866, Geraldine was to help Jane with a tea-party. Mr Carlyle was in Scotland, and

Mrs Carlyle hoped to get through some necessary civilities to admirers in his absence. Geraldine was actually dressing for the occasion when Mr Froude appeared suddenly at her house. He had just had a message from Cheyne Row to say that 'something had happened to Mrs Carlyle'. Geraldine flung on her cloak. They hastened together to St George's Hospital. There, writes Froude, they saw Mrs Carlyle, beautifully dressed as usual,

as if she had sat upon the bed after leaving the brougham, and had fallen back upon it asleep. . . . The brilliant mockery, the sad softness with which the mockery alternated, both were alike gone. The features lay composed in a stern majestic calm. . . . [Geraldine] could not speak.

Nor indeed can we break that silence. It deepened. It became complete. Soon after Jane's death she went to live at Sevenoaks. She lived there alone for twenty-two years. It is said that she lost her vivacity. She wrote no more books. Cancer attacked her and she suffered much. On her death-bed she began tearing up Jane's letters, as Jane had wished, and she had destroyed all but one before she died. Thus, just as her life began in obscurity, so it ended in obscurity. We know her well only for a few years in the middle. But let us not be too sanguine about 'knowing her well'. Intimacy is a difficult art, as Geraldine herself reminds us.

Oh," my dear [she wrote to Mrs Carlyle], if you and I are drowned, or die, what would become of us if any superior person were to go and write our 'life and errors'? What a precious mess a 'truthful person' would go and make of us, and how very different to what we really are or were!

The echo of her mockery, ungrammatical, colloquial, but as usual with the ring of truth in it, reaches us from where she lies in Lady Morgan's vault in the Brompton cemetery.

a – *TLS*: 'attractive – qualities that are almost extinguished in the only portrait we have of her by the flowing skirts and the sweeping tablecloth of the professional photographer. There she'.
b – *TLS*: 'new books – Carlyle's books among them. She gave little parties where she discussed literature rather boldly, with a cigar in her mouth, and life and the relations of the sexes, for she was always being loved or not being loved – whichever it was, passion played a great part in her life.'
c – *TLS*: 'whose lectures she had so'.

d – *TLS*: 'completely. For'.

e – *TLS*: 'complaints and drawn'.

f – *TLS*: 'though it was,'.

g – *TLS*: 'altogether, to be lost in'.

h – *TLS*: 'wrote to cheer her up and'.

i – *TLS*: 'arose. The least moral people, according to Mrs Carlyle, were the most shocked. The most moral, like Erasmus Darwin and Arthur Helps, either admired it or said nothing. A prim Scottish puritan like Miss Wilson owned that, though '*avowedly* the book of an audacious *esprit forte* . . . I think it very clever and amusing,' while 'old and young *roués*'.

j – *TLS*: 'mark or bent that leaf, and what'.

k – *TLS*: 'as one exclaims, one sees, far'.

l – *TLS*: 'then boldly rapped out, a'.

m – *TLS*: 'religion!" "Insincerity has crept into the heart of the most sacred things." "Oh!' See Jewsbury, *Zoe. The History of Two Lives* (3 vols, Chapman & Hall, 1845), vol, ii, ch. iv, p. 69.

n – *TLS*: 'capable." How she hated "the compacted, . . ."! Are women merely to cook, merely to sew, she demanded? And'.

o – *TLS*: 'absurd, tripping about, writing'.

p – *TLS*: 'morality and religion,'.

q – *TLS*: 'again. Through it all it is abundantly clear that Geraldine felt'.

r – *TLS*: 'mind. She had her own views about women. She did not agree with the ugly clever women who came to Manchester preaching the doctrines of women's rights. She did not hold with the professors and the essayists on female education. She thought that their theories and aims were wrong. She thought she could see far off another type of woman arising, a woman something like Jane and herself. ¶ "I believe we are touching on better days [she wrote], when women will have a genuine, normal life of their own to lead. There, perhaps, will not be so many marriages, and women will be taught not to feel their destiny manqué if they remain single. They will be able to be friends and companions in a way they cannot be now . . . Instead of having appearances to attend to they will be allowed to have their virtues, in any measure which it may please God to send, without being diluted down to the tepid 'rectified spirit' of 'feminine grace' and 'womanly timidity' – in short, they will be allowed to make themselves women as men are allowed to make themselves men." ¶ And'.

s – *TLS*: 'contradicted no doubt, but . . . derision, and she'.

t – *TLS*: 'forgetting, of course, like'.

u – *TLS*: 'middle. And when we consider how little we know even of those we live with, how much we must guess of the feelings of those we see constantly, it is difficult to persuade ourselves that we can judge Geraldine Jewsbury and the true nature of her feeling for Jane Carlyle with any certainty. Or if we cherish such an illusion, it is soon destroyed by Geraldine herself. ¶ "Oh,'.

1 – For periodical publication and composition, see 'Geraldine and Jane' above; only material not in that version is annotated here. See also 'The Letters of Jane Welsh Carlyle' and 'More Carlyle Letters', *I VW Essays*. Reprinted: *CE*.

2 – See *Selections from the Letters of Geraldine Endsor Jewsbury to Jane Welsh Carlyle*, ed. Mrs Alexander Ireland (Longmans, Green, 1892), pp. 6–7; there should be an ellipsis between the first and second sentences.

'Aurora Leigh'

By one of those ironies of fashion that might have amused the Brownings themselves, it seems likely that they are now far better known in the flesh than they have ever been in the spirit. Passionate lovers, in curls and side whiskers, oppressed, defiant, eloping – in this guise thousands of people must know and love the Brownings who have never read a line of their poetry. They have become two of the most conspicuous figures in that bright and animated company of authors who, thanks to our modern habit of writing memoirs and printing letters and sitting to be photographed, live in the flesh, not merely as of old in the word; are known by their hats, not merely by their poems. What damage the art of photography has inflicted upon the art of literature has yet to be reckoned. How far we are going to read a poet when we can read about a poet is a problem to lay before biographers. Meanwhile, nobody can deny the power of the Brownings to excite our sympathy and rouse our interest. 'Lady Geraldine's Courtship'[2] is glanced at perhaps by two professors in American universities once a year; but we all know how Miss Barrett lay on her sofa; how she escaped from the dark house in Wimpole Street one September morning; how she met health and happiness, freedom, and Robert Browning in the church round the corner.

But fate has not been kind to Mrs Browning as a writer. Nobody reads her, nobody discusses her, nobody[a] troubles to put her in her place. One has only to compare her reputation with Christina Rossetti's to trace her decline. Christina Rossetti mounts irresistibly to the first place among English women poets. Elizabeth, so much more loudly applauded during her lifetime, falls farther and farther behind. The primers dismiss her with contumely. Her importance, they say, 'has now become merely historical. Neither education nor association with her husband ever succeeded in teaching her the value of words and a sense of form.' In short, the only place in the mansion of literature that is assigned her is downstairs in the servants' quarters, where, in company with Mrs Hemans, Eliza Cook, Jean Ingelow, Alexander Smith, Edwin Arnold, and Robert Montgomery, she bangs the crockery about and eats vast handfuls of peas on the point of her knife.

If, therefore, we take *Aurora Leigh* from the shelf it is not so much in order to read it as to muse with kindly condescension over this token of bygone fashion, as we toy with the fringes of our grand-mothers' mantles and muse over the alabaster[b] models of the Taj Mahal which once adorned their drawing-room tables. But to the Victorians, undoubtedly, the book was very dear. Thirteen editions of *Aurora Leigh* had been demanded by the year 1873. And, to judge from the dedication, Mrs Browning herself was not afraid to say that she set great store by it – 'the most mature of my works,' she calls it, 'and the one into which my highest convictions upon Life and Art have entered'. Her letters show that she had had the book in mind for many years. She was brooding over it when she first met Browning, and her intention with regard to it forms almost the first of those confidences about their work which the lovers delighted to share.

. . . my chief *intention* [she wrote] just now is the writing of a sort of novel-poem . . . running into the midst of our conventions, and rushing into drawing-rooms and the like, 'where angels fear to tread'; and so, meeting face to face and without mask the Humanity of the age, and speaking the truth of it out plainly. That is my intention.

But for reasons which later become clear, she hoarded her intention throughout the ten astonishing years of escape and happiness; and when at last the book appeared in 1856 she might well feel that she had poured into it the best that she had to give. Perhaps the hoarding and the saturation which resulted have something to do with the surprise that awaits us. At any rate we cannot read the first twenty pages of *Aurora Leigh* without becoming aware that the Ancient Mariner who lingers, for unknown reasons, at the porch of one book and not of another has us by the hand, and makes us listen like a three years' child while Mrs Browning pours out in nine volumes of blank verse the story of Aurora Leigh. Speed and energy, forthright-ness and complete self-confidence – these are the qualities that hold us enthralled. Floated off our feet by them, we learn how Aurora was the child of an Italian mother 'whose rare blue eyes were shut from seeing her when she was scarcely four years old'. Her father was 'an austere Englishman, Who, after a dry life-time spent at home In college-learning, law and parish talk, Was flooded with a passion unaware', but died too, and the child was sent back to England to be brought up by an aunt. The aunt, of the well-known family of the Leighs, stood upon the hall step of her country house dressed in black to welcome her. Her somewhat narrow forehead was braided tight with brown hair pricked with grey; she had a close, mild mouth; eyes of no colour; and cheeks like roses pressed in books, 'Kept more for ruth than pleasure, – if past bloom, Past fading also'. The lady had lived a quiet life, exercising her Christian gifts upon knitting stockings and stitching petticoats 'because we are of one flesh, after all, and need one flannel'. At her hand Aurora suffered the education that was thought proper for women. She learnt a little French, a little algebra; the internal laws of the Burmese empire; what navigable river joins itself to Lara; what census of the year five was taken at Klagenfurt; also how to draw nereids neatly draped, to spin glass, to stuff birds, and model flowers in wax. For the aunt liked a woman to be womanly. Of an evening she did cross-stitch and, owing to some mistake in her choice of silk, once embroidered a shepherdess with pink eyes. Under this torture of women's education, the passionate Aurora exclaimed, certain women have died; others pine; a few who have, as Aurora had, 'relations with the unseen', survive, and walk demurely, and are civil to their cousins and listen to the vicar and pour out tea. Aurora herself was blessed with a little room. It was green papered, had a green carpet and there were green curtains to the bed, as if to match the insipid greenery of the English countryside. There she retired; there she read. 'I had found the secret of a garret room Piled high with cases in my father's name, Piled high, packed large, where, creeping in and out ... like some small nimble mouse between the ribs of a mastodon' she read and read. The mouse indeed (it is the way with Mrs Browning's mice) took wings and soared, for^c 'It is rather when We gloriously forget ourselves and plunge Soul-forward, headlong, into a book's profound, Impassioned for its beauty and salt of truth – 'Tis then we get the right good from a book'. And so she read and read, until her cousin Romney called to walk with her, or the painter Vincent Carrington, 'whom men judge hardly as bee-bonneted Because he holds that paint a body well you paint a soul by implication',[3] tapped on the window.

This hasty abstract of the first volume of *Aurora Leigh* does it of course no sort of justice; but having gulped down the original much as Aurora herself advises, soul-forward, headlong, we find ourselves in a state where some attempt at the ordering of our multitudinous impressions becomes imperative. The first of these impressions and the most pervasive is the sense of the writer's presence. Through the voice of Aurora the character, the circumstances, the idiosyncrasies of Elizabeth Barrett Browning ring in our ears. Mrs Browning could no more conceal herself than she could control herself, a sign no doubt of imperfection in an artist, but a sign also that life has impinged upon art more than life should. Again and again in the pages we have read, Aurora the fictitious seems to be throwing light upon Elizabeth the actual. The idea of the poem, we must remember, came to her in the early forties when the connexion^d between a woman's art and a woman's life was unnaturally close, so that it is impossible for the most austere of critics not sometimes to touch the flesh when his eyes should be fixed upon the page. And as everybody knows, the life of Elizabeth Barrett was of a nature to affect the most authentic and individual of gifts. Her mother had died when she was a child; she had read profusely and privately; her favourite brother was drowned; her health broke down; she had been immured by the tyranny of her father in almost conventual seclusion in a bedroom in Wimpole Street. But instead of rehearsing the well-known facts, it is better to read in her own words her own account of the effect they had upon her.

I have lived only inwardly [she wrote] or with *sorrow*, for a strong emotion. Before this seclusion of my illness, I was secluded still, and there are few of the youngest women in the world who have not seen more, heard more, known more, of society, than I, who am scarcely to be called young now. I grew up in the country – I had no social opportunities, had my heart in books and poetry, and my experience in reveries. And^e so time passed and passed – and afterwards, when my illness came . . . and no prospect (as appeared at one time) of ever passing the threshold of one room again; why then, I turned to thinking with some bitterness . . . that I had stood blind in this temple I was about to leave – that I had seen no Human nature, that my brothers and sisters of the earth were *names* to me, that I had beheld no great mountain or river, nothing in fact. . . . And do you also know what a disadvantage this ignorance is to my art? Why, if I live on and yet do not escape from this seclusion, do you not perceive that I labour under signal disadvantages – that I am, in a manner as a *blind poet*? Certainly, there is compensation to a degree. I have had much of the inner life, and from the habit of self-consciousness and self-analysis, I make great guesses at Human nature in the main. But how willingly I would as a poet exchange some of this lumbering, ponderous, helpless knowledge of books, for some experience of life and man, for some . . .

She breaks off, with three little dots, and we may take advantage of her pause to turn once more to *Aurora Leigh*.

What damage had her life done her as a poet? A great one, we cannot deny. For it is clear, as we turn the pages of *Aurora Leigh* or of the *Letters* – one often echoes the other – that the mind which found its natural expression in this swift and chaotic poem about real men and women was not the mind to profit by solitude. A lyrical, a scholarly, a fastidious mind might have used seclusion and solitude to perfect its powers. Tennyson[4] asked no better than to live with books in the heart of the country. But the mind of Elizabeth Barrett was lively and secular and satirical. She was no scholar. Books were to her not an end in themselves but a substitute for living. She raced through folios because she was forbidden to scamper on the grass. She wrestled with Aeschylus and Plato because it was out of the question that she should argue about politics with live men and women. Her favourite reading as an invalid was Balzac and George Sand and other 'immortal improprieties' because 'they kept the colour in my life to some degree'. Nothing is more striking when at last she broke the prison bars than the fervour with which she flung herself into the life of the moment. She loved to sit in a café and watch people passing; she loved the arguments, the politics, and the strife of the modern world. The past and its ruins, even the past of Italy and Italian ruins, interested her much less than the theories of Mr Hume the medium, or the politics of Napoleon, Emperor of the French. Italian pictures, Greek poetry, roused in her a clumsy and conventional enthusiasm in strange contrast with the original independence of her mind when it applied itself to actual facts.

Such being her natural bent, it is not surprising that even in the depths of her sick-room her mind turned to modern life as a subject for poetry. She waited, wisely, until her escape had given her some measure of knowledge and proportion. But it cannot be doubted that the long years of seclusion had done her irreparable damage as an artist. She had lived shut off, guessing at what was outside, and inevitably magnifying what was within. The loss of Flush, the spaniel, affected her as the loss of a child might have affected another woman. The tap of ivy on the pane became the thrash of trees in a gale. Every sound was enlarged, every incident exaggerated, for the silence of the sick-room was profound and the monotony of Wimpole Street was intense. When at last she was able to 'rush into drawing-rooms and the like and meet face to face without mask the Humanity of the age and speak the truth of it out plainly', she was too weak to stand the shock. Ordinary daylight, current gossip, the usual traffic of human beings left her exhausted, ecstatic, and dazzled into a state where she saw so much and felt so much that she did not altogether know what she felt or what she saw.

Aurora Leigh, the novel-poem, is not, therefore, the masterpiece that it might have been. Rather it is a masterpiece in embryo; a work whose genius floats diffused and fluctuating in some pre-natal stage waiting the final stroke of creative power to bring it into being. Stimulating and boring, ungainly and eloquent, monstrous and exquisite, all by turns, it overwhelms and bewilders; but, nevertheless, it still commands our interest and inspires our respect.[g] For it becomes clear as we read that, whatever Mrs Browning's faults, she was one of those rare writers who risk themselves adventurously and disinterestedly in an imaginative life which is independent of their private lives and demands to be considered apart from personalities. Her 'intention' survives; the interest of her theory redeems much that is faulty in her practice. Abridged and simplified from Aurora's argument in the fifth book, that theory runs something like this. The true[h] work of poets, she said, is to present their own age, not Charlemagne's. More passion takes place in drawing-rooms than at Roncesvalles with Roland and his knights. 'To flinch from modern varnish, coat or flounce, Cry out for togas and the picturesque, Is fatal – foolish too.' For living art presents and records real life, and the only life we can truly know is our own. But what form, she asks, can a poem on modern life take? The drama is impossible, for only servile and docile plays have any chance of success. Moreover, what we (in 1846) have to say about life is not fit for 'boards, actors, prompters, gaslight, and costume; our stage is now the soul itself'. What then can she do? The problem is difficult, performance is bound to fall short of endeavour; but she has at least wrung her life-blood on to every page[i] of her book, and, for the rest 'Let me think of forms less, and the external. Trust the spirit . . . Keep up the fire and leave the generous flames to shape themselves.' And so the fire blazed and the flames leapt high.

The desire to deal with modern life in poetry was not confined to Miss Barrett. Robert Browning said that he had had the same ambition all his life. Coventry Patmore's 'Angel in the House' and Clough's 'Bothie' were both attempts at the same kind and preceded *Aurora Leigh* by some years. It was natural enough. The novelists were dealing triumphantly with modern life in prose. *Jane Eyre, Vanity Fair, David Copperfield, Richard Feverel* all trod fast on each other's heels between the years 1847 and 1860. The poets may well have felt, with Aurora Leigh, that modern life had an intensity and a meaning of its own. Why should these spoils fall solely into the laps of the prose writers? Why should the poet be forced back to the remoteness of Charlemagne and Roland, to the toga and the picturesque, when the humours and tragedies of village life, drawing-room life, club life, and street life all cried aloud for celebration? It was true that the old form in which poetry had dealt with life – the drama – was obsolete; but was there none other that could take its place? Mrs Browning, convinced of the divinity of poetry, pondered, seized as much as she could of actual experience, and then at last threw down her challenge to the Brontës and the Thackerays in nine books of blank verse. It was in blank verse that she sang of Shoreditch and Kensington; of my aunt and the vicar; of Romney Leigh and Vincent Carrington; of Marian Erle and Lord Howe; of fashionable weddings and drab suburban streets, and bonnets and whiskers and four-wheeled cabs, and railway trains. The poets can treat of these things, she exclaimed, as well as of knights and dames, moats and drawbridges and castle courts. But can they? Let us see what happens to a poet when he poaches upon a novelist's preserves and gives us not an epic or a lyric but the story of many lives that move and change and are inspired by the interests and passions that are ours in the middle of the reign of Queen Victoria.

In the first place there is the story; a tale has to be told; the poet must somehow convey to us the necessary information that his hero has been asked out to dinner. This is a statement that a novelist would convey as quietly and prosaically as possible; for example, 'While I was kissing her glove, sadly enough, a note was brought saying that her father sent his regards and asked me to dine with them next day'. That is harmless. But the poet has to write:

> While thus I grieved, and kissed her glove,
> My man brought in her note to say,
> Papa had bid her send his love,
> And would I dine with them next day!

Which is absurd. The simple words have been made to strut and posture and take on an emphasis which makes them ridiculous. Then again, what will the poet do with dialogue? In modern life, as Mrs Browning indicated when she said that our stage is now the soul, the tongue has superseded the sword. It is in talk that the high moments of life, the shock of character upon character, are defined. But poetry when it tries to follow the words on people's lips is terribly impeded. Listen to Romney in a moment of high emotion talking to his old love Marian about the baby she has borne to another man:

> May God so father me, as I do him,
> And so forsake me, as I let him feel
> He's orphaned haply. Here I take the child
> To share my cup, to slumber on my knee,
> To play his loudest gambol at my foot,
> To hold my finger in the public ways . . .

and so on. Romney, in short, rants and reels like any of those Elizabethan heroes whom Mrs Browning had warned so imperiously out of her modern living-room. Blank verse has proved itself the most remorseless enemy of living speech. Talk tossed up on the surge and swing of the verse becomes high, rhetorical, impassioned; and as talk, since action is ruled out, must go on and on, the° reader's mind stiffens and glazes under the monotony of the rhythm. Following the lilt of her rhythm rather than the emotions of her characters, Mrs Browning is swept on into generalisation and declamation. Forced by the nature of her medium, she ignores the slighter, the subtler, the more hidden shades of emotion by which a novelist builds up touch by touch a character in prose. Change and development, the effect of one character upon another – all this is abandoned. The poem becomes one long soliloquy, and the only character that is known to us and the only story that is told us are the character and story of Aurora Leigh herself.

Thus, if Mrs Browning meant by a novel-poem a book in which character is closely and subtly revealed, the relations of many hearts laid bare, and a story unfalteringly unfolded, she failed completely. But if she meant rather to give us a sense of life in general, of people who are unmistakably Victorian, wrestling with the problems of their own time, all brightened, intensified, and compacted by the fire of poetry, she succeeded. Aurora Leigh, with her passionate interest in social questions, her conflict as artist and woman, her longing for knowledge and freedom, is the true daughter of her age. Romney, too, is no less certainly a mid-Victorian gentleman of high ideals who has thought deeply about the social question, and has founded, unfortunately, a phalanstery in Shropshire. The aunt, the antimacassars, and the country house from which Aurora escapes are real enough to fetch high prices in the Tottenham Court Road at this moment. The broader aspects of what it felt like to be a Victorian are seized as surely and stamped as vividly upon us as in any novel by Trollope or Mrs Gaskell.

And indeed if we compare the prose novel and the novel-poem the triumphs are by no means all to the credit of prose. As we rush through page after page of narrative in which a dozen scenes that the novelist would smooth out separately are pressed into one, in which pages of deliberate description are fused into a single line, we cannot help feeling that the poet has outpaced the prose writer. Her page is packed twice as full as his. Characters, too, if they are not shown in conflict but snipped off and summed up with something of the exaggeration of a caricaturist, have a heightened and symbolical significance which prose with its gradual approach cannot rival. The general aspect of things – market, sunset, church – have a brilliance and a continuity, owing to the compressions and elisions of poetry, which mock the prose writer and his slow accumulations of careful detail. For these reasons Aurora Leigh remains, with all its imperfections, a book that still lives and breathes and has its being. And when we think how still and cold the plays of Beddoes or of Sir Henry Taylor lie, in spite of all their beauty, and how seldom in our own day we disturb the repose of the classical dramas of Robert Bridges, we may suspect that Elizabeth Barrett was inspired by a flash of true genius when she rushed into the drawing-room and said that here, where we live and work, is the true place for the poet. At any rate, her courage was justified in her own case. Her bad taste, her tortured ingenuity, her floundering, scrambling, and confused impetuosity have space to spend themselves here without inflicting a deadly wound, while her ardour and abundance, her brilliant descriptive powers, her shrewd and caustic humour, infect us with her own enthusiasm. We laugh, we protest, we complain – it is absurd, it is impossible, we cannot tolerate this exaggeration a moment longer – but, nevertheless, we read to the end enthralled. What more can an author ask? But the best compliment that we can pay Aurora Leigh is that it makes us wonder why it has left no successors. Surely the street, the drawing-room, are promising subjects; modern life is worthy of the muse. But the rapid sketch that Elizabeth Barrett Browning threw off when she leapt from her couch and dashed into the drawing-room remains[q] unfinished. The conservatism or the timidity of poets still leaves the chief spoils of modern life to the novelist. We have no novel-poem of the age of George the Fifth.

a – *TLS*: 'animated procession which, thanks to our modern habit of printing letters and writing memoirs and sitting to be photographed, keeps step with the paler, subtler, more obscure shades who, in times gone by, lived solely between the pages of their books. To such immortality the Brownings, of course, laid themselves peculiarly open. Their story appeals to all that is dramatic and romantic in our natures. He must be dull, blind and no better than a bookworm who does not unravel the story of their hearts with enthusiasm and pore with delight over the picture of tiny Miss Barrett issuing one September morning from the dark house in Wimpole-street with Flush under her arm and the maid Wilson following behind to meet Browning, Italy, health and freedom in the church round the corner. ¶ But it cannot be denied that the works of the Brownings have lost lustre even as much as their persons have gained it. "Sordello," "The Ring and the Book," "Men and Women" and the rest are said to have little significance and little resonance in modern ears. Is it worth while, people ask, to sort this tangle of untidy verbiage in order to find the rather dubious treasures of a hearty, cheerful middle-class mind concealed beneath? As for Elizabeth Barrett Browning, her fate as a writer is far worse than her husband's. Nobody reads her, nobody discusses her poems, nobody.'
b – *TLS*: 'over alabaster'.
c – *TLS*: 'way of Mrs . . . and plunged for'.
d – *TLS*: 'relation'.
e – *TLS*: 'reveries. My sympathies drooped to the ground like an untrained honeysuckle. . . . It was a lonely life, growing green like the grass around it. . . . Books and dreams were what I lived in – and domestic life only seemed to buzz gently around, like the bees about the grass. And'.
f – *TLS*: 'arguments and politics and strife'.
g – *TLS*: 'inspires respect.'
h – *TLS*: 'sole'.
i – *TLS*: 'leaf'.
j – *TLS*: 'of'.
k – *TLS*: '"Jane Eyre," "Vanity Fair," "David Copperfield," "Cranford," "The Warden," "Scenes from Clerical Life," "Richard Feverel"'.
l – *TLS*: '. . . whiskers and railway'.
m – *TLS*: 'told, and the'.

n – TLS: 'I kissed her glove in my sadness, a'.
o – TLS: 'go on all the time, the'.
p – TLS: 'general aspects of things, markets, sunsets, scenes in church, owing to the compressions and elisions of poetry have ... continuity which'.
q – TLS: 'complain of a thousand absurdities, but – and this, after all, is a great tribute to a writer – we read to the end enthralled. The best compliment that we can pay "Aurora Leigh," however, is ... sketch which Elizabeth Barrett Browning flung off when she rushed into the drawing-room and met face to face the humanity of her age remains'.

1 – For periodical publication and composition, see 'Aurora Leigh' above; only material not in that version is annotated here. The essay was revised for *CR2*. Reprinted: *CE*.
2 – Elizabeth Barrett, 'Lady Geraldine's Courtship' (1844).
3 – Browning, *Aurora Leigh* (1857), First Book, p. 40 (1873), ll. 1096–8 (1978):

> Whom men judge hardly as bee-bonneted,
> Because he holds that, paint a body well,
> You paint a soul by implication ...

4 – Alfred, Lord Tennyson (1809–92).

The Niece of an Earl

There is an aspect of fiction of so delicate a nature that less has been said about it than its importance deserves. One is supposed to pass over class distinctions in silence; one person is supposed to be as well born as another; and yet English fiction is so steeped in the ups and downs of social rank that without them it would be unrecognisable. When Meredith, in *The Case of General Ople and Lady Camper*, remarks, 'He sent word that he would wait on Lady Camper immediately, and betook himself forthwith to his toilette. She was the niece of an Earl',[2] all of British blood accept the statement unhesitatingly, and know that Meredith is right. A General in those circumstances would certainly have given his coat an extra brush. For though the General might have been, we are given to understand that he was not, Lady Camper's social equal. He received the shock of her rank upon a naked surface. No earldom, baronetage, or knighthood protected him. He was an English gentleman merely, and a poor one at that. Therefore, to British readers even now it seems unquestionably fitting that he should 'betake himself to his toilette' before appearing in the lady's presence.

It is useless to suppose that social distinctions have vanished. Each may pretend that he knows no such restrictions, and that the compartment in which he lives allows him the run of the world. But it is an illusion. The idlest stroller down summer streets may see for himself the charwoman's shawl shouldering its way among the silk wraps of the successful; he sees shop-girls pressing their noses against the plate glass of motor-cars; he sees radiant youth and august age waiting their summons within to be admitted to the presence of King George.[3] There is no animosity, perhaps, but there is no communication. We are enclosed, and separate, and cut off. Directly we see ourselves in the looking-glass of fiction we know that this is so. The novelist, and the English novelist in particular, knows and delights, it seems, to know that Society is a nest of glass boxes one separate from another, each housing a group with special habits and qualities of its own. He knows that there are Earls and that Earls have nieces; he knows that there are Generals and that Generals brush their coats before they visit the nieces of Earls. But this is only the A B C of what he knows. For in a few short pages, Meredith makes us aware not only that Earls have nieces, but that Generals have cousins; that the cousins have friends; that the friends have cooks; that the cooks have husbands, and that the husbands of the cooks of the friends of the cousins of the Generals are carpenters. Each of these people lives in a glass box of his own, and has peculiarities of which the novelist must take account. What appears superficially to be the vast equality of the middle classes is, in truth, nothing of the sort. All through the social mass run curious veins and streakings separating man from man and woman from woman; mysterious prerogatives and disabilities too ethereal to be distinguished by anything so crude as a title impede and disorder the great business of human intercourse. And when we have threaded our way carefully through all these grades from the niece of the Earl to the friend of the cousin of the General, we are still faced with an abyss; a gulf yawns before us; on the other side are the working classes. The writer of perfect judgment and taste, like Jane Austen,[4] does no more than glance across the gulf; she restricts herself to her own special class and finds infinite shades within it. But for the brisk, inquisitive, combative writer like Meredith, the temptation to explore is irresistible. He runs up and down the social scale; he chimes one note against another; he insists that the Earl and the cook, the General and the farmer shall speak up for themselves and play their part in the extremely complicated comedy of English civilised life.

It was natural that he should attempt it. A writer touched by the comic spirit relishes these distinctions keenly; they give him something to take hold of; something to make play with. English fiction without the nieces of Earls and the cousins of Generals would be an arid waste. It would resemble Russian fiction. It would have to fall back upon the immensity of the soul and upon the brotherhood of man. Like Russian fiction, it would lack comedy. But while we realise the immense debt that we owe the Earl's niece and the General's cousin, we doubt sometimes whether the pleasure we get from the play of satire on these broken edges is altogether worth the price we pay. For the price is a high one. The strain upon a novelist is tremendous. In two short stories Meredith gallantly attempts to bridge all gulfs, and to take half a dozen different levels in his stride. Now he speaks as an Earl's niece; now as a carpenter's wife.[5] It cannot be said that his daring is altogether successful. One has a feeling (perhaps it is unfounded) that the blood of the niece of an Earl is not quite so tart and sharp as he would have it. Aristocracy is not, perhaps, so consistently high and brusque and eccentric as, from his angle, he would represent it. Yet his great people are more successful than his humble. His cooks are too ripe and rotund; his farmers too ruddy and earthy. He overdoes the pith and the sap; the fist-shaking and the thigh-slapping. He has got too far from them to write of them with ease.

It seems, therefore, that the novelist, and the English novelist in particular, suffers from a disability which affects no other artist to the same extent. His work is influenced by his birth. He is fated to know intimately, and so to describe with understanding, only those who are of his own social rank. He cannot escape from the box in which he has been bred. A bird's-eye view of fiction shows us no gentlemen in Dickens; no working men in Thackeray. One hesitates to call Jane Eyre a lady. The Elizabeths and the Emmas of Miss Austen could not possibly be taken for anything else.[6] It is vain to look for dukes or for dustmen – we doubt that such extremes are to be found anywhere in fiction. We are, therefore, brought to the melancholy and tantalising conclusion not only that novels are poorer than they might be, but that we are very largely prevented – for after all, the novelists are the great interpreters – from knowing what is happening either in the heights of Society or in its depths. There is practically no evidence available by which we can guess at the feelings of the highest in the land. What does a King feel? What does a Duke think? We cannot say. For the highest in the land have seldom written at all, and have never written about themselves. We shall never know what the Court of Louis XIV looked like to Louis XIV himself.[7] It seems likely indeed that the English aristocracy will pass out of existence, or be merged with the common people, without leaving any true picture of themselves behind.

But our ignorance of the aristocracy is nothing compared with our ignorance of the working classes. At all times the great families of England and France have delighted to have famous men at their tables, and thus the Thackerays and the Disraelis and the Prousts[8] have been familiar enough with the cut and fashion of aristocratic life to write about it with authority. Unfortunately, however, life is so framed that literary success invariably means a rise, never a fall, and seldom, what is far more desirable, a spread in the social scale. The rising novelist is never pestered to come to gin and winkles with the plumber and his wife. His books never bring him into touch with the cat's-meat man, or start a correspondence with the old lady who sells matches and bootlaces by the gate of the British Museum. He becomes rich; he becomes respectable; he buys an evening suit and dines with peers. Therefore, the later works of successful novelists show, if anything, a slight rise in the social scale. We tend to get more and more portraits of the successful and the distinguished. On the other hand, the old rat-catchers and ostlers of Shakespeare's day are shuffled altogether off the scene, or become, what is far more offensive, objects of pity, examples of curiosity. They serve to show up the rich. They serve to point the evils of the social system. They are no longer, as they used to be when Chaucer wrote, simply themselves.[9] For it is impossible, it would seem, for working men to write in their own language about their own lives. Such education as the act of writing implies at once makes them self-conscious, or class-conscious, or removes them from their own class. That anonymity, in the shadow of which writers write most happily, is the prerogative of the middle class alone. It is from the middle class that writers spring, because it is in the middle class only that the practice of writing is as natural and habitual as hoeing a field or building a house. Thus it must have been harder for Byron to be a poet than Keats; and it is as impossible to imagine that a Duke could be a great novelist as that *Paradise Lost*[10] could be written by a man behind a counter.

But things change; class distinctions were not always so hard and fast as they have now become. The Elizabethan age was far more elastic in this respect than our own; we, on the other hand, are far less hide-bound than the Victorians. Thus it may well be that we are on the edge of a greater change than any the world has yet known. In another century or so, none of these distinctions may hold good. The Duke and the agricultural labourer as we know them now may have died out as completely as the bustard and the wild cat. Only natural differences such as those of brain and character will serve to distinguish us. General Ople (if there are still Generals) will visit the niece (if there are still nieces) of the Earl (if there are still Earls) without brushing his coat (if there are still coats). But what will happen to English fiction when it has come to pass that there are neither Generals, nieces, Earls, nor coats, we cannot imagine. It may change its character so that we no longer know it. It may become extinct. Novels may be written as seldom and as unsuccessfully by our descendants as the poetic drama by ourselves. The art of a truly democratic age will be – what?

1 – Originally published in Desmond MacCarthy's *L&L*, October 1928, (*Kp4* C305; see *IV VW Essays*), this essay was slightly revised for *CR2*. Reprinted: *CE, CDML*.
2 – George Meredith (1828–1909), 'The Case of General Ople and Lady Camper' (1890; Memorial Edition of the Works of George Meredith, Constable, 1910), vol. xxi, ch. ii, pp. 130–1. For VW on Meredith, see 'The Novels of George Meredith' below.
3 – George V reigned 1910–36. A young woman of good family was not considered to be an official member of Society until, accompanied by her sponsor, she had been presented to the monarch at Court. The custom was abolished in 1958.
4 – Jane Austen (1775–1817).
5 – Mrs Crickledon in 'The House on the Beach: A Realistic Tale' (1877).
6 – Charles Dickens (1812–70); William Makepeace Thackeray (1811–63); Charlotte Brontë (1816–55), *Jane Eyre* (1847); Austen, Elizabeth Bennet in *Pride and Prejudice* (1813) and Emma Woodhouse in *Emma* (1816).
7 – Louis XIV reigned 1643–1715.
8 – Benjamin Disraeli (1804–81); Marcel Proust (1871–1922).
9 – For VW on Geoffrey Chaucer (c. 1340–1400), see 'The Pastons and Chaucer' in *CR1* and *IV VW Essays*.

10 – George Gordon, Lord Byron (1788–1824); John Keats (1795–1821); John Milton (1608–74), *Paradise Lost* (1667).

George Gissing

'Do you know there are men in London who go the round of the streets selling paraffin oil?'[2] wrote George Gissing in the year 1880, and the phrase because it is Gissing's calls up a world of fog and fourwheelers, of slatternly landladies, of struggling men of letters, of gnawing domestic misery, of gloomy back streets, and ignoble yellow chapels; but also, above this misery, we see tree-crowned heights, the columns of the Parthenon, and the hills of Rome. For Gissing is one of those imperfect novelists through whose books one sees the life of the author faintly covered by the lives of fictitious people.[a] With such writers we establish a personal rather than an artistic relationship. We approach them through their lives as much as through their work, and when we take up Gissing's letters, which have character, but little wit and no brilliance to illumine them, we feel that we are filling in a design which we began to trace out when we read *Demos* and *New Grub Street* and *The Nether World*.[3]

Yet here, too, there are gaps in plenty, and many dark[b] places left unlit. Much information has been kept back, many facts necessarily omitted. The Gissings were poor, and their father died when they were children; there[c] were many of them, and they had to scrape together what education they could get. George, his sister said, had a passion for learning. He would rush off to school with a sharp herring bone in his throat for fear of missing his lesson.[4] He would copy out from a little book called *That's It* the astonishing number of eggs that the tench lays and the sole lays and the carp lays, 'because I think it is a fact worthy of attention'.[5] She remembers his 'overwhelming veneration' for intellect, and how patiently, sitting beside her, the tall boy with the high white forehead and the short-sighted eyes would help her with her Latin, 'giving the same explanation time after time without the least sign of impatience'.[6]

Partly because he reverenced facts and had no faculty it seems (his language is meagre and unmetaphorical) for impressions, it is doubtful whether his[d] choice of a novelist's career was a happy one. There was the whole world, with its history and its literature, inviting him to haul it into his mind; he was eager; he was intellectual; yet he must sit down in hired rooms and spin novels about 'earnest young people striving for improvement in, as it were, the dawn of a new phase of our civilisation'.[7]

But the art of fiction is infinitely accommodating, and it was quite ready about the year 1880 to accept into its ranks a writer who wished to be the 'mouthpiece of the advanced Radical Party',[8] who was determined to show in his novels the ghastly condition of the poor and the hideous injustice of society. The art of fiction was ready, that is, to agree that such books were novels; but it was doubtful if such novels would be read. Smith Elder's reader summed up the situation tersely enough.[e] Mr Gissing's novel, he wrote, 'is too painful to please the ordinary novel reader, and treats of scenes that can never attract the subscribers to Mr. Mudie's Library'.[9] So, dining off lentils[10] and hearing the men cry paraffin for sale in the streets of Islington, Gissing paid for the publication himself. It was then that he formed the habit of getting up at five in the morning in order to tramp half across London and coach[f] Mr M. before breakfast.[11] Often enough Mr M. sent down word that he was already engaged, and then another page was added to the dismal chronicle of life in modern *Grub Street* – we are faced by another of[g] of those problems with which literature is sown so thick. The writer has dined upon lentils; he gets up at five; he walks across London; he finds Mr M.[h] still in bed, whereupon he stands forth as the champion of life as it is, and proclaims that ugliness is truth, truth ugliness, and that[i] is all we know and all we need to know.[12] But there are signs that the novel resents such treatment. To use a burning consciousness of one's own misery, of the shackles that cut one's own limbs, to quicken one's sense of life in general, as Dickens did, to shape out of the murk which has surrounded one's childhood some resplendent figure such as Micawber or Mrs Gamp,[13] is admirable: but to use personal suffering to rivet the reader's sympathy and curiosity upon your private case[j] is disastrous. Imagination is at its freest when it is most generalised; it loses something of its sweep and power, it becomes petty and personal, when it is limited[k] to the consideration of a particular case calling for sympathy.

At the same time the sympathy which identifies the author with his hero is[l] a passion of great intensity; it makes the pages fly; it lends what has perhaps little merit artistically another and momentarily perhaps a keener edge. Biffen and Reardon[14] had, we say to ourselves, bread and butter and sardines for supper; so had Gissing; Biffen's overcoat had been pawned, and so had Gissing's; Reardon could not write on Sunday; no more could Gissing. We forget whether it was Reardon who loved cats or Gissing who loved barrel organs. Certainly both Reardon and Gissing bought their copies of Gibbon at[m] a second-hand book-stall, and lugged the volumes home one by one through the fog.[15] So we go on capping these resemblances, and each time we succeed, dipping now into the novel, now into the letters, a little glow of satisfaction comes over us, as if novel-reading were a game of skill in which the puzzle set us is[n] to find the face of the writer.

We know Gissing thus as we do not know Hardy or George Eliot. Where the great novelist flows in and out of his characters and bathes them in an element which seems to be common to us all, Gissing[o] remains solitary, self-centred, apart. His is one of those sharp lights beyond whose edges all is vapour and phantom. But mixed with this sharp light is one ray of singular penetration. With all his narrowness of outlook and meagreness of sensibility, Gissing is one of the extremely rare novelists who believes in the power of the mind, who[p] makes his people think. They are thus differently poised from the majority of fictitious men and women. The awful hierarchy of the passions is slightly displaced. Social snobbery does not exist; money is desired almost entirely to buy bread and butter; love itself takes a second place. But the brain works, and that alone is enough to give us a sense of freedom. For to think is to become complex; it is to overflow boundaries, to cease to be a 'character', to merge one's private life in the life of politics or art or ideas, to have relationships based partly on them, and[q] not on sexual desire alone. The impersonal side of life is given its due place in the scheme. 'Why don't people write about the really important things of life?'[16] Gissing makes one of his characters exclaim, and at the unexpected cry the horrid burden of fiction begins to slip from the shoulders. Is it possible that we are going to talk of other things besides falling in love, important though that is, and going to dinner with Duchesses, fascinating though that is? Here in Gissing is a gleam of recognition that Darwin had lived, that science was developing, that people read books and look at pictures, that once upon a time there was such a place as Greece. It is the consciousness of these things that makes his books such painful reading; it was this that made it impossible for them to 'attract[r] the subscribers to Mr. Mudie's Library'. They owe their peculiar grimness to the fact that the people who suffer most are capable of making their suffering part of a reasoned view of life. The thought endures when the feeling has gone. Their unhappiness represents something more lasting than a personal reverse; it becomes part of a view of life. Hence when we have finished one of Gissing's novels we have taken away not a character, nor an incident, but the comment of a thoughtful man upon life as life seemed to him.[s]

But because Gissing was[t] always thinking, he was always changing. In that lies much of his interest for us. As a young man he had thought that he would write books to show up the 'hideous injustice of our whole system of society'.[17] Later his views changed; either the task was impossible, or other tastes were tugging him in a different direction. He came to think, as he believed finally, that 'the only thing known to us of absolute value is artistic perfection ... the works of the artist ... remain sources of health to the world'.[18] So that if one wishes to better the world one must, paradoxically enough, withdraw and spend more and more time fashioning one's sentences to perfection in solitude. Writing, Gissing thought, is a task of the utmost difficulty; perhaps at the end of his life he might be able 'to manage a page that is decently grammatical and fairly harmonious'.[19] There are moments when he succeeded splendidly. For[u] example, he is describing a cemetery in the East End of London:

Here on the waste limits of that dread east, to wander among tombs is to go hand-in-hand with the stark and eyeless emblems of mortality; the spirit fails beneath the cold burden of ignoble destiny. Here lie those who were born for toil; who, when toil has worn them to the uttermost, have but to yield their useless breath and pass into oblivion. For them is no day, only the brief twilight of a winter's sky between the former and the latter night. For them no aspiration; for them no hope of memory in the dust; their very children are wearied into forgetfulness. Indistinguishable units in the vast throng that labours but to support life, the name of each, father, mother, child, is but a dumb cry for the warmth and love of which fate so stinted them. The wind wails above their narrow tenements; the sandy soil, soaking in the rain as soon as it has fallen, is a symbol of the great world which absorbs their toil and straightway blots their being.[20]

Again and again such passages of description stand out like stone slabs, shaped and solid, among the untidy litter with which the pages of fiction are strewn.

Gissing, indeed, never[v] ceased to educate himself. While the Baker

Street trains hissed their steam under his window, and the lodger downstairs blew his room out, and the landlady was insolent, and the grocer refused to send the sugar so that he had to fetch it himself, and the fog burnt his throat and he caught cold and never spoke to anybody for three weeks, yet[w] must drive his pen through page after page and vacillated miserably from one domestic disaster to another – while all this went on with a dreary monotony, for which he could only blame the weakness of his own character, the[x] columns of the Parthenon, the hills of Rome still rose above the fogs and the fried-fish shops of the Euston Road. He was determined to visit Greece and Rome. He actually set foot in Athens; he saw Rome; he read his Thucydides in Sicily before he died. Life was changing round him; his comment upon life was changing too. Perhaps the old sordidity, the fog and the paraffin, and the drunken landlady, was not the only reality; ugliness is not the whole truth; there is an element of beauty in the world. The past, with its literature and its civilisation, solidifies the present. At any rate his books in future were to be about Rome in the time of Totila, not about Islington in the time of Queen Victoria.[21][y] He was reaching some point in his perpetual thinking where 'one has to distinguish between two forms of intelligence';[22] one cannot venerate the intellect only. But before he could mark down the spot he had reached on the map of thought, he, who had shared so many of his characters' experiences, shared, too, the death he had given to Edwin Reardon. 'Patience, patience', he said to the friend who stood by him as he died[23] – an imperfect novelist, but a highly educated[z] man.

a – N&A: 'phrase calls ... fourwheelers, of link-boys with flares, of slatternly ... streets and ignoble yellow chapels above which, distant but distinct, as on a clear day one may see some tree-crowned height above the city, rise the columns of the Parthenon and ... sees a face, rather than work.' Selections: 'phrase calls ... fourwheelers, of link-boys with flares, of slatternly ... people.'
b – N&A: 'plenty, dark'.
c – N&A: 'children and there'.
d – N&A and Selections: 'he so reverenced ... impressions, one wonders whether, since he had to make his living and was married, unfortunately, by the time he was twenty, his'.
e – N&A: 'tersely.'
f – Selections: 'London in order to coach'.
g – N&A and Selections: 'Grub Street. For here we run against one of'.
h – N&A: 'he finds M.'. Selections: 'he find Mr. M.'

i – *Ionian*: 'ugliness; that'.

j – *N&A*: 'did, to turn and twist out . . . to use it to fetter the reader's sympathy and curiosity upon your own individual case'. *Selections*: 'did, to shape . . . but to use personal suffering to fetter the reader's sympathy . . . private case'.

k – *N&A* and *Selections*: 'riveted'.

l – *N&A*: 'time sympathy is'.

m – *N&A*: 'bought their Gibbons at'.

n – *N&A*: 'puzzle is'.

o – *N&A* and *Selections*: 'all and not to himself alone, Gissing'.

p – *N&A*: 'in the mind, who'. *Selections*: 'in the power of mind, who'. *Ionian*: 'in the power of the mind – who'.

q – *N&A* and *Selections*: 'based on them partly, and'.

r – *N&A*: 'lived, that the telegraph had been invented, that people read books and talk and look . . . Greece. It is this that makes his books such painful reading that they can never "attract'. *Selections*: 'lived, that the telegraph had been invented, that people read books and talk and look . . . Greece. It is the consciousness of these things that makes his books such painful reading that they can never "attract'.

s – *N&A*: 'novels, what we have taken away is not . . . but a comment upon life.' *Selections*: 'novels what we have taken away is not . . . but a comment upon life, as life seemed to a thoughtful man.'

t – *N&A*: 'Close as he was to his characters, Gissing too commented upon life, and because he was'. *Selections*: 'And because Gissing was'.

u – *N&A*: 'withdraw from it and spend . . . one's sentences into perfection. Writing, Gissing thought, is difficult; . . . "to manage . . . harmonious." Certainly passages in his book stand out like stone slabs, shaped and solid, among the untidy litter with which the pages of fiction are strewn. For'. *Selections*: 'withdraw from it and spend . . . one's sentences into perfection. Writing, Gissing thought, is a task of the utmost difficulty; . . . "to manage . . . harmonious." Certainly passages in his book stand out like stone slabs, shaped and solid, among the untidy litter with which the pages of fiction are strewn. For'. *Ionian*: 'withdraw from the world and spend . . . harmonious." There are moments when he succeeded splendidly. For'.

v – *N&A*: 'For he never'.

w – *N&A*: 'weeks and yet'. *Selections*: 'weeks, and yet'.

x – *N&A*: 'character in this lodging house or that flat, the'.

y – *N&A*: 'landlady was not the only reality; the past with its leisure and its literature and its civilization were perhaps more real to him now. His books . . . Totila, and not Islington under Queen Victoria.' *Selections* as *N&A*, except 'leisure and its civilization' and 'Totila, not'. *Ionian* as *CR2*, except 'the world also. The'.

z – *N&A*: 'venerate intellect . . . reached, he, who shared . . . Reardon, and he died, saying to the friend who stood by him, "Patience, patience," an imperfect novelist, but a highly educated'. *Selections*: 'venerate intellect . . . reached on the map of thought, he, who shared . . . Reardon, and died saying "Patience, patience" to the friend who stood by him, an imperfect novelist, but a highly-educated'.

1 – Originally published in the *N&A*, 26 February 1927, and in the *NR*, 2 March 1927 (see Appendix I), (*Kp4* C280), as a signed review of *Letters of George Gissing* [1857–1903] *to Members of his Family*, collected and arranged by Algernon and Ellen Gissing (Constable, 1927), this essay was revised for *CR2*. Meanwhile, VW was revising her review in November 1928 (see *III VW Diary*, 8 and 10 November 1928) for use as the introduction (*Kp4* B9) to *Selections Autobiographical and Imaginative from the Works of George Gissing*, with Biographical and Critical Notes by his Son (i.e. Alfred Charles Gissing), published by Jonathan Cape on 11 February 1929, for which she was paid ten guineas (WSU). See also '*Arrows of Fortune*', '*The Private Papers of Henry Ryecroft*' and 'The Novels of George Gissing', *I VW Essays*; and 'An Impression of Gissing', *III VW Essays*. Reprinted (*CR2* version): *CE*.

On 17 February 1929 Desmond MacCarthy extensively reviewed *Selections Autobiographical* in his capacity as chief literary critic of the *Sunday Times*. 'Excellent and imaginative as Virginia Woolf's introduction to this book of extracts is,' he noted, 'it does not quite satisfy me.' A brief reply from VW, headed 'The Novelist's Art', was published the following week: 'Whether I am right or wrong in thinking that Gissing had grave disabilities as a novelist, I will not argue; but may I protest that I do not hold that "conception of the novel itself" which Mr. MacCarthy attributes to me and holds that my words imply? Nothing can be further from my belief than that the novelist's art consists in "recording impressions" and in using "charming words" and "metaphors." I am sorry that any carelessness of phrasing on my part should have led Mr. MacCarthy to impute to me a belief which is obviously absurd' (p. 12). See 'Virginia Woolf, Desmond MacCarthy and Literary Character: A Newly-discovered Woolf Letter' by Julia Paolitto, *VWB*, no. 26 (September 2007), pp. 9–18.

Before the reviews of *CR2* appeared, Miss Middlebrook, who was apparently intending to write a biography of Gissing, wrote to VW requesting information about him. VW apologised on 10 October 1932 for being unable to be of much help, and stated: 'I never knew him; my estimate, expressed in my introduction [i.e. to *Selections Autobiographical*], is therefore solely of his work . . . I do not know if any members of his family, save the son, are still alive. My impression is that Gissing lived a good deal shut off from literary society, and was not associated with any group. Except for Mr Wells I have never met anyone who knew him . . . I gather that you wish to deal with his private life, and if so, since he was unfortunate, I believe in his marriage, and other relations no doubt it would be best to consult his son. If you are only dealing with his work, of course he is an interesting writer, and should make a good subject for criticism' (uncollected letter printed in part in bookseller's catalogue, *David J. Holmes Autographs* [NY: Hamilton], no. 81 [Summer 2004], p. 115, item 222).

For 'a fee of five guineas', VW agreed on 18 October 1932 to the *CR2* essay being reprinted as the introduction to Gissing's *By the Ionian Sea* (1901), no. 186 in The Travellers' Library, which was published by Jonathan Cape on 6 March 1933, and she wrote to Cape: 'I would suggest that you should print from the version just issued in the second series of my Common Reader. I have altered it to a certain extent. I do not think that I could alter it any further. I have not read By the Ionian Sea; but I imagine that the introduction is sufficiently general to serve as it stands' (*V VW Letters*, no. 2646). On 21 November, Cape sent her the proofs, including *By the Ionian Sea*, and a cheque for five guineas (and see WSU). She returned the proofs and *By the Ionian Sea* to Cape's office on 25 November 1932 (see list of unpublished letters: [Berg, M 43], no. 119). However, when he received his copies of the book, Gissing's son Alfred complained to Cape. On 2 March 1933 Cape wrote to VW, but he 'reported Alfred Gissing's objections, minus his indignation, so that the echo of the latter's angry protest was made hardly perceptible': see '"A Voice that Spoke Straight and Shapely Words": Gissing in the Works and Papers of Virginia Woolf' by Pierre Coustillas, *Gissing Newsletter*, vol. xxiii, no. 3 (July 1987), p. 15. VW replied to Cape on 3 March: 'I am sorry to hear that Mr Gissing objects to my introduction. I have a vague recollection that he wrote to me when the introduction first appeared and said that I had exaggerated his father's lack of education – or something of the kind. But I did not gather that he objected to the article as a whole; and he certainly did not ask me to alter it or suppress it. Nor did he write to me when I reprinted it in the Common Reader a few months ago. ¶ From what you say I gather that his objections must be much stronger than I realised. And until I see what they are I cant of course say whether I can answer them or not, Certainly I meant no disrespect to his father – and I dont think that any impartial person who read my article would think so. If he should write to the papers, I will see what steps I can take and let you know' (*V VW Letters*, no. 2712). Gissing wrote to the *TLS*, and on the day the letter was published, VW noted: 'A little nip from Gissing which I must answer' (*IV VW Diary*, 13 April 1933). Here is the exchange in the *TLS* (*Kp4* C336):

ACG, 13 April – 'You would do me a favour if you would allow me, through the medium of your columns, to disclaim all responsibility for an introduction which has been attached to a reprint of George Gissing's *By the Ionian Sea* recently issued by Messrs. Jonathan Cape. This introduction was inserted without my knowledge or consent, and I am, therefore, in no way answerable for the errors which it contains.'

VW, 20 April – 'Mr. A. C. Gissing does not mention the fact that I am the writer of the introduction to George Gissing's *By the Ionian Sea*, for which in your last issue he disclaims all responsibility. The introduction is signed with my name and the responsibility is therefore mine. I should be much obliged if Mr. Gissing would inform me what errors of fact it contains, in order that I may correct them, should the opportunity occur.'

ACG, 27 April – 'I am glad to have this opportunity of replying to the question of Mrs. Virginia Woolf regarding the errors to be found in her introduction to *By the Ionian Sea*, more particularly because there are readers of the book who are quite naturally blaming me for the appearance of the introduction. I cannot guarantee that the following list of mistakes and inaccuracies is exhaustive, but at any rate it includes the most obvious of them.

'(1) First sentence of introduction. Inaccurately quoted from a letter of Gissing.

'(2) Page 8, "they [the Gissings] had to scrape together what education they could get." There was at no time a shortage of money for the education of the children. Even the sisters were able to remain at school (the Wakefield High School) until the age of eighteen.

'(3) Page 9, "'Mr. Gissing's novel,' he [Smith, Elder's reader] wrote, 'is too painful to please the ordinary novel-reader . . .' So, dining off lentils . . . Gissing paid for the publication himself. It was then that he formed the habit of getting up at five in the morning. . . ." This passage, which I have abbreviated, refers to the publication of *Workers in the Dawn*. But (*a*) Smith Elder's reader made no such remark in connexion with this novel but about another written a year or two afterwards. (*b*) It was not at this time that Gissing dined off lentils. He had given them up more than a year before the publication of *Workers in the Dawn*. (*c*) It was not at this time that Gissing rose at five in the morning but some time previously.

'(4) Page 11, "certainly both Reardon and Gissing bought their copies of Gibbon at a secondhand book-stall, and lugged the volumes home one by one through the fog." There is no record of Reardon's having done this and Gissing did not carry home the volumes of Gibbon one by one, which would have necessitated six journeys; he carried them home in two journeys, three volumes at a time. There is no mention of any fog.

'(5) Page 15, referring to Gissing's flat in Cornwall Residences – "and the landlady was insolent." There was no landlady; it was a flat furnished by himself.

'(6) Page 16, "he read his Thucydides in Sicily before he died." He never visited Sicily.

'(7) Page 16, "'Patience, patience,' he said to the friend who stood by him as he died. . . ." These words were not said at his death but two days before it, and the friend to whom he said them was not with him when he died.

'May I ask Mrs. Woolf to be good enough not to make further use of her introduction? It would be a kindness to myself and others.'

VW, 4 May – 'I am sorry to find that in my introduction to George Gissing's *By the Ionian Sea* I have left out three dots to indicate that the words "with a cart" are omitted. Otherwise the quotation is accurate. I also regret that I may have led the reader to suppose that Gissing dined off lentils a year after he had given up eating them: still got up at five when he had stopped getting up at five; took six journeys to a bookseller when in fact he took only two: referred to a fog and a landlady when there was not a fog or a landlady: and used the phrase "as he died" instead of "two days before he died." Such mistakes do not seem to me, I admit, of a serious nature. But I apologise for having stated that the Gissings had "to scrape together what education they could get" when it appears that there was no shortage of money for educational purposes.'

2 – *Letters*, to his sister Margaret, 13 January 1880, p. 55: 'Sometimes we never have any daylight. In my study I generally have to burn a lamp all day long. Do you know there are men in London who go the rounds of the streets with a cart selling paraffin oil? I often think they must rub their hands over weather such as this.'

3 – *Demos* (1886); *New Grub Street* (1891); *The Nether World* (1889).

4 – See *Letters*, Appendix C, reminiscences of his sister Ellen, p. 403.

5 – See *Letters*, 'Diary, September 1870', entry '15th. Thursday.', p. 6. The 'little book' (in 21 parts at 2*d.* each) was *That's It, or Plain Teaching*, by the author of *The Reason Why* [i.e. Robert Kemp Philp] (Houlston & Wright, 1860), part iii, p. 93, col. b: 'The number of eggs deposited by certain species . . . is enormous: the *sole* lays 100,000; the *carp*, 200,000; the *tench*, 400,000 . . .'

6 – See *Letters*, Appendix C, reminiscences of Ellen, p. 404, which has: 'give'.

7 – *Ibid.*, to his brother Algernon, 2 January 1880, p. 53, about his *Workers in the Dawn* (June 1880).

8 – *Ibid.*, 8 June 1880, p. 73, on the same subject.

9 – *Ibid.*, quoted 20 September 1882, p. 119. The novel in question is probably 'Mrs. Grundy's Enemies' which was never published: see *The Collected Letters of George Gissing*, ed. Paul F. Mattheisen, Arthur C. Young & Pierre Coustillas (Athens University Press, 1991), vol. ii, 1881–1885, pp. xiii, 98–100.

10 – See *Letters*, from his brother William, 14 March 1879, pp. 43–4: 'How, I repeat, do you get through so much work? and on lentils, too! No, I say that won't do . . . I pray you discard lentils.'

11 – See *ibid.*, 3 November 1879, p. 50: 'I go to M. each morning still, getting up at five so as to be with him at seven. For the last six mornings I have had the walk in vain, being always told he was engaged.'

12 – A reworking of the last two lines of 'Ode on a Grecian Urn' by John

Keats (1795–1821): 'Beauty is truth, truth beauty, – that is all / Ye know on earth, and all ye need to know.' (*OBEV*, no. 625, p. 730).

13 – Charles Dickens (1812–70), Wilkins Micawber in *David Copperfield* (1849–50), Mrs Sarah Gamp in *Martin Chuzzlewit* (1844).

14 – Harold Biffen and Edward Reardon in *New Grub Street*.

15 – For Gissing buying Gibbon, see *Letters*, to Algernon, 7 May 1882, p. 113.

16 – *New Grub Street*, ch. xxvi, 'Married Woman's Property'; the exclamation is Amy Reardon's: 'Best or worst, novels are all the same. Nothing but love, love, love; what silly nonsense it is! Why don't people write about the really important things of life?'

17 – *Letters*, to William, 3 November 1880, p. 83.

18 – *Ibid.*, to his sister Margaret, 12 May 1883, p. 126, in which, discussing Ruskin's 'calm, grave oratory', he concludes: 'Only this, I am growing to feel, that the only thing known to us of absolute value is artistic perfection. The ravings of fanaticism – justifiable or not – pass away; but the works of the artist, work in what material he will, remain, sources of health to the world.'

19 – *Ibid.*, to William, 26 March 1891, p. 317.

20 – *Demos* (Smith, Elder, 1908), ch. xvi, p. 221, which has: 'emblem of mortality' and 'winter sky'. VW also quoted this passage in 'The Novels of George Gissing'.

21 – Totila (d. 552), king of the Ostrogoths; Queen Victoria reigned 1837–1901.

22 – *The Private Papers of Henry Ryecroft* (Archibald Constable, 1903), 'Spring', sec. xvi, p. 48; quoted in Alfred C. Gissing's Preface to the *Letters*, p. v.

23 – *Letters*, Appendix A, p. 398; the friend was the Rev. Theodore Cooper who gave the account in a letter to Gissing's sisters.

The Novels of George Meredith

Twenty years ago[2] the reputation of George Meredith was at its height. His novels had won their way to celebrity through all sorts of difficulties, and their fame was all the brighter and the more singular for what it had subdued. Then, too, it was generally discovered that the maker of these splendid books was himself a splendid old man. Visitors who went down to Box Hill reported that they were thrilled as they walked up the drive of the little suburban house by the sound of a voice booming and reverberating within. The novelist, seated among the usual knick-knacks of the drawing-room, was like the bust of Euripides[3] to look at. Age had worn and sharpened the fine features, but the nose was still acute, the blue eyes still keen and ironical. Though he had sunk immobile into an arm-chair, his aspect was still vigorous and alert. It was true that he was almost stone-deaf, but this was the least of afflictions to one who was scarcely able to keep pace with the rapidity of his own ideas. Since he could not hear what was said to him, he could give himself whole-heartedly to the delights of soliloquy. It did not much matter, perhaps, whether his audience was cultivated or simple. Compliments that would have flattered a duchess were presented with equal ceremony to a child. To neither could he speak the simple language of daily life. But all the time this highly wrought, artificial conversation, with its crystallised phrases and its high-piled metaphors, moved and tossed on a current of laughter. His laugh curled round his sentences as if he himself enjoyed their humorous exaggeration. The master of language was splashing and diving in his element of words. So the legend grew; and the fame of George Meredith, who sat with the head of a Greek poet on his shoulders in a suburban villa beneath Box Hill, pouring out poetry and sarcasm and wisdom in a voice that could be heard almost on the high road, made his fascinating and brilliant books seem more fascinating and brilliant still.

But that is twenty years ago. His fame as a talker is necessarily dimmed, and his fame as a writer seems also under a cloud. On none of his successors is his influence now marked. When one of them whose own work has given him the right to be heard with respect chances to speak his mind on the subject, it is not flattering.

Meredith [writes Mr Forster in his *Aspects of Fiction*] is not the great name he was twenty years ago. . . . His philosophy has not worn well. His heavy attacks on sentimentality – they bore the present generation. . . . When he gets serious and noble-minded there is a strident overtone, a bullying that becomes distressing. . . . What with the faking, what with the preaching, which was never agreeable and is now said to be hollow, and what with the home countries posing as the universe, it is no wonder Meredith now lies in the trough.[4]

The criticism is not, of course, intended to be a finished estimate; but in its conversational sincerity it condenses accurately enough what is in the air when Meredith is mentioned. No, the general conclusion would seem to be, Meredith has not worn well. But the value of centenaries lies in the occasion they offer us for solidifying such airy impressions. Talk, mixed with half-rubbed-out memories, forms a mist by degrees through which we scarcely see plain. To open the books again, to try to read them as if for the first time, to try to free them from the rubbish of reputation and accident – that, perhaps, is the most acceptable present we can offer to a writer on his hundredth birthday.

And since the first novel is always apt to be an unguarded one, where the author displays his gifts without knowing how to dispose of them to the best advantage, we may do well to open *Richard Feverel*[5] first. It needs no great sagacity to see that the writer is a novice at his task. The style is extremely uneven. Now he twists himself into iron knots; now he lies flat as a pancake. He seems to be of two minds as to his intention. Ironic comment alternates with long-winded narrative. He vacillates from one attitude to another. Indeed, the whole fabric seems to rock a little insecurely. The baronet wrapped in a cloak; the county family; the ancestral home; the uncles mouthing epigrams in the dining-room; the great ladies flaunting and swimming; the jolly farmers slapping their thighs: all liberally if spasmodically sprinkled with dried aphorisms from a pepper-pot called the Pilgrim's Scrip – what an odd conglomeration it is! But the oddity is not on the surface; it is not merely that whiskers and bonnets have gone out of fashion: it lies deeper, in Meredith's intention, in what he wishes to bring to pass. He has been, it is plain, at great pains to destroy the conventional form of the novel. He makes no attempt to preserve the sober reality of Trollope and Jane Austen;[6] he has destroyed all the usual staircases by which we have learnt to climb. And what is done so deliberately is done with a purpose. This defiance of the ordinary, these airs and graces, the formality of the dialogue with its Sirs and Madams are all there to create an atmosphere that is unlike that of daily life, to prepare the way for a new and an original sense of the human scene. Peacock, from whom Meredith learnt so much, is equally arbitrary, but the virtue of the assumptions he asks us to make is proved by the fact that we accept Mr Skionar[7] and the rest with natural delight. Meredith's characters in *Richard Feverel*, on the other hand, are at odds with their surroundings. We at once exclaim how unreal they are, how artificial, how impossible. The baronet and the butler, the hero and the heroine, the good woman and the bad woman are mere types of baronets and butler, good women and bad. For what reason, then, has he sacrificed the substantial advantages of realistic common sense – the staircase and the stucco? Because, it becomes clear as we read, he possessed a keen sense not of the complexity of character, but of the splendour of a scene. One after another in this first book he creates a scene to which we can attach abstract names – Youth, The Birth of Love, The Power of Nature. We are galloped to them over every obstacle on the pounding hoofs of rhapsodical prose.

Away with Systems! Away with a corrupt World! Let us breathe the air of the Enchanted Island? Golden lie the meadows; golden run the streams; red gold is on the pine stems.[8]

We forget that Richard is Richard and that Lucy is Lucy; they are youth; the world runs molten gold. The writer is a rhapsodist, a poet then; but we have not yet exhausted all the elements in this first novel. We have to reckon with the author himself. He has a mind stuffed with ideas, hungry for argument. His boys and girls may spend their time picking daisies in the meadows, but they breathe, however unconsciously, an air bristling with intellectual question and comment. On a dozen occasions these incongruous elements strain and threaten to break apart. The book is cracked through and through with those fissures which come when the author seems to be of twenty minds at the same time. Yet it succeeds in holding miraculously together, not certainly by the depths and originality of its character drawing but by the vigour of its intellectual power and by its lyrical intensity.

We are left, then, with our curiosity aroused. Let him write another book or two; get into his stride; control his crudities: and we will open *Harry Richmond*[9] and see what has happened now. Of all the things that might have happened this surely is the strangest. All trace of immaturity is gone; but with it every trace of the uneasy adventurous mind has gone too. The story bowls smoothly along the road which Dickens[10] has already trodden of autobiographical narrative. It is a boy speaking, a boy thinking, a boy adventuring. For that reason, no doubt, the author has curbed his redundance and pruned his speech. The style is the most rapid possible. It runs smooth, without a kink in it. Stevenson,[11] one feels, must have learnt much from this supple narrative, with its precise adroit phrases, its exact quick glance at visible things.

Plunged among dark green leaves, smelling wood-smoke, at night; at morning waking up, and the world alight, and you standing high, and marking the hills where you will see the next morning and the next, morning after morning, and one morning the dearest person in the world surprising you just before you wake: I thought this a heavenly pleasure.[12]

It goes gallantly, but a little self-consciously. He hears himself talking. Doubts begin to rise and hover and settle at last (as in *Richard Feverel*) upon the human figures. These boys are no more real boys than the sample apple which is laid on top of the basket is a real apple. They are too simple, too gallant, too adventurous to be of the same unequal breed as David Copperfield, for example.[13] They are sample boys, novelist's specimens; and again we encounter the extreme conventionality of Meredith's mind where we found it, to our surprise, before. With all his boldness (and there is no risk that he will not run with probability) there are a dozen occasions on which a reach-me-down character will satisfy him well enough. But just as we are thinking that the young gentlemen are altogether too pat, and the adventures which befall them altogether too slick, the shallow bath of illusion closes over our heads and we sink with Richmond Roy and the Princess Ottilia[14] into the world of fantasy and romance, where all holds together and we are able to put our imagination at the writer's service without reserve. That such surrender is above all things delightful: that it adds spring-heels to our boots: that it fires the cold scepticism out of us and makes the world glow in lucid transparency before our eyes, needs no showing, as it certainly submits to no analysis. That Meredith can induce such moments proves him possessed of an extraordinary power. Yet it is a capricious power and highly intermittent. For pages all is effort and agony; phrase after phrase is struck and no light comes. Then, just as we are about to drop the book, the rocket roars into the air; the whole scene flashes into light; and the book, years after, is recalled by that sudden splendour.

If, then, this intermittent brilliancy is Meredith's characteristic excellence, it is worth while to look into it more closely. And perhaps the first thing that we shall discover is that the scenes which catch the eye and remain in memory are static; they are illuminations, not discoveries; they do not improve our knowledge of the characters. It is significant that Richard and Lucy, Harry and Ottilia, Clara and Vernon, Beauchamp and Renée[15] are presented in carefully appropriate surroundings – on board a yacht, under a flowering cherry tree, upon some river-bank,[16] so that the landscape always makes part of the emotion. The sea or the sky or the wood is brought forward to symbolise what the human beings are feeling or looking.

> The sky was bronze, a vast furnace dome. The folds of light and shadow everywhere were satin rich. That afternoon the bee hummed of thunder and refreshed the ear.[17]

That is a description of a state of mind.

> These winter mornings are divine. They move on noiselessly. The earth is still as if waiting. A wren warbles, and flits through the lank, drenched branches; hillside opens green; everywhere is mist, everywhere expectancy.[18]

That is a description of a woman's face. But only some states of mind and some expressions of face can be described in imagery – only those which are so highly wrought as to be simple and, for that reason, will not submit to analysis. This is a limitation; for though we may be able to see these people, very brilliantly, in a moment of illumination, they do not change or grow; the light sinks and leaves us in darkness. We have no such intuitive knowledge of Meredith's characters as we have of Stendhal's, Tchehov's,[19] Jane Austen's. Indeed, our knowledge of such characters is so intimate that we can almost dispense with 'great scenes' altogether. Some of the most emotional scenes in fiction are the quietest. We have been wrought upon by nine hundred and ninety-nine little touches; the thousandth, when it comes, is as slight as the others, but the effect is prodigious. But with Meredith there are no touches; there are hammer-strokes only, so that our knowledge of his characters is partial, spasmodic, and intermittent.

Meredith, then, is not among the great psychologists who feel their way, anonymously and patiently, in and out of the fibres of the mind and make one character differ minutely and completely from another. He is among the poets who identify the character with the passion or with the idea; who symbolise and make abstract. And yet – here lay his difficulty perhaps – he was not a poet-novelist wholly and completely as Emily Brontë[20] was a poet-novelist. He did not steep the world in one mood. His mind was too self-conscious, and too sophisticated to remain lyrical for long. He does not sing only; he dissects. Even in his most lyrical scenes a sneer curls its lash round the phrases and laughs at their extravagance. And as we read on, we shall find that the comic spirit, when it is allowed to dominate the scene, licked the world to a very different shape. *The Egoist* at once modifies our theory that Meredith is pre-eminently the master of great scenes. Here there is none of that precipitate hurry that has rushed us over obstacles to the summit of one emotional peak after another. The case is one that needs argument; argument needs logic; Sir Willoughby, 'our original male in giant form',[21] is turned slowly round before a steady fire of scrutiny and criticism which allows no twitch on the victim's part to escape it. That the victim is a wax model and not entirely living flesh and blood is perhaps true. At the same time Meredith pays us a supreme compliment to which as novel-readers we are little accustomed. We are civilised people, he seems to say, watching the comedy of human relations together. Human relations are of profound interest. Men and women are not cats and monkeys, but beings of a larger growth[22] and of a greater range. He imagines us capable of disinterested curiosity in the behaviour of our kind. This is so rare a compliment from a novelist to his reader that we are at first bewildered and then delighted. Indeed his comic spirit is a far more penetrating goddess than his lyrical. It is she who cuts a clear path through the brambles of his manner; she who surprises us again and again by the depth of her observations; she who creates the dignity, the seriousness, and the vitality of Meredith's world. Had Meredith, one is tempted to reflect, lived in an age or in a country where comedy was the rule, he might never have contracted those airs of intellectual superiority, that manner of oracular solemnity which it is, as he points out, the use of the comic spirit to correct.

But in many ways the age – if we can judge so amorphous a shape – was hostile to Meredith, or, to speak more accurately, was hostile to his success with the age we now live in – the year 1928. His teaching seems now too strident and too optimistic and too shallow. It obtrudes; and when philosophy is not consumed in a novel, when we can underline this phrase with a pencil, and cut out that exhort-ation with a pair of scissors and paste the whole into a system, it is safe to say that there is something wrong with the philosophy or with the novel or with both. Above all, his teaching is too insistent. He cannot, even to hear the profoundest secret, suppress his own opinion. And there is nothing that characters in fiction resent more. If, they seem to argue, we have been called into existence merely to express Mr Meredith's views upon the universe, we would rather not exist at all. Thereupon they die; and a novel that is full of dead characters, even though it is also full of profound wisdom and exalted teaching, is not achieving its aim as a novel. But here we reach another point upon which the present age may be inclined to have more sympathy with Meredith. When he wrote, in the seventies and eighties of the last century, the novel had reached a stage where it could only exist by moving onward. It is a possible contention that after those two perfect novels, *Pride and Prejudice* and *The Small House at Allington*,[23] English fiction had to escape from the dominion of that perfection, as English poetry had to escape from the perfection of Tennyson. George Eliot, Meredith, and Hardy[24] were all imperfect novelists largely because they insisted upon introducing qualities, of thought and of poetry, that are perhaps incompatible with fiction at its most perfect. On the other hand, if fiction had remained what it was to Jane Austen and Trollope, fiction would by this time be dead. Thus Meredith deserves our gratitude and excites our interest as a great innovator. Many of our doubts about him and much of our inability to frame any definite opinion of his work comes from the fact that it is experimental and thus contains elements that do not fuse harmoniously – the qualities are at odds: the one quality which binds and concentrates has been omitted. To read Meredith, then, to our greatest advantage we must make certain allowances and relax certain standards. We must not expect the perfect quietude of a traditional style nor the triumphs of a patient and pedestrian psychology. On the other hand, his claim, 'My method has been to prepare my readers for a crucial exhibition of the personae, and then to give the scene in the fullest of their blood and brain under stress of a fierce situation',[25] is frequently justified. Scene after scene rises on the mind's eye with a flare of fiery intensity. If we are irritated by the dancing-master dandyism which made him write 'gave his lungs full play' instead of laughed, or 'tasted the swift intricacies of the needle'[26] instead of sewed, we must remember that such phrases prepare the way for the 'fierce situations'. Meredith is creating the atmosphere from which we shall pass naturally into a highly pitched state of emotion. Where the realistic novelist, like Trollope, lapses into flatness and dullness, the lyrical novelist, like Meredith, becomes meretricious and false; and such falsity is, of course, not only much more glaring than flatness, but it is a greater crime against the phlegmatic nature of prose fiction. Perhaps Meredith had been well advised if he had abjured the novel altogether and kept himself wholly to poetry. Yet we have to remind ourselves that the fault may be ours. Our prolonged diet upon Russian fiction, rendered neutral and negative in translation, our absorption in the convolutions of psychological Frenchmen, may have led us to forget that the English language is naturally exuberant, and the English character full of humours and eccentricities. Meredith's flamboyancy has a great ancestry behind it; we cannot avoid all memory of Shakespeare.

When such questions and qualifications crowd upon us as we read, the fact may be taken to prove that we are neither near enough to be under his spell nor far enough to see him in proportion. Thus the attempt to pronounce a finished estimate is even more illusive than usual. But we can testify even now that to read Meredith is to be conscious of a packed and muscular mind; of a voice booming and reverberating with its own unmistakable accent even though the partition between us is too thick for us to hear what he says distinctly. Still, as we read we feel that we are in the presence of a Greek god though he is surrounded by the innumerable ornaments of a suburban drawing-room; who talks brilliantly, even if he is deaf to the lower tones of the human voice; who, if he is rigid and immobile, is yet marvellously alive and on the alert. This brilliant and uneasy figure has his place with the great eccentrics rather than with the great masters. He will be read, one may guess, by fits and starts; he will be forgotten and discovered and again discovered and forgotten like Donne, and Peacock, and Gerard Hopkins.[27] But if English fiction continues to be read, the novels of Meredith must inevitably rise from time to time into view; his work must inevitably be disputed and discussed.

1 – Originally published in the *TLS*, 9 February 1928, and (as 'George Meredith: Feb. 12, 1828') in the *NYHT*, 12 February 1928, (*Kp4* C297; see *IV VW Essays*), this essay was considerably revised for *CR2*. See also 'On Re-Reading Meredith', *II VW Essays*; 'Small Talk About Meredith' and 'Memories of Meredith', *III VW Essays*; 'On Re-reading Novels', *III* and *VI VW Essays*, Appendix; 'Phases of Fiction' above. Reprinted: *CE*.
2 – Written in January 1928 (VW's fn. in *CR2*). For VW on George Meredith (1828–1909) 'twenty years ago', see *IV VW Essays*, p. 535, n. 2.
3 – Euripides (c. 480–406 BC), the last of the three great tragedians of classical Athens (the others being Aeschylus and Sophocles).
4 – E. M. Forster (1879–1970), *Aspects of the Novel* (Edward Arnold, 1927), ch. v, 'The Plot', pp. 120–1, which has: 'twenty or thirty years ago . . . home counties'.
5 – *The Ordeal of Richard Feverel: A History of Father and Son* (3 vols, Chapman & Hall, 1859).
6 – Anthony Trollope (1815–82); Jane Austen (1775–1817).
7 – Character in *Crotchet Castle* (1831) by Thomas Love Peacock

(1785–1866). Peacock was Meredith's father-in-law.

8 – *Ordeal*, vol. ii, ch. iv, 'A Diversion Played on a Penny-Whistle', p. 41. Richard Feverel and Lucy Desborough are mentioned in the next line.

9 – *The Adventures of Harry Richmond* (3 vols, Smith, Elder, 1871), which first appeared in Leslie Stephen's *Cornhill Magazine*, 1870–1.

10 – Charles Dickens (1812–70).

11 – Robert Louis Stevenson (1850–94).

12 – *Adventures*, vol. i, ch. vi, 'A Tale of a Goose', p. 103.

13 – Dickens, *David Copperfield* (1849–50).

14 – Richmond Roy, the hero's father, and Princess Ottilia of Eppenwelzen-Sarkeld in *Adventures*.

15 – Clara Middleton and Vernon Whitford (drawn from Leslie Stephen) in *The Egoist: A Comedy in Narrative* (3 vols, C. Kegan Paul, 1879); Nevil Beauchamp and Renée de Croisnel in *Beauchamp's Career* (serialised in *The Fortnightly*, 1874–5).

16 – See *Adventures*, vol. ii, ch. iv, 'On Board a Yacht'; *Egoist*, vol. i, ch. xi, 'The Double-Blossom Wild Cherry-Tree'; *Ordeal*, vol. i, ch. xviii, 'Ferdinand and Miranda'.

17 – *Adventures*, vol. ii, ch. ix, 'A Summer Storm, and Love', p. 101, which has: 'were satin-rich; shadows perforce of blackness had light in them, and the light a sword-like sharpness over their edges. It was inanimate radiance. The laurels sparkled as with frost-points; the denser foliage drooped burning brown: a sickly saint's-ring was round the heads of the pines. That . . . thunder, and . . .'

18 – *Ibid.*, ch. xii, 'What came of a Shilling', p. 145, which has: 'Those winter . . . if awaiting. A . . . the lank drenched brambles; hill-side opens green; elsewhere is mist, everywhere expectancy. They bear the veiled sun like a sangreal aloft to the wavy marble flooring of stainless cloud.'

19 – For VW on Stendhal (Marie-Henri Beyle, 1783–1842), see 'Stendhal', *III VW Essays*, and 'Some French Books', *VI VW Essays*, Appendix. For VW on Anton Chekhov (1860–1904), see 'Tchehov's Questions', *II VW Essays*; 'The Russian Background' and 'The Cherry Orchard', *III VW Essays*; 'The Russian Point of View', *IV VW Essays*.

20 – Emily Brontë (1818–48).

21 – *Egoist*, vol. ii, ch. v, 'Treats of the Union of Temper and Policy', p. 108, which has: 'The Egoist, who is our original male in giant form, had no bleeding victim beneath his paw, but there was the sex to mangle.'

22 – See 'Lord Chesterfield's Letters to his Son' above, n. 1.

23 – Austen, *Pride and Prejudice* (1813); Trollope, *The Small House at Allington* (1864). VW wrote to Hugh Walpole on 28 February [1932]: 'I think the Small House at Allington perhaps the most perfect of English novels along with Jane Austen – I cant explain now why' (*V VW Letters*, no. 2537).

24 – Alfred, Lord Tennyson (1809–92); George Eliot (1819–80); Thomas Hardy (1840–1928).

25 – *Letters of George Meredith* (2 vols, Constable, 1912), vol. ii, Letter to G. P. Baker, 22 July 1887, p. 398, which has: 'a fiery situation'.

26 – *Ordeal*, vol. i, ch. vii, 'Arson', p. 111, which has: 'Richard gave his lungs loud play'; and *ibid.*, ch. xiv, 'In Which the Last Act of the Bakewell Comedy is Closed in a Letter', p. 202, which has: 'Mama Thompson and her submissive brood sat tasking the swift intricacies of the needle, and emulating them with the tongue . . .'

27 – John Donne (1572–1631); Gerard Manley Hopkins (1844–89).

'I am Christina Rossetti'

On the fifth of this December[2] Christina Rossetti will celebrate her centenary, or, more properly speaking, we shall celebrate it for her, and perhaps not a little to her distress, for she was one of the shyest of women, and to be spoken of, as we shall certainly speak of her, would have caused her acute discomfort. Nevertheless, it is inevitable; centenaries are inexorable; talk of her we must. We shall read her life; we shall read her letters; we shall study her portraits, speculate about her diseases – of which she had a great variety; and rattle the drawers of her writing-table, which are for the most part empty. Let us begin with the biography – for what could be more amusing? As everybody knows, the fascination of reading biographies is irresistible. No sooner have we opened the pages of Miss Sandars's careful and competent book (*Life of Christina Rossetti*, by Mary F. Sandars. (Hutchinson)) than[a] the old illusion comes over us. Here is the past and all its inhabitants miraculously sealed as in a magic tank; all[b] we have to do is to look and to listen and to listen and to look and soon the little figures – for they are rather under life size – will begin to move and to speak, and as they move we shall arrange them in all sorts of patterns of which they were ignorant, for they thought when they were alive that they could go where they liked; and as they speak we shall read into their sayings all kinds of meanings which never struck them, for they believed when they were alive that they said straight off whatever came into their heads. But once you are in[c] a biography all is different.

Here, then, is Hallam Street, Portland Place, about the year 1830; and here are the Rossettis, an Italian family consisting of father and mother and four small children. The street was unfashionable and the home rather poverty-stricken; but the poverty did not matter, for, being foreigners, the Rossettis did not care much about the customs and conventions of the usual middle-class British family. They kept themselves to themselves, dressed as they liked, entertained Italian exiles, among them organ-grinders and other distressed compatriots, and made ends meet by teaching and writing and other odd jobs. By degrees Christina detached herself from the family group. It is plain that she was a quiet and observant child, with her own way of life already fixed in her head – she was to write – but all the more did she admire the superior competence of her elders. Soon we begin to surround her with a few friends and to endow her with a few characteristics. She detested parties. She dressed anyhow. She liked her brother's friends and little gatherings of young artists and poets who were to reform the world, rather to her amusement, for although so sedate, she was also whimsical and freakish, and liked making fun of people who took themselves with egotistic solemnity. And though she meant to be a poet she had very little of the vanity and stress of young poets; her verses seemed to have formed themselves whole and entire in her head, and she did not worry very much what was said of them because in her own mind she knew that they were good. She had also immense powers of admiration – for her mother, for example, who was so quiet, and so sagacious, so simple and so sincere; and for her elder sister Maria, who had no taste for painting or for[d] poetry, but was, for that very reason, perhaps more vigorous and effective in daily life. For example, Maria always refused to visit the Mummy Room at the British Museum because, she said, the Day of Resurrection might suddenly dawn and it would be very unseemly if the corpses had to put on immortality under the gaze of mere sight-seers – a reflection which had not struck Christina, but seemed to her admirable. Here, of course, we, who are outside the tank, enjoy a hearty laugh, but Christina, who is inside the tank and exposed to all its heats and currents, thought her sister's conduct worthy of the highest respect.[e] Indeed, if we look at her a little more closely we shall see that something dark and hard, like a kernel, had already formed in the centre of Christina Rossetti's being.

It was religion, of course. Even when she was quite a girl her life-long absorption in the relation of the soul with God had taken possession of her. Her sixty-four years might seem outwardly spent in Hallam Street and Endsleigh Gardens and Torrington Square, but in reality she dwelt in some curious region where the spirit strives towards an unseen God – in her case, a dark God, a harsh God – a God who decreed that all the pleasures of the world were hateful to Him. The theatre was hateful, the opera was hateful, nakedness was hateful – when her friend Miss Thompson painted naked figures in her pictures she had to tell Christina that they were fairies, but Christina saw through the imposture – everything in Christina's life radiated from that knot of agony and intensity in the centre. Her belief regulated her life in the smallest particulars. It taught her that chess was wrong, but that whist and cribbage did not matter. But also it interfered in the most tremendous questions of her heart. There was a young painter called James Collinson, and she loved James Collinson and he loved her, but he was a Roman Catholic and so she refused him. Obligingly he became a member of the Church of England, and she accepted him. Vacillating,*f* however, for he was a slippery man, he wobbled back to Rome, and Christina, though it broke her heart and for ever shadowed her life, cancelled the engagement. Years afterwards another, and it seems better founded, prospect of happiness presented itself. Charles Cayley proposed to her. But alas, this abstract and erudite man who shuffled about the world in a state of absent-minded dishabille, and translated the gospel into Iroquois, and asked smart ladies at a party 'whether they were interested in the Gulf Stream', and for a present gave Christina a sea mouse preserved in spirits, was, not unnaturally, a free thinker. Him, too, Christina put from her. Though 'no woman ever loved a man more deeply', she would not be the wife of a sceptic. She who loved the 'obtuse and furry' – the wombats, toads, and mice of the earth – and called Charles Cayley 'my blindest buzzard, my special mole', admitted no moles, wombats, buzzards, or Cayleys to her heaven.

So one might go on looking and listening for ever. There is no limit to the strangeness, amusement, and oddity*g* of the past sealed in a tank. But just as we are wondering which cranny of this extraordinary territory to explore next, the principal figure intervenes. It is as if a fish, whose unconscious gyrations we had been watching in and out of reeds, round and round rocks, suddenly dashed at the glass and broke it. A tea-party is the occasion. For some reason Christina went to a party given by Mrs Virtue Tebbs. What happened there is unknown – perhaps something was said in a casual, frivolous, tea-party way about poetry. At any rate, suddenly there uprose from a chair and paced forward into the centre of the room a little woman dressed in black, who announced solemnly, 'I am Christina Rossetti!' and having so said, returned to her chair.

With those words the glass is broken. Yes [she seems to say], I am a poet. You who pretend to honour my centenary are no better than the idle people[b] at Mrs Tebbs's tea-party. Here you are rambling among unimportant trifles, rattling my writing-table drawers, making fun of the Mummies and Maria and my love affairs when all I care for you to know is here. Behold this green volume. It is a copy of my collected works. It costs four shillings and sixpence.[3] Read that. And so she returns to her chair.

How absolute and unaccommodating these poets are! Poetry, they say, has nothing to do with life. Mummies and wombats, Hallam Street and omnibuses, James Collinson and Charles Cayley, sea mice and Mrs Virtue Tebbs, Torrington Square and Endsleigh Gardens, even[i] the vagaries of religious belief, are irrelevant, extraneous, superfluous, unreal. It is poetry that matters. The only question of any interest is whether that poetry is good or bad. But this question of poetry, one might point out if only to gain time, is one of the greatest difficulty. Very little of value has been said about poetry since the world began. The judgment of contemporaries is almost always wrong. For example, most of the poems which figure in Christina Rossetti's complete works were rejected by editors. Her annual income from her poetry was for many years about ten pounds. On the other hand, the works of Jean Ingelow, as she noted sardonically, went into eight editions. There were, of course, among her contemporaries one or two poets and one or two critics whose judgment must be respectfully consulted. But what very different impressions they seem to gather from the same works – by what different standards they judge! For instance, when Swinburne read her poetry he exclaimed: 'I have always thought that nothing more glorious in poetry has ever been written', and went on to say of her New Year Hymn

that it was touched as with the fire and bathed as in the light of sunbeams, tuned as to chords and cadences of refluent sea-music[j] beyond reach of harp and organ, large echoes of the serene and sonorous tides of heaven.

Then Professor Saintsbury comes with his vast learning, and examines *Goblin Market*, and reports that

The metre of the principal poem ['Goblin Market'] may be best described as a dedoggerelised Skeltonic, with the gathered music of the various metrical progress since Spenser, utilised in the place of the wooden rattling of the followers of Chaucer. There may be discerned in it the same inclination towards line irregularity which has broken out, at different times, in the Pindaric of the late seventeenth and earlier eighteenth centuries, and in the rhymelessness of Sayers earlier and of Mr. Arnold later.

And then there is Sir Walter Raleigh:

I think she is the best poet alive. . . . The worst of it is you cannot lecture on really pure poetry any more than you can talk about the ingredients of pure water – it is adulterated, methylated, sanded poetry that makes the best lectures. The only thing that Christina makes me want to do, is cry, not lecture.

It would appear, then, that there are at least three schools[k] of criticism: the refluent sea-music school; the line-irregularity school, and the school that bids one not criticise but cry. This is confusing; if[l] we follow them all we shall only come to grief. Better perhaps read for oneself, expose the mind bare to the poem, and transcribe in all its haste and imperfection whatever may be the result of the impact. In this case it might run something as follows: O Christina Rossetti, I have humbly to confess that though I know many of your poems by heart, I have not read your works from cover to cover. I have not followed your course and traced your development. I doubt indeed that you developed very much. You were an instinctive poet. You saw the world from the same angle always. Years and the traffic of the mind with men and books did not affect you in the least. You carefully ignored any book that could shake your faith or any human being who could trouble your instincts. You were wise perhaps. Your instinct was so sure, so direct, so intense that it produced poems that sing like music in one's ears – like a melody by Mozart or an air by Gluck. Yet for all its symmetry, yours was a complex song. When you struck your harp many strings sounded together. Like all instinctives you had a keen sense of the visual beauty of the world. Your poems are full of gold dust and[m] 'sweet geraniums' varied brightness'; your eye noted incessantly how rushes are 'velvet-headed', and lizards have a 'strange metallic mail' – your eye, indeed, observed with a sensual pre-Raphaelite intensity that must have surprised Christina the Anglo-Catholic. But to her you owed perhaps the fixity and sadness of your muse. The pressure of a tremendous faith

circles and clamps together[n] these little songs. Perhaps they owe to it
their solidity. Certainly they owe to it their sadness – your God was a
harsh God, your heavenly crown was set with thorns.[o] No sooner have
you feasted on beauty with your eyes than your mind tells you that
beauty is vain and beauty passes. Death, oblivion, and[p] rest lap round
your songs with their dark wave. And then, incongruously, a sound of
scurrying and laughter is heard. There is the patter of animals' feet and
the odd guttural notes of rooks and the snufflings of obtuse furry animals
grunting and nosing. For you were not a pure saint by any means. You
pulled legs; you tweaked noses. You were at war with all humbug and
pretence. Modest as you were, still you[q] were drastic, sure of your gift,
convinced of your vision. A firm hand pruned your lines; a sharp ear
tested their music. Nothing soft, otiose, irrelevant cumbered your pages.
In a word, you were an artist. And[r] thus was kept open, even when you
wrote idly, tinkling bells for your own diversion, a pathway for the
descent of that fiery visitant who came now and then and fused your
lines into that indissoluble connection which no hand can[s] put asunder:

> But bring me poppies brimmed with sleepy death
> And ivy choking what it garlandeth
> And primroses that open to the moon.

Indeed so strange is the constitution of things, and so great the miracle
of poetry, that some of the poems you wrote in your little back room
will be found adhering in[t] perfect symmetry when the Albert Memorial
is dust and tinsel. Our remote posterity will be singing:

> When I am dead, my dearest,

or:

> My heart is like a singing bird,[4]

when Torrington Square is a reef of coral perhaps and the fishes shoot
in and out where your bedroom window used to be; or perhaps the
forest will have reclaimed those pavements and the wombat and the
ratel will be shuffling on soft, uncertain feet among the green undergrowth that will then tangle the area railings. In view of all this, and
to return to your biography, had I been present when Mrs Virtue
Tebbs gave her party, and had a short elderly woman in black risen

to her feet and advanced to the middle of the room, I should certainly have committed some indiscretion – have broken a paper-knife or smashed a tea-cup in the awkward ardour of my admiration when^u she said, 'I am Christina Rossetti'.

a – N&A: 'book than', but a footnote gives details for *Christina Rossetti & her Poetry*, following 'We shall read her life' above.
b – N&A: 'sealed up as . . . tank, and all'.
c – N&A: 'once in'.
d – N&A: 'so quiet, so . . . simple, and . . . painting and none for'.
e – N&A: 'conduct admirable.'
f – N&A: 'refused him; obligingly . . . accepted him; vacillating,'.
g – N&A: 'strangeness and terror and oddity'.
h – N&A: 'women'.
i – N&A: 'Gardens, and even'.
j – N&A: 'sea of music'.
k – N&A: 'are many schools'.
l – N&A: 'cry. Yet if'.
m – N&A: 'dust and poppies and'.
n – N&A: 'your song. One feels the pressure . . . faith circling and clamping together'.
o – N&A: 'was uncertain.'
p – N&A: 'Death and oblivion and'.
q – N&A: 'means. Did not Watts Dunton realize that fact with relief when for the first time he heard your voice behind the door? You pulled . . . pretence. In a word, you were an artist. Modest as you were, you'.
r – N&A: 'pages. And'.
s – N&A: 'hand it seems can'.
t – N&A: 'adhering together in'.
u – N&A: 'a teacup – from sheer gratitude and respect when'.

1 – Originally published in the *N&A*, 6 December 1930, and (with variants) in the *NYHT*, 14 December 1930 (*Kp4* C328), as a review of *The Life of Christina Rossetti*. It was later revised for *CR2*. The reader is referred to p. 208 above, where the *NYHT* version is printed in its chronological order; only material not in that version is annotated here.

Following publication in the *N&A*, Ottoline Morrell wrote and praised the article. VW replied: 'How extraordinarily nice of you to write! It is a surprise to find these little articles liked – especially by you. I was impressed by Christina – but what nonsense these lives of her are!' (*IV VW Letters*, no. 2285, [12 December 1930]). Then Edmund Blunden, the literary editor of the *N&A* (who had replaced LW in February 1930), sent VW Dorothy Margaret Stuart's *Christina Rossetti* (English Men of Letters series, Macmillan,

1930) for review. VW replied: 'Many thanks for sending me the little book on Christina Rossetti, which I shall like to read. I felt some hesitation in writing of a poet, with you as editor, but am very glad if you liked the article' (*ibid.*, no. 2289). In the event, she decided not to write a review (*pace Kp4 Cb35*), although she began a holograph draft (Berg, M 1.4) which reveals her problems with the book (for editorial conventions, see p. 608 below):

'Miss Stuart's volume in the English men of letters series possesses ~~enjoys~~ so many merits – is so well informed, so discreet, so witty & so well written – that one hesitates to ~~formulate any grievance~~. lay any charge against it. Indeed the ~~only~~ <the> charge ~~is~~ against Christina for being a woman, & against the founder of the men of letters series for being a man & not against the ~~abli ability of~~ Miss Stuart who ~~must of course conform~~ has had to conform to an impossible conditions. How should the nebulous, ~~difficult~~ <profoundly introspective>, unformulated ~~feminine~~ Christina lend herself to the system of of pigeon holes & tabulation which is ~~con~~ so convenient <when the [intent?] is of the sex that loves [clarification?]> for most male writers? How can her development, her life, her poetry be made to ~~square & to circle & to:~~ tied up in neat packets? The series, we are reminded at every turn, was devised by Lord Morley in the middle of the 19th century; & inevitably much that we have now come to look upon as character & life escape. Perhaps the system fails from the beginning. ~~There is no [such?] [con?]~~ To give an example of the difficulties with wh. Miss Stuart has has t struggle one need only run over the points of the two following sentences. Here is the end of one paragraph:— ~~here is the~~ the next begins . . . Somehow, the mind does not make the connection easily. ¶ And then Christina's life was mysterious in the extreme.'

As she was coming to the end of her revisions for *CR2*, VW wrote: 'I should now attack Ch. Rossetti. But Lord, how tired one gets of one's own writing' (*IV VW Diary*, 3 July 1932). See also 'Letters of Christina Rossetti', *I VW Essays*. Reprinted: *CE*.

2 – 1930 (VW's fn. in *CR2*).

3 – VW owned the 1924 edition of Rossetti's *Poetical Works* (sold at Sotheby's on 27 April 1970). According to *Macmillan's Complete Catalogue* of January 1928, their standard edition of Rossetti's *Complete Poetical Works* did indeed cost 4*s*. 6*d*. (p. 198).

4 – See p. 133, n. 8, above.

The Novels of Thomas Hardy

When we say that the death of Thomas Hardy leaves English fiction without a leader, we mean that there is no other writer whose supremacy would be generally accepted, none to whom it seems so fitting and natural to pay homage. Nobody of course claimed it less. The unworldly and simple old man would have been painfully embarrassed by the rhetoric that flourishes on such occasions as this. Yet it is no less than the truth to say that while he lived there was one novelist at all events who made the art of fiction seem an honourable calling; while Hardy lived there was no excuse for thinking meanly of the art he practised. Nor was this solely the result of his peculiar genius. Something of it sprang from his character in its modesty and integrity, from his life, lived simply down in Dorsetshire without self-seeking or self-advertisement. For both reasons, because of his genius and because of the dignity with which his gift was used, it was impossible not to honour him as an artist and to feel respect and affection for the man. But it is of the work that we must speak, of the novels that were written so long ago that they seem as detached from the fiction of the moment as Hardy himself was remote from the stir of the present and its littleness.

We have to go back more than a generation if we are to trace the career of Hardy as a novelist. In the year 1871 he was a man of thirty-one; he had written a novel, *Desperate Remedies*, but he was by no means an assured craftsman. He 'was feeling his way to a method',[2] he said himself; as if he were conscious that he possessed all sorts of gifts, yet did not know their nature, or how to use them to advantage. To read that first novel is to share in the perplexity of its author. The imagination of the writer is powerful and sardonic; he is book-learned in a home-made way; he can create characters but he cannot control them; he is obviously hampered by the difficulties of his technique and, what is more singular, he is driven by some sense that human beings are the sport of forces outside themselves, to make use of an extreme and even melodramatic use of coincidence. He is already possessed of the conviction that a novel is not a toy, nor an argument; it is a means of giving truthful if harsh and violent impressions of the lives of men and women. But perhaps the most remarkable quality in the book is the sound of a waterfall that echoes and booms through its pages. It is the first manifestation of the power that was to assume such vast proportions in the later books. He already proves himself a minute and skilled observer of nature; the rain, he knows, falls differently as it falls upon roots or arable; he knows that the wind sounds differently as it passes through the branches of different trees. But he is aware in a larger sense of Nature as a force; he feels in it a spirit that can sympathise or mock or remain the indifferent spectator of human fortunes. Already that sense was his; and the crude story of Miss Aldclyffe and Cytherea[3] is memorable because it is watched by the eyes of the gods, and worked out in the presence of Nature.

That he was a poet should have been obvious; that he was a novelist might still have been held uncertain. But the year after, when *Under the Greenwood Tree* appeared, it was clear that much of the effort of 'feeling for a method' had been overcome. Something of the stubborn originality of the earlier book was lost. The second is accomplished, charming, idyllic compared with the first. The writer, it seems, may well develop into one of our English landscape painters, whose pictures are all of cottage gardens and old peasant women, who lingers to collect and preserve from oblivion the old-fashioned ways and words which are rapidly falling into disuse. And yet what kindly lover of antiquity, what naturalist with a microscope in his pocket, what scholar solicitous for the changing shapes of language, ever heard the cry of a small bird killed in the next wood by an owl with such intensity? The cry 'passed into the silence without mingling with it'.[4] Again we hear, very far away, like the sound of a gun out at sea on a calm summer's morning, a strange and ominous echo. But as we read these early books there is a sense of waste. There is a feeling that Hardy's genius was obstinate and perverse; first one gift would have its way with him and then another. They would not consent to run together easily in harness. Such indeed was likely to be the fate of a writer who was at once poet and realist, a faithful son of field and down, yet tormented by the doubts and despondencies bred of book-learning; a lover of old ways and plain countrymen, yet doomed to see the faith and flesh of his forefathers turn to thin and spectral transparencies before his eyes.

To this contradiction Nature had added another element likely to disorder a symmetrical development. Some writers are born conscious of everything; others are unconscious of many things. Some, like Henry James and Flaubert,[5] are able not merely to make the best use of the spoil their gifts bring in, but control their genius in the act of creation; they are aware of all the possibilities of every situation, and are never taken by surprise. The unconscious writers, on the other hand, like Dickens and Scott,[6] seem suddenly and without their own consent to be lifted up and swept onwards. The wave sinks and they cannot say what has happened or why. Among them – it is the source of his strength and of his weakness – we must place Hardy. His own word, 'moments of vision',[7] exactly describes those passages of astonishing beauty and force which are to be found in every book that he wrote. With a sudden quickening of power which we cannot foretell, nor he, it seems, control, a single scene breaks off from the rest. We see, as if it existed alone and for all time, the wagon with Fanny's dead body inside travelling along the road under the dripping trees; we see the bloated sheep struggling among the clover; we see Troy flashing his sword round Bathsheba where she stands motionless, cutting the lock off her head and spitting the caterpillar on her breast.[8] Vivid to the eye, but not to the eye alone, for every sense participates, such scenes dawn upon us and their splendour remains. But the power goes as it comes. The moment of vision is succeeded by long stretches of plain daylight, nor can we believe that any craft or skill could have caught the wild power and turned it to a better use. The novels therefore are full of inequalities; they are lumpish and dull and inexpressive; but they are never arid; there is always about them a little blur of unconsciousness, that halo of freshness and margin of the unexpressed which often produce the most profound sense of satisfaction. It is as if Hardy himself were not quite aware of what he did, as if his consciousness held more than he could produce, and he left it for his readers to make out his full meaning and to supplement it from their own experience.

For these reasons Hardy's genius was uncertain in development, uneven in accomplishment, but, when the moment came, magnificent in achievement. The moment came, completely and fully, in *Far from the Madding Crowd*. The subject was right; the method was right; the poet and the countryman, the sensual man, the sombre reflective man, the man of learning, all enlisted to produce a book which, however fashions may chop and change, must hold its place among the great English novels. There is, in the first place, that sense of the physical world which Hardy more than any novelist can bring before us; the sense that the little prospect of man's existence is ringed by a landscape which, while it exists apart, yet confers a deep and solemn beauty upon his drama. The dark downland, marked by the barrows of the dead and the huts of shepherds, rises against the sky, smooth as a wave of the sea, but solid and eternal; rolling away to the infinite distance, but sheltering in its folds quiet villages whose smoke rises in frail columns by day, whose lamps burn in the immense darkness by night. Gabriel Oak tending his sheep up there on the back of the world is the eternal shepherd; the stars are ancient beacons; and for ages he has watched beside his sheep.[9]

But down in the valley the earth is full of warmth and life; the farms are busy, the barns stored, the fields loud with the lowing of cattle and the bleating of sheep. Nature is prolific, splendid, and lustful; not yet malignant and still the Great Mother of labouring men. And now for the first time Hardy gives full play to his humour, where it is freest and most rich, upon the lips of country men. Jan Coggan and Henry Fray and Joseph Poorgrass gather in the malt-house when the day's work is over and give vent to that half-shrewd, half-poetic humour which has been brewing in their brains and finding expression over their beer since the pilgrims tramped the Pilgrims' Way; which Shakespeare and Scott and George Eliot[10] all loved to overhear, but none loved better or heard with greater understanding than Hardy. But it is not the part of the peasants in the Wessex novels to stand out as individuals. They compose a pool of common wisdom, of common humour, a fund of perpetual life. They comment upon the actions of the hero and heroine, but while Troy or Oak or Fanny or Bathsheba come in and out and pass away, Jan Coggan and Henry Fray and Joseph Poorgrass remain. They drink by night and they plough the fields by day. They are eternal. We meet them over and over again in the novels, and they always have something typical about them, more of the character that marks a race than of the features which belong to an individual. The peasants are the great sanctuary of sanity, the country the last stronghold of happiness. When they disappear, there is no hope for the race.

With Oak and Troy and Bathsheba and Fanny Robin we come to the men and women of the novels at their full stature. In every book three or four figures predominate, and stand up like lightning conductors to attract the force of the elements. Oak and Troy and Bathsheba; Eustacia, Wildeve, and Venn; Henchard, Lucetta, and Farfrae; Jude, Sue Bridehead, and Phillotson.[11] There is even a certain likeness between the different groups. They live as individuals and they differ as individuals; but they also live as types and have a likeness as types. Bathsheba is Bathsheba, but she is woman and sister to Eustacia and Lucetta and Sue; Gabriel Oak is Gabriel Oak, but he is man and brother to Henchard, Venn, and Jude. However lovable and charming Bathsheba may be, still she is weak; however stubborn and ill-guided Henchard may be, still he is strong. This is a fundamental part of Hardy's vision; the staple of many of his books. The woman is the weaker and the fleshlier, and she clings to the stronger and obscures his vision. How freely, nevertheless, in his greater books life is poured

over the unalterable framework! When Bathsheba sits in the wagon
among her plants, smiling at her own loveliness in the little looking-glass,
we may know, and it is proof of Hardy's power that we do know,
how severely she will suffer and cause others to suffer before the end.
But the moment has all the bloom and beauty of life. And so it is,
time and time again. His characters, both men and women, were creatures to him of an infinite attraction. For the women he shows a more
tender solicitude than for the men, and in them, perhaps, he takes a
keener interest. Vain might their beauty be and terrible their fate, but
while the glow of life is in them their step is free, their laughter sweet,
and theirs is the power to sink into the breast of Nature and become
part of her silence and solemnity, or to rise and put on them the
movement of the clouds and the wildness of the flowering woodlands.
The men who suffer, not like the women through dependence upon
other human beings, but through conflict with fate, enlist our sterner
sympathies. For such a man as Gabriel Oak we need have no passing
fears. Honour him we must, though it is not granted us to love him
quite so freely. He is firmly set upon his feet and can give as shrewd
a blow, to men at least, as any he is likely to receive. He has a previ-
sion of what is to be expected that springs from character rather than
from education. He is stable in his temperament, steadfast in his affections, and capable of open-eyed endurance without flinching. But he,
too, is no puppet. He is a homely, humdrum fellow on ordinary occasions. He can walk the street without making people turn to stare at
him. In short, nobody can deny Hardy's power – the true novelist's
power – to make us believe that his characters are fellow-beings driven
by their own passions and idiosyncrasies, while they have – and this
is the poet's gift – something symbolical about them which is common
to us all.

And it is when we are considering Hardy's power of creating men
and women that we become most conscious of the profound differences that distinguish him from his peers. We look back at a number of
these characters and ask ourselves what it is that we remember them
for. We recall their passions. We remember how deeply they have
loved each other and often with what tragic results. We remember
the faithful love of Oak for Bathsheba; the tumultuous but fleeting
passions of men like Wildeve, Troy, and Fitzpiers; we remember the
filial love of Clym[12] for his mother, the jealous paternal passion of
Henchard for Elizabeth Jane. But we do not remember how they have
loved. We do not remember how they talked and changed and got

to know each other, finely, gradually, from step to step and from stage to stage. Their relationship is not composed of those intellectual apprehensions and subtleties of perception which seem so slight yet are so profound. In all the books love is one of the great facts that mould human life. But it is a catastrophe; it happens suddenly and overwhelmingly, and there is little to be said about it. The talk between the lovers when it is not passionate is practical or philosophic, as though the discharge of their daily duties left them with more desire to question life and its purpose than to investigate each other's sensibilities. Even if it were in their power to analyse their emotions, life is too stirring to give them time. They need all their strength to deal with the downright blows, the freakish ingenuity, the gradually increasing malignity of fate. They have none to spend upon the subtleties and delicacies of the human comedy.

Thus there comes a time when we can say with certainty that we shall not find in Hardy some of the qualities that have given us most delight in the works of other novelists. He has not the perfection of Jane Austen, or the wit of Meredith, or the range of Thackeray, or Tolstoy's amazing intellectual power.[13] There is in the work of the great classical writers a finality of effect which places certain of their scenes, apart from the story, beyond the reach of change. We do not ask what bearing they have upon the narrative, nor do we make use of them to interpret problems which lie on the outskirts of the scene. A laugh, a blush, half a dozen words of dialogue, and it is enough; the source of our delight is perennial. But Hardy has none of this concentration and completeness. His light does not fall directly upon the human heart. It passes over it and out on to the darkness of the heath and upon the trees swaying in the storm. When we look back into the room the group by the fireside is dispersed. Each man or woman is battling with the storm, alone, revealing himself most when he is least under the observation of other human beings. We do not know them as we know Pierre or Natasha or Becky Sharp.[14] We do not know them in and out and all round as they are revealed to the casual caller, to the Government official, to the great lady, to the general on the battlefield. We do not know the complication and involvement and turmoil of their thoughts. Geographically, too, they remain fixed to the same stretch of the English country-side. It is seldom, and always with unhappy results, that Hardy leaves the yeoman or farmer to describe the class above theirs in the social scale. In the drawing-room and clubroom and ballroom, where people of leisure and education come together, where comedy is bred and shades of character revealed, he is awkward and ill at ease. But the opposite is equally true. If we do not know his men and women in their relations to each other, we know them in their relations to time, death, and fate. If we do not see them in quick agitation against the lights and crowds of cities, we see them against the earth, the storm, and the seasons. We know their attitude towards some of the most tremendous problems that can confront mankind. They take on a more than mortal size in memory. We see them, not in detail but enlarged and dignified. We see Tess reading the baptismal service in her nightgown 'with an impress of dignity that was almost regal'. We see Marty South, 'like a being who had rejected with indifference the attribute of sex for the loftier quality of abstract humanism',[15] laying the flowers on Winterbourne's grave. Their speech has a Biblical dignity and poetry. They have a force in them which cannot be defined, a force of love or of hate, a force which in the men is the cause of rebellion against life, and in the women implies an illimitable capacity for suffering, and it is this which dominates the character and makes it unnecessary that we should see the finer features that lie hid. This is the tragic power; and, if we are to place Hardy among his fellows, we must call him the greatest tragic writer among English novelists.

But let us, as we approach the danger-zone of Hardy's philosophy, be on our guard. Nothing is more necessary, in reading an imaginative writer, than to keep at the right distance above his page. Nothing is easier, especially with a writer of marked idiosyncrasy, than to fasten on opinions, convict him of a creed, tether him to a consistent point of view. Nor was Hardy any exception to the rule that the mind which is most capable of receiving impressions is very often the least capable of drawing conclusions. It is for the reader, steeped in the impression, to supply the comment. It is his part to know when to put aside the writer's conscious intention in favour of some deeper intention of which perhaps he may be unconscious. Hardy himself was aware of this. A novel 'is an impression, not an argument', he has warned us, and, again

Unadjusted impressions have their value, and the road to a true philosophy of life seems to lie in humbly recording diverse readings of its phenomena as they are forced upon us by chance and change.[16]

Certainly it is true to say of him that, at his greatest, he gives us impressions; at his weakest, arguments. In *The Woodlanders*, *The Return of the Native*, *Far from the Madding Crowd*, and, above all, in *The Mayor of Casterbridge*, we have Hardy's impression of life as it came to him without conscious ordering. Let him once begin to tamper with his direct intuitions and his power is gone. 'Did you say the stars were worlds, Tess?' asks little Abraham as they drive to market with their beehives. Tess replies that they are like 'the apples on our stubbard-tree, most of them splendid and sound – a few blighted'. 'Which do we live on – a splendid or a blighted one?' 'A blighted one',[17] she replies, or rather the mournful thinker who has assumed her mask speaks for her. The words protrude, cold and raw, like the springs of a machine where we had seen only flesh and blood. We are crudely jolted out of that mood of sympathy which is renewed a moment later when the little cart is run down and we have a concrete instance of the ironical methods which rule our planet.

That is the reason why *Jude the Obscure* is the most painful of all Hardy's books, and the only one against which we can fairly bring the charge of pessimism. In *Jude the Obscure* argument is allowed to dominate impression, with the result that though the misery of the book is overwhelming it is not tragic. As calamity succeeds calamity we feel that the case against society is not being argued fairly or with profound understanding of the facts. Here is nothing of that width and force and knowledge of mankind which, when Tolstoy criticises society, makes his indictment formidable. Here we have revealed to us the petty cruelty of men, not the large injustice of the gods.[18] It is only necessary to compare *Jude the Obscure* with *The Mayor of Casterbridge* to see where Hardy's true power lay. Jude carries on his miserable contest against the deans of colleges and the conventions of sophisticated society. Henchard is pitted, not against another man, but against something outside himself which is opposed to men of his ambition and power. No human being wishes him ill. Even Farfrae and Newson and Elizabeth Jane whom he has wronged all come to pity him, and even to admire his strength of character. He is standing up to fate, and in backing the old Mayor whose ruin has been largely his own fault, Hardy makes us feel that we are backing human nature in an unequal contest. There is no pessimism here. Throughout the book we are aware of the sublimity of the issue, and yet it is presented to us in the most concrete form. From the opening scene in which Henchard sells his wife to the sailor at the fair to his death on Egdon

Heath the vigour of the story is superb, its humour rich and racy, its movement large-limbed and free. The skimmity ride, the fight between Farfrae and Henchard in the loft, Mrs Cuxsom's speech upon the death of Mrs Henchard, the talk of the ruffians at Peter's Finger with Nature present in the background or mysteriously dominating the foreground, are among the glories of English fiction. Brief and scanty, it may be, is the measure of happiness allowed to each, but so long as the struggle is, as Henchard's was, with the decrees of fate and not with the laws of man, so long as it is in the open air and calls for activity of the body rather than of the brain, there is greatness in the contest, there is pride and pleasure in it, and the death of the broken corn merchant in his cottage on Egdon Heath is comparable to the death of Ajax, lord of Salamis.[19] The true tragic emotion is ours.

Before such power as this we are made to feel that the ordinary tests which we apply to fiction are futile enough. Do we insist that a great novelist shall be a master of melodious prose? Hardy was no such thing. He feels his way by dint of sagacity and uncompromising sincerity to the phrase he wants, and it is often of unforgettable pungency. Failing it, he will make do with any homely or clumsy or old-fashioned turn of speech, now of the utmost angularity, now of a bookish elaboration. No style in literature, save Scott's, is so difficult to analyse; it is on the face of it so bad, yet it achieves its aim so unmistakably. As well might one attempt to rationalise the charm of a muddy country road, or of a plain field of roots in winter. And then, like Dorsetshire itself, out of these very elements of stiffness and angularity his prose will put on greatness; will roll with a Latin sonority; will shape itself in a massive and monumental symmetry like that of his own bare downs. Then again, do we require that a novelist shall observe the probabilities, and keep close to reality? To find anything approaching the violence and convolution of Hardy's plots one must go back to the Elizabethan drama. Yet we accept his story completely as we read it; more than that, it becomes obvious that his violence and his melodrama, when they are not due to a curious peasant-like love of the monstrous for its own sake, are part of that wild spirit of poetry which saw with intense irony and grimness that no reading of life can possibly outdo the strangeness of life itself, no symbol of caprice and unreason be too extreme to represent the astonishing circumstances of our existence.

But as we consider the great structure of the Wessex novels it seems irrelevant to fasten on little points – this character, that scene, this phrase of deep and poetic beauty. It is something larger that Hardy had bequeathed to us. The Wessex novels are not one book, but many. They cover an immense stretch; inevitably they are full of imperfections – some are failures, and others exhibit only the wrong side of their maker's genius. But undoubtedly, when we have submitted ourselves fully to them, when we come to take stock of our impression of the whole, the effect is commanding and satisfactory. We have been freed from the cramp and pettiness imposed by life. Our imaginations have been stretched and heightened; our humour has been made to laugh out; we have drunk deep of the beauty of the earth. Also we have been made to enter the shade of a sorrowful and brooding spirit which, even in its saddest mood, bore itself with a grave uprightness and never, even when most moved to anger, lost its deep compassion for the sufferings of men and women. Thus it is no mere transcript of life at a certain time and place that Hardy has given us. It is a vision of the world and of man's lot as they revealed themselves to a powerful imagination, a profound and poetic genius, a gentle and humane soul.

1 – Originally published (entitled 'Thomas Hardy's Novels') in the *TLS*, 19 January 1928, (*Kp4* C294; see *IV VW Essays*), this essay was revised for *CR2*. VW footnoted the title in *CR2*: 'Written in January 1928.' Thomas Hardy (1840–1928). She wrote on 3 July 1932 that she had 'just finished [revising] Hardy'; then on 21 July: 'Mrs Hardy writes that she has often wished, after my wonderful article on Hardy, that she had asked me to write his life. Had I consented she would have given me all the materials. And how proud I was to be asked to do the T.L.S. article!' (*IV VW Diary*). See also 'Half of Thomas Hardy', *IV VW Essays*; 'The Art of Thomas Hardy', *VI VW Essays*, Appendix. Reprinted: *CE*.

2 – *Desperate Remedies. A Novel* (1871; Wessex Novels, Osgood, McIlvaine, vol. xii, 1896), Prefatory Note, dated January 1889, p. v: 'The following story, the first published by the author, was written nineteen years ago, at a time when he was feeling his way to a method. The principles observed in its composition are, no doubt, too exclusively those in which mystery, entanglement, surprise, and moral obliquity are depended on for exciting interest . . .' VW owned a copy of this edition.

3 – Cytherea Graye, the heroine, and lady's maid to Miss Aldclyffe whose illegitimate son Æneas Manston she marries in *Desperate Remedies*.

4 – *Under the Greenwood Tree: A Rural Painting of the Dutch School* (1872; Wessex Novels, Osgood, McIlvaine, vol. xvi, 1896), Part the Fourth: Autumn, ch. ii, 'Honey-taking, and Afterwards', p. 207: 'Dick said nothing; and the stillness was disturbed only by some small bird that was being killed by an owl in the adjoining wood, whose cry passed into the silence without mingling with it.'

5 – Henry James (1843–1916); Gustave Flaubert (1821–80).

6 – Charles Dickens (1812–70); Sir Walter Scott (1771–1832).

7 – 'Moments of Vision', the title of a poem and of a volume of poems by Hardy (Macmillan, 1917).

8 – Fanny Robin, Sergeant Troy and Bathsheba Everdene in *Far from the Madding Crowd* (1874), a novel originally serialised in Leslie Stephen's *Cornhill Magazine*.

9 – Gabriel Oak in *Far from the Madding Crowd*.

10 – Coggan, Fray and Poorgrass in *Far from the Madding Crowd*. George Eliot (1819–80).

11 – Eustacia Vye, Damon Wildeve and Diggory Venn in *The Return of the Native* (1878); Michael Henchard, Lucetta Le Sueur and Donald Farfrae in *The Mayor of Casterbridge* (1886), also Elizabeth-Jane Henchard, Michael Henchard's daughter, and Richard Newson, mariner (below); Jude Fawley, Sue Bridehead and Richard Phillotson in *Jude the Obscure* (1894–5).

12 – Edred Fitzpiers in *The Woodlanders* (1887); Clym Yeobright in *Return*.

13 – Jane Austen (1775–1817); for VW on George Meredith (1828–1909), see above; William Makepeace Thackeray (1811–63); Leo Tolstoy (1828–1910).

14 – Pierre Bezuhov and Natasha Rostov in Tolstoy's *War and Peace* (1865–9); Becky Sharp in Thackeray's *Vanity Fair* (1847–8).

15 – *Tess of the D'Urbervilles: A Pure Woman* (1891; Wessex Novels, Osgood, McIlvaine, vol. i, 1895), 'Phase the Second: Maiden No More', ch. xiv, p. 119, which has: 'dignity which was'; and *The Woodlanders* (Wessex Novels, Osgood, McIlvaine, vol. vii, 1896), ch. xlviii, p. 459, which has: 'almost like'.

16 – *Tess*, Preface, dated July 1892 (a view that VW said she shared: see V *VW Letters*, no. 2622); *Poems of the Past and the Present* (Harper & Bros, 1902), Preface, dated August 1901.

17 – *Tess*, 'Phase the First: The Maiden', ch. iv, p. 35, which has: 'stubbard-tree. Most' and 'a splendid one'.

18 – Cf. *III VW Diary*, 18 December 1928: 'He [Max Beerbohm] talked of Hardy, & said he couldnt bear Jude the Obscure: thought it falsified life, for there is really more happiness than sorrow in life, & Hardy tries to prove the opposite. And his writing is so bad.'

19 – Ajax, mythological Greek hero, cousin of Achilles, and King of Salamis, plays an important role in Homer's *Iliad*.

How Should One Read a Book?

In the first place, I want to emphasise the note of interrogation at the end of my title. Even if I could answer the question for myself, the answer would apply only to me and not to you. The only advice, indeed, that one person can give another about reading is to take no advice, to follow your own instincts, to use your own reason, to come to your own conclusions. If this is agreed between us, then I feel at liberty to put forward a few ideas and suggestions because you will not allow them to fetter that independence which is the most important quality that a reader can possess. After all, what laws can be laid down about books? The battle of Waterloo was certainly fought on a certain day; but is *Hamlet* a better play than *Lear*? Nobody can say. Each must decide that question for himself. To admit authorities, however heavily furred and gowned, into our libraries and let them tell us how to read, what to read, what value to place upon what we read, is to destroy the spirit of freedom which is the breath of those sanctuaries. Everywhere else we may be bound by laws and conventions – there we have none.

But to enjoy freedom, if the platitude is pardonable, we have of course to control ourselves. We must not squander our powers, helplessly and ignorantly, squirting half the house in order to water a single rose-bush; we must train them, exactly and powerfully, here on the very spot. This, it may be, is one of the first difficulties that faces us in a library. What is 'the very spot'? There may well seem to be nothing but a conglomeration and huddle of confusion. Poems and novels, histories and memoirs, dictionaries and blue-books; books written in all languages by men and women of all tempers, races, and ages jostle each other on the shelf. And outside the donkey brays, the women gossip at the pump, the colts gallop across the fields. Where are we to begin? How are we to bring order into this multitudinous chaos and so get the deepest and widest pleasure from what we read?

It is simple enough to say that since books have classes – fiction, biography, poetry – we should separate them and take from each what it is right that each should give us. Yet few people ask from books what books can give us. Most commonly we come to books with blurred and divided minds, asking of fiction that it shall be true, of poetry that it shall be false, of biography that it shall be flattering, of history that it shall enforce our own prejudices. If we could banish all such preconceptions when we read, that would be an admirable beginning. Do not dictate to your author; try to become him. Be his fellow-worker and accomplice. If you hang back, and reserve and criticise at first, you are preventing yourself from getting the fullest possible value from what you read. But if you open your mind as widely as possible, then signs and hints of almost imperceptible fineness, from the twist and turn of the first sentences, will bring you into the presence of a human being unlike any other. Steep yourself in this, acquaint yourself with this, and soon you will find that your author is giving you, or attempting to give you, something far more definite. The thirty-two chapters of a novel – if we consider how to read a novel first – are an attempt to make something as formed and controlled as a building: but words are more impalpable than bricks; reading is a longer and more complicated process than seeing. Perhaps the quickest way to understand the elements of what a novelist is doing is not to read, but to write; to make your own experiment with the dangers and difficulties of words. Recall, then, some event that has left a distinct impression on you – how at the corner of the street, perhaps, you passed two people talking. A tree shook; an electric light danced; the tone of the talk was comic, but also tragic; a whole vision, an entire conception, seemed contained in that moment.

But when you attempt to reconstruct it in words, you will find that it breaks into a thousand conflicting impressions. Some must be subdued; others emphasised; in the process you will lose, probably, all grasp upon the emotion itself. Then turn from your blurred and littered pages to the opening pages of some great novelist – Defoe, Jane Austen, Hardy.[2] Now you will be better able to appreciate their mastery. It is not merely that we are in the presence of a different person – Defoe, Jane Austen, or Thomas Hardy – but that we are living in a different world. Here, in *Robinson Crusoe*,[3] we are trudging a plain high road; one thing happens after another; the fact and the order of the fact is enough. But if the open air and adventure mean everything to Defoe they mean nothing to Jane Austen. Hers is the drawing-room, and people talking, and by the many mirrors of their talk revealing their characters. And if, when we have accustomed ourselves to the drawing-room and its reflections, we turn to Hardy, we are once more spun round. The moors are round us and the stars are above our heads. The other side of the mind is now exposed – the dark side that comes uppermost in solitude, not the light side that shows in company. Our relations are not towards people, but towards Nature and destiny. Yet different as these worlds are, each is consistent with itself. The maker of each is careful to observe the laws of his own perspective, and however great a strain they may put upon us they will never confuse us, as lesser writers so frequently do, by introducing two different kinds of reality into the same book. Thus to go from one great novelist to another – from Jane Austen to Hardy, from Peacock to Trollope, from Scott to Meredith[4] – is to be wrenched and uprooted; to be thrown this way and then that. To read a novel is a difficult and complex art. You must be capable not only of great fineness of perception, but of great boldness of imagination if you are going to make use of all that the novelist – the great artist – gives you.

But a glance at the heterogeneous company on the shelf will show you that writers are very seldom 'great artists'; far more often a book makes no claim to be a work of art at all. These biographies and auto-biographies, for example, lives of great men, of men long dead and forgotten, that stand cheek by jowl with the novels and poems, are we to refuse to read them because they are not 'art'? Or shall we read them, but read them in a different way, with a different aim? Shall we read them in the first place to satisfy that curiosity which possesses us some-times when in the evening we linger in front of a house where the lights are lit and the blinds not yet drawn, and each floor of the house shows us a different section of human life in being?[5] Then we are consumed with curiosity about the lives of these people – the servants gossiping, the gentlemen dining, the girl dressing for a party, the old woman at the window with her knitting. Who are they, what are they, what are their names, their occupations, their thoughts, and adventures?

Biographies and memoirs answer such questions, light up innumer-able such houses; they show us people going about their daily affairs, toiling, failing, succeeding, eating, hating, loving, until they die. And sometimes as we watch, the house fades and the iron railings vanish and we are out at sea; we are hunting, sailing, fighting; we are among savages and soldiers; we are taking part in great campaigns. Or if we like to stay here in England, in London, still the scene changes; the street narrows; the house becomes small, cramped, diamond-paned, and malodorous. We see a poet, Donne,[6] driven from such a house because the walls were so thin that when the children cried their voices cut through them. We can follow him, through the paths that lie in the pages of books, to Twickenham; to Lady Bedford's Park, a famous meeting-ground for nobles and poets; and then turn our steps to Wilton, the great house under the downs, and hear Sidney read the *Arcadia* to his sister;[7] and ramble among the very marshes and see the very herons that figure in that famous romance; and then again travel north with that other Lady Pembroke, Anne Clifford,[8] to her wild moors, or plunge into the city and control our merriment at the sight of Gabriel Harvey in his black velvet suit arguing about poetry with Spenser.[9] Nothing is more fascinating than to grope and stumble in the alternate darkness and splendour of Elizabethan London. But there is no staying there. The Temples and the Swifts, the Harleys and the St Johns beckon us on;[10] hour upon hour can be spent disentangling their quarrels and deciphering their characters; and when we tire of them we can stroll on, past a lady in black wearing diamonds, to Samuel Johnson and Goldsmith and Garrick;[11] or cross the channel, if we like, and meet Voltaire and Diderot, Madame du Deffand;[12] and so back to England and Twickenham – how certain places repeat themselves and certain names! – where Lady Bedford had her Park once and Pope lived later, to Walpole's home at Strawberry Hill.[13] But Walpole introduces us to such a swarm of new acquaintances, there are so many houses to visit and bells to ring that we may well hesitate for a moment, on the Miss Berrys' doorstep, for example, when behold, up comes Thackeray; he is the friend of the woman whom Walpole loved;[14] so that merely by going from friend to friend, from garden to garden, from house to house, we have passed from one end of English literature to another and wake to find ourselves here again in the present, if we can so differentiate this moment from all that have gone before. This, then, is one of the ways in which we can read these lives and letters; we can make them light up the many windows of the past; we can watch the famous dead in their familiar habits and fancy sometimes that we are very close and can surprise their secrets, and sometimes we may pull out a play or a poem that they have written and see whether it reads differently in the presence of the author. But this again rouses other questions. How far, we must ask ourselves, is a book influenced by its writer's life – how far is it safe to let the man interpret the writer? How far shall we resist or give way to the sympathies and antipathies that the man himself rouses in us – so sensitive are words, so receptive of the character of the author? These are questions that press upon us when we read lives and letters, and we must answer them for ourselves, for nothing can be more fatal than to be guided by the preferences of others in a matter so personal.

But also we can read such books with another aim, not to throw light on literature, not to become familiar with famous people, but to refresh and exercise our own creative powers. Is there not an open window on the right hand of the bookcase? How delightful to stop reading and look out! How stimulating the scene is, in its unconsciousness, its irrelevance, its perpetual movement – the colts galloping round the field, the woman filling her pail at the well, the donkey throwing back his head and emitting his long, acrid moan. The greater part of any library is nothing but the record of such fleeting moments in the lives of men, women, and donkeys. Every literature, as it grows old, has its rubbish-heap, its record of vanished moments and forgotten lives told in faltering and feeble accents that have perished. But if you give yourself up to the delight of rubbish-reading you will be surprised, indeed you will be overcome, by the relics of human life that have been cast out to moulder. It may be one letter – but what a vision it gives! It may be a few sentences – but what vistas they suggest! Sometimes a whole story will come together with such beautiful humour and pathos and completeness that it seems as if a great novelist had been at work, yet it is only an old actor, Tate Wilkinson, remembering the strange story of Captain Jones;[15] it is only a young subaltern serving under Arthur Wellesley and falling in love with a pretty girl at Lisbon;[16] it is only Maria Allen[17] letting fall her sewing in the empty drawing-room and sighing how she wishes she had taken Dr Burney's good advice and had never eloped with her Rishy. None of this has any value; it is negligible in the extreme; yet how absorbing it is now and again to go through the rubbish-heaps and find rings and scissors and broken noses buried in the huge past and try to piece them together while the colt gallops round the field, the woman fills her pail at the well, and the donkey brays.

But we tire of rubbish-reading in the long run. We tire of searching for what is needed to complete the half-truth which is all that the Wilkinsons, the Bunburys and the Maria Allens are able to offer us. They had not the artist's power of mastering and eliminating; they could not tell the whole truth even about their own lives; they have disfigured the story that might have been so shapely. Facts are all that they can offer us, and facts are a very inferior form of fiction. Thus the desire grows upon us to have done with half-statements and approximations; to cease from searching out the minute shades of human character, to enjoy the greater abstractness, the purer truth of fiction. Thus we create the mood, intense and generalised, unaware of detail, but stressed by some regular, recurrent beat, whose natural expression is poetry; and that is the time to read poetry when we are almost able to write it.

Western wind, when wilt thou blow?
The small rain down can rain.

> Christ, if my love were in my arms,
> And I in my bed again![18]

The impact of poetry is so hard and direct that for the moment there is no other sensation except that of the poem itself. What profound depths we visit then – how sudden and complete is our immersion! There is nothing here to catch hold of; nothing to stay us in our flight. The illusion of fiction is gradual; its effects are prepared; but who when they read these four lines stops to ask who wrote them, or conjures up the thought of Donne's house or Sidney's secretary; or enmeshes them in the intricacy of the past and the succession of generations? The poet is always our contemporary. Our being for the moment is centred and constricted, as in any violent shock of personal emotion. Afterwards, it is true, the sensation begins to spread in wider rings through our minds; remoter senses are reached; these begin to sound and to comment and we are aware of echoes and reflections. The intensity of poetry covers an immense range of emotion. We have only to compare the force and directness of

> I shall fall like a tree, and find my grave,
> Only remembering that I grieve,[19]

with the wavering modulation of

> Minutes are numbered by the fall of sands,
> As by an hour glass; the span of time
> Doth waste us to our graves, and we look on it;
> An age of pleasure, revelled out, comes home
> At last, and ends in sorrow; but the life,
> Weary of riot, numbers every sand,
> Wailing in sighs, until the last drop down,
> So to conclude calamity in rest,[20]

or place the meditative calm of

> whether we be young or old,
> Our destiny, our being's heart and home,
> Is with infinitude, and only there;
> With hope it is, hope that can never die,

> Effort, and expectation, and desire,
> And something evermore about to be,[21]

beside the complete and inexhaustible loveliness of

> The moving Moon went up the sky,
> And nowhere did abide:
> Softly she was going up,
> And a star or two beside —[22]

or the splendid fantasy of

> And the woodland haunter
> Shall not cease to saunter
>   When, far down some glade,
> Of the great world's burning,
> One soft flame upturning
> Seems, to his discerning,
>   Crocus in the shade,[23]

to bethink us of the varied art of the poet; his power to make us at once actors and spectators; his power to run his hand into character as if it were a glove, and be Falstaff or Lear; his power to condense, to widen, to state, once and for ever.

'We have only to compare' – with those words the cat is out of the bag, and the true complexity of reading is admitted. The first process, to receive impressions with the utmost understanding, is only half the process of reading; it must be completed, if we are to get the whole pleasure from a book, by another. We must pass judgment upon these multitudinous impressions; we must make of these fleeting shapes one that is hard and lasting. But not directly. Wait for the dust of reading to settle; for the conflict and the questioning to die down; walk, talk, pull the dead petals from a rose, or fall asleep. Then suddenly without our willing it, for it is thus that Nature undertakes these transitions, the book will return, but differently. It will float to the top of the mind as a whole. And the book as a whole is different from the book received currently in separate phrases. Details now fit themselves into their places. We see the shape from start to finish; it is a barn, a pig-sty, or a cathedral. Now then we can compare book with book as we compare building with building. But this act of comparison means that our attitude has changed; we are no longer the friends of the writer, but his judges; and just as we cannot be too sympathetic as friends, so as judges we cannot be too severe. Are they not criminals, books that have wasted our time and sympathy; are they not the most insidious enemies of society, corrupters, defilers, the writers of false books, faked books, books that fill the air with decay and disease? Let us then be severe in our judgments; let us compare each book with the greatest of its kind. There they hang in the mind the shapes of the books we have read solidified by the judgments we have passed on them – *Robinson Crusoe, Emma, The Return of the Native.*[24] Compare the novels with these – even the latest and least of novels has a right to be judged with the best. And so with poetry – when the intoxication of rhythm has died down and the splendour of words has faded, a visionary shape will return to us and this must be compared with *Lear*, with *Phèdre*,[25] with *The Prelude*; or if not with these, with whatever is the best or seems to us to be the best in its own kind. And we may be sure that the newness of new poetry and fiction is its most superficial quality and that we have only to alter slightly, not to recast, the standards by which we have judged the old.

It would be foolish, then, to pretend that the second part of reading, to judge, to compare, is as simple as the first – to open the mind wide to the fast flocking of innumerable impressions. To continue reading without the book before you, to hold one shadow-shape against another, to have read widely enough and with enough understanding to make such comparisons alive and illuminating – that is difficult; it is still more difficult to press further and to say, 'Not only is the book of this sort, but it is of this value; here it fails; here it succeeds; this is bad; that is good'. To carry out this part of a reader's duty needs such imagination, insight, and learning that it is hard to conceive any one mind sufficiently endowed; impossible for the most self-confident to find more than the seeds of such powers in himself. Would it not be wiser, then, to remit this part of reading and to allow the critics, the gowned and furred authorities of the library, to decide the question of the book's absolute value for us? Yet how impossible! We may stress the value of sympathy; we may try to sink our own identity as we read. But we know that we cannot sympathise wholly or immerse ourselves wholly; there is always a demon in us who whispers, 'I hate, I love',[26] and we cannot silence him. Indeed, it is precisely because we hate and we love that our relation with the poets and novelists is so intimate that we find the presence of another person intolerable. And even if the results are abhorrent and our judgments are wrong, still our taste, the nerve of sensation that sends shocks through us, is our chief illuminant; we learn through feeling; we cannot suppress our own idiosyncrasy without impoverishing it. But as time goes on perhaps we can train our taste; perhaps we can make it submit to some control. When it has fed greedily and lavishly upon books of all sorts – poetry, fiction, history, biography – and has stopped reading and looked for long spaces upon the variety, the incongruity of the living world, we shall find that it is changing a little; it is not so greedy, it is more reflective. It will begin to bring us not merely judgments on particular books, but it will tell us that there is a quality common to certain books. Listen, it will say, what shall we call *this*? And it will read us perhaps *Lear* and then perhaps the *Agamemnon*[27] in order to bring out that common quality. Thus, with our taste to guide us, we shall venture beyond the particular book in search of qualities that group books together; we shall give them names and thus frame a rule that brings order into our perceptions. We shall gain a further and a rarer pleasure from that discrimination. But as a rule only lives when it is perpetually broken by contact with the books themselves – nothing is easier and more stultifying than to make rules which exists out of touch with facts, in a vacuum – now at last, in order to steady ourselves in this difficult attempt, it may be well to turn to the very rare writers who are able to enlighten us upon literature as an art. Coleridge and Dryden[28] and Johnson, in their considered criticism, the poets and novelists themselves in their unconsidered sayings, are often surprisingly relevant; they light up and solidify the vague ideas that have been tumbling in the misty depths of our minds. But they are only able to help us if we come to them laden with questions and suggestions won honestly in the course of our own reading. They can do nothing for us if we herd ourselves under their authority and lie down like sheep in the shade of a hedge. We can only understand their ruling when it comes in conflict with our own and vanquishes it.

If this is so, if to read a book as it should be read calls for the rarest qualities of imagination, insight, and judgment, you may perhaps conclude that literature is a very complex art and that it is unlikely that we shall be able, even after a lifetime of reading, to make any valuable contribution to its criticism. We must remain readers; we shall not put on the further glory that belongs to those rare beings who are also critics. But still we have our responsibilities as readers and even our importance. The standards we raise and the judgments we pass steal into the air and become part of the atmosphere which writers breathe as they work. An influence is created which tells upon them even if it never finds its way into print. And that influence, if it were well instructed, vigorous and individual and sincere, might be of great value now when criticism is necessarily in abeyance; when books pass in review like the procession of animals in a shooting gallery, and the critic has only one second in which to load and aim and shoot and may well be pardoned if he mistakes rabbits for tigers, eagles for barndoor fowls, or misses altogether and wastes his shot upon some peaceful cow grazing in a further field. If behind the erratic gunfire of the press the author felt that there was another kind of criticism, the opinion of people reading for the love of reading, slowly and unprofessionally, and judging with great sympathy and yet with great severity, might this not improve the quality of his work? And if by our means books were to become stronger, richer, and more varied, that would be an end worth reaching.[29]

Yet who reads to bring about an end, however desirable? Are there not some pursuits that we practise because they are good in themselves,[30] and some pleasures that are final? And is not this among them? I have sometimes dreamt, at least, that when the Day of Judgment dawns and the great conquerors and lawyers and statesmen come to receive their rewards – their crowns, their laurels, their names carved indelibly upon imperishable marble – the Almighty will turn to Peter and will say, not without a certain envy when He sees us coming with our books under our arms, 'Look, these need no reward. We have nothing to give them here. They have loved reading.'[31]

1 – Originally published in the *Yale Review*, October 1926, (*Kp4* C277; see *IV VW Essays*), this essay was very considerably revised for *CR2*. VW footnoted the title in *CR2*: 'A paper read at a School.' The essay derives from a lecture VW delivered at a private school for girls at Hayes Court in Kent on 30 January 1926. It seems that the *Yale Review* was thinking of reprinting the article, for VW wrote to Helen McAfee, the managing editor, on 27 July 1930: 'I cannot find my copy of the article on Reading which you want to reprint. My memory of it is that I thought there were a good many alterations needed – if they should be too many I might of course be unable to let you have it, as my time is very full. But I will let

you know as soon as I get the copy which you say you are sending' (*IV VW Letters*, no. 2213). She wrote in her diary on 6 July 1932 that 'the CR I confess is not yet quite done. But then – well I had to re-write the last article, which I had thought so good, entirely. Not for many years shall I collect another bunch of articles' (*IV VW Diary*). See 'The Love of Reading' above, an abridged version. See also 'Reading', 'On Re-reading Novels' and 'Byron & Mr Briggs', *III VW Essays*. For a transcript of a draft of the lecture, dated 18 November [1925], and a guide to the various drafts, see Beth Rigel Daugherty, 'Virginia Woolf's "How Should One Read a Book?"', *WSA*, vol. iv (1998), 123–85. Part of a draft dated 'Sunday | June 5th' 1932 (MHP, B 2e). Reprinted: *CE*.

2 – Daniel Defoe (1660?–1731); Jane Austen (1775–1817); Thomas Hardy (1840–1928); for VW on their novels, see above.

3 – For VW on Defoe, *The Life and . . . Adventures of Robinson Crusoe* (1719), see 'Robinson Crusoe' above.

4 – Thomas Love Peacock (1785–1866); Anthony Trollope (1815–82); for VW on Sir Walter Scott (1771–1832), see 'Scott's Character' and '*The Antiquary*' in *III VW Essays*, and 'Gas at Abbotsford' in *VI VW Essays*; George Meredith (1828–1909), for VW on his novels see above.

5 – Cf. 'Street Haunting: A London Adventure', *IV VW Essays*.

6 – For VW on John Donne (1572–1631), see above.

7 – See Philip Sidney (1554–86), 'The Countess of Pembroke's Arcadia' above.

8 – See 'Donne After Three Centuries', p. 357.

9 – See 'The Strange Elizabethans' above.

10 – See 'Swift's *Journal to Stella*' above.

11 – Samuel Johnson (1709–84); Oliver Goldsmith (1730–74); David Garrick (1717–79), actor, theatre manager and dramatist.

12 – Voltaire (François Marie Arouet, 1694–1778); Denis Diderot (1713–84), philosopher and writer; Marie Anne de Vichy-Chamrond, marquise du Deffand (1697–1780).

13 – Alexander Pope (1688–1744); Horace Walpole (1717–97).

14 – Mary (1763–1852) and Agnes Berry (1764–1852); William Makepeace Thackeray (1811–63) became friends with the Miss Berrys late in their lives. Walpole's relationship with the Miss Berrys, particularly the elder, 'appears to have been one of amiable badinage and warm affection laced by a characteristic sexless flirtation on Walpole's side' (*ODNB*).

15 – Tate Wilkinson (1739–1803), actor and provincial theatre manager, who enjoyed some short-lived celebrity for his 'imitations' of the leading performers of his day. See *Memoirs of his Own Life* (1790) and 'Jones and Wilkinson', *IV VW Essays*.

16 – See Anon [i.e. Thomas Bunbury], *Reminiscences of a Veteran. Being Personal and Military Adventures in Portugal . . .* (3 vols, Charles J. Skeet,

1861), vol. i, pp. 55–7; cf. pp. 209–12. Arthur Wellesley, 1st Duke of Wellington (1769–1852).

17 – Maria Allen, who married Martin Rishton, was Dr Burney's stepdaughter by his second wife Mrs Allen; see 'Fanny Burney's Half-Sister' above.

18 – Anon, sixteenth century. *OBEV* has: 'O western wind, when wilt thou blow / That the small rain down can rain? / Christ, that my love were in my arms / . . .' (no. 27, p. 53).

19 – Francis Beaumont (1584–1616) and John Fletcher (1579–1625), *Beaumont and Fletcher*, ed. J. St Loe Strachey, *The Mermaid Series: The Best Plays of the Old Dramatists, Unexpurgated Edition* (2 vols, Vizetelly, 1887), vol. i, *The Maid's Tragedy* (1610), iv, i., p. 66, spoken by Amintor.

20 – John Ford (1585–1640?), *John Ford*, ed. Havelock Ellis, in *The Mermaid Series: The Best Plays of the Old Dramatists, Unexpurgated Edition* (Vizetelly, 1888), *The Lover's Melancholy* (1628), iv, iii., p. 72, spoken by Eroclea.

21 – William Wordsworth (1770–1850), *Prelude, or Growth of a Poet's Mind: An Autobiographical Poem* (Edward Moxon, 1850), bk vi, 'Cambridge and the Alps', p. 160.

22 – Samuel Taylor Coleridge (1772–1834), *The Rime of the Ancient Mariner* (1798), ll. 255–8; *OBEV*, no. 549, at p. 637.

23 – Ebenezer Jones (1820–60), 'When the World is burning', *OBEV*, no. 745, p. 883. Cf. *Mrs. Dalloway* (Hogarth Press, 1925), p. 50: 'Then, for that moment, she had seen an illumination; a match burning in a crocus; an inner meaning almost expressed.'

24 – Austen, *Emma* (1816); Hardy, *The Return of the Native* (1878).

25 – Jean Racine (1639–99), *Phèdre* (1677).

26 – Catullus (c. 84–c. 55 BC), *Carmina*, no. 85 ('Odi et amo'). See also *The Waves* (Hogarth Press, 1931), pp. 14, 149, 243, 271; and *Between the Acts* (Hogarth Press, 1941), pp. 60, 82, 109, 111, 252.

27 – *Agamemnon*, the first of the three surviving *Oresteia* plays by Aeschylus (525/4–456 BC).

28 – John Dryden (1631–1700).

29 – Cf. 'Reviewing', *VI VW Essays*.

30 – See G. E. Moore, *Principia Ethica* (Cambridge University Press, 1903), e.g., ch. vi, 'The Ideal', sec. 113, p. 166: 'By far the most valuable things, which we know or can imagine, are certain states of consciousness, which may be roughly described as the pleasures of human intercourse and the enjoyment of beautiful objects. No one, probably, who has asked himself the question, has ever doubted that personal affection and the appreciation of what is beautiful in Art or Nature, are good in themselves . . .'

31 – Judith Sloman suggests that this passage is a rewriting of the final stanza of Dryden's 'Ode' (*OBEV*, no. 398, at pp. 466–7): see her 'The Opening and Closing Lines of "To . . . Mrs. Anne Killigrew": Tradition and Allusion', *Notes and Queries*, vol. xxvi (February 1979), pp. 12–13.

Leslie Stephen, the Philosopher at Home: A Daughter's Memories

By the time that his children were growing up the great days of my father's life were over. His feats on the river and on the mountains had been won before they were born. Relics of them were to be found lying about the house – the silver cup on the study mantelpiece; the rusty alpenstocks that leant against the bookcase in the corner; and to the end of his days he would speak of great climbers and explorers with a peculiar mixture of admiration and envy. But his own years of activity were over, and my father had to content himself with pottering about the Swiss valleys or taking a stroll across the Cornish moors.

That to potter and to stroll meant more on his lips than on other people's is becoming obvious now that some of his friends have given their own version of those expeditions. He would start off after breakfast alone, or with one companion. Shortly before dinner he would return. If the walk had been successful, he would have out his great map and commemorate a new short cut in red ink. And he was quite capable, it appears, of striding all day across the moors without speaking more than a word or two to his companion. By that time, too, he had written the *History of English Thought in the Eighteenth Century*, which is said by some to be his masterpiece: and the *Science of Ethics* – the book which interested him most: and *The Playground of Europe*, in which is to be found 'The Sunset on Mont Blanc' – in his opinion the best thing he ever wrote.[2]

He still wrote daily and methodically, though never for long at a time. In London he wrote in the large room with three long windows at the top of the house. He wrote lying almost recumbent in a low rocking chair which he tipped to and fro as he wrote, like a cradle, and as he wrote he smoked a short clay pipe, and he scattered books round him in a circle. The thud of a book dropped on the floor could be heard in the room beneath. And often as he mounted the stairs to his study with his firm, regular tread he would burst, not into song, for he was entirely unmusical, but into a strange rhythmical chant, for verse of all kinds, both 'utter trash,' as he called it, and the most sublime words of Milton and Wordsworth[3] stuck in his memory, and the act of walking or climbing seemed to inspire him to recite whichever it was that came uppermost or suited his mood.

But it was his dexterity with his fingers that delighted his children before they could potter along the lanes at his heels or read his books. He would twist a sheet of paper beneath a pair of scissors and out would drop an elephant, a stag, or a monkey, with trunks, horns, and tails delicately and exactly formed. Or, taking a pencil, he would draw beast after beast – an art that he practised almost unconsciously as he read, so that the fly-leaves of his books swarm with owls and donkeys as if to illustrate the 'Oh, you ass!' or 'Conceited dunce,' that he was wont to scribble impatiently in the margin. Such brief comments, in which one may find the germ of the more temperate statements of his essays, recall some of the characteristics of his talk. He could be very silent, as his friends have testified. But his remarks, made suddenly in a low voice between the puffs of his pipe, were extremely effective. Sometimes with one word – but his one word was accompanied by a gesture of the hand – he would dispose of the tissue of exaggerations which his own sobriety seemed to provoke. 'There are 40,000,000 unmarried women in London alone!' Lady Ritchie once informed him. 'Oh, Annie, Annie!' my father exclaimed in tones of horrified but affectionate rebuke. But Lady Ritchie, as if she enjoyed being rebuked, would pile it up even higher next time she came.[4]

The stories he told to amuse his children of adventures in the Alps – but accidents only happened, he would explain, if you were so foolish as to disobey your guides[5] – or of those long walks, after one of which, from Cambridge to London on a hot day, 'I drank, I am sorry to say, rather more than was good for me,' were told very briefly, but with a curious power to impress the scene. The things that he did not say were always there in the background. So, too, though he seldom told anecdotes, and his memory for facts was bad, when he described a person – and he had known many people, both famous and obscure – he would convey exactly what he thought of him in two or three words. And what he thought might be the opposite of what other people thought. He had a way of upsetting established reputations and disregarding conventional values that could be disconcerting, and some-times perhaps wounding, though no one was more respectful of any feeling that seemed to him genuine. But when, suddenly opening his bright blue eyes, and rousing himself from what had seemed complete abstraction, he gave his opinion, it was difficult to disregard it. It was a habit, especially when deafness made him unaware that his opinion could be heard, that had its inconveniences.

'I am the most easily bored of men,' he wrote,[6] truthfully as usual: and when, as was inevitable in a large family, some visitor threatened to stay not merely for tea but also for dinner, my father would express his anguish at first by twisting and untwisting a certain lock of hair. Then he would burst out, half to himself, half to the powers above, but quite audibly, 'Why can't he go? Why can't he go?'[7] Yet such is the charm of simplicity – and did he not say, also truthfully, that 'bores are the salt of the earth'?[8] – that the bores seldom went, or, if they did, forgave him and came again.

Too much, perhaps, has been said of his silence; too much stress has been laid upon his reserve.[9] He loved clear thinking; he hated sentimentality and gush; but this by no means meant that he was cold and unemotional, perpetually critical and condemnatory in daily life. On the contrary, it was his power of feeling strongly and of expressing his feeling with vigour that made him sometimes so alarming as a companion. A lady, for instance, complained of the wet summer that was spoiling her tour in Cornwall. But to my father, though he never called himself a democrat, the rain meant that the corn was being laid; some poor man was being ruined; and the energy with which he expressed his sympathy – not with the lady – left her discomfited. He had something of the same respect for farmers and fishermen that he had for climbers and explorers. So, too, he talked little of patriotism, but during the South African War – and all wars were hateful to him – he lay awake thinking that he heard the guns on the battlefield. Again, neither his reason nor his cold common sense helped to convince him that a child could be late for dinner without having been maimed or killed in an accident. And not all his mathematics together with a bank balance which he insisted must be ample in the extreme, could persuade him, when it came to signing a cheque, that the whole family was not 'shooting Niagara to ruin,' as he put it. The pictures that he would draw of old age and the bankruptcy court, of ruined men of letters who have to support large families in small houses at Wimbledon (he owned a very small house at Wimbledon)[10] might have convinced those who complain of his under-statements that hyperbole was well within his reach had he chosen.[11]

Yet the unreasonable mood was superficial, as the rapidity with which it vanished would prove. The cheque-book was shut; Wimbledon and the workhouse were forgotten. Some thought of a humorous kind made him chuckle. Taking his hat and his stick, calling for his dog and his daughter, he would stride off into Kensington Gardens, where he had walked as a little boy, where his brother Fitzjames[12] and he had made beautiful bows to young Queen Victoria and she had swept them a curtsey, and so, round the Serpentine, to Hyde Park Corner, where he had once saluted the great Duke himself; and so home. He was not then in the least 'alarming'; he was very simple, very confiding; and his silence, though one might last unbroken from the Round Pond to the Marble Arch, was curiously full of meaning, as if he were thinking half aloud, about poetry and philosophy and people he had known.

He himself was the most abstemious of men. He smoked a pipe perpetually, but never a cigar. He wore his clothes until they were too shabby to be tolerable; and he held old-fashioned and rather puritanical views as to the vice of luxury and the sin of idleness. The relations between parents and children today have a freedom that would have been impossible with my father. He expected a certain standard of behaviour, even of ceremony, in family life. Yet if freedom means the right to think one's own thoughts and to follow one's own pursuits, then no one respected, and indeed insisted upon freedom more completely than he did. His sons, with the exception of the Army and Navy, should follow whatever profession they chose; his daughters, though he cared little enough for the higher education of women, should have the same liberty. If at one moment he rebuked a daughter sharply for smoking a cigarette – smoking was not in his opinion a nice habit in the other sex – she had only to ask him if she might become a painter, and he assured her that so long as she took her work seriously he would give her all the help he could. He had no special love for painting; but he kept his word. Freedom of that sort was worth thousands of cigarettes.[13]

It was the same with the perhaps more difficult problem of literature. Even today there may be parents who would doubt the wisdom of allowing a girl of 15 the free run of a large and quite unexpurgated library. But my father allowed it. There were certain facts – very briefly, very shyly he referred to them. Yet 'Read what you like,'[14] he said, and all his books, 'mangy and worthless,' as he called them, but certainly they were many and various, were to be had without asking. To read what one liked because one liked it, never to pretend to admire what one did not – that was his only lesson in the art of reading. To write in the fewest possible words, as clearly as possible, exactly what one meant – that was his only lesson in the art of writing. All the rest

must be learnt for oneself. Yet a child must have been childish in the
extreme not to feel that such was the teaching of a man of great
learning and wide experience, though he would never impose his own
views or parade his own knowledge. For, as his tailor remarked when
he saw my father walk past his shop up Bond Street, 'There goes a
gentleman that wears good clothes without knowing it.'

In those last years, grown solitary and very deaf, he would sometimes call himself a failure as a writer: he had been 'jack of all trades
and master of none.'[15] But whether he failed or succeeded as a writer,
it is permissible to believe that he left a distinct impression of himself
on the minds of his friends. Meredith saw him as 'Phoebus Apollo turned
fasting friar'[16] in his earlier days; Thomas Hardy, years later, looked at
the 'spare and desolate figure' of the Schreckhorn and thought of

> him,
> Who scaled its horn with ventured life and limb,
> Drawn on by vague imaginings, maybe,
> Of semblance to his personality
> In its quaint glooms, keen lights, and rugged trim.[17]

But the praise he would have valued most, for though he was an agnostic
nobody believed more profoundly in the worth of human relationships,
was Meredith's tribute after his death: 'He was the one man to my
knowledge worthy to have married your mother.'[18] And Lowell, when
he called him 'L. S., the most lovable of men,'[19] has best described the
quality that makes him, after all these years, unforgettable.

1 – A signed centenary essay in *The Times*, 28 November 1932, (*Kp4* C335),
introduced: 'Sir Leslie Stephen, philosopher, man of letters, editor of the
Dictionary of National Biography, and mountaineer, was born on November
28, 1832.' In an article entitled 'Philosophy of Comfort', in the *New York
Times*, 18 December 1932, the essay was referred to as 'a charming piece'
and passages were quoted; the *New York Times* also described VW as
'Thackeray's granddaughter', but this was corrected in a letter from Mary
Poore published on 25 December. In *The Times*, a photograph of Sir Leslie
appeared on p. 18; there was a brief article, 'Loans for Training of Women.
Increasing Demand for University Degree'; and from *The Times* of 28
November 1832, quoting *Tait's Magazine*: 'Every man who works nine hours
a-day is employed during three of these hours to enable him to pay his taxes.'
Four years earlier VW had famously written: 'Father's birthday. He would
have been . . . 96, yes, today; & could have been 96, like other people one

has known; but mercifully was not. His life would have entirely ended mine. What would have happened? No writing, no books; – inconceivable. I used to think of him & mother daily; but writing The Lighthouse, laid them in my mind. And now he comes back sometimes, but differently. (I believe this to be true – that I was obsessed by them both, unhealthily; & writing of them was a necessary act.) He comes back now more as a contemporary. I must read him some day. I wonder if I can feel again, I hear his voice, I know this by heart?' (*III VW Diary*, 28 November 1928). On 12 April 1931 she wrote to her sister Vanessa: 'Many thanks for the cheque – father's books do remarkably well, I think, considering it will be his centenary next year' (*IV VW Letters*, no. 2348). On 2 September 1932 she wrote: 'here I am, asked to write about "my father" in the Times. No' (*IV VW Diary*). She expressed her doubts to two correspondents: 'I've been asked to write in the Times about my father for his Centenary. Shall I or shall I not? I cant resist trying because he was such a very remarkable figure: but you wont see it: indeed I cant make it visible, in only 1500 words, so I shall give up, I think; but at the moment my head is full of him. One thing you would have liked – his extreme sincerity; also unless I'm partial, he was beautiful in the distinguished way a race horse, even an ugly race horse, is beautiful – And he had such a fling with his hands and feet. Also he was a great climber. Also he was completely unworldly. Also he begot me: but then you prefer Vanessa' (*V VW Letters*, no. 2629, 7 September, to Ethel Smyth); 'By the way, it is my father's Centenary in Novr. and the Times want me to write an article about him – but I dont think I can. Anyhow, do tell me what you thought of him. Was he very alarming? charming? eccentric? rude? or what?' (*ibid.*, no. 2630, 8 September, to Nelly Cecil). But she changed her mind: 'I've just polished up the L. S. for the Times – a good one, I think, considering the currents that sway round that subject in the Times of all papers' (*IV VW Diary*, 2 November 1932). Finally, on 10 November: 'I am taking a morning off, having done the child scene – the man exposing himself – in the Pargiters [later *The Years*]: to polish my LS. (done) & then to write letters' (*ibid.*).

After the essay was published VW received a letter of praise from her cousin, H. A. L. Fisher, and she replied: 'I am greatly pleased that you liked my article, and it was very good of you to say so. I was reluctant to write it, but Vanessa and Adrian wanted me to – and I did it in the fear that I should make a complete failure of it' (*V VW Letters*, no. 2673, 29 November). Referring to an anonymous review (by Percy Lubbock), entitled 'Cambridge and Leslie Stephen', in the *TLS* of 1 December 1932, VW wrote on 22 December: 'Quite good I thought, in its surface way: but then they'd no space. It is ironical that my father thought nothing of his criticism, and secretly believed himself a great philosopher. No one mentions the philosophy; all the criticism' (*V VW Letters*, no. 2683, to Ethel Smyth). On 1 February 1939 VW wrote to Elizabeth E. Nielsen: 'Thank you very much for sending me your essay upon my father. I will not attempt to criticise it, for I find it very difficult to read my father's books critically, as one should in order to have an opinion. But it is interesting to me to have your view of him for that very reason. I feel that I see him as a whole through unfamiliar eyes. I am very glad that he seems to you a figure of such importance. I suspect that it is as a figure that he means most nowadays. He stood for a point of view which I believe to be rare and very valuable. You have not of course dealt with his philosophical books which he himself took much more seriously than his literary criticism. The English Thought in the 18th century is generally felt to be his most important work; but he told me that he was most interested himself in The Science of Ethics. Perhaps you will go on to this side of him. I am too ignorant of philosophy to know where he stands in the eyes of the moderns. But I am sure he is a healthy subject for study; for he was extremely truthful, serious, and aware of the lasting side of life. I write without trying to be intelligent; knowing that you destroy my hasty notes; nor is this worth sending, save as token of gratitude to you for thinking of him and of me so kindly' (uncollected letter in *Modern Fiction Studies*, vol. xxx, no. 2 [Summer 1994], p. 199).

The essay was reprinted in the Boston *Atlantic [Monthly]*, March 1950, as 'My Father: Leslie Stephen', and introduced: 'The daughter of Sir Leslie Stephen, Virginia Woolf was one of four children. The family divided its time between the London house in Hyde Park Gate and their summer home on the coast of Cornwall near St. Ives. Her father was a delightful host, and of his intimate friends, the children came to know James Russell Lowell, Dr. Holmes, Hardy, Meredith, Stevenson, Ruskin, and John Morley. No formal schooling was imposed upon the young Virginia; she was allowed the unrestricted freedom of her father's magnificent library. This portrait will appear in a volume entitled *The Captain's Death Bed and Other Essays* (Harcourt, Brace).' See also 'Impressions of Sir Leslie Stephen', *I VW Essays*. Reprinted: *CDB, CE*.
2 – Followed by subheading, 'Chanted the Poets'. Leslie Stephen, *History of English Thought in the Eighteenth Century* (1876), *The Science of Ethics* (1882), *The Playground of Europe* (1871). See *Sir Leslie Stephen's Mausoleum Book*, ed. Alan Bell (Clarendon Press, 1977), p. 21: 'In 1873 . . . I climbed Mont Blanc to see the sunset and think – forgive an author's vanity! – that my description in the Cornhill [1873], reprinted in the last edition of the Playground [1894] – is the best thing I ever wrote and a good bit of Alpine literature.'
3 – John Milton (1608–74); William Wordsworth (1770–1850).
4 – Followed by subheading, 'Persons and Places'. Anne Isabella Ritchie, *née* Thackeray (1837–1919), sister of Leslie Stephen's first wife, Harriet Marian ('Minny', 1840–75), and daughter of William Makepeace Thackeray (1811–63).
5 – See F. W. Maitland, *Life and Letters of Leslie Stephen* (Duckworth, 1906), p. 93.
6 – See *Mausoleum Book*, p. 89: 'I am, I think, one of the most easily bored

of mankind; I cannot bear long sittings with dull people and even when alone in my family I am sometimes as restless as a hyena.' Quoted in *Life*, p. 434.

7 – See *MoB*, pp. 165–6: 'my father groaned beneath his breath but very audibly, "Oh Gibbs, what a bore you are!" . . . Repenting of his irritation he would press poor Gibbs warmly by the hand and beg him to come soon again – which needless to say, poor Gibbs did.' Cf. *Mausoleum Book*, p. 105: 'His [Gibbs's] love of information and consequent cross-questioning used to bore me, and I fear . . . that I did not always conceal the fact.' For Stephen's habit of twisting and untwisting a lock of hair, see *Life*, p. 439.

8 – See Stephen's biography of Robert Owen (1771–1858) in the *DNB*: 'Owen may be described as one of those intolerable bores who are the salt of the earth'; quoted in *Life*, p. 371.

9 – In praising VW's essay, the *New York Times*, 18 December 1932, ignored her opinion: 'Edmund Gosse records that most of the walks on which he accompanied Stephen were "speechless." Once, dining at Stephen's, his host said scarcely a word, absorbed in contemplation of his beard and the universe.' See James Sully, *My Life & Friends: A Psychologist's Memoirs* (T. Fisher Unwin, 1918), p. 297: 'Stephen had recently lost his first wife, and I was warned that he was just now very much of a recluse.' See also *Life*, pp. 90, 103, 168, 268, 361.

10 – See Henrietta Garnett, *Anny: A Life of Anne Isabella Thackeray Ritchie* (Chatto & Windus, 2004), p. 193: in 1876 Stephen bought a house in 'Wimbledon for Anny's mother to move to with her caretaker'. It was called Kingsley Lodge (now Kingsley Court, 35 Lingfield Road).

11 – Followed by subheading, 'A Walk'.

12 – Sir James Fitzjames Stephen (1829–94), writer and judge. Queen Victoria reigned 1837–1901. Arthur Wellesley, 1st Duke of Wellington (1769–1852).

13 – Followed by subheading, 'Free of the Library'.

14 – See Stephen, 'The Study of English Literature', *Cornhill Magazine*, vol. lv (1887), p. 508: 'read what you really like and not what some one tells you that you ought to like; let your reading be part of your lives'. Cf. 'How Should One Read a Book?' above.

15 – See *Mausoleum Book*, p. 93: 'The sense in which I do take myself to be a failure is this: I have scattered myself too much. I think that I had it in me to make something like a real contribution to philosophical or ethical thought. Unluckily, what with journalism and dictionary making, I have been a jack of all trades; and instead of striking home have only done enough to persuade friendly judges that I could have struck.'

16 – George Meredith (1828–1909), *The Egoist* (1879), ch. ii, where Leslie Stephen is pictured as Vernon Whitford; quoted in *Life*, p. 423.

17 – Thomas Hardy, 'The Schreckhorn (With thoughts of Leslie Stephen)' (dated June 1897), in *Life*, p. 278; collected in *Satires of Circumstance: Lyrics and Reveries, with Miscellaneous Pieces* (Macmillan, 1914). VW wrote to Hardy on

17 January 1915: 'I have long wished to tell you how profoundly grateful I am to you for your poems and novels, but naturally it seemed an impertinence to do so. When however, your poem to my father, Leslie Stephen, appeared in *Satires of Circumstance* this autumn, I felt that I might perhaps be allowed to thank you for that at least. That poem, and the reminiscences you contributed to Professor Maitland's Life of him, remain in my mind as incomparably the truest and most imaginative portrait of him in existence, for which alone his children should be always grateful to you' (*II VW Letters*, no. 719).

18 – *Letters of George Meredith*, collected and ed. by his son (2 vols, Constable, 1912), Letter to Vanessa Stephen, 23 February 1904, vol. ii, p. 556, which has: 'He was the one man in my knowledge worthy of being mated with your mother.'

19 – James Russell Lowell, 'On a Certain Condescension in Foreigners', in *My Study Windows* (1871); quoted in *Life*, pp. 129, 494.

Portrait of a Londoner

Nobody can be said to know London who does not know one true Cockney – who cannot turn down a side street, away from the shops and the theatres, and knock at a private door in a street of private houses.

Private houses in London are apt to be much of a muchness. The door opens on a dark hall; from the dark hall rises a narrow staircase; off the landing opens a double drawing-room, and in this double drawing-room are two sofas on each side of a blazing fire, six armchairs, and three long windows giving upon the street.[2] What happens in the back half of the drawing-room which looks upon the gardens of other houses is often a matter of considerable conjecture. But it is with the front drawing-room that we are here concerned; for Mrs Crowe always sat there in an armchair by the fire; it was there that she had her being; it was there that she poured out tea.

That she was born in the country seems, though strange, to be a fact: that she sometimes left London, in those summer weeks when London ceases to be London, is also true. But where she went or what she did when she was out of London, when her chair was empty, her fire unlit and her table unlaid, nobody knew or could imagine. To figure Mrs Crowe in her black dress and her veil and her cap, walking in a field among turnips or climbing a hill where cows were grazing, is beyond the scope of the wildest imagination.

There by the fire in winter, by the window in summer, she had sat for sixty years – but not alone. There was always someone in the armchair opposite, paying a call. And before the first caller had been seated ten minutes the door always opened, and the maid Maria, she of the prominent eyes[3] and prominent teeth, who had opened the door for sixty years, opened it once more and announced a second visitor; and then a third, and then a fourth.

A *tête-à-tête* with Mrs Crowe was unknown. She disliked *tête-à-têtes*. It was part of a peculiarity that she shared with many hostesses that she was never specially intimate with anyone.[4] For example, there was always an elderly man in the corner by the cabinet – who seemed, indeed, as much a part of that admirable piece of eighteenth-century furniture as its own brass claws. But he was always addressed as Mr Graham – never John, never William: though sometimes she would call him 'dear Mr Graham' as if to mark the fact that she had known him for sixty years.

The truth was she did not want intimacy; she wanted conversation. Intimacy has a way of breeding silence, and silence she abhorred. There must be talk, and it must be general, and it must be about everything. It must not go too deep, and it must not be too clever, for if it went too far in either of these directions somebody was sure to feel out of it, and to sit balancing his tea-cup, saying nothing.

Thus Mrs Crowe's drawing-room had little in common with the celebrated salons of the memoir writers. Clever people often came there – judges, doctors, members of parliament, writers, musicians, people who travelled, people who played polo, actors and complete nonentities, but if anyone said a brilliant thing it was felt to be rather a breach of etiquette[5] – an accident that one ignored, like a fit of sneezing, or some catastrophe with a muffin. The talk that Mrs Crowe liked and inspired was a glorified version of village gossip. The village was London, and the gossip was about London life. But Mrs Crowe's great gift consisted in making the vast metropolis seem as small as a village with one church, one manor house and twenty-five cottages. She had first-hand information about every play, every picture show, every trial, every divorce case. She knew who was marrying, who was dying, who was in town and who was out. She would mention the fact that she had just seen Lady Umphleby's car go by, and hazard a guess that she was going to visit her daughter whose baby had been born last night, just as a village woman speaks of the Squire's lady driving to the station to meet Mr John, who is expected down from town.

And as she had made these observations for the past fifty years or so, she had acquired an amazing store of information about the lives of other people. When Mr Smedley, for instance, said that his daughter was engaged to Arthur Beecham, Mrs Crowe at once remarked that in that case she would be a cousin twice removed to Mrs Firebrace, and in a sense niece to Mrs Burns, by her first marriage with Mr Minchin of Blackwater Grange. But Mrs Crowe was not in the least a snob. She was merely a collector of relationships; and her amazing skill in this direction served to give a family and domestic character to her gatherings, for it is surprising how many people are twentieth cousins, if they did but know it.

To be admitted to Mrs Crowe's house was therefore to become the member of a club, and the subscription demanded was the payment of so many items of gossip every year. Many people's first thought when the house caught fire or the pipes burst or the housemaid decamped with the butler, must have been 'I will run round and tell that to Mrs Crowe.' But here again distinctions had to be observed. Certain people had the right to run round at lunchtime; others, and these were the most numerous, must go between the hours of five and seven. The class who had the privilege of dining with Mrs Crowe was a small one. Perhaps only Mr Graham and Mrs Burke actually dined with her, for she was not a rich woman. Her black dress was a trifle shabby; her diamond brooch was always the same diamond brooch. Her favourite meal was tea, because the tea-table can be supplied economically, and there is an elasticity about tea which suited her gregarious temper. But whether it was lunch or tea, the meal had a distinct character, just as a dress and her jewellery suited her to perfection and had a fashion of their own. There would be a special cake, a special pudding – something peculiar to the house and as much part of the establishment as Maria the old servant, or Mr Graham the old friend, or the old chintz on the chair, or the old carpet on the floor.

That Mrs Crowe must sometimes have taken the air, that she did sometimes become a guest at other people's luncheons and teas, is true. But in society she seemed furtive and fragmentary and incomplete, as if she had merely looked in at the wedding or the evening party or the funeral to pick up some scraps of news that she needed to complete her own hoard. Thus she was seldom induced to take a seat; she was always on the wing. She looked out of place among other people's chairs and tables; she must have her own chintzes and her own cabinet and her own Mr Graham under it in order to be completely herself. As years went on these little raids into the outer world practically ceased. She had made her nest so compact and so complete that the outer world had not a feather or a twig to add to it. Her own cronies were so faithful, moreover, that she could trust them to convey any little piece of news that she ought to add to her collection. It was unnecessary that she should leave her own chair by the fire in winter, by the window in summer. And with the passage of years her knowledge became, not more profound – profundity was not her line – but more rounded, and more complete. Thus if a new play were a great success, Mrs Crowe was able next day not merely to record the fact with a sprinkle of amusing gossip from behind the scenes, but she could cast back to other first nights, in the eighties, in the nineties, and describe what Ellen Terry had worn, what Duse had done, how dear Mr Henry James had said[6] – nothing very remarkable perhaps; but as she spoke it seemed as if all the pages of London life for fifty years past were being lightly shuffled for one's amusement. These were many; and the pictures on them were bright and brilliant and of famous people; but Mrs Crowe by no means dwelt on the past – she by no means exalted it above the present.

Indeed, it was always the last page, the present moment that mattered most. The delightful thing about London was that it was always giving one something new to look at, something fresh to talk about. One only had to keep one's eyes open; to sit down in one's own chair from five to seven every day of the week. As she sat in her chair with her guests ranged round she would give from time to time a quick bird-like glance over her shoulder at the window, as if she had half an eye on the street, as if she had half an ear upon the cars and the omnibuses and the cries of the paper boys under the window. Why, something new might be happening this very moment. One could not spend too much time on the past: one must not give all one's attention to the present.

Nothing was more characteristic and perhaps a little disconcerting than the eagerness with which she would look up and break her sentence in the middle when the door opened and Maria, grown very portly and a little deaf, announced someone new. Who was about to enter? What had he or she got to add to the talk? But her deftness in extracting whatever might be their gift, her skill in throwing it into the common pool, were such that no harm was done; and it was part of her peculiar triumph that the door never opened too often; the circle never grew beyond her sway.

Thus, to know London not merely as a gorgeous spectacle, a mart, a court, a hive of industry, but as a place where people meet and talk, laugh, marry, and die, paint, write and act, rule and legislate, it was essential to know Mrs Crowe. It was in her drawing-room that the innumerable fragments of the vast metropolis seemed to come together into one lively, comprehensible, amusing and agreeable whole. Travellers absent for years, battered and sun-dried men just landed from India or Africa, from remote travels and adventures among savages and tigers, would come straight to the little house in the quiet street to be taken back into the heart of civilisation at one stride. But even London itself could not keep Mrs Crowe alive for ever. It is a fact that one day Mrs Crowe was not sitting in the armchair by the fire as the clock struck five; Maria did not open the door; Mr Graham had detached himself from the cabinet. Mrs Crowe is dead, and London – no, though London still exists, London will never be the same city again.

1 – A signed essay in *Good Housekeeping*, December 1932, (*Kp4* C335.1), the sixth and final essay in 'The London Scene'. It was accompanied by illustrations in tomato and grey by Robert Nicholl and was introduced: 'Even London itself could not keep Mrs. Crowe alive for ever – but over her tea-table she reigns once more in the vivid phrases of this essay by Virginia Woolf'. The issue also contained: Walter de la Mare's poem, 'Memory'. See also 'The Docks of London' above, and Appendix VIII. A final typescript draft, entitled 'A London Character', together with the proofs (Berg, M 135). Reprinted: *LSc* (Snowbooks and Ecco editions only).

2 – Typically, the London houses in which the Woolfs lived had 'three long windows giving upon the street' at first-floor level: see the illustrations by Leonard McDermid in Jean Moorcroft Wilson's *Virginia Woolf: Life and London: A Biography of Place* (Cecil Woolf, 1987).

3 – A physical characteristic that VW noted and recreated in her fiction. Fanny Burney had 'rather prominent gnat-like eyes' (see 'Dr Burney's Evening Party' above). Christina Rossetti had 'prominent eyes' (*I VW Letters*, no. 331, [25 December 1906]). By the '1908' chapter in *The Years*, the old servant Crosby is 'more shrivelled, more gnat-like, and her blue eyes were more prominent than ever' (Hogarth Press, 1937), p. 160; while on the first page of *Between the Acts* (Hogarth Press, 1941) Mrs Haines is 'a goosefaced women with eyes protruding as if they saw something to gobble in the gutter'.

4 – VW considered that the hostess, Lady Colefax (1874–1950), shared these traits: e.g. 'She is a woman of the world: Sybil Colefax. To me, an almost unknown type. Every value is different. Friendship, let alone intimacy, is impossible' (*III VW Letters*, no. 1687, [19 November 1926]); and

see *IV VW Diary*, 15–16 August 1931, and 'Am I a Snob?', *MoB*, pp. 210–20.

5 – Cf. *O*, ch. iv, pp. 180–3.

6 – For VW on Ellen Terry (1848–1928), see *VI VW Essays*. Eleanora Duse (1858–1924), Italian actress. Henry James (1843–1916) was a friend of VW's parents; for Sybil Colefax and James, see 'Am I a Snob?, pp. 219–20.

Appendices

APPENDIX I

George Gissing

The following review in the *NR*, 2 March 1927, (*Kp4* C280), varies too considerably from the *CR2* version printed above for its substantive difference to be sensibly accounted for other than by reproducing it in its entirety. See Editorial Note, p. xxiii.

'Do you know there are men in London who go the round of the streets selling paraffin oil?' wrote George Gissing in the year 1880, and the phrase calls up a world of fog and four-wheelers and horse omnibuses, of link-boys with flares, of slatternly landladies, of struggling men of letters, of gnawing domestic misery, of gloomy back streets and ignoble yellow chapels above which, distant but distinct, as on a clear day one may see some tree-crowned height beyond the city, rise the columns of the Parthenon and the hills of Rome. For Gissing is one of those writers of stubborn individuality whose chance phrases have power to bring them back to us. He has a world of his own, and yet it is not our world; it remains his world. He is one of those imperfect writers with whom we establish a personal rather than an artistic relationship. Their books are half-transparent; while we read them we are looking at a face, so that now, taking up Gissing's letters, we feel that we are filling in a design which we began to trace out when we read Demos and New Grub Street and The Nether World.

Yet here, too, there are gaps in plenty, dark places left unillumined. Much information has been kept back, many facts necessarily omitted. The Gissings were poor, and their father died when they were children, and there were many of them, and they had to scrape together what education they could. George, his sister said, had a passion for learning. He would rush off to school with a sharp herring bone in his throat for fear of missing his lesson. He would copy out from a little book called That's It, the astonishing number of eggs that the tench lays, 'because I think it a fact worthy of attention.' She remembers his 'overwhelming veneration' for intellect, and how patiently this tall boy with the high white forehead and the short-sighted eyes would sit beside her and help her with her Latin, 'giving the same explanation time after time without the least sign of impatience.'

Partly because he so reverenced facts and had no faculty it seems (his language is meagre and unmetaphorical), for impressions, one wonders whether, since he had to make his living and was married unfortunately by the time he was twenty, his choice of a novelist's career was a happy one. There was the whole world with its history and its literature inviting him to haul it into his mind, to give it shape and coherency, and he must sit down in hired rooms and spin novels about 'earnest young people striving for improvement in, as it were, the dawn of a new phase of our civilisation.'

But the art of fiction is infinitely accommodating, and it was quite ready, about the year 1880, to accept into its ranks a writer who wished to be the mouthpiece of the 'advanced Radical Party,' who was determined to show in his novels the ghastly condition of the poor, and the hideous injustice of society. The art of fiction was acquiescent; such novels, that is to say, might be written, but it was doubtful if such novels would be read. Smith Elder's reader summed up the situation tersely. Mr. Gissing's novel, he wrote, 'is too painful to please the ordinary novel reader, and treats of scenes that can never attract the subscribers to Mr. Mudie's library.' So, dining off lentils and hearing the men cry paraffin for sale in the streets of Islington, Gissing paid for the publication himself. It was then that he formed the habit of getting up at five in the morning, in order to tramp half across London and coach Mr. M. before breakfast. Often enough Mr. M. sent down word that he was already engaged. Gissing had to tramp back half across London again, and another page was added to the dismal chronicle of life in modern Grub Street. And here we run against one of those problems with which literature is sown so thick. The writer has dined upon lentils; he gets up at five; he walks half across London; he finds M. still in bed, whereupon he stands forth as the champion of life as it is, and proclaims that ugliness is truth, truth ugliness, and that is all we know and all we need to know. But there are signs that the novel resents such treatment. To use a burning consciousness of one's own misery and of the shackles that cut one's own limbs to quicken one's sense of life in general, as Dickens did, to turn and twist out of the murk some resplendent figure, such as Micawber or Mrs. Gamp, is admirable; but to use suffering to fetter the reader's sympathy and curiosity upon your own individual case is harmful. Imagination is at its freest when it is most generalised; it loses something of its sweep and power when it is riveted to the consideration of a particular case calling for sympathy.

At the same time, sympathy is a passion of great intensity; it makes the pages fly; it lends what has perhaps little merit artistically another and momentarily a keener edge. Biffen and Reardon had, we say to ourselves, bread and butter and sardines for supper; so had Gissing; Reardon could not write on Sunday; no more could Gissing. We forget whether it was Reardon who loved cats or Gissing who loved barrel organs. Certainly both Reardon and Gissing bought their Gibbons at a second-hand book stall and lugged the volumes home one by one through the fog. So we go on capping these resemblances, and each time we succeed, dipping now into the novel, now into the letters, a little glow of satisfaction comes over us, as if novel reading were a game of skill in which the puzzle is to find the face of the writer.

We know Gissing thus as we do not know Hardy or George Eliot. Where the great novelist flows in and out of his characters and bathes them in an element which seems to be common to us all and not to himself alone, Gissing remains solitary, self-centred, apart. His is one of those sharp lights beyond whose edges all is vapour and phantom. But mixed with this sharp light is one ray of singular penetration. With all his narrowness of outlook and meagreness of sensibility, Gissing is one of the extremely rare novelists who believes in the mind, who makes his people think. They are thus differently poised from the majority of fictitious men and women. The awful hierarchy of the passions is slightly displaced. Social snobbery does not exist; money is desired almost entirely to buy bread and butter; love itself takes a second place.

But the brain works and that alone is enough to give us a sense of freedom. For to think is to become complex; it is to overflow boundaries, to cease to be a 'character,' to merge one's private life in the life of politics or art or ideas, to have relationships based on them partly and not on sexual desire alone. The impersonal side of life is given its place in the scheme. 'Why don't people write about the really important things of life?' Gissing makes one of his characters exclaim, and at the unexpected cry the horrid burden of fiction begins to slip from the shoulders. Is it possible that we are going to talk of other things besides falling in love, important though that is, and trying to dine with duchesses, fascinating though that is? Here in Gissing is a gleam of recognition that Darwin had lived, that the telegraph had been invented, that people read books, that friendship exists, that once upon a time there was such a place as Greece. It is this that makes his books such painful reading that they can never 'attract the subscribers to Mr. Mudie's library.' They owe their peculiar grimness to the fact that the people who suffer most are capable of making their suffering part of a reasoned view of life. The thought endures when the feeling has gone. Their unhappiness represents something more lasting than a personal reverse; it becomes part of a view of life. Hence, when we have finished one of Gissing's novels, what we have taken away is not a character nor an incident, but a comment upon life.

Like his characters, Gissing commented upon life, and because he was always thinking, he was always changing. In that perpetual change, that incessant comment, lies much of his interest for us. As a young man he had thought that he would write books to show up the 'hideous injustice of our whole system of society.' Later, his views changed; either it was not possible, or other tastes tugged him in a different direction. He came to think, as he believed, finally, that 'the only thing known to us of absolute value is artistic perfection . . . the works of the artist . . . remain sources of health to the world.' So that if one wishes to better the world, one must, paradoxically enough, withdraw from it and spend more and more time fashioning one's sentences into perfection. For writing, in Gissing's view, was a difficult art. At the end of his life he thought that he might perhaps be able 'to manage a page that is decently grammatical and fairly harmonious.' Certainly, passages in his books stand out like stone slabs, shaped and solid, among the untidy litter of prose fiction. For example, he is describing a cemetery in the East End of London: 'Here on the waste limits of that dread east, to wander among tombs is to go hand in hand with the stark and eyeless emblems of mortality; the spirit fails beneath the cold burden of ignoble destiny. Here lie those who were born for toil; who, when toil has worn them to the uttermost, have but to yield their useless breath and pass into oblivion. For them is no day, only the brief twilight of a winter's sky between the former and the latter night. For them no aspiration; for them no hope of memory in the dust; their very children are wearied into forgetfulness. Indistinguishable units in the vast throng that labours but to support life, the name of each, father, mother, child, is but a dumb cry for the warmth and love of which fate so stinted them. The wind wails above their narrow tenements; the sandy soil, soaking in the rain as soon as it has fallen, is a symbol of the great world which absorbs their toil and straightway blots their being.'

For he never ceased to educate himself. While the Baker Street trains hissed their steam beneath his windows, and the lodger downstairs blew the room out, and the landlady was disobliging, and the grocer refused to send the sugar, so that he had to fetch it himself, and the fog burnt his throat and he caught cold and vacillated weakly from one domestic disaster to another in one dreary lodging after another – while all this went on with a dismal monotony which caused him to reflect bitterly upon the weakness of his own character, he still doggedly went on learning. The columns of the Parthenon and the hills of Rome still rose above the fogs and fried-fish shops of the Euston Road. At last he actually set foot in Athens; he saw Rome, he read his Thucydides in Sicily, before he died. His comment upon life was always changing. Perhaps the old sordid reality was not the only reality; the past with its leisure and its literature and its civilisation were equally real. His books in future were to be about Rome in the time of Totila and not Islington in the time of Queen Victoria. But he could only mark down the spot he had reached and the conclusions he saw before him, when death – the same death he had given to Edwin Reardon – came upon him and he died, saying to the friend who stood by his side: Patience, patience. That comment was his last.

APPENDIX II

Notes of a Day's Walk

This is a transcript of VW's typescript 'Notes of a Days Walk' (MHP, B 7e), a version of 'The Truth-Tellers' section of 'Phases of Fiction' (see above), cast in fictional form. This version – although unpolished – can be read as a discrete sketch where the story throws light on the argument. It is thus an especially valuable document. There is a three-page manuscript fragment that begins a notebook of about 1938–9 in the Berg (M 1.8); it is headed 'A Days Walk' and mentions Maupassant; another typescript fragment, which mentions a hair merchant, is in the MHP (B 5b). Although the typescript is undated, it is likely that it was produced between August and October 1934: VW wrote on 11 July 1934 that she was 'writing about belief in a city church' (*IV VW Diary*), but did not read Maupassant's *Une Vie* (see n. 4 below) until 21 August (see *IV VW Diary*). For VW's attempts during this year to produce her 'never completed book on Fiction', see *IV VW Diary*, 19, 21 July, 10, 14–17 October, and 1 November 1934.

The 'ancient city church' is a composite of two churches. One is St Mary the Virgin, Aldermanbury, a medieval church destroyed in the Great Fire and rebuilt by Sir Christopher Wren. It was badly damaged by an incendiary bomb in the Second World War and not rebuilt, and the ruins were shipped to Westminster College in Fulton, Missouri, where the church was re-erected in 1964–9 as a memorial to Sir Winston Churchill. In the churchyard in the City of London there is a late-nineteenth-century monument to the Shakespearean actors, John Hemming and Henry Condell, who published the First Folio and were buried there. It is said that the need for a monument arose because there was no memorial in the church to identify them. The other church is St Bartholomew the Great, which dates from the twelfth century and is near Smithfield Meat Market. VW wrote on Monday, 16 November

1931: 'I'm disoriented; have been to the City & seen St Bartholomew's' (*IV VW Diary*); and see 'Monday, Tuesday, Wednesday', *CSF*, Appendix C. In the floor of the north aisle, there is a white marble slab: 'Under this Stone I Lies Interr'd the Body of Mᴿ JONATHAN THORNELL I *Hair Merchant* of this Parish I Who died Novembʳ yᵉ 14ᵗʰ 1757. I In the 57ᵗʰ Year of His Age. I A Man whose Piety and Virtues I Were worthy of Imitation.' See also 'Friday, 13 November 1931', *VWB*, no. 26 (September 2007), pp. 39–41.

The double-spaced typescript consists of twenty-three pages, numbered 2–6 and 8–22 by VW; pages 1, 7 and 23 are unnumbered. A mixture of blue and black typewriter ribbons is used. VW's emendations are made in ink, lead pencil and coloured pencil, which are not differentiated below. Additions and revisions are reproduced between <angled brackets> whether these occur in the text or its margins and whether they are typed or holograph. Every effort has been made to divine and represent the sequence of VW's alterations, although this has sometimes been a matter of intelligent guesswork or, in the last resort, practicability. Cancelled words, including those exed out by the typewriter, are marked through with a fine line. Cancelled passages are reproduced between {wavy brackets}. Editorial interventions, including page numbers and [?doubtful readings], are contained in square brackets, with the exception of all apostrophes added for clarity's sake. Mistypings of words (including French words) have usually been silently corrected, and spacing regularised. Single quotation marks are employed throughout. The footnotes are editorial.

Notes of a Day's Walk.

'It is to be lamented that we judge of books by books, instead of referring what we read to our own experience.'

S. T. Coleridge. Lectures on Shakespeare, &c. p.213[1]

.....I.....

A little old lady was selling cards and lavender in the doorway of an ancient city church in order to raise funds for its restoration. But there were very few visitors; the church indeed was almost empty, robed in the gray green light which seemed its natural hue. In some places the shadow was so profound that those ignorant of the building could fancy that there were statues in niches, ~~or~~ where there were none; or ignore tombs that were in fact there. A few little lights burnt high up in the roof, not <so much> to illumine but only <as> to testify to the fidelity, the enduringness of light. The body of sound in the street outside was here reduced to the ghost of sound, just as daylight was reduced to the ghost of light by the immense thickness of the medieval walls.

As it happened two young men had come in and sat down sinking at once into the attitude of prayer. They seemed at once to become engaged in some intensity of supplication. <That the effort was exhausting was obvious.> At intervals, as if the effort of prayer wore them out, now one would lie back for a moment with his eyes closed; then he would return again to his task. They Their created all round them an [*p*. 2] an atmosphere <island> of peace and concentration.

It was natural to think about belief. to try to pin down and describe this profound human instinct. What did it spring from – this universal desire to believe in something that cannot be seen or touched? In the first place the human mind is of vast antiquity; far older than this church; it is full of graves and memories; It may be that when it is born into a particular body, it half remembers other experiences, and tries to escape from the limits of its own single existence by supplementing it with recollections of what it can half remember. {We wish to fill out and supplement; to make our single thread of life many plaited,} and so do <We do> our utmost to believe in another world, or in another race of beings, in order to enrich what seems too by itself seems too single and separate. But owing to the extreme age of the human mind, and the consequent weakness of its memories, we find it necessary to support this belief upon something actual; hence the emblems hung up in churches; pictures of saints and madonnas. Hence too our habit of writing words upon tombs.

A few paces to the right lay a slab of purplish stone cut with a few worn letters too distant to be deciphered. But as the church is known to be the burial place of some of Shakespeare's actors it was possible that they lay [*p*. 3] under that particular stone. The very bones that once wore the cloak of Hamlet or the robes of Lear lay a few paces to the right. Then a doubt from the difficulty of reading them arose. Suppose they were not buried there? The doubt took the edge of the pleasure of believing – the ghosts which had been about to rise sank back again. If the little old woman who sold cards at the door had been able to say for certain The bones are there. The grave was opened on the fifth of April last; the Rector held the thighbone in his hand; I myself actually saw a white face with a red pointed beard, then the power of belief would have been greatly helped. Nourished on an actual thigh bone it would have been strong enough to create – belief would have become fruitful.

How strange a thing then is this b<B>elief – <there is> this desire <But> to believe, <a faculty> which can draw up out of the inane whole worlds and divine beings, and yet shies and unseats its rider at the least touch of doubt! The Here a ray of sun came through the window and, falling on the purple slab, illumined the words Frek. Cripps, Hair merchant of this parish, died Decr. 1705. The piece of information thus volunteered changed the current of thought; This not only changed the current of thought; but gave pleasure. <& it was amazing to watch ideas assembling now that they had something hard to form with> <One world was dismissed; another rose. And the [last?] that it was now certain that Cripps was revealed. But what was he [made?] [of?]> But why should it be pleasant to think of a man who had no existence two minutes before? It must be because the mind [p. 4] <scattered [?]> is stored with wandering sounds, <enjoys putting them in [?],> <(>li[k]e those of a summers day. with birds songs, and the barking of dogs; the rumble of wheel and motor horns, and the confused sounds of voices far away.<)> Drop a fact in and these wandering ideas coalesce; close round; combine and form the figure of a man called Cripps; who stood in his shop handling hair, selling wigs to the citizens of this parish two centuries and a half ago. The act of crystallisation is pleasant. For a moment we have a real relationship also with this man. We have endowed him with enough humanity to rouse a sense of difference; to set in motion <action> the give and take of emotion which is so exciting; he is like that he we are like this. We can perhaps feel as much about him as we feel about a complete stranger who is talking to the conductor in an omnibus. Yet there is a certain difference. For if we drop into the mind the fact 'Fredk. Cripps, hair merchant, died Decr. 1705' the ideas that it attracts to it from the wandering hordes in the brain are received not from life, since we cannot see him opposite us in the flesh with houses and shops behind him, but from history from literature. The name of the dead hair merchant will attract ideas about Queen Anne, Marlborough, Blenheim, full bottomed wigs, Pepys, the lice that Mrs Pepys found on her husband's body when she combed his hair,[2] Defoe, Moll Flanders – according to the lumber previously stored the mind. Again there is another source of suggestion that will colour our imaginary portrait – that [*p.* 5] supplied by the dark and the quiet of the church, the stained glass, the altar, and the two young men who all this time are praying so assiduously that sight seers passing them will instinctively avoid their line of vision and tread on the tips of their toes. Again if the organ were ab[out] to begin to play, if some clerk were to take this occasion to begin practising <his Sunday anthem>, other ~~ideas~~ <emotions> would rush out incited by the music and bury the name of Cripps under ~~other~~ ideas – probably of a general kind, about the shortness of life and its perils; of the peace and solitude of the dead.

<(>Thus the doubtfulness of all belief became apparent; Here in this church it was natural to think about rh dead. Yet of all the effort in spite of all the effort we make to b[ri]n[g] them back to us, to reclothe bones with flesh in words instead of flesh – and think how many people spend their lives in the attempt – what success waits us? <[?] to all this [?] what success> The two young men were praying; yet near a[s] they were to it was impossible to be sure of any fact about them Their characters, their occupations, let alone what stress ha[d] brought them here, – all this was doubtful, yet we shared the identical morning and the church. The dubiousness of it all was depressing; and the folly of the attempt, and the wrong we do the dead by thus furbishing them up again, and making them take the form of our words. Often words are born of private spite private desire; we make them up for money or for our own [*p.* 6] advancement.

Altogether the sponge or lump of matter that lies in the little box at the top of the head is a most capricious faulty undefined and perhaps indefinable piece of machinery; what with its extreme antiquity, its porous nature, and its close connection with the body that <is for ever interrupting, [composing?]; &> has to be cared for, flattered, kept in health, fed. It would be interesting to discover whether there was a plan in it all. ~~If the origin of~~ <To discover, under all these shifting lights <layers> & shadows, some ~~grain~~ thing to lay hands upon was impossible.>
<But the question – what does the desire to believe spring from, is [?] flushing it or [staining?] it,>

<flushing it ~~with~~ interrupting & interfering.>
[*p.* 7] ~~Yet~~ <But> to discover under all these shifting layers something that could be called the origin of the desire to believe was clearly impossible. Yet if that were so, it might be possible to discover some more superficial system of which some account could be given <some map or plan directing the [mere?] superficial operations of the mind> – can we say for instance that one wish will follow another? Do the desires proceed crabwise, each one seeking its contrast, by way of antidote; ~~and does~~ it is it impelled to take this course by the wish to form some final combination? Certainly the <2> mirage of a final combination, of some whole to which we move perpetually believing that we shall there attain rest, comprehension, is very commonly met with among human beings. There was old Miss Milligan,[3] the irish lady in the pension, who derived comfort in all the disillusions and disappointments of her life by holding an ordinary pebble in her hand and gazing at it fixedly. All the sting went out of the day she said; She became she said looking ahead of her with a curious expression of glazed ecstasy one with the universe.

[*p.*8] <I>
As for the other idea that we make our way crabwise, always seeking out the opposite, the contrast, <This was a question that the little old woman reading by the door might help to solve> perhaps the little old woman reading a book in the doorway <seemed accidentally> might throw some light on the problem. She was reading a lively jaunty novel about the adventures of a very beautiful girl in a punt on the river. More could scarcely be said. It was not possible to stop and read over her shoulder. <But it seemed probable> Evidently it seemed she was balancing the sepulchral nature of a calling which compelled her to spend so much of her time among tombs with as much gaiety, and and love, and luxury as a novel could give her. At any rate she was reading with such intensity that she gave a great start when two sight seers asked her where they could find the tombs of the Elizabethan actors.

Belief then is clearly a very strange and mixed sensation. The young men prayed; the woman read; even the tourists had an idea that it would help them to attain to a state which must be very delightful if they could be assured that certain bones actually lay beneath a certain spot.

But although various kinds and degrees of belief are possible for the greater part of the day we believe nothing except that there is a pavement under our feet and that by lifting one foot after another we shall find ourselves in Holborn.

[*p. 9*] These speculations however were suddenly put an end to. A boy on a bicycle <coming out of a side street> was suddenly upset by a taxicab; the boy sprawled to the ground; bottles of milk were spilt; the cab swerved and hit the lamp post on the other side; the boy jumped up; the milk spread in white rivers to the gutter; ~~traffic was stopped~~; the sight was ~~enthralling~~ everybody stood still and gazed. They stopped thinking what they had been thinking; they stopped going where they had been going. It ~~felt as if~~ <seemed that> some faculty that had been dormant suddenly rushed down a channel cut for it by the accident and every other feeling was obliterated. ~~It was an extraordinary relief~~. This rapt gazing ecstasy continued to feed upon the sight of the boy, the cabman, the milk flowing and the policeman arguing <making notes in a pocket book> until just as suddenly as the accident had happened it seemed to be over; what was to come would be lost interest; it became a repetition merely. It was over; nothing new was going to happen; and the crowd began to move on, as if slowly we again remembered what we had been thinking, where we were going.

The sight of the accident had caused such a strong feeling that it was natural to ask what the nature of it was – Had it given so much pleasure because it supplied a drama; because it banished all other thoughts so masterfully; because it was heaven sent, provided without our own effort; without any pain to us, or to the actors;<)> Most of us would have liked to see another [*p. 10*] accident, on the same terms at the next turning. It was rather flat to walk on without an accident; and to realise that everybody, rather further along the street, was indifferent, and ignorant that anything out of the way had happened. <One wd. have liked to stop the first comer & say, I have just seen an accident. But that was impossible.>

Partly to prolong the pleasure, partly to try to explain it, I thought ~~of~~, stopping at a book stall, where there were cheap books an a stall outside, marked one shilling or one and sixpence, how the same sort of experience w[as] provided by the great truth tellers – Defoe, for example, one of whose books – Roxana – happened to be on sale in a cheap edition. Was there not some likeness between reading Defoe < Roxana > and seeing an accident? ~~He at least produces something of the same~~ The old feelings that the book used to arouse stole out again. Soon they produced the same state of acquiescence that the accident had produced – the orderly matter of fact sentences cut a channel down which belief flowed with smoothness, with satisfaction, obliterating whatever opposed them. It was remarkable how ~~he soothed certain senses sound asleep and stimulated others. For exa~~ ~~For~~ how naturally and quietly he insisted that his reader should believe in the story he was telling; ~~should accept his own belief in Roxana~~. This he did partly at least by emphasising ~~what is~~ <the> solid, matter of fact in life; ~~Persistently~~ <dwelling> naturally with a curious unconscious iteration ~~he makes us dwell~~ upon money and furniture and food. [*p.* 11] Roxana had veal and turnips for dinner. It was an actual day in an actual month. Soon he had brought the eyes entirely to his focus. The intrusion of another kind of idea would be foolish. <(>Try to think of sliding streams, forest glooms, solitary riders on midnight roads – it is impossible. For the other side of the page, the thing that is not said but that completes the world of the book, is there in our minds as clearly as the actual page. it is of a piece with what is said. All that he has taken into his mind has become saturated with his own belief, a proof of greatness. For how few novelists can keep this large <conviction> <maintain this [~~stenth~~?] intensity of conviction> grasp of their world throughout. Again and again belief flags; realities are mixed; and instead of a final clarity we get a baffling and shifting confusion.

Yet if he were to go on adding fact to fact that nerve would soon be satiated. He must devise some change to distract us, and yet it must be one that does not disturb us. <Here his genius came to his help.> On with the story he says; and on it moves; and the mind moves on too, rested, relieved, <inspired> with a fresh spurt of belief. <~~To change the [form~~?] & [refine?] & [?] wd change {He does not want} to refine & [?] [the?] [form?]. That [must?] have been the [puzzle?]: & it was solved by his [genius?].> And then it becomes obvious that the simplicity of Roxana's character was intentional. She must be kept simple in order that she may move freely. His people must travel light since they must travel far.

[*p.* 12] But at this point – that is to say when some noise in the shop interrupted – further evidence of his power was given. Everything had come under his sway. Look out of the window; the houses were Defoe's; the lorries were Defoe's; the cloud now darkening the sky was his. Should one frame a sentence it would be after his manner. The old book seller, writing with a fine pen dipped in a little penny bottle of ink was one of his characters. Should one frame a sentence it would be after his manner. That perhaps might serve as a rough and ready test of a book's greatness – its power to shape the present, and its thoughts and its figures, to its own likeness. To try the experiment, it was only necessary to open another book; and here was one by a writer once well known and immensely prolific – The Triumphs of Sara, by W.E. Norris. <Chance dictated the choice. It w> <A vast number of books were collected under his name.>

He was no mean craftsman either. The story was under way in a trice. Girls and boys; cricketing and shooting; dancing and riding; love making; quarrelling – green fields and grey manor houses, clubs and streets, all took shape and being. But as they cantered past, Stop! I said. I can believe much more than you are asking me to believe. But he could not stop. All his powers were fully stretched to keep the scene as it was moving past. [p. 13] There was nothing beyond. And, lacking the power to suggest, he is dead beyond recall. He can cast no spell. Even the elderly cat washing its face in the corner seemed to protest, I am not Mr Norrises cat. I am my own cat. And therefore the book was put back on the shelf; and, <since the desire to believe had <been roused but> not ~~been~~ gratified> as illusion had not been created, it was put back with a keen sense of frustration, of deception, of having asked for bread, and been given ashes.

Such a feeling is extremely lowering. ~~If the body were affected~~. <The mind [receives?]> <exposed to disease.> The government takes care of its citizens' bodily health, but it leaves their minds exposed to infection from bad books without compunction. The difficulty of course arises from the fact that <the> infectious books are not the violent immoral books, but the smug respectable books; the books that smear the mind's surface and leave it dulled and torpid. a prey to disease. In this predicament, the best thing to do is to snatch some antidote – and since a foreign language is efficacious, it was natural to turn to the yellow backed novels in the corner <for help>. French words are new and bright; the sentences take hard new shapes instead of flopping softly into the old creases. Nothing could be more instantly efficacious than a dose of Maupassant, and happily there was a copy [p. 14] of Boule de Suif for sale at a shilling. And even if we have to stand to read, still read we must. Each sentence like quick rilling wave, hands us on to the next. And at the end – to change the metaphor – the whole thing explodes; it is summed, stated, done with.

The end is always the explanation. And when this is so, there cannot be a great complexity of character to explain. Obviously Maupassant was far less successful in the long novel – like Une Vie – than in a short story, because the novel tempted him to introduce subtleties in his figures of which he was by no means sure. The last words of Une Vie are by no means so satisfactory as the last words of Boule de Suif.[4] But in the short story everything is effective. He rourses He keeps us in the presence of reality – the reality of the body, of the senses. ~~He uses~~ similes <are used> that nei bring things close and make them brighter; not metaphors that enlarge and remove. For example, 'Elle restait inerte, ne sentant plus sons corps, et l'esprit dispersé, comme si quelqu'un l'eût d'échiqueté avec un de ces instruments dont se servent les cardeurs pour effiloquer la laine des matelas.' Or if he wishes us to see tears drying on a girl's cheeks he says 'comme des gouttes d'eau sur du fer rouge'. It is all concrete; all visualised; ringed, encircled, encircled, cut off in a bright circle of [p. 15] ringed round in a bright circle. Within that circumference, there is a world in which the eyes the nose and the fingers can believe; and that form of belief, whether among the most satisfying or not, is certainly among the most vivid. Undoubtedly, if we use again the test already applied, Maupassant has the power to impose himself upon real life.

For a girl had come in with the book seller's dinner on a tray. Under the influence of Maupassant she changed; she became sensual. Her relation with the bookseller was by no means moral. It was the simple human relation of one body with another body. The shop became fuller of bodies than of books. But although there was something in this that was disturbing, ~~although~~ pictures at once became visible from the book of servants girls seduced by their masters, of illegitimate children born all of a sudden while the girl does the bed, the sensation was not enervating, as Robert Elsmere enervates or Norrises book, the Triumphs of Sara. Maupassant after all was telling the truth, by which we mean that <we felt that he had cleared> he opened a space in the mind to the shock of experience. What had been insensitive before [one?] felt. The shock was pleasant, though the feeling itself – that the girl, in the story or out of it, [p. 16] was bearing an illegitimate child – was unpleasant. ~~But then, clearly, p~~<P>leasure <then> is not a simple emotion; but a sum of many feelings.

But again, as one of the elements in the pleasure that Maupassant produces, was barred to the Victorian ~~English~~ novelist of English birth, by the censor – it is scarcely fair to charge Mrs Ward or Mr Norris or Mr James Payn[5] with a crime causing anaemia, influences, or whatever the a crime which was imposed <[by?] the respectable> upon them by law <public opinion>. <Thackeray somewhere complains that> To deal with all the facts of a servant girl's life was then out of the question. {A great writer like Thackeray had to bow} to the law which made <said that it was> made it impossible for him to write the true story of his heroes life. <But tho' he complained, he obliged.> He was forced to bow to the convention.

Trollope bowed too. And Trollope, belonged, even more by nature than Thackeray, to the natural truth [?] school of truth tellers. He was far less cultivated, urbane, and civilised than Thackeray. In real life, so Lady Violet Greville records in her Memoirs, he was 'a big, blustering, spectacled, loud voiced hunting man whose language in male society was, I believe, so lurid that I was not admitted to breakfast with him.' But Lady Violet was perforce admitted to his novels, and it would be [p. 17] interesting to see in what way this restriction affected him when he came to write. It had, little effect upon his popularity it seems. For they are printed and reprinted; a new edition was here on the booksellers shelf.

At first sight, glancing into the pages of the Barchester novels, the English truth seems to be as plain featured as prosaic, as impressive too as her French sister. He spares us nothing of the prose and the dulness and the smallness and the life in clerical society. Mr Slope is a hypocrite with 'a pawing, greasy with way with him.' Mrs Proudie is a domineering bully. The Bishop is a weak man. None of the Stanhope family has an heart. The Archdeacon is well meaning but coarse grained and thick cut. All these people, these well fed, black coated unimaginative men and women of the fifties go through their daily eating and drinking and worshipping and marrying with a thoroughness that leaves us no loop hole of escape. This is the truth about Barchester, beyond a doubt; and the truth about Barchester, the truth of the Slopes and the Proudies, the truth of the evening party where Mrs Proudie has her dress torn off her back by the light of eleven gas jets is entirely acceptable. <To that [extent?]> He is a great novelist, there is a profound pleasure in our belief.

[p. 18] But then we are aware of a difference. For some reason, the clear cold truth which lay before us in Moll Flanders, or in La maison Tellier is here disguised. We become aware of some bias, some indirectness. Trollope for one thing, cannot keep himself out of his story. He cannot help telling us that he loves pretty girls and hates oily humbugs. I will keep nothing from you, Trollope seems to say to the reader, who is seated at his right hand; I will not mislead you for a moment into thinking that 'my Eleanor' is going to marry Slope or Bertie Stanhope – both of whom I detest heartily. Thus though we believe in Barchester we believe through the medium of Trollope's temperament; Another relationship is set up, with Trollope himself, with the shrewd sensible man, who is too well, acquainted with human foibles to judge them [heartily?]; other than tolerantly; and is not above the human weakness of liking one person a good deal better than another. Therefore the truth is a little qualified and confused. The story becomes a screen, over which we peep, and see a number of interesting but rather distracting objects <on the other side>. Is it not for this reason that we throw down these English novels and complain that we are tired of being treated like children? Is it not for this reason that we cannot keep our on pld <that we [?] so often at> plodding through their slack diversity?

[p. 19] But before we utter the usual verdict, that no English novelist in the Victorian age was an artist, let us glance once more at the power of the censor. The artistic instinct is extremely susceptible plant. And if the censor – not merely the individual man, but the whole public spirit to which Lady Violet reveals when she says that she was not allowed to meet Trollope at breakfast, – blew upon the novel, probably iy the whole always from the same direction, probably its whole shape was affected. Forbidden to say this, the novelist was forced to say that. His book instead of growing freely as the sap ran, was lopped on this side, flourishing <& [thriving?]> on that <the other> <to sprout & flower on the other>. Hence the <overblown> familiar shape; the happy ending shape; the plot shape; the amiable kindly garrulous garrulity. So Trollope fills chapter after chapter; and, unconsciously <comes to [suppers?] [&?] [acts?] a part,> acts the part of the benevolent kind man, when in fact he would far rather write <out boldly> as he used to talk in male society at breakfast.

Here the bookseller interposed. His dinner was done, and like most of his calling he had the agreeable habit of liking to pass the time of days with his customers. <He named> The price of these first editions of Trollope<; it> was very high, he said. All the cry was for the Victorian novelists now. [p. 20] So fashions chop and change, without rhyme or reason that he could discover he added, with a touch of the cynicism that is natural to a man who has sold books in Holborn these fifty years without making enough to retire upon.

Fashions chop and change – the remark served to rouse into being a host of questions; The Victorians are cried down; the Victorians are cried up. That is easy to understand, if we consider for a moment – <waiting to cross the road & [so?] [enter?] the [?]> while the waitress goes off to bring us too our luncheon – upon what fleeting impressions, upon what due direct impulses, we too at the present time form our opinions of Defoe, <[boule?],> Maupassant, Trollope. Maupassant is a good writer because he imposes himself upon life; Norris is a bad writer because he leaves the book sellers act untouched. <(>Here <again> we must draw a distinction – there is one kind of life for novelists; shall we call it Monday or Tuesday, everyday life that is; another for poets; Saturday and Sunday; the life of contemplation, of dusk and stars.<)> Then again, what meaning do we attach to the word 'reality'? In what sense is a brothel more real than a pink carnation? Is it not as foolish to limit 'reality' to the indecent, and to endow that with superior intensity, as to limit reality to what can be said to Lady Violet Greville at breakfast?

[*p.* 21] All that we can justly ask whether as reader or writer is that the writer shall have free run of all experience. The harm is done when through suppression, the brothel becomes more real than the carnation – more desirable, more of a luxury; just as a piece of meat, when it is hung up out of reach, becomes the envy of all flies, so that they buzz and buzz and buzz round the forbidden joint, and fill the whole room with their buzzings.

But as this image was clearly suggested by the fact that the 'I' who made it, was sitting at a table in a restaurant, it was ~~clear~~ <obvious> that ~~another accident must be~~ such accidents too must be ~~allowed for in~~ given their weight. The instrument with which we judge books, <is loaded by personal accidents –> the instrument which is at the mercy of ~~accidental~~ innumerable accidents and influences. The 'I' that makes these judgments is <not by any means [?] [?]> shaped by a thousand to to birth, <That is [from?]> education, experience. Yet the 'I' which comes in contact with books is obviously a different 'I' from the one that assembles itself before a plate a plate of beef at a restaurant. It is far less personal. It attempts to put on immortality. It tries to rise above what is bodily. Indeed one of the pleasures of reading is that it anesthetises certain elements in 'I' and gives scope to others. Under the influence of words it expands; it wings [*p.* 22] up and down the world in and out of all minds at all times, of all qualities. Yet it always keeps some print of the particular body at a particular moment, and that necessary idiosyncrasy is the prime cause of the chops and changes of fashion, of the fact, to which the book-seller testified, that the Victorian novels are now all the rage but will again be neglected tomorrow.

Therefore ~~all~~ one can say of a morning spent in dipping here and there into the truth tellers is that a particular '<I>' has been made aware of a world that is very visible; very tangible; very clear to senses of touch and taste and feeling. that it much resembles the world of Monday and Tuesday; that after a time this reality palls; that it is then broken up by action; that all realists are also story tellers; that they use plain language; that they avoid metaphors; that they shut out what is subtle, ambiguous, difficult and indefinite in human character. Before long therefore it is precisely for those qualities that we begin to crave.

Was this then some confirmation of the idea that was suggested by the old woman in the church, who read a novel of river life because she spent her day among the tombs; for do we take our way crab wise, from one desire to its opposite? Are we driven by the

[*p.* 23] Did this then confirm the idea which was suggested by the woman in church that we take our way crabwise impelled by one desire to another, its opposite? in the effort to find that marvellous land where we hold the magic pebble in our hands and say like the poor spinster in the Italian pension 'I am one with the universe.'?

Was it becoming desirable down there in the dark underworld where desires have their rise, to rate[6] this experience with one among writers of a very different kind?

1 – Samuel Taylor Coleridge, *Lectures and Notes on Shakespere and Other English Poets*, now first collected by T. Ashe (George Bell and Sons, 1885), 'The Drama generally and Public Taste', pp. 208–18. VW owned Leslie Stephen's copy of this edition.

2 – For Pepys and his lice, see *The Diary of Samuel Pepys . . .* , ed. Henry B. Wheatley (8 vols in 3, George Bell & Sons and Harcourt, Brace, 1923), vol. iii (i.e. vol. viii), 23 January 1668–9, p. 196.

3 – VW may have had in mind Alice Milligan (1880–1953), Irish poet, author of *Hero Lays* (1908); see 'Caution and Criticism', *II VW Essays*.

4 – Guy de Maupassant, *Une Vie (l'humble vérité)* (Victor Havard, 1883), p. 337: 'La vie, voyez-vous, ça n'est jamais si bon ni si mauvais qu'on croit'

(spoken by Rosalie, the maid); 'Boule de suif', *Boule de suif et autres contes normands*, ed. M.-C. Bancquart (Éditions Garnier Frères, 1971), p. 43: 'Et Boule de suif pleurait toujours; et parfois un sanglot, qu'elle n'avait pu retenir, passait, entre deux couplets, dans les ténèbres.'

5 – James Payn (1830–98), novelist and miscellaneous writer; he was a friend of Leslie Stephen whom he succeeded as editor of the *Cornhill*, 1883–96.

6 – VW typed 'kate'.

APPENDIX III

The Essays of Augustine Birrell

The following review in *L&L*, July 1930, (*Kp4* C323), varies too considerably from the *Yale Review* version printed above as 'Augustine Birrell' for its substantive difference to be sensibly accounted for other than producing it in its entirety. See Editorial Note, p. xxiii. The issue also contained: 'Dorothy Osborne' by F. L. Lucas, and 'Nobody Loves Me' by D. H. Lawrence. A French translation by Jeanne Fournier-Pargoire of this version, (*Kp4* D57), entitled 'Les Essais d'Augustin Birrell', appeared in *Le Figaro* on 28–9 August 1930.

'But it is not bedtime,' a lady was heard to protest the other night. When assured that the clock had already struck twelve, she murmured that the clock might say what it liked, but that she must finish her book. And what was her book? It was a book by Mr Birrell. In fact, our friend had strewn the floor – like the learned pig in the picture[1] – with three robust red volumes containing The Collected Essays and Addresses of Augustine Birrell. It was these that she was engaged in sampling; it was these that kept her from her bed when the chimes of midnight were ringing and the voice of duty called.

Such being the truth and nothing more than the truth, it may be worth while to attempt to justify her defiance of discipline; to try to discover what are the qualities that make us slip from the end of one essay by Mr Birrell to the beginning of another, and so on through page after page when not only is the hour late, but when, to tell the truth, more serious and more learned volumes are shut with a snap on the stroke of eleven. In those words, perhaps, some glimpse of the reason sought for is to be found. One reads Mr Birrell for pleasure. Nobody has ever, in the mercantile sense of the term, read Mr Birrell for profit. It seems doubtful whether tutors bent on steering young men into the safe pasturage of scholarships and fellowships have ever counselled them to commit *Obiter Dicta* to memory. There is very little talk in Mr Birrell's pages of schools and influences, and origins and developments, and how one style grew out of another; no new theory of poetry is advanced, no key warranted to unlock all the doors of poetry is struck out. And since Nature has so contrived it that we only feel highly virtuous when we are also feeling slightly uncomfortable, there has been a note of apology in the tones of Mr Birrell's admirers as if to be found reading *Obiter Dicta* or *Res Judicatae* or *Men, Women and Books* was to be caught drinking champagne in the middle of the morning – a proceeding too pleasant to be right. If, on the other hand, one has muddled one's wits for an hour by the clock over some philosophical treatise, and come to feel that all Shakespeare is a matter of mathematics, then very justly one bruits the fact abroad, claims the esteem of one's friends, and leaves the book lying about with a marker stuck in the middle.

So, then, Mr Birrell is no philosophical critic. But once that is said we have to explain why it is that one feels, nevertheless, no lack of substance in his pages – they are not airy flimsy gossip – they are not dainties made to serve up with the *soufflé* at luncheon parties. They have, on the contrary, a bluffness, a toughness, even a grittiness about them which makes one suspect that if it be true that Mr Birrell has not mined deeply in the darker galleries of thought, he has, it may be, done a day's work in the open air. There is something of the man of action in his style. He comes in with his hair slightly rumpled and a splash of mud on his boots. If we turn to the first pages of the collected edition, we shall find our surmise confirmed. 'I became an author', he writes, 'quite by accident. I had never dreamt of such a thing. Some time in 1883, while pursuing in Lincoln's Inn, after a dimmish but not wholly unremunerative fashion, the now decayed profession of an equity draughtsman and conveyancer, it occurred to me' – that he might, perhaps, print certain manuscripts which had been read aloud in friendly coteries and put back in the desk. This he did, and the little book – it was the famous *Obiter Dicta* – had an instant and remarkable success. But though when he had found his way into print he never lost it again, he yet went on, as everybody knows, to pursue the law, to fight cases, to win seats, to sit in Parliament, to enter the Cabinet, to rule Ireland, and so to become, in course of time, the Right Honourable Augustine Birrell of varied and happy fame.

Thus the life of letters and the life of action were lived simultaneously, and there can be no doubt that the politician influenced the author, and that the author influenced the politician. With the politician we have no concern: it is the author only who comes within our scope. But it is plain that the author gained something of great value from his partnership with the man of affairs. In the first place he gained an unprofessional air, a holiday spirit. To sit down and write an essay was, it seemed, a treat that Mr Birrell had promised himself, not a duty that had to be got through. A zest clings to the performance. He would have been, one feels, as much put out at missing a day's writing as most people are annoyed at losing a day's sport. But the advantage of the connection between the man of action and the man of letters goes deeper than that. The substance of Mr Birrell's essays, the point of view that collects them and makes them, however disconnected in subject, of one spiritual texture, is the result of knowing the world and of passing judgement upon human life. It is the moral sense, not the literary, that makes a unity of these scattered papers. We know, as we look back, what men Mr Birrell has liked, rather than what books he has admired. And since the moral sense has gone abroad and taken the air, whether the sun shone or the rain poured, it is a healthy and active moral sense, genial and shrewd, without a trace of that sour and leathery constitution which afflicts the moral sense of those who live indoors passing judgement upon their fellows from the seclusion of a library. He has rubbed up with men and women in daily life; the incessant friction of affairs has kept him brisk; and when, therefore, he goes amongst the dead he goes with his sympathy and shrewdness as much on the alert as if he were meeting his friends at dinner, or had some point of business to settle with men of diverse character and pronounced opinion. There is not a trace of the pedagogue or of the dictator about him. And it is this elastic and humane quality that has kept his essays – some were written in the remote 'eighties – so much fresher than the mass of their contemporaries. For it is no uncommon experience to be pulled up in the middle of the brilliant and authoritative essay by a great Victorian – a Thackeray, a Carlyle, a Matthew Arnold – by some harsh and, as it seems to us, merely trivial and conventional judgement passed in a fit of the spleen upon the character or conduct of some great man. Thackeray's judgement upon Sterne, Carlyle's upon Lamb, Matthew Arnold's on Shelley, throw far more light upon the Victorian critics than upon their victims. We see in a flash how the critics of those days sat surrounded, for all their vigour, by keepsakes in dark rooms with draped mantelpieces; how much that we talk of openly was wrapped up in brown paper and hidden away behind plush curtains. But when we read Mr Birrell it is strange how seldom he speaks as an elder; how seldom we are reminded of Victorian prejudices and limitations. And this is due very largely to his robust powers of enjoyment. If there is one quality that alienates us more than another from the Victorians, it is their censorious habit of mind; their moral righteousness; their preference for pain to pleasure; for work to play. They had but to discover that Lamb drank, that Shelley was immoral, that Sterne, though a married man, was capable of flirting with a girl, and their hands fly up in dismay. We, they insinuate, could never have behaved like that. From this sin Mr Birrell is free – astonishingly so, if we remember, what we have already said, that his chief concern is with character and not with art. He summons up man after man, woman after woman, the big, the small, the wise, the foolish, and yet in passing judgement his voice never loses its cordiality, his temper is almost consistently unruffled. Even if, as will happen, a pretentious fool comes across him, he buffets his victim so genially across the stage that even that great goose, Hannah More herself, must have taken the process in good part. For this, again, credit must be given to politics. Life in the House of Commons, as Mr Birrell says, makes it difficult to maintain aloofness, 'You hob-nob at luncheon, you grumble together over your dinner, you lament the spread of football clubs and brass bands in your constituencies.' And so, what with lunching here and dining there, it has been very difficult for Mr Birrell to pull a long face over human failings, if at least they are such as proceed from good fellowship or hot-bloodedness, or a warm appreciation of the pleasures of life. It is the prigs and the censors and the timid water-drinkers whom he wholeheartedly despises, and he can be trusted to trounce them much to our delectation whenever they raise their voices to deplore Lamb's drunkenness or the sinful extravagance of Sir Walter Scott.

Yet, to be honest, it is somewhere about this point that we become aware of divergence. We begin to catch now and again a note of irritation in his voice, to hear some echoes of the sonorous Victorian trumpet. His love of charity and good sense and good temper lead him on little by little to declaim not only against their opposites, but against those whom he takes to be their allies – speculation and introspection, and all those other vices of the new age which he fears will lead to the clouding of the clear stream of English literature and the paralysis of healthy human activity. Already, early in the 'eighties, he had scented the coming of change. He complained that 'The ruddy qualities of delightfulness, of pleasantness, are all "sicklied o'er with the pale cast of thought". The varied elements of life . . . seem to be fading from literature.' Indeed, even in the 'eighties things had come to such a pass that he was about to make up his mind 'to look for no more Sir Walters, no more Thackerays, no more Dickenses. The stories have all been told. Plots are exploded. Incident is over', when, miraculously, *Treasure Island* appeared, and the honour of English literature was saved.

Thus, for all his tolerance and catholicity, Mr Birrell, it would appear, has his notion of what literature should be, and the fact that he eschews æsthetic criticism by no means implies that he has not a code of his own, and a will of his own, and a taste of his own, so that, though one seldom finds him splitting hairs, or sifting phrases, one does find as time goes on that there are whole tracts of literature, and we make bold to say, of very good literature at that, which he very surprisingly and completely ignores. He has nothing to say about the great Russians or the great Frenchmen. His essays, though they embrace the years between 1880 and 1930, make no mention of Meredith or Henry James or Hardy or Conrad. For all he tells us to the contrary, one might suppose that English literature, in some terrific catastrophe, had fallen over a precipice about the year 1900, and lay in fragments not worth picking up and examining on the stones beneath. That, perhaps, is the disadvantage of treating books as if they might at any moment turn into people. One detects in them qualities that are distasteful to one in real life – gloom, self-analysis, morbidity, sexual aberration – and because such a character would nauseate one at a dinner party, one has nothing to say about a book, the fruit of a corrupt society and of an introspective temperament, called *La Recherche du Temps Perdu*. About this Mr Birrell is perfectly plain spoken. 'We want Lambs,' he writes, 'not Coleridges. The verdict to be striven for is not "Well guessed" but "Well done".' And so with a great sweep of his arm he throws into the wastepaper basket such trifles as *The Egoist*, and *The Wings of a Dove*, *The Return of the Native*, *The Possessed*, and *Lord Jim*. That done, he heaves a sigh of relief and returns to the past; to his Borrow, his Lamb, and his Scott.

Thus we must accept the fact that Mr Birrell will neither illumine the present nor acknowledge the future, save as a disagreeable necessity which it is the part of a wise man not to anticipate. But once that fact is faced – and it need not surprise us, seeing that a politician is in partnership with a writer – there still remain three fine volumes, and if another of autobiography could be added nothing would please us more, of witty, varied and most entertaining criticism. Let us for a moment dwell upon the quality which kept our friend so unrepentantly out of bed – the charm, the seductiveness of Mr Birrell's writing. It is just and right so to pause, for it is, perhaps by this quality rather than any other, that the books are destined to endure. Yet how are we to define the word that is so easily and sometimes so condescendingly pronounced? 'It is not easy to define charm which is not a catalogue of qualities but a mixture.' So Mr Birrell says himself; and there is much in the saying that applies to him. Open Mr Birrell where you will, and there is this mixture in operation; there is this blending of many often mutually destructive gifts in one effervescence – irony and feeling; sound sense and fantasy; caustic humour and sunny good temper. Hence the iridescence and sparkle and varied movement of his prose. It never forms into one smooth wave that comes crashing down upon our heads: it is forever rippling and dancing, giving and withholding, like a breeze-stirred lake. And when this is said we have also said by implication that Mr Birrell is a born writer – not one of our great writers, certainly not one of our professional writers, but one of those writers who spring as naturally from our literature as the dog-rose from the hedge, and scent it with as true a fragrance. How lightly and easily he casts the line of his sentence! How the images come flocking to his pen, and how pleasant and sometimes more than pleasant they are to the ear! 'So obviously genuine, so real, though so quiet, was his pleasure in our English lanes and dells,' he wrote of Matthew Arnold, 'that it is still difficult to realize *that his feet can no longer stir the cowslips or his ear hear the cuckoo's parting cry*'[2] – but to underline what is so natural is to spoil it. And then beneath the wit and the sparkle there lies, not dormant by any means, but never obtruded, something pungent as the smell of good tobacco and as pervasive – that profound love of books which some good critics have lacked, perhaps, but would be all the better critics for possessing. 'No man of letters knew letters better than he. He knew literature in all its branches – he had read books, he had written books, he had sold books, he had bought books, and he had borrowed them. . . . He loved a catalogue; he delighted in an index. . . .' What Mr Birrell says of Johnson we might say of Mr Birrell. Everything about a book smells sweet in his nostrils, from the leather of the binding to the print upon the page.

So, then, if one seeks an excuse for reading Mr Birrell – and pleasure is still a little suspect – it is that he makes books seem lovable objects and reading an entrancing pursuit. Literature, when he writes of it, ceases to be an art and a mystery, and becomes instead a vast and varied assembly of all sorts of interesting people. Books turn into men and women, and men and women turn into books. There are Johnson and Scott, and George Eliot and Lamb; there are also Miss Hannah More and Arthur Young, and Arthur Young's little Bobbin. Some of the books are very rare and some of the people are very queer. There are many theological volumes among them and a good many lawyers. Then suddenly Mr Browning or Mr Matthew Arnold appears in the flesh, or 'Keep your eyes open,' says Mr Birrell's father, 'for the author of the *Wonder Book* will pass us in a moment,'[3] and behold, we see Hawthorne himself through the eyes of little Augustine Birrell in a street in Liverpool seventy years ago. Whether they are alive or dead, whether they are books or people, it is a splendid entertainment, call it what you will. To have created so varied a prospect, to have brought together out of the dimness so many shapes, the queer and the hunchbacked as well as the stately and the splendid, to have led us up to the great writers in a mood of warmth and happy expectation yet critically too, and by no means ready to tolerate fustian or humbug – that is a great task to have accomplished. It tempts us, indeed, to take a liberty with one of Mr Birrell's sentences without asking his permission. 'Even that most extraordinary compound, the rising generation of readers, whose taste in literature is as erratic as it is pronounced, read their Lamb', says Mr Birrell, and here we interpose 'read their Birrell', and then go on in concert 'with laughter and with love'.

1 – For more information about the learned pig and an illustration of 1787 for Philip Astley's Circus, showing a ringmaster with a pig choosing the letter 'A' from a pile of alphabet cards, see *VWB*, no. 26 (September 2007), pp. 42–4. VW also mentioned the 'learned pig' in *I VW Letters*, no. 263, [end March 1906], and *III VW Letters*, no. 1626, 29 March 1926.

2 – *The Collected Essays & Addresses of the Rt. Hon. Augustine Birrell, 1880–1920* (3 vols, J. M. Dent, 1922), 'Matthew Arnold' (1892), vol. ii, p. 196 (emphasis VW's).

3 – Birrell, *Et Cetera: A Collection* (Chatto and Windus, 1930), 'Nathaniel Hawthorne' (1928), p. 199; *A Wonder Book for Girls and Boys* (1852). Hawthorne (1804–64) was United States Consul in Liverpool, 1853–7.

APPENDIX IV

The Women's Co-operative Guild

This article, signed L. S. Woolf, appeared in *Jus Suffragii: Monthly Organ of the International Woman Suffrage Alliance*, vol. x, no. 12 (1 September 1916), 177. There are a number of points in common with VW's 'Memories of a Working Women's Guild' and 'Introductory Letter to Margaret Llewelyn Davies' above. Sybil Oldfield notes: 'It is curious that . . . Margaret included this article in her Commonplace Book but inserted Virginia's name as its author over Leonard's. It is difficult to believe that Leonard would ever have put his name to anything he had not himself written, but possibly Margaret recognized one or two turns of phrase as Virginia's. Both Leonard and Virginia had attended the London Congress in 1916' ('Margaret Llewelyn Davies and Leonard Woolf', *Women in the Milieu of Leonard and Virginia Woolf: Peace, Politics, and Education*, ed. Wayne K. Chapman and Janet M. Manson [Pace University Press, 1998], p. 30, n. 34). This may account (*pace Kp4 Cb15*) for the postscript to Davies's undated letter in which she wrote: 'Virginia *has* written charmingly about our Congress in the Suff. Mag.' (MHP, A, letter to LW).

The Annual Congress of the Women's Co-operative Guild met the other day in a building not a stone's throw from the Houses of Parliament, and many points of likeness between the two assemblies were bound to occur to one. The women, like the men, come from all parts of England; each is the representative of a certain group of human beings; both bodies are met to deliberate upon matters of public interest; and of the two, we imagine, the woman is almost prouder of the charge entrusted to her. You will often be told by a delegate that she looks forward to Congress more than to any event in the whole year. The eagerness, the interest, the vitality of these working women overflowed even into the busy Westminster street. There was no need for asking one's way to the Central Hall. Women seemed to be making straight from all points of the compass to the door, and gathering in little knots on the pavement for a final interchange of views before taking their seats inside. There was no mistaking them: there is something in the look of a member of the Women's Guild by which you may know her, something homely, competent, and genuine, as if her lot had always called for courage and initiative, and she had never known, as one of the speakers at the Congress put it, much pleasure, treasure or leisure.

Inside the hall these impressions were confirmed and solemnised, for no one, however ignorant of all that the Women's Guild has done, could fail to be moved by the sight of this vast congregation of women. It was impressive far more than most assemblies of middle-class people are impressive, because the delegates seemed met for business. The hall, it is true, was hung with their banners, but otherwise there was neither decoration nor paraphernalia, and of ceremony only as much as was necessary for the bare conduct of business. The President raised her hand, and instantly the tumult of talk and laughter was stilled. Certainly in the prompt and sensible and orderly conduct of their business this assembly of 800 working women could have given lessons to that older and more pompous assembly across the road. One speaker after another stepped out from her place on the floor, and, turning her back upon the President and platform, addressed her fellow-Guildswomen in a speech which was limited to a few minutes by the clock. If one happened to be a member of the middle classes with a seat on the platform, there was something in this little proceeding symbolical of the whole Congress. It seemed as if the working-women of England were gathered together and become articulate. Working-women were addressing working-women about the questions that interest them, and not to have shared their experiences seemed for the first time perhaps to set a woman, or even a man, apart in a way that was curiously humiliating. Certainly, no middle-class woman could speak with anything like the knowledge and conviction with which these women spoke upon one question after another. They demanded that Maternity Committees, on which working-women organisations should be adequately represented, should be made compulsory; they demanded that a municipal service of trained midwives should be instituted; that day nurseries should be established for the children of mothers who were compelled to go out to work. All these questions touched them more nearly than it is possible for a well-to-do woman to conceive. They spoke with conviction, singularly clearly and fluently, and with an absence of rhetoric which increased the air of democratic simplicity of the meeting. It seemed as if every woman who mounted the little flight of steps had something which she genuinely felt and wanted to say as forcibly as she could; and the audience listened, pencil in hand very often, as though in their eagerness they were actually helping her to get at the meaning. When she had done, the pencils were set to work, and here and there you could see delegates jumping up in their keenness to carry on the discussion. The most eloquent of orators would not have disdained the applause which some simple statement of fact called forth, or the rapture of laughter which seized the audience when one speaker imitated the mincing manner of a lady visitor who had required her to 'wash up the pots.'

It was laughter, however; not bitterness or indignation. The Congress, despite its eagerness and quickness in taking points, gave one the impression that it was a very broad-minded and tolerant assembly. 'We ought not to be hard on the ladies,' one of the delegates observed, and this largeness of view was shown in the discussion of questions of a less domestic and a more broadly political nature. They passed a resolution unanimously in favour of adult suffrage, and the discussion on this point was particularly good. Again, there was an overwhelming majority urging the Government to seek the earliest opportunity of promoting negotiations with the object of securing a just and lasting peace, and another overwhelming majority against the adoption of conscription by this country. Whatever the question was, it seemed at the hands of this democratic assembly to lose its academic dulness, and to become something with a very direct bearing upon life.

But when one left the Hall, and read the newspaper placards with their latest news from the trenches, and looked upon the immense pile of the Houses of Parliament, one realised with a shock that all of this force of women's experience and brain power was being allowed to waste itself upon the air. They come, pass their resolutions, and go away again, and what difference does it make to the gentlemen talking over there? Without votes they are without a weapon by which they can ensure that they shall be listened to and their knowledge made use of. For days after the Congress the visitor will be haunted by the sense of the lop-sidedness of the world, in which trivial things and trivial people are given the first place, and things and people of enormous importance find no place at all.

APPENDIX V

Speech to the London and National Society for Women's Service

This is a clean text of VW's speech of 21 January 1931. A full transcription, to which I am indebted, of VW's untitled typescript, with her deletions and second and third thoughts, was published by the late Mitchell A. Leaska in *The Pargiters by Virginia Woolf: The Novel-Essay Portion of 'The Years'* (Hogarth Press, 1978), pp. xxvii–xliv. The typescript in the Berg (M 70) consists of twenty-five pages, the first two unnumbered and the remainder numbered 2–8, 8–10, 10–22 by VW. Editorial interventions, including one [?doubtful reading], are given in square brackets; the exceptions are the occasional quotation mark and apostrophes added for clarity's sake. Mistypings of words have usually been silently corrected, and spacing regularised. Single quotation marks are employed throughout. The footnotes are editorial, and indebted to Leaska and to *CDML*.

In 'A Woman's Notebook' column in the *N&A* on 31 January 1931, Vera Brittain reported: 'Two functions on the same day last week gave additional prominence to three women who in their diverse fashions are among the greatest of this generation. From the At Home arranged on the eve of her seventy-third birthday by Mrs. Sidney Webb, where several of the older guests recalled the Fabian-Socialist group described in the final chapter of "My Apprenticeship," I went on to a delicious entertainment provided for a large audience by Dame Ethel Smyth and Mrs. Virginia Woolf. This hilariously serious party was organized, incidentally, by the Junior Council of the London Society for Women's Service, that lively body of young professional women which includes Miss Amy Johnson, and somehow captures exciting visitors who will not so much as put their distinguished noses into the offices of other associations. Dame Ethel, whose superb humour gives the lie to the common belief that all women are heavy and conscientious speakers, told us that, having expressed in her diary at the age of nine the ambition "to be made a Peeress in my own right because of music," she accepted her D.B.E. with alacrity, "especially as it was all due to an absurd row in the Woking Golf Club." I was interested, in view of what I said on this page a fortnight ago about the poverty of women, to hear both Dame Ethel and Mrs. Woolf attribute their success largely to the possession of a private income, which enabled the one to take up a non-lucrative career, and the other to flout the displeasure of authors and editors by writing honest reviews. Women, Mrs. Woolf maintained, had succeeded better in literature than in other arts because paper was cheap and pens made no noise. I am delighted to record, from the internal evidence of a quotation in her speech, that Mrs. Woolf is a reader of this Notebook' (p. 571; and see n. 9 below).

VW recorded: 'The speech took place; L. I think slightly exacerbated: an interesting observation if a true one. Two hundred people; well dressed, keen, & often beautiful young women. Ethel in her blue kimono & wig. I by her side. Her speech rollicking & direct: mine too compressed & allusive. Never mind. Four people wish the speeches printed' (*IV VW Diary*, 23 January 1931). The following day she wrote to Ethel Smyth (1858–1944): 'About the speech – I dont think I shall print mine, as it stands, because as you doubtless perceived, with your supernatural apprehensiveness, it was clotted up, clogged, partly owing to the rush I was in – no time to comb out – partly because, the very last morning in my bath I had a sudden influx of ideas, which I want to develop later, perhaps in a small book, about the size of a Room – But this must wait – Lord – if only I could finish the Waves!' (*IV VW Letters*, no. 2314). In February 1933 VW wrote: 'I have it at the back of my mind that I will re-write a paper on professions that I read a year or two ago' (uncollected letter quoted by Marion Shaw in her Preface to Winifred Holtby, *Virginia Woolf: A Critical Memoir* [1932; Continuum, 2007], p. xvii). VW's revision of the speech, 'Professions for Women', was published posthumously in *DoM*: see *VI VW Essays*, Appendix.

When your Secretary[1] invited me to come here, and I so rashly agreed, she told me that your Society is concerned with the employment of women, and she suggested that I might perhaps tell you something about my own professional experiences. Well of course I am a woman; and I am employed but I wonder what professional experiences I have had?

None at any rate to compare with those of Dame Ethel Smyth. After what she has told us – after what she has not told us but we can guess for ourselves – I feel rather like an idle and frivolous pleasure boat lolloping along in the wake of an ironclad. She is of the race of pioneers, of path makers. She has gone before and felled trees and blasted rocks and thus made a way for those who come after her. Thus we honour her not only as a musician and as a writer – and when I read her books I always feel inclined to burn my own pen and take to music – for if she can toss off a masterpiece in my art without any training why should not I toss off a symphony or two without knowing a crotchet from a quaver? – we honour her not merely as a musician and a writer, but also as the blaster of rocks and the maker of bridges. It seems sometimes a pity that a woman who only wished to write music should have been forced also to make bridges, but that was part of her job and she did it.

But in my own profession – literature – the way was cut long ago. I have no doubt that I owe a great [deal] to some mute and inglorious Ethel Smyth. I have no doubt that there were women two hundred years ago who drew upon themselves hostility and ridicule in order that it might not be wicked or ridiculous for women nowadays to write books. But when I came to hold a pen there were very few obstacles of that sort in my way. Writing was a reputable, a harmless accomplishment. The family peace was not broken by the scratching of a pen. No great demand was made upon the family purse. And pens and paper are cheap. For ten and sixpence one can buy enough paper to write – if one has a mind – all the tragedies of Shakespeare. Pianos, models, studios, north lights, masters and mistresses are not needed. Berlin, Paris, Vienna and all the rest of it are not needed. One has only got to sit down and write. The cheapness of writing materials is of course the reason why women have succeeded as writers before they succeeded as painters or musicians.

Thus you see my story is compared with Dame Ethel's a very tame one. You have only got to figure to yourselves a girl sitting and writing in a bed-room with a pen in her hand, a girl who had plenty of pens and paper at [her] command. Then it occurred to her to do what again only costs a penny stamp – to slip an article into a pillar-box to a newspaper; and to suggest to the editor of that newspaper that she might be allowed to try her hand at reviewing a novel. He replied that Mrs Humphry Ward[2] had just written her fifty-sixth masterpiece and that it would not matter a straw to her or anybody else if an uneducated and probably incompetent young woman said what she thought of it. Hence I became a reviewer. Hence, on the first day of the following month I received a cheque for one pound seven and sixpence; and it will show you how little I deserve to be called a professional woman, or a working woman – it will show you how very little I know of life and its reality when I confess that instead of spending the money on bread and butter, on shoes and stockings, I went out – flown with glory – and bought a cat – a beautiful cat, a Persian cat; a cat which being of the male sex soon involved me in rows with all the neighbours.

What could be easier, simpler and [in] its way more delightful than to review Mrs Humphry Ward's novels and to buy Persian cats with the proceeds? But after all the story is not quite as simple as all that. There is a villain in the piece. That villain was not, I grieve to say, our old friend the other sex – or at least only indirectly. The villain of my story was a woman, and I propose to call her, after a figure in a well known poem, the Angel in the House.[3] You who come of a younger and happier generation may not have heard of the Angel in the House. Therefore I will describe her. She was intensely sympathetic. She was immensely charming. She was utterly unselfish. She excelled in the difficult arts of family life. She soothed, conciliated, sacrificed herself, took the hash if there was only chicken enough for one, and in short was so constituted that she never had a wish or a mind of her own but preferred to sympathise with the wishes and minds of others. Above all – I hope I need not say it – she was pure. There were a great many things that one could not say without bringing a blush to her cheek. Almost every respectable Victorian house had its angel. And when I came to write – though I was not an angel myself – I had five hundred a year and angels never have a penny – there was an Angel in the house with me. The shadow of her wings fell upon the page; I heard the rustling of her skirts in the room. Now this creature – it was one of her most annoying characteristics – never had any real existence. She had – what is much more difficult to deal with – an ideal existence, a fictitious existence. She was a dream, a phantom – a kind of mirage like the pools and the palm trees which nature places in the desert to lure the caravan across. The angel in the house was the ideal of womanhood created by the imaginations of men and women at a certain stage of their pilgrimage to lure them across a very dusty stretch of the journey. They agreed to accept this ideal, because for reasons I cannot now go into – they have to do with the British Empire, our colonies, Queen Victoria, Lord Tennyson, the growth of the middle class and so on – a real relationship between men and women was then unattainable. If you disbelieve me, let me quote you this scrap of dialogue between men and women in the age of Victoria. Tennyson speaks first. He addresses his ideal of woman-hood – She, he says,

> On tiptoe seemed to touch upon a sphere
> Too gross to tread, and all male minds perforce
> Swayed to her from their orbits as they moved

Then Lowell said

> It is not woman leaves us to our night
> But our brute earth that glories from her sun.

To which Christina Rossetti in duty bound replied,

> Woman was made for man's delight
> Charm O woman be not afraid;
> His shadow by day, his moon by night
> Woman was made.[4]

Those words seem to me to imply a relationship between men and women that was both false and disagreeable.

At any rate when I came to write reviews the Angel in the House stole behind me and said 'You have got yourself into a very queer position. You are young and unmarried. But you are writing for a paper owned by men, edited by men; you are even reviewing a book that has been written by a man – one Mr Arnold Bennett[5] – therefore whatever you say let it be pleasing to men. Be sympathetic; be tender; flatter; use all the arts and wiles which I, Heaven help me, have used till I am sick of the whole thing (the Angel did sometimes speak like this to women when she was alone) but believe me it is absolutely necessary. Never disturb them with the idea that you have a mind of your own. And above all be pure.' With that she made as if to guide my pen.

I now record the one act for which I take some credit – though the credit belongs rather to my income than to me – if one has five hundred a year there is no need to tell lies and it is much more amusing to tell the truth – I turned upon that Angel and caught her by the throat. I did my best to kill her. My excuse – if I were to be had up in a law court and charged with murder – would be that I acted in self defence.

If I had not killed her, she would have killed me – as a writer. That woman – but she was not a woman, she was an Angel – has more blood on her hands than all the murderers who have ever been hanged. Writer after writer, painter after painter and musicians I dare say too she has strangled and killed. One is always meeting their corpses laid out in biographies. But she has a special hatred for writers and with good reason. Her province, you see, is the House. Painters and musicians – it is one of their chief assets – have very little to do with the house. When Vanessa Bell paints a picture it is as often as not a picture of red apples on a plate. That's all right, says the Angel. It may be a pity to waste your time painting; but if you must paint there is no harm in apples. Ethel Smyth writes a Mass.[6] It's a pity, says the Angel. But music doesn't much matter – music is only sound after all – no nasty meaning is attached to it. And so she lets them be.

But writing is a very different matter – you cannot even review a novel without expressing an opinion upon charac[ter,] morality, human relations – all matters of vital importance in the conduct of the house, and thus coming directly under the notice of its Angel. Young and ignorant and unmarried as I was, I did have to say for example that I thought that Mr Carlyle ought to have had a child and that Mrs Carlyle ought to have written a novel; I did have to say that there was a good deal more to be said for Fanny Brawne as a lover than for Keats; I did have to [say] that it did not matter a straw whether George Eliot – Mrs Lewes – wore a wedding ring or not.[7] In short I was forced to attack many of the most sacred objects in the house and that the Angel did not like. Therefore I did my best to kill her. Whenever I felt the shadow of her wings or the radiance of her halo upon the page I took up the inkpot and flung it at her. But though I flatter myself that I did kill her in the end, the struggle was severe; it took up much time that had better have been spent in learning Greek grammar or in roaming the world in search of adventures. Well, that is one professional experience – killing the Angel in the House.

And now when the Angel is dead, what remains? You may think that what remains is something quite simple and common enough – a young woman. Having rid herself of falsehood, so we might put it, she has now only to be herself and write. But what is 'herself'? I mean, what is a woman? I assure you, I don't know; I do not believe that you know; I do not believe that anybody can know until she has expressed herself in all the arts and professions open to human skill. What a woman is [is] a discovery which you here are in process of making – a piece of very important knowledge which we shall owe to you. But I am limited to my own experience, which as I began by saying is narrow. All I can tell you is that I discovered when I came to write that a woman – it sounds so simple, but I should be ashamed to tell you how long it took me to realise this for myself – is not a man. Her experience is not the same. Her traditions are different. Her values, both in art and in life are her own.

To show you how this difference works out in my own profession, I will take a practical example – one is provided, as it happens, by the current number of the Nation. If you will look at that number, you will find Mr Keynes there reviews a book – a history of Clare College Cambridge. Mr Keynes begins by saying that this book cost it is rumoured six thousand pounds to produce. He goes on to say that Clare is a very ancient and famous college; he dwells upon the beauty of its buildings, the fame of its butler, and the excellence of its claret. And he ends with an eloquent description of this book and all that it implies which I will read you. 'Clothed in the finest dress of paper and black buckram, armed with intellect and learning, adorned with curiosity and fancy, there is here embodied the Sentiment of one of those of the ancient foundations of the country which have outlived the centuries with least loss of the past and least sacrifice of the present, a college. It is a gracious sight – worthy, but difficult of imitation.' That is the way that Mr Keynes reviews that book.[8]

Had the Editor of the Nation sent it to me, I should have been compelled by that different sense of values to write in a very different strain.

O you old humbugs, I should have begun. O you who have enjoyed for all these centuries comfort and prosperity – O you who profess devotion to the lady of Clare and love for the Sentiment of colleges, would it not be better to spend your six thousand pounds not upon a book, clothed in the finest dress of paper and buckram, but upon a girl, whose dress allowance is very meagre, and who tries to do her work, as you will read if you turn the very next page in the Nation, in one cold gloomy ground floor bedroom which faces due north and is overrun with mice.[9] A college I entirely agree with Mr Keynes is a gracious sight; worthy but difficult of imitation. If the members of Clare college handed over the six thousand pounds that they have spent upon a book to Girton, some of the difficulties of imitation would be removed, and what is more I am sure that the lady of Clare would rise from her grave and say Gentlemen you have done my will honour.

That is more or less how I should be forced to write that review, if the editor had sent me the book; but I doubt that that review would be printed; for I am a woman. My sense of values would differ too much I am afraid from that of a very celebrated economist. Now that difference is bound to show itself in all kinds of ways. And you are bound to find when you come to practise your innumerable professions that your difference of outlook is bringing you to loggerheads with some respected chiefs of your professio[ns.] But one of your most amusing and exciting experiences will be precisely on this account – that you will have to make your profession adapt itself to your needs, your sense of values, your common sense, your moral sense, your sense of what is due to humanity and reason. As a member of the general public, who sometimes has to employ lawyers, then architects, then builders, then doctors, stock brokers and so on – I can assure you that I think it is high time that these ancient and privileged professions came more in touch with human needs.

Well now, to go on with the tame story of my professional career. I suppose that the Persian cat which I bought out of the proceeds of my first review did not satisfy me. I grew ambitious. I desired not merely a cat but a motor car. You cannot afford a car on five hundred a year; but it is a strange fact that people will provide you with a motor car if you will tell them a story. That is one reason for writing novels. And then to imagine and to create would seem to be an easier, a simpler occupation than to reason and to criticise. Ignorance does not so much matter. I could let my heroes and heroines be born when they liked in a novel; but if I said in the Times or elsewhere that Shakespeare was born in May when he was born in April it roused a storm of indignation in every capital in Europe. Hence, along these natural avenues of greed and laziness I reached the next stage in my professional career – that is to say novel writing. Now your secretary asks me to tell you what experiences of a professional nature did I have as a novelist?

That is an extremely difficult question to answer. A novelist is not nearly so conscious; or so reasonable a person as a critic. Fiction is not nearly so conscious, or so reasonable an art as criticism. I do not wish you to infer from this that a novelist is in a perpetual state of inspiration. I mean rather that the novelist is in a perpetual state of lethargy. It is his desire to be as unconscious as possible. He wants life to proceed with the utmost quiet and regularity. He wants to see the same faces, to read the same books, to do the same things day after day and month after month so that nothing may break the illusion; that nothing may disturb the flow, that nothing may interrupt the mysterious nosings about, feelings round, darts and dashes and sudden discoveries of that very shy and illusive fish the imagination.

Therefore I find it very difficult to describe to you what happens to a novelist, what are the incidents of her professional career. Outwardly I can perhaps sketch her for you. That ignorant girl who used to sit scribbling reviews and now and again getting up to shy an inkpot at an angel, now spent her time mooning. She mooned and mooned. I figure her really in an attitude of contemplation, like a fisherwoman, sitting on the bank of a lake with her fishing rod held over its water. She was not thinking; she was not reasoning; she was not constructing a plot; she was letting her imagination down into the depths of her consciousness while she sat above holding on by a thin but quite necessary thread of reason. She was letting her imagination feed unfettered upon every crumb of her experience; she was letting her imagination sweep unchecked round every rock and cranny of the world that lies submerged in our unconscious being.

Then suddenly this fisherwoman gave a cry of dismay. What had happened? The line had suddenly slackened; her imagination had floated limply and dully and lifelessly upon the surface. The reason hauled the imagination on shore and said What on earth is the matter with you? And the imagination began pulling on its stockings and replied, rather tartly and disagreeably; its all your fault. You should have given me more experience to go on. I cant do the whole work for myself.

And I – the reason – had to reply: Many forms of experience are lacking to me because I am a woman.

Well, that is one experience – quite a common one if you are a woman – of the novelist's profession.

But there is another. The novelist is sitting on the shores of the lake, holding the little line of reason in her hands when suddenly there is a violent jerk; she feels the line race through her fingers. The imagination has rushed away; it has taken to the depths; it has sunk – heaven knows where – into what dark pool of extraordinary experience. The reason has to cry 'Stop!' The novelist has to pull on the line and haul the imagination to the surface. The imagination comes to the top in a state of fury.

'Good heavens' she cries – 'how dare you interfere with me! How dare you pull me out with your wretched little fishing line?' And I – that is the reason – have to reply, 'My dear you were going altogether too far. Men would be shocked.' Calm yourself, I say, as she sits panting on the bank – panting with rage and disappointment. We have only got to wait fifty years or so. In fifty years I shall be able to use all this very queer knowledge that you are ready to bring me. But not now. You see I go on, trying to calm her, I cannot make use of what you tell me – about women's bodies for instance – their passions – and so on, because the conventions are still very strong. If I were to overcome the conventions I should need the courage of a hero, and I am not a hero. I doubt that a writer can be a hero. I doubt that a hero can be a writer. And then I point out to her that the moment I become heroic, I become shrill and hard and positive – in short I cease to be a writer [but] become a preacher; and that, I say, is extremely unpleasant for you, poor imagination. And I go on to tell her that even men, who can let their imaginations go much further than women can, because the convention allows men to be much more open in what they say than women – even men, I tell her, have to say Stop. Thackeray for instance.[10] And in our time, though things are better, still there are conventions, even for men; and if a man like Lawrence,[11] I tell her, runs against convention he injures his imagination terribly. She becomes shrivelled and distorted; and you would not like to become shrivelled and distorted, would you? I say. It is your nature to understand and to create.

Very well, says the imagination, dressing herself up again in her petticoat and skirts, we will wait. We will wait another fifty years. But it seems to me a pity.

This then is another incident, and quite a common incident in the career of a woman novelist. She has to say I will wait. I will wait until men have become so civilised that they are not shocked when a woman speaks the truth about her body. The future of fiction depends very much upon what extent men can be educated to stand free speech in women. But whether men can be civilised, what capacities lie dormant in them, how far their condition is the result of education or of nature, whether given a better environment the results might be such that women too can be artists lies on the lap of the Gods, no not upon the laps of the Gods, but upon your laps, upon the laps of professional women.

Here then I am really come to an end of my professional experiences – I have told you how I tried to murder the Angel in the House – I have recorded the little dialogue between the reason and the imagination, which sometimes breaks the peace of our solitary hours of contemplation. That these are very tame experiences I know. But as I explained to you, I have had two peculiarities which made it unnecessary for me to go through many of the experiences which fall to the lot of you who are pioneers – I had five hundred a year of my own, and my profession is the one profession which, owing to the cheapness of writing paper, and the fact that pens scarcely make any noise, women have practised for many years with some success. When people said to me 'What is the use of your trying to write?' I could say, truthfully, I write, not for use, but for pleasure. When they said, Women cannot write, I downed them with the sacred name of Sappho – a very difficult writer whom few people have read.

But for you it is very different. You who are now for the first time practising as barristers, architects, decorators, solicitors, – you have no Sappho, no Jane Austen[12] to fall back upon. You must be the Sappho and the Jane Austen of your profession. Therefore you will meet with much more ridicule than ever fell to my lot. And then, you have, I imagine, to make your livings – which I never did. And therefore you will meet with an opposition much sterner than any I could [have] had to face, because you are trying to make men pay you for work which no woman has ever done before [and] they have hitherto done themselves. Now I cannot delude myself into thinking that you have an easy task before you. You are bound I am afraid to meet with a great deal of derision and opposition. You will want all your strength and courage. And for this reason it is of the highest importance that you should not add to your burdens a very heavy and unnecessary burden, the burden of bitterness. If you are always comparing your lot with the lot of men, if you are always thinking how much easier it is for them to earn a living than for you – you will have an enemy within who is always sapping your strength and poisoning your happiness. Here I would beg of you, speaking from the very comfortable easy armchair position of a woman who need not earn her living, but can spend her time imagining how other people earn theirs – speaking as a novelist, I would ask you to use a novelist's prerogative – to use your imaginations and to try that [imagination?] as a specific against bitterness. Imagine what it is like to be a man. Put yourselves into his shoes for a moment. Now directly that you try to put your selves into the shoes of a man, I think you will find that those shoes change their size: they become very large. A delicious sense of weight and importance pervades you. You feel that you are a very respectable and responsible human on whose shoulders rests the burden of providing for that house and servants. This large and important and responsible person is being put by you into a very difficult position. Let us imagine how it appears to him. He has been out all day in the city earning his living, and he comes home at night, expecting repose and comfort, to find that his servants – the women servants – have taken possession of the house. He goes into the library – an august apartment which he is accustomed to have all to himself – and finds the kitchen maid curled up in the arm chair reading Plato.[13] He goes into the kitchen and there is the cook engaged in writing a Mass in B flat. He goes into the billiard room and finds the parlourmaid knocking up a fine break at the table. He goes into the bed room and there is the housemaid working out a mathematical problem. What is he to do? He has been accustomed for centuries to have that sumptuous mansion all to himself, to be master in his own house. Well of course his first instinct is to dismiss the whole crew. But he reflects that then he would have to do the work of the house himself, and he has not been trained to do it. – Nature has denied him certain quite essential gifts. He therefore says that these women servants may practise their silly little amusements in their spare time, but that if he finds them neglecting the sacred duties which nature has imposed upon them he will do something very dreadful indeed. But what can he do? It is difficult to say. It is extremely amusing to see. He can stand upon his dignity. He can appeal to precedent. He can say that nature intended servants to be servants, and that there is no getting over nature. He can make the most cutting and disagreeable remarks about housemaids playing the piano and scullerymaids reading Plato; he can turn them out of the library, lock the billiard room door, and put the key of the cellar in his pocket – because after all he pays the rent and the house is his property. But there is a spirit in the house not by any means an Angel – a very queer spirit – I don't know how to define it – it is the sort of spirit that is in Dame Ethel Smyth – you have only got to look at her and you will feel it for yourselves – and this spirit of adventure and daring it is impossible to lock up – or to lock out. Hence the man came home one day to find that although the servants had managed to keep the house going all the time – and that is really one of the most [blank space] they had yet contrived, by practising their silly little accomplishments, to have saved enough money to hire rooms of their own. Therefore they need not go on living in his house any more. That did place the man in a very awkward predicament.

His deepest instincts were outraged – and his most cherished traditions were flouted. He had thought that nature had meant women to be wives, mothers, housemaids, parlourmaids and cooks. Suddenly he discovers that nature – but he did not call it nature – he called it sin – had made them also, into the bargain, doctors, civil servants, meteorologists, dental surgeons, librarians, solicitors' clerks, agricultural workers, analytical chemists, investigators of industrial psychology, barristers at law, makers of scientific models, accountants, hospital dieticians, political organisers, store keepers, artists, horticultural instructors, publicity managers, architects, insurance representatives, dealers in antiques, bankers, actuaries, managers of house property, court dress makers, aero engineers, history instructors, company directors, organisers of peace crusades, newspaper representatives, technical officers in the royal airships works, – and so on.

That is the sort of position that you have put this man into, and it is an extremely difficult one. Remember what a tremendous tradition of mastery man has behind him – consider what prestige and power he has enjoyed. And reflect, as I think in all honesty you can, that there are men who have triumphed over all the difficulties of their very lopsided education, of their very specialised and arduous careers, men of generous and wide humanity, [of] civilisation, not only of education, men with whom a woman can live in perfect freedom, without any fear. Men too can be emancipated. Do not therefore be angry; be patient; be amused. It is a situation of extraordinary interest and amazing possibilities both for the present and for the future. You have earned your room; you have paid the rent for it. It is a little bare at present I agree. I suspect that the sofa turns into a bed; and the wash stand is covered with a check cloth by day to look as much like a table as possible. You picked up the carpet at the Caledonian market for half a crown or so on condition that you carried it home under your arm. And I convict you of eating poached eggs instead of mutton chops – because poached eggs are cheaper. But these things are your own – you have bought them with your own money. There, in the privacy of your own room, you can sit and write or paint, or compose music, design houses or aeroplanes – or whatever it is. There you must work, because you have your livings to earn. That is perhaps enough at the moment. But, then as Dame Ethel asks, what will be the next step? There will have to be one. And I predict that the next step will be a step upon the stair. You will hear somebody coming. You will open the door. And then – this at least is my guess – there will take place between you and some one else the most interesting, exciting, and important conversation that has ever been heard. But do not be alarmed; I am not going to talk about that now. My time is up.

1 – Philippa Strachey (1872–1968); see *IV VW Diary*, 20 January 1931.

2 – Although VW made reading notes on *Fenwick's Career* by Mrs Humphry [Mary Augusta] Ward (1851–1920), her published review has not been traced with certainty: see *I VW Essays*, Appendix II.

3 – Coventry Patmore (1823–96), *The Angel in the House* (first part published anonymously, 1854; subsequent parts, 1856, 1860 and 1862).

4 – Queen Victoria (1819–1901); Alfred, Lord Tennyson (1809–92), 'The Princess; a Medley', canto vii; James Russell Lowell (1819–91), 'Das Ewig-Weibliche'; Christina Rossetti (1830–94), 'A Helpmeet for Him'.

5 – Strictly speaking, the only book by Arnold Bennett (1867–1931) that VW reviewed was *Books and Persons* in 1917: see *II VW Essays*.

6 – Smyth's 'Mass in D' was written in 1891 and revised in 1925. In *Streaks of Life* (Longmans, Green, 1921), which VW reviewed (see 'Ethel Smyth', *III VW Essays*), Smyth wrote: 'be the worth of my music what it may, I shall never do anything better [than the Mass]! But if, even after one's own death, anyone thinks it worth producing, it will not have been written in vain' (p. 110). VW heard the Mass on 3 March 1934: see *IV VW Diary*.

7 – Thomas Carlyle (1795–1881); Jane Welsh Carlyle (1801–66); Fanny Brawne (1800–65); John Keats (1795–1821); George Eliot (1819–80); George Henry Lewes (1817–78).

8 – J. M. Keynes, 'Clare College', *N&A*, 17 January 1931, p. 513.

9 – Vera Brittain, 'A Woman's Notebook', *ibid.*, pp. 508–9: 'The poverty of the women's colleges bears hardest upon those who have to live out . . . When I lived out during my last year at Somerville, my one room was a cold, gloomy, ground-floor bedroom, which faced due north and was overrun with mice, but others in the same house fared even less enviably . . . Women undergraduates . . . need more space, more food, more comfort, more scholarships, more opportunities in more professions. To provide these things they require, above all, money. Virginia Woolf's little masterpiece, "A Room of One's Own," is the classic expression of this need' (p. 509). In *Three Guineas* (Hogarth Press, 1938, n. 18 to ch. i, pp. 272–3), VW cited Keynes's review, drew upon Brittain's account of her room and quoted her (anonymously) on the financial plight of Somerville college.

10 – William Makepeace Thackeray (1811–63).

11 – D. H. (David Herbert) Lawrence (1885–1930).

12 – Sappho (b. c. 612 BC); Jane Austen (1775–1817).

13 – Plato (428/7–348/7 BC).

APPENDIX VI

As a Light to Letters

This review in the *NYHT*, 26 July 1931, (*Kp4* C331), varies too considerably from the *Fortnightly Review* version printed above as 'Edmund Gosse'
for its substantive difference to be sensibly accounted for other than producing
it in its entirety. See Editorial Note, p. xxiii. Max Beerbohm's caricature of
'Max Beerbohm and Austin Dobson at the Board of Trade', taken from Evan
Charteris's *The Life and Letters of Sir Edmund Gosse* (facing p. 150), was
reproduced on the second page of VW's article.

When famous writers die it is remarkable how frequently they are
credited with one particular virtue – the virtue of kindness to the
young. Every newspaper article contained that eulogy upon Arnold
Bennett. And here is the same tribute paid to another writer who
differed in every possible way from Arnold Bennett – Sir Edmund
Gosse. He, too, it was said, was generous to the young. Of Bennett
it was certainly, although on some occasions rather obliquely, true.
He might, that is to say, have formed a very low opinion of a book;
he might have expressed that opinion bluntly and emphatically in
print; and yet if he met the writer he made it by his own candour
and simplicity perfectly easy for that unfortunate person to feel that
they both cared so much for the craft of letters that it was quite
possible to say, 'But Mr Bennett, you cannot possibly hate my books
more than I hate yours' – after which a frank discussion of fiction
and its nature was possible; and a very obscure writer was left with
the feeling that a very famous one was the most magnanimous of
men. That certainly is one way of being generous and not the worst.

But what would have happened if, taking advantage of Sir Edmund's generosity, one had said 'You cannot possibly hate my books, Sir Edmund, more than I hate yours'? Instant death would have been the only and the happiest solution of the situation. But nobody who had ever seen Sir Edmund even at a distance would have risked such folly. Bristling, brilliant, formal, yet uneasy, he radiated even across a room all the qualities that make younger writers draw in their horns. Magnanimous was not the adjective that sprang to the lips at the sight of him, nor is it one that frequently occurs on reading the life of him by Mr Charteris. He could be as touchy as a housemaid and as suspicious as a governess. He could smell out an offence where none was meant and hoard a grievance for years. He could quarrel permanently because a lamp wick was snuffed out too vigorously in his presence and an apology was not forthcoming. Hostile reviews threw him into paroxysms of rage and despair. His letters are full of phrases like 'Mr. Clement Shorter in terms of unexampled insolence speaks of me as "the so-called critic." . . . If that insolent notice in *The Times* is true . . . it is better I should know it. . . . I feel I shall never have the heart to write another sentence.' It seems possible that one severe review by Churton Collins gave him more pain than he suffered from any private or public sorrow in the course of seventy-nine years. All this must have made him the most prickly of companions and the young must have been possessed of greater tact and greater discretion than the young usually possess to reach the kindness that no doubt lay hid behind the thorns. For the great merit of the present life is that it does not attempt to conceal the fact that Sir Edmund was a complex character composed of many different strains. Plain virtue was no sure passport to his affection. He could disregard genius and ignore merit if they trod clumsily upon his toes. On the other hand, the House of Lords possessed a distinct glamour for him; the rigours of high society delighted him; and to see the words 'Marlborough Club' at the head of his note paper did, it seems, shed a certain lustre upon the page.

But these foibles, amusing and annoying as they are, become more interesting and less irritating when we learn that there lay behind them a very good cause. His upbringing was responsible. 'Far more than might be supposed of his conduct in life,' writes Mr Charteris, 'was due to unconscious protest against . . . the things which had darkened his childhood.' Readers of *Father and Son* know well what things those were – the narrowness[,] the ugliness of his upbringing; the almost insane religious mania of his father; the absence of culture[,] beauty, urbanity[,] graciousness – in fact, of all those elements in life which Edmund Gosse turned to as instinctively and needed as profoundly as a flower the sun. What could be more natural than that the flower, once transplanted, should turn, almost violently, the other way, should climb too high, should twine too lavishly, should – to drop these metaphors – order clothes in Savile Row and emerge from behind the form of Dr Fog uttering what appear at this distance of time rather excessive praises of the now little known Danish poet, Paludan-Müller?

Few people can have been pitchforked, as Mr Charteris calls it, into the world by a more violent propulsion than that which Gosse was given by the bleakness and bareness of his upbringing. It was no wonder that he overshot the mark, never quite got his equilibrium in society, which he loved, required to know the maiden names of married guests, and observed formalities punctiliously which are taken as a matter of course by those who have never lived in dread of the coming of the Lord, and have ordered their clothes in Savile Row for generations. But the impulse itself was generous and the tokens of kindling and expansion more admirable than ridiculous. The 'sensual sufficiency in life' delighted one who had been starved of it. Happiness formed the staple of what he would certainly not have called his creed. 'To feel so saturated with the love of things,' to enjoy life and 'suck it as a wasp drains a peach,' to 'roll the moments on one's tongue and keep the flavour of them,' above all to cherish friendship and exalt the ideal of friendship – such were the beliefs that his nature, long repressed, stretched out to, generously, naturally, spontaneously. And yet—

Those who are acquainted with Sir Edmund's lively portraits know what demure but devastating qualifications he would insinuate after those two small words 'and yet.' 'He possessed the truth and answered to the heavenly calling,' he wrote of Andrew Lang, 'and yet' . . . And yet, we echo, how much better Gosse would have written, how much more important a figure he would have been if only he had given freer rein to his impulses, if only his pagan and sensual joy had not been dashed by perpetual caution. The peculiarity which Mr Charteris notes in his walk 'curiously suggestive at once of eagerness and caution' runs through his life and qualifies his intelligence. It twinkles rather than glows; trips rather than strides. He hints, he qualifies, he insinuates, he suggests, but he never speaks out, for all the world as if some austere Plymouth brother were lying in wait to make him do penance for his audacity. Yet it seems possible, given the nature of his gifts, that if only he had possessed a greater boldness, had pushed his curiosity further, had incurred wrath instead of irritation, and complete confusion instead of some petty social tribulation he might have rivalled the great Boswell himself. When we read how young Edmund Gosse insinuated himself, under cover of Dr Fog, into the presence of an irascible poet and won the day by the adroitness of his flattery, we are reminded of the methods of Boswell in pursuit of Paoli or Voltaire or Johnson. Both men were irresistibly attracted by genius. Both had a medium-like power of drawing other people into the open. Both were astonishingly adept at reporting the talk and describing the appearance of their friends. But where Boswell is drawn headlong by the momentum of his hero and his own veneration beyond discretion, beyond vanity, beyond his sense of what people will say, down into the depths, Gosse is kept by his respect for decorum, by his decency and his timidity dipping and ducking, fingering and flattering upon the surface. Thus we never know his sitters intimately; we never plunge into the hidden parts of their minds or into the more profound regions of their hearts. But we know all that can be known by somebody who is always a little afraid of being found out.

But if Gosse's masterpiece and his portraits suffer from his innate regard for caution much of the fault must be laid upon his age. Even the most superficial student must be aware that in the nineteenth century literature had become, for one reason or another, a profession and an institution. It had its organisation, its functions, its emoluments and a host of people, not primarily writers, attached to its service. Among them Gosse, of course, was one of the most eminent. 'No public dinner where literature was involved,' writes Mr Charteris, 'was complete without Gosse to propose or to return thanks for the cause.' He welcomed strangers, addressed bodies, celebrated centenaries, presented prizes, and represented letters indefatigably and with unction. Then again some intellectual stir had risen in the nineties and ardent if uninstructed ladies wished to be enlightened. Here again Gosse was invaluable. By an odd irony while Churton Collins, his deadly foe, was lecturing in St James's Square, Gosse was serving up Matthew Arnold to 'some of the smartest women in London' in Bruton Street. After this, says Mr Charteris, he became 'a much more frequent guest in Mayfair' and his appetite for social life was whettened. Nothing would be more foolish than to sneer at a natural love of ceremony and society, and yet it seems possible that this concern with the ritual of literature, this scrupulous observance of the rites of society encouraged Edmund Gosse in his natural decorum. Friendship had been his ideal; and yet when one of his friends, Robert Ross, was involved in a famous scandal and had need of friends, Gosse could write 'I miss your charming company in which I have always delighted. . . . I would say to you, – be calm, be reasonable, turn for consolation to the infinite resources of literature. . . . Write to me when you feel inclined, and however busy I am I will write in reply, and in a more happy season you must come back to be truly welcomed in this house.' Is that the voice of friendship, or is that the voice of Mayfair? And later his decorum seems to have drawn a film even over his wonted perspicacity as a critic. He was terribly shocked by an incident in *Howards End*. 'I should like to know,' he wrote to Mr Marsh, 'what you think of the new craze for introducing into fiction the high-bred maiden who has had a baby? . . . I do not know how an Englishman can calmly write of such a disgusting thing, with such sang-froid. . . . I cannot help hoping that you may be induced to say something that will redeem him.' But when Sir Edmund goes on to say that no high-bred maiden has ever had a baby in a French novel one can only suppose that he was, not unnaturally, thinking of the House of Lords.

But if Gosse was not Boswell and still less St Francis, he was himself, and perhaps we have no right to ask more. He was able to fill a place and create a legend. He stored himself in book after book of history, criticism and biograph[y]. For over fifty years he was busily concerned as he put it 'with the literary character and the literary craft.' There is scarcely a figure of any distinction in modern letters, or a book of any importance upon which we cannot have Gosse's opinion if we wish it. For instance one may have a curiosity about Disraeli's novels, and hesitate which to begin with. Let us consult Gosse. Gosse advises *Coningsby* on the whole. He gives his reasons. He drops a suggestive remark. He defines Disraeli's quality by comparing him with Bulwer, and Mrs Gore, and Plumer Read.

He tells an anecdote about Disraeli told him by his friend the Duke of Rutland. He breaks off a phrase here and there for our amusement or admiration. All this he does with perfect suavity and precision, so that by the time he has done, Disraeli is left glowing and mantling like an old picture lit up by a dozen bright candles. To illumine, to make visible and desirable was his aim as a critic. Literature to him was an incomparable mistress and it was his delight. 'To dress her charms and make her more beloved.' Lovers, of course, sometimes go farther and a child is the result. Critics, too, sometimes love literature creatively, and the fruit of their passion is very different from the smooth strains of Sir Edmund's platonic devotion. Like all critics who judge without creating he forgets the danger, the effort, the agony that attend the act of childbirth. His criticism runs too smoothly, too glibly, too currently to be quite credible. He is a critic for those who read rather than for those who write. But then no creator possesses Gosse's impartiality, his urbanity, the width of his reading, or the lightness and freedom of his mind, so that if you want to hold a candle to some dark face in the long portrait gallery of letters there is no better illuminant than Edmund Gosse.

As for his own face, his own idiosyncrasy, only those who saw him at home among his books, or in one of those club corners that he made his own, can bring the odds and ends of this vivid, cautious, excitable, worldly, kindly yet malicious man into one complete synthesis. It was only in company that he expressed himself. 'I was not born for solitude,' he wrote. He lived on the tip of his tongue. It is a cruel fate that makes those who only come fully into being in the raptures of talk, fall silent. It is a harsh necessity that brings these warm and mobile characters into the narrow confines of the grave. 'You speak of "the peace which the years bring",' he wrote, 'but they bring no peace for me.' Life continued to be very pleasant. 'I am not without terror sometimes at the idea of this sensual sufficiency in life coming to an end; I have no idea how the spiritual world would look to me, for I have never glanced at it since I was a child and gorged with it.' He by no means wished to die when at length he died at seventy-nine.

APPENDIX VII

The Text of *The Common Reader:*
Second Series

None of VW's proofs appears to have survived. She almost certainly followed her usual practice of asking for at least two sets of proofs from R. & R. Clark (the printers of the Hogarth Press editions), correcting both, returning one copy to Clark and sending the other to Harcourt, Brace to be used as the text for the American edition. The first impression of the first English edition has been used as the copy-text for this edition. It has been lightly emended as indicated below, principally to correct misprints and supply missing punctuation. No attempt has been made to resolve inconsistencies (e.g. 'high road' and 'highroad'). Where there was doubt as to whether an endline hyphen in the copy-text should be hard or soft, this has usually been resolved on the basis of other occurrences of it; where doubt remained, the decisions are reported under 'Emendations'; disagreements with the first American edition are not reported. The following abbreviations have been used:

1E The first English edition, first impression (Hogarth Press, 13 October 1932)

1E2 The first English edition, second impression (Hogarth Press, November 1932)

1EU The first English edition, photo-offset reprint of the first impression, Uniform Edition (Hogarth Press, 25 October 1935)

1A The first American edition, first impression (Harcourt, Brace, 27 October 1932)

Emendations to 1E Incorporated in This Edition

The emended reading is given first, preceded by the page and line numbers for this edition. The reading of the copy-text follows the right square bracket. A vertical bar indicates the end of a line in the original text when this may have affected a variant. Editorial explanations are enclosed within wavy brackets. See also Editorial Note, p. xxiv.

342.35	learning] lean-ling 1E.19.15–16 (cf. 1A.14.22–3)
343.33	this – .We] this—We 1E.20.24 (cf. 1A.16.4)
350.32	outthinks] out-|thinks 1E.25.31–2 (cf. 1A.22.8: outthinks)
351.28–9	to the *Satyres*] to *Satyres* 1E.27.4 (cf. 1E.25.18 and 350.20 above)
351.33–6 and 352.1–8	{poetry inset}] {poetry not inset} 1E.27.9–13 and 15–22
377.6	Paraguay] Paraquay 1E.52.7 (cf. *IV VW Essays*, 332.3)
379.36–7	middle-class] middle | class 1E.55.31–2 (cf. 1E.55.24 and 379.30–1 above)
418.19	speak the] speak of the 1E.94.10 (cf. *IV VW Essays*, 442.7)
420.19	baptise] baptize 1E.96.34
421.31	Parsonage] parsonage 1E.98.26 (cf. 1E.98.6 and 29 and 421.15 and 34 above)
426.19	Diodorus] Diodorum 1E.105.3 (cf. 1E2.105.3)
449.26	horses] hourses 1E.131.10 (cf. 1A.140.1)
463.10	charm, some] charm | some 1E.145.6–7 (cf. 1A.155.26–7)
476.22	roof?] roof. 1E.162.29 (cf. 1A.175.17)
496.1	philosophy. There] philosophy, There 1E.174.32 (cf. 1A.188.6)
497.14	Lambs'] Lambs 1E.176.27
517.16	death-bed] death-|bed 1E.201.17–18 (cf. *TLS* version)
521.19	aunt] Aunt 1E.204.34 (cf. *Yale Review* version, 260.12 above)
523.4	some . . . | She] some. . . . | She 1E.207.7–8 (cf. *Yale Review* version, 262.9 above, and 1A.223.28–9)
532.37	prerogative] prerogatives 1E.218.17 (cf. 1E2.218.17)
551.27	If we] It we 1E.235.9–10 (cf. 1A.255.8–9)
557.6	Tebbs's tea-party] Tebb's | tea-party 1E.240.29–30 (cf.

NYHT, 211.9 above, and N&A versions: 'Tebbs's tea party')

567.40 clubroom] club-lroom 1E.253.11–12 (cf. 1A.275.11: clubroom)

571.2 Wessex novels] Wessex Novels 1E.257.15 (cf. 1A.279.31)

Textual Variants between 1E and 1E2

378.27–8 1E(54.8–9) born. ¶ *Robinson* 1E2 born ¶ *Robinson*

401.24 1E(79.1) "SENTIMENTAL JOURNEY" 1E2 "SENTIMENTAL JOURNEY'

426.19 1E(105.3) Diodorum 1E2 Diodorus

449.4 1E(130.18) Mytton with 1E2 Mytton wtih.

449.15 1E(130.32) Sophocles 1E2 Soph ocles

510.10 1E(191.28) Mudieism' {comma above line} 1E2 Mudieism,

513.12 1E(195.32) expatiating, 1E2 expatiating, {comma broken and faint}

532.37 1E(218.17) prerogatives 1E2 prerogative

1E and 1EU

1EU is identical with 1E and was photo-offset from 1E 'by the Replika Process' by Percy Lund, Humphries & Co. Ltd., 12 Bedford Sq., London, WC1, and at Bradford. The printing is uneven in places, notably 'Tory' (1EU[68.13]) which looks like 'Torv'. The May 1945 and March 1948 printings are much more consistent, although they have only been spot-checked. However, in all three printings, there is no full stop after 'heaven' (1EU[241.29]) and the full stop after 'hid' (1EU[253.34]) is slightly raised.

Selected Textual Variants between 1E and 1A

There are some 150 variants between the two texts, most of which concern punctuation, capitalisation and the splitting of words. Many

variants are attributable to house style: 1A has fewer commas than
1E; 1A prefers 'today' rather than 'to-day', 'some one' rather than
'someone', and 'any one' rather than 'anyone'.

331.1–3	1E.[3].1–3	THE	COMMON READER	SECOND SERIES
	1A.[iii].1–2	THE SECOND	Common Reader[1]
331.6	1E.[3].8	subtilty
	1A.[iii].8	subtility
339.15	1E.14.27	Philip
	1A.9.18	Phillip
339.27	1E.15.6	But let {blank line precedes}
	1A.10.1	But let {no blank line}
342.35	1E.19.15–16	lean-ling
	1A.14.22–3	learn-ling
343.33	1E.20.24	If only I had done this—We
	1A.16.4	If only I had done this— We
345.36	1E.23.16	Perne
	1A.19.6	Pern
357.18	1E.34.6	*Faery*
	1A.31.10	*Faërie*
357.35	1E.34.26	*Faery*
	1A.31.30	*Faërie*
359.21	1E.36.32	to day
	1A.34.13	today
366.25	1E.40.14	dog's-eared
	1A.38.15	dog-eared
369.27	1E.44.12	while
	1A.42.28	wile
372.9	1E.47.23	tree.
	1A.46.14	tree
374.11	1E.50.11	while
	1A.49.11	wile
392.26	1E.69.6	He scribbled {new line but not ¶}
	1A.70.14	He scribbled {¶}
421.11–12	1E.98.2	to-day boiled . . . rosted."
	1A.102.24	today . . . rosted".
422.13	1E.99.16	'et cetera'. Look . . . 'et cetera'
	1A.104.10	"et cetera". Look . . . "et cetera"

422.16	1E.99.20	'visiting or being visited'.
	1A.104.14	"visiting or being visited".
424.23	1E.102.16	coal-mines
	1A.107.20	coal-miners
435.9–10	1E.114.8	"Yes, Sir," or "No, Sir,"
	1A.120.30	"Yes, Sir", or "No, Sir",
440.3	1E.120.23	Brighthelmstone
	1A.128.2–3	Brightelm-|stone
446.38	1E.127.19	Channel
	1A.135.26	channel
449.26	1E.131.10	hourses
	1A.140.1	horses
463.10	1E.145.6–7	charm	some
	1A.155.26	charm, some
463.25	1E.145.24	fabric
	1A.156.12	fabrics
467.10	1E.150.15	dirty – beside
	1A.161.21	dirty beside
473.8	1E.158.14	been refused
	1A.170.18	was refused
476.22	1E.162.29	roof.
	1A.175.17	roof?
496.1	1E.174.32	philosophy, There
	1A.188.6	philosophy. There
496.27–8	1E.175.29–30	"Essay on the Principles of Human Action"
	1A.189.6–7	*Essay on the Principles of Human Action*
520.26	1E.203.32	become
	1A.220.9	became
521.23	1E.205.4	few who have
	1A.221.19	few have
523.4–5	1E.207.7–8	some. . . .	She
	1A.223.28–9	some . . .	She
535.18	1E.221.27	London and coach
	1A.240.4	London in order to coach
551.27	1E.235.9	It we
	1A.255.8	If we
555.19	1E.238.23	what was said
	1A.258.30	what she said

562.33–4 1E.246.10–11 sound of a waterfall that echoes | and booms
through its pages.

1A.267.18–19   sound that echoes and booms through
its | pages of a waterfall.

571.2   1E.257.15   Wessex Novels

1A.279.31   Wessex novels

1 – According to Selma Meyerowitz, 'in January 1932, when Virginia was finishing the second collection of Common Reader essays, Brace was involved in selecting the final title. Virginia had tentatively chosen "The Common Reader: Second Series," but when Brace suggested "The Second Common Reader," she consented. Although she liked this title less than her working title, she recognized that Brace's title was clearer than hers' ('Virginia Woolf's American Publisher', *Virginia Woolf Miscellany*, no. 7 [Spring 1977], p. 7).

APPENDIX VIII

Notes on the Journals

VW continued to receive commissions to write for, or requests to co-publish articles in, a wide range of journals, especially in the USA and increasingly through literary agents. As in the preceding volumes of this edition, this appendix provides notes on the editors and their editorial policies as available from the journals themselves, from the *Newspaper Press Directory*, from biographical studies, including the *DNB*, the *ODNB*, and from John Gross's *The Rise and Fall of the Man of Letters* (Weidenfeld & Nicolson, 1969). Information has also been taken from Frank Luther Mott, *A History of American Magazines* (5 vols, Harvard University Press, 1930–68); Edward E. Chielens (ed.), *American Literary Magazines* (Greenwood Press): *The Eighteenth and Nineteenth Centuries* (1986) and *The Twentieth Century* (1992); and Alvin Sullivan (ed.), *British Literary Magazines* (Greenwood Press): *The Victorian and Edwardian Age, 1837–1914* (1984) and *The Modern Age, 1914–1984* (1986). Against each periodical are given details of VW's contributions and often of the payments she received as recorded in her account book (WSU).

Bookman (New York)

Founded in 1895, it was bought by Seward Collins in 1927, who chose to renovate the magazine by combining the features of a literary review with a general magazine. He appointed Burton Rascoe as editor, but he left shortly afterwards. Collins edited the magazine until he ended its publication in 1933. VW's contributions, for which she received £37 for the former and £106 9s. 8d. (i.e. $575, less 10% to her agent Curtis Brown, at $4.86 = £1) for the latter (LWP Ad. 18; WSU): 1929: 'Geraldine and Jane' (February) [*TLS*]: 'Phases of Fiction' (April–June).

Figaro (Paris)

Originally founded as a satirical weekly in 1826, it became a daily in 1866, was bought by the perfume millionaire François Coty in 1922, and by the beginning of the Second World War had become France's leading newspaper. In *CR2* VW acknowledges that some of her 'papers' appeared in this newspaper. In a letter of 9 December 1928 to André Chaumeix, editor of *Le Figaro*, VW wrote: 'I heard from Miss Halford and told her that I should be ready to give the French rights of my articles from time to time to the Figaro on the terms that you suggest', and she offered to send him an article of 1500–2000 words the following month; in a letter of 16 January 1929, she enclosed an article and wrote: 'I have arranged that it will not appear here before Feb. 7th. I hope this suits you, and that the article is the kind that you wish for' (uncollected letters in Michael Silverman's *Manuscripts, Autograph Letters & Historical Documents: Some Recent Acquisitions*, Catalogue no. 3 [London, 1998], items 51–2). VW was usually paid £8 per article (WSU). VW's contributions (all but the first are identified as translated by Jeanne Fournier-Pargoire): *1929*: 'Quand on ne sait pas le français . . .' (10 February): 'La Soirée du docteur Burney' (19, 20, 22–23 August): 'Cowper et Lady Austen' (22–23 September): 'Le beau Brummell' (14–15 October): 'Mary Wollstonecraft' (26–27 December); *1930*: 'Dorothy Wordsworth' (5–6 May): 'Les Essais d'Augustin Birrell' (28–29 August); *1931*: 'La Demi-soeur de Fanny Burney' (16–18 February): 'Edmond Gosse' (5 August); *1932*: 'Un Roman-poème "Aurora Leigh"' (5–7 January).

Fortnightly Review

Founded in 1865 as a review of politics, literature, etc., it soon became a monthly but maintained its high reputation under the editorship of William Leonard Courtney (1850–1928) until his death, but then its quality dropped off sharply. VW's contribution, for which she was paid £9 0s. 3d. (WSU): *1931*: 'Edmund Gosse' (1 June) ['As a Light to Letters', *NYHT*].

Forum (New York)

A quarterly review, founded in 1886, and edited 1923–40 by Henry Goddard Leach (1880–1970), author and educator. Concerned with contemporary national and international questions, it also published general articles and, during 1925–36, fiction. According to S. P. Rosenbaum, it 'was a distinguished New York review that took its title seriously and tried to provide a non-partisan medium for intellectual debate and contemporary literature' (*W&F*, p. xxi). VW's contribution, for which she received £40 (WSU): *1929*: 'Women and Fiction' (March).

Good Housekeeping

A weekly magazine, founded in March 1922, aiming 'to teach middle-class women how to run their homes, especially after the First World War' ('in these days of servant shortage'), and then later, in the 1930s, when 'a businessman with two children lived comfortably on £1000 pa' (*Ragtime to Wartime: The Best of Good Housekeeping 1929–1939*, compiled by Brian Braithwaite, Noëlle Walsh and Glyn Davies [Ebury Press, 1986], pp. 7, 11, 108; and see 'Budgeting the Income', pp. 122–5, from the December 1931 issue; see also facsimiles of the opening spreads of 'The Docks of London' and 'Oxford Street Tide', pp. 126–7 and 138–9). It was edited 1924–1939 by Alice Maude Wood. VW's contributions were the six essays listed below. *Good Housekeeping* 'apparently had expressed interest in "more than one article"' (Naomi Black, *Virginia Woolf as Feminist* [Cornell University Press, 2004], p.132, quoting an uncollected letter of 10 February 1931). For this series, she received £50 per article less 10% to her agent, Curtis Brown. When Curtis Brown sent her the payment for the last article on 7 December 1932, they still referred to it as 'A London Character' (LWP Ad. 18; and see WSU). VW's contributions: *1931*: 'The Docks of London' (December); *1932*: 'Oxford Street Tide' (January); 'Great Men's Houses' (March); 'Abbeys and Cathedrals' (May); '"This is the House of Commons"' (October); 'Portrait of a Londoner' (December).

Life and Letters

A monthly financed by Oliver Brett (later 3rd Viscount Esher), founded in 1928 and edited until 1934 by Desmond MacCarthy (1877–1952), with Brett as his sub-editor. In his opening editorial MacCarthy told readers they could not expect 'to perceive any marked tendency in its pages' and could anticipate 'a varied diet'. From about 1929, however, figures associated with modernism received a great deal of space either as the subjects of essays or as contributors themselves. VW's contributions, for which she was paid £30 for the former and £10 for the latter (WSU): *1929*: 'Dr Burney's Evening Party' (September) [*NYHT*]; *1930*: 'The Essays of Augustine Birrell' (July) ['Augustine Birrell', *Yale Review*].

Listener

The British Broadcasting Corporation's weekly literary journal. VW's contribution, for which she was paid £4 14s. (WSU): *1929*: 'Beau Brummell' (27 November – see *VI VW* Essays, Appendix) [*N&A, NYHT*].

Nation and Athenaeum

A Liberal weekly journal of politics, literature, science, art, the drama and finance, edited by Hubert Henderson (see Appendix IV, *III VW Essays*), with LW as his (increasingly reluctant) literary editor until February 1930, and succeeded by Edmund Blunden. It merged with the *New Statesman* in 1931. VW's contributions, for which she appears to have been paid £42 in total for the first four and £7 10s. for the sixth (WSU): *1929*: 'Cowper and Lady Austen' (21 September)

[*NYHT*]; 'Beau Brummell' (28 September) [*NYHT, Listener*]; 'Mary Wollstonecraft' (5 October) [*NYHT*]; 'Dorothy Wordsworth' (12 October) [*NYHT*]; 'Women and Leisure' (16 November); *1930*: '"I am Christina Rossetti"' (6 December) [*NYHT*].

New Republic (New York)

A weekly journal of opinion and liberal views, founded in 1914 by Willard D. Straight, and edited by Herbert Croly (1869–1930) until his death and then by Bruce Bliven, 1930–46. VW's contributions, for each of which she received between £14 and £15 (WSU): *1929*: 'On Not Knowing French' (13 February); *1931*: 'All About Books' (15 April) [*NS&N*]; 'The Pundit of the Quarterly' (15 July) ['Lockhart's Criticism', *TLS*].

New Statesman and Nation

The *New Statesman* was founded as a Fabian weekly in 1913. Basil Kingsley Martin (1897–1969) was the first editor of the merged *NS&N* and retained the post until his retirement in 1960; his first literary editor was R. Ellis Roberts, whom he inherited from the *New Statesman*: 'Kingsley Martin lunched with us ... & said that the Nation & the N.S. are to amalgamate; & he is to be editor (highly secret, like all nonsense) & would L. be literary editor? No; L. wd. not' (*III VW Diary*, 20 December 1930, and see fn. 13). The *NS&N* was a weekly review of politics and literature and its first issue was on 28 February 1931. VW was usually paid seven guineas per article (WSU). VW's contributions: *1931*: 'All About Books' (28 February) [*NR*]; *1932*: 'The Rev. William Cole: A Letter' (6 February).

New York Herald Tribune

A major newspaper with an extensive 'Weekly Book Supplement', edited 1926–63 by Irita van Doren (1891–1966). 'It aint so much

that I'm a bad writer though that I am, as that I'm a sold soul . . .
to Mrs Van Doren', VW wrote on 2 September 1927 to Vita Sackville-
West. 'Here am I bound hand and foot to write an article on the
works of a man called Hemingway. There are three more to follow.
For this I shall be paid £120. Not a penny more do I earn as long
as I live; so help me God . . . write for the Americans again, write
for money again, I will not' (*III VW Letters*, no. 1805). She received
£30 for 'A Sentimental Journey', published on 23 September 1928
(WSU). However, she wrote on 13 April 1929: 'I have just agreed
to do another 4 articles for Mrs Van Doren, because she has raised
her price to £50 an article – so that, whatever the cost, I can have
my new room' (*III VW Diary*). By 5 August she was 'in the thick
of my four Herald articles'; on 19 August she had 'written my four
little brief hard articles'; and on 22 August 1929 she noted: 'Now
my little tugging & distressing . . . articles are off my mind' (*III VW
Diary*). As indicated, VW usually received £50 per article, but she
received £60 for 'Dr Burney's Evening Party' and £30 for 'As a Light
to Letters'; she recorded two payments of £50 for '"Evelina's" Step
Sister', but this may just possibly be an error (WSU). VW's contributions: *1929*: 'Dr Burney's Evening Party' (21 and 28 July) [*L&L*];
'Cowper and Lady Austen' (22 September) [*N&A*]; 'Beau Brummell'
(29 September) [*N&A, Listener*]; 'Mary Wollstonecraft' (20 October)
[*N&A*]; 'Dorothy Wordsworth' (27 October) [*N&A*]; *1930*: 'Wm.
Hazlitt the Man' (7 September) ['William Hazlitt', *TLS*]; '"Evelina's"
Step Sister' (14 September) ['Fanny Burney's Half-Sister', *TLS*]; 'I am
Christina Rossetti' (14 December) ['"I am Christina Rossetti"', *N&A*];
1931: 'As a Light to Letters' (26 July) ['Edmund Gosse', *Fortnightly
Review*].

Nineteenth Century and After

A monthly founded in 1877 by Sir James Thomas Knowles
(1831–1908) as owner/editor. It changed its name in 1901, and its
prominence and reputation declined after his death. It aimed to publish
original signed articles on topics of the day by eminent authors. VW's
contribution, for which she was paid £5 (WSU): *1929*: 'The
"Censorship" of Books' (April).

Time and Tide

An independent weekly founded in 1920, and for many years from 1928 edited, by Margaret Haig, Viscountess Rhondda (1883–1958), a feminist who sought to change the nation's 'habit of mind' and establish 'a fresher, more liberal climate of opinion'. In 1956 Lady Rhondda wrote: 'A first-class weekly review . . . is read by comparatively few people, but they are the people who count, the people of influence, the people who make the universities, the people who teach the young, the people who make the laws and the people who administer them. The good weekly review is in fact amongst the unacknowledged legislators' (Introduction to *Time and Tide Anthology*, ed. Anthony Lejeune [André Deutsch, 1956], p. 11). VW's contribution, for which she was paid eight guineas (WSU): *1929:* 'An Excerpt from "A Room of One's Own"' (22 and 29 November).

The Times

Edited by Geoffrey Dawson (1874–1944), 1912–19 and 1923–41. VW's contribution, for which she was paid £15 (WSU): 1932: 'Leslie Stephen, the Philosopher at Home: A Daughter's Memories' (28 November).

Times Literary Supplement

Still under the editorship of Bruce Lyttelton Richmond (1871–1964), the *TLS* published fewer pieces by VW in 1929–32 than in 1925–8. She was usually paid between £28 and £32 15*s.* for each article, but received only £4 16*s.* for 'Lockhart's Criticism'. VW's contributions: *1929:* 'Geraldine and Jane' (28 February) [*Bookman*]; *1930:* 'Fanny Burney's Half-Sister' (28 August) ['"Evelina's" Step Sister', *NYHT*]; 'William Hazlitt' (18 September) ['Wm. Hazlitt, the Man', *NYHT*]; *1931:* 'Lockhart's Criticism' (23 April) ['The Pundit of the Quarterly', *NR*]; 'Aurora Leigh' (2 July) ['"Aurora Leigh"', *Yale Review*].

Yale Review (New Haven)

A quarterly published by Yale University Press. Founded in 1892 and reorganised in 1911, it was edited from 1911 by Wilbur Lucius Cross (1862–1948). His objective was to publish articles of exceptional quality in literature, art, history, religion, public issues, and the social and natural sciences. The untiring assistance of Helen McAfee (or MacAfee; 1884–1956), who joined the staff in 1912, contributed to its success. VW appears to have dealt only with McAfee, the review's managing editor from 1925. See 'Letters to Helen MacAfee', *VWB*, no. 9 (January 2002), pp. 4–11. See also Phyllis Rose, 'Virginia Woolf and the Yale Review: Material in the Beinecke Library', *Virginia Woolf Miscellany*, no. 2 (Spring 1974), pp. 7–8. VW now received £50 for each article, but £68 14s. for 'Letter to a Young Poet' (WSU). VW's contributions: *1930*: 'Augustine Birrell' (June) ['The Essays of Augustine Birrell', *L&L*]; 'Memories of a Working Women's Guild' (September); *1931*: '"Aurora Leigh"' (June) ['Aurora Leigh', *TLS*]; *1932*: 'Letter to a Young Poet' (June) [*A Letter to a Young Poet*, Hogarth Press].

Bibliography

For bibliographical details concerning other works by Virginia Woolf, and for related reference works, see Abbreviations, p. xxvii.

Bloomsbury Guide to English Literature: The New Authority on English Literature (Bloomsbury, London, 1989), ed. Marion Wynne-Davies

The Library of Leonard and Virginia Woolf: A Short-title Catalog (Washington State University Press, Pullman, Washington, 2003), compiled and ed. Julia King and Laila Miletic-Vejzovic

The London Encyclopædia (revised ed., Macmillan, London, 1995), ed. Ben Weinreb and Christopher Hibbert

Major Authors on CD-ROM: Virginia Woolf (Primary Source Media, Woodbridge, Connecticut, 1997), ed. Mark Hussey

The Times Digital Archive 1785–1985

The Times Literary Supplement Centenary Archive

Virginia Woolf A to Z: A Comprehensive Reference for Students, Teachers, and Common Readers to her Life, Work and Critical Reception (Facts On File, New York, 1995), by Mark Hussey

The Virginia Woolf Manuscripts: From the Henry W. and Albert A. Berg Collection at the New York Public Library (Research Publications, Woodbridge, Connecticut, 1994), microfilms

The Virginia Woolf Manuscripts: From the Monk's House Papers at the University of Sussex (Research Publications, Woodbridge, Connecticut, 1994), microfilms

Virginia Woolf's Literary Sources and Allusions: A Guide to the Essays (Garland, New York, 1983), by Elizabeth Steele

Virginia Woolf's Rediscovered Essays: Sources and Allusions (Garland, New York, 1987), by Elizabeth Steele

Wikipedia, the Free Encyclopedia, http://en.wikipedia.org

Index

This index has been compiled upon the same principles as those employed and outlined in the previous volumes of *The Essays*. Thematic entries have been included under the following heads: America; Biography (and autobiography); *Complete Shorter Fiction*; Elizabethans; France; Illness; Impressions; Letter-writing; Literature; Novels (and fiction); Perspective; Poetry; Prose; Reading; Women; Working classes; Writers (and writing). References to places in London have been grouped together under London.

xi; few contemporary writers in *CR2*, xiv; partnership between reader and writer, xvii; and the extraordinary woman, 29; and the man's sentence, 32; average citizen quite frequently a writer, 36–7; slightly ridiculous in a girl, 89, 431; tradition and its lack on, 132; in close touch with reality, 182, 232; anyone can write, 184, 233; taught in universities, 222; unknown writers dangerous, 242, 244; Gosse and the young, 248–9; and their possessions, 294; writing about other people, 315–17; write by the ream, 318; escaping the present, 366–7; and the reader, 377, 573–4; period and perspective, 377–8; 'not writing', 418; the writer's psychology, 453; the famous, and the great, 532; and education, 532–3; Gissing on writing, 537; seldom great artists, 575; and biography, 576; Leslie Stephen's advice on, 588; and Ethel Smyth, 637; cheapness of writing materials, 637, 645; and the Angel

in the House, 638–40; as a woman, 641–2; cannot be a hero?, 644
Wylie, Eleanor, 35n1

Yale Review, periodical, 668
Years, The, x, 590n1, 597n3
Yeats, William Butler: riches held in reserve, 317
Yeobright, Clym, Hardy's character, 566
York, Archbishop of: and Sterne, 401–2
Young, Arthur: and his little Bobbin, 148, 151n19
Young, Dolly: and Fanny Burney, 89, 152, 431
Young, G. M.: 'A Word for Gabriel Harvey', 346n1

Zelmane, Arcadian character, 370, 372, 375n26
Zemgulys, Andrea P.: '"*Night and Day is Dead*" . . .', 299n1
Zetland, Marquis of: ed. *The Letters of Disraeli* . . ., 490n1
Zoe, Geraldine Jewsbury's character, 16–17, 512